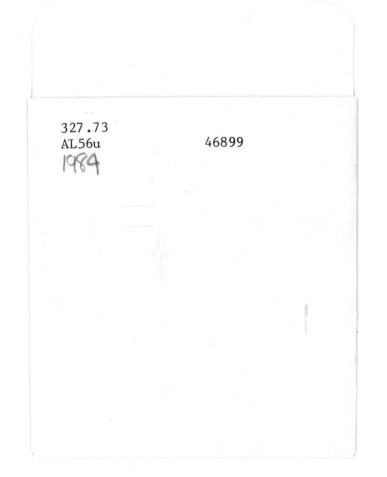

Unmanifest Destiny

Unmanifest Destiny

MAYHEM AND ILLUSION IN AMERICAN FOREIGN POLICY—
FROM THE MONROE DOCTRINE
TO REAGAN'S WAR IN EL SALVADOR

T. D. ALLMAN

The Dial Press
DOUBLEDAY & COMPANY, INC.
GARDEN CITY, NEW YORK
1984

Library of Congress Cataloging in Publication Data

Allman, T. D.
  Unmanifest destiny.

  Bibliography: p. 443
  Includes index.
  1. Developing countries—Foreign relations—United
States. 2. United States—Foreign relations—Developing
countries. 3. United States—Foreign relations—
1945–   . I. Title.
D888.U6A45 1984   327.73   84-4224
ISBN 0-385-27464-5

Published by The Dial Press
Copyright © 1984 by T. D. Allman
Manufactured in the United States of America
All rights reserved
First printing

Acknowledgments

Thanks to Professor William LeoGrande for his valuable comments on the
manuscript and to Walter Karp for his expert reading of Chapter IV, and to
the editors of *Harper's Magazine* and *Penthouse* for permission to reprint
sections of this book that originally appeared in those publications.

For
Pamela, Stephen—and Cousin Joan—Allman

Because of
Joyce Johnson

Waw yung yuan ai ni, Lap Fu.

Wherever the standard of freedom and Independence, has been or shall be unfurled, there will [America's] heart, her benedictions and her prayers be. But she goes not abroad, in search of monsters to destroy. . . . She well knows that by once enlisting under other banners than her own, were they even the banners of foreign Independence, she would involve herself beyond the power of extrication, in all the wars of interest and intrigue, of individual avarice, envy, and ambition, which assume the colors and usurp the standard of freedom. . . . The frontlet upon her brow would no longer beam with the ineffable splendor of Freedom and Independence; but in its stead would soon be substituted an Imperial Diadem, flashing in false and tarnished lustre the murky radiance of dominion and power.

—John Quincy Adams, on proposals that President Monroe intervene in Latin America, 1821.

Contents

If you want war, nourish a doctrine. Doctrines are the most frightful tyrants to which men ever are subject, because doctrines get inside a man's own reason and betray him against himself. . . .

—William Graham Sumner, on President Theodore Roosevelt's interventions in the Caribbean and Central America, 1903.

[A]t this moment conditions [there] are said to be worse than at any time within the memory of man. Constitutional government is as far off as it ever was. The needed land reforms are not in the least likely to be carried out, foreigners are not safe . . . and the country is prostrate. What have we accomplished? For what purpose did American soldiers . . . die . . . ? To what end did we intervene?

  —Walter Lippmann, on President Woodrow Wilson's intervention in Mexico, 1914.

We are the last domino. . . .

  —Ronald Reagan on El Salvador, 1980.

Unmanifest Destiny

Prologue
The Clearing in the Forest

It was as though America had converged in that forest clearing, looking for some explanation of itself.

Father Paul Schindler, a missionary priest from Ohio, was the first to locate it, but by midafternoon so many other Americans had arrived that the clearing in the forest might have been an American parking lot. There were vans, cars, Jeeps, American television crews and press correspondents, and U.S. officials. Around one-thirty, a convoy led by a limousine had appeared. The big car flew an American flag on its right front fender.

Possibly no U.S. citizen ever before had set foot on the Hacienda San Francisco, near the remote village of Santiago Nonualco; now it seemed half the fair-skinned foreigners in El Salvador were impelled by some common force to search out this place where normally only a few scrawny cattle grazed. A curious crowd gathered to watch the spectacle of these Americans, who could go anywhere and do anything and yet had chosen to come here. One Salvadoran youth in a green shirt had wrapped a white handkerchief around his face. It made him look like a bandit, but it was only to keep away the flies, the smell. Most of the rest just stood and stared.

The Americans themselves adopted various postures. Teresa Alexander, Madeline Dorsey and Elizabeth Kochik, all Catholic nuns, knelt down in the yellow dirt. Their lips moved in prayer, but their eyes, wide open, looked straight ahead into the patch of upturned earth in front of them.

Ambassador Bob White—everyone called him Bob, even though he was the U.S. Ambassador—strode from the flag car into the center of the clearing. With his clenched fists pressed against his hips, he stood looking straight down.

Father Schindler, who had been searching for this spot for more than twenty-four hours, later remembered rocking back and forth "and just saying 'uhuh, uhuh, uhuh, uhuh. . . .' I was in shock by then," he recalled.

The press photographers and TV cameramen, unlike the others, had no time to kneel or stand. There were too many pictures to take, too many images to capture—and then broadcast to the world. It was December 4, 1980; by the next day, nearly a hundred million Americans, and millions of other people around the world, would turn on their television sets and see what Schindler, Bob White and the others were seeing now. The horror of this one Salvadoran village would become a momentary horror everywhere. An image that would never entirely disappear would be seared into the minds of people thousands of miles away.

Four Americans—Jean Donovan, Dorothy Kazel, Ita Ford and Maura Clarke—had arrived at the forest clearing long before the others.

Jean, Dorothy, Ita and Maura had been, respectively, an American volunteer worker, an Ursuline nun, and two members of the Maryknoll order. Jean and Dorothy, along with Father Schindler and other Americans from the Cleveland area, had lived and worked in La Libertad, a provincial capital on the road between San Salvador and the country's international airport. Ita and Maura had worked in the northern province of Chalatenango. But, for all four, the task had been the same. El Salvador, by December 1980, was already undergoing an ordeal of mass murder. The women were trying, as best they could, to alleviate the terrible suffering all around them. "Their concern was with the people," Ambassador White later said, "not with politics."

Jean, Dorothy, Ita and Maura had been brought to the Hacienda San Francisco about thirty-six hours before the other Americans finally found them.

They all knew the search was over, even before they got out of their cars. "There were flies all around," Ambassador White remembered two and a half years later. "That was the first thing you saw." With White was Patricia Lasbury, the American consul in San Salvador. As they drew closer, she recognized a pair of blue slacks and grabbed White's arm.

"It's Jean," she said.

Villagers were pulling the bodies of Jean Donovan, Dorothy Kazel, Ita Ford and Maura Clarke out of the hole with ropes. What surprised Father Schindler was that "we could have four bodies in that small hole. It was only about three feet wide. They had put them in there two by two. Jean was on top of Dorothy and the two of them were on top of Ita and Maura. Jean's skull had exploded."

As the second body was pulled out, Lasbury said to White: "The underwear is not on her." Later a State Department report to the White House observed that

All four women had been shot in the head. The face of one had been destroyed. The underwear of three was found separately. Bloody bandanas were also found in the grave.

People at the grave site saw bruises and other signs of abuse on the bodies. "You could tell from the blood and the underwear," White said. "They had been raped."

Who had committed what the State Department report called "this appalling crime"?

The full details would never be known. But what was known, even then, cast a dark shadow over the conscience of America, an even darker shadow over all the efforts of the U.S. Government to support the government of El Salvador against a guerrilla insurgency. The four churchwomen had not been murdered by "terrorists," of either the Left or the Right.

They had been abducted and killed by the armed forces of the U.S.-backed Salvadoran Government itself.

On the evening of the first of December, Jean Donovan and Dorothy Kazel, along with some other American Catholics, including Father Schindler, had gone to the American embassy residence for dinner. Though Jean Donovan and the others had, as Ambassador White put it, "a proper skepticism about the ability of the United States to carry through an intelligent program in El Salvador," the dinner party was long and pleasant.

For a time, they discussed the problems refugee relief workers faced in El Salvador. White remembered Jean Donovan asking, "What do you do when even to help the poor, to take care of the orphans, is considered an act of subversion by the government?"

Serious talk, however, gave way to camaraderie. "We had a great time, a wonderful time," White said later. At 1 A.M., Ambassador White and his wife, Marianne, invited their guests to spend the night. They offered to leave, but Ambassador White insisted.

"There's real danger out there," he told them. "I'm not having someone leave the embassy residence and getting killed."

The next day, following breakfast with Mrs. White, Jean and Dorothy left the embassy residence and drove their white Toyota van to El Salvador's international airport. There they planned to meet four Maryknoll nuns returning from a religious conference in Nicaragua and then spend the night in La Libertad. Two of the nuns did arrive, as planned, on the early-afternoon flight. But Ita Ford and Maura Clarke could get seats only on a later flight. Jean and Dorothy returned to the airport to meet them about six that evening.

There already were signs that a well-planned assassination plot was unfolding. The only question was who the intended victims were. Following the arrival of the first flight from Nicaragua, for example, the ten transit passengers were ordered to remain on board the airplane, rather than enter the transit lounge, which is the usual procedure. Uniformed Salvadoran soldiers boarded the aircraft and closely questioned the passengers.

Singled out for special attention was the only American woman among the transit passengers, Sister Marie Rickelman. A Maryknoll psychiatrist who also had attended the religious conference in Nicaragua, Rickelman was now on her way back to the United States. She later told Pacific News Service correspondent John Dinges that "the soldiers scrutinized her closely and instructed the stewardess to question her twice about where she was going."

A little later, the following radio communication, between Salvadoran Government security forces at the airport, was intercepted and ultimately passed on to Ambassador White:

"No, she didn't arrive on that flight," it said. "We'll have to wait for the next."

Outside the airport, too, there were strong indications the Salvadoran military were searching for a particular North American woman, or group of women. As they left the airport, a party of Canadian missionaries, the last foreigners to see the four women alive, were interrogated so thoroughly that they considered their lives in danger and appealed to Ambassador White for help.

Heather Foote, a member of the Washington Office on Latin America, a church-founded organization, also passed the airport checkpoint late that afternoon, after having seen Jean and Dorothy in the terminal. "Usually the soldiers just glance inside the car or open the trunk," Foote later recalled. "This time they checked our identities and questioned us carefully. It was the most thorough check I've ever seen in El Salvador."

Around six-thirty, Jean, Dorothy, Ita and Maura left the airport in the white Toyota van. At the airport checkpoint, soldiers were flagging down all vehicles, ordering them to stop and be searched. But as the four women approached the checkpoint, the soldiers waved them on. In another twenty minutes, if all went well, Jean and Dorothy would be home in La Libertad, hearing about Ita's and Maura's adventures in Nicaragua, as they prepared for dinner.

Around six, shortly after it had been verified that Jean and Dorothy had returned to the airport and that Ita and Maura had disembarked from the plane, a member of the airport security forces, Sergeant Luis Antonio Colindres Aleman, had given the command that, in El Salvador, normally precedes a planned assassination: he ordered five of his subordinates to change from their uniforms into civilian clothes and to report to him with their government-issue G-3 rifles. Then, as the four women prepared to leave the airport, Colindres had radioed another command, this one to the airport checkpoint. All vehicles, he ordered, were to be stopped from leaving the airport for the moment—except the white van with the four American women in it.

Colindres and the five national guardsmen jumped into a National Guard jeep, raced down the airport access road, and intercepted the van. One of the soldiers got into the van and, following Colindres' orders, began driving it toward the nearby town of Rosario de la Paz, with the National Guard jeep following just behind. Just outside Rosario de la Paz, the jeep had a flat tire.

One soldier was left with the jeep. Colindres and the three other soldiers boarded the van.

Several miles beyond the town, Colindres ordered the guardsman driving the van to head down a secondary road. When they reached the Hacienda San Francisco, the van stopped.

It was at this point, according to the findings of an investigation by the Lawyers Committee for International Human Rights, "that the guardsmen murdered the women, after sexually abusing them." Then the guardsmen got back into the van, drove back to the airport to pick up a Customs Police truck, drove the Toyota van to an isolated spot twenty miles from the scene of the murders, unloaded the van's contents into the truck, removed the van's license plates, poured kerosene on the van and set it on fire.

The fire so totally disfigured the vehicle that the next day, when he found it, Father Schindler was able to identify it only by the engine number. This confirmed what Schindler, in La Libertad, and others, in San Salvador and Chalatenango, had begun to suspect on the morning of the third of December when Jean, Dorothy, Ita and Maura were not to be found at any of the places where they usually lived and worked. "Something horrible had happened," Schindler then realized. But what?

In El Salvador the tropical heat works nearly as fast on human corpses as burning kerosene works on glass, plastic and steel. The exact fate of the four women might never have been known had it not been for one curiosity of El Salvador: in that feudal nation there is a hierarchy of death, as well as of life, extending down from the oligarchs and generals through the sergeants and enlisted men to the campesinos.

Those who give the orders to kill do not do the killing. Those who do the killing do not bury the victims; that task is left for the lowest of the low. Had Colindres and his men buried the four women after they murdered them, the burned van might have decoyed Schindler, White and the others into searching that area for days—while the bodies of the women decomposed twenty miles away.

Instead they had left the bodies where they had fallen. Villagers heard shots about eleven-thirty; the next morning, as a U.S. embassy cable to the State Department put it, "The driver of a milk truck discovered the bodies of four women in a ditch beside a field close to the hacienda." The clothes of all four were in disarray. One was naked from the waist down. Out of respect for the dead, the villagers replaced some of the clothes, though even later, when the bodies were disinterred, several of them were clad, above the waist, only in bras. National guardsmen arrived and ordered the villagers to dig a shallow, common grave. While the bodies were being placed in the hole, a Salvadoran justice of the peace, Jorge Plutarco Dominguez, arrived with his secretary. On the guardsmen's orders, Dominguez certified that the four women were "unknowns," but already too many people had seen too much.

One of the villagers had recognized that the women were foreign; he told his parish priest, who told the archdiocesan office in San Salvador, who informed the archbishop, who informed, among others, Heather Foote. El Salvador is one of those Third World countries where high technology coexists with the primeval. Illiterate peasants try to grow a few beans in a field next to an earth-satellite station; members of the death squads play video games when they are off duty. When, more than a year later, Francisco Orlando Contreras, one of the guardsmen accused of murdering the women, was photographed by the press, he looked as if he were headed for a discotheque in Queens, not a courtroom in San Salvador. A muscular, darkly handsome man with thick curly hair and a bushy mustache, Contreras was wearing a tight-fitting pair of blue jeans and a Mickey Mouse T-shirt.

It was a similar kind of culture and technology warp that, after more than twenty-four hours of fruitless searching, of doubt and anguish, finally brought Father Schindler's quest to an end. In San Salvador, Heather Foote happened to be talking on the telephone to a Catholic nun in Washington named Peggy Healy when the message was passed to her saying the bodies of the four women had been found and giving the exact location. After Heather read the details to her over the telephone, Peggy Healy picked up a telephone and dialed 503, the area code for El Salvador, and then a seven-digit number. The phone rang in Father Schindler's house in La Libertad; a second later he found himself learning the exact position of the bodies from a person nearly two thousand miles away.

And so, by the afternoon of the fourth of December, a combination of conspiracy and happenstance, some mixture of dark inevitability and luck, had brought all the Americans to the Hacienda San Francisco. The bodies of the women, partly covered with branches, were spread out on the ground, their limbs pointing out from the center. They formed a kind of star. This photo—of the bodies and the people around them—was the one that was reproduced most often.

A second photograph was nearly as widely published. It showed Ambassador White staring down into that hole where the bodies had been placed. Some time later I asked White what he had been thinking.

"We already knew they would be dead," White answered, "but when you saw the flies, the ropes, when you saw them uncovered, it was so horrible and pitiable. The face of Jean Donovan had been destroyed; it was a mask." Only two and a half days earlier, Jean Donovan had been sitting at Bob White's dinner table. She had been laughing.

"You see people you love beaten and broken, and you realize something important about El Salvador," the ambassador said. "They'll kill anybody."

By "they" White meant the forces of the very government to which he was accredited: the government to which the outgoing Carter administration had given crucial support, support that the incoming Reagan administration would escalate into a full-scale U.S. military intervention in Central America.

Whatever Bob White had been thinking as his picture was taken, everyone who was there remembered what he was saying: "The bastards won't get away with it, the bastards won't get away with it." Schindler remembered White saying it over and over again.

Meanwhile, not far away, Colindres Aleman, the Salvadoran National Guard sergeant who was accused of the murders, was on a spending spree. In the days following the deaths of Jean, Dorothy, Ita and Maura, it was rumored, Sergeant Colindres purchased a television set, a new set of living room furniture and other luxuries. Guardsmen stationed at the airport later testified that, in early December, Colindres had suddenly come into some five thousand dollars in cash. What, his neighbors and co-workers wondered, was the source of this good fortune?

It certainly had not come from the possessions the murdered women had been carrying in the van. "On the basis of careful research," the Lawyers Committee later reported, "the Maryknoll Order has established that the two Sisters arriving in El Salvador were carrying only $175 in cash." Dorothy and Jean (whose monthly stipend for her work in El Salvador was only $200) had been carrying only pocket money.

The inference was inescapable: Colindres had been paid to murder the four women.

In La Libertad, Father Schindler recalled, even the most completely nonpolitical, church-related activities had incurred official ire, including the training of Salvadoran lay workers to perform pastoral duties in villages where priests and nuns seldom appeared.

"The reality is that you train leaders," the local commander had told Schindler. "The Communists will come in and take over your leaders, and we can't allow that." The missionaries' telephones had been tapped, and a little after this conversation two of their Salvadoran co-workers were murdered. "They clearly were trying to scare us into leaving," Schindler recalls. "But we just could not walk out on the people we had tried to help."

In Chalatenango, where Ita Ford and Maura Clarke worked, circumstances also strongly suggested an official Salvadoran assassination plot. Less than a month before they were murdered, a sign was posted on the house where they and their Salvadoran colleagues lived.

"Anyone who enters this house," it read, "will die." Threatening letters were also sent in the mail. Then, on the night of the second of December—the night the women were killed—an even more ominous event occurred: A member of the Chalatenango church was approached by a man in a local movie house. He told Father Efrain Lopez, of the parish, that the man had shown him a piece of paper and said, "Here is a list of the people we are going to kill—and today, this very night, we will begin."

The names of Ita Ford and Maura Clarke were on the list, along with the priest's own name, and several others. The next day, still unaware the women had been killed, Father Lopez went to visit the Chalatenango commander,

Colonel Ricardo Arbaiza. "He harangued me for an hour," the priest later told Pacific News Service, "accusing me . . . and the nuns. He said we were inciting the popular movement. . . . I thought they could kill me at any moment."

The hostility toward Maura Clarke and Ita Ford was surprising. Ita had worked in Chalatenango only since the previous April. Maura had been there only about three months when they were killed. What could have given the local authorities the idea that these newcomers, with so little experience in the area, were part of some deep-seated conspiracy of subversion? One possible explanation was that the highest-ranking military authorities in El Salvador had decided that the work of the missionaries must be stopped, through murder if necessary.

About two weeks before the killings, in the presidential palace in San Salvador, in a speech to high-ranking civilian and military officials, Defense Minister Jose Guillermo Garcia, who had been named to his post with U.S. embassy support, had accused the Chalatenango missionaries of supporting the antigovernment guerrillas and inciting people to join them. Among those present at the presidential palace in San Salvador were leaders of some of the country's most notorious death squads.

Certainly by then the Salvadoran high command needed some explanation for its failure to control the province of Chalatenango. A full-scale peasant insurrection was erupting there, following months of government massacres. What could explain this popular resistance?

In late February 1981, less than three months following the murders of the four American women, the Reagan administration would offer its explanation for the widening uprising in El Salvador. In an official State Department white paper entitled "Communist Interference in El Salvador," it was asserted that the rebellion had been instigated by the Soviet Union and was part of a conspiracy in the Kremlin to subvert the western hemisphere and undermine the national security of the United States.

It is clear [the State Department stated] that over the past year the insurgency in El Salvador has been progressively transformed into another case of indirect armed aggression against a small Third World country by the Communist powers acting through Cuba.

It was as a result of "the clandestine military support given by the Soviet Union, Cuba and their Communist allies to Marxist-Leninist guerrillas now fighting to overthrow the established government of El Salvador," the Reagan administration maintained, that the rural population of Chalatenango and several other Salvadoran provinces were up in arms against the government in San Salvador.

At the meeting in the presidential palace, however, Defense Minister Garcia had offered another explanation.

The American missionaries were behind it all, Garcia said. Furthermore, he told the meeting, he had proof.

Then, to the astonishment of many of those present, a weeping young boy, about ten years old, was led into the room. The Defense Minister of El Salvador asked the child a question, and yes, the child answered, the priests and nuns were responsible for it all. Then the little boy, still crying, was led away.

This dialogue between the Defense Minister and the child was not, in the Salvadoran hierarchy of death, as bizarre as it might seem to outsiders. Just as those who order the killings do not kill, so those who decide who is to be killed seldom explicitly give the order. Instead they make the identities of their intended victims indirectly known, and—in the world of the Salvadoran death squads—the hint is quickly taken.

Even before reaching the clearing in the forest, Ambassador White had come to the conclusion that the murder of the four American women was no random event, that higher-ranking officials of the U.S.-supported government were implicated and that "the cover-up had begun."

White's alarm bells had begun to ring on the afternoon of the third of December, nearly a full day before the bodies were finally recovered, when Patricia Lasbury informed him of a telephone conversation she had had with Colonel Lopez Nuila, chief of the Salvadoran National Police.

The American consul, on White's instructions, had contacted the police chief, informed him the four American religious women were missing, and asked the cooperation of the National Police in finding them. But Nuila himself had a question to ask the Americans. "Were they wearing habits?" the chief of the national police had asked.

"I could see them building a case from the beginning," said White. "The implication was that if they weren't wearing habits, they weren't 'real' nuns." Two telephone contacts with Defense Minister Garcia also left White apprehensive. "I emphasized to him that it was terribly important to the U.S. Government that the four women turn up healthy and sound," White recalled. But, during the second conversation, Garcia had started quibbling about what time the first call had come. "Maybe he already knew they were dead," says White. "At any rate he was suddenly making excuses."

Both Nuila and Garcia had promised a full military alert and a nationwide search for the women. But over the next twenty-four hours, one thing became clear: the Salvadoran military was doing nothing to help find either the women or the killers. When Father Schindler, for example, visited military headquarters in La Libertad to seek information about the missing women, the officer in charge asked, "What women?" Other searchers discovered the same thing, and this approach would continue even after the bodies were recovered. When White contacted Colonel Jaime Abdul Gutierrez, a senior member of the ruling junta, and asked him to ensure that autopsies be performed, Gutierrez, like Garcia and Nuila, pledged his full cooperation. But no autopsies of the victims would ever be performed in El Salvador.

"[A]lthough the forensic surgeons arrived within an hour, they refused to perform the autopsy," a State Department report to the White House later stated. "The reason given was that no surgical masks were available." "The Salvadorans never performed any ballistics tests either," said Michael Posner, who headed the Lawyers Committee investigation of the case. "When you asked about it, it would seem there was no one in the entire country capable even of doing that."

Had the Chalatenango authorities, following Garcia's lead, engaged Colindres Aleman to kill Ita and Maura? Had the La Libertad authorities, themselves eager to close down the mission in their province, hired him to murder Jean and Dorothy? Or did some entirely different sequence of events explain the actions leading up to the murders of the women, including the search of the airplane and the radio communication at the airport?

Even as the bodies were being exhumed at the Hacienda San Francisco, one thing was evident: There was not one level in the entire Salvadoran military chain of command—from the soldiers who had pulled the triggers all the way up to the Defense Minister himself—that was not possibly implicated, directly or indirectly, in the crime. If justice really was going to be done, it would have to involve more than a search for the killers. It would have to involve an inquiry into the entire nature and operation of the Salvadoran regime the United States was supporting. It would have to involve an inquiry into all the assumptions underlying America's efforts to stop "armed aggression" there.

The ambassador swung into action right there at the grave site: interviewing bystanders, dispatching an embassy car to get the justice of the peace, Dominguez, and his secretary. Then he took the two Salvadoran officials back with him in his car to the capital.

"It was vital to get statements from them," White explained in another statement that proved prophetic, "before they were either terrorized into silence or killed." What had started as a clandestine assassination was now a full-fledged international incident; the murder of four "unknowns" in El Salvador was now the subject of an investigation initiated by the ambassador of the most powerful nation on earth.

But it was more than that. It was, as White believed, a crucial test of America's whole intervention in Central America. Would the Salvadoran authorities the United States supported have either the interest or the capacity to punish even the most grotesque crimes its own forces committed? Even more important, did the government of the United States really care whether justice was done or not?

The journalists and photographers dashed back to San Salvador to transmit their stories and pictures. Ambassador White and the other American officials hurried back to the embassy to report to Washington, to get the investigation started. It was one of those moments in El Salvador when events seemed to have some meaning other than mere terror, mere death, when actions seemed to have a purpose. Soon the only Americans left there besides Schindler were Sister Elizabeth Kochik and another American priest named John Spain.

Arrangements had been made for Salvadoran funeral workers to come from the capital, to get the bodies and take them to the morgue. And so the three Americans were left there to stand vigil over the bodies of Jean Donovan, Dorothy Kazel, Ita Ford and Maura Clarke until the hearse arrived.

As they waited with the bodies in the clearing in the forest, one immense truth was apparent to Schindler and the others: the four dead Americans had come to El Salvador, as so many Americans have gone to so many countries, because their faith—not only in God, but in America—had convinced them they could accomplish great good in the world. Sister Dorothy Kazel, a friend later recalled, "was a flag-waver. She was terribly proud to be an American." The friend, Martha Owen, who was also an Ursuline nun, had worked with Dorothy in El Salvador, and she remembered a particular instance of her friend's patriotism. "It was back in 1976, during the Bicentennial," she remembered. "Dorothy and I were so proud of our country's two-hundredth birthday that we climbed the tallest mountain in El Salvador and hoisted a big American flag there."

Jean Donovan had been the politically conservative daughter of a politically conservative family. Her parents, Patricia and Ray, who lived in Sarasota, Florida, and her brother, Michael Donovan, who lived in Connecticut, had voted, exactly four weeks before she was murdered, for Ronald Reagan. "I remember Jean defending Nixon during the Watergate crisis," her friend Deborah Miller later told me. A few months before her death, while visiting friends and relatives in Cleveland, Jean Donovan also had taken a hard line on the Iranian hostage crisis. For the Donovan family, indeed, the Reagan victory was almost a family triumph. For more than twenty years, Ray Donovan had designed helicopters, including some helicopter gunships of the kinds used in U.S.-supported counterinsurgency wars in places like Vietnam and El Salvador, for Sikorsky Aircraft. Now Reagan was naming Alexander M. Haig, the president of Sikorsky's parent corporation, United Technologies, to be his Secretary of State. It seemed as if Americans like the Donovans at last were taking charge.

Ita Ford and Maura Clarke also had come from one hundred percent American backgrounds. Ita's brother, William Ford, was a Wall Street lawyer; many of Maura Clarke's friends and relatives lived in Locust Valley, New York. It was the values of places like Locust Valley these women had brought to the terror-stricken, impoverished barrios of El Salvador. In the months preceding their murders, as repression by the Salvadoran armed forces became more and more intolerable, some young Salvadorans had confided to Jean Donovan they intended to join the Frente Democrático Revolucionario

—the Democratic Revolutionary Front, or FDR, as the opposition coalition in El Salvador was usually called.

"If you join the Frente," she told them, "don't come back here."

In Chalatenango, Ita Ford and Maura Clarke also had carefully avoided involvement in politics, as a high-level, bipartisan report to the White House soon confirmed. It explicitly dismissed "unconfirmed suspicions that Catholic missionaries are assisting leftist groups." The report also explicitly reported to the White House the other great salient fact in the case: that evidence existed of "possible security force involvement in the murders or their aftermath."

In El Salvador itself, the realization that not even U.S. citizens were immune from official mistreatment was not new. Indeed for months it had confronted the four American women and their co-workers with what truly was a life-and-death dilemma. "Everyone was fully aware of the growing threat," Father Schindler remembered. "But what could we do? Abandon the people we had tried to help—and just go home to America?"

Dorothy Kazel's family several times had urged her to come home. " 'Next year, maybe next year,' " her brother, James Kazel, later told me, "that was always Dorothy's answer. She felt she had made a commitment to helping those people which she could not forsake." "Dorothy loved life. She didn't want to die," added her mother, Malvina Kazel. "But she would say, 'I must go back. They need me too much.' "

Months before their own rendezvous with Colindres Aleman's death squad, the four women were well aware that a reign of terror had descended on El Salvador that respected nothing and no one. They had seen women, even small children, tortured and murdered. Then, in March 1980, the most grotesque act of terrorism of all had occurred: Archbishop Oscar Arnulfo Romero, the Roman Catholic primate of El Salvador, had been gunned down by an "anti-Communist" assassin while he said mass, and the Salvadoran Government, by then receiving military support from the Carter administration, had failed to see that justice was done. Would the death squads stop at nothing?

Only a few days before Jean, Dorothy, Ita and Maura were murdered, El Salvador's "anti-Communists" gave a stunning answer to that question. In the midst of a press conference being held in a Catholic school in San Salvador, right-wing gunmen burst in and abducted a wealthy, U.S.-educated critic of the regime named Enrique Alvarez Cordova, and five other moderate leaders of the FDR. Later, their tortured, mutilated bodies were recovered; the funeral was held in San Salvador the same day the four American women were killed. This wanton violation of religious sanctuary, this brutal kidnapping conducted in full view of the press, showed what the murders of the four women a short time later would also show. To El Salvador's "anti-Communists," a "Communist" was anyone they happened to decide to kill.

Alvarez Cordova had been educated at Hackley Preparatory School, in

Tarrytown, New York, and had studied economics at Rutgers. His personal fortune was believed to exceed $2 million. "He was a Christian, not a Marxist," a priest who had known Alvarez for nearly twenty years told Raymond Donner, of the New York *Times*. It might have been the epitaph for almost all the Salvadorans the women had seen tortured and killed.

The day before she and Maura Clarke returned to El Salvador from Nicaragua, Ita Ford had addressed the terrible question their continuing work in El Salvador raised. What if they, too, became, like those they were trying to help, victims of the terror? Speaking to fellow members of the Maryknoll Order, Ita Ford chose to quote the following words of Archbishop Romero:

> Christ invites us not to fear persecution because, believe me, brothers and sisters, [we] who [are] committed to the poor must run the same fate as the poor, and in El Salvador we know what the fate of the poor signifies: to disappear, be tortured, to be captive—and to be found dead.

For the three nuns, the decision to stay in El Salvador had been, perhaps, inevitable. "Dorothy had taken her vows," observed Martha Owen. "Ita and Maura were professional missionaries." But Jean Donovan was a lay worker, a kind of Catholic Peace Corps volunteer, whose time in El Salvador would soon be up. Her friends at home often had considered her not merely a fun-loving, but a self-indulgent young woman. Jean Donovan had a fiancé in California she said she intended to marry when her time in El Salvador was finished. What kind of a commitment could have led a young American individualist like Jean to stay on in El Salvador as terror enveloped the land?

Only a few weeks before the women were murdered, I had one of those odd journalistic encounters whose full significance becomes clear only later. I had been visiting a refugee camp in San Salvador. The condition of the people there was wretched. Most of them were women and young children who had sought sanctuary on the grounds of the Catholic cathedral. There were no men there, and very few boys. And whenever I asked these homeless, frightened women where their husbands, sons and brothers were, they had the same answer: the government soldiers had taken them, tortured them, killed them.

It began to rain; many of the refugees began to huddle under pieces of plastic. I was late for my next appointment, I realized, and there were no taxis. So I introduced myself to the two American women I had seen distributing food and medicine. They had a white Toyota van, I had noticed. When I explained my predicament, they gave me a ride to my next interview.

One of the women said her name was Jean Donovan, and that her friend's name was Dorothy Kazel. Dorothy drove, as perhaps she was driving a few weeks later when the van headed out from the airport. Jean talked to me about her work.

Jean and Dorothy, it struck me at the time, were just about the only happy people I had met in El Salvador.

A few weeks later, after the bodies were recovered, I tried to put down on paper what had made that short drive in the white Toyota van so memorable:

Why does Jean's face remain so clear to me [I wrote in December 1980]? She was big and blond and cheerful, the kind of girl the boys in Ohio would have called bouncy or peppy. In this land of despair she seemed made up of all the bright pastel colors, all the blankets of flowers one associated with the peculiarly Christian belief in the Resurrection. It was not the catastrophe all around her that Jean found astonishing. It was the possibility that she herself might actually be able to help alleviate it that seemed to fill her constantly with amazement, and joy.

Jean herself had summed up the nature of her commitment, two weeks before her death, in a letter to a friend in Connecticut. She wrote:

Several times I have decided to leave El Salvador. I almost could except for the children. The poor bruised victims of this insanity. Who would care for them? Whose heart would be so staunch to favor the reasonable thing in a sea of their tears and helplessness? Not mine dear friend, not mine.

Now the bodies lay on the ground, as Father Schindler and the others waited. The four women had been exceptional Americans even before this terrible thing had been done to them. But, in another way, Jean, Dorothy, Ita and Maura were not exceptional at all, at least among the Americans living and working in El Salvador.

The truth was that it was virtually impossible in this land of rampaging evil to find any Americans who did not say they were there because it was their destiny, as Americans, to do good.

The U.S. embassy shipped supplies to the Salvadoran armed forces; it gave the Salvadoran Government money which was used to pay soldiers like Colindres Aleman. Yet, inside his office, Ambassador White spoke, as his successors would speak, of the real job of the U.S. embassy being to build democracy and bring a better life to El Salvador. The military attachés said the same thing.

U.S. involvement in El Salvador's civil war had only just begun. Yet already Americans were deeply involved in El Salvador's internal affairs. Among them were two young Americans named Michael Hammer and Mark Pearlman, who were helping to run El Salvador's land-reform program. They, too, considered themselves idealists. For all these official Americans, the effort to "stop Communist aggression" was only a means to an end.

The end was that El Salvador, through the help of us Americans, would become a decent, democratic, happy land. President Carter had said that, even as he had started sending military aid to the Salvadoran armed forces. And President Reagan would say it again, many times, as he escalated our military commitment there.

Yet in that forest clearing on the Hacienda San Francisco, one found oneself face to face with a great enigma, with some dark riddle—not just about El Salvador and the Salvadorans, but about the United States and us Americans.

If it truly was the destiny of Americans to do good, how was it that they found themselves ensnared by such evil? The flies, the ropes, the cadavers had no answer, but Ambassador White thought he had one.

The murder of the four American women in El Salvador, horrible as it was, he decided, would help American good prevail in El Salvador. There was no doubt in Ambassador White's mind as he stared at the bodies. Now the United States of America would see that justice was done—not just in the case of the four dead women, but for the Salvadorans themselves. The United States would not only see that the murderers of these Americans were punished; it would use its immense power, wealth and influence to help ensure that those Salvadorans who were as committed to justice in their own land as we Americans were would prevail.

"It was clear to me," White later said, "that we were up against a real test. If there could be no justice for U.S. citizens in El Salvador, there could be no justice for the Salvadorans, and everything the United States did there would be a joke."

In the United States, however, officials higher-ranking than White perceived an entirely different kind of test than he did in the events in El Salvador. From this perspective, the murders did not suggest that the United States should reevaluate, let alone redirect, its policy in El Salvador. So far as they were concerned, the murders showed that the United States had not given the Salvadoran armed forces enough military support.

Two weeks after the murders, for example, President Reagan's nominee for ambassador to the United Nations, Jeane Kirkpatrick, discussed the murders with a reporter from the Tampa *Tribune.* By then, high-ranking American investigators already had returned from El Salvador. The transition teams already were in place in the State Department and the White House. The findings that the murdered women were uninvolved in politics and that Salvadoran Government forces seemed implicated in the murders were freely available to officials of the incoming Reagan administration. Yet when asked about the murders, and who might be responsible for them, Kirkpatrick had the following to say:

I think it's meaningful to ask: Do you think the government [of El Salvador] was responsible or brought about the murders? The answer is unequivocal. No. I don't think the government was responsible.

She then turned to an assessment of the activities of Jean, Dorothy, Ita and Maura in El Salvador:

The nuns were not just nuns. The nuns were also political activists. We ought to be a little more clear about this than we actually are. They were political activists on behalf of the Frente and somebody who is using violence to oppose the Frente killed these nuns.

"The death squads are not agents of the Salvadoran Government," Ambassador Kirkpatrick emphasized.

Ambassador Kirkpatrick had given her interview on December 16, 1980. But the Tampa *Tribune,* which has a large circulation in the Sarasota area, where Jean Donovan's parents lived, waited nine days to publish the interview. So it was only on Christmas Day that first the Donovans, then the other families of the slain women learned that a high-ranking U.S. official had accused Jean, Dorothy, Ita and Maura of being "activists on behalf of the Frente," that is, enemies of their own country.

At the Hacienda San Francisco, the cameras saw only what Father Schindler saw: flies, ropes, blood-soaked clothes. How could high-ranking U.S. officials read so many other, so many different things into that one small scene? White and Kirkpatrick represented, as it were, opposite poles in a single continuum of official American perception. They saw what U.S. officials always saw, to one extent or another, when they looked at El Salvador, Central America, the world.

For Kirkpatrick the murders bespoke a conspiracy of Communist aggression—which the United States must combat in El Salvador and everywhere else it could, because, she believed, it must be the foreign policy of the United States to defend and, if possible, expand freedom around the world.

For White the murders represented a violation of human rights—which the United States must combat in El Salvador and everywhere else it could, because, he believed, it must be the foreign policy of the United States to defend and, if possible, expand freedom around the world.

Should the United States have a policy of human rights, as it had under President Carter? Should the United States have a policy of fighting Communist aggression, as it would have under President Reagan? Not just for White and Kirkpatrick, but for millions of Americans, these had been vital questions in the recent presidential election. Yet, much as they disagreed on many matters, White and Kirkpatrick—like Carter and Reagan and many other Americans—had one thing in common.

They could conceive of no alternative to U.S. intervention. As Ambassador White saw it, the United States must intervene to assure justice was done. As Ambassador Kirkpatrick saw it, the United States must intervene to stop communism, which was one reason why, even after administrations changed in Washington, very little changed in El Salvador. President Carter had sent U.S. money, U.S. military aid, U.S. advisers, to defend human rights in El Salvador. President Reagan would send more U.S. money, more U.S. military aid, more U.S. advisers, to defeat communism in El Salvador. But, under both presidents, El Salvador would remain a country of forest clearings where, every morning, bodies would be found.

Ambassador Kirkpatrick's comments were not an isolated statement. All during the presidential campaign, Reagan and his closest advisers had said "anti-Communists" everywhere, not just in El Salvador, could count on much greater U.S. support if he was elected. Following the election, all Reagan's major foreign-policy appointees were sending the same message. The United States would take a strong stand against communism now.

In El Salvador, where the Communist subversives, in the eyes of the "anti-Communists," included Archbishop Romero and the four slain women, the Reagan victory was greeted with jubilation. Now that Carter was defeated, their hands were untied: with President Reagan's support, a real war could be waged, and won.

In fact the difference between the two American presidents was much less than such Salvadorans assumed. Jimmy Carter had been just as committed to preventing a "Communist" victory in El Salvador as Ronald Reagan was; the Reagan administration would continue the Carter policy of supporting domestic reform and national elections.

The change in rhetoric in Washington nonetheless did produce one concrete change in El Salvador. "A reckless statement made in the domestic American context is not just a reckless statement in the context of El Salvador," White said later, referring to Kirkpatrick's comments and those of other Reagan appointees. "It is an incitement to murder."

Between Reagan's election, in November 1980, and his inauguration, in January 1981, the "anti-Communist" forces in El Salvador went on the rampage—not just against other Salvadorans, but against Americans in that country. In addition to Jean, Dorothy, Ita and Maura, Thomas Bracken, a U.S. citizen living in El Salvador, and John Sullivan, a free-lance journalist, were murdered. Then, on the third of January—the week after Ambassador Kirkpatrick's remarks had received wide publicity in El Salvador—perhaps the most outrageous murders of all occurred. The two U.S. land-reform advisers, Michael Hammer and Mark Pearlman, along with the Salvadoran head of the U.S.-sponsored program, were gunned down in the coffee shop of the Sheraton Hotel. Their crime was the same as the four women's, though they had worked, under U.S. Government contract, for the government of El Salvador itself. Those Americans also had tried to do good in that country, in this case by working in the land-reform program.

Neither then nor later was it ever seriously suggested that any of these Americans had been killed by the guerrillas, whom both the Carter and the Reagan administrations said threatened both El Salvador and the security of the United States. Instead all these U.S. citizens had been murdered by those who were committed to stopping a "Communist takeover" in El Salvador.

Should the United States, in its desire to prevent a guerrilla victory, support a regime that condoned and even participated in such crimes? Should the United States withdraw its support from a government whose forces murdered Americans, even if it meant the "loss" of El Salvador?

Later the debate would swirl noisily through Washington, sometimes ebbing, sometimes gaining new momentum, yet never ending, like some persistent tropical storm. But all that would come later. In the clearing in the forest there was only silence now. Father Schindler looked at his watch.

It had been hours since the officials and journalists had rushed away to convey to Washington, to give the world, the impression that great and important events were unfolding in El Salvador. But as the hours passed and the afternoon shadows lengthened, it gradually became clear to Father Schindler: In reality, nothing was happening. In the furor following the murders the bodies—and the three Americans guarding them—had been forgotten. The hearse and the funeral workers would never arrive. It was the metaphor for everything that, over the next four years, would follow: While the journalists and the TV crews, the U.S. officials and U.S. troops and U.S. gunships dashed about Central America creating the impression that something was happening, the friends and families of the dead American women—like the people of El Salvador they had tried to save—would be left standing, so to speak, with the bodies in a darkening forest.

Something else was also apparent to Father Schindler and the other two Americans: Salvadoran troops had staked out the place, and from a distance of about 150 yards they were watching and waiting. All the soldiers had guns. Some had begun to drink. In another hour or so, it would be dark. It was as though the American ambassador had never stood here, as though the American press had never taken photographs, as though America had never touched this place. Like everywhere else in El Salvador, there was only the approaching darkness, the nearby soldiers, the guns.

The three Americans made their decision. First they wrapped the bodies in sheets. Then they covered them with branches, "to keep the bugs off," Schindler remembered. Then, struggling with the dead weight, they managed to get the four bodies into the back of Schindler's mustard-yellow Toyota pickup truck.

They drove past the soldiers toward La Libertad, a town of terror named for liberty.

I
The War Against the Children

The vulture is from the beginning the journalist's guide in El Salvador. In time the vultures come to seem like philosophers, too.

They circle meditatively, as though considering the subtle complexity of this chain of Central American being in which they, no less than the campesinos and the colonels and the American ambassador and the TV crews, play their essential part. Finally the vultures alight, as if to indulge in more careful cerebration. Their shoulders are hunched; their hunched shoulders are garbed in black. They might be a congregation of scholastics bent low over some disputed text. They are unhurried, careful. It is only after lengthy meditation that a beak flashes, a talon claws the flesh.

An eye for the vulture; a tooth for the vulture. If Providence is beneficent, it is at this moment that a few children or some old women appear, waving sticks. They are scarecrows to this harvest, holding the birds of carrion at bay until the searching mothers, wives and daughters arrive. They pick over the bodies, turning a face to the light in hopes enough of it will remain to recognize a husband, a father, a son. Suddenly one of the searching women cries out. It is the kind of ejaculation—part penance, part absolution—that ends a long novena.

The body is gathered up, and carried to one of those churches where the requiem masses scarcely leave the priests time for the celebrations of baptism and marriage and confirmation. The body goes to its grave with more ceremony, in greater material comfort, than it knew in life. It is washed, and dressed in clean clothes; the bier is covered with flowers. It is attended by a procession led by a priest in a white alb—color of hope, color of death. The women weep. The men say nothing. "Ask, and it shall be given; seek, and ye shall find; knock, and it shall be opened unto you." The priest chants the words from Matthew, and those behind him repeat the incantation, like a hymn of Thanksgiving. The unfortunate are not these mourners following the priest, and the body, through some dirt-poor village or down an alley in a barrio of San Salvador. The unfortunate are those who follow the vultures, and never find. In El Salvador they call those whose bodies are never found the *desaparecidos*, which should never be translated into English as "the missing," though it often is. The English word connotes a certain ambiguity. The missing, it is assumed, may still possibly be alive. For the desaparecidos of El Salvador, however, the only ambiguity concerns where and when death came.

For the victims, death is final. Yet even after they are dead, the distinctions of Salvadoran caste continue to apply, because one of the privileges of the privileged in El Salvador is medical care, and doctors keep records. Even after a son or lover is only a skull in a mass grave, or a jawbone in a gully, these relics can be photographed, and the photographs sent for verification to the hospital or clinic. Thus some of the Salvadoran dead live on, even when they are among the desaparecidos, in the X rays of a childhood soccer injury or in the dental plates of cavities filled years ago. But what of that category of desaparecidos who live and die without entering a hospital? Of them, there are no remains. It is as though they had never lived, which in a sense is quite correct.

"Ah, the poor. They are the misfortune of my country," a cultivated and wealthy Salvadoran man of letters once told me when I visited him at his home. Bougainvillea clung to the patio walls, but beneath the purple blossoms, the stucco was embedded with slivers of broken glass.

At the time he spoke, El Salvador was considered to be a nation of great strategic, military, political and ideological significance. Yet, to the visitor, El Salvador seemed notable for another reason. Just beyond the bougainvillea-covered walls, the slums and shanties of the city of San Salvador extended in every direction. The vast multitude of unmarked graves were only the logical continuation of unmarked lives. Millions of Salvadorans were born without birth certificates; they grew up without schooling. One could search all the land titles and electoral rolls of the republic and never find their names. They wed without registry; they worked almost without pay. Their homes were no more than huts in the countryside, shanties in the cities; their funerals were attended only by vultures.

Neither great eagles nor majestic condors inhabit this land of low, eroded coastal ranges punctuated here and there with volcanic peaks. Instead, *Carogyps atratus*, the commonest of the vultures, acts as the universal scavenger. Even in its scavengers, El Salvador seemed a land of perpetual inadequacy.

And so events asked a question about El Salvador one never heard in the United States: could the birds of carrion keep up with the feast that, every night, under the cover of curfew, the soldiers prepared for them?

Hoping to find friends, kinfolk, lovers, the Salvadorans follow the vultures. The journalists follow the vultures for a different reason—in search of a photo caption, a lead sentence, a paragraph, some illuminating vignette.

"The bodies of 16 youths with their throats slit were found dumped along a deserted highway on the outskirts of San Salvador," one wire service report began, in June 1980. "Authorities said none of the youths had been identified. They said the bodies, dressed only in underpants, were dumped early yesterday from a van on a highway near the town of San Ramon, 6 miles northwest of San Salvador."

"According to El Salvador's Human Rights Commission, more than 13,000 people were killed in the political violence last year," a photo caption explained in January 1981. "Women as well as men are victims. The bodies of these two women, their hands tied behind their backs, were dumped along a rural road."

"Residents of a suburb of San Salvador looking at the bodies of some of the civilians killed in a raid Tuesday" was the line under a photo published in April 1981. The picture itself showed a sight many Salvadorans see almost every day: a few broken and tortured corpses tossed into the street as though they were the refuse from some abattoir of history.

While officials in Washington fostered the impression that El Salvador was the victim of some Tet-style guerrilla onslaught, the real war in El Salvador went on. This consisted of the U.S.-supported forces' attempting to terrorize a nation of five million people into utter submission.

In Washington, officials described El Salvador as a vital test case for U.S. foreign policy. El Salvador was on the television news programs almost nightly. Americans were intermittently fascinated by the conflict in the tiny, overpopulated Central American nation which, except for a few island states in the Caribbean, is the smallest and by far the most densely inhabited nation in the western hemisphere. In El Salvador, the visitor might see only a feast fit for vultures. But when one came home, one discovered that gargantuan issues were considered to be at stake.

What was really happening there? Was El Salvador "the next Vietnam"? My answers, I am afraid, often disappointed those who asked.

Uprisings such as the one that began in 1980 had occurred frequently throughout the history of the country. With equal frequency, the oligarchs and the military had retaliated. On one level, the whole history of El Salvador was the history of the conflict between a vicious and selfish elite and people who were denied even the most basic human necessities.

"It was as if nature had gone mad," one American student of Salvadoran affairs observed. "The peasants had chosen . . . to launch one of the bloodiest revolts in the history of Latin America." And in an effort to protect their own privileges, the oligarchs and the armed forces were responding with a brutality that made the insurgents seem almost like pacifists in comparison. "Before this revolt was ended untold thousands would lose their lives, unspeakable outrages would be committed, the nation's economy would be set back for years, and the entire personality of the nation of El Salvador would be changed."

That description of the state of affairs in El Salvador, which any visitor to the country could have written in the early 1980s, had been published a full decade before the current slaughter began, in 1971, by Thomas P. Anderson, a professor of history in Connecticut. And the situation he was describing had unfolded even earlier—in 1932. That year, in the depths of the Great Depression, a revolt had broken out that was, in its origins, ends and general results, virtually identical to the conflict that overtook El Salvador half a century later.

Like the killings of the 1980s, the killings in El Salvador in the 1930s were not exceptional. They were only the recurrence of a historical norm, for in Latin America, as Juan Vasquez, an experienced observer of events there, wrote in the Washington *Post* in 1980, "the ghost of history never sleeps. It is a phantom that haunts the memory of the living as they attempt to construct the puzzle of the future from the shattered mosaic of the past." A second, more terrible phantom, Vasquez pointed out, haunts El Salvador: "It is the specter of death."

To place what was happening, with U.S. support, in El Salvador in the 1980s in the context of Salvadoran history, one had to learn only one word of Spanish. That word is *matanza,* which means slaughter. In fact La Matanza would be a much more appropriate name for the Central American republic than El Salvador. It always has been a land of slaughter, and redemption has played no part in its national life at all.

In 1524 the Spanish conquistador Pedro de Alvarado, a lieutenant of Cortes, marched south from Mexico to act out, one more time, that dismal pageant of murder and destruction that was the history of the Spanish conquest of the New World. In June 1524 the feathered Mayan warriors stood, and fought, and were—as their descendants would be for the next 460 years —slaughtered. It was a day, as Alvarado wrote, of *"muy grande matanza y castigo"*—of great slaughter and punishment. It was not until two years later, after the enslavement of the Mayan and other tribes was complete, that Alvarado surveyed his handiwork and presumed to christen it "El Salvador." He thus applied to his carnage the name of the Messiah Himself.

Although the killings in El Salvador in the 1930s claimed far fewer lives than the carnage of the 1980s, Salvadorans use the same word Alvarado used to describe the terrible events of early 1932. They call that chapter in their history La Matanza.

The name is important not only for what it describes, but for what it leaves out. Salvadorans do not refer to "The Uprising," "The Insurrection" or "The Revolt." This is because the initial attempt of the Salvadorans to overthrow a repressive government quickly paled into insignificance in comparison to what followed. In the course of the brief 1932 uprising, "the total number of those who fell to the machetes and guns of the rebels could not have been more than thirty-five," as Professor Anderson has concluded from extensive interviews with those who witnessed, and helped to put down, the revolt.

In fact it was only after the insurgents were defeated that the real matanza began. Over the next few months, in reprisal for the killing of at most thirty-five Salvadoran landowners, government officials and troops, the landowners, government officials and troops slaughtered an absolute minimum of ten thousand campesinos, though some accounts suggest that very many more, perhaps as many as forty thousand, were killed.

"The roadways were littered with bodies in many areas, the drainage ditches along the side serving as expeditious burial places," Anderson writes of the events of 1932. "In some cases burial was too shallow or nonexistent and 'the pigs and buzzards ate well for a while,' as one person interviewed put it."

In El Salvador in the 1980s, one frequently could see a macabre play unfold. Government troops would arrive in a village and invite the campesinos to come to an American-supplied "refugee camp," built as part of the U.S. embassy's program of "humanitarian relief." In these camps, the soldiers said, the campesinos would be "protected from the communist guerrillas." As for those who refused to go to the camps, their refusal was considered proof they were "communist sympathizers," and therefore they would be killed. The problem was that those who went to the camps faced a similar fate. Once inside the government stockade, men and boys would be rounded up. Their thumbs would be tied behind their backs, and they would be marched away, hacked to death with machetes or, as the U.S. military aid shipments began to arrive, shot with new American M-16 rifles, and their bodies left for the vultures to consume.

Anderson provides the following description of Salvadoran "justice" fifty years earlier:

All those who were found carrying machetes were guilty. All those of a strongly Indian cast of features, or who dressed in a scruffy, campesino costume were considered guilty. To facilitate the roundup, all those who had *not* taken part in the uprising were invited to present themselves at the comandancia to receive clearance papers. When they arrived they were examined and those with the above-mentioned attributes were seized. Tied by the thumbs, in the customary Salvadoran manner, groups of fifty were led to the back wall of the church [and] were cut down by firing squads. In the plaza in front of the comandancia, other selected victims were made to dig a mass grave and then shot. . . . In some cases, women and children refused to leave their menfolk and shared their fate. An old Izalco resident, who was then a soldier in the army, says that there is no doubt that the guardia behaved much worse than the rebels, "shooting anyone they came across."

"Seated on sacks of rice and powdered milk at a refugee camp," a June 1981 article in the New York *Times* began, "the farmer from the embattled northern state of Cabanas said he had been an army sympathizer until troops came to his town in March, burned a man alive on a pyre of sticks in the main square and killed a pregnant woman with a machete." Once again El Salvador had become a land where life was as worthless as garbage, as one American witness discovered when he visited a municipal dump in the city of San Salvador: "[B]odies [were] dumped over the cliff, where they fell amid rotting food, plastic bottles, tin cans and other garbage. On the narrow shoulder between the road and the ravine, a tree branch marks the grave of a young woman buried there recently. Funeral home workers said that more than 500 bodies, many decapitated and showing signs of having been tortured, were dumped along this stretch in the last six months. A 23-year-old man who lives along the road said last week that he hears trucks at night, after 11 P.M., and finds bodies the next morning."

That account was written in 1981. In 1932, the following description of the situation was written by a Salvadoran:

Martial law . . . was applied excessively in the cities. How many vengeances took place on that occasion! A mere joke against so-and-so was enough to send one to the cells of the policia and thence to oblivion. [One person] was killed taking a little house dog for a walk, and two boys in El Coror, who went to bathe early in the morning, were cut down by the civicos. That martial law of 1932 . . . converted the capital into a cemetery. . . . No one went out because of fear.

In 1981, a wire service report began:

The body of Felix Banjamun Granados Montano was discovered by family members who went looking for him after he took his dog for a walk and the dog returned home alone. Granados Montano's head was cut off and then placed on top of his stomach.

"The Guardsmen threw the children into the water," one witness reported of another incident around the same time, "and boasting of their marksmanship, shot them with their machine-guns. Others were thrown into the air and shot. I saw them cut off the palomita ["dove," the slang word for penis] of a little boy. They shot at that, too."

What could possibly justify such a grotesque slaughter? In the 1930s, as in the 1980s, officials explained that the people who had their heads chopped off for walking their dogs, and all the other desaparecidos of El Salvador were not the real target. The real target, as the killers and those who supported them saw it, was international communism and its conspiracy to subvert free nations everywhere.

No evidence of any kind suggests Soviet Russian involvement, direct or indirect, in the 1932 uprising, and El Salvador's home-grown Communists were hardly a serious subversive force.

In 1932, even U.S. State Department officials complained that General Maximiliano Hernandez Martinez—the Salvadoran dictator who crushed the revolt and then ran El Salvador as his personal fief until 1944—had "greatly exaggerated" the uprising "and used [it] for political ends." "From Martinez's point of view," Anderson observes, "the communist uprising was a godsend." It allowed the Salvadoran general—as the "communist uprising" in 1981 would later allow the Salvadoran colonels—to solve a wide range of very serious problems, not the least consequential of which was a growing threat to the general's own position.

Like El Salvador's rulers half a century later, General Martinez had come to power as the result of a coup d'état just as the State Department was going through one of its phases of distaste for Latin American military dictatorships. The U.S. refusal to recognize the Martinez regime threatened Martinez's position far more than "Communist" subversion. As would be the case fifty years later, the Martinez regime also had big problems with the Yankee bankers. As a result of the Great Depression, the price of coffee, El Salvador's principal export, had collapsed. El Salvador had been obliged to suspend payments of its foreign debts—a situation which, in those days, frequently led to intervention by the U.S. Marines and the replacement of the debtor regime with one that could be counted on to pay back its loans on time.

General Martinez, in brief, found himself in a most vulnerable situation. This vulnerability had little to do with either foreign or domestic subversion, though the population was desperate and ready to revolt. Instead it flowed from the fact that the regime was repressive, brutal and unpopular and had no real claim to legitimacy. Morally as well as economically, it was bankrupt.

To this day, many Salvadorans are convinced that Martinez himself deliberately provoked the 1932 revolt in order to win U.S. recognition and loans and to unite the armed forces and the oligarchy behind him as the only possible savior of the country, and their privileges, from "communism."

In both the 1930s and the 1970s, as economic conditions worsened and political repression increased, there was a proliferation of mass popular organizations in El Salvador. In our own time, these groups have tended to draw their inspiration from the Christian-democratic and social-democratic movements of Europe and South America. Above all, these recent Salvadoran popular movements were inspired by the Roman Catholic Church, which, following the 1968 conference of bishops in Medellin, Colombia, had begun to place its immense authority behind the demands of poor Latin Americans for social justice, rather than using the power of the Church to support the Army and the oligarchy, as it usually had before.

With names like the Christian Federation of Salvadoran Campesinos, the Pastoral Reflexion Group, the National Coordinating Committee of the Peoples' Church, the Unified Salvadoran Workers' Confederation, the

Landworkers' Union and the Popular Revolutionary Bloc, the new mass organizations in El Salvador represented one of the most promising responses to both political dictatorship and economic injustice in the modern history of Latin America. Previously the choice in such countries had seemed to be between right-wing dictatorship and Communist revolution. Inevitably the United States had chosen to back the dictators. Nonetheless, in the late 1970s the Salvadorans began to develop a third way. Opposed to violent revolution because of their Christian and democratic philosophies, and with the political process closed to them because of the nature of the Salvadoran dictatorship, these groups found a political and economic desert, and began to turn it into a garden of popular participation. The village church, the Catholic school, the public plaza, even open fields where peasants gathered to discuss their problems, became parliament and free press for a people to whom the most elementary constitutional and human rights had been denied. Peaceful demonstrations and nonviolent campaigns for labor rights, living wages and freedom of expression steadily undermined the power of the dictator of the moment, General Carlos Humberto Romero.

Then, in autumn 1979, this spontaneous upsurge of peaceful, popular protest produced a dramatic and momentarily hopeful result. On October 15, the Romero regime collapsed from within, without a single shot being fired or a single person being killed. All over El Salvador there was euphoria.

It seemed for a moment that a coalition of idealistic young army officers, rural organizers, urban intellectuals, Catholic activists and other Salvadoran democrats might lead the country out of its long nightmare. But within a few months, it would be the members of these same groups that the Salvadoran right would set out to exterminate in their entirety, with the growing support of the United States.

Back during the Great Depression, dictatorship and hunger had borne similar fruit in El Salvador. From the poorest barrios to the classrooms of the national university, where even the children of the rich called for radical reform, the winds of change had briefly blown through El Salvador. San Salvador became a city of mass demonstrations; even the poorest villages were the scenes of political ferment. El Salvador was not being subverted, but the privileges of the oligarchs and the power of the Army clearly were in danger.

In 1932, as in 1979, the landowners, the rich and their allies within the armed forces thus faced a choice that, for them, was hardly a choice at all: they could accept a peaceful liberalization of the national society, or they could fight reform with every rifle, machete and grenade at their disposal. Then, as later, when faced with a threat to their privileges, the Salvadoran elite opted instinctively for violence. Like the killings in El Salvador today, the mass killings of La Matanza, in 1932, were much less a case of a military offensive against insurgents than a program of mass political murder designed to destroy completely the popular organizations that—much more than the brief uprising—threatened the foundations of a repressive, military regime.

After the 1932 uprising had failed and the slaughter had run its course, it would be purported that the revolt had amounted to nothing less than an effort by Stalin to establish a beachhead in the western hemisphere. In fact, the Soviet Union, for almost all Salvadorans in 1932, was as remote as Tibet or New Guinea. There were other, much more important examples of successful revolution much closer to home. Only a year earlier, in 1931, the oldest autocracy in the Hispanic world had fallen and the Spanish republic been proclaimed in Madrid. Much more important, Mexico, El Salvador's colossus to the north, had undergone a chaotic but ultimately successful revolution, beginning in 1910. By the 1930s, it was clear that Mexico had managed to put behind it many of the problems—ranging from military dictatorship in the capital to virtual serfdom in the countryside—that afflict many other Latin American countries even today. Mexico also was weathering the Depression much better than its Central American neighbors, who then, as now, were utterly dependent on wild fluctuations in foreign demand for their exports—chiefly coffee and bananas. Whatever its limitations, the Mexican revolution, like the Cuban revolution later, instilled in many Latin Americans the faith that even in countries as poor, backward and unhappy as El Salvador, people could struggle successfully for political freedom and human dignity. But the parallels did not end there. Mexico in that period also instilled in U.S. foreign-policy officials the same kind of dread Cuba later did. To read the State Department cable traffic of the time is to learn that there seemed to be Mexican subversives lurking behind every coffee bush.

Whatever the influence of the Mexican revolution on El Salvador in the 1930s, two conclusions are historically indisputable. The Salvadoran radicalism of that time—like the Salvadoran radicalism of today—was generated by conditions inside El Salvador itself. And the vast majority of both the popular organizations and their members, as is also the case today, were in no sense Communists. As John Gunther observed, following a flying visit to El Salvador:

> The official story is that this was a "communist" revolt, inspired by Mexican agents; in actuality the poverty-blighted peasants, no more communists than Martinez is an Eskimo, agitated for a land reform, and were shot for their pains. . . .

Gunther, who placed the death total in the 1932 matanza at "between 8,000 and 11,000 people," provided a description of the lot of the average Salvadoran that still is valid today. In spite of Martinez's promises of reform, he noted, "there has been no substantial land reform in El Salvador. The peons are penniless agrarian workers, a landless proletariat, working a few miserable months a year." Nonetheless, the Department of State had reason for satisfaction.

"El Salvador under Martinez is thoroughly pro-United States," Gunther reported.

In the 1930s, the mass organizations in El Salvador ranged from American-style labor unions to *cofradías,* or Indian religious and social brotherhoods. But at least one of the most important groups was led by a self-proclaimed Marxist. This was a group called the Socorro Rojo Internacional, or the International Red Aid Society. The group sought to provide the kinds of social and human services the Salvadoran Government totally neglected. It also was active on behalf of El Salvador's many political prisoners and used tactics such as peaceful marches, hunger strikes and written petitions in an attempt to achieve national reform. According to one of its own manifestos, Socorro Rojo Internacional was

a vast organization, without party affiliation, which accepts the idea of class struggle. It proposes to defend all the workers who are persecuted by imperialism, capitalist governments, and all other agencies of oppression. . . .

The leader of this organization dedicated to "class struggle" in what remains the most class-ridden national society in the western hemisphere was a young radical named Agustin Farabundo Marti, whose name the current guerrillas in El Salvador have adopted, in the form of the Farabundo Marti National Liberation Front. Though Marti had never visited the Soviet Union, and his knowledge of Marxist doctrine seems to have been at best rudimentary, he described himself as a Communist.

But was Marti a Communist in any sense of the word that either Stalin would have understood then, or one would use now to describe the agent of foreign subversion? And what role did Marti and his organization play in the 1932 "Communist" revolt in El Salvador? As Professor Anderson points out, Marti's emphasis on organizing peasants, as opposed to concentrating, in keeping with Marxist doctrine, on the industrial proletariat, was "heresy in Moscow" at this time. He adds that "it would be wrong to think of this temperamental and passionate Salvadoran as a Stalinist." Marti often "wore a red star on his lapel with a picture of Leon Trotsky on it."

In his emphasis on social work among the rural poor, peaceful protest and free speech, and open membership in his movement, Marti's "communism" in fact was the antithesis of the Moscow communism of the identical period. Had he actually gone to the Soviet Union in the 1930s, one can easily imagine this Salvadoran "Communist" disappearing into the Gulag.

Whatever Marti's real ideology and ultimate goals, he played no role in the 1932 "Communist" uprising for a very simple reason. He was arrested, on the orders of General Martinez, on January 18, 1932—four days before the uprising occurred. Held incommunicado, Marti did not learn of the insurrection until after it had been crushed.

Who, then, did participate in the brief, failed Salvadoran uprising against the Martinez dictatorship in 1932? Then, as now, the trajectory of every stone thrown at every police post was supposed to be plotted by foreign subversives. The truth was that the revolt in the capital was limited to a partial mutiny by Martinez's own troops, which was quickly put down. In the countryside, peasants—chiefly Indians led by the heads of the traditional *cofradías,* not by members of Communist cells—seized a couple of towns for a couple of days before they, too, were crushed.

There was another similarity to the future. Although Martinez had been in serious trouble with the United States before the uprising, as soon as it occurred a U.S. flotilla appeared on the scene to demonstrate U.S. support for the threatened regime. Like Jimmy Carter forty-five years later, Herbert Hoover faced an uphill reelection campaign. Whatever chances he had of winning a second term would not be enhanced by "losing" another republic in Latin America.

With the revolt crushed and the risk of "subversion" from Washington— the only real external threat the Martinez dictatorship had really faced— eliminated, the matanza of 1932 was followed by an American-supported "political solution" eerily reminiscent of the one the Carter and Reagan administrations later pursued there as well.

A program of banking and land reform was loudly proclaimed, just as a similar program, at U.S. behest, was proclaimed in 1980. To complete El Salvador's rehabilitation, Martinez himself, while retaining all power, actually resigned the presidency and held national elections. His "pseudosuccessor," as one authority puts it, was "Andres Ignacio Menendez, a man of upright character and liberal sentiments," just as the Christian Democrat Jose Napoleon Duarte would later become head of the Salvadoran Government. Renegotiation of El Salvador's loans and full U.S. recognition followed, even though the "land reform" benefited only Martinez and the oligarchs, and Martinez used the discovery of yet another "Communist conspiracy" as the pretext for taking back the presidency as well.

El Salvador had been "saved"—for the oligarchs, for the United States, above all for General Martinez, who ruled until 1944, when he was overthrown, not by "Communists" but by his own officers.

In June 1981, President Reagan's ambassador to El Salvador, Deane R. Hinton, announced, "Things are moving in the right direction." El Salvador (the ambassador seems not to have intended the historical irony) was on the way to having "a government of a kind this country hasn't seen in 50 years." What of the twenty thousand Salvadorans murdered by the U.S.-backed government? The human rights situation, the ambassador maintained, was "better than it was." The vital thing, he explained, was to stand by "the commitment of the United States government to see to it that the junta is not taken over by an armed insurrection supported in Havana, from Managua or anywhere else."

By then, the progress of the second matanza of the twentieth century in El

Salvador resembled one of those Hollywood remakes of a 1930s cinema classic. The cast was larger. This time the blood flowed in living color, but the plot was the same, and many of the same names reappeared. Most prominent among them was the name of Agustin Farabundo Marti.

On the surface, Marti was an unlikely candidate for patron saint of a guerrilla war. If, indeed, Marti had been planning an insurrection against Martinez, he was a most inept conspirator, as both the fate of the uprising and his own fate demonstrated. Far from leading his country to reform and liberation, Marti—however unwittingly—had helped bring upon his countrymen even greater repression, exploitation and privation. Like the Mayan chiefs Alvarado slaughtered, Marti was a victim, not a victor. He was no ruthless revolutionary, only a voice crying out in the wilderness of Salvadoran national life. The judgment of an American Communist editorial writer, made in March 1932, seems, historically, harsh but just. Marti, the supposed "Communist," had succumbed to "putschist and 'left' sectarian tendencies." He had confused manifestos and marches with a real revolution.

If Marti makes a very poor model for leaders of a successful war of national liberation, he nonetheless is an archetypical Salvadoran. In the 1980s, as in the 1930s, the victims of the mass slaughter in El Salvador were not the shock troops of the invincible hordes of Havana and Moscow, but hapless campesinos, workers, students, professionals and religious activists who were powerless to defend themselves. Whatever the alarums in Washington, they clearly lacked the power to overthrow a brutal regime that, by every standard of decency, deserved to be repudiated by its own people as well as by the United States.

The collapse of the military dictatorship in October 1979 had allowed a small group of civilian and military reformers to assume office for the moment. But how would the real powers in El Salvador—the death squads, the oligarchs, above all the armed forces—react? In early 1980 the "anti-Communists" of El Salvador began doing exactly what the forces of Martinez had done in the 1930s. Faced with peaceful demonstrations in the streets, they machine-gunned the demonstrators and turned the capital into a morgue. Confronted with peaceful agitation, they began murdering every Salvadoran who dared raise a voice on behalf of justice.

This decision to crush peaceful dissent with violence was also a decision to goad the dissenters themselves into violence. As a report prepared for the State Department candidly put it in December 1980, the repression had "forced" the "social democrats and the dissident Christian democrats and independents" as well as "the mass organizations . . . to endorse the vía armada (armed struggle) as their only realistic option." This official State Department report also pointed out what the State Department and the rest of the U.S. Government at that time were strongly denying: Far from being fanatical revolutionaries, most of the "subversives" Washington was denouncing were "not comfortable in the role of armed opposition." Behind the public rhetoric of 1980, the private prognosis for a "Communist takeover" in El Salvador was also the same as it would have been in 1932. "Clearly," the State Department investigators pointed out, "the extreme Left lacks, at the present time, the fire power to match that available to [the anti-Communist] paramilitary organizations." "In summary," the State Department investigators concluded, "the prospects for the Left are not very bright."

In early 1981, as in early 1932, an uprising against the government nonetheless occurred. Spokesmen for the opposition naïvely called it their "final offensive." But its significance was quite the opposite. It turned out to be a most opportune "godsend" for the government in El Salvador.

Following the murders of so many U.S. citizens in El Salvador, the Carter administration had briefly suspended military aid to the armed forces; in December 1980 it had also used its influence to have Jose Napoleon Duarte named head of the ruling junta. Not even Duarte himself purported to control the armed forces, let alone to have the capacity to punish the death squads. Nonetheless these actions were an experiment in the approach Ambassador White had vowed to pursue. After more than a year of mayhem in El Salvador, the United States was not just singling out for support figures who, like Duarte, were unimplicated in the murders; it was withholding support from those who were.

Could such an approach bring about justice? The question would never be answered, because, even before President Reagan took office, President Carter restored military aid to the armed forces of El Salvador. Stopping "a Communist takeover" in El Salvador, even under Carter, had always been the overriding priority of the United States. So even as the "final offensive" failed to shake the Salvadoran Government, the United States rushed aid to the forces commanded by officers like Defense Minister Garcia; it sent more guns, more ammunition to soldiers like Colindres Aleman.

The four American women had been killed in early December; by late January the Salvadoran armed forces had a blank check from the U.S. embassy once again. El Salvador's "anti-Communists," it turned out, did not even have to wait for Ronald Reagan to move into the White House to have proof that the fundamental maxim of U.S. policy there was unchanging, and completely bipartisan.

This maxim, quite simply, was that the U.S. opposition to a guerrilla victory in El Salvador would always take priority over U.S. opposition to government violations of human rights—even when those humans were Americans and the right that had been taken away from them was the right to life. Over the next four years, the talk of fostering freedom would never stop in Washington, just as the slaughter in El Salvador never stopped, and for an interrelated reason: the Salvadoran killers knew the policy makers in Washington would do everything on behalf of justice in El Salvador except deny them guns, money and support.

Watching the opposition's doomed "final offensive" play into the hands of the junta in 1981, just as the 1932 uprising had played into Martinez's hands, it was difficult not to see Agustin Farabundo Marti as a paradigmatical Salvadoran figure—though hardly for the reasons his admirers supposed. The worst in El Salvador were killers, the best were hapless martyrs. In El Salvador, the talent for killing, like the gift for dying, simply overwhelmed any capacities either the good or the bad possessed for dealing with the complexities of life.

Another important reason Marti lived on in Salvadoran history was that General Martinez had deliberately made him a national figure. Though Marti had spent the entire 1932 insurrection in one of the general's jails, after it was over, he was put on highly publicized trial, quickly convicted, and shot. General Martinez "set out to make Marti a legendary folk villain," as Anderson put it.

In the long run, however, Martinez and his successors achieved an opposite result. They transformed Marti into a national figure who—much more than Martinez himself—would dominate the later history of El Salvador, serving as an inspiration to its downtrodden and rebellious, as a specter haunting the armed forces and the rich. By explaining away every challenge to their privileges as a "Communist" plot, the Salvadoran generals and oligarchs also gave "communism" a far better name in El Salvador than it has in most countries. But was Marti a "Communist," and was the 1932 uprising a "Communist revolt"? Lest any doubt remain, it is best to let the U.S. Government itself speak:

"The disorders were attributed to Communist agitators," the Defense Department's official *Area Handbook for El Salvador* conceded in its 1971 edition, "but there was scant evidence to substantiate this accusation. The unrest was, nevertheless, vigorously suppressed by the new president, and order was restored, though at the cost of considerable loss of life." What really had been behind El Salvador's first matanza? "The unrest," the *Handbook* added with admirable hindsight, "stemmed primarily from the worldwide economic depression that had brought a sharp decline in the world coffee market and seriously impeded the nation's prosperity."

No doubt the Pentagon, in the fullness of time, will come to an equally temperate judgment of the Salvadoran matanza of the 1980s. By 1980, the year the killings started in earnest in El Salvador, the world market price for Salvadoran coffee was only one third of what the dollar price of it had been a decade earlier. Factoring in inflation and devaluations, the real price of coffee was perhaps only a fifth of what it had once been. Meanwhile outlets for both Salvadoran manufactures and for the country's excess population had been largely closed off by the collapse of the Central American Common Market and the 1969 "soccer war," with Honduras (which previously had taken in many Salvadoran immigrants).

El Salvador also lacked oil, and so the consequences of the plunging price for coffee had been multiplied by the rising cost of foreign petroleum products. In 1971, a hundred-pound bag of coffee could be exchanged on the world market for eighteen barrels of oil. By 1981, a hundred-pound bag of coffee could buy only two barrels.

As in the 1930s, El Salvador in the 1980s was less the scene of an international crisis than an economic disaster zone. And once again the Salvadoran military (this time with far greater U.S. support) had decided to fight hunger, joblessness, landlessness and desperation with machine-gun fire. There was another similarity between the latest matanza and the earlier one. Once again the slaughter was being justified through recourse to the "big lie." This time, however, it was not the Salvadorans who led the chorus of disinformation. It was the State Department, in Washington. The problem, the State Department announced in February 1981, was that

> Cuba, the Soviet Union and other Communist states . . . are carrying out
> . . . a well-coordinated, covert effort to bring about the overthrow of El
> Salvador's established government and to impose in its place a Communist
> regime with no popular support.

It was as though General Maximiliano Hernandez Martinez—who studied theosophy when he was not butchering his people, and strongly believed in such things—had been reincarnated fifty years later in America.

The following report, published on an inner page of the New York *Times* in 1981, conveyed the truth of the situation far better than the official explanations ever did:

> SAN SALVADOR, Jan. 10—Salvadoran soldiers dumped the bodies of 22 young people in a pile on the asphalt parking lot behind the six-story judicial center in the capital last night.
>
> The victims, who appeared to be in their early 20's, were dressed in civilian clothes. Many were barefoot, others were wearing rubber thongs or tennis shoes.
>
> A civilian guard said there were 18 men and 4 women. He said the women had been raped. Several showed signs of having been shot at close range.
>
> Military sources said the victims were subversives.
>
> The killings occurred yesterday afternoon in a gully of mud and stucco shanties just off the main highway, seven miles north of the center of the city. Witnesses said today that the victims were eating in a house when a patrol of soldiers surrounded it at about 3:30 P.M. yesterday. The stucco house is situated at the base of a 20-foot dirt wall at the end of a dusty alley.
>
> Standing in front of her house across the alley, a neighbor said soldiers had fired automatic weapons and had thrown two grenades. There were thick pastes of dirt and blood on the cement floors in two of the five rooms.

Clothes and papers were strewn about two other rooms. The walls were filled with bullet holes. There was no evidence that the victims had returned the fire. A pool of blood in the dirt behind the house suggested that one person had been killed while trying to escape.

The military reported no casualties of its own in the attack. . . .

It often seemed to me that the clerks of death in El Salvador—those dedicated churchmen and human rights activists who spent their time simply adding up the toll, rather than trying to impute any meaning to it—told more truths, more eloquently, than any journalist ever could. Consider the random tally of a random month—September 1980—in the Salvadoran slaughter:

* During the first two weeks of the month, the legal assistance department of the archdiocese of San Salvador reports, government troops killed 247 persons for "political" reasons. The victims include 152 peasants, 23 students, 25 public employees (of the very government the armed forces supposedly are defending), 6 businessmen and "25 persons whose professions are unknown." This tally does not include "military" casualties in operations against the guerrillas.

* On Friday, September 12, between five and six in the morning, elements of the National Guard and Army sweep through the villages of Plan del Pito, San Roque and Notificacion Guadalupe, northwest of San Salvador. Eyewitnesses describe "a large massacre," but the exact toll is unknown.

* The next day, "members of paramilitary organizations" bomb the Catholic radio station, known as "The Voice of Truth," for the fourth time this year.

* On Sunday the fourteenth, the Army enters Huizucar. It seizes members and leaders of the Federation of Farm Workers, who are then reported to have "disappeared."

* September 15 is uneventful, perhaps because it is the one hundred and fifty-ninth anniversary of El Salvador's independence.

* In the town of Spaentique the next day, the general secretary of a union is arrested and taken away. Members of the National Guard arrest his wife and family as well.

* On September 17, nonviolent demonstrators begin a hunger strike, "in support of the demands of political prisoners," in the cathedrals of San Miguel and San Salvador. In retaliation, troops harass and beat political prisoners being held without formal charges or trial at the Santa Tecla jail.

* The following day, soldiers enter San Miguel cathedral, beat the hunger strikers and drive them from the church. Nine of the protesters are arrested

by the military and handed over to the "paramilitary" forces. The nine bodies, all tortured and mutilated, later are dumped in a public place.

* On September 19, combined forces of the Army and the Guardia kill thirty-six Catholic laymen in the Church of Santa Lucia in Sacatecoluca. Later that night the power plant of the Catholic radio station is bombed again, and just before midnight seventy members of the security forces attack the Domus Mariae refugee camp in Mejicanos. They blow up the front gate with a bomb, severely wound a seven-year-old child, and then proceed to the radio station and bomb it again, destroying the transmitter and equipment completely. Four trucks of uniformed soldiers arrive while the demolition is underway. They cordon off the area, preventing efforts to save the station. When the demolition is completed, they withdraw. Later the junta states the explosion is the work of "unknown terrorists." Defense Minister Garcia cites such incidents as proof of the need for more American aid.

* On September 20, it is reported that over the previous six days, there have been verified assassinations of 224 persons by the security forces. The victims include 53 peasants, 12 workers, 18 students, 6 of the U.S.-backed government's own employees, 5 businessmen, 4 professors, 1 professional "and 125 unidentified individuals," some of whom are unidentifiable because they have been beheaded or had their faces so disfigured that they are unrecognizable.

* At the end of the month it is reported that the verified number of assassinations committed by the Army, the National Guard and other "organizations under the protection of the military junta" is 637. "Figures exist stating that even more people were killed," a document from the San Salvador archdiocese explains, "but in some areas of the country it is impossible to prove this."

* A random selection of the desaparecidos for the month of September includes: Salvador Martinez Cardona, 18 years old; Ismael Funes, 17, and his brother Carlos Alfredo Funes, 15; Milagro Fuentes Villatoro, 16; Luis Fernando Hernandez Aguilar, 17; Juan Lemos Calderon, 14; Ricardo Ruiz Orellana, 14; Jorge Alberto Argumido, 14; Pedro Ros, 18; Edgar Ernesto Lopez, 17; Jose Santos Serrano Garcia, 20; Adan Ramirez, 19; the brothers Edwin and Roque Chavez, 15 and 16; Jose Antonio Palacios, 18; Jose Antonio Mena, 19; Mario Anibal Victoriano Enriquez, 20; Aristides Wilfredo Garcia Alfaro, 18; Hernan Flores, 19; Manuel de Jesus Torres, 21; Carlos Guzman, 20; Francisco Gomez, 20; Jose Luis Hernandez, 18; Maria Isabel Escoto de Quintanilla, 20.

These youngsters are among the privileged of the Salvadoran war. Like the dismembered victims who bequeath a dental plate or a mended bone, they are among that minority of Salvadorans whose names are ever written down, either by themselves or others—whose misfortune attracts any notice at all. Most of them are students; almost all are devout Catholics involved in diocesan work. In short they are—unlike the anonymous dead—people who were not desaparecidos from birth.

Such chronicles tell the truth of El Salvador. But they also reveal a truth about our own capacity, as human beings, to react to even the most gruesome crimes our fellow human beings commit. If a single killing of a single person is a catastrophe, an obscenity, a crime, is it not, then, ten thousand times worse to kill ten thousand people? The intellect agrees this is the case, but the problem is that the emotions cannot keep up with the mathematics. Often in El Salvador it seemed that if it were only possible to show the face and name the name of every victim, as the human rights workers tried to do, then the simple truth of the situation there would become known to everybody, and perhaps then the killing would stop.

But that is not the way human sensibilities work, perhaps because to murder someone is to turn a living person from flesh and blood into the ultimate abstraction. As the numbers of the dead mount, the living are overwhelmed not with grief and shock, but by the numbness of rote. The personal catastrophe of thousands of individual human beings is subsumed into the cold statistics of the body count, until not even those who do the counting have the capacity to ache with grief any more. Once, a member of El Salvador's Human Rights Commission was asked how he continued to go about his terrible business.

Every morning this person—like the relatives of the desaparecidos—would follow the vultures. He was determined that not a single murder go unrecorded, and unreported to other human rights organizations around the world. So, every day, he would inspect and try to identify dozens and sometimes scores of bodies. He conducted this task quickly, systematically, as you or I might keep a running tally of our bank account.

When he was asked how he could do this work with so little emotion, he replied that for many months he had wept at the sight of the corpses, and dreamed of their faces when he went home at night and tried to sleep. But then, one day, in the course of unearthing the shallow mass grave of some massacre, he had found among all the other bodies the body of his own father. Thereafter a terrible calmness overcame him.

One Sunday morning in El Salvador, I went out in search of vultures with Ian Mates, a young South African photographer. Mates never tired of counting the lost ones. Nor did he silently watch the dead. In fact, he was one of the most enterprising and tireless journalists of the entire Salvadoran War. His searing films of the carnage looked death straight in the face and, for a time, communicated the reality of El Salvador with a total lack of abstraction that shocked the world. But we had no luck that particular day. The only desaparecidos Ian and I found were the living: children with no shoes or milk, women with no food for their children, illiterate men with no jobs and no money for their wives and children. There seemed not a ravine on the hilly outskirts of El Salvador that was not filled with cardboard packing crates which whole families had covered with plastic and tried to turn into shelters against the rain. The parks were filled with idle, jobless men and women. And everywhere we drove, we were almost lost in the crowds of teenagers and children.

The statistics of El Salvador had been illuminating, but it was much more illuminating to see these statistics come to life. One half the population was illiterate; perhaps 80 percent of all Salvadorans had no real fluency in reading and writing. More than half the national wealth went to less than 9 percent of the population. That is to say some 400,000 Salvadorans received more income every year than the other 4,600,000 Salvadorans combined.

In the city of San Salvador this last statistic took architectural as well as human form. In its affluent sections, the Salvadoran capital resembled some unlicensed franchise of Beverly Hills. The signs of an American-style affluence—Sheraton, Holiday Inn, Kodak, Colonel Sanders—were everywhere. But in these modern shopping centers emaciated children held out their hands to chic passersby, and for every Salvadoran youth wearing designer jeans and ordering a hamburger in an American-style fast-food restaurant there were a hundred in rags, who never in their lives had known the taste of meat. As for the rest of the city, it was no more or less than an endless slum.

In the countryside, conditions were even worse. A hundred thousand people owned 60 percent of all the arable land. Two million Salvadoran campesinos had no productive land at all, and most of the rest possessed only a tiny scrap of hillside or ravine—insufficient to sustain themselves, let alone their children and all the children their children would have. The national unemployment rate at that time was 25 percent. The underemployment rate (a far more accurate indicator of a country's desperation) was 84 percent. Only one Salvadoran in six had a full-time, year-round job. Less than a quarter of the peasants had access to tap water. In rural areas, only one house in a hundred had a toilet. There were only three doctors for every ten thousand Salvadorans (as opposed to about twenty for every ten thousand Americans).

One could drive for hours and never see schoolchildren carrying books. But armed men were everywhere—stopping cars, surveying *cantinas,* watching those who dared attend Mass or buy a newspaper or speak with a foreigner. Everywhere in this tropical, sunlit country was the cold shadow of fear. Not including the guerrillas, this tiny country had no fewer than ten different armed forces. Besides the regular Navy, Air Force and Army, there were the National Guard, the National Police and the Treasury Police (which was actually an American-trained "counterterrorism" force). Then there was ORDEN, the paramilitary organization, founded with U.S. encouragement, to act (as the official explanation ran) as "a barrier against the attempts of the communists to provoke subversion in the countryside." ORDEN was augmented by the unofficial "anti-Communist" security forces. One of these, the White Warriors, was dedicated to purging El Salvador "of Jesuits and other communists." "Be patriotic," ran one of its slogans, "and kill a priest." Another Salvadoran paramilitary force, the Organization for Liberation from Communism, took a more ecumenical, almost secular approach, dedicating "our entire war" to the destruction of all "Communists and their followers, [who] are our country's worst enemies." But the full name of FALANGE, a death squad consisting of active, retired and off-duty members of the Salvadoran armed forces, explained both the philosophy and the strategy of the conflict in El Salvador best. FALANGE stood for "Fuerzas Armadas de Liberacion Anticommunista—Guerra de Eliminacion," or "Anti-Communist Armed Forces of Liberation—War of Elimination."

At the time it became U.S. policy that only U.S. guns, ammunition and helicopters could deflect the menace El Salvador posed to the entire hemisphere, perhaps a hundred thousand heavily armed men were already working actively in that small nation to pursue their "war of elimination" against "Communists and their followers." Even before U.S. arms began arriving in large quantities, El Salvador was about as lacking in soldiers and weapons as it was deficient in coffee beans. To send weapons there was like shipping petroleum to Kuwait. How could it possibly be necessary?

The most fascinating statistic of El Salvador helped provide an answer. This statistic was not economic or political or military. It was demographic. All those guns and soldiers and vigilantes and all that American military aid were evidently needed to save El Salvador from an onslaught by its own children.

Less than 5 percent of all Salvadorans had managed to live to the age of sixty. More than half of all Salvadorans were under fifteen years of age. Two thirds were under twenty-one. And this nation of children had faced a dire calculus, even before the latest matanza had begun. Among the children of El Salvador, sixty-three out of every thousand were destined to die before their first birthday of disease or malnutrition (as opposed to ten in the United States). Of those that survived, 73 percent were severely undernourished. By the tim : puberty was reached, the average Salvadoran youngster was landless, jobless, homeless, and functionally illiterate.

In such a country, was not every teenager a potential guerrilla, every youth the military killed, as the official statements explained, a "subversive"? As Ian Mates and I toured the barrios of San Salvador, the mass killings of the junta —like the big plans in Washington for shipments of M-16s and helicopters and U.S. advisers—suddenly made much more sense. These throngs of hungry children, these masses of brown-skinned, skinny, shoeless youths, clearly were far too numerous to be kept under control by the traditional implements of Salvadoran authority: the machete, the handgun, the electric shocks, the garrote and the grenade. One could slit the throats of teenagers forever, and dump their bodies in downtown San Salvador morning, noon and night, and still not make much headway against this menace.

What was the use of killing even thirteen thousand people a year when that many Salvadorans were born, and nearly that many reached the age of eighteen, every month? The only really effective way to ensure "that the junta is not taken over," and thus fulfill the U.S. "commitment" to El Salvador, was to give the Salvadoran military the kind of aid that would permit it to kill its people much more quickly, more efficiently and in far greater numbers than it was able to do without the benefit of American advisers and technology.

What, Americans asked, was the real nature of the conflict in El Salvador? In time it seemed to me the only adequate answer was a simple one. It was only a war against a nation's children and their allies in subversion, that is to say all those—their teachers, priests, parents—who worked, as the slain American women had worked, to give them any hope. To the extent that the government of El Salvador had a policy to deal with the poverty, hunger, ignorance and unemployment that were the real forces of subversion in that country, it was a policy of infanticide. This was no war on poverty, in spite of the populist tinge the American advisers tried to give to the programs of the junta; it was a war on the poor. It was not hunger that was being eliminated, only the hungry, along with the ignorant and the dispossessed. The beneficiaries of the present had decided to declare war on the future. The current *matanza* resembled nothing so much as a program of postpartum birth control.

By the end of 1980, even massacres were no longer news, unless they were particularly large, dramatic and gruesome ones. Only Amnesty International bothered to print the names of forty-nine Salvadorans who became *desaparecidos* in the space of eight days. Of these, nine—including Jesus Palacios, 15, and Herbert Rivas Aguilar, 17—all disappeared from the town of San Antonio Abad in the space of forty-eight hours. In another unnoticed incident, the National Guard entered the town of Cojutepeque and, the week before Christmas, killed eight persons, including a husband and wife, in the space of an hour. Mass killings that once might have made headlines now consisted only of endless lists of mimeographed names. "DIS/KILLED. CALDERON, Rafael Amilcar. 17 Dec 80. Body found 22 Dec 80," read a typical entry in an Amnesty report in which the names, in single space, ran page after page.

Gradually the war in El Salvador became like a telephone book, and one needed a kind of yellow pages to sort the victims out. Academics? At least ninety teachers "murdered by security forces in El Salvador" in one 10-month period in a government offensive "aimed at eliminating the leadership of the National Association of Salvadoran Educators." Nine parish priests killed; twenty-eight children killed as part of the agrarian reform program in Cuscatlan Department alone; forty trade unionists abducted from a meeting, and never seen again. The reports were all the same—as boring as the yellow pages, finally. "Maria Magdalena Enriquez," read one, "has been found dead in a shallow grave near the port of La Libertad, about 20 miles from San Salvador. She had been shot four times in the head and twice in the chest. She appears to have been killed the day after she was abducted on 3 October while shopping with her young son in San Salvador. Witnesses have now confirmed that two of the heavily armed men who detained Sra. Enriquez were uniformed members of the National Police. Despite evidence confirming her detention by government security forces, representatives of the junta that leads the government of El Salvador have denied that police carried out the detention, and have stated the government 'was not implicated' in the matter. Maria Magdalena Enriquez," the report elaborated, "was the press secretary of the El Salvador Human Rights Commission, an independent human rights monitoring group that provides assistance to victims of human rights abuse, and publicizes their cases."

By January 1981, when President Carter made his decision to restore military aid to the Salvadoran military, about seventy persons a week were being killed for political reasons by the Salvadoran military (not including, as always, those killed in military operations). Among the desaparecidos for that month, Amnesty International noted, were two sisters, "Carolina Concepcion, aged 7, and Sandra Guadalupe, aged 5" and a relative, "Angelica Perez, aged 13," along with four adults, including the girls' parents. A report explained:

On January 28, 1981, at 9:40 P.M., uniformed members of the security forces and the army violently burst into the house of Marianella Garcia Villas, President of the El Salvador Human Rights Commission. She was not at home at the time of the attack, but her home was ransacked. The seven people named above were staying in the house at the time of the attack and were questioned about the whereabouts of Marianella Garcia Villas. When the attackers did not receive the information they wanted, they started to beat and torture the adults in front of the children, who cried and begged them to stop. The children were then also beaten. They were all taken to the central barracks of the National Police in San Salvador.

Despite government claims that those killed by its forces are guerrillas and guerrilla sympathizers [Amnesty added], victims of torture and death in the hands of the security forces were not generally shown to have any direct involvement in armed guerrilla activity.

In another report, Amnesty noted "a consistent pattern of killing by the security forces of peasants, young people and other victims who have not been involved in guerrilla activities." Atypical only because of the size of the massacre was an incident at the Sumpul River, along the border between El Salvador and Honduras, on May 14, 1980, when Salvadoran troops fired on peasant refugees trying to swim the river to safety. According to Father

Alberto Gallagher and Jose Leon Ayala, a Catholic priest and teacher living in Guarita, Honduras, a town near the scene of the killings, 320 bodies were found on the riverbanks. Later the Episcopal Conference of Honduras estimated that as many as six hundred Salvadorans had been killed as they tried to flee the "security forces" of their own country. According to one Honduran witness, Antonia Guardado, Salvadoran troops attacked "hundreds of campesinos, women, old people and children." Describing the "barbarity of the National Guard," she added, "The victims came covered with mud. I still have one of the blankets covered with blood. We gave them what we could."

One Salvadoran woman, aged sixty, who managed to reach the opposite bank, described how her two children were killed. She also told how members of the National Guard raped a woman, then cut her throat, leaving a great pool of blood. "And they were not satisfied with that," she added. "They also hung her body on a barbed-wire fence, and warned that no one go near her. That was shameful, as we could not even cover her private parts with a rush mat."

By June 1981—as the Reagan administration sought to provide the junta with up to $523 million in direct and indirect military and economic aid—all this had been going on, day after day, for more than twenty months. For anyone with any firsthand experience of it, the defining characteristic of the Salvadoran War—besides the killing—was its sameness. Nothing ever changed, except for the rising total of the dead, which by then was about twenty-five thousand, or five times the largest official U.S. estimate of the guerrilla force. Yet in spite of all these killings, subversives still seemed to be everywhere, as numerous as the crowds of young people Ian Mates and I saw everywhere in the barrios of San Salvador. In a new effort to combat the threat, the Salvadoran military—evidently heeding the counsel of its U.S. advisers on the need for "getting more intelligence from the public than before"—began broadcasting death lists of priests, human-rights activists, educators and former members of the government. Salvadorans were invited to expose these subversives, or to kill them themselves if they preferred.

Meanwhile, El Salvador had some new statistics, in addition to the mounting body counts and the soaring total of official U.S. aid. According to the Salvadoran Catholic Church, the "anti-Communist" forces of El Salvador by mid-1981 were killing as many as 2,000 people a month—1,244 farmers, 40 workers, 39 students, 84 government employees, 17 merchants, 2 health workers, 3 professionals and 504 other persons (whose occupations could not be ascertained) was the toll during a typical month. According to the junta's own Ministry of the Interior, more than 200,000 peasants had been displaced from their homes and lands in the time since the slaughter had begun. As for the American-designed land-reform program, by mid-1981, not only its leaders but most of its other Salvadoran employees were dead, in hiding or in exile. Who had murdered these administrators of U.S.-backed reform? According to studies by the Salvadoran land institute itself, the guerrillas played at most a minor role in the disruption of the program designed "to take the revolution away from the Communists." Instead, William Doherty, Jr., the executive director of the American Institute for Free Labor Development, which had been advising the land-reform program on a U.S. Government contract, told a U.S. congressional subcommittee that "at least 70 percent of these killings are attributable not to 'leftist' forces, but to Salvadoran government troops or paramilitary organizations."

While the junta's U.S.-armed troops were killing off the junta's U.S.-paid land-reform workers, El Salvador's anti-Communist elite was busy destroying the free-enterprise system U.S. aid was supposed to defend from the Communist threat. According to no less an authority than President Jose Napoleon Duarte, members of the Salvadoran business community had removed some $1.2 billion in assets, mostly to U.S. banks in Miami and New York, since the American aid program had begun. This was four times the national budget; it was nearly three times what even the immense Reagan aid proposals hoped to provide. According to the junta's own economics minister, Guillermo Dian Salazar, Salvadoran industry was operating at only 50 percent capacity and the junta faced a balance-of-payments deficit on the order of a quarter-billion dollars a year. The unemployment rate, according to United Nations statistics, had risen in the months following the arrival of the first "lethal" U.S. military aid from the 25 percent cited earlier to 50 percent.

In the guise of a struggle to "defend" El Salvador from communism, not only was the military killing off the nation's children, but, with growing American assistance, the country was cannibalizing itself economically, politically and socially. Meanwhile the daily vignettes of the war continued to repeat themselves, like summer reruns of some violence-packed series on TV.

The same day, in March 1981, that three labor leaders are killed, bringing the number of union organizers murdered in the first five months of the year to a total of 193, and the naked, raped and decapitated bodies of two women are also discovered in a garbage heap in San Salvador, an event of considerably more significance occurs: two hundred people are slaughtered as they try to cross the Lempa River to reach Honduras and safety. These massacres along the borders are not news. They have been going on for months. The news is that the new American reconnaissance planes and helicopter gunships and other weapons at last are beginning to change the tactics, if not the substance, of the Salvadoran War. The fleeing refugees are spotted by Salvadoran personnel flying a U.S.-provided helicopter, which is also maintained by U.S. "advisers" in El Salvador. Returning fully armed a short time later, the aircraft machine-guns children in the water and directs ground fire from the bank of the river. The American gunship hovers so close over the fleeing women and children that they can see the pilot's face.

Massacre by machete had become a matanza in which the killers could stalk their victims with the best weapons systems the Pentagon could supply, and fly back to San Salvador in time for a siesta.

El Salvador, both the officials of the junta and their American supporters claimed, was a nation besieged by external aggression. Yet, month after month, a continuing refrain nonetheless filled the reports emanating from El Salvador.

"The government reported no casualties in the attack," ran the sentence which one read over and over again. In 1981, a number of independent observers attempted to form a realistic assessment of the government toll the "Communist onslaught" had inflicted. It was well known that between five hundred and two thousand Salvadoran "subversives," depending on the vicissitudes of the conflict, were being killed every month. But how many Salvadoran men in uniform had fallen victim to the "Communist" assault?

There turned out to be a surprising degree of correlation in the totals various observers had amassed. I found I was on the high side, having come to the conclusion that the toll on the junta's side might be running as high as three hundred. Others placed government fatalities as low as one hundred. Tom Buckley, writing in *The New Yorker* in mid-1981, found his estimate to be the median. "There is no official count of casualties in the armed forces," he wrote, "but the 'In Memoriam' notices that appear in the press suggest there may be something like a hundred and fifty or two hundred dead"—not each month, but "so far," that is to say, in the entire course of the first eighteen months of the war.

At most three hundred—perhaps as few as one hundred—Salvadoran forces killed in the course of what the junta and Washington alike purported was a nation's life-and-death struggle against revolutionary subversion. At least twenty thousand Salvadoran civilians murdered by those same forces over the same period of time. Of all the statistics in El Salvador, that mathematical relationship illuminated the true nature of what was happening there. With between twenty thousand and twenty-five thousand Salvadorans killed by government forces, the ratio of government dead to Salvadorans killed by their own government was, at the absolute minimum, a ratio of one hundred to one, and quite possibly even higher than that. This in fact was a ratio of the same order of magnitude that had informed the matanza of 1932, when—as we have seen—losses to the insurgents were at most thirty-five, but that did not stop the forces of "law and order" from murdering at least ten thousand, and possibly as many as thirty thousand, Salvadorans in return.

In truth the real war in El Salvador had not yet begun. For besides helping to expand and deepen the matanza, the shiploads of American weapons had another effect neither President Carter nor President Reagan intended. Gradually the hapless people the government troops drove into the hills learned to survive, and then, equally gradually, they learned how to fight, both with captured American weapons and weapons of their own. Every massacre produced a double body count: the count of the dead, and the count, even harder to enumerate, of the living who, having seen their friends and families killed, decided to join the guerrillas. All over El Salvador, young men, in the face of oppression by their government, made the same decision the young man of La Libertad had confided to Jean Donovan.

By the beginning of 1984, after four years of slaughter, there were still at most only eight thousand antigovernment insurgents. They were still ill equipped and not really united. After nearly four years of talk in Washington about the Communist threat in El Salvador, the Farabundo Marti Liberation Front was still very far from the gates of San Salvador.

But the years of killing had produced a new development in Salvadoran history. For the first time, there existed a force of peasant insurrectionaries the armed forces of El Salvador could not eradicate—no matter how many U.S. weapons they were given. Gradually, as the guerrilla force grew, government casualties also mounted. Hundreds of government troops were now being killed and wounded every month. The slaughter was no longer one-sided, as it had been in 1932. With the U.S. arms shipments acting as midwife, this latest matanza had given birth to a real insurrection. Four years after the United States had set out to "stop communism" in El Salvador, there was real war there. And no one in Washington or San Salvador knew how either to win or end it. Meanwhile, the slaughter, as opposed to the war, continued.

Often, it seemed to me that even to write logically about the slaughter was to contribute to the obscenity. Was it not dishonest and misleading to write a story with a beginning, a middle and an end about killings that had no beginning, no middle, no end? The very abstraction of words, in such circumstances, becomes a kind of lie, because in the end words are like statistics: they do not show the faces of the dead; they are inadequate to the moral and spiritual corruption of what is taking place.

One had to be a cameraman, it seemed, to really show the tortured face of El Salvador, which perhaps explains why I felt closest to the reality of El Salvador in the company of a photographer like Ian Mates. When I watched him working, and then again when I saw his film, I felt he had done what neither a writer nor the statisticians of death could do. In celluloid at least, the desaparecidos do not disappear. Their faces still gaze out, to haunt us forever. As for the larger meaning of this slaughter, perhaps one had to be a saint to reveal what had happened to the Salvadoran soul.

"Beloved brothers and sisters," Archbishop Romero told his congregation on March 23, 1980:

No government can be effective unless it is rooted in the people, much less so when it seeks to impose itself at the cost of blood and pain.

The archbishop went on to describe the efforts of the U.S.-backed forces "to eliminate the leadership of the popular organizations" and destroy the freedoms "longed for by the people." What could be done to deal with "these horrifying situations"? "The Church, defender of the rights of God, of the law of God, of human dignity and of the human person," Romero told his congregation, "cannot remain silent in the case of so much abomination." From the altar of San Salvador cathedral, the primate of the Salvadoran Catholic Church therefore addressed the following words to "the men of the armed forces, and especially, to the troops of the National Guard, of the police, and of the military posts":

> Brothers, you belong to our people; you kill your own brother peasants; and in the face of an order to kill which comes from a human person, the law of God shall prevail which says DO NOT KILL! No soldier is obliged to obey a command which goes against the law of God. No one is required to comply with an immoral law. It is time now that you recover your conscience, and that you obey your conscience first, rather than the sinful command.
>
> In the name of God, then, and in the name of this suffering people, whose laments reach up to the heavens every day with greater intensity, I BEG OF YOU, I BESEECH YOU, I COMMAND YOU in the name of God, STOP THE REPRESSION!

As always in El Salvador, the price of speaking the truth, like the price of looking truth in the face, was death.

The next day, as he turned to bless his congregation in the course of another mass, Archbishop Romero was shot through the heart with a single bullet fired by a single marksman from a single high-powered rifle.

Romero's killer, ballistics experts agreed, no doubt was an expert who had benefited from the most professional military training that could be had. A vignette of Salvadoran justice followed worthy of General Martinez and the earlier matanza. The killer was never apprehended. The judge assigned to investigate the killings fled the country. The case was closed, and a few days after Romero's murder the U.S. Congress moved to provide the junta with more military assistance to counter "the Communist threat."

"Because you are a Christian and because you have shown that you want to defend human rights," Romero had written to President Carter the month before his murder, "I ask you, if you truly want to defend human rights, to prohibit the giving of military aid to the Salvadoran government." U.S. military aid, Romero warned, would only "sharpen the injustice and repression," strengthen an "unscrupulous military" and "promote the interests of the Salvadoran oligarchy." "In these moments," the archbishop explained, "we are living through a grave economic and political crisis in our country." "It would be unjust and deplorable" for the United States "to frustrate the Salvadoran people, or to repress them and block their autonomous decisions about the economic and political form that our country ought to follow." "I hope," Romero concluded in his letter to the American President, "that your religious sentiments and your feelings for the defense of human rights will move you to accept my position, avoiding by this action worse bloodshed in this suffering country."

Ian Mates photographed the archbishop's funeral, at which tens of thousands of Salvadorans mourned one of the few voices of truth the country had ever known. When the immense crowd was gathered in front of the cathedral, a bomb exploded; soldiers began firing on the unarmed civilians. A terrible melee followed, in which dozens of people were killed. When one saw the film Mates took of the funeral, one saw El Salvador for what it was: children being shot, women being trampled underfoot, bodies falling everywhere. The fate of every anonymous desaparecido had become the fate of the reigning prince of the Salvadoran church. Even the cathedral of San Salvador now was no different from the slums of the capital, the ravines of the countryside and the rivers along the Honduran border: it was only another place pockmarked with bullets and smeared with blood. These images which Mates recorded were broadcast all over the world, and when people saw them, they saw, if only for an instant, what they also would see as the bodies of Jean Donovan and the others were taken from the earth: the true face of El Salvador.

The murder of the archbishop and the attack on his funeral, combined with the influx of American money and arms, marked a turning point in El Salvador. By silencing the archbishop, the junta made the guerrillas the voice of the people. By killing Romero, they resurrected Agustin Farabundo Marti. By driving peaceful demonstrators from the streets of the capital, they also did what General Martinez had done in the 1930s. They established, for the benefit of their American patrons, a clear-cut choice between the "Communists" of the countryside, and themselves. Once again the political agitation of the city was ended. Once again the war against the countryside—with American guns and helicopters and advisers this time—had begun, and as the scene of the war changed, Ian Mates followed the war from the cathedral to the villages. He was there that day, at the Hacienda San Francisco. It was his films of the clearing in the forest that hundreds of millions of people saw; and as the murders of Jean, Dorothy, Ita and Maura were replicated everywhere in El Salvador, Mates seemed to be everywhere too. He pursued the slaughter —he never let the slaughter escape his camera—until January 1981, when the car he was driving hit a mine on a rural road. He died very slowly in a hospital in San Salvador.

It was the death of a cameraman, I thought when I heard about it, in a country where every living person seemed to have a predestined place in the hierarchy of death. For the campesinos, death was a ravine or river crossing. For priests and nuns and bishops, death was an altar. All across El Salvador history was repeating itself, but in another sense it was as though history had never happened, as though the conquistadors had never conquered, as though the Mayan priests still practiced their cults: El Salvador once again was a land of human sacrifice.

What possibly could come out of all this killing? The Americans, like the colonels, said they were fighting for stability: the perennial Salvadoran status quo of death. Though I have no idea what Ian Mates believed, Archbishop Romero had believed the fruit of death was redemption. "As a Christian," he once remarked, "I don't believe in death without resurrection. If they kill me, I will rise again in the Salvadoran people. . . . My hope is that my blood will be like a seed of liberty."

Marti had gone to his rendezvous with General Martinez's firing squad in the 1930s with similar hopes. As in the past, El Salvador was not just a land of murderers who styled themselves a government. It was a country where, it seemed to me, the murdered died with too much grace. Romero was succeeded by another bishop (who spoke more cautiously from the pulpit). Ian Mates's place was taken by other cameramen. The truth was that even the most dramatic events seemed to leave the underlying processes of El Salvador unaffected.

So the voices of El Salvador were muted; the television images seemed fuzzier; but little else changed. For all the talk of subversion, El Salvador, at least for the time being, was safe once again—safe for the junta, safe for President Reagan's stand against worldwide communism, safe for the slaughter to go on. In America, as the months passed, El Salvador gradually was demoted from a human and moral tragedy to a persistent and complex foreign-policy debate. The official statements and congressional speeches and academic analyses became endless, as intrusive and distorting as static on a television tube. One could read the official statements and watch the official spokesmen forever and never glimpse the face of El Salvador, which was only a Salvadoran soldier firing an American gun, and then the vulture plucking the eye from the face of a child.

II
The Last Domino

From the beginning, in Central America, a grim but intelligible logic animated the matanza. But what drove the United States to immerse itself in a bloodbath in which, initially at least, it had not been implicated?

As the U.S. intervention deepened, the mystery only grew deeper and posed questions that were more moral than military, less political than philosophical: Why had the government in Washington chosen to impute such significance to the uprising? Why was it so unswerving in its "commitment" to a regime whose forces were murdering thousands?

To these questions the vultures had no answers, but officials in Washington had a ready reply: there was a great "threat" to the United States in Central America. As the death toll mounted and the destruction expanded, that was one contention no one could dispute. But to one who did not inhabit the official world of security clearances, who had to make do with what one could hear and see in Central America itself, the "threat," while more and more alarming, was quite different from the one the White House and the State Department described.

From this perspective, the great danger confronting the United States was not the "loss" of a small Latin American republic to a few thousand badly armed insurgents; it was that the United States would diminish its own prestige, influence and credibility—in a fundamental way diminish itself—by backing a regime that possessed no legitimacy, legal, moral or human.

Even the newly arrived American military advisers were appalled by what they saw. The countryside was in a state of "anarchy," a U.S. major reported, with roving bands of soldiers indiscriminately "terrorizing the population." An American colonel described a condition resembling war less than it did a general collapse of civilization. The interminable violence had led "to an abandonment of the fields, and the crops . . . would be lost if the war did not end."

Since no substantive U.S. interests would be threatened whichever side won, and since even those opposing the U.S.-backed regime said they wanted friendly relations with the United States, was not a peaceful settlement preferable to perpetuating pointless carnage?

Such might have seemed the logical conclusion to one not privy to the inner workings of American foreign policy. But at the State Department another logic—a veritable doctrine of coercion as an end in itself in the conduct of U.S. foreign policy—dictated American actions.

Heretofore, the Secretary pointed out, in a stern directive designed to scatter the doves and ensure compliance with his own, hard-line approach, it had been the inalterable U.S. policy to "control the destinies of Central America." "Until now," the State Department memorandum stated, "Central America has always understood that governments which we recognize and support stay in power, while those which we do not recognize and support fall." The uprising, however justified politically or morally, was utterly impermissible on U.S. strategic grounds, because it amounted to "a deliberate attempt to undermine our position and set aside our special relationship in Central America." By presuming to resist a tyrannical regime, the guerrillas, as seen through the official U.S. prism, were not attacking tyranny; they were committing aggression against the United States. The United States had "to decide whether we shall tolerate the interference of any other power in Central American affairs or insist upon our own dominant position."

Having defined the choice, the Secretary laid down the law. U.S. intervention on behalf of one of the most uncivilized regimes in the world not only was justifiable; it was necessary "for the simple reason that the national interest absolutely dictates such a course." If, in spite of those considerations, America shirked its responsibilities and the uprising "succeeds it will take many years to recover the ground we shall have lost."

With great accuracy, this memorandum thus described U.S. actions in El Salvador as well as the motives, methods and ends of those actions. It also documented the fact that, by the beginning of the 1980s, the Salvadorans were not the only ones fated to reenact the catastrophes of the past.

Although it reads as though it were composed in 1982 by one of President Reagan's policymakers, the document in question was written in 1927. Its author was Robert Olds, President Coolidge's under secretary of state, and he was prescribing American policy toward Nicaragua, not its neighbor El Salvador. Fifty-three years before the second matanza of the twentieth century began in El Salvador, current U.S. policy in Central America already had been established, and the strategic and ideological doctrine justifying it already had been ordained.

Olds's edict had its intended effects. It silenced internal policy dissent and fixed the United States on a steadfast course of military intervention. Later the consequences of the policy would stir up much criticism, and the State Department would vary its tactics from time to time in an effort to cloak its actions in the mantle of defense against foreign aggression and support for social and economic reform. But U.S. policy remained inflexible. First, the slaughter would be perpetuated—at whatever cost in innocent life—until a "Communist triumph" was prevented, that is to say until the killings eradicated all opposition of any kind. Meanwhile U.S. advisers, training programs and weapons shipments would make the armed forces even more powerful than they were before the killings began, so that the local military could dominate the country after U.S. advisers were withdrawn. Finally, once the U.S.-supported troops had "pacified" the country, they would oversee and thus ensure acceptable results of closely controlled elections. Then, if all went according to plan in the culmination of this final phase, a triumph for American-style liberties would be proclaimed.

In 1927 as in 1982, the subversives the United States set out to destroy in Central America were not Communists. They were supporters of Nicaragua's Liberal Party who had been driven to rebellion by a Conservative dictatorship. But then as later, that did not matter. What mattered, from the perspective of American power, was that these insurgents not only dared to defy U.S. wishes; they were, in the estimation of the State Department, the agents of a conspiratorial outside power whose real objective was not just the conquest of a single small Central American republic, but the defeat and humiliation of the United States.

By the 1980s, the Soviet Union—whether it was involved in El Salvador or not—was not just an American rival. It was a superpower with the capacity, directly or indirectly, to involve itself in Central America if it chose. In the time of Ronald Reagan, Latin America did possess, in the form of Cuba, at least one state closely allied to Moscow. But none of that had been true back in 1927. What could have caused U.S. officials to assume then that U.S. failure to control one small republic inevitably would lead to the loss of all Central America to an outside aggressor, with incalculable consequences for the United States itself?

"The action of Mexico in the Nicaraguan crisis," Secretary Olds declared, "is a direct challenge to the United States." Just as the Mexicans, five years later, would be accused of manufacturing the uprising against General Martinez in El Salvador, so also, in the late 1920s, was the Mexican conspiracy believed to explain every problem the United States faced in Nicaragua as well.

As Professor Millett observes in his study of U.S. intervention in Nicaragua *Guardians of the Dynasty*, peace back then—like peace in El Salvador in the 1980s—was inadmissible, because it would have "conflicted with the State Department's insistence" on putting the exercise of American might ahead of every local consideration of justice. Then as later, the devastation of a small Central American republic was a small price to pay for preventing "a Mexican triumph," as the State Department described it in 1927, or a "Cuban breakthrough," as it was defined in 1981.

Would the United States forsake its principles, shirk its duty and let "a deliberate attempt to undermine our position and set aside our special relationship in Central America" pass unresisted? Or would it act with "due regard for our own safety and protection" and the safety and protection of the Central Americans as well?

Secretary Olds had circulated his memorandum of force the day after New Year's 1927. Just ten weeks later, U.S. troops were in full control of all opposition centers in Nicaragua, as well as the Caribbean and Pacific ports and the national capital. To some, this U.S. occupation of a small and defenseless nation might seem to constitute an act of interference in its internal affairs, indeed a clear-cut act of aggression.

But as in El Salvador fifty-five years later, U.S. officials were quick to point out this was not the case at all. Explaining his Nicaraguan intervention, President Coolidge used words virtually identical to those heard from President Reagan in our own time. American troops were not on the offensive; they were only helping Nicaragua defend itself against a "serious threat to stability and constitutional government." Nor, whatever were the appearances to the contrary, was the United States intervening in Nicaragua's internal affairs. It was helping the Nicaraguans resist aggression "brought about by outside influences." Lest thousands of U.S. troops be insufficient to protect Nicaragua from Bolshevik-Mexican aggression, the U.S.-supported regime soon became the beneficiary of an El Salvador-style military aid program as well.

President Coolidge, like President Reagan later on, was a well-known adversary of "Bolshevism," whether that conspiracy took the form of insurrection in Latin America or subversion at home. In 1919, Coolidge, then governor of Massachusetts, had become a national figure by crushing the Boston police strike. As Samuel Eliot Morison observes, "This caught the imagination of a public jittery about the Red Menace," assured Coolidge's vice presidential nomination in 1920, and thus, by 1927, following Harding's death, had made Coolidge commander in chief of the U.S. forces sent to Nicaragua to stamp out subversion there as well.

Reflexive anticommunism, however, was by no means the sole motive for sending in the Marines. As in El Salvador later, the U.S. purpose was, as U.S. officials saw it, political and social reform. "Control of venereal disease," Professor Millett relates, was a major U.S. policy objective—one that proved as elusive as land reform would in El Salvador, as U.S. officers discovered after handing out prophylactic kits, when they found Nicaraguan "enlisted men using the contents to polish their shoes." Other U.S. advisers busied themselves, as one diarist recorded, preventing the Nicaraguans from "blow[ing] their whistles all nite." This was one reform that seems to have lost more hearts and minds than it won over. "Well," the marine responsible for enforcing the policy concluded, "one cannot satisfy all the people. Some like to sleep."

By what right did Americans decide whether the Nicaraguans blew whistles or not? The State Department, as Dexter Perkins notes in *A History of the Monroe Doctrine,* might choose "to rest its case upon the danger of Bolshevism," but as most Americans saw it, our purpose in Nicaragua was selfless. Had it not always been our duty, as Americans, not merely to defend our freedoms, but to share them with others? And going back to the days of President Monroe, had not an idealistic and generous America been the champion of liberty throughout the western hemisphere?

Like so many of our foreign wars, the intervention in Nicaragua, at least in the beginning, seemed not only a prudent defense of our national security against external conspiracy, but a moral duty dictated by our national role of promoting liberty around the world.

Whatever the rationales, the results, at least at first, were indisputable. The Mexican menace was thwarted. Indeed, were it not for the proclamations from Washington, one never would have suspected the conspiracy existed at all. The advancing U.S. troops met no resistance. Nicaragua was "saved"— but only at a price both we and the Nicaraguans are still paying today. The first bill came due immediately—though it was payable on a seemingly eternal installment plan. It was one thing to get into Nicaragua, but as Washington quickly rediscovered in 1927, it was quite another thing to find a way out. One must say "rediscovered," because Nicaragua already had taught the United States the same lesson, even though it was a lesson the Coolidge administration had not learned. Back in 1912, President Wilson also had sent the Marines down to Nicaragua. Like Wilson's similar interventions in Mexico, Haiti and the Dominican Republic, it was all part of an American effort "to teach the South Americans to elect good men." The problem was that in Nicaragua, as in so many other Latin American nations, "good men" seemed to be elected only when U.S. troops counted the votes. The U.S. Marines had been obliged to remain in Nicaragua until 1925, and scarcely were they withdrawn when the little republic reverted to the anarchy that had led Wilson to send them in thirteen years earlier.

Wilson's war for democracy in Central·America is now as utterly forgotten in the United States as Coolidge's crusade against the Bolshevik conspiracy— as the similar effort in El Salvador no doubt will be in the fullness of time. Yet just as the current El Salvador intervention provides a case study in all the American illusions that have informed much vaster catastrophes of American foreign policy, so Wilson's Central American adventure was a dress rehearsal in miniature for the tragedy of presumptuousness that later would grow out of Wilson's "war to end war," and to confer democracy on Europe through the Fourteen Points.

In both cases the key to making the world safe for democracy, as Colonel House, Wilson's closest adviser, instructed one American proconsul in Latin America, was U.S. "insistence on orderly, constitutional democratic government." But what if this insistence was ignored?

The day when U.S. armies and CIA agents would be on permanent patrol, from one end of the "free world" to the other, was not yet at hand. But long before the United States became a superpower, our presidents were accustomed to "defending democracy" in Latin America the same way they later defended it in many other parts of the world. The Marines were there to overthrow governments that did not correspond to our idea of democracy and to occupy Latin American nations lest their freedom from foreign intervention be subverted. As in the future, this policy was thoroughly bipartisan. Democrats like Wilson, Republicans like Taft, progressives like Theodore Roosevelt and conservatives like Coolidge all concurred that our right, indeed our duty, to intervene in our neighbors' affairs was as old as the Monroe Doctrine, that is to say nearly as old as the republic itself.

For some six years, before the Great War in Europe diverted his attention to an even vaster stage, President Wilson acted as though he were a professor of democracy—and the nations of Latin America unruly undergraduates. Would the United States recognize one regime? Would it lend money to another? Not unless these adolescent Latin nations followed the American textbook of democracy. The former president of Princeton University was now President of the United States—first Latin America, then the whole world became the great lecture hall where he gave his civics lessons. Eventually Wilson's classroom would be Versailles's Hall of Mirrors, where the minefields of World War II would be laid. Later still, the members of the U.S. Senate would be Wilson's students—and like the ungrateful Europeans, those selfish "isolationists" would also fail the final exam.

But, long before these much vaster catastrophes unfolded, Wilson's war for freedom in Central America revealed what many later American wars for freedom also would show: the American urge to "save" others leads often only to perdition, for both them and us.

Not that Wilson's intervention seemed anything less than a resounding triumph for democracy at first. In 1912, as in 1927, the Marines quickly put down the Nicaraguan uprising and restored to power the American-supported President. Having democratized Nicaragua with bayonets, President Wilson did not fail to reward the United States for its good works. Two years after the Marines had restored "orderly, constitutional democratic government" to Nicaragua, the State Department presented to that government for signature the Bryan-Chamorro treaty, by which Nicaragua surrendered to the United States nothing less than its entire national destiny.

Even though it was a poor, small nation, with no important natural resources, Nicaragua had always seemed a country with an important future because of its privileged geographical location.

Ever since the Spanish Conquest, Nicaragua's ideal situation as the site of a canal across the Central American isthmus, linking the Caribbean Sea with the Pacific Ocean had been its most obvious asset. Nicaragua in fact provided, even more than Panama, the most feasible route for a path between the seas. In Nicaragua the isthmus was wider than in Panama, but where in Panama high mountains divided the two oceans, a series of rivers and lakes almost linked them in Nicaragua.

Generations of Nicaraguans grew up, as a result, believing that their country was as much a land of destiny as the United States. But as John A. Booth points out in *The End and the Beginning,* his study of the Sandinista revolution, the arbitrary decision in Washington to build the canal in Panama "shattered Nicaragua's hopes for a waterway and set in motion in Nicaragua events from which that country has yet to recover."

The Panama Canal, then under construction, would not be completed until 1914. In the meantime, there was nothing to prevent Nicaragua, as a sovereign nation, from constructing a canal of its own, though that could be accomplished only with massive foreign financial and technical assistance. The Nicaraguans would have derived all the benefits that would have flowed from such an immense project, and the world as a whole would have enjoyed the benefits of two canals in Central America: the system of locks the Americans were constructing across Panama, and the sea-level canal Nicaragua would provide.

But, in Washington, any such project was perceived to pose a "threat" to the United States as dire as any the Bolsheviks were later supposed to present. A Nicaraguan canal would have undercut the U.S. dominion over interocean traffic the Panama Canal was soon to provide. And if a canal in Nicaragua were to be built with "outside" assistance, Japan or some European power might suddenly rival the United States as an influential power in Central America.

In 1909 the United States disposed of that "threat" the same way it has dealt with many similar "threats" in Latin America. When the longtime Nicaraguan President, Jose Santos Zelaya, sought foreign support for the construction of a canal, the outgoing Roosevelt and incoming Taft administrations engineered a revolt against the Nicaraguan Government—and then landed marines on the Caribbean coast and occupied Bluefields, the principal port there, in order to provide the dissidents a secure base of operations.

This was one Bay of Pigs invasion that achieved its intended results. Under intense U.S. military, economic and diplomatic pressure, Zelaya was forced to flee the country. A widespread revolt soon broke out against the new President the Americans had put in power. Faced with the choice of supporting an unpopular protégé or changing its policy, Taft chose to send in the Marines again, and it was that intervention which Wilson in turn escalated into a full-scale counterinsurgency war.

The Taft administration had disposed of Zelaya. The 1914 treaty the Wilson administration imposed on Nicaragua disposed of the "threat" of a Nicaraguan canal once and for all. For the sum of $3 million, most of which went to its American creditors, the indebted regime the Marines had installed ceded to the United States the exclusive right to build a canal in its own country. The exclusive right to build a canal in Nicaragua, of course, was the exclusive right not to build a canal as well. The country that once seemed on the way to becoming a crossroads of the world remains a strategically irrelevant backwater to this day.

Wilson's war for democracy in Central America, like his later crusade for freedom in Europe, thus had the principal result of deeply embittering its supposed beneficiaries. Indeed it kindled a nationalist reaction to American hegemony that would find its complete fulfillment only in the triumph of the Sandinista revolution in 1979.

One of the victims of Wilson's attempt to teach the Nicaraguans "to elect good men" was Benjamin Zeledon, a former teacher, journalist, district judge and representative to the Central American Court of Justice. When the young insurgent leader was captured, the Americans were in a position to show magnanimity, and spare his life. Instead the U.S. commander suggested that "through some inaction on our part someone might hang him." With Washington's approval, Zeledon was hanged. Then his body was desecrated and dragged through the streets.

Before his death, however, this victim of exemplary justice had handed down a verdict of his own. The United States, Zeledon declared, would suffer "eternal infamy" for "having employed your arms against the weak who have been struggling for the reconquest of the sacred rights of [their] fatherland." President Wilson took no notice. Of what import was Nicaragua, now that a whole world waited to be made safe for democracy? But the fate of Zeledon, and the U.S. role in it, was not lost on others. As Thomas W. Walker relates in his book *Nicaragua: The Land of Sandino:*

> There, by historical coincidence, a short, skinny, seventeen-year-old boy was among those who witnessed government troops kicking [Zeledon's] lifeless form. This seemingly insignificant teenager—who later commented that the scene had made his "blood boil with rage"—was Augusto Cesar Sandino.

One wonders what Salvadoran teenagers are watching today, as the mutilated bodies are dumped from trucks; what "aggression" they will commit against us in the fullness of time, and what defensive measures we will take in return.

Zeledon's death, in 1912, like Marti's execution, in 1932, and Archbishop Romero's assassination, in 1982, demonstrated the power of bullets to stifle dissent. But by 1927, Nicaragua, like El Salvador later, proved another truth. Not even massacre can permanently expunge the human desire for freedom; sometimes, in fact, armies only ignite the flames of resistance they are supposed to stifle. When President Coolidge sent in the Marines, Nicaragua had not been in the throes of real revolution, only in its usual state of political anarchy. But by mid-July 1927 a real Nicaraguan revolt had broken out, and by the end of the year the United States found itself bogged down in an indecisive and evidently endless ground war in Central America. It had become necessary to run search-and-destroy missions against the Nicaraguans in order to save them, also to shell them with heavy artillery. Wilson's war in Nicaragua had been a kind of New Haven tryout production of his approach to World War I.

Coolidge's war in Nicaragua soon seemed like a work in progress for World War II. During the battle of Ocotal, Sandino's guerrillas were fighting U.S.-supported national guardsmen when a formation of five U.S. warplanes appeared overhead. As Bernard Diederich recounts in his book on the Somoza dynasty:

> The planes formed a column and made reconnaissance flights, quickly locating concentrations of Sandinistas. And then began the first organized dive-bombing attack in history—long before the Nazi Luftwaffe was popularly credited with the "innovation."

Only one U.S. marine was killed in the battle; more than a hundred Nicaraguans died in the U.S. air attack. On one side were thousands of U.S. marines, with the best equipment the military arsenals of the time could provide. Opposing them was a shadowy force, commanded by an equally shadowy leader, Augusto Cesar Sandino, whose name would dominate the future of Nicaragua the same way the name of Agustin Farabundo Marti dominates El Salvador today. The United States could drop bombs on Nicaragua, but the problem there was the same one the United States would later encounter in other countries. Air raids, even superior numbers on the ground, were ineffective against a resourceful and dedicated guerrilla force that believed it was defending liberty against a foreign aggressor.

In Washington some dismissed Sandino as a bandit chieftain holding out for the biggest bribe in Yankee dollars he could get to lay down his arms. Others, as always, perceived the sinister hand of the Mexican-Bolshevik conspiracy. But the truth of the matter is that Sandino, like his Salvadoran contemporary Marti—and like the guerrillas still fighting in their names in Central America today—was a product both of his times and of the constant impulses of the human heart. "Quite simply," as Walker observes, Sandino "found the U.S. occupation and domination of his country to be offensive and unacceptable." As the guerrilla leader himself put it, "The sovereignty and liberty of a people are not to be discussed, but rather, defended with weapons in hand."

Sandino might have explained his resistance in terms the Founding Fathers had used during our own War of Independence. And he might have been fighting outrages we Americans also would have considered it our duty to resist, were they ever inflicted on us. But in Washington in the 1920s, such statements had no more influence on the Coolidge administration than Zeledon's comments, before going to the firing squad, had on President Wilson, or Archbishop Romero's entreaties, before his assassination, had on President Carter. The fundamental maxim of Olds's policy had been force.

And so, then as later, U.S. calculations were insensible to the human yearnings, among the Central Americans, for liberty.

It had been as easy, in 1927, for the Marines to occupy Nicaragua as it had been in 1912. But President Coolidge soon discovered what President Wilson earlier had, and what many future presidents would come to learn as well. Occupying a foreign nation, even a small one, year after year, is expensive. Yet the foreign military and financial costs are minuscule in comparison to the domestic political costs when the occupation must be sustained in the face of armed revolt by the very people our intervention is supposed to help. For nearly six years, the marines would chase Sandino up the slopes of volcanoes —and then down the other sides—with no more success than our helicopter gunships would later have as they pursue the Salvadoran guerrillas.

Newspapers became suddenly as skeptical of the State Department's tales of Mexican subversion as the media later would be of the State Department "White Paper" on Communist interference in El Salvador. Will Rogers made fun of the great crusade in the little country, and where some saw a bad joke, other Americans saw a moral issue. Leftists held rallies to raise funds for medical supplies for Sandino's forces, just as the American television actor Edward Asner would for the Salvadoran guerrillas in 1982. In Congress, as Millett points out, the Marines—so recently lauded as the missionaries of civilization—were now denounced as "ambassadors of death." Soon some normally responsible politicians were going so far as to suggest that strafing Nicaraguan campesinos from airplanes was a moral obligation not ordained by the Monroe Doctrine at all. "The Monroe Doctrine," declared Senator William E. Borah, of Idaho,

> has nothing whatever to do and furnishes us no guide with reference to dealing with different factions or different conditions internal in any Central American country. . . . Those who believe in the Monroe Doctrine, and think it of vital importance to the people of this country, are doing it a great disservice by undertaking to invoke it in aid of any kind of interference in those countries, either Central or South American.

There followed a dress rehearsal for both the Pentagon Papers and President Reagan's 1983 decision to send former Secretary of State Henry Kissinger to search for solutions in Central America. At President Coolidge's behest, a high-level group, headed by future Secretary of State Henry L. Stimson, went down to Nicaragua on its fact-finding mission. It came back with a Vietnamization program in its steamer trunks.

The U.S. would soldier on in Nicaragua, even escalate the war if necessary —but only until the Nicaraguans themselves were sufficiently trained to carry on the killing by themselves. One side in Nicaragua called itself the Conservatives, the other the Liberals. They might as well have called themselves the Montagues and the Capulets. Beneath the chronic Nicaraguan civil wars lay ancient feudal vendettas, between the rival towns of Granada and Leon. As

58 UNMANIFEST DESTINY

the U.S. intervention persisted, however, even the significance of those obscure rivalries faded. It no longer mattered who was a Hatfield, who a McCoy. The only real struggle now was between those who were in the pay of the Americans, and those the Americans chose to bomb.

The people the State Department saw as Bolshevik subversives were only illiterate peasants trying to scratch a subsistence living from the soil. As for the "friends of freedom," they were only the same parasitic coterie, swarming like flies around the American arms shipments and handouts of money, that one has seen in our own time from Saigon to San Salvador. Poverty, exploitation, foreign domination were the real subversives in Nicaragua. And far more than any other factors, they successfully conspired to make Nicaragua a country which, both materially and morally, had, in the early-twentieth century, no obvious claim to superiority over the state of the country half a millennium earlier, before the conquistadors had arrived.

Certainly so far as the United States was concerned, the most vexing problem was the same problem that so complicated U.S. policy in El Salvador half a century later. This was the chronic militarization of politics. Political warfare was the permanent condition in Nicaragua.

How to end this militarization of national life? Stimson, a former colonel, hit upon the same solution that Secretary Haig, a former general, later would devise for El Salvador. The way to end all those *coups d'état* and civil wars was to build up the armed forces. The way to promote constitutionalism in Central America was to concentrate all power in an American-trained officer corps. The Marines had saved Nicaragua from the Bolsheviks. Surely the way to make Nicaragua safe for democracy forever was to assure a permanent military occupation of the country—not by the U.S. Marines, but by the Nicaraguans themselves. As Stimson later explained it, after he became Hoover's Secretary of State, the key to peace with honor was

> the establishment of an absolutely non-partisan, non-political Guardia which will devote its entire attention to the preservation of peace, law and order.

There was only one problem with this "solution": it was based on the utter fantasy that the military, which was the essential problem, could be used to solve all the problems the military itself had created.

Even under Coolidge, the Nicaraguan War had been no more popular than our Salvadoran intervention is today. "There is a great deal of criticism in this country," complained Frank B. Kellogg, Coolidge's second Secretary of State, in 1928, "about the way in which these operations are being dragged out with constant sacrifice of American lives and without any concrete results." The advent of the Great Depression generated even less public enthusiasm for a war in Central America.

But how could the United States extricate itself from a pointless, divisive war without admitting that America had made a mistake? Whatever its deficiencies so far as Central America was concerned, the Stimson Plan possessed the same domestic advantages that the Vietnamization program, forty years later, would have. It allowed the Administration in Washington to prolong an unpopular war while seeming to end it. It created the impression of power being handed over to the Nicaraguans while in fact U.S. domination of Nicaragua became greater than ever before.

The American creation of the Nicaraguan National Guard nonetheless raised a question as old as Plato. Who would guard the guardsmen? A semblance of civilian supremacy prevailed in Nicaragua so long as its armed forces were commanded by Americans. But what would happen when the Yankees went home? Providentially, Stimson, on his brief visit in 1928, had happened upon just the kind of American-style Nicaraguan that was needed to maintain respect for American-style liberties.

"Somoza is a very frank, friendly, likeable young Liberal," wrote Stimson, "and his attitude impresses me more favorably than almost any other." Somoza spoke a colloquial American that would astonish American visitors for decades. He had translated for Stimson during his "fact-finding" tour—and Somoza had been careful to give the American dignitary only the answers he wanted to hear. Because they found him "likeable," the Americans placed in charge of the National Guard the man whose family would oppress the nation for more than fifty years.

Thus metaphor was added to prophecy. Until 1979, Somoza and his sons, along with their wives, children, in-laws, relatives and hangers-on would never cease to translate for the Americans. The United States had but to ask, in Nicaragua, to receive from the Somozas answers it wanted. In return, all the Somozas asked was the liberty of their country—that is to say, the liberty a horde of locusts takes with an unguarded field.

Having barged into Nicaragua in 1927, the United States bugged out in early 1933. The Republican "defense" of Central America against revolution, like everything else connected with the Hoover administration, had been repudiated in the 1932 elections. The age of Franklin Roosevelt's "Good Neighbor Policy" was at hand. The Stimson mission was soon forgotten, except as a footnote to U.S. diplomacy. Yet this was a most instructive chapter in the history of the Monroe Doctrine and all the other doctrines U.S. presidents later would try to enforce around the world. What had begun as an American effort, under Wilson, to teach the Nicaraguans democracy had led to the creation of an American-supported dictatorship that would last until the presidency of Jimmy Carter. Nicaragua was the greatest long-term success for a policy we have pursued—in the end, no matter how prolonged, with disastrous consequences—from Vietnam to Iran to El Salvador. This has consisted in the attempt to crush revolution and so "stabilize" a foreign country, through use of an American-chosen leader and a surrogate army, so as to avoid the military and financial, above all the domestic political, costs of occupying the country ourselves.

In a strict military sense, however, the long American war in Nicaragua was a complete failure. For even as the Marines pulled out, leaving Nicaragua in the hands of Somoza and his guardsmen, one thing was clear: "In more than five years of warfare," as Millett points out, "the Guardia and the Marines failed to eliminate Sandino, leaving him as great a threat in January 1933 as he had been at any previous point in his career."

A month after the Marines withdrew, in February 1933, it became clear the entire American war in Nicaragua had been fought for nothing. Once the Americans were gone, Sandino showed he was no revolutionary (a statement the Sandinistas would consider sacrilege today), only that most paradigmatical of American foreign-policy victims, an honest nationalist. The erstwhile agent of the Bolshevik-Mexican conspiracy wired Managua, offering to negotiate. Within days, the guerrilla leader the Marines had chased in vain for nearly six years was riding around Managua in Somoza's limousine. A peace settlement was negotiated in less than a day. To quote Millett: "Sandino even declared that he had never believed that United States actions in Nicaragua represented the actual sentiments of most Americans and that he had no hostility toward Americans who came to Nicaragua to work, providing they did not come as bosses." It seemed time for a good-neighbor policy not just in Washington, but in Managua, too.

There was only one problem: U.S. policy had created a monster, in this case the Nicaraguan National Guard. A little more than a year later, during one of Sandino's visits to Managua, troops of the National Guard kidnapped the guerrilla leader, took him to an airfield just outside Managua and murdered him in cold blood.

"[N]o one denies that Somoza was the one who eventually gave the order to shoot Sandino," Millett writes, just as fifty years later no Salvadoran officer would ever be punished for the murders of U.S. citizens in El Salvador, let alone for the wholesale massacre of their own countrymen.

Somoza, in his capacity as head of the National Guard, had been effective dictator of Nicaragua since the day he had replaced the Americans, which was New Year's 1933. The murder of Sandino had removed the last possible counterbalance to his dictatorship. But Somoza—ever wary of antagonizing his American patrons—waited until 1936 to overthrow the civilian President the U.S.-supervised elections had placed in office, just as in El Salvador General Martinez for a time ruled through a civilian figurehead in deference to U.S. sensibilities. But these civilians in presidential sashes—like Duarte and Magana in El Salvador—were only department-store mannequins, to be removed from the window once the Americans had come inside and bought. On New Year's 1937—exactly a decade, minus a day, since Secretary Olds had circulated his memo about sending in the Marines because "the national interest absolutely dictates such a course"—Somoza installed himself as President of the Republic of Nicaragua as American diplomats looked on.

By 1937, the State Department had more substantial problems to engage its attention than Central America: The Japanese were overrunning China; the Italians had overrun Ethiopia; the Nazis had reoccupied the Rhineland. The Four Horsemen of the Apocalypse, less than twenty years after Wilson had carried democracy to Versailles in his briefcase, were loose again. And as the diplomats scurried from Berchtesgaden to Munich, laboring to bolt barn doors, one of the most important costs of our long intervention in Nicaragua was revealed: We Americans had been too busy resisting Bolshevism in Nicaragua to help defend China against the Japanese—too committed to defending democracy against the "threat" Sandino posed to help defend democracy against the threat of Mussolini, Franco and Hitler. And so now the United States, like the rest of the world, was teetering toward another global war. It will be interesting, in due course, to see what problems our leaders' obsession with "saving" El Salvador also have left us unprepared to meet.

By 1937, Franklin Delano Roosevelt had far too many problems on his hands to waste his time making and unmaking regimes in the Latin American tropics. Nonetheless, Somoza's shameless usurpation of power with U.S. guns was a flagrant insult—"a direct challenge," as both Olds and Haig would have put it—to every tenet of U.S. policy in Latin America. Woodrow Wilson certainly would not have recognized such a regime. Even the laconic Coolidge probably would have had it overthrown and the constitutional President restored by U.S. bayonets.

Roosevelt would indeed prove himself a good neighbor—to the dictators of Latin America, if not to those they repressed. In 1939, he received Somoza, quite literally, like a king in the course of a state visit to the United States. But beneath all the pageantry, there were no illusions. Like the Great Depression and the growing crisis in Europe, Somoza and his army of U.S.-trained thugs were only another legacy of all the real foreign-policy opportunities the United States had squandered between Versailles and the stock-market crash of 1929, and Roosevelt knew it. "He's a sonofabitch, but he's ours," he wrote of Somoza, using the same words later American presidents would apply to leaders like Chiang Kai-shek, Diem and Batista.

Much later, the Somozas were supposed to be vital to U.S. interests in Latin America because, whatever their deficiencies, they possessed the virtue of being such staunch "anti-Communists." But it would be a mistake to elevate Somoza to the status of a man of principles. His real talent was his ability to sense whatever "threat" was agitating the American imagination at any one moment and then jump on the bandwagon even before the Americans themselves fully realized it was rolling.

At the time of Somoza's 1939 visit, for example, he was able to exploit the groundless "threat" of a Nazi fifth column taking over Latin America as successfully as, earlier, he had played on America's fear of Bolshevism. "I consider every Nicaraguan aviator and soldier as a potential fighting man for the U.S.," he declared, two and a half years before the attack on Pearl Harbor brought the United States into the war. The man who had seen Henry Stimson coming down the gangplank twelve years earlier could recognize an even bigger opportunity in the offing. No matter that Somoza's official flatterers were wont, with his own encouragement, to compare his greatness to the greatness of Hitler and Mussolini. No matter that Somoza's youth gang, called the Blue Shirts, was modeled on Hitler's Brownshirts. Suddenly Somoza was Washington's own little sentinel against fascism in Central America. Japan attacked Pearl Harbor on December 7, 1941. Somoza issued a declaration of war on the Axis twenty-four hours after Roosevelt did.

The Axis, whatever its capacities elsewhere, posed no more of a threat to Central America than the Bolsheviks had in 1927 or the "Sino-Soviet bloc" did later. But, for a figure like Somoza, there were manifest advantages in being, by turns, more anti-Bolshevik than Secretary Olds, more anti-Nazi than Roosevelt and more anti-Communist than John Foster Dulles later on. In fact, Somoza derived the same advantages the Salvadoran military later gained by being more right-wing than Ronald Reagan.

First, Somoza got from Roosevelt what he also had been given by Coolidge and Hoover: lots of American money, and American guns. Lend-lease weapons poured into the arsenals of the Nicaraguan National Guard at the very moment the Luftwaffe was bombing London and U.S. troops were being overwhelmed by the Japanese at Corregidor. Giving Somoza even more weapons for the repression of his people might seem a grotesque diversion of American resources, but Henry Stimson was now Roosevelt's Secretary of War, and Somoza continued to interpret for the Americans in Nicaragua. The U.S. arms shipments, Somoza explained, would assure that "neither expatriate Nicaraguans nor resident Nazis make any kind of diversion for the United States in this country."

From this initial blank check, a second and even more important advantage flowed. Every opponent of Somoza was now a "Nazi," just as, earlier, Sandino had been a "Bolshevik," and after World War II every Nicaraguan who opposed Somoza and his heirs would be a "Communist." In the 1940s, American journalists searched Central America as tirelessly for fifth columnists and Nazi agents as they earlier had sought out Bolsheviks and Mexican subversives—as tirelessly as they seek out Marxist guerrillas and Cuban agents today. From Nicaragua, John Gunther had good news to report: One of Somoza's rivals in the military had been fired because his "son-in-law was German." The Somoza family had taken over German firms and real estate in Nicaragua. A German businessman had been arrested and a Nicaraguan thrown in prison for criticizing President Roosevelt. Somoza "passionately admires Mr. Roosevelt," Gunther explained. "Economically as well as politically," he added, "Nicaragua is closely dependent on the United States."

America's willingness to consider any Latin American dictator a good neighbor so long as he was an anti-Nazi dictator consolidated Somoza's grip on Nicaragua during World War II. Our fear of "losing" Central America to the Russians and the Cubans would assure U.S. support for Somoza's sons into the 1970s. In the end, the Somozas would be removed from power only by a national uprising in which three hundred thousand people, more than 10 percent of Nicaragua's 2.5 million people, would be killed or mutilated as a result of the U.S. effort to promote "stability and constitutional government" there. No doubt just as many Salvadorans will pay the same price in the current matanza, though that will be only the first installment if, as seems entirely possible, we "win" in El Salvador the same kind of victory we won in Nicaragua fifty years ago.

Though no Americans died in combat in Nicaragua after 1933, the United States, too, paid a very high price for "saving" Nicaragua in 1927 and keeping it "safe" for the next fifty-two years. The great illusion was that Somoza (or Diem in South Vietnam or the Shah in Iran or the generals in El Salvador) could "stabilize" such a country, instead of only manufacturing a time bomb sure, sooner or later, to blow up in America's face.

But the even more dangerous illusion was that we Americans could let Somoza do the killing without getting blood on our own hands. What became manifest in El Salvador later had already been manifest in Nicaragua long before: to commit the United States to a regime of torture and murder in a foreign country is to taint ourselves, as well, with the most loathsome corruptions.

Somoza's most shameless flatterer, the silent partner in the giant scam he had made of a whole nation, was Thomas E. Whelan, the ambassador of the United States—an official the Nicaraguans called "Somoza's shadow." Assassination? Torture? Bribery? Rigged elections? Electric shocks and laundered money became the stock-in-trade not just of the Nicaraguan Government, but of the government of the United States. These costs, however, proved to be trivial in comparison to the most important result: by the 1960s, our long collusion with the Somozas helped bring the United States, and the rest of the world, closer to annihilation than at any other moment in history, either before or since.

In 1961 the United States once again faced the consequences of its support for dictatorship; only, this time the uprising erupted even closer to home, in Cuba, where that country's Somoza-like dictator, Fulgencio Batista, had been overthrown.

Like the lessons of Sandino's uprising in Nicaragua, the lessons of Castro's revolution in Cuba were there to be learned. The main lesson, quite simply, was that precisely because they are dictators, dictators, even when we support them, almost always are eventually brought down by revolution—because their suppression of peaceful political process means revolution is the only way left to get rid of them. If the United States really did wish to forestall revolution, the logical policy would be not to support dictatorship in the first place.

When it came to Cuba, that logic had no more influence on the Kennedy administration in 1961 than it had had on the Coolidge administration in 1927 or would have on the Reagan administration in 1981. Since the "loss" of Cuba could not flow from U.S. mistakes, surely it must be the product of some sinister, extra-hemispheric plot. As earlier in Nicaragua and later in El Salvador, the fundamental questions were not even really debated. The only question was how, and from where, the U.S. invasion might be mounted.

Nicaragua, the Somozas informed their American friends, would be only too delighted to provide the CIA with training camps, airfields and secret bases for the Bay of Pigs invasion. In one sense, history was repeating itself; in another sense, history was sliding toward an abyss.

The CIA's mercenaries would be no more able to eliminate Castro than the Marines had been able to eliminate Sandino. But the American illusion that all the factors producing revolution in Latin America could be undone with bullets and bombs was setting the stage for the Cuban missile crisis of 1962.

A kind of domino theory was at work, although it did not operate as the State Department supposed. Coolidge's invasion of Nicaragua had paved the way for Kennedy's invasion of Cuba, just as Johnson's intervention in Vietnam would lead to Nixon's Cambodia "incursion," and the eventual "loss" of Nicaragua itself under Carter would lead to Reagan's intervention in El Salvador. The dominoes that would topple were successive U.S. presidential administrations, not little countries in Latin America or Asia. And what pushed them over in each case was the American refusal to look reality squarely in the face. Had later presidents learned the lesson of Sandino and Somoza, they might not have made the same mistake in Cuba; and had they learned the lesson of Castro and Batista, perhaps the Vietnam "mistake" would never have been made.

But we Americans are a forgetful people, with the result that a dismal pattern constantly repeats itself. Like Secretary Olds, we suddenly consider countries like Nicaragua great "test cases." Then, like Secretary Stimson, we find the test not to our liking and so manufacture illusory plans to transfer the catastrophes we have created to others. Finally we pretend that the country in question never much mattered, one way or the other, to us at all—often because some new "test case" has begun to excite our obsessions.

In 1927 the consequence was American dive bombers killing Nicaraguans. In 1962 it was a nuclear confrontation that brought the whole world to the brink of annihilation. Later the consequence was nearly sixty thousand American—and many more than a million Indochinese—war dead, just as today it is our implication—all in the name of the defense of democracy—in the murder of tens of thousands of human beings in El Salvador. These various melodramas fitfully attract our attention. But we seldom notice an even more pervasive consequence of this pattern of attempting to defend ourselves against illusory "threats" by killing those who have done us no harm.

It is, quite simply, that for every Zeledon or Sandino we Americans help destroy, we also give at least one Somoza a historical lease on life.

When it comes to choosing our friends, or deciding who our enemies will be, our secretaries of state and presidents almost always apply a political, indeed an ideological, test. Are the Salvadoran colonels—or the Somozas, or the Shah or Thieu or Lon Nol—sufficiently "anti-Communist" to merit our support?

We might spare others—and even more important, we might spare ourselves—many catastrophes if we applied quite a different test in the choice of our "test cases": one of human character, honesty, decency and integrity. We shall never know what a man like Sandino might have made of a nation like Nicaragua, just as we shall never know what might have become of El Salvador had Archbishop Romero lived. But it is beyond dispute that Sandino was a leader as honorable as the Somozas were corrupt. Even his American adversaries developed a deep respect for Sandino, and an admiring appreciation for the sense of honor, and humor, he retained even while his forces were being bombed by American planes. So respected by his troops was Sandino that they called him San Digno, a play on words that transformed his surname into a phrase meaning "worthy saint." There is a surviving photograph of Sandino and the elder Somoza together. Somoza resembles a New World Mussolini. Sandino, in his ten-gallon hat, bears an astonishing resemblance to Gene Autry, though with a difference. When Sandino headed for a shoot-out, he would pluck a tropical flower from a tree and tuck it into the brim of his sombrero. For all his skill in battle, Sandino clearly was a man of peace, who believed politics need not involve violence. It was that faith, of course, that gave Somoza the opportunity to kill him.

Compare the portrait of Sandino that emerges from such glimpses of the past with Bernard Diederich's description of Sandino's murderer receiving American officials following his own usurpation of the presidency:

[Somoza] delighted in cheap, gaudy things. A jukebox, with all its flashing lights, occupied a place of honor in the reception hall of his palace, next to a fourteen-foot stuffed alligator on the floor. His favorite sport was cock-fighting, although he sometimes liked to have a calf thrown into the Tip-itapa River and then watch the freshwater sharks fight over it.

Nor was he always happy simply rummaging around in the disorderly pile of papers on his desk, looking for his collection of dirty pictures to show visitors. He sometimes took his cabinet and friends to his ranch to watch the bulls servicing cows. They sat on the corral fence and rooted like football fans for a home team defending its own five-yard line.

Callers to [his] office were likely to come away a little dazed after hearing two or three specimens from his collection of dirty stories, followed by a good-bye pat on the back with the admonition: "Be good, and if you can't be good, be careful, and if you can't be careful, goddammit, at least be sanitary."

It was no accident that the Bay of Pigs invasion, and all the enormous consequences it entailed, should originate in Somoza's Nicaragua. Only a regime utterly lacking in legitimacy, only a government whose sole origin and survival was bound up in the betrayal of its country's sovereignty and true national interests, would have let its territory be used to launch such an adventure. No leader with the slightest sense of responsibility to its neighbors or with any sense of real friendship for the United States—in short, no leader with any character and sense of honor—would have let himself and his country be used the way Somoza did.

But such irresponsibility was precisely why the Somozas were so highly valued for so long in Washington. Uncorrupt allies neither ask for blank checks nor give them in return. Though it is almost never noticed in Washington, that is their greatest value: they are true enough friends not merely to support us when we are right, but to oppose us when we are wrong.

So the invasion of Cuba was unleashed, thirty-four years after Olds wrote his memorandum, from its Nicaraguan bases. The Wilson domino in due course had toppled the Coolidge domino, and now the Kennedy domino was falling too.

The CIA's mercenaries had attempted, in 1961, to break into Cuba; by 1972 the veterans of the Bay of Pigs were breaking into Watergate. In little more than a decade the "dirty tricks" used against Castro were being used against the Democratic National Committee, and the White House had an "enemies list" not just for Latin America but for the United States as well.

Back in 1939 the elder Somoza had been received like a king at the White House. In April 1971 his second son, Anastasio Somoza Debayle, had flown to Washington for his own state reception. By this time, so intertwined had relations between the two countries become, that the visit literally took the form of a class reunion. Over the decades since Stimson's visit, the American blank check for the Somozas had not only included guns but free tuition. The Somoza sons had been educated at West Point, at U.S. taxpayers' expense. The White House gala in Somoza's honor therefore was arranged by another general who eventually would help write a whole new chapter in the history of U.S.-supported repression in Central America: Alexander M. Haig, who had been one of Somoza's classmates at the military academy. One official photograph of the visit shows President Somoza and President Nixon, both in dinner jackets, engaged in cordial conversation. Each has the look of a man who, quite literally, considers himself above the law. The long process of political convergence was now moving, in both Washington and Managua, toward a kind of culmination. Nearly sixty years after Woodrow Wilson had set out to Americanize Nicaragua, the Nicaraguanization of the American presidency was almost complete.

Americans by then, of course, had long since forgotten our role in creating a permanent dictatorship in Nicaragua. But very soon they would be asking themselves a question familiar enough in Managua. Was our own constitution as worthless as the constitution of some banana republic? Would we Americans accept the same kind of abuses of power we asked the Nicaraguans to accept? Or would we in our own way, no less than Zeledon and Sandino in theirs, resist the attempt to make a mockery of our liberties?

Within months the ground would be shaking under both the Nixon and the Somoza presidencies, and in Nicaragua the ground would shake quite literally. Two days before Christmas 1972, at twenty-seven minutes past midnight, both Somoza and Turner B. Shelton—Nixon's ambassador to Nicaragua—were jolted out of bed. As the earthquake struck Managua, it was as though the earth itself finally had risen up against the Somoza dictatorship. Within moments, Somoza's capital fell to the assault. Today many buildings in Managua still bear the scars they suffered during the 1979 Sandinista uprising against the Somozas. But these bullet holes and bomb craters are minor blemishes in comparison to the havoc nature wrought on the Nicaraguan capital in 1972.

As with man-made catastrophes like the matanza in El Salvador, natural catastrophes like the Managua earthquake bring out both the best and the worst in human beings. By 1972, the Nicaraguan National Guard, which had enjoyed the benefits of U.S. training, arms and support for no less than forty-five years, was face to face with a crisis far greater than any Nazi or Bolshevik menace. Though hardly in the manner U.S. officials had supposed, the hour of judgment was at hand—and not just for Somoza and the National Guard. The earthquake presented a "test case" of all we Americans had made of Nicaragua too.

The earthquake had leveled Managua in minutes; within hours it was evident that the earthquake had demolished another edifice as well. Somoza's National Guard completely disintegrated; even the dictator's personal bodyguard deserted. As in El Salvador later, the problem was not merely that the local military was powerless to deal with the catastrophe. The problem was that the military itself was making the catastrophe worse. By dawn the streets of Managua were filled with Somoza's troops—looting the capital of the country they were supposed to defend. For days, Nicaraguans died beneath the rubble because no one bothered to rescue them; no food or medicine was distributed. Fires burned out of control.

In societies where military dictators decide how the money is spent, there seldom is any money left over for fire engines. All Somoza's tanks, bombers and machine guns combined could not rescue a single child trapped in a burning building.

Not that this latest national catastrophe troubled the Somozas any more than all Nicaragua's previous catastrophes had. While people were dying in downtown Managua, Somoza lounged beside his swimming pool in the suburbs, as reporters discovered when they visited him, partaking of one of his usual gargantuan lunches. On the same visit, journalists found Mrs. Somoza whiling away the afternoon studying American fashion magazines and mail-order catalogues.

At the American embassy, too, it was business as usual. One of Ambassador Shelton's many services for the Somozas had been to use his diplomatic skills to persuade Howard Hughes—drug addict, billionaire, psychotic, and close collaborator with CIA clandestine operations—to seek refuge, from both U.S. legal processes and his own phobias, in Nicaragua.

Tens of thousands of Nicaraguans had been made homeless by the earthquake. But the tremors also had interrupted the sleep of Howard Hughes, even though the Intercontinental Hotel, where he had been living as a recluse, was undamaged. Just across the street, buildings had collapsed; fires had broken out. In the city beyond, thousands were injured and dying. Surely this terrible disaster provided an opportunity not just for the U.S. embassy, but for one of the richest men in the world, to put into practice our American ideals?

Instead Hughes packed while embassy officials busied themselves assuring that the road to the Managua airport stayed open and that protection and gasoline were provided for the convoy of the American billionaire. Within hours of the earthquake, after all his documents, money and personal possessions were loaded, U.S. officials saw Hughes aboard a private airplane. The plane taxied down the runway where, thirty-eight years earlier, Somoza's guardsmen had dumped Sandino's body, and flew north—leaving thousands of dying people behind.

Having protected the life and property of at least one U.S. citizen, the American embassy turned to its most important task: assuring that the earthquake, whatever else it did, left the Somozas' control of Nicaragua unshaken. President Nixon telephoned Somoza from Key Biscayne to express his personal concern for the safety of the dictator and his family. Five hundred U.S. troops were flown in to guard the Somoza residence, and a U.S. field hospital set up there too. Somoza and his family were uninjured, but they had good use for their American bodyguards. For days, the U.S. troops were all that stood between Somoza himself and the anarchy that had overtaken the capital.

Not that U.S. troops were the sole manifestations of American largesse. Soon boxes of American cornflakes were raining down on Nicaragua the way U.S. bombs rain down on El Salvador today. The only problem in Nicaragua in 1972 was the same problem afflicting the U.S. aid program in El Salvador later. This American "aid" was of no help to the people whose hearts and minds it was supposed to win. Instead, everything from toilet paper to antibiotics went into the warehouses of the Somozas and their underlings.

Like all their country's disasters for so many decades, the earthquake would only make the Somozas richer. Fast as the U.S. supplies arrived, they were put on sale, at enormous markups, on the Managua black market; the devastation also meant that most of Managua's businesses, and much of its population, had to be relocated—onto property the Somozas owned, into new buildings Somoza's construction companies built. The Somozas seem simply to have stolen nearly $16 million of the $32 million in cash the U.S. Government provided for emergency relief, but the long-term profits the Somozas made on their country's catastrophe no doubt were many times greater.

As for the United States, our relief effort had the same result as all our previous efforts to come to the rescue of the Nicaraguans. The travails of that unfortunate land were not ended. They were made worse, for to the cruelty of nature was added the depravity of U.S.-backed forces that fed off their country's suffering like ghouls. Thanks to our aid, a regime now revealed to be not merely oppressive but utterly incompetent was spared, at least for the time being, the consequences of its own irresponsibility.

While the United States, the richest and most powerful nation on earth, was manifesting its priorities in Nicaragua, the earthquake also gave one of the weakest and least consequential nations on earth the opportunity to put its principles into practice. For years prior to the 1972 earthquake, Nicaragua actually had been involved in a Central American struggle between democracy and tyranny—though it was not the struggle against Bolshevism, Nazism or "Communist aggression" to which the State Department manifestoes periodically referred.

This struggle pitted the Somozas, Central America's most corrupt dictators, against Costa Rica, Nicaragua's southern neighbor and Latin America's most successful democracy. When the Somozas were not locking up "Nazis" or "Communists," depending on the prevailing fashion in Washington, they were trying, by one means or another, to turn back the democratic menace Costa Rica posed to the prevailing order of dictatorship in Central America. In the early 1950s, for example, precisely at the moment anti-Communist hysteria was approaching its peak in the United States, the Somozas had welcomed with open arms the leadership of the Costa Rican Communist Party, because the Costa Rican Communists, no less than Somoza himself, opposed the democratic constitution adopted in Costa Rica in 1948.

Not that Somoza's attempts to subvert democracy in Costa Rica were limited to harboring Communists. In 1948 and 1955, Somoza's National Guard invaded Costa Rica, in hopes of helping to install a Somoza-style regime there. As late as November 1959, the National Guard crossed the border, destroying property and kidnapping Costa Rican civilians.

By the early 1970s, Nicaragua and Costa Rica had more than twenty years of bad blood between them. Both countries were "pro-American," but in quite different ways. Costa Rica actually put into practice the freedoms the United States constantly preached in Latin America, while Nicaragua, under the Somozas, was the inevitable confederate in the U.S. policy of force. Even today the success of democracy in Costa Rica continues to astonish many American officials, and even disturb them a bit. Perhaps Costa Rica's most shocking experiment in democracy, for many U.S. officials, was its decision to abolish its armed forces altogether.

Armies in Latin America were at best useless, Jose Figueres, the leader of the struggle for democracy in Costa Rica, argued. And at worst they turned whole nations into economic and political bordellos, as Somoza and the National Guard had in Nicaragua. Under the circumstances, an army in Costa Rica could have only two real effects: it would drain resources away from peaceful national development, and it would pose a constant threat to democracy itself.

The way—indeed the only way—to do away with chronic coups d'état, endless military dictatorships and the revolutions they inevitably incite, the Costa Ricans understood, was to do away with the military itself. Even today, in a time when Costa Rica's economic problems easily are as severe as those of many of its neighbors, it is the simple fact that Costa Rica has no plotting generals, no barracks full of soldiers waiting to march on the presidential palace, that explains why that country creates so few problems either for itself or for the United States. "If we had an army," as one Costa Rican politician pointed out in late 1981, "we long ago would have had a coup."

Logical as the Costa Rican approach might seem, it has never had much influence on U.S. policy, because it violates the entire logic of our long-standing approach to Latin America. As a high-ranking State Department official remarked early in the Reagan administration, "We must preserve the Salvadoran military as institution at all costs." Such, of course, was the U.S. policy for half a century in Nicaragua—the policy we have pursued even longer in other countries, and which we apply, generation after generation, almost instinctively to the El Salvadors of the world.

Costa Rica is less than two thirds the size of Maine. In 1972 its population was less than 1.8 million and its per capita income was about five hundred dollars a year. Yet in the course of its brief "intervention" in Nicaragua following the earthquake, Costa Rica gave more Nicaraguans more real help than we Americans had over the previous sixty years combined. While the Nicaraguans waited in vain for their own government to act, the Costa Ricans jumped in their fire engines and drove north. Today there is hardly a fire station in Costa Rica that does not have its bronze plaque honoring the firemen who gave their lives saving Nicaraguan lives following the earthquake.

Less than seven years later, Sandinista guerrillas converged on Managua as Somoza cowered in his bunker calling down air strikes on the capital nature already had destroyed. Having grabbed Cuba, as the State Department saw it, the "Communists" were now taking over Nicaragua.

The truth was that the Somoza domino already had fallen. The earthquake had shown the Nicaraguans what more than half a century of U.S. support for the Somozas had made of that country. Even more important, it had revealed to the Nicaraguans the liberty even the humblest people can achieve when they take their own destiny into their own hands.

Nicaragua had not been in the throes of revolutionary upheaval when the catastrophe struck. But, once unleashed, the earthquake's consequences were revolutionary, because it gave hundreds of thousands of people no choice except to lie down and die—or stand up and fight.

While Somoza took his ease beside his swimming pool, attended by his American bodyguards, while his national guardsmen looted their compatriots' few possessions with one hand and sold them U.S. powdered milk with the other, all over the country, a spontaneous relief effort sprang up. Neighbors banded together to save neighbors; whole towns took in the straggling lines of refugees fleeing the rubble.

Years later, about the time El Salvador began to make headlines, I visited one of the refugee encampments outside Managua to which, so many years earlier, the homeless had fled. Over the years it had transformed itself from a refugee camp into a shantytown, and from a shantytown into a little city. The most striking thing about this place, which the residents, following Somoza's overthrow, had renamed Barrio Sandino, was that everything they had there these people had created for themselves. The church, the school, the *cantinas* and shops, the gravel streets, the electricity and sewerage systems had all been planned and constructed by the people who used them.

"People in the United States," one young Nicaraguan told me, "talk as though the revolution happened when we drove Somoza out, that a revolution is something you make by firing a gun. Actually our revolution began the night of the earthquake, when we discovered that if anyone was going to save us, it would have to be ourselves." He had been twelve years old the night of the earthquake. Now, at the age of twenty-one, he was a tested battlefield commander, the veteran of successful guerrilla war.

Such were the origins and the nature of the "Communist aggression" that befell Somoza's Nicaragua in 1979. By then, of course, no doctrinaire anti-Communist was in the White House. Indeed, to listen to some of Jimmy Carter's critics, his human rights policy had emasculated both our own strength and that of our allies all over the western hemisphere. In truth, President Carter pursued the same policy toward Somoza that all his predecessors had—and as Carter himself also did with the Shah of Iran, whose own U.S.-backed dynasty was soon to disintegrate for many of the same reasons the Somoza dynasty fell. Even after the Sandinista insurrection had broken out, Carter had clung, without realizing it, to the policy of Coolidge and Stimson: praising the dictator in a warm personal letter, but also counseling him to use the National Guard "to ensure fair and free elections in which all political parties could compete fairly." As Bernard Diederich recounts it, even after all the many crimes he had committed against his country, Somoza was still deemed "worthy of support," because, in the U.S. view, there was "no visible alternate leader" to prevent Nicaragua from becoming "a second Cuba."

Even before President Carter wrote his friendly letter to Somoza about free elections, Somoza's most prominent critic—the distinguished newspaper editor Pedro Joaquin Chamorro—had been murdered. The Nicaraguan uprising had its martyr, just as the murder of Archbishop Romero a little later would give the Salvadoran insurrection its martyr too. Somoza's ensuing bombing raids, tank assaults and other acts of terrorism against his own cities and citizens soon went on to reveal that whatever the recurring fantasy in Washington, "fair and free elections" can never be assured through supporting dictators like Somoza and gangs of thugs like the Nicaraguan National Guard. It only led to the mass slaughter of the very people we imagine it is our duty, as Americans, to show the way to liberty.

Not that Nicaraguans were the only "Communists" Somoza's guardsmen murdered. In July 1979, a year after President Carter had praised Somoza for his "constructive actions," Americans witnessed the spectacle of U.S.-trained and -supplied Nicaraguan national guardsmen murdering a U.S. citizen, ABC news correspondent Bill Stewart, on the nightly network news.

The Stewart murder—like the murders, less than nineteen months later, of the four American churchwomen in El Salvador—generated the usual notoriety. But, as always, the underlying pattern in this tapestry of U.S.-supported violence was invisible in Washington, and so the fundamental lesson went unlearned. Stewart's murderer "was never convicted," as Diederich notes, even though a complete videotape of the murder existed. But even that travesty of justice was no more sufficient to change the Carter administration's basic approach to Nicaragua than the later murders of the churchwomen sufficed to change the Reagan administration's basic policy in El Salvador. Even after Somoza's overthrow was militarily certain, even after our own Latin American allies, notably democratic Costa Rica and Venezuela, but also military regimes like the one in Panama, had thrown their support behind the Sandinistas, the Carter administration strove to prolong the fighting, in hopes of preserving what Nicaraguans called "Somozism without Somoza." This Thomas Walker describes as

> a political system in which a slightly broader spectrum of traditional privileged elites would have participated in a superficially democratic system under the watchful eye of a cosmetically reorganized National Guard. Not until just before Somoza fell [Walker concludes], when it had exhausted all other alternatives, did the Carter administration face reality and begin serious communication with the popular Sandinist Front of National Liberation.

Following Somoza's resignation, in July 1979, history repeated itself. After months of fighting, there was no final Sandinista assault on the capital, no decisive battle of Managua, and the National Guard dissolved into a rabble. As it turned out, the Sandinistas stormed an American rampart that already had been abandoned. The Nicaraguan National Guard did not defend Managua because, no matter how successfully Americans had deluded themselves into believing the contrary, it never had been the function of these U.S.-created forces to "defend" anything. Their essential function always had been offensive: to overrun, occupy and loot the very nation generations of U.S. officials had imagined it was their purpose to defend, indeed to uplift and liberate. Yet, until the end, U.S. officials continued to project onto Nicaragua the same utterly illusory antithesis they later projected onto El Salvador. Even following its defeat, the National Guard had to be supported, because it was "anti-Communist."

The truth—manifestly evident to anyone who took the trouble to look— was that no conspiracy in Moscow was necessary to conjure up a revolution in Nicaragua, because Wilson, Coolidge, Roosevelt and Nixon—not Marx, Engels, Lenin and Stalin—already had made revolution inevitable there. For generations, the American ambassadors, Marine Corps commandants and CIA station chiefs had imagined they were the masters of Nicaragua, when they were only the sorcerer's apprentices of Central American history. By overthrowing Zelaya, they had only created Zeledon, and by killing Zeledon they had only conjured up Sandino. Now, out of the Nicaraguan earth where Sandino's corpse had been thrown, hundreds of thousands of Sandinistas had arisen—and they constituted a force not even all of Somoza's machine guns and dive bombers could quell. Calling these authentic Central American revolutionaries "Communists" might help the United States deceive itself yet again about its own historical responsibility for the carnage in Nicaragua, but it could not deprive the Sandinistas of a strength they seemed to derive from the soil of Nicaragua itself.

Following the Sandinista victory, Nicaragua did not become a paragon of American-style liberty. But neither did it become, in spite of all the State Department's attempts to make it seem so, "another Cuba." In fact there were a number of similarities to the old Mexican revolution—which initially had instilled such dread in the United States but which, by the early 1980s, practically no one remembered at all. Of these perhaps the most important was the emergence in Nicaragua of a pluralistic political system in which one party dominated but did not entirely monopolize power, and in which no one individual was allowed to dominate the government permanently.

Nicaragua was a "Communist" country where several of the most important government posts were held by American-trained Catholic priests. It was a "totalitarian dictatorship" where, besides the Sandinistas, more than half a dozen other political parties, ranging from Conservatives to self-avowed

Communists, also functioned. Not that Nicaragua, following Somoza's down-fall, had become another Costa Rica. While dissent, and even "opposition within the framework of the revolution" was tolerated, the Sandinista security apparatus regularly arrested, and exhibited to the press, "counterrevolutionaries" ranging from what appeared to be real plotters to hapless amateurs. The independent press did survive, contrary to official U.S. predictions, but it was often censored.

What were the most important characteristics of this revolution that bore the name not of Marx, not of Lenin, nor even of Fidel Castro but, nearly fifty years following his murder, of Augusto Cesar Sandino? Whatever its various faults under the Sandinistas, Nicaragua was no longer a land of sheer, unbridled terror. The average Nicaraguan, perhaps for the first time in history, had the chance to own land, to go to school—above all, to exist without being harassed and killed by the forces of his very own government. For the foreign visitor, there were also advantages: you could fly into Managua and take a taxi to the hotel—without wondering, as you always did in El Salvador, if the government troops you encountered on the airport road would kill you, whether you had an American passport to show them or not. There were other amenities for the visitor: one could go for a stroll at night in Nicaragua —and be quite sure one would not be abducted, tortured and murdered.

In El Salvador, even if you were an American, you feared to mention political topics, even in English, in the back of a taxi cab. The driver might belong to a death squad. You also feared to leave your address book in your hotel room. The maid might be part of the "security forces," and even if you were not harmed after your notes had been photocopied, Salvadorans who had trusted you suddenly might find themselves arrested, abducted, subjected to the kind of unspeakable tortures from which death itself was only a welcome relief.

One afternoon in 1983, with some friends, I drove to the old colonial town of Granada. We skirted the center of Managua, where thousands had died in the earthquake of 1972. The Somozas had banked the American "emergency relief" funds and left the center of the city a desolate ruin. Now even U.S. officials conceded the Sandinistas were taking the right approach. Parks and playgrounds were being gradually laid out where, before, there had been only rubble. New housing was being built; the city was slowly coming to life again.

From there the main road to Granada ran through the barrios on the eastern outskirts of Managua, where thousands of civilians had died in 1979, when Somoza's bombers had indiscriminately attacked the main population centers. We passed the airport, where Sandino had been murdered. Then the road began to climb. It left Lake Managua behind and passed the Masaya volcano. Today the volcano is a tourist attraction; before 1979 the volcano also attracted many visitors, though for a different reason. Somoza's guardsmen would throw "subversives," some of them still alive, off cliffs into the crater, and so the volcano had been a mecca for both the American television crews and the searching Nicaraguan families.

A little beyond Masaya the road passed an old Spanish fort. It was there, in President Wilson's time, that Zeledon was captured and killed by the Nicaraguan "security forces" and their American allies. From the same fort, during Jimmy Carter's presidency, the Somoza forces shelled the surrounding towns, including the local railroad station and provincial market, killing hundreds.

The fort commanded a watershed; thereafter the road descended to Granada and the shores of Lake Nicaragua—that vast inland sea, more than three thousand square miles in extent, that the Nicaraguans once imagined would be part of an interocean waterway conferring wealth, progress and power on their nation. At Granada a dilapidated pier extended a few hundred yards into the lake. But no steamers docked there any more; there were only a few small fishing boats. The port—like the city of Granada, indeed like Nicaragua itself—had been in a state of decline for generations, ever since the opening of the Panama Canal terminated trade and transportation across the isthmus there.

An atmosphere of sleepy quaintness enveloped Granada. On the main square the Sandinistas, in hopes of exploiting Granada's charm, if not its geographical potential, had opened a tourist hotel. Locals drank beer on the terrace, and at sunset people gathered, for the sake of the lakeshore breezes, in the park beside the empty pier.

"Life under the Sandinistas is very hard," a woman told me. "My husband is a doctor; yet now nurses are paid nearly as much as he is. We are expected to help in community projects. Imported goods were plentiful under Somoza. Now things are rationed, and we cannot visit Miami any more, because it is so difficult to get foreign exchange." She and her husband and I continued our conversation for about a half hour, there in the public park. People milled about; once, a policeman passed.

It was a revealing interview—not because of the discontent with the Sandinistas that was expressed, but because it had occurred at all. In El Salvador, people would not have dared to discuss such issues so openly.

All Nicaragua's past and present, and perhaps much of its future, were there to be discovered in Granada. But the Nicaraguan town also contained its revelations about the United States.

It was at Granada, as long ago as October 1855, that America's chronic state of relations with Nicaragua first assumed its present form. That month, an American named William Walker, along with some Nicaraguan followers and their American advisers, seized a steamship on Lake Nicaragua and used it to capture Granada. After shooting a number of local notables, Walker set the city ablaze.

Why was this U.S. citizen engaged in piracy, arson and murder? For Nicaraguans, it was only the first of countless times Americans would appear among them firing guns and taking lives. But, for many Americans, Walker was no criminal. He was "the grey-eyed man of destiny"—ordained to confer American-style freedom on Central America. Walker's goals were the very goals of Woodrow Wilson, Calvin Coolidge and Ronald Reagan. He wanted to establish in Nicaragua the same institutions that then flourished in the United States.

In June 1856, Walker proclaimed himself President of Nicaragua. A few months later—hoping to attract American settlers and investors—he reinstated slavery, which the Nicaraguans, "backward" as they were considered, had abolished, long before it was terminated in the United States. He also made English the official language.

Walker was not a paid agent of the United States. But at home he was widely regarded not as a plunderer and pirate, but as much a hero of the expanding American civilization as the defenders of the Alamo were in Texas. As one account written in the nineteenth century points out, Walker's

> government was formally recognized at Washington by President Pierce, and . . . the Democratic national convention expressed its sympathy with the efforts being made to "regenerate" Nicaragua.

Though President Monroe had issued his famous statement on hemispheric liberty more than thirty years earlier, no U.S. Government acted to save Nicaragua from this usurpation of its sovereignty by a U.S. citizen. Instead, help, when it finally arrived, came, as in the future, from the opposite direction. In 1857, the Costa Ricans raised an army and marched north to the aid of their neighbors. In order "to avoid capture by the natives," as the same account puts it, Walker boarded a U.S. Navy frigate, which carried him safely back to the United States. Not that Walker's adventures in Central America ended there. The final chapter in this bizarre story of an American ego rampant in the tropics came only in August 1860, when Walker, following several attempts to restore himself to power, fell into the hands of the Honduran authorities and was shot.

Like Wilson's and Coolidge's wars, Walker's adventure in Nicaragua was soon utterly forgotten in the United States. But like Stimson's later apparition there, Walker's own intervention in Nicaragua helped establish a pattern that prevails until this day. Over the past century and a quarter there hardly has been a moment in Nicaraguan history when one kind of American or another —filibusters, marines, CIA agents—has not been involved in expanding Nicaragua's ceaseless political violence.

From Granada we drove back to Managua by night—another expedition that was unremarkable under the Sandinistas but would have been ill-advised, possibly fatally reckless, either in El Salvador or during the final period of the Somoza regime. Nonetheless, to listen to high U.S. officials around that time, one might have assumed the Sandinistas had turned Nicaragua into a vast concentration camp. Less than two months earlier, in April 1983, President Reagan had accused the Sandinistas of imposing a "Marxist-Leninist dictatorship" on Nicaragua. But the President did find signs of hope in Central America: "Meanwhile," he told Congress, "the government of El Salvador [is] making every effort to guarantee democracy, free labor unions, freedom of religion, and a free press."

Two years before, I had taken a similar excursion in El Salvador—to Aguilares, a dusty, terror-stricken little district town an hour's drive up the Troncal del Norte from the American-style shopping centers of San Salvador.

It was my last full day in El Salvador, and I had traveled to Aguilares in hopes of meeting some "guerrillas" and making contact with "the revolutionary front." The campesinos around Aguilares had a saying. If Christ landed at El Salvador's modernesque new international airport on the Pacific slope, their maxim ran, He would be arrested before He reached Aguilares. It seemed my last chance to come face to face with that momentous struggle that, back then, had just started to make front-page headlines in the United States.

Near the center of Aguilares, there was the outpost of the Guardia Civil, which people passed hurriedly, with their eyes averted, lest some involuntary gesture excite the curiosity of the police and thus spell their doom. There was the dusty square filled with listless men, the few begging children, the "motel"—the Salvadoran term for the local brothel—near the main highway, with the Mercedes of one of the district notables parked outside. There were the police spies stationed outside the church, peering through black sunglasses, carefully noting those so reckless as to compromise themselves in the eyes of the regime by attending mass. On the outskirts of town stood a small wooden cross, marking the place where the local priest had been murdered when he tried to organize the town's landless farm laborers. After the priest's death, I was told, the cross had taken root, and then the cross had sprouted leaves—surely this, the campesinos agreed, bespoke the invincibility of faith, the inevitability of salvation, the certainty of resurrection.

When we reached our destination, we abandoned the car in a blind of bamboo stalks and began picking our way through a no-man's-land composed of felled trees and drainpipes laid across the dirt road, and of pungi sticks made of sharpened branches and planted, like some experimental crop, in shallow excavations. Anything they could find in their huts or fields, or take from the forest that might be of use, the campesinos had gathered together and attempted to interpose between themselves and the Jeeps and armored cars of the soldiers who periodically descended on them, like blight on the coffee harvest, for reasons of which they had no understanding. After a few minutes I was able to sense that we were not walking alone. The rustling of the trees became a rustling apart from the trees; then the rustling became a series of shadows and the shadows grew into silent forms, appearing on the trail in front of us, behind us, and on both sides. The "insurgent forces," as they usually are described in the official communiqués, had a few flintlocks among them, but their main weapons were machetes. One youth had tried to fashion a kind of uniform from an old pair of khaki pants and a safari shirt. He wore a beret and had a tin crucifix strung around his neck. Like most of the others, he had no boots.

The trail led to a clearing, and at the head of the clearing, many years ago, during the time the Americans had said El Salvador must have an Alliance for Progress, the government had built a one-room cinder-block building here and called it a school. But years had passed since the government had sent books or a teacher. All that remained now were a few broken school benches and a rusted plaque proclaiming the devotion of a forgotten dictator to the emancipation of his people. We sat on one of the benches, waiting, and then, quite rapidly, the reverse of what happens when the Salvadoran Army mounts one of its counterinsurgency offensives occurred: A whole village—old men, grandmothers leading boys and girls, mothers carrying infants, more men with machetes—emerged out of the forest, from every direction, and converged around us. A few came on horseback; all the rest walked; most had no shoes.

"What is this thing you call a 'guerrilla'?" one of the men wanted to know. When it was explained to him, he said, "I would like to become a guerrilla, and have boots and a uniform to wear and a gun. Then, when the soldiers came, I could fire back. I would not have to run and hide in the forest." Another of the men had heard that beyond the mountains where El Salvador becomes Honduras, beyond even the other sea on the other side of Honduras there existed a country that might give them boots and uniforms and guns, called Cuba. But how could one get to that place? Even when one went to Aguilares to attend mass or to try to buy a little salt, the guardias took you, and tortured you and killed you, and Cuba was much more distant—farther away than the capital, even than the Pacific Ocean. Perhaps our apparition there—the apparition of our shoes with their leather soles, of our clean, unpatched clothing and our cameras and tape recorders—might be, like the leaves sprouting from the cross, the sign of a miracle. "Can you tell us, please, sir," an old man asked, "how we might contact these Cubans, and inform them of our need, so that they might help us?"

The child standing next to me was so blond I took him for the descendant of some conquistador from Castile until I looked into his shrunken, dark eyes. Everywhere around us the forest was a profusion of stout-limbed trees, exuberant vines, gaudy flowers preening themselves in the midmorning sun, but it was a childhood of no meat, no vegetables, no milk, not even *frijoles*, that had turned his hair white at seven and given him the look of some grave little Bourbon duke, peering out from a gilt-framed canvas hung on a Prado wall.

The old man who was speaking had been tortured twice, and so his face had a tic, and it was the tic that made me realize as I listened to him that the only really pretty places I had seen in El Salvador were the graveyards. Whether they were the crypts of the murdered wealthy—as ostentatious as the fortified villas of the San Salvador oligarchs—or the wooden markers, as humble as the shanties where they lived in life, of the murdered poor, the cemeteries of El Salvador glistened with color, and sparkled with life. The tombs were painted bright pink, or deep green or pastel blue, and even the graves of the humblest peasants were blanketed in bright tropical flowers. In a land where death waited at the bus stop, and sat next to you in darkened cinema halls and rang doorbells every night, the graveyards had become celebrations of life—places where children at last could be near their fathers, and friends be reunited, and lovers at last lie together with nothing to fear in this world.

"The last time, they came in a helicopter," a woman was explaining, "and used it to show the soldiers on the ground where we were. They also threw grenades out the windows, and pushed bombs out the door of the helicopter that made the fields burn." Only the campesinos' poverty made them different from the well-informed sources of the capital; these people were the same as others everywhere in El Salvador, even those who owned automobiles and had university degrees. Outsiders might perceive some pattern in their catastrophe; they only knew that to be a Salvadoran was to be born with a ticket in a national lottery of death. One woman had given birth four hours before the soldiers came. She had hidden under leaves in the rain for three days without food; the infant had died. Another woman told about her sister, raped and mutilated before they let her die. We heard of the boys marched away and killed, of the stolen chickens and the smashed photographs of Archbishop Romero, of the Bible used as toilet paper, before the soldiers finally seemed to spend themselves and followed the helicopter to another place.

In San Salvador the liberals spoke of human rights and the United Nations charter, of manifestoes appealing to American public opinion: the priests and nuns and lay activists debated Vatican II and the theology of liberation; the intellectuals gathered data on the killings, as though out of columns of statistics some meaning could emerge. The campesinos of Aguilares were different. In their lives, abstraction played no part at all.

When, for example, I asked them if they were revolutionaries, the villagers all raised their hands. "To be a revolutionary," one man explained, "is to fight against the soldiers who kill people who have committed no crime." They were asked for a definition of social justice, and another person said, "With that thing we would be paid for the work we do, and if we had to walk very far to work in some field, we would have some place to sleep there, and something to eat if it was too far to walk home again and back before the next day's work began." "If we had a revolution," a woman added, "even people like us could eat meat sometimes, on feast days or at weddings." An older man said that if El Salvador had a revolution it would be possible to go to mass without being killed, and a young mother said that with a revolution the hospital in Aguilares would be open to all children, not just those whose parents had military identity cards. "For example," she elaborated, "if your child had diarrhea, you could take him to the pharmacist, and the pharmacist could sell you medicine without getting into trouble with the guardias."

"That is why we would like to be guerrillas," the man with the tic concluded. "We need guns to get things like that."

Like so many other people in El Salvador these campesinos had been pushed across a threshold. They had begun as a group of devout Catholic laity, organizing themselves into what in Spanish is called a *comunidad de base,* which might best be translated as a grassroots congregation, in order to pray, and study the Bible, and use Christian principles to organize their lives. Using nonviolent means, they had sought to organize farm workers, with the objective, never attained, of a daily wage of three dollars and fifty cents.

At first only their leaders were harassed, beaten and tortured. Then, as one of them put it, "the strict repression began." Whole families were driven from their homes, into the marginal forest they inhabited now. Men who sought work, even at the landowners' wages and under the landowners' conditions, were killed on sight. "At first we could still go into town from time to time," the youth in the beret explained, "to get food or medicine, but then they began killing any man who showed his face in the market, so we would send our sisters or wives. They started killing them, so we sent the children, and last week they killed an eight-year-old girl. Her brother was sick, and her mother had sent her to the market with the few coins she had left. She had hoped to buy an egg." Of the original 150 members of this *comunidad de base,* they told me, 23 had been killed in the preceding nine months. The parish priest in Aguilares said that of 45,000 parishioners, some 4,500 had been murdered over the same period of time. "The Bible is considered a subversive document in El Salvador," he explained. "Anyone who worships God openly takes his life into his hands."

"There is this myth that revolution is inevitable in Central America," a Maryknoll nun later remarked, when I told her the story of the boy in the beret, of the murdered girl and the egg. "The astonishing thing is that revolutions ever occur at all. The truth is that even the most oppressed people will do everything they can to avoid having to fight. I've heard both peasants and university professors say the identical thing, over and over again: 'There must be some other way, there must be some other way.'" She added: "Then one day you hear that person has joined the guerrillas. I wonder if that kind of decision creeps up on you gradually, or if suddenly it comes all at once?"

In that forest clearing in Aguilares, I had asked the campesinos if they had not forsaken Christ, who preached peace and love, and embraced Marx, who believed progress could come only through violence and conflict. "I do not know what Marx did," one man replied. "I know Our Lord and Saviour drove the Pharisees from the temple when they desecrated it with their iniquities and crimes. Have we not the duty to imitate Him, even here in Aguilares?"

As I walked back down the trail, I think I had for the first time the sense of what it means to grasp the realities of the world as a campesino understands them. What were the patterns I typed on pieces of paper, let alone the State Department's grand strategic doctrines, to people like these? They were only the same unimaginable abstractions that working eighteen hours in a cane field for a few dollars was to me, or being hunted down in the forest by an American helicopter gunship was to President Reagan. I said I regretted I had brought them no food or medicine. "It doesn't matter," the man with the tic replied, "your presence is proof we are not alone." But of course they were alone—figures turning back into shadows, and shadows turning back into rustlings in the forest even before our car jolted down the gravel road, away from them.

The next day, from El Salvador I had taken a flight to Nicaragua. A little later I found myself walking down another forest trail, to another forest clearing, where another group of campesinos were waiting. This place was not far from the provincial town of Esteli—still partly in ruins thanks to the American bombs Somoza's American-trained pilots had dropped on the town during the insurrection—in the rolling plateau country between Lake Managua and the Honduran border. But the campesinos I met near Esteli were really no different from those I had met near Aguilares.

It was only their circumstances that were different, so I asked them the same questions, and found the same lack of abstraction in their lives. No, one man replied, they did not want to be guerrillas. They had too much other work to do. I asked them what a revolution was, and they showed me: It was rows of beans and acres of maize and plots of vegetables. It was the bamboo suspension bridge they had built across the river to reach the previously untilled fields they now cultivated. It was being able to walk home from their fields, even after dark, without being afraid—and being able to keep for themselves or sell the crops they grew.

I had never imagined that a group of grown men could be so clearly excited about a field full of pumpkins, beans and corn, but they became even more animated as they showed us how they could sign their names. They took great, simple pride writing out their names and ages in my red-covered notebook, taking especial care to make sure the letters sat properly on the blue lines running across the page. It was as though being able to render their names conferred on these people a dignity they had not possessed before, and I found myself keeping their signatures in my files long after I had discarded the other notes from my visit to Esteli.

As we took our leave, the Nicaraguan campesinos stood out in the middle of their field, waving and smiling, until we were out of sight.

Despite such encounters with hope, and even happiness, Nicaragua under the Sandinistas never struck me, as it did some foreign visitors, as some euphoric fulfillment of Central American liberation. The Sandinista authorities, while certainly more responsive than many Latin American officials, could be heavy-handed. The country remained littered with the wreckage of the insurrection, and no change of regime could make the Nicaraguans rich. The wooden shanties on the outskirts of Managua, like those in San Salvador, were still shanties—whatever the ideology of those who ran the government. If Nicaragua was no tropical version of the Soviet Union, neither was it, following "the triumph," some Latin fulfillment of the American dream. Even if the Sandinistas were left in peace, it would take years, probably decades, to construct a new society atop the rubble.

But how did Nicaragua, after 1979, compare with the norms of Latin America? By any objective standard, the Nicaraguans lived in a society that was freer, more just and far less repressive and exploitative than many of its neighbors, including El Salvador and Guatemala. And in terms of Nicaraguan norms, even U.S. embassy officials agreed: whatever the limitations of the Sandinistas, Nicaragua had the best government it had had in generations, perhaps in its entire history. If, as the State Department and the White House purported to believe, the only choice in Central America was between reigns of right-wing terror like the one in El Salvador and left-wing revolutions like the one in Nicaragua, there was no doubt which was the preferable alternative. Certainly the vast majority of all Central Americans (and people in the United States as well, if confronted with that choice) would have chosen revolution over terror.

Inside the U.S. embassy in Managua, however, one found quite a different atmosphere than the one encountered on the streets outside: an atmosphere of deep bitterness. Even before the Reagan administration embarked on a policy of total hostility toward the Nicaraguans, our officials looked upon the Sandinistas with unconcealed disfavor. In fact, U.S. diplomats in Nicaragua professed themselves appalled by conditions similar, though infinitely milder, than those their counterparts in El Salvador condoned. The press, though not terrorized the way it was in El Salvador, was under constant pressure, they lamented. The opposition, though not abducted, tortured and murdered as it was in El Salvador, was increasingly deprived of real power. Even they, however, acknowledged one important difference between Nicaragua and El Salvador: Where the Salvadorans we supported murdered tens of thousands, the Sandinista victory had been followed by no bloodbath. Instead of being killed, the remnants of Somoza's National Guard had been interned in camps that foreigners were free to visit. In private interviews, the prisoners stated they had not been mistreated. Even members of Somoza's secret police faced a maximum penalty of only thirty years' imprisonment, because Nicaragua had no death penalty.

The Americans nonetheless found themselves most deeply offended by an undeniable fact of Nicaraguan life: the continuing role of the military in politics. "The men with guns are everywhere," complained Lawrence A. Pezzullo, who was President Reagan's first ambassador there and who earlier, at

President Carter's behest, had attempted to negotiate a continuing role in the Nicaraguan Government for Somoza's National Guard. "Underneath all the talk about power to the people," he said, "this is nothing but another police state."

Ambassador Pezzullo was right. Though the Sandinista government was less repressive than many of the military regimes the United States supported in Latin America, the overthrow of Somoza certainly had not ended the militarization of Nicaraguan politics. To the contrary, it had only entered a new phase. In their long effort to prevent revolution in Nicaragua, the Americans not only had made revolution inevitable, they had forgotten that it takes an army to overthrow an army and so helped assure that the militarization of Nicaraguan politics would continue long after the National Guard was gone, by forcing the opposition to take military, as opposed to political, form.

Nicaragua would never know true democracy until some unforeseeable day when the military was at last excised from politics. Though they would be the last to admit it, the Sandinistas were not just the grandsons of Sandino. They were also the descendants of Henry Stimson—just as the ayatollah's revolutionary guards in Iran were the children of John Foster Dulles and the CIA coup that had restored the Shah to power there in 1953.

From Nicaragua I went to Costa Rica to meet Jose Figueres—the leader who, more than any other, had turned Costa Rica into one of those rare Latin American nations where fire engines outnumber tanks. By the beginning of the 1980s, Figueres' glory days were long gone. He was old now, and by Somoza standards the former Costa Rican President was a contemptible failure. Figueres had no immense personal fortune: no villas and haciendas at home, no numbered bank accounts abroad. No coterie of flatterers applauded his speeches; uniformed men carrying submachine guns did not spring to attention whenever he entered a room. In fact, as he strolled through a quiet residential neighborhood of San Jose, the former Costa Rican President was indistinguishable from his fellow citizens.

This was one Central American leader whose equestrian statue would never lord it over the central plaza. Yet all around Figueres extended a monument to what he had accomplished. On the street corners of San Jose, one could buy a dozen different newspapers, all expressing differing viewpoints. In El Salvador and Nicaragua, soldiers carrying guns were everywhere. In Costa Rica one also saw many uniforms—but they were only the uniforms the throngs of schoolchildren wore.

Strolling the tidy streets of San Jose, where even the homes of the richest were only large bungalows unprotected by walls, and even the poor had electricity and running water, one yet again felt oneself confronted by a mystery. In Washington the spokesmen talked as though all that differentiated the Central American republics were lines drawn on maps. To most people in the United States, these countries, and the rest of Latin America as well, were no more than sinkholes of violence and desperation, and hence—whatever the political philosophy—the same grand theorems could be applied to them all: revolution was inevitable in Latin America; revolution could be averted only if we Americans showed sufficient military resolve (or social compassion).

Yet Costa Rica contradicted all these notions. It was as different from Nicaragua as Nicaragua was from El Salvador, and all three of them were different from Guatemala and Belize, Honduras and Panama. What was the likelihood that, if El Salvador was "lost," the rest of Central America would "fall" too? And how should one react to President Reagan's assertion that the "national security of all the Americas is at stake in Central America"?

No one can foresee the future, but one conclusion was historically indisputable. If the domino theory did prove applicable in Central America in the 1980s, it would be in utter defiance of all that had gone before. The whole history of the region was the history of entropy prevailing, of local idiosyncrasies, not grand doctrines, triumphant. In spite of Secretary Olds's alarums, the Mexican revolution had not spread throughout Latin America, any more than, half a century later, the Cuban revolution did. And even within Central America, the same theorem of diversity had prevailed. The Somoza dictatorship had not prevented democracy from taking root in Costa Rica—yet democracy in Costa Rica had not spread to neighboring Panama. Matanzas were the historical norm in El Salvador, but in spite of its backwardness and poverty, notable even by Central American standards, mass slaughter was virtually unknown, happily enough, in neighboring Honduras.

No tidal waves of historical inevitability coursed through this part of the world. Instead, a democracy thrived adjacent to a left-wing dictatorship, which in turn abutted a right-wing reign of terror; the truth in 1983, as in 1927 and 1912, was that events in countries like Costa Rica, Nicaragua and El Salvador were remarkable precisely for the lack of influence they had on each other. Like Southeast Asia, Central America was one of those parts of the world where history flowed down a dozen channels, in nearly as many directions.

Amid the intractable heterodoxies of Central America, I found one especially intriguing pattern: among the seven countries of the region, only Costa Rica and Belize were completely democratic.

Costa Rica has been independent from Spain since 1823; Belize was a British colony until 1981. At times Costa Rica seemed more like a part of Europe than of Central America; as for Belize, it could have been part of the West Indies, or even Africa. What could mostly white, Spanish-speaking Costa Rica and mostly black, English-speaking Belize have in common to explain the success of democracy, contrary to all stereotypes, within their borders?

To fly from El Salvador to Costa Rica, or from Guatemala to Belize, was not like hopping from one domino to another. It was like traveling between different worlds; the whole texture of public discourse changed. In the military-dominated nations, the talk was all of Communist subversion and military "solutions." But people in the democratic countries saw things in quite a different light.

The problems troubling their countries, people in both Costa Rica and Belize said, derived neither from foreign nor home-grown subversion. And the only possible effect of U.S. guns, U.S. military training and U.S. advisers could be to make those problems much worse. That, they explained, was why they had asked for no U.S. military assistance.

In fact, both Figueres. in Costa Rica, and George Price, the Prime Minister of Belize, had the same thing to say. The hurricane bearing down on their societies was economic: the more raw materials they produced, the less they were paid; and the more they tried to develop, the costlier became the bills for American technology and OPEC oil. "People find it a boring subject," Price said, "but the only issue that counts in Central America is the north-south dialogue. If you don't bring stability and justice to the markets in sugar or coffee, you will never have stability and justice in the countries that produce them." In Costa Rica, where the price of coffee had declined from three hundred dollars a bag in 1977 to one hundred dollars a bag by the end of 1980, Figueres said, "I am a foolish old man who remembers the Depression. I saw people freezing in New York and when I came home to Costa Rica I saw people with no clothes to wear, who were hunting squirrels in the forest because there was nothing else to eat. We didn't build a democracy in this country for abstract reasons," he added, "but because we wanted a better life. The issue here in Costa Rica is simple. If democracy fails here economically, people would be quite correct to seek out something else."

Neither Costa Rica nor Belize had an army. By the beginning of the 1980s, they were the only two countries in Central America never to have been subject to U.S. military intervention. No Henry Stimson had chosen their leaders for them. No Marine Corps commandants or U.S. advisers had taught the Belizans and Costa Ricans to run search-and-destroy operations against their own people. President Wilson had not sent in U.S. troops to teach them "to elect good men." And neither President Reagan nor President Coolidge had shipped them millions of rounds of ammunition to help them defend their freedoms.

And of all the Central American patterns invisible there in the United States, this surely was the most revealing, not only of the Central Americans, but of us: democracy tended to perish and dictatorship to flourish, precisely to the extent we Americans made military "commitments" to their governments to defend freedom. Only in countries that were spared the ordeal of U.S. intervention did liberty prosper.

More than half a century following the formulation of the Olds-Coolidge policy, very few Americans recalled the long U.S. military occupation of Nicaragua which led to the rise, and ultimately to the fall, of the Somoza dynasty, and hence to a renewed sense of Central American menace in Washington in our time. Even fewer had any suspicion that the Sandinista uprising was generated far more by the legacy of American intervention than by the Russians or Cubans or any other external factor. Yet the "crisis" the United States faced in Central America at the beginning of the 1980s clearly was, on many levels, a crisis of its own invention. Historically the Olds-Coolidge policy begat the Nicaraguan National Guard; the National Guard begat the Somoza dictatorship and the Somoza dictatorship begat the Sandinista uprising, which, by 1979, brought the United States—and Central America as well —back full circle to the same unfortunate situation that had prevailed in 1927. Both then and in our own time, the United States mistook an uprising against dictatorship and injustice in Latin America as an attack on itself. It confused the internal events in a single Latin American country with an external threat to the entire hemisphere.

Psychologically it was the "loss" of Nicaragua that, more than any other single factor, determined the U.S. reaction to the crisis in El Salvador, just as it was the "loss" of Mexico that, in the 1920s, dictated the American intervention in Nicaragua. On both occasions, as on many others in our history, it was the American insistence on drawing an illusory line against an illusory aggressor that made U.S. officials imagine they had "no choice" but to transform an obscure foreign conflict into a war of their own.

The cyclical nature of events in countries like El Salvador is obvious. In such countries, history often resembles a linear progression less than it does a static affliction. Along with malnutrition and malaria, massacre is only one more of the permanent catastrophes infesting the unchanging human condition there.

But what of the United States? When El Salvador began to make news, many Americans wondered if it would become "another Vietnam." Others, seeing the American advisers and helicopters, remembered other U.S. attempts to "stop communism": in Chile in the 1970s, in the Dominican Republic and in Cuba in the 1960s, and in Guatemala in the 1950s.

Yet even among the harshest critics of our actions in El Salvador, few Americans questioned what the sameness, the endless repetition of it all implied—not for Latin America, but for the United States and our cherished national belief in ourselves as a people embodying the forces of historical progress. Most Americans, even as they watched the Salvadoran carnage on television, did not doubt what Americans, throughout their history, have never doubted: that, whatever the occasional lapses, both American actions and the consequences of those actions were, like America itself, intrinsically good. Peoples like the Salvadorans might be doomed, periodically, to relive and thus propagate into the future a gruesome past. But we Americans were, and always had been, different. It was not just that we were gifted, educated and "developed" enough to learn both the lessons of history and the lessons of our past mistakes; it was that the course of American history inevitably flowed from good to greater good—both for ourselves and for those on whom we chose to confer our grace.

Yet to visit the mass graves of El Salvador was to confront the same questions that events in so many other countries have posed about the United States and the nature of our actions in the world. If we Americans really are the champions of liberty, why do we so often support the forces of dictatorship? If our object really is peace and our only motive our own defense, why do we so often make war on those who have done us no harm? If the problem really is "Communist aggression," why in so many countries is the most obvious problem the United States itself?

Above all, if we and our nation really do provide the best model for a better, freer life for human beings everywhere, how is it that we Americans so often find ourselves the accomplices of repression and torture, the accomplices of death?

It certainly is not too early to state explicitly the great theme underlying our chronic abuse of so many small, poor, weak nations, and thus the principal theme of this book: the similarity of the Coolidge approach to Nicaragua in the 1920s to the Reagan approach to El Salvador in the 1980s, and of them both to so many other incidents in our history is no coincidence, no accident, no "mistake"—as the catastrophes we Americans visit on others are usually called when we wish to forget them.

Like the Vietnam "mistake," such destructive adventures establish a powerful, permanent—and unadmitted—theme running through most of American history. For generations, we Americans have been like President Reagan and Secretary Olds: confusing repression with liberation, conquest with philanthropy, perceiving the attempts of others to defend themselves as attacks upon us. Like them, we have perceived conspiracies where none existed, and read falsely into the most obscure events the portents of universal menace. Long before we had helicopters, indeed even before communism existed, we Americans were out pursuing phantoms, as though by doing that we could find some inner vindication of ourselves.

For Salvadorans and Nicaraguans, history may be a closed circle. But are we Americans capable of escaping the prison of history? By the beginning of the 1980s, the United States did indeed face a most serious threat, though the threat was not in Central America. Instead this threat gnawed, like some enemy within, at every decision made in the White House, the Pentagon, the State Department and the CIA.

Would the United States and its leaders have the wisdom to confront the realities of places like El Salvador? Or would the government in Washington, once again, opt for a fantasy confrontation? Would it have the courage to face one of the great unadmitted truths of American nationalism: that the United States itself is capable of visiting just as much gratuitous and wanton grief on its neighbors as the Soviet Union or any other country? Or would the United States once again fall prey to the illusion that unpalatable events always can be explained in terms of sinister conspiracies against us, to the fantasy that the most intractable foreign problems are always amenable to an American military "solution"?

The definitive answer came just a month after President Reagan took office —less than three months after the four American women had been killed in El Salvador, less than two months after the two American land-reform workers had been murdered there. In late February 1981, the Administration published, with great publicity, the official U.S. explanation for the growing crisis in Central America.

The State Department white paper on El Salvador offered the same explanation Secretary Olds had offered for our problems in Nicaragua in 1927, the same explanation Ambassador Kirkpatrick had offered for the murders of U.S. citizens in El Salvador two and a half months earlier.

A Communist conspiracy explained it all. The policy prescription was the same too: the United States must intervene, before all the dominoes fell. Were it not for the machinations of Moscow and Havana, the white paper argued, El Salvador would be a tranquil, even prosperous land.

American guns the insurgents had purchased from American arms dealers in Miami were laboriously traced to Cuba, to Vietnam, even to Marxist Ethiopia. Even Salvadoran nuns and priests, through an equally tortuous process, were "proven" to be agents of the Kremlin. From reading the white paper, one gained no sense at all that El Salvador was a land of social injustice, economic exploitation and unparalleled political brutality, let alone that the United States itself was arming, supplying and advising the forces of repression.

Indeed, when refracted through the prism of American policy, even the U.S.-supported death squads underwent a dramatic transformation. No longer were they murderers and torturers; they were forces of freedom striving to "create jobs, feed the hungry, improve health and housing and education and support the reforms that are opening and modernizing El Salvador's economy."

"The United States," the white paper concluded, "will continue to work with the Salvadoran Government toward economic betterment, social justice and peace."

Many Americans, including much of the press, initially accepted the white paper at face value, including its assertion that it provided "definitive evidence" of clandestine military aggression in El Salvador "by the Soviet Union, Cuba and their Communist allies." But others, later including some high State Department officials, pointed out, after studying the white paper in its entirety, that this supposedly factual U.S. official document was nothing more or less than the projection of an official fantasy on Central America. The charges that "Cuba and other Communist countries" were providing "military direction, and arming the insurgent forces in El Salvador" were unproved. Indeed, like many of the State Department's other allegations, they were actually contradicted by the documents the white paper presented.

"The State Department's white paper on El Salvador," the Washington *Post* later reported, "contains factual errors, misleading statements and unresolved ambiguities that raise questions about the administration's interpretation of participation by communist countries in the Salvadoran civil war." "[T]he documents," it added, "do not support conclusions drawn from them by the administration."

Earlier, Pacific News Service and *The Wall Street Journal* had come to the same conclusion. "Several of the most important documents, it's obvious," the *Journal* reported, "were attributed to guerrilla leaders who didn't write them. Statistics of armament shipments into El Salvador, supposedly drawn directly from the documents, were extrapolated. . . . Much information in the white paper can't be found in the documents at all." John Dinges, the Pacific News Service reporter who first pointed out the discrepancies in the Administration's attempt to prove "Communist Interference in El Salvador," called the white paper a "Rube Goldberg machine."

The Washington *Post* summed up the single most important misrepresentation in the white paper:

> The contention . . . that the Salvadoran rebels were enjoying the benefits of "nearly 200 tons" of communist-supplied arms and materiel is not supported anywhere in these documents, and is implicitly refuted by many of them. In document after document there are reports of rebels short of arms, or looking for ways to buy arms, or exhorting comrades to produce home-made arms. . . .

Even the State Department's own raw intelligence, in sum, suggested the same conclusion a visit with the campesinos of Aguilares did. The Salvadoran insurgents were not armed and directed by some external conspiracy; they were hapless victims of repression trying to defend themselves by whatever means they could—a conclusion also supported by military events. As Jonathan Kwitny pointed out in *The Wall Street Journal*, "the dire circumstances described in the white paper seem to have little bearing on what has subsequently happened in El Salvador this year. Far from being overwhelmed by the power of imported Soviet arms, the Salvadoran government put down a desperate rebel offensive in January. . . . [T]here haven't been successful large-scale attacks indicating big new arms supplies."

Even the principal author of the white paper, a State Department official named Jon D. Glassman, later conceded that parts of the white paper were "misleading." But few asked the most important question: how was it that the U.S. Government had been so misled?

At a meeting at the Center for Inter-American Relations, in New York, in May 1981, Glassman provided the answer: He had found "definitive evidence" that the Soviet Union was behind the Salvadoran uprising for two

reasons: his superiors in Washington had instructed him to find such evidence
—and when the request was relayed from Washington, the Salvadoran high
command had provided it.

Glassman's own account of how the American Government assembled its
evidence that El Salvador was not the scene of a civil war, but a victim of
"armed aggression against a small Third World country by Communist powers" is worth quoting for a number of reasons:

> The origins of this paper [the State Department official explained] were in
> January of this year 1981. On January 10, you will recall, El Salvador
> insurgents launched a so-called general offensive or final offensive against
> the government of El Salvador. . . . On January fourteenth, about four
> days after the offensive started, I was in Mexico City and I received a
> telephone call from [the] Assistant Secretary of State for Latin American
> Affairs. [He] asked me to proceed to El Salvador to see if there was any
> further information regarding foreign involvement in support of the insur-
> gents. . . . I proceeded to El Salvador arriving around January sixteenth
> of this year. January eighteenth we met with Colonel Garcia, who is Minis-
> ter of Defense of the Salvadoran government and explained what we had
> been sent there for. He agreed to provide us any documents, any weapons
> they had captured which dealt with this issue.

Defense Minister Garcia previously had offered the Americans documents
that would prove, as he claimed, that the guerrillas his troops were fighting
were receiving aid from the Soviet Union. He gave new copies of these documents to Glassman, and over the next week, at intervals, provided Glassman
with others.

A week after his arrival in El Salvador, Glassman came to his conclusion.
Thanks to Defense Minister Garcia, "we had discovered the details of a very
complicated scheme to bring in weapons to El Salvador with the participation
of many countries and confirming all the earlier indications we had on the
basis of the [earlier documents Garcia had provided]." "At this point," Glassman added, "we reported this to Washington." Following his report to Washington that he had unearthed nothing less than a far-flung conspiracy to
subvert El Salvador, Glassman went back to Garcia with a new request from
Washington:

> We then asked if the General Staff could once again review the archives to
> ensure that we had in fact received all the documents because of the obvi-
> ously important nature of the information that these documents contained.
> They subsequently reviewed their documents and produced another ten or
> fifteen, including one of which you'll see in this collection here.

Somoza had translated for Stimson in Nicaragua in 1927; now Garcia was
translating for Glassman in El Salvador. This tale of the eager State Department official and the Salvadoran Defense Minister equally eager to provide

him the "definitive evidence" of Communist conspiracy his superiors in Washington wanted, no doubt, had its charming side. This fable of American naïveté and Salvadoran guile in which the wolf fed the lamb was worthy of Aesop—and should be required reading at both the State Department and the CIA.

But its charm was totally overshadowed by the elements of the sinister. Only two months before he met Glassman, the Salvadoran Defense Minister had denounced the Chalatenango missionaries at the presidential palace. Less than six weeks before Garcia passed his first batch of documents to Glassman, Jean Donovan, Dorothy Kazel, Ita Ford and Maura Clarke had been murdered. By the time their meetings unfolded, Garcia himself was already suspected by members of the State Department of involvement either in the murders of U.S. citizens or in a cover-up. Glassman's mission to San Salvador in fact pointed up a revealing anomaly: a regime that lacked the wherewithal to conduct autopsies or ballistics tests when its own troops killed U.S. citizens possessed a truly impressive capacity for generating documents "proving" its Salvadoran victims were really the agents of a Moscow conspiracy.

How would the United States Government interpret the documents Garcia had given to Glassman and which Glassman had given to the Department of State? The "proof" that the January 1981 guerrilla offensive was really a Soviet-Cuban offensive played a major role in the decision of the outgoing Carter administration to resume military aid to Garcia's forces. But the real effects on U.S. policy were only beginning. As Glassman himself explained:

> So this is the sum total of the documents we had. We subsequently returned to Mexico, the following week proceeded to Washington—after the new administration [took office. R]emember that this starts, it's all proceeding in the very first days of the new administration—they decided that they were going to give these findings publicity.

"Subsequently," Glassman concluded, "this document, this white paper was elaborated." Nor was the American press alone in being told the white paper contained irrefutable proof that the United States faced a "test case" of Soviet aggression in El Salvador. A high-ranking American diplomatic mission was dispatched to Europe with the white paper, and so Defense Minister Garcia's documents were soon on the desks of the foreign ministers of our most important NATO allies as well.

The most important effect, however, was on the leaders of the new administration. A week after the white paper was released, Secretary of State Haig informed Congress that the Administration possessed "overwhelming and irrefutable" proof that the insurgents in El Salvador were controlled and directed by foreign agents. The new director of Central Intelligence, William Casey, declared, "This whole El Salvador insurgency is run out of Managua by professionals experienced in directing guerrilla wars." Among those the

CIA director said were behind the insurgency in El Salvador were "Cuba, Vietnam, the Palestinian Liberation Organization and the Soviet Union."

Then, on March 7, 1981, President Reagan gave his own assessment of the uprising in El Salvador. It was not an internal revolt, the President said, but an act of external aggression. It would be the policy of his administration, the President added, "to halt the infiltration of the Americas by a destabilizing force of terrorism and guerrilla warfare and revolution exported in here, backed by the Soviet Union and Cuba." Within days of the publication of the white paper, the National Security Council had announced its approval of plans to provide the government of El Salvador with an additional $65 million in U.S. aid, and that was only the first installment of a "commitment" to U.S. military intervention in Central America that would escalate throughout the Reagan presidency.

"We completely screwed it up," Glassman himself later conceded, and that might have been the epitaph not merely for the white paper, but for the entire Reagan policy. For even after the white paper was discredited, its unfounded assumptions remained the cornerstone of U.S. actions in Central America. And so, as the first half of the decade slipped by and the body count in El Salvador multiplied, that national crisis became a regional crisis, and the headlines about the "threat" in Central America became a permanent feature of our daily newspapers, just as the films of the expanding carnage became a permanent image on the nightly network news. Would El Salvador "fall"? Would Honduras and the others "fall" too? One could read and watch such reports forever and never suspect that the only dominoes that really mattered —the White House, the Pentagon, the CIA, the State Department—had toppled long ago.

It was not merely the Salvadorans who, whether as victims or victimizers, were sharing the destiny of Marti and Martinez, and reenacting catastrophes going back to Alvarado; we Americans, too, once again were acting out a half-forgotten pageant of murder and desolation. That we were blind to the realities of El Salvador, as we have been blind to the realities of so many other countries, was obvious to anyone who took the trouble to look at that unfortunate nation. But if one looked closely enough at El Salvador, something else was also visible: a blindness to ourselves, to the contradictions in our own national character, and to the true effects of our actions on others, that was even more destructive than all our illusions about El Salvador.

It was the fate of the white paper, like many of the most revealing documents in our history, to be almost completely forgotten. Even after its discrepancies were established, many Americans continued to accept implicitly its fundamental allegation: that the turmoil in Central America had to be caused by an external conspiracy, directed not just against the Central Americans but against the United States.

But whether they rejected or accepted the Administration's claims, most Americans missed the real revelation of the white paper. Like our El Salvador intervention as a whole, the white paper was an exercise in illusion, a case of the most powerful government on earth imagining it could coerce the facts to conform to its fantasies, just as it imagined American helicopter gunships could transform oligarchs into constitutionalists and harassed campesinos into loyal supporters of the regime that terrorized them.

"The idea that the war in El Salvador is an internal, factional struggle," the Washington *Post* observed at the time, "does not appear in the Reagan administration's white paper." Nor, over the next four years, would the idea that the whole of Central America was anything but a simplistic "test case" of U.S. resolve against Communist aggression appear in the Reagan policy for the region.

Precisely because of its errors, misinterpretations and complete fabrications, the white paper was the single most important, the single most revealing document of the entire Salvadoran crisis up to that time.

What are the consequences of a foreign policy of fantasy? By the end of 1982, three years after Somoza's downfall, the Reagan administration had made the same discovery about El Salvador that the Coolidge administration earlier had made about Nicaragua. Even in tiny Central American countries, the quest for a quick, easy victory over the forces of "conspiracy" and "subversion" led to no signal triumph of American arms. It only immersed the United States in another quagmire. The search for a vindication of American liberties was even more illusory, as the continuing slaughter daily demonstrated. Less than two years after Secretary Haig had proclaimed El Salvador a "test case" for U.S. foreign policy, his successor as Secretary of State, George Shultz, was as impatient with the latest interminable and pointless U.S. intervention in Central America as Coolidge's Secretary of State earlier had become.

Not that the U.S. disenchantment with democracy in the Salvadoran manner by then was unfounded. By then, the U.S.-sponsored land reform was running in reverse: the landlords were busy evicting the campesinos from the farmlands that had been handed over to them with so much fanfare only a little while earlier. The highly publicized, U.S.-sponsored 1982 elections also had produced results unanticipated in the State Department and the White House: Far from producing any liberalization of Salvadoran politics or ending terrorism, they had provided the most ruthless of the right-wing terrorists with a claim to political legitimacy. The authors of the Salvadoran matanza now ruled not just with the bullet and the machete, but with a National Assembly to legitimize their opposition to all the reforms the Americans had imagined could "take the revolution away from the Communists." The bloom was gone from the great American attempt to make freedom flower.

What to do? One thing that was not done was to question the whole basis of an American policy that perpetually aligned the United States with the forces of repression and savagery. Instead, U.S. arms continued to flow to the

Salvadoran military, but, as in the past, the most important corollary of the domino theory was a wider war: escalation. If El Salvador was not the ideal place to "defend democracy" and "stop communism," then a more appropriate "test case" must be found. By the end of 1983, U.S. flotillas were prowling both the Caribbean and Pacific coasts of Central America, and thousands of U.S. troops, in an eerie reenactment of the past, had landed in Honduras.

This repetition of history did not end with the gunboats, with the Marine Corps training camps, where homilies on human rights were handed out with the rifles and boxes of ammunition. For while the Honduran intervention did nothing to "stop communism" in El Salvador or to overthrow the Sandinistas in Nicaragua, it did produce some important results inside Honduras. Between 1981 and 1984, indeed, the Reagan administration succeeded in transforming that backward but previously tranquil republic into a mirror image of what the white paper had accused the Soviets and Cubans of making of Nicaragua. Honduras had become a springboard for the United States' own military interference in El Salvador, the sanctuary for a major U.S. campaign of subversion against Nicaragua—the base for an entire campaign of "outside" interference that was destabilizing the whole of Central America. The only difference was that the "outside" power in question was not the Soviet Union; it was the United States. Whatever the results elsewhere, the consequences for Honduras itself were alarming. Previously well insulated from its neighbors' crises, Honduras now was increasingly the center of an expanding regional crisis. Internally the result was a deepening polarization between the CIA's protégés in the Honduran armed forces and the Honduran opposition, which was increasingly radicalized by U.S. intervention in that country's affairs. If Honduras ever did "fall," there would be no doubt as to who started it toppling.

Why had the United States, as Beth Nissen, of *Newsweek*, aptly summarized it, unleashed a "plot [which] now threatens . . . to destabilize Honduras, to fortify the Marxists in Nicaragua and to waste U.S. prestige along the tangled banks of the Coco River"? President Reagan had a ready answer— one as revealing of America's illusions about Central America, above all, of America's illusions about itself, as the white paper had been.

"Violence," the President explained in April 1983, "has been Nicaragua's most important export to the world." "If the Nazis during World War II," he added in the same speech, "could recognize the Caribbean and Central America as vital to our interest, shouldn't we also?"

Where some saw our growing intervention in Central America as a timely defense of U.S. interests against the Nicaraguan menace, others perceived the fulfillment of an American commitment that went much farther back than the 1930s and '40s. The United States had no choice but to intervene in Central America, former President Nixon argued in 1981, because the most hallowed principles of our national history demanded it. The author of the Nixon Doctrine elaborated:

The first major foreign policy statement by an American President was the Monroe Doctrine, and it is just as important now as it was then. We cannot allow the Soviet Union to get a further foothold in Latin America. Cuba and Nicaragua is enough.

Administrations passed; even the countries changed, but in a sense nothing did. Nixon might have been defending his invasions of Cambodia and Laos, his bombings of Hanoi, not Reagan's interventions in El Salvador and Honduras and his expanding campaign against Nicaragua. Beneath the growing Central American turmoil there lay a constant—though it was not a Central American constant. It was the belief, which not even Nixon's own debacle in Indochina had been able to eradicate, that if only the United States sailed enough flotillas across enough oceans, and landed enough troops in enough countries, then it could find the right battlefield, where American good finally could fight—and win—a war for freedom over the forces of conspiratorial evil.

"Two years ago it was El Salvador," a U.S. official remarked to Bernard Weinraub, of the New York *Times,* in the autumn of 1982, "but that's not the key any more, is it? It's Honduras."

In 1927 it had been Krag rifles and prophylactic kits we conferred on the Nicaraguans. By 1982 it was M-16s and cluster bombs we were giving to teen-aged Honduran conscripts, many of them shorter than their rifles. Why was so much killing necessary, in such a small part of the world? U.S. officials spoke of the Cuban menace, the Soviet "threat." But even when they found their mark, the bullets only hit the numberless offspring of Farabundo Marti, the countless reincarnations of Augusto Sandino.

Bullets had not been able, in 1912, 1932 or 1934, to quell the revolutionary constant in Central America, even when they riddled the bodies of Zeledon, Marti and Sandino. Nor, it was equally evident, had a Honduran firing squad, back in 1860, been able to quell some recurring constant in the American spirit. Whether they wore U.S. Army uniforms or carried security clearances from the CIA, the descendants of William Walker were also loose, once again, in Central America.

How does one come to terms with American fantasy? Just as it took a saint to do full justice to the matanza in El Salvador, so perhaps only a literary genius, some master of the surreal, could do full justice to the self-repeating, self-perpetuating absurdities of destruction the United States has constantly visited on the innocent, the poor, the hungry, the unlettered and the weak.

Our adventures in such countries as Nicaragua, El Salvador and Honduras might all be short stories in some anthology of futility, decades, centuries long —an anthology exploring the labyrinth of violence and illusion through which not just the Nicaraguans and Salvadorans, but we Americans seem fated ceaselessly to wander.

The material is there. But what kind of maestro with words and images could bring it to life? Such an author is Jorge Luis Borges, the Argentine writer whose genius it is to be able to evoke in a paragraph, sometimes in a mere sentence, nearly half a millennium of ceaselessly self-repeating futility. Borges's stories are of the knife with which brother stabs brother in one generation, of sons killing sons with the same knife in the next. The human beings in Borges's stories are mortal, but the knife in his writings, as in the history of our interventions in Latin America, lives forever. In one story there is an infinite encyclopedia. Its pages are numberless; once read, the same page never can be found again, so information never becomes knowledge. Experience never yields wisdom. Like the long history of our actions, for example against Nicaragua, this not only is a book with no end and no beginning; it is a volume without an index, a drama without reference points, a journey from nowhere to nowhere, without maps; the past has no meaning, and all the future does is recapitulate the past.

In Borges's stories, there is no difference between 1912, 1927 and 1984. Time is illusory, and the only real meaning to be found in the labyrinth is that the labyrinth has no meaning. All that counts is the ceaselessly repeating pattern. Names, even whole histories, are no more than incantations of the pattern: Taft, Wilson, Coolidge, Carter, Reagan; Zelaya, Zeledon, Sandino, Chamorro, Romero. History is nothing more than a rhythmic babble of half alliterations, a dyarchy in which neither killer nor killed is king, because both are only the playthings of a monarchy even more powerful and inscrutable than the bullet.

"Fate takes pleasure in repetitions, variants, symmetries," Borges observes. One of his most famous stories, "Death and the Compass," might provide the title for all our own ceaseless searches for the right "test case" for our guns and bombs. The tale takes the form of a murder mystery, part Talmudic, part geometric. But, by the end, it is evident this is one mystery that never will be solved; it will only go on posing its puzzle forever:

It was already night [Borges concludes]; from the dusty garden arose the useless cry of a bird. For the last time, Lönnrot considered the problem of symmetrical and periodic death.

"In your labyrinth there are three lines too many," he said at last. "I know of a Greek labyrinth which is a single straight line. Along this line so many philosophers have lost themselves that a mere detective might well do so too. Scharlach, when, in some other incarnation you hunt me, feign to commit (or do commit) a crime at A, then a second crime at B, eight kilometers from A, then a third crime at C, four kilometers from A and B, halfway en route between the two. Wait for me later at D, two kilometers from A and C, halfway, once again, between both. Kill me at D, as you are now going to kill me at Triste-le-Roy."

"The next time I kill you," said Scharlach, "I promise you the labyrinth made of the single straight line which is invisible and everlasting."

He stepped back a few paces. Then, very carefully, he fired.

Sometimes in our story the labyrinth is Nicaragua, at others El Salvador. Sometimes the labyrinth is not even in Central America, but in Iran or Cambodia or some other place with a meaningless name. The significance of the single straight line is not that it leads in one variation of the pattern to Honduras, or that another of its manifestations takes the form of Vietnam. It is that the line, because it is invisible and everlasting, leads nowhere.

"He is killed and never knows he dies so that a scene may be reenacted," Borges writes elsewhere. Certainly this is true of the execution of Agustin Farabundo Marti and the Farabundo Marti Liberation Front, of Augusto Sandino's murder and the Sandinistas.

But they were not the only ones trapped by history. We Americans, no less than any Salvadoran oligarch or Nicaraguan national guardsman, might also have been Borges's inventions, with only slight paraphrase.

For it is our fate, whether in Nicaragua yesterday, El Salvador today or someplace else tomorrow, to kill and never know we kill so that a scene may be reenacted.

III
The Barren Gesture

A history of conquest, oppression and massacre is easy enough to relate. But how does one come to grips with the progression through time and across foreign lands of an illusion, a fantasy, a kind of hallucination?

From the floor of the House of Representatives to the most exalted echelons of the American foreign policy establishment, there was agreement.

This time, it was the "Cuban question," in the judgment of the Secretary of State, that posed a threat of "deeper importance and greater magnitude" than any "since the establishment of our Independence."

America itself, one elder statesman informed the President, faced a crucial test "in the great struggle between liberty and despotism." Would the Russians and their allies be permitted to take over Latin America? Or would we Americans stop them?

The President, for the moment, kept his own counsel, but the intelligence community had made its judgment. The Caribbean was only the beginning. The "general expectation," the President's chief military adviser warned, was that the Russians and their surrogates were plotting to "employ force against South America" as well.

As the President made his decision, and prepared his message to Congress, a sense of crisis gripped Washington. Would the President stand up for America? Or would he let aggression be its own reward?

Then, as suddenly as it had arisen, the crisis abated. No dominoes fell in Latin America. No U.S. troops went into battle.

It was as though nothing had happened, and in a sense that was true. This crisis had not unfolded in Cuba or Russia. It was one of those crises that periodically grips the official American brain, and then, like some fit of governmental epilepsy, runs its course. The real test American statesmanship had faced was not that of standing up to some foreign conspirator. The real test was subtler, more difficult.

Would our leaders be able to differentiate between simplistic doctrines and the manifold complexities of the world? Would they be able to distinguish between reality and fantasy?

The best way to come to grips with our fantasies about others is to come to grips with our fantasies about ourselves. Yet just how deep those fantasies go, how far back into our history they run, and how intractable they are can be illustrated with a single fact: this particular Cuban crisis occurred in 1822 and 1823, not 1961 and 1962. John Quincy Adams was the Secretary of State who found himself grappling with the "Cuban question." It was Secretary of War John C. Calhoun who alerted the Cabinet to the Russian conspiracy. James Madison was the elder statesman who wrote of "the great struggle of the Epoch between liberty and despotism." Henry Clay was the "hawk" in Congress, eager for a war for freedom in Latin America even if it meant, he told Adams, "a war for it against all Europe."

The man in the White House back then, of course, was not John F. Kennedy; it was James Monroe. And we all know what Monroe did.

Or do we?

More than 160 years later, it revealed much about both the limitations and the selectivity of the American historical memory that the Monroe Doctrine was still very much with us. In 1981, as we saw earlier, former President Nixon invoked the Monroe Doctrine to justify U.S. military action in El Salvador and against Nicaragua. It soon became clear that President Reagan and supporters of his Central America policy agreed. In 1982, Senator Steven Symms of Idaho proposed a resolution committing the United States to stopping Marxism-Leninism in the Western Hemisphere by "whatever means necessary," "including the use of arms." A few senators fretted that the Symms measure would be a new Gulf of Tonkin resolution. But the resolution's backers did not see it that way. The Senate was only "reinstituting the 1823 Monroe Doctrine to protect the Western Hemisphere," a Symms spokesman explained. The new "Monroe Doctrine" passed both houses of Congress by overwhelming majorities.

The Monroe Doctrine, according to some of Reagan's supporters, not only empowered the President to make war in Central America. As the crisis there deepened, it forbade the United States to make peace. Negotiating with "Communists" in the Western Hemisphere "is a direct contradiction of the Monroe Doctrine," Howard Phillips, national director of the Conservative Caucus, announced in July 1983. Earlier that year, William Safire urged the President "to update the Monroe Doctrine." Defending countries like El Salvador was not enough, he argued. The United States should go on the offensive against "the subverting countries." Safire called for a "Reagan Corollary" to the Monroe Doctrine. He did not have long to wait. With the invasion of Grenada, supporters of the Monroe Doctrine soon had their Reagan Corollary.

Neither the President nor his supporters, it seems fair to say, sensed any moral or legal contradiction between "saving" El Salvador and subverting

Nicaragua—between defending the hemisphere and invading a hemispheric neighbor. For many Americans these actions embodied a return to the values of a safer, surer time—the reassertion of principles going back to the Founding Fathers. Senator Jesse Helms caught this mood well when he called for "reinstituting" the Monroe Doctrine. "It's time America starts acting like America again," he declared.

Nixon was wrong when he suggested that the Monroe Doctrine was the "first major foreign-policy statement by an American President." That distinction belongs to Washington's Farewell Address. It nonetheless is impossible to overstate the importance of the Monroe Doctrine.

For more than a century, our vision of Monroe proclaiming his doctrine has shaped the nature of our relations with the external world, the same way our vision of the Founding Fathers propounding the Declaration of Independence, or of Lincoln handing down the Emancipation Proclamation, has shaped our domestic life as a nation. For generations, Monroe and his doctrine have been models of how our presidents and secretaries of state believe they should act if they, too, are to achieve greatness in foreign affairs.

The specifics of the Monroe Doctrine, as almost every American understands them, are well known: President Monroe liberated the entire western hemisphere by terminating the era of European colonization. Having done that, he protected the independence of our sister republics by establishing a U.S. shield against extra-hemispheric aggression that has guarded the New World ever since. Above all, as we Americans see it, the Monroe Doctrine proclaimed liberty the length of the hemisphere—and by doing that, not only assured the emancipation of Latin America but thwarted the aggressive designs of Russia and the other European autocracies of the Holy Alliance, who were forced to abandon their schemes of extending their repressive empires to the New World. In 1823 James Monroe took the same American stand—against tyranny, in defense of freedom—that much more recent presidents have told us they were taking in Vietnam, Cambodia, Cuba, Guatemala and El Salvador itself.

The principles behind the Monroe Doctrine are equally familiar, though we seldom stop to consider how thoroughly they condition our perception of the world and what they reveal about the way we see ourselves as Americans.

The prime axiom, from which all the doctrine's other corollaries are derived, is that we Americans really do inhabit a "New World," separated from the Old World not merely by oceans, but by some immutable natural, above all moral, law. This faith that we are the inheritors of a New World, untainted by the corruptions of Europe, and predestined to inhabit not just a new world, but a better one, has determined the way we see the world, and our own place in it, for nearly 350 years.

There has hardly been a moment in American history when our faith in ourselves as a people with a New World birthright has not been a powerful motor force behind what we do and say. But the continuing influence of this belief was demonstrated with particular force by President Reagan in February 1982, shortly after he "certified" to Congress that the Salvadoran junta was making "steady progress" in the achievement of human rights.

"I have always believed," Reagan told the Organization of American States, as he defended U.S. military intervention in El Salvador,

> that this hemisphere was a special place with a special destiny. I believe we are destined to be the beacon of hope for all mankind. With God's help, we can make it so. We can create a peaceful, free and prospering hemisphere based on our shared ideals and reaching from pole to pole of what we proudly call the New World.

By the time President Reagan spoke, at least thirty thousand Salvadorans had been murdered. His audience consisted in large part of the representatives of military dictatorships. If El Salvador resembled anything then, it was no New World utopia; it was a medieval chamber of horrors. President Reagan, like so many of his predecessors, however, chose to treat El Salvador, indeed the whole of Latin America, as an extension of our most cherished American beliefs about ourselves.

In its attempt to reconcile the belief that we Americans are the inevitable protagonists of "economic betterment, social justice and peace" with the gruesome facts of our intervention, the State Department, in the form of the white paper, had already conjured up an entirely illusory El Salvador. But President Reagan went even further—back to the metaphysics of the Founding Fathers—as he strove to make Latin America, and what we were doing there, conform to our own national faith that whatever we Americans do, and wherever we do it, our participation transforms even the El Salvadors of the world into "a special place with a special destiny."

Our vision of President Monroe proclaiming his doctrine is not just one of the oldest, and most important, of the precedents for how we seek to deal with the contradictions of the world; it is the paradigm of how we Americans, generation after generation, have sought to resolve not only the world's contradictions, but our own—as one can see by conjuring up that vision of Monroe proclaiming his doctrine that all of us remember from our grade-school history books. Let us go back to that great moment when the last of the Founding Fathers strides to the podium and a tense hush of suspenseful apprehension falls over the joint session of Congress. A sinister, powerful and far-reaching conspiracy threatens the liberties and independence of the entire western hemisphere. Will the kings and emperors of autocratic Europe crush the freedom of our sister republics? Will they go on to threaten the United States itself? What will—what can—the United States do to turn aside the threat?

Slowly, simply, forcefully, President Monroe announces America's commitment to defending its neighbors. He goes beyond that: he dedicates this nation to ridding the New World of the scourge of imperialism forever. The fifth President of the United States does not just proclaim a doctrine. He pulls down the curtain on the epoch of New World subservience to Europe, and inaugurates an entirely new epoch in the history of the Americas—a new age of national, constitutional and human rights.

When President Monroe finishes speaking, there is a moment of stunned silence. Then there is thunderous applause. There is not a person in the chamber who does not appreciate that he has been the eyewitness to a turning point in history. The Europeans know now that if they invade the Americas, it will not just be the Colombians or Argentines that they will be fighting. They will be up against the power and might of the United States itself.

Thanks to the Monroe Doctrine, our Latin American neighbors are at last free. They know that not just now, but forever, every American President will honor this solemn commitment.

It is one of the classic dramas of American nationalism—this vision of the heir of Washington and Jefferson completing their work of independence by ringing freedom the length and breadth of the entire hemisphere. To the left of Monroe in this great cyclorama of our unfolding national destiny, the Founding Fathers write the Constitution just as in an earlier panel they pledge their lives, fortunes and sacred honors to the cause of independence. Farther on in time, Lincoln frees the grateful slaves, Theodore Roosevelt proclaims his corollary to the Monroe Doctrine, while Wilson confers on a benighted Europe the Fourteen Points—really an expansion of the Monroe Doctrine, making not just the Americas, but the Old World, too, safe for democracy. As this epic of unfolding American virtue approaches our own era, Franklin Roosevelt tells us there is nothing to fear but fear itself. He goes on to proclaim the Four Freedoms to the four corners of the globe.

It has been a stunning metamorphosis: In little more than a century and a half, we Americans have grown from the benefactors of the hemisphere to the benefactors of the universe—become that nation destined, as President Kennedy still later proclaims, to "pay any price, bear any burden, meet any hardship, support any friend, oppose any foe to assure the survival and success of liberty." It is at this point, if not before, that for most Americans this pageant of liberty triumphant begins to merge into the difficult realities of our own lives as we must live them in the real world today.

But certainly for many this series of heroic tableaux is—like our own national destiny—endless, limitless, and oddly self-repeating. Truman, Eisenhower, Nixon and Carter all proclaim their own doctrines to the world, while Lyndon Johnson confers the Great Society not just on his own country but on South Vietnam, too.

In the latest panel, Ronald Reagan strides to the podium of the Organization of American States. Slowly, simply, forcefully, he reiterates America's commitment to defending its neighbors. Not only does he pledge U.S. resistance to those "attempting to impose a Marxist-Leninist dictatorship on the people of El Salvador"; the fortieth President promises "to overcome injustice, hatred and oppression, and to build a better life for all the Americas." The year is 1982, but it might be any year, any President.

Although these events span centuries and traverse continents, these paradigms of American history are all identical. In each tableau, America solemnly consecrates itself to a high moral purpose. But, in each case, the essence of the action—and often of the commitment—is exclusively rhetorical, not in the sense of being verbose, but in the belief that when America speaks, history obeys. From the Mayflower Compact to the War on Poverty, we Americans have had the same faith that still lies behind our proclamations of land reform in El Salvador. Even before we called ourselves Americans, we believed that if only we could get the words right, and then "let the word go forth, from this time and place," that what we Americans chose to proclaim would somehow cause other times and other places to conform to our notion of what they should be.

In Washington, near the Capitol, is a bronze statue of Abraham Lincoln freeing the slaves. The Great Emancipator gazes down on the slaves with divine beneficence. They gaze upward in simian adoration, and—however much we deny it—this is how we Americans perpetually see ourselves and our relationship with the rest of the world. Did we not create—out of parchment and wilderness—not only the richest and most powerful, but also the most virtuous and generous nation history has ever seen? Is it not our duty to do the same for others—whether it is proclaiming the freedom of South Vietnam or proclaiming the Shah of Iran "a pillar of stability" or proclaiming democracy for El Salvador?

Even today, America's inner vision of itself is that of the beneficent lawgiver bringing liberty, goodness and order to a world of slavery, evil and chaos. At least to ourselves, the quality of our destiny is biblical. In the beginning is always the Word—the American Word, with which it is the duty of history (and the destiny of others) to comply. The Declaration of Independence, the Preamble to the Constitution, the Emancipation Proclamation, the Monroe Doctrine itself—on one level we Americans constantly perceive our national experience as a series of epochal, virtually divine pronouncements in which America separates the darkness from the light.

One reason our vision of Monroe proclaiming his doctrine is important is that it so perfectly mirrors our belief that we Americans are not merely prophets of freedom, but veritable Jehovahs of liberty.

There is, however, another, even more important reason why the "Monroe Doctrine," as Richard Nixon put it, "is just as important now as it was then."

President Monroe never proclaimed a Monroe Doctrine. He rejected the calls for alarms and war, and adopted a policy of negotiation with Russia and strict U.S. nonintervention in Latin America's internal affairs. In fact, Monroe's policy in almost all respects was the opposite of what we now imagine the Monroe Doctrine to be. Far from hurling defiance at the emperor of Russia and his fellow members of the Holy Alliance, Monroe informed Congress of "the great value" he and his Cabinet "invariably attached to the friendship of the Emperor" and their "solicitude to cultivate the best understanding with his government," and explicitly recognized Russia's "rights and interests" in Alaska, which the United States had previously contested. Monroe propounded a doctrine of U.S. respect for the colonial rights of other European powers as well. "With the existing colonies or dependencies of any European power," he assured Congress, "we have not interfered and shall not interfere."

Nor did the President liberate Latin America, which, by the time he made his statement, already had liberated itself. Least of all did Monroe protect, or even pledge to protect, that independence.

President Monroe never "proclaimed" anything to anyone. (The document in question was a written message, addressed to Congress, delivered in an envelope.) Monroe neither called nor considered his message a "doctrine." (Americans only started invoking the "Monroe Doctrine," and the kind of foreign policy it supposedly ordained, long after Monroe was dead.) His message did not even deal principally with Latin American affairs. Nor did President Monroe proclaim liberty the length of the hemisphere. (No unalienable right to freedom is suggested in his message at all.) He did not hurl defiance at Europe. (Monroe's message was one of conciliation, indeed of almost servile ingratiation, to the autocrats of the Old World.) The Monroe "doctrine" did not change Europe's policy with respect to the Americas, which was already settled before his message was published. Monroe did not even introduce any major changes in U.S. foreign policy.

But perhaps the greatest (and most revealing) illusion about the "Monroe Doctrine" is the belief that it was a veritable model of the United States speaking and the rest of the world obeying, once we Americans had shown them the light. In his message, Monroe committed the United States to policies that had been proposed from Europe, indeed pressed by Europeans upon the United States. Indeed, were it not for the insistence of these European outsiders, President Monroe might never have composed his message at all.

The most important reason our vision of Monroe proclaiming his doctrine is so revealing both of us and of what we Americans do to others is that, like many other truths—about the world, about ourselves—that we Americans consider self-evident, it is entirely a product of our own fantasies.

Quite simply, the Monroe Doctrine is to the entire history of our relations with Latin America what the white paper was to our intervention in El Salvador and what the Olds memorandum was to the reality of Nicaragua in 1927. It is a hallucination of ourselves we Americans have gone on to try to impose upon the world.

"The story that the President prevented a terrible danger," observes Dexter

Perkins, the premier historian of the Monroe Doctrine, "is legend and nothing more."

When James Monroe, utterly unaware of the uses future presidents would make of what he was doing, composed his message to Congress, his world, of course, was in many ways completely different from our own. In a number of other ways, it was also surprisingly similar. That, too, was an age of ideology, and then, as now, the world demonstrated a tenacious capacity for rebutting all the doctrines human beings liked to make up—even when it was we Americans who invented them. Less than fifty years earlier, the Founding Fathers had proclaimed it "self-evident" that all men were created equal. Even more recently, the French Revolution had shown that the doctrine of the rights of man could shake a thousand years of European absolutism to its foundations. Yet, by 1823, there was substantial evidence that nothing in this world is inevitable, not even revolution. Two years earlier, Napoleon had died in the treeless wastes of St. Helena; a Bourbon king once again sat on the throne of France. Just thirty-four years after the storming of the Bastille, the conservative European dynasties, restored to their sovereignty by the Congress of Vienna, were preaching their own doctrine—the doctrine of the divine right of kings—as earnestly, sometimes as hysterically, as Marat and Robespierre had preached their doctrines to the French National Assembly.

In the United States, at least three doctrines held sway that would be quite familiar to us today: The first was that America incarnated liberty. The second was that the New World was a world apart from the wars and chaos that so recently had ravaged Europe. The third was that the liberties of the Americas were imperiled by a sinister conspiracy emanating from the opposite side of the Atlantic Ocean. And as in our own time, reality rebutted all these suppositions. Nearly half a century following the Declaration of Independence and its stirring proclamation of human equality, the United States was still a land of slavery and not yet a democracy in the sense we understand it today. The President, the Vice President and the Senate were all indirectly elected, in keeping with the Founding Fathers' deep conviction that the popular will, as expressed in the House of Representatives, must be kept in firm check. Not that the "people," even when it came to electing their own representatives, were entirely trusted. Women, blacks and Indians remained outside the formal political process. Property qualifications also excluded practically all white, male adult Americans who were not at least, in today's idiom, "middle class."

If equality was an illusion in the United States in 1823, even more illusory was any belief that the Atlantic Ocean separated us from the quarrels and crises of Europe. European arms, European fleets and foreign military "advisers" from half the nations of the old continent had been deeply, crucially involved in our own War of Independence. Indeed without the kind of "foreign military intervention" we now denounce in countries like El Salvador, our own revolution might well have been crushed. Not that Old World involvement in the New World, even in the United States, ended with independence. During the War of 1812, a British fleet had bombarded Baltimore, provoking Francis Scott Key to write the national anthem. British marines had burned Washington, turning President James Monroe into the highest-ranking refugee in American history, and a British army had occupied New Orleans, which led to the battle that made Andrew Jackson a national hero.

The strategic reality—the same reality that prevails today—was that our national security was intimately connected with Atlantic and European affairs. In comparison, the affairs of the rest of the New World, especially Latin America, were inconsequential, and both President Monroe and his Secretary of State and successor in the White House, John Quincy Adams, knew it. In fact Monroe and Adams had to deal with a foreign calculus oddly similar to our own.

For all the talk about new worlds and immutable freedoms, indeed, the options confronting a President and a Secretary of State in 1823 were easily as convoluted as those we confront today, because Monroe and Adams also operated in a "trilateral" or "multipolar" world, to use some phrases of current fashion.

Of central concern were events in Europe, where, then as now, the maintenance of a fragile but surprisingly durable peace was at the center of all world events. On the periphery was Latin America, where, as in our own time, chaos, indeed revolution, was afoot.

Finally, and most important, there was the United States itself, which had interests that were neither European nor Latin American, but exclusively its own, just as is true today.

The early-nineteenth century resembled the late-twentieth century in another way as well. The global multiplicity of problems was too subtle, too complex and too dangerous for exercises in dogma. What was required, on the contrary, was what we so often need these days and lack: a "combined system of policy," as Secretary of State Adams aptly put it. One reason President Monroe and his Cabinet proclaimed no "doctrine" in 1823 is that they appreciated what their successors have so often forgotten: that grand American pronouncements are no substitute for dealing pragmatically with problems as they really exist.

In 1823, the most important fact about Europe was the same fact that, once again, dominates our lives. After generations of warfare, that continent of seething nationalisms and perpetual bloodshed was more or less at peace, and would remain so until the outbreak of World War I, in 1914.

But, as in the future, the problems of war had been solved only at the cost of creating other enormous problems, of peace. Napoleon's defeat and the Congress of Vienna in fact had produced results quite similar to those produced by Hitler's defeat and the Yalta arrangements at the end of World War II. In both eras, the victorious allies superimposed a political settlement over the human geography of Europe that was arbitrary, unjust and illogical. Some countries were partitioned; other nations were fused together in unstable, unwanted union. Popular governments were removed, unpopular governments imposed. One consequence was that the nineteenth century, like our own, was punctuated by revolutions within and wars of national liberation on the periphery of this generally stable international system. As President Monroe prepared his message, revolution in Greece and counterrevolution in Spain squalled across the horizon of international events the same way revolt and repression constantly do today. Later the quests for national unification in Italy and Germany, for national independence in the Balkans and Eastern Europe, and for social justice practically everywhere would make nineteenth-century Europe a place of perpetual crisis—yet somehow, the center would always hold. Like our own, it was an age of ceaseless upheaval and basic stability. The great-power settlement that had ended the last general conflict was, at once, the pervasive solution and the particular problem almost everywhere.

In another striking way, Europe in 1823 resembled the world of our own time. After the Napoleonic Wars, the allies—Great Britain on one side and the major continental powers on the other—had a falling out. Responsibility for the breach was complex. But the underlying reason for the breakup of the great anti-Napoleonic alliance was the same one that explained the collapse of the anti-Nazi alliance following World War II. After defeating the common enemy, the victors had no common agenda for the postwar world.

By 1823, indeed, Europe was in the midst of a kind of cold war. On one side were Russia and its fellow members of the Holy Alliance, including Metternich's Austria and the restored Bourbon monarchies of France and Spain. On the other was liberal England and its maritime allies. There was nearly as much talk back then about "freedom" confronting "tyranny" as there is now. But beneath all the rhetoric lay the same fears and rivalries that infest international relations even today.

Beneath its bold, antirevolutionary doctrine of dynastic legitimacy, the Holy Alliance in fact was held together by a common sense of threat to its members. The guillotine still overshadowed Versailles, just as the French Revolution still overshadowed every dynasty in Europe; and with some justification, the European dynasties had a domino theory of their own. If revolution was not stopped in one country, they feared, it would inevitably spread to others and eventually consume them all. Although their own divisions had often drenched the battlefields of Europe with blood, the autocrats of the Old World were at last united in the realization that if they did not hang together —as Benjamin Franklin had once put it—they might all hang separately. The principle of monarchical legitimacy must prevail, they agreed, not only over the forces of nationalism and revolution, but over their own divisions as well.

All over Europe, advocates of reform quite correctly perceived in this combination of expediencies an unholy alliance against all the great principles of liberty that so recently had swept the continent. In the United States, and also in Britain, others, with far less justification, looked at the Holy Alliance and saw a conspiracy of aggression threatening the whole world. It was quite true, in 1823, that the Holy Allies were no more willing to let the genie of revolution out of the bottle again in their own realms than the brittle Soviet autocracy is willing today to let Solidarity take over in Poland, or spring return to Prague. Yet the Holy Alliance was not only conservative, but fundamentally defensive. It was not dreams of worldwide conquest that united the monarchies of Europe and guided their actions, but a well-founded sense of their own vulnerabilities.

By 1823, Great Britain also considered itself to be facing a threat, though with far less justification. Napoleon's defeat had assured Britain's continuing world primacy into the twentieth century. Yet Britain, in the years following Waterloo, was like the United States following Hiroshima. Total victory had brought with it a nagging sense of menace.

In part this was because while alliances changed and revolutions and restorations came and went, Britain's strategic vision of the world, and of its own place in it, had remained changeless. Whatever the time or circumstances, it was Britain's fixed objective to maintain the "balance of power" on the continent of Europe. Europe divided, according to this deeply ingrained British belief, assured British security. Europe united posed an unacceptable threat. We Americans are hardly the only ones to let ourselves be governed by doctrine. The emergence of the Holy Alliance thus excited, in at least some quarters in Britain, the same reflex of deep alarm that revolution in Latin America habitually provokes in the United States. It mattered not, according to this perspective, that the pathetic Louis XVIII was no Napoleon, that the objective of the Holy Alliance was to prevent change, not produce revolution in world affairs. That such a potential unity of opposition to Britain's supremacy existed at all was sufficient to revive specters dating back to the Spanish Armada, if not to the Norman Conquest, which brings us to another similarity with our own time.

In 1823, both Britain and the Holy Alliance, by any objective standard, were infinitely more secure than they had been when Napoleon's armies were on the march from the Straits of Gibraltar to the gates of Moscow. Yet eliminating Napoleon no more had liberated the world from its fears and suspicions than eliminating Hitler later did.

The early-nineteenth century was also a time when the great powers constantly perceived threats to themselves in the travails of the weak, and sought to "defend" themselves by intervening in nations manifestly lacking the power to threaten others. In fact it was a crisis in Europe not unlike the El Salvador crisis that set in motion the events that ultimately led President Monroe to compose the message that anachronistically and erroneously would become the "Monroe Doctrine" of U.S. military intervention in the western hemisphere.

One of the many side effects of the French Revolution had been the disintegration of Spain's three-hundred-year-old New World empire and the demotion of Spain itself to the ranks of a minor European nation. From Mexico to Argentina, Spain's colonies had risen up in revolt, and the Spanish were impotent to crush them. Then, in 1820, revolution erupted in Spain itself, and the party of reform, after years of conservative repression and misrule, briefly gained ascendancy.

Spain by then manifestly lacked the capacity to menace its neighbors, let alone to harm a superpower like Great Britain. Yet, as in our own time, the great powers nonetheless managed to read great things into this minor crisis. In the cause of the Spanish liberals the Holy Alliance perceived an insidious threat to itself. If the germs of revolution were allowed to infect Spain, what was to prevent them from starting an epidemic of revolution everywhere in Europe? Britain perceived an equally insidious threat. If the Spanish conservatives regained power and Spain was "lost" to the Holy Alliance, was not the loss of much else inevitable?

Then, in April 1823—eight months before President Monroe finally composed his "doctrine"—a French army, with the full approval of the Holy Allies and over the vociferous objections of Great Britain, marched into Spain, deposed the liberals, and restored the conservatives to power. The last shred of the old wartime unity between Britain and the continental powers was torn away. Behind an obscure, local struggle there suddenly now seemed to lurk a far grander confrontation—between Great Britain and Europe—which could determine the fate of much of the whole world. Having restored the divine right of kings in Spain, would the Holy Alliance continue its offensive . . . and restore the Spanish king to power in the Americas as well? And if Spain and the Americas were "lost," would not Great Britain itself suddenly be outflanked, surrounded . . . defeated?

As so often in international affairs, there was less there than met the eye. The crisis in Spain led to no breakthrough for the Holy Alliance, no strategic reversal for Great Britain. Least of all did it produce any threat to the New World and to the United States.

All that did not, however, prevent some from perceiving a general menace where none existed. Nor was the alarmism confined to Britain. "There is a general expectation that the Holy Alliance will employ force against South America," Secretary of War Calhoun told the Cabinet, in Washington.

Calhoun urged President Monroe "to sound the alarm to the nation," and in the House of Representatives, Henry Clay urged even stronger measures. The United States, he urged, should commit itself to defend the independence of Latin America even if it meant "a war for it against all Europe."

The alarums of Clay and Calhoun, the "hawks" of 1823, fit in quite well with our supposition about the "threat" Europe supposedly posed to the Americas in 1823—and with our vision of how President Monroe supposedly dealt with it. Indeed had Henry Clay been President then, a "Clay Doctrine" might well have been proclaimed.

But as in future American foreign-policy debates, the doves marshaled their forces too, and the most influential doves were President Monroe and Secretary Adams. Completely contrary to what we Americans have imagined for generations. Monroe not only carefully avoided risking a war "against all Europe" on behalf of Latin American freedom, he successfully blocked all efforts to hand down some American "doctrine" for the hemisphere.

Although Britain's interests were much more directly affected by the Holy Alliance's intervention in Spain, even George Canning, the British Foreign Minister, "conceive[d] the recovery of the Colonies by Spain to be hopeless" —and said so in a letter that the American minister in London forwarded to the White House four months before the Monroe message was written. This conviction was shared by most of the world, including the Holy Allies themselves. There was no "chance of success whatsoever" of regaining that "immense part of the American continent which Spain formerly possessed as colonies," Metternich observed, even though today he is vaguely remembered as the mastermind of that wicked cabal the Monroe Doctrine so courageously stood down. "In deeming it possible to regain all," he cautioned, "Spain would be practically sure to lose all."

"From whom can Spain expect aid to reconquer her colonies?" the French Foreign Minister, Chateaubriand, wrote more than a month before President Monroe issued his statement. "Surely she cannot think that France would furnish her money, vessels or troops for such an exercise." The truth of the matter, Metternich concluded, was that the Holy Alliance in its entirety "lack[ed] arms to reach America, or even a voice to make themselves heard there."

Even before the "Monroe Doctrine" was written, therefore, Spain had no possibility of menacing Latin America, and Spain's allies had absolutely rejected any possibility of an attack on the New World. The chief reason our vision of Monroe bravely defying the threat of "outside" aggression is illusory is that, quite simply, no such threat ever existed—and both President Monroe and Secretary of State Adams knew it.

The hawks in Washington might claim otherwise, but, as usually was the case with the affairs of his time, it was John Quincy Adams who had the last word. There was no more danger, Adams exclaimed to the Cabinet, "that the Holy Allies will restore the Spanish dominion upon the American continent than that the Chimborazo will sink beneath the ocean." Chimborazo, 20,561 feet high, is the tallest mountain in Ecuador.

If one looked only at the surface of events, one might have been led to say that in 1823 Latin America was being swept by a revolutionary storm. Certainly by the time President Monroe prepared his message, the political formalities of that region had undergone an extraordinary change. In 1822, a

Spanish grandee named Juan O'Donoju, had arrived in Mexico to play his brief role in history—that of a punctuation mark. He had been named viceroy of New Spain by the court in Madrid, but since Spain had not the slightest chance of restoring its authority, O'Donoju signed a treaty with Mexico formally terminating Spanish rule.

From Mexico's independence flowed, almost as an afterthought, the independence of Spain's Central American provinces, including El Salvador. In South America, from Chile to Venezuela, Bolivar, O'Higgins, San Martin and their largely Indian armies routed the Spanish.

Everywhere in Latin America the banners of liberation were flying. To many in the United States, it seemed that the history of our revolution was repeating itself in these wars of independence.

Beneath the surface, however, lurked one of the determinant ironies of Latin American history.

Independence from Spain had not ushered in a new era of life, liberty and happiness. Most of Latin America had only suffered a new kind of conquest, as local conquistadors seized power, and new elites, no less avaricious than the Spaniards, looted Latin America's resources and treated its vast indigenous population like serfs. For all the talk of a shared New World destiny, Latin America, even following its independence, remained as fundamentally different from President Monroe's America as the bloodstained barrios of El Salvador are from an American suburb today.

Latin America was born of the sword in the sixteenth century. Today it still remains a region where the formal institutions of government are largely, and often totally, irrelevant to the actual governance of society. Whereas in the United States power is channeled through institutions; in Latin America power has historically been largely extragovernmental, often extralegal. Local elites, private death squads, the banks, peasant syndicates, sometimes even labor unions, but above all the Catholic Church and, most important, the military, are the real sources and conduits of power. Even today, with some notable exceptions, Latin America remains ruled by the machete and the machine gun. In fact, the early-nineteenth-century wars of independence, by casting off the restraints on unchecked abuses of local power fitfully provided by the Spanish monarchy and Catholic theocracy, greatly strengthened the militarization of Latin American politics.

From the time of the conquistadors, most of Latin America has also been a region of economic exploitation. Latin America was born of the quest for cities of gold to plunder. It remains a region where coffee, bananas, tin, oil, copper and nitrates are no more than some latter-day version of Moctezuma's ransom—trinkets to be wrenched from those who produce them, then melted down for the gratification of a tiny elite. Though the wars of independence changed the forms of this exploitation, just as they replaced the Spanish autocracy with a different form of repression, the substance was unaltered by even the most famous battlefield victories of Bolivar and the others.

Previously, Spain had imposed an utterly irrational and counterproductive economic monopoly on its colonies, as a single example will illustrate. Then as now, the great River Plate estuary was the natural outlet for the incalculable wealth of the pampas; Buenos Aires was the natural port and capital of that veritable empire. But because the court in Madrid had ordained that Argentina was a dependency of Peru, all Argentina's trade had to be conducted through Lima. That is to say, everything that Argentina exported had to be packed across the Andes to Chile, transferred up the long Pacific coast to Lima, then trans-shipped to Panama, where it was carried across the jungles of the isthmus and placed on Spanish galleons, then, finally, transported across the Atlantic, by way of Havana or Santo Domingo, to Cadiz. Everything the Argentines imported—from sextants to crystal—had to follow the same tortuous route in reverse. Before independence, the Argentines—inhabitants of one of the naturally richest nations on earth—lived in penury, because Buenos Aires—one of the world's great natural ports—was closed to oceangoing commerce. It was such absurdities of exploitation that underlay the decision, all over Latin America, to throw off the Spanish yoke.

With the victories of Bolivar and the others, the Spanish keys to the coffer were thrown away and the Latin American treasure chest opened to all comers. In the course of the nineteenth century, European and American capital surged into Latin America. Everywhere, foreign bankers and investors made killings—with the eager cooperation of the local elites. This new form of extractive exploitation—oligarchic and multinational, rather than monopolistic and colonial—still impoverishes much of Latin America today.

One reason the campesinos of El Salvador, for example, are so hungry even in times of peace is that so little land there is devoted to the production of food. Instead, the best land is used to cultivate cash crops—notably coffee, but also cotton and sugar—which can be exported, mostly to the United States, and sold for money (which in turn is mostly spent on imported consumer goods or placed in U.S. banks or real estate, rather than being invested in El Salvador). Thus the average Salvadoran faces a situation similar to that the average Argentine faced 175 years ago. Even before the truckful of soldiers rumbles into his village, or the helicopter gunship appears overhead, the campesino knows the taste, in the pit of his stomach, of a system that takes everything from him, for the enrichment of others.

Back in 1823, as in so much of Latin America now, government did not exist for the benefits of the governed, nor was the purpose of production to benefit the producers. To the contrary, the categorical imperative of politics was repression, and plunder was the first law of economics. Then as now, this was a hemisphere divided, not united, by destiny.

Nearly half a millennium after the discovery of America, the peoples of the Americas remain far more divided by their Old World origins, and the circumstances of their colonial pasts, than they are united by either New World geography or some two centuries of shared independence.

If only inadvertently, President Reagan drew attention to these crucial divisions when he proclaimed his Caribbean Basin Initiative in the speech, quoted earlier, to the OAS. "Most of our forebears came to this hemisphere seeking a better life for themselves; they came in search of opportunity and, yes, in search of God," the President said. That comment certainly applies, in the profoundest possible way, to the United States, even when full emphasis is given to that great exception, African slavery. Our ancestors' search for economic (and social) opportunity and religious (and political) liberty is one of those inheritances of the past whose importance it is simply impossible to exaggerate. Our land was born as the refuge of heretics; it remains so even today.

In Latin America, however, it was not merely the "opportunity" to loot that propelled the conquistador, it was the opportunity to crush heresy that caused the cross to follow the sword. Even today, Latin America (with some notable exceptions) remains deeply intolerant of nonconformism; from El Salvador to Chile, the torture chamber remains as much a part of the reigning orthodoxy as it was four hundred years ago. One might as well equate the Quakers with the Inquisition—or political terrorism with "a triumph for democracy"—as to imagine that the "search for God" unites, rather than profoundly divides, the two sections of the hemisphere.

Yet such differences are almost insignificant in comparison to that even greater difference which President Reagan accentuated if only by denying its existence. I am referring to his statement that "Most of our forebears *came* to this hemisphere," whatever the political, economic or religious reasons for their migration. In the United States that statement is certainly almost universally true. Whether they came as pilgrims or slaves, from seventeenth-century Britain or from Poland or Russia or the Third World, we remain a nation of immigrants and their descendants, no matter if we are illegal aliens or descendants of signers of the Declaration of Independence.

The forebears of so many modern Latin Americans, on the other hand, never "came to this hemisphere" at all. They were already here when Columbus arrived, when the captains of Castile and the priests of Rome marched inland to subject whole peoples and civilizations to the auto-da-fé. It is true that in some Latin American countries—notably Costa Rica, Uruguay, Chile and Argentina—the ancestors of almost the entire present population were immigrants. In Brazil and the Caribbean, these European migrants were joined—as in the United States—by African slaves. But in almost every other Latin American country, the population is largely—and in some cases almost entirely—descended from the same Indian populations that Cortes, Alvarado and Pizarro conquered, and which their successors, with our help, still rule by the sword today.

Latin America thus does share with the United States one common fact of genesis: Everything both we and the Latin Americans have become over the past four hundred years derives from the subjugation by our Old World ancestors of the only real "Americans": those hapless American Indians whose own birthright both British Protestant and Spanish Catholic did not hesitate, in the name of God, to trample into dust. In the two halves of the hemisphere, however, the nature of the crime visited on the indigenous population was very different—depending on whether those committing them came from the British Isles or from the Iberian Peninsula.

Leaving aside, as always, the great exception of the plantation South and African slavery, our country was basically built by settlers whose chief objective was not the exploitation of others, but freedom from exploitation for themselves. The American frontiersman never saw himself as a European lord in the making—and thus never saw in the Indians potential serfs. Since the American vision always was essentially egalitarian, not hierarchical, our forebears created a nation in which, for the Indians, there was no place at all. So successful was this eradication of the original inhabitants from the face of our country that most of us have never set eyes on an American Indian— except on a movie screen.

But in most of Latin America, the face, along with the texture, of human events is entirely different. From southern Paraguay to northern Mexico, one inhabits a world of bootblacks and peasants, even major generals and cabinet ministers, whose faces Incan, Mayan and Aztec artisans might have sculptured a thousand years ago. Our ancestors exterminated the Indians; in Latin America the Indians faced a different destiny: conquest and enslavement, a bondage that in many ways continues now.

The historical consequences, in at least half of Latin America, dominate, and explain, events even today. In Paraguay, the Amazon basin and Guatemala, along the entire spine of the Andes north of Chile, in large parts of Mexico and Nicaragua, from the tin mines of the Bolivian *altiplano* to the coffee *fincas* of El Salvador, the confrontation between native American and European (or Europeanized) interloper is no relic of history. It remains the essential conflict of contemporary history.

In some areas, this confrontation still takes the form of a direct political or military clash between unassimilated Indian tribesmen and the Spanish-speaking state. This is the case in right-wing Guatemala, as it combats "Communist" insurrection; it is equally true of the Sandinistas in Nicaragua as they cope with "CIA-backed" dissidents along the Miskito Coast. In many more areas, this continuing conflict assumes the form of a clash of cultures, as rural Indians, crowding the barrios of such cities as La Paz, Quito and Bogota, encounter the Ladino civilization of the whites and Hispanicized *mestizos*. In the Brazilian and Peruvian Amazon, it is anthropological—a veritable collision of the neolithic world with modern technology. And everywhere, this confrontation is economic—as Latin America's elites manipulate a subject population that often, most notably in El Salvador, has been robbed not only of land and opportunity, but of its dignity and indigenous culture as well.

For nearly half a millennium now, North America and Latin America have had not merely quite different, but in many cases utterly divergent, histories. Events, even when superficially very similar, have an entirely different significance in Latin America from that in the United States. Looking at the matanza in El Salvador, for example, Americans see bloodshed, terror, devastation—and perceive a significance in those events that simply does not exist. In the guerrillas, we (or at least our leaders) see dedicated revolutionaries, determined, in President Reagan's words, to impose "Marxist-Leninist dictatorship" on the Salvadorans. But even our own military allies in El Salvador know that their adversaries really are the same peasant insurrectionaries it has been the function of the Salvadoran armed forces to terrorize into submission since time immemorial.

In the Salvadoran military, similarly, we perceive an army which, for all its corruptions and indisciplines, is engaged, as our own armed forces periodically are, in the attempt to achieve certain national goals on the battlefield—in this case, "defeating Communist insurgency." But all, on both sides, in El Salvador know that the writ of Clausewitz does not apply there. This war is no "political act." It is the means by which the military maintains its own supremacy over the state, by which it pursues its own objectives—ranging from the murder of its critics to the use of American military aid for the enrichment of its officers.

In these two utterly different worlds, and systems of history, even the same words have entirely different meanings. For most Americans, for example, the word "Communist" connotes external aggression. In El Salvador the definition could not be more different. For the oligarchs and colonels, it matters not at all whether those wanting land reform, free elections and human rights happen to receive external support or not—useful as that accusation may be in acquiring U.S. assistance. It does not even matter to them whether their victims are Marxist. To them, everyone opposed to the status quo, from militant revolutionaries to reform-minded Catholics, is a "Communist" and therefore a legitimate military target—even when the "Communists" happen to be U.S. land-reform workers and nuns.

What is true today was equally true back in 1823. The only difference, so far as U.S. foreign policy is concerned, was that both Monroe and Adams fully appreciated what many later presidents and secretaries of state have entirely forgotten: An immense void separates the significance of events, even superficially similar events, in the two different worlds of the western hemisphere, which no amount of doctrinizing could bridge.

In Monroe's time from about 1810 into the 1830s, both the countryside of El Salvador and the American wilderness west and south of the Appalachians were the stages of two superficially similar but fundamentally different melodramas. In both countries, white men on horseback hunted and harassed, massacred and dispossessed the Indian population, and in both cases one consequence was a series of abortive Indian uprisings, quelled in both the United States and El Salvador with merciless, unrelenting brutality.

Then, in 1832, a full-scale Salvadoran insurrection broke out, quite similar in its origins and results to the matanzas of 1932 and our own time. In the end the Indian leader, Anastasio Aquino—like Agustin Farabundo Marti, exactly a century later—was captured, killed and turned into a gruesome example of the determination of the oligarchs and armed forces to exploit the entire country as their private hacienda, whatever the human costs. Aquino's head was cut off and exhibited on a spike. With the insurrection crushed, the Indians were reduced from free tribesmen to serfs. As in the future, El Salvador had been "saved"—this time for the cultivation of indigo, coffee's predecessor as the most profitable cash crop in El Salvador, and for those this plantation system enriched. The basic historical process in El Salvador was the same as it is today: a process of repression, enslavement and exploitation utterly different from our own, for all our attempts to impute our own meanings to it.

On the surface, the events in the United States were very similar to those in El Salvador. But the results—and the significance for our future—could not have been more different: while the Salvadorans (and many others in Latin America) were turning the Indians into a downtrodden, subject population, there was hardly an American leader during the first half of our independence who was not an accomplice, to one extent or another, in a veritable campaign of genocide. It is a most illuminating comment on our national illusions that most Americans back then perceived no more of a moral issue in the massacre of the Indians than the Salvadoran military sees in the massacre of campesinos today. To the contrary, the attacks on the Indians were so popular they helped turn two of the most merciless Indian fighters into American presidents.

One was William Henry Harrison, who died after only a month in office. But the other was Andrew Jackson, who left a greater mark on his time than any other American and gave his name to one of the most decisive eras of our history. In both cases the path to national eminence was a trail of Indian blood and tears. In 1811, the same year the first Indian uprisings occurred in El Salvador, Harrison and eleven hundred U.S. troops, in the Battle of Tippecanoe, destroyed an Indian encampment and drove the survivors off into a swamp. Two years later, the Indians' leader, Tecumseh, was killed in battle and thus became to the farm lands of the Midwest what Anastasio Aquino was to the plantations of El Salvador. Thereafter his followers were deprived of everything and scattered to the winds.

This slaughter made William Henry Harrison a national hero—the "Savior of the West" as many called him—for reasons that still resonate in the events of our own time. For, in the American view, Tecumseh and his confederation were the agents of an insidious outside conspiracy—the tools of external aggression aimed at destroying the United States itself. In this case the conspiratorial aggressor was Britain; its lair was Canada. If only the wicked British could be forced from their sanctuaries just north of the border, the Indian "threat" would disappear. It was inconceivable that the Indians' hostility to us might flow from our own countless crimes against them. To the contrary, most Americans in 1811, as Samuel Eliot Morison observes,

> believed that Britain was behind Tecumseh's confederacy. That was not true; the confederacy would have been formed if there had been no white men in Canada.

Belief in the British-Indian conspiracy, and the "red scare" it produced, nonetheless had effects very similar to those produced by our belief in the Mexican-Bolshevik, Sino-Soviet and Havana-Moscow conspiracies in later times. It helped propel the United States into a long, pointless, frustrating and ultimately unsuccessful war, in this case the War of 1812. If only we could conquer Canada, this particular American doctrine ran, and drive the British out, then all our problems in the Ohio Valley would disappear. The Indians of the Midwest thus became the first of the many peoples we have hounded not only into the earth, but into a self-fulfilling prophecy of our phobias. For following Tippecanoe, and the outbreak of war with Britain, Tecumseh and his allies did side with the British. Their reasons were obvious. Only the British offered them any hope of salvation from the Americans. But, as in the future, this alliance only "proved" to Americans what they had already believed: our problems did not flow from our own misdeeds; they were work of sinister "outsiders."

Farther south, in the present-day states of Alabama and Mississippi, the sense of foreign conspiracy was equally strong. It was not the Indians, but "the British scalping knife" that threatened our settlers along the frontier. As a test of American honor, "The blood of our murdered heroes," vowed Andrew Jackson, "must be revenged." Only twenty-six Americans died in one attack in which 557 Creeks were slaughtered; in each Indian cadaver the Americans perceived a dead British agent. Long before the phrase came into use, the body count was a calibration of U.S. military "success," but Jackson's counterinsurgency war against the Indians proved disastrously irrelevant to the defense of our real national security. For while Jackson was killing Indians in Alabama, the British had invaded Louisiana and seized New Orleans, the biggest American city and most vital port and center of communications outside the Atlantic coast.

Eventually Jackson rode to the rescue, but by the time his forces finally did reach New Orleans, it made no difference who won or lost. More than a month earlier, in faraway Belgium, the British and the Americans had already signed a peace treaty. Now both British and American soldiers died for no objectively valid military or political reason. The British would have evacuated New Orleans, and returned it to us, whether the battle of New Orleans had been fought or not.

Like the Battle of Tippecanoe, the Battle of New Orleans was a meaningless victory—except for its significance, like so many of our battles, as a triumph for American illusion.

The slaughter of a few hundred Indians at Tippecanoe in 1811 had "proved" to the nation that a sinister foreign conspiracy really did threaten us along the banks of the Wabash. The War of 1812 was an American military disaster second only in our history to the war in Vietnam. The Americans not only failed to conquer Canada but failed to prevent British occupation of our own territory. More than that, the war deeply divided the nation and created such bitter dissension that New England nearly seceded. Not one of our principal aims was achieved, and in that sense the War of 1812 was a clear-cut American defeat.

Who bore the greatest responsibility for this military disaster? Few of our leaders were without blame, but slaughtering Indians while a British armada seized New Orleans was hardly a model of astute generalship. For that matter, fighting battles in times of peace is seldom considered the mark of a great military leader. In another time or country, Andrew Jackson might have been court-martialed.

Instead, the slaughter of a few thousand British at New Orleans in 1815 made him "the hero of New Orleans"—and an even more commanding national figure than the "hero of Tippecanoe." Even more important, the battle of New Orleans "proved" to Americans something they had always liked to fervently believe: that we Americans always triumph, even when we lose. Prior to the battle of New Orleans, observes Thomas A. Bailey, the war had gone so badly, and the prospective peace terms had been so unsatisfactory, that "many people were confidently predicting the disruption of the United States." Then came the news from Louisiana, and "the flagging American spirit bounded to extravagant heights of rejoicing."

"Who would not be an American? Long live the republic!" ran one panegyric to the victory at New Orleans. "All hail! last asylum of oppressed humanity!" Americans, Bailey adds, now "believe[d] that the United States had beaten the British into submission and extorted a victor's terms. . . . Without even waiting to read the treaty the populace burst into the wildest demonstrations of joy."

But the Indians continued to resist our attacks on them even after our "victory" over the British "conspiracy." What possibly could explain this continuing hostility? This time, it was decided, the Spanish were to blame. By providing "sanctuary" for the Indians in Florida, were not the Spanish really committing aggression against us?

So Jackson's outrages against the Indians inside American territory were soon followed by outrages against international law. In a series of "incursions" into Spanish territory, Jackson and his troops marauded across Florida, hanging Englishmen, imprisoning the Spanish governor, putting Indian villages to the torch and the Indians themselves to the sword. A century and a half before another contemporary military phrase came into vogue, U.S. troops were running search-and-destroy missions into neutral foreign territory, the better to "defend" this country against the British-Indian-Spanish cabal. As in the future, the "enemy" proved to be only a primitive and defenseless population. In 1819, the Spanish Government, recognizing it was as powerless in the face of American encroachment as any Indian tribe, meekly ceded Florida to the United States.

Spain was a sovereign nation that had done us no harm, which in fact had rendered us useful assistance during our own War of Independence. The United States nonetheless had taken advantage of Spain's own travails, including intervention in its internal affairs by foreign troops, to wrest away from it lands to which Spain's claim in international law was incontestable. Yet as with Tippecanoe and New Orleans—and the "Monroe Doctrine" itself —our seizure of Florida was destined to be transformed into a triumph of American virtue. Even today we are taught in school that the United States "purchased" Florida for $5 million, as though we Americans only fight for what is rightly ours, and always pay a fair price for what we acquire from others.

In truth, all the Spanish negotiators had been able to elicit from the Americans was a U.S. pledge to settle any claims our own citizens might have against the Spanish Government in Florida up to that sum. But in a completely different area the Spanish had extracted one meaningful concession from the United States: in the Florida treaty, the Monroe administration unequivocally renounced all our claims to Texas, which was soon to become the northeasternmost province of an independent Mexico. Jackson's incursions into Florida thus set the stage for another hallucinatory U.S. "defense" of what would be called the "area of freedom": our war with Mexico over the "American territory" of Texas, in 1846.

On one level, what happened in our own country back in the time of President Monroe was very similar to what was happening at the same time in El Salvador. In each case, the destruction of the Indians' rights profoundly shaped the national future. In both countries, the men on horseback rode back from the Indian wars to dominate, and fundamentally change, their countries' entire national lives.

But in terms of specific results, the significance of these separate episodes could not have been more different. The Indian wars made our country safe for white, freehold agriculture, and this egalitarian homogeneity was the foundation of the boisterous Jacksonian democracy that soon would sweep away Monroe's aristocratic republic and pave the way for the popular mass culture of a later day. One reason we Americans have seemed like such a blessed people is that our forebears did the dirty work of our history with such ruthless effectiveness.

El Salvador, in contrast, had been saved for feudalism—a feudalism that nation is still trying to transcend, so far without success. What is true of El Salvador, for all its many idiosyncrasies, has been true of much of the rest of Latin America. The Iberian conquest of the New World from the beginning was essentially a process of cyclical repression and revolution superimposed on a society stratified by a system of class, which in turn very often still mirrors the original confrontation of the conquistador, with his feudal ambitions, and the Indians, whom he instinctively saw as serfs.

The development of the United States, in contrast, has been essentially linear. Things did not endlessly repeat themselves. They moved, through war or peace, to solutions, including the "final solution" that was imposed on the Indians. In that sense, our national history does indeed embody "progress." Quite unlike the history of El Salvador, it has essentially been a process of extermination and settlement, tending toward a politics of liberty, in which the main cleavage lines were determined much less by class than by geographical sectionalism, and by race.

It is no exaggeration to state that the Salvadoran oligarchs and military, even now, are still fighting the battles of Alvarado—while we Americans, heedless of the battlefield, are still fighting our own very different kind of Indian wars. History teaches Salvadoran landowners and generals that, if they kill enough campesinos, the rest may well remain their serfs forever—or at least until the next matanza becomes necessary. Our tendency not just to mythologize, but to universalize our own history periodically provokes us to a different kind of vendetta. Surely, once the "Communists" are hounded from the face of the earth, the earth will at last be safe for our ideals, our principles —for people like us.

"We, the peoples of the Americas," President Reagan proclaimed in 1982,

> have much more in common than geographical proximity. For over 400 years, our peoples have shared the dangers and dreams of building a new world. From colonialism to nationhood, our common quest has been for freedom.

"We are all Americans," the President declared—as the representatives of Baby Doc and Pinochet, of the politics of the matanza in many more countries than El Salvador, gave him a standing ovation.

John Quincy Adams knew better: that to base U.S. policy on a hallucination of Latin America would not change Latin America, only condemn the United States to act out a kind of fantasy.

"As to an American system," Adams observed in a conversation with Monroe, "there is no community of interests or of principles between North and South America." He added, in a comment equally valid of the White House and State Department in our own time: "Bolivar and O'Higgins talk about an American system . . . but there is no basis for any such system."

Once again Adams had the last word. Just as they proclaimed no "Monroe Doctrine" to Europe because they knew no threat to the Americas existed, so Monroe and Adams propounded no "Monroe Doctrine" for Latin America, because they recognized that all the talk of "our shared identity" was hallucinatory too.

Confronting the Monroe administration in 1823 was, in some ways, the same international triangle our leaders faced 160 years later. At the center of world events was a brittle though surprisingly stable balance of power in the heartland of Europe. This, of course, was not the balance of nuclear terror that simultaneously buttresses and threatens the very destruction of world order today. But our cities back then were as vulnerable to naval bombardment as they are to nuclear missiles today. Then as now it was on a system of armed peace in Europe that the security, perhaps even the survival, of the United States depended. Latin America also impinged on our national calculations in many of the same ways. Geographically proximate, but in so many ways a world apart, Latin America was poor, chaotic, possibly vulnerable to manipulation by powers hostile to the United States itself. Monroe and Adams had to grapple with the same problems of "revolution" and "underdevelopment" on our doorstep that still complicate our foreign policy.

But what of the third side of this triangle? In 1823, the United States was more different from the country we know today than perhaps any of us can imagine.

At the fourth national census, conducted in 1820 at a cost of less than $250,000, the population of the United States stood at less than ten million—9,638,453 to be exact. More than half the population was under sixteen years of age. One quarter of the population consisted of black slaves. All in all, the national life of the country in 1823 was in the hands of that small minority of the population, numbering no more than 1.5 million, that happened to be free, white, male and over twenty-one. Demographically, not just historically, the United States was a child of a nation. It was only 160 years ago, but, in many ways, the Washington of Monroe's time had more in common with the classic Greek polis of antiquity—with both its enfranchised elite and its subject population of artisans and slaves—than to the Washington of today. Although the first sailing ship equipped with a steam engine, the *Savannah*, had crossed the Atlantic in 1819, the full brunt of the Industrial Revolution would transform our country only much later. No less than the ancients, the Americans of 1823 inhabited a world propelled by wind and rushing water, above all by straining muscle, both animal and human. Overland travel between our major cities was measured in weeks, communications with Europe in months, and when explorers and fur traders headed West, across the immensity of the Great Plains, toward the fabled Oregon country, they measured their expeditions not just in miles, but in years. The bustling little metropolises on the fringe of this vast, empty New World—ranging from Boston in the Northeast, through New York, Philadelphia, Baltimore and

Charleston to New Orleans in the distant Southwest—really were a world away from the great capitals of Europe. But they were even more remote from the interior wilds of the continent, and from the military melodramas then unfolding in Latin America. Though, geographically, the United States in 1823 was immense by European standards, the total area of the United States, then 1,752,347 square miles, was less than half of what it is now, despite Jefferson's acquisition of Louisiana and Monroe's own acquisition of Florida.

In spite of its immense hinterland, the United States was still essentially a North Atlantic nation, not the continental, let alone the hemispheric and global, power it later became. Not only was the United States almost inconceivably weak by present standards, the stage on which our country performed in international affairs was far smaller and more constricting than the one on which our leaders perform now.

One result was that our leaders were far less provincial in their worldview back then than in later times, when our immense power allowed so many of our presidents to imagine the United States to be at the center of all events. In the early-nineteenth century, provincialism was a luxury the world denied our presidents and secretaries of state, because a cosmopolitan worldview was a vital national necessity in a world dominated by others. All the living American presidents in 1823—Monroe and his predecessors Madison, Jefferson and Adams—knew Europe, and understood European affairs from the perspective of longtime, firsthand experience. Secretary of State Adams—son of the second President, destined to succeed Monroe in the White House—had spent the formative years of his life abroad. None of these quintessentially American figures, it is illuminating to note, had ever laid eyes on the Mississippi River, let alone on the Pacific Ocean or the nations of South America. Even when they addressed the problems of the hemisphere and the world, they did so from a perspective that was essentially European and Atlantic. Behind them, the nation stretched across mostly untracked wilderness to the Rockies, where it stopped. But, like the nation they governed, these men still faced east—toward Europe—as they conducted the affairs of the nation, because the reality of the world gave them no other choice.

Chronologically the United States was almost at midpoint between the ratification of the Constitution, in 1789, and the outbreak of the Civil War, in 1861, and in terms of domestic, as well as foreign, affairs, it showed.

Three years earlier, the Missouri Compromise had papered over the national divisions created by the antithetically different economic and social systems prevailing in the freehold North and the slaveholding South. But sectionalism was already tearing at the heart of the Union by 1823, signaling the approaching end of Monroe's Era of Good Feeling. Already, the Age of the Common Man was struggling to overturn the age of aristocratic politics personified by New England dynasties like the Adamses, and by Virginia gentlemen like Washington, Jefferson, Madison and Monroe. At the end of

1823, as Monroe prepared to begin his last full year in office, nothing so aptly personified the growing cleavages in the United States as the intense personal rivalry between Secretary of State John Quincy Adams—scion of the Puritan aristocracy, a man whose veins pulsed with the blood of American tradition —and Henry Clay, Kentuckian, self-made man, apostle of both the rights of the frontier and the frontiersman. The quondam Speaker of the House of Representatives, as one nineteenth-century observer noted, had "trained himself in the art of speech-making in the forest, the field and even the barn, with horse and ox for audience."

The wide differences between Adams and Clay on foreign policy were only one item on an entire agenda of disputes which amounted to a kind of distant rehearsal for the Sun Belt and Frost Belt rivalry of today. Adams personified the traditions and interests of the East, Clay the newness and ambition of the West—and both aimed to succeed James Monroe in the White House.

Yet as history would have it, the contest was irrelevant. Adams would have his one, unhappy term in the White House; Clay would seek the presidency for a quarter century, but never win it. The War of 1812 may have been a military disaster, but the illusion of victory had changed U.S. politics forever. The new age—the Age of Jackson—would belong to the "hero of New Orleans," the scourge of the Indians, the marauder of Florida. Here at home, the future belonged to the prophets of force.

So far as the "Monroe Doctrine" and our entire relationship with Latin America was concerned, however, the Adams-Clay debates had produced one result that is still of stupendous importance.

Clay might have called for a crusade for New World freedom, but the caution of John Quincy Adams had prevailed. For all its rhetoric about freedom, the United States had played no part in the great Latin American struggle for emancipation, which had consumed more than a decade as well as countless lives. No American Lafayettes or Kosciuskos had fought alongside O'Higgins or Bolivar. No U.S. fleet had sailed to the rescue of the Latin Americans, the way a French fleet had sailed to our assistance—and thus ensured our ultimate victory over the British—at Yorktown. Instead we maintained full diplomatic relations with Spain, and recognized the Latin American states only after all the battles were won.

This point is absolutely critical to any understanding of the Latin American reaction to our periodic pretensions that we Americans, going back to the time of Monroe, always have been the great champions of liberty in the western hemisphere.

Philosophically, Monroe and Adams were advocates of a foreign policy that they called Abstention. They were opposed to our involvement in other peoples' internal affairs as a matter of principle. Expediency, for neither the first nor the last time, also played a very important role in an American decision to spurn the appeals of those fighting for their liberty. Recognition of Latin American independence, let alone direct U.S. support for the independence forces, would have involved a diplomatic breach with Spain. And a rupture with Spain would have interfered with Secretary of State Adams's diplomatic campaign—pursued as relentlessly as Jackson's own military campaign—to gain Florida for the United States. Only after Florida had been successfully wrested away from the Spanish did any question of U.S. recognition of the Latin Americans arise. And even then, recognition was withheld for years, and no effective aid was ever given at all.

But the fact is that even if the United States had been willing to fight for the liberty of our neighbors, it could have helped the Latin Americans very little. By 1823 the military might of the United States was sufficient to overwhelm Indian tribesmen, even to hound the Spanish out of Florida. But as the War of 1812 had made manifest, larger military ambitions were still beyond our grasp. We Americans tend to consider ourselves the one fixed point in a chaotic world. The truth is that over the past 160 years we have changed, almost unrecognizably, while the foreign problems that bedevil us have stayed, in some cases at least, oddly unchanging. One reason we seem perpetually unable to solve the permanent problems of the world is that we march through events so totally unaware of our own national metamorphoses. One of the most important formative facts of our history is often totally forgotten.

Long after the United States won paper independence, we were like many Third World countries today. We were an "underdeveloped," indebted nation, with artificial borders, pursuing a republican experiment in a world of kings and emperors. Our own revolution was considered as controversial—and outright subversive at times—as we now consider Third World experiments in "revolution" and "national liberation."

The War of Independence itself in many ways had been an example of that fusion of civil war and great-power conflict that has ravaged so many nations in our own time. It was a war that had cost some seventy thousand American lives and exhausted and divided us. The losers were in many cases no loyal opposition; the victors, in most cases, were vengeful. For a time, our own offshore waters were full of "boat people"—as those Americans who had sided with Britain fled to Bermuda, the West Indies and the maritime provinces of Canada. Once formal independence was achieved, the struggle to establish a workable national union was as long, arduous and full of pitfalls as it is in many newly independent countries today.

We tend to regard the War of Independence as one of the seminal liberation struggles of human history—a model of self-determination that, like so much of the rest of our history, the rest of the world should gratefully copy. The truth of the matter is that those we so often accuse of engaging in "subversion," or even abetting "Communist aggression," are imitating us more faithfully than we suspect. Our struggle for independence was not merely characterized by massive foreign intervention on both sides. It was only an incident in a far vaster struggle between maritime, parliamentary Britain and continental, absolutist (and later revolutionary) France, for nothing less than domination of the world.

Democracy, as we understand it today, may not have existed back then. But the moral and ideological issues at stake in that contest were at least as clear-cut as the issues of freedom versus tyranny we perceive in our own rivalry with the Soviet Union today. By any objective standard, Great Britain —with its parliamentary system, rule of law and economic liberalism—came as close as any nation to meeting today's standards of "freedom," not the least in the governance of its colonies. As for France, it was not just the embodiment, with its system of royal absolutism, of all we might condemn as "totalitarianism" today. It had a government so corrupt, so unjust, so repressive and so contemptuous of its own citizens' aspirations that it soon would drive its own people to popular revolt.

It is therefore instructive to note which side our Founding Fathers chose. All the injustices that soon would produce the French Revolution had not prevented Benjamin Franklin from kissing Marie Antoinette's hand, or a whole chorus of American revolutionaries from dancing attendance on Louis XVI as assiduously as, in our own times, revolutionary leaders make the rounds of Communist capitals—seeking loans, advisers and guns.

Of course, according to the British, Versailles was only trying to use the revolution for its own ends, which was no less than the truth. Employing the Americans as surrogates in its struggle with Britain in North America, much as we (and the Soviets) use similar groups today, France won a great battle in its world war with Britain at Yorktown in 1781, when Cornwallis' British forces, trapped by a French fleet, surrendered to the Americans. The very achievement of our independence thus had flowed from configurations of great-power politics we neither created nor controlled.

What of the maintenance of that independence? Today when leaders of newly independent nations try to pursue a foreign policy of nonalignment, our leaders often consider them suspiciously "un-American," little suspecting that the father of our country has an equally valid claim to paternity of the modern nonalignment movement in the Third World.

"It is our true policy," George Washington said in his Farewell Address of 1796, "to steer clear of permanent alliances with any portion of the foreign world." In later times, Washington's sage counsel to the young republic would undergo as fantastic a metamorphosis in the American imagination as the "Monroe Doctrine" or the Battle of Tippecanoe. Washington, however revered for his other accomplishments, would be remembered as the purveyor of antiquated, indeed pernicious foreign-policy theorems. James Monroe, on the other hand, would be venerated as the originator of a policy of strong American, above all strong presidential, intervention in struggles all over the globe.

But Washington was no isolationist and Monroe no interventionist. In a frequently ignored passage in the Farewell Address, Washington had emphasized the need for foreign alliances. Permanent foreign entanglements, Washington pointed out, threatened U.S. independence; even more dangerously, they aggravated domestic divisions. But "temporary alliances for extraordinary emergencies" were both justified and necessary. Unlike so many of his modern successors, the first President appreciated that the only constant in international affairs is national interest. He also understood the folly of attempting to superimpose on the constant flux of the world some rigid structure of American commitments.

Though they differed on domestic policies, Monroe was in profound agreement with Washington on foreign policy, because Washington's advice was so obviously correct. What Washington called "[t]he duty of holding a neutral conduct" was the only logical choice if the United States was to develop the substance, not just the form, of true independence. Only by minimizing both our own involvement in great-power struggles and foreign intervention in our internal affairs, as Washington put it in a statement that might be made at any nonaligned conference today, could the United States

> gain time . . . to settle and mature its yet recent institutions, and to progress without interruption to that degree of strength and consistency, which is necessary to give it, humanly speaking, the command of its own fortunes.

In 1823, for all the talk of the "threat" from the Holy Alliance, the new and overriding geopolitical fact of life was the utter supremacy in world affairs of Great Britain. France had won the battle of Yorktown (and many other famous victories) in the course of its long struggle with Britain. But with Napoleon's defeat at Waterloo, as we have seen, France definitively lost the war. When all was said and done, Metternich, in faraway Vienna, had a keener grasp of the strategic dilemma confronting Monroe and Adams than those in Washington who talked of aggression from Europe and the need for New World doctrines to counter it. Not just France—our traditional ally against Britain—but the whole of Europe, lacked the arms to reach America, or even a means to have its voice heard there. Instead, after forty years of paper independence, it was Great Britain, more than ever, that, in the western hemisphere as in most parts of the world, was incontestably the dominant power.

What did this all mean for the United States? Quite simply it meant that the entire foundation of the foreign policy that had won us our independence had been overturned by Napoleon's defeat at Waterloo. Even before Napoleon's defeat, Britain had experienced little difficulty in containing the United States militarily during the War of 1812. But now the United States found itself a nation surrounded—by a vise of British might.

Britain was master of Canada to the north and the Caribbean to the south, and unchallenged master of the seas surrounding the United States. A generation after independence, the United States still looked through a British window on a world that was now even more thoroughly a British dominion than it had been in colonial days.

This raised a question for Monroe and Adams very similar to the question the Brezhnev Doctrine poses for the Eastern Europeans, and our own "Monroe Doctrine" approach to this hemisphere poses so often for the Latin Americans. How can a weak nation maintain its nonalignment, its independence, when—at least in its own region of the world—one great power is so extraordinarily powerful and all the others are so comparatively weak? Indeed, in the case of the United States in 1823, it raised the danger of gradual incorporation into the sphere of influence of the nearest great power—in America's case, Great Britain.

All through 1823, Monroe consulted his fellow Virginians Jefferson and Madison about what policy he and Adams should adopt toward Britain, the Europeans and the Latin Americans—above all, toward our own national aspirations in relation to them all. From Monticello, Jefferson offered his usual sage advice. At the center of everything had to be our relations with London, because Great Britain was "the nation which can do us the most harm of any one, or all on earth." Jefferson, along with Monroe and Adams, no doubt would have considered all our later suppositions about the "Monroe Doctrine" nothing more than an absurd travesty of the problems they really faced and the policy the United States actually followed.

As A. P. Whitaker points out, the prime concern of Monroe and Adams in Latin America was not "to promote the independence of that region but to prevent Britain from adding it to her already overgrown empire." It was fear that Great Britain—not the Holy Alliance—would acquire Cuba from an enfeebled Spain that, in 1822, had caused Adams to call the "Cuban question" the most serious one facing the nation "since the establishment of our Independence." And it was Adams's concern the following year, as he wrote in his own diary, that events in Latin America might "throw them completely into [Great Britain's] arms, and in the result make them her colonies instead of those of Spain," that convinced him of the necessity of issuing the declaration later so inaccurately called the "Monroe Doctrine."

Today Monroe's and Adams's pervasive concern with Britain and with Britain's power to harm us may seem as fantastic as our own fantasies about the Monroe Doctrine no doubt would seem to them. But in 1823, far away from Latin America, British and American ambitions were already on a collision course. Both nations claimed Oregon—a vast territory stretching from California to Alaska, of which the present state of that name was only part. Monroe and Adams favored territorial compromise. But Britain spurned all such proposals and maintained its claim to the entire region. For the time being, London and Washington had agreed to joint occupation of Oregon. But a Britain newly dominant in South America would be even more unlikely to compromise in North America. For the United States, therefore, the most pressing danger in 1823 was not that the Holy Alliance would conquer Latin

America; it was that Great Britain would halt our own national expansion by clinging as stubbornly to Oregon as it had to Canada and that the United States would never fulfill its national destiny, but forever remain a small North Atlantic nation surrounded by a ring of British naval power and British client states.

South of Oregon, of course, lay the immensity of California, only recently transformed from a Spanish territory into a province of our newly independent sister republic of Mexico. Monroe and Adams contemplated no conquest of California, but territorial purchases in the manner of Jefferson's acquisition of Louisiana were considered not just possible but entirely likely in the fullness of time. And as Monroe himself had shown with his annexation of Florida, even this classic American noninterventionist was not averse to a little meddling in a neighbor's territory if the territorial ambitions of the United States were adequately served.

Yet here, again, the reality of British power rebuked any American illusion that our national destiny could be fulfilled easily, let alone inevitably. A system of independent Latin American republics "protected by the guarantee of Great Britain," as Adams put it in his diary, would establish a far stronger barrier to our national expansion than the Spanish had in Florida, because the world's greatest power would be behind them.

Thus, to all our other illusions about the "Monroe Doctrine" must be added a culminating one: it was our national ambitions in North America, not some philanthropic urge to help the Latin Americans, and our own quite justified sense of vulnerability to British power, not some threat of the European powers' harming our neighbors, that produced the document later revered as the "Monroe Doctrine."

Practical realists that they were, Monroe and Adams never let the American tendency to interpret events in terms of grand doctrines deflect them from the proper function of foreign policy, which is not to fulfill fantasies, but to protect real national interests. In the end, they acted as they did only because the United States—not Latin America—faced a serious challenge from the opposite side of the Atlantic. This challenge, emanating from both Britain and Russia, turned out to be diplomatic and peaceful. It was only friendly cooperation with the United States that both countries wanted. Yet each diplomatic initiative presented a challenge to American principles.

In August of 1823, the British Foreign Secretary, George Canning, had sent a very important message to Washington. In his message, the British Foreign Secretary made five general points about the prevailing state of affairs in Latin America, the possible ambitions of Spain, France and the other members of the Holy Alliance there, and Britain's own position. The full text of these five points is worth quoting in full, because the British note was nothing less than a first draft of the American "doctrine" Monroe supposedly proclaimed to the European colonial powers, including Britain, the following winter. Canning's observations were as follows:

1. We conceive the recovery of the Colonies by Spain to be hopeless.
2. We conceive the question of the recognition of them as Independent States, to be one of time and circumstances.
3. We are, however, by no means disposed to throw any impediment in the way of an arrangement between them and the mother country by amicable negotiations.
4. We aim not at the possession of any portion of them ourselves.
5. We could not see any portion of them transferred to any other Power, with indifference.

"[T]hese opinions and feelings are," as Canning himself wrote at the time, "common to your Government with ours," and Canning was, for the most part, entirely correct.

Since American and British objectives in Latin America were substantively identical, Canning added,

> why should we hesitate mutually to confide them to each other; and to declare them in the face of the world?
>
> If there be any European Power which cherishes other projects, which looks to a forcible enterprise for reducing the colonies to subjugation . . . by cession or conquest; such a declaration on the part of your government and ours would be at once the most effectual and least offensive mode of intimating our joint misapprobation of such projects.

In his effort to win American acceptance of his proposal, the British diplomat was not above grossly flattering the former colonists when it came to the importance such a joint initiative might have:

> Nothing could be more gratifying to me than to join with you in such a work [Canning concluded], and I am persuaded, there has seldom, in the history of the world, occurred an opportunity when so small an effort of two friendly Governments might produce so unequivocal a good and prevent such extensive calamities.

The cordiality of Canning's note demonstrated that any belief that Britain intended us harm was as hallucinatory as any belief the Holy Alliance would invade South America. Canning's notification that Great Britain "aim[ed] not at the possession of any portion" of Spain's former empire also laid to rest Adams's fear that "the independence of the South Americans" would only "result [in Great Britain's making] them her colonies instead of those of Spain."

Even more important, Canning's words about how "gratifying" it would be for the "two friendly Governments" to "join . . . in such a work" suggested a major turning point in the history of U.S. foreign policy, if not "in the history of the world." Ever since 1776, Britain's capacity to harm us had been the central fact of national life in the United States. Now Canning seemed to be making a proposal that would not merely serve U.S. interests in Latin America, but solve the central foreign-policy problem, confrontation with Britain itself, that had dominated the first two generations of our national life. For that reason, Jefferson counseled acceptance of Canning's proposal. Jefferson's observation that Britain "is the nation which can do us the most harm of any one, or all on earth" was no more than a case of stating the obvious in 1823. But his corollary observation—that "with her on our side we need not fear the whole world"—was a perception that would become a keystone of American policy only generations later. Jefferson's acute comment in fact may constitute the first real inkling in American strategic thinking that, once the legacy of two British-American wars faded away, and the other disputes, mostly territorial, dividing the two English-speaking nations were resolved, a special Anglo-American relationship could not only serve U.S. interests, but reshape the world.

All that, of course, lay far in the future. Nothing speaks more eloquently of the real position of the United States in the world in 1823, and of the real concerns of the Monroe administration, than that Jefferson's advice was rejected—unless it is the even more illuminating fact that Canning's friendly proposal generated considerably more apprehension in the White House and the State Department than talk of the Holy Alliance invading South America ever did. President Monroe, in his own words, was completely "averse to any course which would have the appearance of taking a position" of the kind Canning proposed, and Secretary of State Adams was equally opposed to the British proposal. The mere suggestion that the United States align itself with its former colonial ruler was sufficient to excite, in both the President and the Secretary of State, a reaction of prickly American national pride.

But they had even more substantive reasons for being suspicious of Canning's proposal. At worst, they feared, Canning's cordial suggestion was a ploy to entice the United States, through diplomacy, into an imperial design for the Americas that Britain had been unable to impose on us through war. And at best, from their perspective, Canning was offering the United States a partnership in which we would be, without question, a completely subordinate member.

Not that the American suspicions were entirely unfounded. Canning's motives were largely benign, but not even the most positive kind of joint action with the United States in the Americas could be separated from Britain's prime strategic concern of that time, its rivalry with the Europeans. For more than a year before President Monroe finally issued his statement, Canning had not just been sending the Americans friendly notes. He had been wooing the United States as assiduously as our own diplomats attempt, from time to time, to court nonaligned countries in the Third World today.

What was Canning up to? Our foreign missions back then had no electronic listening devices and parabolic antennas on the roof. But in 1823, our minister in London, Richard Rush, applied quill pen to parchment, put the parchment in an envelope, sealed the envelope with wax, and put it on a sailing ship. More than a month later, there arrived in Washington the kind of pithy, right assessment that not even the entire "intelligence community" seems capable of producing these days.

"It is France that must not be aggrandized," Rush observed of Canning's purpose, "not South America that must be made free." Even after the American, French and Latin American revolutions, a principle as old as warfare itself still guided British diplomacy: the enemy of Britain's enemy was its friend—or at least should be made so through deft maneuver. Britain thus was now the patron of Latin American liberation and the ardent suitor of the United States for the same reason that, less than fifty years earlier, it had gone to war against our own independence. Our Declaration of Independence, in 1776, had threatened, indeed had helped, to aggrandize France, and thus impeded Britain's efforts to sustain the "balance of power" in Europe. But, by 1823, independence in the New World could not help but serve the opposite purpose. An independent Latin America was by definition a place that garrisoned no Spanish armies, harbored no French fleets, did not contribute to Europe's weight in the balance of world affairs—and was thus an asset to Britain itself.

More than three quarters of a millennium after the Battle of Hastings, British policy, as it would be into our own time, was infused with that visceral sense that the defense of England begins and ends in France, no matter how far-flung and convoluted the route in between. And thus, in the loss of its American empire by France's ally, Spain, Canning perceived a magnificent opportunity, as both Rush, in London, and Monroe and Adams, in Washington, fully recognized, for Britain itself. For Canning, the beauty of independence was not that it liberated the Mexicans or the Argentines. It was that it liberated Britain itself from garrisoning, administering and defending yet another pink patch on the map of the world.

At a stroke, Britain's rivals were deprived of any chance to inflict on Britain a two-front war. Yet, at the same time, independence freed Britain itself from acquiring any new imperial obligations—obligations which by then spanned the globe from Oregon to India, and from the Caribbean to Burma.

As Jefferson's reaction demonstrated, Canning's proposal had been well baited, but that did not stop it from being a kind of trap, for it amounted to a classic case of a great power attempting to charm a small, nonaligned nation onto its team, the better to help it in its rivalry with the other great powers. Whatever other benefits Canning offered the United States, his proposal therefore threatened the basic principle of American foreign policy. As Monroe and Adams fully realized, to join with the British in the declaration Canning proposed would undermine our entire approach to the world as an independent nation, going back to Washington's Farewell Address.

Not that the potential snares of Canning's proposal ended there. In spite of its cordial, diplomatic tone Canning's letter also threatened America's future national ambitions as well.

Certainly it was gratifying to our President and Secretary of State that Britain was renouncing any territorial ambitions of its own in Latin America. But what of the ambitions of the United States itself? By 1823, it was an established tenet of American national faith that immense new lands would fall to us, as President James Madison had put it, through the "manifest course of events."

For Americans of all political tendencies, therefore, it was as much of an absurdity to suggest that our territorial expansion, as opposed to European expansion, was at an end in the Americas as it was to suggest that our national interests could be served by abandoning Washington's revered principle of nonalignment. Yet Canning was urging that the United States itself declare, along with Britain, that *"[w]e aim not at the possession of any portion"* of Spain's empire "ourselves."

By 1823, as Canning was well aware, the United States already had taken advantage of European weakness in the New World to acquire Louisiana and Florida, and few Americans doubted that Spain's only significant remaining New World colony, Cuba, would eventually fall into our hands like a ripe avocado.

Indeed, the threat of Cuba's following Florida into the American fold alarmed the British Foreign Secretary at least as much as the threat that Spain might transfer Cuba to France. U.S. expansion into the Caribbean could outflank the British position in Jamaica. Thus by the time Canning sent his message to Washington, Cuba was nearly as central to U.S. foreign-policy concerns as it would be 139 years later, during the Cuban missile crisis.

It is illuminating that not even in Washington was Cuban independence considered an option. Instead, as Canning himself recognized, and Adams and Monroe quickly came to appreciate, the most practical way to defuse a potential international crisis over Cuba was, in spite of all the talk about human liberty and national self-determination, to leave the island under the colonial rule of Spain. Enfeebled as it was, Spain could pose no threat to the rest of the hemisphere even if it kept Cuba. But a continuing Spanish presence there would serve to keep more powerful nations from using Cuba to further their own ambitions.

Tactically, therefore, Canning's proposal fitted in well with U.S. interests of the moment. The big problem was that the British were asking the United States to elevate expediency into principle—in this case the very principle (nonintervention in Latin American affairs and respect for Latin America's independence and territorial integrity) that we suppose it was the achievement of the "Monroe Doctrine" to have proclaimed to the world. We thus arrive at one of the greatest ironies of the "Monroe Doctrine." "Without entering now into the enquiry of the expediency of our annexing Texas or Cuba to our Union," Adams told the Cabinet, "we should at least keep ourselves free to act . . . and not tie ourselves down to any principle which might immediately afterwards be brought to bear against ourselves."

We shall momentarily see precisely how Monroe and Adams managed to sidestep Canning's attempt to bind the United States to the very principles later supposed to be the gift of the "Monroe Doctrine" to the world. But what of the other power whose ambitions potentially threatened Canning's New World design? Canning was not idle in any direction in 1823. Indeed, that September, two months in advance of Monroe's own statement, the British Foreign Secretary made the identical proposal to France that he had dispatched the previous month to the United States. And the Bourbon France of Louis XVIII—unlike the republican United States of James Monroe—immediately, unhesitatingly, totally, and with no signs of regret, committed itself to the very "Monroe Doctrine" principles the Monroe administration itself was so loath to embrace.

In the Polignac memorandum of October 9, 1823, the French Government formally confirmed

> That [it] believed it to be utterly hopeless to reduce Spanish-America to the state of its former relation to Spain.

> That France disclaimed, on her part, any intention or desire to avail herself of the present state of the Colonies, or of . . . Spain, to appropriate to herself any part of the Spanish Possessions in America. . . . That she abjured, in any case, any design of acting against the colonies by force of arms.

Nearly two months in advance of Monroe's own statement, France had joined Britain in issuing a "Monroe Doctrine" of its own. The difference was that the French, like the British, formulated a much firmer and more thorough commitment to Latin America's independence than any the United States was prepared to undertake. Indeed, by then, the only real question in Washington was not whether President Monroe would "sound the alarm" and so save the western hemisphere from invasion, but whether the United States itself could overcome its own reluctance to issue a broad declaration on behalf of hemispheric freedom—and bring itself to join a veritable stampede, on the other side of the Atlantic, to the cause of noninterference in Latin American affairs.

Canning had urged the Americans not to "hesitate." But, for months, hesitation was the only policy the Monroe Cabinet, unlike the ministers of Louis XVIII, could muster. Yet inaction also contained important dangers, the greatest of which was that a unilateral British pronouncement could be even more wounding of U.S. pretensions to an independent role in the world than a joint declaration. And a combined British-European pronouncement on behalf of the Latin Americans would "threaten" both our principles and our ambitions in the New World even more. In London, Canning had not informed Rush of the French declaration, but the American minister had informed Washington that Canning's earlier eagerness for a joint U.S.-British declaration had waned, indeed that the British Foreign Secretary now considered the matter of hardly any importance at all.

This time, it was President Monroe himself who divined the real significance of events. "Probably some inducement has been presented, after the French triumph in Spain, to quiet [Canning's] apprehensions," Monroe told Adams, quite correctly. As in Europe during the Cold War, so it also was in Europe following the defeat of Napoleon. The great powers might have had a falling out, but none of them had any desire to precipitate another general conflict. On the contrary, France was only too willing to sign on the dotted line, and thus let Canning's design for the Americas prevail, so long as Britain itself left France free to pursue its own design—the design of containing revolution—in Spain.

It was fear that the United States would be preempted by the British initiative—not solicitude for the freedoms of the Latin Americans—that finally prompted the Monroe administration to act. Were it not for the British Foreign Secretary, it is no exaggeration to state, there never would have been, for better or worse, a "Monroe Doctrine."

Even today it is the Russian czar who is remembered as the most avaricious of the aggressors whose conspiracies the Monroe Doctrine supposedly scotched. But that belief, too, is only a historical hallucination. The czar had liked Americans, and had had friendly feelings toward the United States ever since John Quincy Adams had served as our minister to Russia, during the War of 1812. Like the dispatches from London, the diplomatic notes from St. Petersburg fairly dripped with cordiality in 1823. The czar wanted no New World conquests in the Latin American tropics. He only desired peaceful negotiations, and an amicable settlement of the conflicting Russian, British and American claims to the cold and empty Pacific Northwest.

At their most extravagant, the claims of the Russian czar embraced not only Alaska, but Oregon and northern California as well. But the czar had made it clear he was quite willing to severely curtail his previous claims. By then our ambitions in the northwest only overlapped those of the Russians. They did not directly conflict, as our claims did with those of the British.

Yet the Russian diplomatic initiative raised nearly as many knotty problems as the British proposal, not the least of which was that Great Britain itself already had agreed to negotiate with Russia. For if Britain and Russia negotiated their own settlement in the northwest, we would be left out. Britain's claims to Oregon would be strengthened by an amicable settlement with Russia. And our own claims in the northwest might be imperiled if we refused to negotiate.

Expediency therefore dictated U.S. recognition of Russia's claims in Alaska. But Secretary of State Adams was just as opposed in principle to colonialism in the Arctic as he was to European rule much closer to home. In July 1823—nearly five months before the "Monroe Doctrine" was finally issued—he had let the Russian minister in Washington know in no uncertain terms

> that we should contest the right of Russia to any territorial establishment on this continent, and that we should assume distinctly the principle that the American continents are no longer subjects for any new European colonial establishments.

The Russian claims, distant as they were from our own interests, thus faced the Monroe administration with the same conflict of expediency and principle that our ambitions in Florida and the appeals of the Latin American independence forces for our recognition and help also had. Should we seek territorial advantage in our dispute with Britain over Oregon through peaceful compromise with the Russians over Alaska, even if it meant compromising our anticolonial principles? Or should we stand up to Russia's imperial pretensions right here in North America, whatever the risks and costs to ourselves?

It was these two peaceful initiatives from Europe that set in motion the events in Washington that, on the second of December 1823, would produce the document now known as the "Monroe Doctrine." And it was from the paramount concerns of U.S. foreign policy at that time—relations with Britain, and our own ambition to extend our boundaries to the Pacific—and certainly not from any desire to proclaim a doctrine for the Andes or the Amazon, that the statement flowed. It bespeaks a national capacity for fantasy, if nothing else, that such a statement should be remembered as the moment the United States defied the autocrats of Europe and propounded a doctrine of liberty for Latin America.

Much later, American historians not only would conceal Monroe's real message in a veritable mausoleum of scholarship; they would find themselves riven into warring factions over who deserved the real credit for the construction of their imposing edifice: Monroe, Adams, Madison and Jefferson (along with a whole host of minor figures) all would have their partisans.

In the form it finally took, Monroe's message flowed from many quill pens, dipped in many pots of ink.

To John Quincy Adams, however, must belong the strongest claim for drafting the entire structure of the message, and for the conception of its most important features. The czar had proposed negotiations in the northwest, but his proposal had not mentioned Latin America. Canning had proposed a joint declaration on Latin America, but had not linked it to the negotiations with the Russians. It was Adams who recognized that all these responses fell short of the real task at hand, which was not to say yes or no to the British and the Russians, but to lay out a coordinated policy for the United States. Where others saw crisis, Adams perceived a most useful opportunity to reaffirm

America's most important foreign policy principle of all: its nonalignment with both blocs. "It affords," he told Monroe and the Cabinet, "a very suitable and convenient opportunity to take our stand against the Holy Alliance and at the same time to decline the overture of Great Britain."

Rather than meekly accede to the principles of others, Adams added, "[i]t would be more candid, as well as more dignified, to avow our principles explicitly. . . ." In spite of his own, earlier strong words, Adams also counseled against any rash or intemperate American pronouncements. Rather than shaking a fist at anyone, the United States should announce its position in a "moderate and conciliatory manner, but with a firm and determined spirit."

The ensuing avowal of American principles contained four main points. Two of them did not deal with Latin America at all. One did deal with Latin America, though its central concern was not the freedoms of the Latin Americans, but the national interests of the United States. The most famous of the provisions—even today considered the cornerstone of the "Monroe Doctrine"—chiefly concerned the ambitions of the United States, and dealt almost exclusively with North America, indeed with the Arctic and the northwest, not with South and Central America.

This first provision, in fact, was not a U.S. initiative at all, but an acquiescent American response to the Russian diplomatic proposal. It pledged U.S. friendship for Russia, heaping fulsome praise on Czar Alexander I, the autocrat of three continents and the most powerful member of the Holy Alliance. "At the proposal of the Russian Imperial Government," the message announced, instructions had "been transmitted to the minister of the United States at St. Petersburg to arrange by amicable negotiation" the settlement the Russians sought.

"By this friendly proceeding," as Monroe himself described it, the United States hardly terminated the age of European colonialism in the Americas. To the contrary, it explicitly recognized Russia's "rights and interests . . . on the northwestern coast of this continent"—territories a third the size of the United States itself.

Practical diplomats that they were, Monroe and Adams had chosen the path of expediency. By explicitly recognizing Russia's "rights and interests . . . on the northwest coast of this continent," the Monroe administration assured that our own rights and interests there would not be left out of any settlement. Thus, they not only gratified the czar but served notice on Canning that the United States was not about to let any separate British-Russian settlement strengthen London's hand in Oregon.

What this first provision implied, the subsequent provisions of the message made explicit: Russia might be free to extend its system of government to North America. But that did not mean the United States would assume any reciprocal obligation to propagate its own principles in the Old World. "Our policy in regard to Europe," the message emphasized (following a lengthy digression into domestic affairs), ". . . remains the same, which is, not to interfere in the internal concerns of any of its powers." This was a point Monroe took pains to reiterate in his statement. "In the wars of the European powers in matters relating to themselves," he argued elsewhere in his text, "we have never taken part, nor does it comport with our policy to do so."

What was the significance of this second cardinal provision of the "Monroe Doctrine"—the only provision President Monroe had any power to enforce? While Monroe's pledge to keep the United States out of European affairs was important, his argument that "we have never taken part" in "the wars of the European powers in matters relating to themselves" was disingenuous. By the time Monroe wrote his message, the United States—willingly or not—had been deeply embroiled in European conflicts for nearly fifty years, as we have seen. The U.S. strategic relationship to Britain, since the Declaration of Independence, often had been a little like the strategic relationship of Cuba to the United States today. While Britain dueled with its European rivals, notably France, we had been a nettlesome annoyance, and sometimes a strategic threat, in Britain's rear.

With this pledge of U.S. noninvolvement in European conflicts, President Monroe gave the British something they had been seeking for decades. He laid the specter of Yorktown to rest at a moment when Britain once again was facing a coalition on the continent of Europe it considered hostile to its own interests.

Britain was not the only beneficiary of Monroe's strong reaffirmation of Washington's principles. The Holy Allies also benefited, and, even farther away, in the seraglios of the Sublime Porte, so did the Turks. From Spain to Greece, in 1823, local nationalists were fighting against imperial repression, and like the Latin Americans, the partisans of liberty in Europe looked to the United States for support.

Many Americans, including President Monroe himself, deeply sympathized with these struggles. As Samuel Flagg Bemis points out, both "Monroe and Calhoun initially favored reprov[ing] France for her invasion of Spain" and also including in Monroe's message "a broad acknowledgement of the revolted Greeks as an independent nation." Whatever else such a statement might accomplish, it would be sure to offend all the major nations of Europe. And as usual, it was Secretary of State Adams who checked the initial impulses of his colleagues and steered U.S. policy away from broad declarations of principle back onto the narrow path of practicality and national interest.

Interjecting the United States into the crises in Spain and Greece, Adams argued, could turn the whole of Europe against us and even create strong opposition at home to what manifestly would be a renunciation of Washington's nonalignment principle. The message, he warned, "would have an air of open defiance to all Europe" and undercut efforts to "carry the opinion of the nation with us, and the opinion of the world." Ironically enough, since "open defiance to all Europe" later was supposed to be the whole point of the "Monroe Doctrine," Adams's arguments carried the day.

To the extent this second provision of the message propounded any doctrine, it was Washington's Farewell Address that it elevated into a dogma—a dogma of American aloofness from the squabbles of the Europeans that would guide U.S. foreign policy for generations and not be fully discarded until our entry into World War I. Not that this desire to stay out of foreign conflicts was limited to Europe. Both Monroe and Adams were equally opposed to "permanent alliances" in the western hemisphere. The United States had steered clear of involvement in the Latin American wars of independence before the message was delivered. Following proclamation of the "Monroe Doctrine," its authors also rejected proposals for alliances from Brazil, Haiti, Colombia and other New World nations. "Abstention" was the real doctrine that guided U.S. foreign policy back then, and it was a doctrine Monroe and Adams applied to both hemispheres.

The first of Monroe's four points had rendered much to Russia, while serving U.S. interests by putting a great deal of daylight between us and Great Britain. The second point had offended no one except the embattled partisans of liberty in Europe, while serving the interests of potentates from Versailles to Constantinople.

The third provision of the "Monroe Doctrine" offered something for everyone—with the exception of those who imagine President Monroe proclaimed a doctrine of New World liberty. This section of the message did indeed deal with the question of colonial rule, both in Latin America and, equally important, in North America itself—but hardly in the manner later generations supposed. The truth is that President Monroe did not so much come to bury colonial rule in the New World as to praise it. Far from making the United States the champion of the struggle for freedom in the western hemisphere, the Monroe message reiterated a U.S. policy which, had France adopted such a policy a half century earlier, might well have left the Founding Fathers all hanging—together or separately, depending on the verdicts of British military courts.

Stressing "our neutrality" in the struggle between Spain and the independence forces in Latin America, President Monroe formally committed the United States to respect for the American empires of the European powers— ranging from France's island remnants of empire off Newfoundland and in the Caribbean, to Britain's own vast American empire, at that time far larger than the United States itself. More than that, the "Monroe Doctrine" fully acknowledged all of Europe's rights in the New World while avoiding any assertion of any inherent right to self-determination on the part of the colonized. Independence might be an "unalienable" and "self-evident" right for us, as the Declaration of Independence asserted. But in Latin America, at least from the U.S. perspective, such a right was not obvious at all.

"With the existing colonies or dependencies of any European power," President Monroe pledged, "we have not interfered and shall not interfere." This statement, too, was disingenuous. The United States certainly had "interfered" in Canada during the War of 1812, and General Jackson's "incursions" into Spanish Florida, under President Monroe himself, also had constituted interference of the most blatant sort. Thus, to the extent President Monroe inaugurated a new U.S. policy in this section of the "Monroe Doctrine," it was one of retreat from the anticolonialist policies that previously had guided U.S. actions.

Such are the two middle provisions of the "Monroe Doctrine," which subsequent presidents have largely preferred to forget as they enmeshed the United States in European affairs and attempted to justify, among other things, the U.S. seizure of Spain's remaining colonies in the New World.

It is the final provision of Monroe's statement that most Americans still have in mind when they remember the "Monroe Doctrine" as having proclaimed the right of the Latin Americans to independence from European control—and having guaranteed that right by pledging U.S. protection for the newly independent Latin republics.

Yet just as one searches in vain, in President Monroe's message, for any assertion of any intrinsic Latin American right to independence, so one also searches without result for any concrete U.S. pledge to help defend it, even after the Latin Americans had won it for themselves.

In fact, Monroe established a three-part test for Latin American independence—a test the United States itself certainly would have failed had it been applied on the Fourth of July, 1776. It was not enough, by Monroe's standards, for a country to have declared its independence. Before U.S. recognition (not actual support) could be forthcoming, the country in question must have "maintained it," that is, successfully defeated any attempts by the colonial ruler to retain control. In other words, if a European nation like Spain or Portugal was capable of putting down an independence movement, even after its colonial subjects had declared their right to be free, that was no concern of the Monroe administration.

Nor was it even enough for a Latin American country to have declared and "maintained" its independence. To fall within the purview of the policy President Monroe was outlining, such states had to be countries "whose independence we have . . . acknowledged." Only then would the United States consider "any interposition for the purpose of oppressing them or controlling them" by any European power unjustified—not because such "interpositions" harmed the Latin Americans, but because, as President Monroe bluntly put it, they would be interpreted as "the manifestation of an unfriendly disposition *toward the United States.*"

This provision was based exclusively on U.S. *Realpolitik,* not on Latin American rights. It made no explicit American commitment of any kind to aid any Latin American states whose independence might be endangered by

European aggression. The message merely stated that the United States would not "behold such interposition in any form with indifference"—the kind of diplomatic language that, fully in keeping with the Monroe administration's caution in foreign affairs, risked nothing, because it committed the United States to nothing:

> We owe it, therefore, to candour, and to the amicable relations existing between the United States and those [European] powers, to declare that we should consider any attempt on their part to extend their system to any portion of this hemisphere as dangerous to our peace and safety. With the existing colonies or dependencies of any European power we have not interfered and shall not interfere. But with the governments who have declared their independence and maintained it, and whose independence we have on great consideration and on just principles acknowledged, we could not view any interposition for the purpose of oppressing them or controlling in any other light than as the manifestation of an unfriendly disposition toward the United States. . . .

Monroe's message left the United States free to express its lack of "indifference" in any manner it chose—from breaking diplomatic relations to a formal declaration of war. But, as we shall see, when such contingencies arose—when "outsiders" actually did attempt to crush the independence of Latin American states and did seize their territories—the United States in fact did what the message also allowed it to do. That is to say, nothing at all. And since Monroe's caution against European "interposition" applied only to those nations "whose independence we have . . . acknowledged," the "Monroe Doctrine" excluded many Latin Americans from even the vague assurances Monroe's message did contain. By 1823, the United States had not yet recognized the independence of Brazil, Peru, Central America or Haiti.

The "Monroe Doctrine," so far as the Latin Americans were concerned, was thus informed by a triple irony from its very inception. Far from ridding the hemisphere of European tyranny, it pledged U.S. recognition of Europe's New World colonies. Far from protecting those nations that had won their independence, it offered no U.S. support at all. Beyond all that, it excluded from its provisions, ineffective as they were, those nations whose independence was most fragile or controversial. So far as the actual provisions of President Monroe's message were concerned, Portugal was free to restore its union with Brazil, Spain to fight on in Peru. Even France—which first had lost control of Haiti a full generation earlier, in 1791—was free to crush the world's first black republic.

Of course the Monroe message did the Latin Americans no harm, unlike later U.S. efforts, under the "Monroe Doctrine," to "defend" Latin America from what President Reagan in our time calls "forces not of this hemisphere." Yet to suggest such U.S. military interventions are authorized—let alone necessitated—by the "Monroe Doctrine" is not merely a misrepresentation, but a perversion of Monroe's actual words and his administration's real intent.

Is the belief that President Monroe closed the western hemisphere to European colonialism an entire fabrication? The answer is that it is *almost* entirely a myth. Immediately following his paean to the czar, in the course of discussing the conflicting U.S., Russian and British claims in the Pacific Northwest, President Monroe made the famous statement that later supposedly would have such millennial import for Latin America:

> In the discussions to which this interest has given rise and in the arrangements by which they may terminate [the President informed Congress], the occasion has been judged proper for asserting, as a principle in which the rights and interests of the United States are involved, that the American continents, by the free and independent condition which they have assumed and maintain, are henceforth not to be considered as subjects for future colonization by any European powers. . . .

Taken out of context (as later they always were) these are strong words, even audacious ones. In fact the statement marked a substantial retreat from the much broader anticolonialist position Adams had taken less than five months earlier with the Russians. At that time, the United States had opposed "the right of Russia to any territorial establishment on this continent." This most famous dictum of the "Monroe Doctrine," like most of its other provisions, reflected a tendency, hardly new to the Monroe administration, to limit the American impulse to proclaim doctrines to the world, in proportion to our manifest limitations there.

The words about "future colonization" were of the most limited importance for another reason. By the time the United States made its avowal, "as a principle," future colonization simply was not the main, or even a major, issue either in Latin America or Europe. Spain and Portugal were unable, the other European powers unwilling, to attempt "future colonization" there—and one and all, on both sides of the Atlantic, knew it. And even had the Europeans been able or willing, the scope for "future colonization" would have remained very small, because by then almost all of Latin America was either long colonized or already independent—and the powerful independence armies of Latin America, which already had defeated the Spanish, now also had Canning and the Royal Navy as their de facto ally.

Monroe and Adams were quite right to describe their opposition to future colonization "as a principle in which the rights and interests of the United States are involved" and to avow it in the course of their discussion of the northwest, because for all practical purposes, the only major parts of the New World where "future colonization" was likely to occur, by December 1823, were not in Latin America at all. They were in North America, and consisted of those immense northwestern lands, west of the Rockies and stretching from California to Alaska, which the United States, still lacking a Pacific coastline nearly fifty years after the Declaration of Independence, coveted for itself. Since these lands were virtually unsettled, and in many cases unexplored, what rights possibly could be violated even if they did become the scene of "future colonization" by European powers?

President Monroe made no attempt to cloak U.S. ambition in moral principle. The "rights and interests of the United States are involved," the message bluntly stated—making very clear the motivation behind this provision of the message. Having pledged respect for Europe's colonies in the Americas, promised U.S. noninterference in Europe's affairs, and bowed in the direction of Latin American independence in his message, President Monroe did not neglect to proclaim something on behalf of the United States—no "doctrine" of hemispheric liberty, but some clear-cut territorial ambitions of America's own.

Canning had managed, after all, to elicit a broad U.S. statement opposing European colonization in Latin America—but only as a throwaway line in a declaration whose central purpose was to reiterate U.S. opposition to Britain's own expansion right here in North America.

Few phrases in American history have been used to justify more—and to excuse more—than Monroe's dictum against "future colonization." Yet no amount of ex post facto mythmaking can change either the reality or the circumstances Monroe's message addressed. This, quite simply, is that President Monroe and his collaborators had absolutely no intention of propounding a doctrine for Latin America, no desire to impose some immutable hemispheric order. They never imagined for a moment that their statement later would be used to justify a United States system of chronic military intervention in its neighbors' internal affairs, let alone that it would assume the proportions of some immutable national principle in the United States:

> [W]e should emphasize the fact [Perkins writes] that there is no evidence that Monroe was in any degree aware that he was enunciating maxims which should govern in perpetuo, or at least for a long time to come, the foreign policy of the United States. The language of the message related to a specific situation. . . .

Future events would shortly make it manifest that not even opposition to colonization was an immutable principle, so far as the authors of the "Monroe Doctrine" were concerned. Great Britain, as Canning assured the Monroe administration, may not have aimed at future colonization in Latin America, but events soon vindicated the maxim that the British Empire was acquired in a fit of absent-mindedness. Less than three years after President Monroe issued his statement, Great Britain began to expand a few logging settlements on the Caribbean coast of Guatemala into a full-scale colony. By 1836, Britain had seized almost the entire eastern coast of Guatemala and turned "British Honduras"—known as Belize today—into an integral part of the British Empire. The Central Americans, at that time linked together in an unstable and weak confederation, were powerless to stop the British, much as they protested the action.

These British encroachments posed no general menace to Latin America, let alone to the whole western hemisphere. But they did prove the point on which Monroe, Adams and Jefferson all had agreed. Great Britain, not the Holy Alliance, was the power with the greatest capacity to threaten, indeed to undo, the work of independence in the New World. More than that, British encroachment constituted a clear-cut violation of the "Monroe Doctrine" as Monroe had actually formulated it. Surely the United States, as the habitual champion of New World freedom, would ride to the rescue—or at least make clear its "lack of indifference"?

Both President John Quincy Adams, who presumably recognized a violation of the "Monroe Doctrine" when he saw one, and President Andrew Jackson, never averse to a scrap with the British, failed even to protest, let alone give the Central Americans any effective support. For a century and a half, indeed, the United States would remain as neutral in the dispute between Britain and Guatemala over Belize as it had remained neutral in the Latin American wars of independence. Finally, in the late 1970s, the United States did change its policy of neutrality—to one of direct support for Britain's plans to grant Belize independence, over Guatemala's protests.

Even today our historic insensitivity to Guatemala's claims is, along with our overthrow of its government in 1954, one of the two major elements in the pathology of our relations with that country. American presidents come and go; our protestations of hemispheric solidarity are eternal. Yet the Guatemalans for nearly 160 years have known what most other Latin Americans also have learned: that we Americans apply the "Monroe Doctrine," like all our other principles, only where and when it suits our convenience.

Again, in 1833, in the distant South Atlantic, there occurred one of those trivial events that plant the seeds of enormous melodrama in the distant future. A British flotilla appeared in the Malvinas Islands and evicted the Argentine population, including its governor. This was a case of European "interposition" even more blatant than the expansion of Britain's settlements in Central America. Again the United States did nothing. Argentina vainly protested the British seizure of the Falkland Islands for no less than 149 years —until 1982.

The Falkland Islands War is vivid enough in most peoples' memories not to require recapitulation here. Yet even as it was unfolding, few people in the United States appreciated how starkly that obscure and overblown clash of nationalisms illustrated the true nature of our habitual policy toward Latin America. For more than two years before the Argentines seized the islands, the United States had been citing El Salvador as a classic case of extrahemispheric aggression, against which the entire Organization of American States should rally. Yet, less than six weeks following President Reagan's speech about "our common destiny" and "our shared ideals," Latin Americans were witnessing the spectacle of the United States, erstwhile defender of the hemisphere against outside intervention, taking Britain's side in the dispute.

The United States had not applied the "Monroe Doctrine" against Britain's encroachment on Guatemala in the 1830s, because the national interests of the United States were not involved. It actively supported Britain in the 1980s, in defiance of the "Monroe Doctrine," for the opposite reason. The trans-Atlantic alliance with Britain, for all our talk about a hemispheric unity, manifestly transcended the value of good relations with Argentina.

The "Monroe Doctrine" was never intended to impose, and certainly did not have the effect of imposing, some absolute U.S. ban on "future colonization" in Latin America. Nor did it obligate the United States, as later presidents purported, to intervene militarily in "defense" of the hemisphere. The truth is that in 1823 the objective was exactly the opposite: to issue a U.S. statement, as Adams put it, "*disclaiming* all intention of attempting to propagate [U.S. principles] *by force.*"

The full text of Adams's statement to the Cabinet, which President Monroe approved, merits quotation, because it perfectly summarizes both the actual contents of the 1823 message and its utter discrepancy from the "Monroe Doctrine" conjured up in later years:

> My purpose [the Secretary of State told the Cabinet] would be in a moderate and conciliatory manner, but with a firm and determined spirit, to declare our dissent from the principles avowed in these communications [from Europe]; to assert those upon which our own Government is founded, and, while disclaiming all intention of attempting to propagate them by force, and all interference with the political affairs of Europe, to declare our expectation and hope that the European powers will equally abstain from the attempt to spread their principles in the American hemisphere, or to subjugate any part of these continents to their will.

On the opposite side of the Atlantic, the reaction was principally one of indifference. The members of the Holy Alliance took neither particular umbrage nor satisfaction in this American statement that so diplomatically and tactfully expressed opposition to a course of action they never had intended anyway.

Even in Washington, reaction was muted. "It seems to be the work of several hands," Clay remarked to Adams, in obvious reference to the message's disorganization and the variety of subjects it mentioned. "The War and Navy Departments make a magnificent figure in it," Clay dryly added, "as well as the Post Office."

Adams found it necessary to remind Clay that the message had touched on foreign affairs at all. "There is an account of a full treasury," the New England diplomat informed the orator from Kentucky, "and much concerning foreign affairs, which is the business of the Department of State." Adams's rival for the presidency acknowledged that "the part relating to foreign affairs is the best part of the message."

Then Clay delivered a most illuminating statement—considering the significance the "Monroe Doctrine" was supposed to have had in later years. "The Government had weakened itself and the tone of the country," he remarked, "by withholding so long the acknowledgment of South American independence." Far from seeing the message as an audacious charter of New World freedom, Clay recognized it for what it was, a message fully in keeping with the caution Monroe and Adams habitually brought to the conduct of U.S. foreign affairs—a belated pronouncement that was still infused with a deep reluctance to take real risks for the cause of our neighbors' freedom.

For reasons of their own, the Latin Americans—the supposed beneficiaries of the "Monroe Doctrine"—took even less notice of the message than people in Europe and the United States. As repeatedly would be the case in future U.S. hemispheric initiatives, the Latin Americans had not been consulted before the Monroe administration issued its unilateral declaration. Nor did the message provide what the Latin Americans really wanted from the United States in 1823 and so often in the future: constructive cooperation, not rhetoric. At that time, Latin American leaders such as Bolivar and O'Higgins dreamed of establishing an "American System," in which the republics of the New World would band together to defend their principles of liberty, just as the Holy Allies had united to defend the principles of monarchical legitimacy. But, far from responding to Latin American aspirations for a concert of the Americas to balance the concert of Europe, the northern, English-speaking republic was going it alone.

The United States for years had rebuffed Latin American efforts to establish closer ties. This policy would only grow stronger after the "Monroe Doctrine" was issued. Less than three years later, Simon Bolivar convoked the Congress of Panama, hoping the congress would create a hemispheric system of liberty, not force, and of equality, not hegemony, and "act as a Council in great conflicts, to be appealed to in case of common dangers." If the nations of the New World did cooperate, Bolivar believed, the result could be a brilliant future, for both Americas, in which New World justice merged with might. "What then," he asked, "shall be the Isthmus of Corinth, compared with that of Panama?" But John Quincy Adams—by then in the White House—sent only observers to Panama and with strong instructions to avoid involvement in any such visionary schemes.

Only generations later, after it had become the dominant power of the hemisphere, did the United States show any interest in such hemispheric institutions as the Pan-American Union and the Organization of American States—and then only as rubber stamps for such actions as the U.S. seizure of Panama for itself, and invasions of Guatemala, the Dominican Republic and Cuba. By then the dream of hemispheric concord, like the "Monroe Doctrine" itself, had become the nightmare of repression and foreign intervention that continues in El Salvador today.

In 1823, it was Simon Bolivar, not James Monroe, who was the commanding personality of the western hemisphere. Bolivar's stunning battlefield victories, above all his visionary policies in fields ranging from the abolition of slavery to the formation of an American System, had made him the hero of the Americas and a figure of immense prominence in Europe as well. Bolivar's unification of the northwestern quadrant of South America promised the emergence of a third American republic that, along with the United States and Brazil, would be virtually continental in extent, and equally consequential in world affairs.

Mexico, too, at that time, seemed destined for a greatness as manifest as our own. The United States and Mexico in 1823 in fact were virtually identical in extent—and Mexico's provinces of Texas and California clearly were naturally richer and of much greater potential than Oregon, even if we managed to make our claims there prevail against British might. Our theft of half Mexico's national territory—in an equally real sense, our theft of its national future—lay a quarter century away. Argentina, too, seemed destined for an important role in world affairs, and Brazil already was a power of far greater consequence than its erstwhile colonial master, Portugal.

By then the former colonial rulers of Latin America were minor powers. As every major statesman of the time agreed, even the combined might of the Iberian monarchies would have been insufficient to attempt, let alone realize, the reconquest of even a significant fraction of the New World.

But what of the United States? The truth is that where the Latin Americans were safe, we were vulnerable. Our own former colonial ruler—unlike Spain and Portugal—was still a great power, in fact the greatest power in the world, and no Iberian armadas stood between the United States and the Royal Navy. Instead, as we saw earlier, British sea power and British territory formed a vast arc nearly encircling the United States to the north, east, south—and even to the west.

In such a situation it was not merely unrealistic, but, as Adams and Monroe themselves fully realized, absurd, to suppose that any doctrine the United States might formulate could be of much significance in Latin America. The Latin Americans took little notice of what the United States chose to say in 1823 for the simple reason that, at that time, it would have made more sense, in strategic terms, for them to propound a "Bolivar Doctrine" on our behalf than for us to proclaim a "Monroe Doctrine" for them.

What was true of Latin America was true of the whole world. As Perkins points out, in a chapter ironically enough subtitled "Monroe Hurls Defiance at Europe," the general indifference to the message derived not just from the mildness of its provisions, but much more fundamentally from "a sense of American weakness, rather than American strength." Any notion that

Monroe's message assured Latin America liberty, like any supposition it turned aside a European threat, he observes,

> is legend and nothing more. It assumes a material strength on the part of the United States which close examination reveals not to have existed; it assumes that the United States was a great power, in the modern sense of the word, in 1823. It assumes this country was listened to then with the same respect which it commands today.

In one quarter, at least, the message did elicit satisfaction—and it was in the very place where the Monroe administration was most interested in not presenting the impression of American ingratiation.

"With this message, Great Britain was in hearty agreement," runs the pithy assessment of one nineteenth-century source. In fact, Monroe and Adams had provided all that Canning had hoped to gain from them, and more. The United States, not merely the Latin American republics, had become a part of his grand design for the Americas. For by pledging abstention from involvement in European conflict, the United States in fact was promising Britain not to ally itself with Britain's continental rivals, as the United States, either formally or effectively, had during both the War of Independence and the War of 1812. Never again, after 1823, would American ports harbor fleets hostile to the Royal Navy. Never again would American armies threaten Britain's rear while Britain fought a European war. Canning was right: in world terms, the most important strategic result of Spain's loss of its empire was not that Latin America was made free; it was that France and the rest of Europe were not aggrandized. Never again would Britain have to fight a two-front war in the Atlantic Ocean.

By promising to respect "existing colonies and dependencies," the American message also fell in with Canning's design that Cuba, rather than falling into the hands of either France or the United States, be left in the custody of Spain, where it would stay until the end of the century. But the long-term effect of this American pledge not to interfere with existing European colonies in the Americas was of much greater importance than that, for it amounted to a formal renunciation of the long-standing U.S. ambition to incorporate Canada into the Union.

Of course, Monroe and Adams took pains not to exclude eventual union by voluntary and peaceful means. Indeed, during the first half of the nineteenth century, most Americans were so trustful of our continental destiny that they believed all we wanted for ourselves would be rendered unto us not merely inevitably, but without our even having to fight for it. But this was only another national hallucination, as future events in Canada, Oregon, Texas and California would demonstrate—and the British knew it. Just as the chief practical effect of Monroe's reassertion of Washington's principle of nonalignment was to bar Britain's adversaries from the western hemisphere, so the chief historical result of this U.S. pledge not "to interfere" with Europe's existing colonies was to assure the peaceful consolidation of Britain's North American empire. Monroe's pledges to abstain from involvement in European wars and to avoid U.S. intervention in Europe's New World empires, in fact, amounted to a belated U.S. recognition of America's own strategic defeat in the War of 1812.

The final provision—the statement that the United States would not view European "interposition" in Latin America, at least in Latin American countries whose independence we recognized, with "indifference"—equally suited Canning's purpose, for effectively, if not formally, the United States had done what Canning asked and joined Britain in open opposition to European intervention in Latin America.

Historically, however, the main importance of this provision was what it implied for U.S.-Latin American relations. By issuing a unilateral declaration, rather than joining in one with Canning, the Americans had not merely failed to recognize any inherent right to Latin American independence or to pledge any specific U.S. support for maintaining that independence; by acting as they did, Monroe and Adams successfully *evaded* Canning's attempt to elicit a commitment of United States respect for the independence and territorial integrity of the Latin American republics.

The fact is of such monumental importance for the whole history of our relationship with Latin America that it must be reemphasized: Far from pledging U.S. support for the principle of Latin American liberty, Monroe's message committed the United States to the preservation of Spain's remnant New World dominions. Far from pledging U.S. respect for those former colonies that had won their independence, Monroe's message avoided committing the United States to nonintervention in the Latin American republics. The message urged only that the Europeans avoid such "interposition."

In this sense—and this sense alone—did the message contain the tiny acorn that ultimately would grow into a mighty "Monroe Doctrine" of constant U.S. violation of Latin America's sovereign and human rights. Even as early as 1823, Monroe's message—like the "Monroe Doctrine" later, and our own action in El Salvador today—was informed by a monumental double standard, both moral and political.

Over the past 160 years, the United States has changed enormously. But to read the "Monroe Doctrine" as President Monroe actually formulated it is to discover one constant of American nationalism. Then as now the United States was unwilling to commit itself to practicing what it so earnestly preached to others.

Unlike the "Monroe Doctrine" conjured up in later times, Monroe's message was above all a document of realism. The only sensible course for a vulnerable, newly independent nation that really valued its independence was a policy of nonalignment, whatever name for such a policy such a nation happened to choose. Future presidents and secretaries of state, notably in our time, would have served their nation, and us, far more effectively had they shared the talent of Monroe and Adams for trimming the sails of U.S. principle to the winds of change that course constantly not just around the western hemisphere but throughout the entire world.

Great things did flow from the diplomatic events of 1823—though not in the sense the mythology of the "Monroe Doctrine" later led Americans to believe. President Monroe's own fears, that the policy his administration was adopting "would have the appearance of taking a position subordinate to that of Great Britain," went to the nub of the matter. It was all the more important that the United States seem to be asserting an independent policy, precisely because the "Monroe Doctrine," far from ordaining a U.S. order for the western hemisphere, so manifestly was a case of the United States acquiescing to a British order for the whole world.

With his statement, Monroe in fact wiped the slate of British-American relations clean—eliminating with a few hundred words almost all the issues of contention that had pitted the two nations against each other for nearly fifty years. Forty-seven years after we had declared ourselves independent, Monroe liberated the United States from what might almost be called its postcolonial Oedipus fixation—so characteristic, even today, among newly independent nations—with the former fatherland. Never again (in spite of a number of future confrontations with Britain which the "Monroe Doctrine," in yet another irony, would be used to justify) would it be the principal purpose of U.S. foreign policy to murder England and marry Canada. For all his pains to avoid the appearance of alignment with Britain, Monroe's message, to the extent it was the origin of anything, was one of the seminal documents of the Anglo-American special relationship.

No one was more impressed by Canning's accomplishment than George Canning. Indeed his main complaint with the American message was that it might lead some to suppose that Monroe and Adams, not he, had been the real masters of events. Lest anyone suppose the contrary, Canning made public his own correspondence with the French soon after the Monroe message was sent to Congress; thereafter he publicly scoffed at all pretensions that the upstart Americans, not the British Foreign Secretary, had assured the emergence in the western hemisphere of a system of independent nations detached strategically from Britain's continental rivals: "I called the New World into existence," the British statesman boasted, "to redress the balance of the Old."

Modesty may not have been one of Canning's virtues; historical accuracy was. Canning's grandiloquent but accurate boast penetrates all the later mythology of the "Monroe Doctrine" the way a needle punctures a hot-air balloon. There is no statement in the history of diplomacy more wounding of America's imagination of itself as the creator of a "New World" order.

What did it matter to Canning if the Americans, instead of joining the British declaration, insisted on issuing a declaration of their own? What did it matter if Spain kept Cuba, if the Emperor of Russia was confirmed in the possession of his immense Alaskan icebox? Britain's unchanging objective, which Rush had so aptly defined, was fulfilled: *France* was not aggrandized.

Canning, of course, could no more foresee what ultimately would come of calling "the New World into existence to redress the balance of the Old" than Monroe could imagine what "doctrines" ultimately would be ascribed to his name. But even today, Canning's boast to Parliament holds true: Over the past 160 years, France has been replaced by Germany as the great continental weight on one side of the world balance of power, and then Germany has been replaced by Russia (once again). Britain itself has declined to a status not much more consequential than that of the United States in 1823.

Yet the Canning calculation still holds sway everywhere in the world, even as the principles of Monroe and Adams fail to prevail even in New World nations as tiny as El Salvador. If anything, Canning's diplomacy has shaped our century even more fundamentally than it shaped his own. Whether it is on the western front in 1918, or on the Normandy beaches in 1944, or at the Berlin Wall today, the New World ceaselessly redresses the balance of the Old. And thus—even as we cope with the nuclear balance of power—our mythology of the "Monroe Doctrine" is informed by its most stupendous irony, in this case an irony possibly fatal not just for such peoples as the Salvadorans, but for us as well: Far from being a bill of divorcement of the two hemispheres, Monroe's declaration enlisted (permanently, as it turned out) the New World in the ceaseless process of European balance-of-power politics. This supposed separation of the two hemispheres, this mythical ordination of a unique New World system, in reality was a milestone in the history of our own irretrievable enmeshment in the ceaseless quarrels and confrontations of the old, blood-drenched continent we imagine it has been the principal achievement of our history to transcend.

Later American historians would never cease to write as though some stupendous threat to the Americas had arisen in 1823—just as Americans later repeatedly would conjure up similar threats, into our time. Even today, it is a cardinal tenet of American mythology that the threat was turned aside only by some heroic feat of American diplomacy. Such overdramatizations do great injustice both to the subtlety of the game Canning was playing back in 1823 and to the ingeniousness of the response of Monroe and Adams to it. Even more important, such melodramatizations (like so many of our portrayals of international events today) grossly misrepresent the motives of the supposed "aggressor." Although the Holy Alliance still looms in our mythology as some precursor of the Axis, of the "Sino-Soviet Bloc," of the "larger imperialistic plan" President Reagan perceived in the Salvadoran matanza in 1982, the truth is that it is difficult to imagine how the Holy Alliance could have been more reasonable and less aggressive when it came to the major diplomatic issues affecting the western hemisphere in 1823. The czar, far from unleashing the Cossacks on North America, sought peaceful negotiations over Russian claims to Alaska that were at least as well founded as Britain's claims to Canada, or our own to Louisiana. France, far from seeking to avenge the loss of Quebec or the defeat at Waterloo, both renounced its American ambitions and refused to aid Spain. Even Metternich was a model of "Monroe Doctrine" principles when it came to the affairs of the New World.

Not until 1846, a full twenty-three years later, would any Latin American nation be threatened by foreign invasion. And when that threat arose it would not come from Europe. Instead, in yet another of the many ironies infesting our image of ourselves as the defenders of liberty in the western hemisphere, that threat would come from the United States itself.

Monroe's "assertion of the noncolonization principle accomplished nothing," Perkins acknowledges. "[A] harsh critic might even go so far as to describe it as a barren gesture."

Of all the continuities that do link the 1820s with the 1980s, the most important, so far as our foreign policy is concerned, is the one Americans always find it most difficult to accept: the continuing, no doubt insuperable, limitation we face whenever we attempt to make the world comply with our principles.

The United States was weak back then, of course; today a single U.S. battalion commands more firepower than all the nations of the earth could muster in 1823. But, as we have seen, not just Monroe and Adams, but the czar of Russia, Metternich, the ministers of Louis XVIII and even George Canning—brilliantly though he manipulated the affairs of the world's greatest power—all inhabited a world of limitations. Not only that, all of them recognized it. That is the chief reason the potential crises of 1823 were followed not by another general war, involving both Europe and the Americas, but by a generation of peace in the western hemisphere and three generations of (relative) peace on the opposite side of the Atlantic.

The truth of the matter is that today most Americans—liberals and conservatives alike—would not know what to make of the authors of the "Monroe Doctrine," because Monroe and Adams fervently believed it was not the business of the United States either to police the world or to redeem it. Our fifth President and his Secretary of State would have considered both our arms shipments to El Salvador and our land-reform programs there, both Ronald Reagan's counterinsurgency campaign and Jimmy Carter's human-rights campaign, not just absurdities but morally wrong—indeed totally contrary to the real interests of both the Salvadorans and the United States.

Quite simply, they believed it was in no sense the function of the United States Government—of its presidents, its secretaries of state, its diplomats, secret agents and armies—to charge around the hemisphere, let alone the world, conferring "freedom" on foreign peoples. To them the very idea of the United States doing this was not only absurd; it amounted to a contradiction in terms. How can one nation or people confer—let alone impose by force of arms—"freedom" on another? Invisible as this contradiction so often is to us today, it is a contradiction—the same one that still infests so much of what we do in foreign countries, notably El Salvador—that, to Monroe and Adams, was manifest.

Just as the meaning of morality changes with time, so do the meanings of words. Liberal and conservative alike today would dismiss Monroe and Adams as "isolationists" even though, as we have seen, they were far less isolated from the flux of international events than many subsequent leaders were.

But one period's craven "isolationism" can be the most noble principle of another age. Certainly that was the case with the principle of "abstention," which Monroe and Adams regarded not merely as an expediency, but as a moral imperative. The nuance is worth emphasizing. They were, to be exact, noninterventionists, as opposed to isolationists. For them, belief in abstention from involvement in other peoples' internal affairs in no sense implied any indifference, moral or political, to foreign struggles—whether they unfolded in Europe or in our own hemisphere.

In his message, President Monroe not only made clear his belief in the correctness of the struggle for liberation in the New World. He made no attempt to conceal where his sympathies lay in similar struggles in Europe. Considering the efforts "in Spain and Portugal to improve the condition of the people in those countries," he observed:

> Of events in that quarter of the globe, with which we have so much intercourse and from which we derive our origin, we have always been anxious and interested spectators. The citizens of the United States cherish sentiments the most friendly in favor of the liberty and happiness of their fellow-men on that side of the Atlantic.

But when it came to other people's struggles for freedom, President Monroe considered the only proper role for the United States to be that of "spectator," no matter how important the issues involved.

Many years earlier, the man who was to become Monroe's Secretary of State had expressed the identical principle in only a slightly different way. In 1794, Adams, then only twenty-seven, had surveyed the revolutionary upheavals on the other side of the Atlantic and enunciated the principle that would guide him during the Latin American wars of independence and shape his approach to foreign affairs until the end of his extraordinarily long and fruitful public career, which came only in 1848, at the age of eighty-one.

Anticipating by two years the foreign-policy principles of Washington's Farewell Address, the young diplomat argued in his "Marcellus" letters that "it is our duty to remain, the peaceful and silent, though sorrowful spectators of the European scene."

Explicitly Adams reavowed this same principle even as he and President

Monroe were composing the "Monroe Doctrine." It was the function of U.S. diplomats, the Secretary of State instructed his envoys, to be "tranquil but deeply attentive spectators" of the Latin Americans' struggle against Spain. Under no circumstances were they to involve themselves in the struggle for liberation, no matter how much they—and the U.S. Government—sympathized with the partisans of liberty. Thus the cautious rhetoric of the "Monroe Doctrine" mirrored the equally cautious approach of the Department of State to the daily conduct of foreign affairs.

Why were Adams and Monroe so opposed to the United States' taking a stand on behalf of what they so earnestly believed was right for the Latin Americans?

The truth of the matter is that they were far less fearful of "losing" Latin America to the Holy Alliance than they were of the United States' losing its own soul. They feared that use of American force abroad inevitably would coarsen and compromise our concepts of liberty at home.

On the Fourth of July of 1821, in the course of his long public debate with Henry Clay over foreign policy, Adams delivered one of the most prescient (and ignored) analyses of the relationship between foreign policy and domestic affairs in the whole of American history. Responding to Clay's urgings that the United States directly intervene in the Latin American struggles, and to suggestions from Europe that the United States involve itself in the struggles for reform and independence there as well, Adams—as he had done and would for more than half a century—argued that the only correct policy for the United States was to be "the well-wisher to the freedom and independence of all" but "the champion and vindicator only of her own." He based his argument on the general principle of abstention and on the rights of others to work out their own destinies free from "interposition" by us or anyone else.

Adams had seen in his countrymen's earlier impulse to help the French storm the Bastille that same danger to our own internal liberties that, in much more recent times, has been greatest precisely at those moments when we Americans have imagined that we and we alone can "stop communism" or "defend the Free World." As Bemis puts it, Adams "sensed in the South American revolution the same temptation that had beset his fellow countrymen in the time of the French Revolution: to rush into a foreign conflict to save somebody else's liberty—and perhaps to lose their own."

This was a strange fear by our present standards, indeed an entirely contradictory one in terms of all the "doctrines" we have followed in the twentieth century. Did not President Wilson involve us in World War I to "make the world safe for democracy"? Has not the same premise—that our own freedoms are safe only when we fight for the freedom of others—guided us in World War II and all our subsequent wars and been the great doctrine of our foreign policy in this, the age of our greatest power? From Korea to Indochina to El Salvador, we Americans have died—and even more often we have killed—because our faith that freedom is indivisible has given us no other choice.

Behind all our latter-day "doctrines" lies the American doctrine that by making war abroad—by visiting death and destruction on foreign countries—we somehow are not only defending their freedoms, but our own.

We thus now stand at the edge of the moral and philosophical abyss separating the authors of the "Monroe Doctrine" from our own "Monroe Doctrine" approach to El Salvador, and to so much of the rest of the world. It is a chasm even wider and even deeper than the abyss separating the actual provisions of the Monroe message from what Americans later have pretended them to be.

Today the principles of the early-nineteenth century seem not just quaint but without tangent to the ethical choices facing our leaders. What could some Fourth of July homily more than 160 years ago have to do with the foreign-policy dilemmas we face today? What relationship could there possibly be between the diplomacy of Monroe and Adams, no matter how much it has been mythologized, and the diplomatic conundrums of the nuclear age?

Occasionally there occur moments, insignificant though they may be, in which all our illusions of the past converge with all our illusions of the present—when, if only we take the trouble to notice, we can perceive the real continuities that run through our whole history and the whole of our relations with the external world.

A number of such moments occurred in mid-1981, as U.S. officials struggled to reconcile their rhetoric of liberty with the policy of force they were pursuing in El Salvador. In congressional hearings, for example, Secretary of State Haig had been arguing for closer ties with the military dictatorships of Argentina, Chile and Guatemala, as well as for increased military appropriations for El Salvador, when he was asked why the United States should support such regimes.

"We share the same values," he replied. And as our growing support for the Salvadoran matanza by then demonstrated, this had come to be no less than the truth. Ambassador Kirkpatrick's explanation for the murders of U.S. citizens in El Salvador had been the same as Defense Minister Garcia's explanation. The State Department's "proof" of Communist aggression there had been Garcia's proof as well. By then it was already clear that the U.S. objective in El Salvador was not justice—either for Americans or for the Salvadorans themselves. Instead, the values of Garcia and Colindres Aleman were the values of the White House and the U.S. embassy: The "Communists" must be eradicated at all costs.

Why has the United States backed so many regimes that have murdered so many people? In May 1981, Richard Nixon was asked the same question. Of course, by then, his removal in disgrace from the White House was nearly seven years in the past. His illegal bombings of Cambodia, on the grounds that they were necessary to "save" South Vietnam, his illegal wiretaps of those involved in the publication of the Pentagon Papers on the grounds that "national security" made such violations of our liberties necessary, to say nothing of the entire Watergate affair, long ago had removed the former President from the high councils of U.S. foreign policy.

Yet—like Haig, Kirkpatrick and President Reagan himself—Nixon saw our intervention in Central America not merely as a strategic necessity but as a moral duty. The United States had no choice but to intervene, in Nixon's view. In his judgment, "the Monroe Doctrine" was "just as important now as it was then," and so a war in Central America was necessary, just as a war in Indochina earlier had been. The history of one war, or even a dozen wars, is easy enough to relate. But to repeat the question that began this chapter, how does one come to grips with the progression through time and across foreign lands of an illusion, a fantasy, or a kind of hallucination?

Though we Americans seldom appreciate it, most of our foreign-policy disasters over the past seventy years can be traced to the illusion that the whole world now is no more to us than we suppose Latin America was back in 1823. We have believed that if only twentieth-century presidents proclaim the right doctrines to Europe and Asia, then the entire globe will vindicate our hallucinations, just as we imagine Latin America did back when President Monroe proclaimed his "doctrine."

The Nixon presidency is only the most melodramatic manifestation of certain truths that have dominated both our foreign policy and our domestic politics for much of the twentieth century: the greater the illusion of the man in the White House that he can confer liberty on foreigners, the more real becomes the threat to our own liberties here in the United States. The greater the fantasy of the man in the White House that he has but to proclaim a doctrine for the world to obey, the greater the likelihood the President himself will be undone by his own efforts to acquit himself as a hallucinatory Monroe.

Since 1917, six American presidents have sent U.S. troops to fight in major foreign wars. In each case the justifications were the same as those the Reagan administration marshaled for its intervention in Central America, the same arguments Monroe and Adams dismissed as "absurdities" back in 1823.

America incarnates good; the world is menaced by conspiratorial evil; if the conspiracy is allowed to prevail anywhere, it will triumph everywhere. But in each case the real doctrine was a notion both Monroe and Adams would have considered pernicious: that U.S. bombs and bullets could not merely destroy buildings, lay waste crops and maim human beings, but make the world, or at least large tracts of it, "safe for democracy."

On two of these six wartime presidents no complete historical judgment is possible. Would Kennedy, had he lived, have grasped that Indochina was only the Bay of Pigs on a gargantuan scale and spared both the United States and Southeast Asia the catastrophe his Vice President and Cabinet unleashed, following his death? Would Franklin Roosevelt, had he lived, have managed to avert the Cold War, the McCarthy inquisitions, to have redefined the debate on "who lost China" into a valid consideration of the realities of Asia and the rest of the Third World? The Roosevelt presidency also is a great exception, because World War II was a great exception: for all our reluctance to recognize it at the time, and for all our initial unwillingness to become involved, it was perhaps the only foreign war in American history in which the adversary did embody evil, in which the survival of freedom may well have been at stake.

In the case of the four other wartime presidents—Wilson, Truman, Johnson and Nixon—a dismal pattern clearly prevails. Their crusades for democracy overseas failed, even when the enemy, in Wilson's and Truman's case, did not prevail. But in all four cases the greatest defeat came at home. All four presidents began their wars with grand incantations of America's destiny to defend liberty around the world. All four presidencies ended with violations of liberty here at home that were unprecedented. Each President, at first, acquitted himself as though he were the commander of light in a battle against darkness, not merely the Commander in Chief of the United States forces. Though fate was least vindictive to Harry Truman, each, by the end, was impotent, even in Washington, D.C.

Woodrow Wilson's historical writings provide as useful a primer for understanding the ultimate fate of his crusade to "make the world safe for democracy" as his military adventures in Central America do. A History of the American People, which Wilson published at the turn of the century, is a mythology of the American people—in which the Founding Fathers, Monroe and Adams, and Abraham Lincoln all speak and history springs to attention.

"No one could mistake the meaning of the words," Wilson writes of the effect of the Monroe message on Latin America, "and Spain's plans in the south were given up." The czar of Russia also quakes in his boots when Monroe and Adams apply pen to parchment, in Wilson's account. Writing of Monroe's ingratiating message to the czar, Wilson comes to the following historical judgment: "These decisive words proved sufficient. Whatever may have been Russia's plans, she did not care to force them now." In Wilson's account of why "the revolted colonies of South America" were never restored to Spain, neither Simon Bolivar nor any other Latin American leaders figure.

What happens when Americans not only write down myths, but try to act them out in the world? It was Wilson's destiny, though he seems never to have appreciated it, to demonstrate that American manifestoes were incompetent to instill democracy in either Nicaragua or Europe—that just because the President of the United States spoke, neither Clemenceau nor Senator Henry Cabot Lodge necessarily saw the light. So widespread was the myth of Monroe by then, in fact, that when the United States entered World War I, President Wilson repeatedly was asked what was, in reality though not in the national mythology, a very odd question:

Did our involvement in the Great War in Europe mean the end of the Monroe Doctrine? No, the President assured the press and Congress, it did not. The United States remained committed to the principles of President Monroe. America would continue to be guided by the great doctrine he had laid down for the future conduct of our national affairs so long ago.

In terms of historical fact, of course, President Wilson could not have been more wrong. Whatever it had sought from the Europeans, Monroe's message had laid down only two rules of conduct for the United States itself. The first rule was noninterference in Europe's New World colonies. The second rule was nonintervention in Europe's wars.

President McKinley's conquest of Cuba and Puerto Rico, during the Spanish-American War, had turned Monroe's first rule into a dead letter. Now Wilson's war in Europe laid to rest the last surviving tenet of the doctrine of abstention. Not that either action violated the "Monroe Doctrine," because Monroe had never meant his message to govern the conduct of U.S. policy in perpetuity. But, rather than acknowledge the new historical reality our involvement in the European war created, Wilson—like so many of our presidents—chose to pretend, even when the Four Horsemen of the Apocalypse galloped across the world, that America was changeless, forever true to immutable principles.

The Fourteen Points were no repudiation of the "Monroe Doctrine," only an expansion of it, Wilson argued. We had defended the freedom of Latin America in 1823. Would we shirk our duty to make Europe safe for democracy in 1917?

"Cambodia is the Nixon Doctrine in its purest form," another American President would declare, more than half a century later.

"Fifty years ago, in this room and at this very desk," he told the nation, "President Woodrow Wilson spoke words which caught the imagination of a war-weary world. He said, 'This is a war to end wars.' "

Nixon added: "I have initiated a plan which will end this war in a way that will bring us closer to that great goal to which Woodrow Wilson, and every American President in our history, has been dedicated: the goal of a just and lasting peace."

Historically wrong as he was in one sense, President Wilson had been right in another. The myth that we Americans are always the champions of liberty has been one of the great consistent "doctrines" of American history.

"During the long months of the Paris Peace Conference," Harold Nicolson later wrote of President Wilson, "I observed him with interest, admiration and anxiety, and became convinced that he regarded himself, not as a world statesman, but as a prophet designated to bring light to a dark world. It may have been for this reason," Nicolson concluded, "that he forgot all about the American Constitution. . . ."

In Europe, Wilson's dream of bringing "light to a dark world" had helped pave the way for Hitler, but what might be the consequences for the President himself?

"His dream for peace after World War I was shattered on the hard realities of great power politics and Woodrow Wilson died a broken man," Nixon observed in 1969, little suspecting a similar fate might grow out of his own quest to prove that the writ of American doctrine was limitless.

A great consistency did run through American history, though it was not the "Monroe Doctrine." Illusion began catastrophe—as surely as our Stimson plans and Vietnamization programs began dictatorships, as surely as the "freedom fighters" at the Bay of Pigs were transposed by American circumstance into the burglars at Watergate.

Monroe and Adams, of course, could not foresee the witch-hunts of President Wilson's Attorney General, A. Mitchell Palmer, which so quickly followed Wilson's proclamation of the Fourteen Points to the world. They could not prophesy the fervor of the McCarthy witch-hunts, which destroyed the freedoms of so many Americans precisely at the moment we imagined the external threat to our freedom was greatest. They had no way of predicting Lyndon Johnson's crusade for freedom in Vietnam—or his COINTELPRO operations at home. Least of all could they foresee the crimes of terror, mutilation, torture and rape in El Salvador that their names would be used to justify.

For Americans living in the early-nineteenth century, the "defense of freedom" was not the rhetorical abstraction it has become in our own time. Twice, during their own lifetimes, these men had seen foreign armies occupy our cities, burn our buildings, destroy our crops—and kill our sons. They knew no good ever comes from war, only greater or lesser amounts of suffering and misfortune. They had seen patriot turn against loyalist, American kill American and the entire nation threaten to fly apart—all in the name of a war for freedom. And because they had seen what war did to the United States, they had no illusions about what war could achieve for peoples like the Salvadorans.

This deep-seated appreciation that war is the natural enemy of liberty, not its ally, ran through everything Monroe and Adams did in foreign policy, including the preparation of the "Monroe Doctrine." The very day the message was delivered to Congress, Adams and Clay discussed the threat foreign wars posed to liberty at home—and, for all their disagreements on other matters, the two men found themselves in broad agreement on that matter.

Reacting to Clay's calls for an American war, even against "all Europe," for hemispheric liberty, Adams conceded that such a war

under certain circumstances might be expedient, but I view war [he told Clay] in a different light from you—as necessarily placing high interests of different portions of the Union in conflict with each other, and thereby endangering the Union itself.

Clay, like a number of later American statesmen, imagined victory could swallow up division. But he, too, was aware of the dangers even victory posed to freedom. Referring to Adams's fear that war created disunion, Clay replied:

Not a successful war, but a successful war, to be sure, creates a military influence and power, which I consider the greatest danger of war.

By then, of course, the Latin American wars of independence already had "create[d] a military influence and power" from which most of Latin America remains unliberated even today. And though, happily enough, our history and Latin American history already tended in quite opposite directions, even the United States would hardly escape the influence and power war bestowed on its offspring, as both Adams and Clay would discover, less than a year later, when Andrew Jackson won the popular vote for President.

No one in 1823 could have imagined the extravaganzas of destruction we Americans later would visit on others in the name of freedom. But long before our first clear-cut war of aggression was fought, they would have understood that the Cold War and the McCarthy hearings, the Cambodia invasion and Watergate were not separate foreign and domestic crises, but only separate manifestations of a single crisis of American liberty.

Some months after an American Secretary of State condoned the murders of American citizens in El Salvador on the grounds of our shared values with the dictators of Latin America, and a former American President excused the Salvadoran *matanza* on the grounds that the Monroe Doctrine made it necessary, an American journalist called on an American diplomat in San Salvador. President Reagan had just given his speech in which he enunciated the real doctrine that has guided our wars of intervention in so many countries: the doctrine that it is possible to create liberty through force. The President had asked his audience to view our intervention in Central America—the helicopter gunships, the heavy artillery, the countless M-16s and cases of ammunition—as

not an end in itself, but a means to an end. It is a means toward building representative and responsive institutions, toward strengthening pluralism and free private institutions—churches, free trade unions and an independent press. It is a means to nurturing the basic human rights freedom's foes would stamp out.

It was one of those moments of optimism about our war in El Salvador, both in the U.S. embassy and in Washington. The elections were approaching. Who could foresee that this American-style exercise in "democracy" would confer on the worst terrorists great power, that it would undo even the entirely ineffective land-reform program the Americans told themselves was "taking the revolution away from the Communists"? If one tried hard enough, it seemed one could almost see a triumph of New World liberty rising from the graves of the murdered Americans and all the others murdered in El Salvador.

The journalist and the diplomat nonetheless found themselves discussing another subject besides liberty. It was El Playon, "a lava field 15 miles outside the capital where death squads used to dump so many bodies that feasting vultures became too fat to fly."

"It still gives me a funny feeling," the U.S. official told Warren Hoge of the New York *Times*. "Sometimes I sit here defending our policy and suddenly I think about El Playon. It gets me sick in the heart."

The same specter had haunted John Quincy Adams. That was why he argued so strongly that America should not go abroad "seeking monsters to slay." In the end, Monroe's Secretary of State recognized, the only freedom worth having—whether it was in Latin America or the United States—was the freedom a free people wins, holds and practices for itself. What would happen if we in the United States—even for the best of motives—took matters into our own hands? Whatever the advantages to others, Adams understood, the price the United States paid would be immense.

America "might become the dictatress of the world," Adams conceded, but she "would no longer be the ruler of her own spirit."

"The fundamental maxims of her policy," he warned, "would insensibly change from *liberty* to *force*."

IV
From Liberty to Force

"President Monroe, in his famous message to Congress, denounced the expansionist and despotic system of Czarist Russia and its allies." Dared the United States forsake Monroe and his principles now that, once again, there was "loose in the world a fanatic conspiracy" whose goal was nothing less than "conquering the world"?

John Foster Dulles spoke the first words, President Eisenhower the second. This time the country in question was Guatemala, the year 1954. But so far as the reaction in Washington to events in Latin America was concerned, it was as though time was meaningless, the foreign policy of the United States only some fable by Borges. Even when it came to official pronouncements, fate seemed to take "pleasure in repetitions, variants, symmetries."

On the twenty-eighth of June, 1954, John E. Peurifoy, Eisenhower's ambassador to Guatemala, angrily left a meeting with high Guatemalan officials. Only a day earlier, there had been euphoria in the American embassy. A U.S. campaign of economic and military harassment and diplomatic and psychological intimidation had forced the resignation of Jacobo Arbenz Guzman, who was only the second freely elected President in Guatemala's 131-year history as an independent nation. The meeting nonetheless had not gone well. Arbenz's successor, Carlos Enrique Diaz, intended to continue a policy of reform in Guatemala—and in the meeting with the American ambassador he had been indiscreet enough to let his true intentions show.

Accordingly the representative of the United States, when he returned to the embassy, composed a five-word message and dispatched it to the CIA operations center at the Opa-Locka airfield, near Miami. By the end of the day, a P-47 Thunderbolt, on the orders of the American ambassador, was bombing the capital of the nation to which he was accredited.

This exercise in fighter-bomber diplomacy had its intended effect. By dawn the next day, Diaz had been removed, at gunpoint, from office. A U.S.-supported military reign of terror began in Guatemala which continues to this day. Like El Salvador under Martinez and Nicaragua under Somoza, Guatemala had been "saved."

In Washington, they called the U.S. destabilization campaign that destroyed democracy in Guatemala Operation Success. But Ambassador Peurifoy's five word message to Opa-Locka summed up the price we Americans pay whenever we let an obsession with power outweigh our commitment to liberty.

"WE HAVE BEEN DOUBLE-CROSSED," the message had read. "BOMB!" What had Guatemala—a nation the size of Tennessee, with a population, in 1954, of less than three million—done to "menace . . . the security of the United States"?

Back then, Guatemala found itself in a predicament President Monroe would have understood: The national flag flew over Guatemala's ponderous and ornate presidential palace. Guatemala had a national assembly and a national currency, but of what value were they when a great foreign power was as free to blockade Guatemala's ports and bomb its capital as the British had been to intercept our shipping and burn our own capital during the War of 1812—when, beneath all the appurtenances of independence, there was a void of sovereignty?

Guatemala menaced no one in 1954, because it lacked the capacity even to defend itself, as the ease with which the United States violated its sovereignty and overthrew its government demonstrated.

In their study of the U.S. overthrow of the Guatemalan Government, Stephen Schlesinger and Stephen Kinzer describe the Eisenhower-Dulles policy as "a sort of warmed-over Monroe Doctrine." In fact, few events in recent times have so starkly epitomized the American abandonment, in foreign affairs, of Monroe and his principles. Whatever else it revealed, our 1954 intervention in Guatemala bespoke the changes in moral perspective that had overtaken the United States since the time when Monroe and Adams had opposed such adventures not merely because the United States was weak, but because they recognized our values were vulnerable too.

Spanish rule had ended in Guatemala in 1821, almost at the moment Adams was expatiating on the antithesis of liberty and force. Full independence, following a brief union with Mexico, came in September 1823. The newly independent nation of Central America, with Guatemala City as its capital, was larger than Spain itself—the size of California and New York combined. It included all the present nations of Central America except Panama, as well as what is now the southern Mexican state of Chiapas. The Pacific coastlands were fertile, the central highlands cool and verdant. The forests of the Caribbean coast were full of hardwoods, and the prospect of an interocean canal already excited both the dreams and the rivalries of men. A visitor to Guatemala City in 1823 would have found another similarity, besides the sense of potential, to the United States. In 1779 the Guatemalans had built themselves a new, planned capital, just as the Americans would later. Even today, Guatemala City, with its numbered, linear avenues perpendicularly intersected by numbered, linear streets, retains that capacity to confuse the visitor that most planned capitals have. But as Adams had foreseen, declarations of independence, federal constitutions, even rectilinear street plans, would not suffice to bridge the chasm dividing the two Americas. Over the following 160 years, the histories of the two nations never ceased to diverge; there was hardly a trend in the United States that did not have its countertrend in Guatemala.

In 1877, nine years after the adoption of the Fourteenth Amendment in the United States, Guatemala legalized peonage. Fifty-three years after President Monroe proclaimed his "doctrine," serfdom in the manner of the czars was the law of the land in an American republic. Even today, involuntary servitude—forced labor for little or no pay—prevails in much of Guatemala, and the constitutional guarantees are meaningless for high and low alike.

A Guatemalan President was overthrown by force for the first time in 1829; the most recent coup d'état occurred in 1983. In between, some Guatemalan Presidents were assassinated; others were hacked to pieces in battle; others were marched before firing squads. But the presidential blood was only a drop in a river of blood that has never stopped flowing. Political murder was the norm in Guatemala in 1823, and a visitor there in 1980 would have found that norm, like so much else, changeless. Between January and November that year, Amnesty International reported, "some 3,000 people described by government representatives as 'subversives' and 'criminals' were either shot on the spot in political assassinations or seized and murdered later." "[T]hese tortures and murders are part of a deliberate and long-standing program of the Guatemalan government," the report added, conducted "under the direct control of the president of the republic." Since 1966, perhaps 30,000 Guatemalans have been murdered by their own government. As in Alvarado's time, the only real law is the law of the sword.

Politically speaking, the history of the United States has been a history of the triumph of the national principle over sectionalism—at times, notably during the Civil War, a triumph won only at terrible cost. But here, too, history in Guatemala from the beginning ran in the completely opposite direction. The fruits of independence were only civil war, repression and disintegration. Britain's annexation of Belize was an insult to Guatemalan pride that still deeply rankles that country today, but its effect did not end there. Internally it provided another rationale, in addition to the ceaseless Indian wars and chimeral crusades to reunite Central America by force, for continuing military domination of the Guatemalan state. Economically the consequences were equally disastrous, for British Belize soon came to dominate Central America's commerce with the outside world. By 1840, about 80 percent of Guatemala's imports came from Great Britain, three quarters of that total coming through Britain's Central American colony. And as Ralph Lee Woodward notes in his history of Central America, "Loans furthered the

British domination of the Central American international economy, adding the bond of debt to that of commerce between the two nations."

These external problems, however, were secondary to Central America's essential problem: Even provincial governors had no difficulty defying the authority of the capital. One by one, El Salvador, Nicaragua, Honduras and Costa Rica went their separate ways. Entropy—not historical inevitability—was the master of events in Central America, as it remains to this day.

For years, Central America was caught up in a war in which the forces of sectionalism battled the forces of unity. Then, in 1842, Francisco Morazon, the leading proponent of the Central American union, was captured and executed. It was as though first George Washington had been overthrown in a coup d'état and then Abraham Lincoln captured and shot, all in the space of twenty years. Later attempts to reunite Central America would be made; all would fail.

In less than a generation of independence, Central America had rebutted the domino theory definitively. Guatemala, once the capital of an empire, became what it is today: a city with imperial pretensions lording it over a small and hapless backwater, a place where even presidents and generalissimos are the victims of history.

In 1954, U.S. officials spoke of Guatemala the way they spoke of Nicaragua in 1927, the way they later spoke of El Salvador. But beneath all the talk of a shared destiny of freedom there was "no community of interests or of principles"—only a widening gulf.

Today the skyscraper office blocks of Guatemala City might be in Miami. In the lobbies of the deluxe hotels the air conditioning is as chilly as in any Hilton or Sheraton, and even when the bill arrives, the American visitor feels he might be at home. The quetzal, the Guatemalan unit of currency, is worth, at the official rate of exchange, exactly one American dollar.

Not far from the broad boulevards and tall buildings, however, the rectilinear street plan breaks down into a morass of mud and squatter huts, and one enters a different world. Children run naked or, in the cold months, clutch dirty pieces of coarsely spun wool to their bodies. One has not just traversed a city. One has gone back in time and is very close now to the Guatemala the Spaniards ruled.

Here doors are padlocked and the kerosene lanterns extinguished early, as though darkness can make a victim invisible to those who hunt him. And the same is true in the neighborhoods of the rich, because the fear, like the killing, is both calculated and pervasive.

Such is the Guatemala City the visitor discovers in the 1980s. Such it also was in the 1950s as the CIA bombers sought, as the death squads do today, targets of opportunity. In almost every decade, the fantasy—inside the presidential palace, inside the American embassy—is that a conspiracy threatens the security of the state. The reality, for nearly two centuries in Guatemala, has been that fear breeds fear, that terror begets terror.

Just as one flies an American jet to Guatemala City and finds one has arrived at some outpost of the Age of the Propeller, where the Cold War never stopped, so one drives a new rental car over the mountains to Antigua Guatemala and finds oneself surveying all the depravities and retributions of the eighteenth century.

Almost everywhere in Latin America, especially in Central America, one lives in a world shaped by humanity's capacity for inhumanity. But at Antigua one encounters an even more formative element: the capacity of nature to be unnaturally cruel. In our world, Mount Olympus is an extinct volcano, but in Central America it is as though the gods of the Mayans, even the blood-lusting gods of the Toltecs, are only sleeping. Dictators raise themselves up on the backs of their people; in the torture chambers, the men in black frocks and the men with security clearances bend low over the rack, the better to "save" the heretic, the nation pinioned there. The debased are raised up. That great fearful center of humanity extinguishes its lanterns and locks its doors from the inside.

Then the dormant gods awaken. The very first capital of Guatemala, now called Ciudad Viejo, was founded in 1527 by the same Pedro de Alvarado who laid waste the country he presumed to christen El Salvador. The Inquisition passed no judgment on that sacrilege, but, fourteen years later, Central America itself rose up in retribution, and like some biblical prophet, called down punishment first by fire, then by flood. In 1541 the quiet mountain overlooking Alvarado's capital exploded—an explosion that foreshadowed death by drowning. The rains of the millennia had turned the crater of the volcano into a lake; the lake burst. A wall of water swept down the mountain, transforming all Alvarado had built from adobe into mud, and from conquest into death.

Mountains of Mayan corpses had not stopped Alvarado before. The vengeance of nature did not deter him now. For far longer than Washington has been our capital, Alvarado's second city, Antigua Guatemala, reigned over Central America like a jealous mistress. In subterranean caverns, naked *peones* clawed stone—for the gold and silver that filled Antigua's glistening mansions. From the rain forests of the Caribbean came mahogany—for her rococo altars. In a valley deep in the mountains of tropical America arose a fantasy metropolis of the Iberian baroque. At its apogee The Most Noble and Most Loyal City of Santiago of the Caballeros of Antigua had thirty-two churches, eighteen convents, fifteen monasteries, seven schools, five hospitals and, long before Harvard or Yale was founded, a university.

The capital of Guatemala was outshone, in the western hemisphere, only by Mexico City and Lima. It reveals much about what has happened in Latin America in the past two centuries, even more about what has happened to us, that in 1770 Antigua, with its seventy thousand inhabitants, was as populous as our three largest cities—Boston, Philadelphia and New York—combined. Would not the world of Alvarado prevail forever?

In 1972, in Nicaragua, the earthquake shook Somoza's capital so hard it disinterred Sandino. The Guatemalan earthquake of 1773, which transformed Antigua from a capital into a necropolis, produced an equally dramatic metamorphosis. It turned a city built on torture and peonage into a tourist attraction. There, today, fifteen kilometers off the Pan-American Highway, lies embalmed amid the bougainvilleas and poinsettias, that fantasy Central America that otherwise only exists in Hollywood films and State Department scenarios.

The traffic jams of the capital have no place in the cobblestone streets of Antigua, nor does the poverty of the surrounding mountains, because this is a museum city. Saints no one venerates any more gaze benignly on ruined chapels where no one prays. The dungeons and arsenals are empty around the Plaza de Armas. It is as though one civilization was destroyed, and then another built on its ruins, and then destroyed in turn only in order to fill a valley with picturesque ruins.

But just as the skyscrapers of Guatemala City are the monuments to one kind of fantasy, so the ruins of Antigua are only the expressions, in carved stone, of another. At Patzun, less than an hour's drive from Antigua, the world of Alvarado is as remote as the world of the American embassy. It is as though the Spaniards never conquered, the CIA never sponsored a coup. The Indians gaze at passersby neither with hostility nor with envy, only indifference. At Lake Atitlan, one stands high on a cliff, staring down into depths no conqueror has ever plumbed.

Aldous Huxley called this prospect of volcanic peaks and blue volcanic waters the fairest vista on earth. Whatever the century, visitors never cease to remark upon the beauty of Guatemala, and the violence. On a winding mountain road, the car enters a forest of orchids; at a bridge, soldiers are interrogating a line of campesinos at gunpoint. It is the 1980s, but one is reminded of a description published in 1911: "In character the Indians are, as a rule, peaceable, though conscious of their numerical superiority and at times driven to join in the revolutions which so often disturb the course of local politics." The orchids, the soldiers, the bridge, the peasants, the guns, the commingling of beauty and terror—are all elements in a tableau vivant that never stops unfolding. At Chichicastenango, the great white cathedral lords it over the mud-colored town the way the soldiers lord it over the Indians. But, as in Antigua, one is in the presence of a façade. The figure on the cross resembles Christ, but penitent chanting aloud in Quiche knows it is really the god of maize. The effigies of Roman saints are pre-Columbian gods and goddesses. The throngs of Indians are lighting votive candles before idols the Jesuits imagined they toppled nearly half a millennium ago.

In the market that spills down the hill in front of the cathedral, the homespun textiles, like the costumes of the Indians themselves, resemble those the mountain tribesmen of Laos and Burma weave and wear. It is as though the ancestors of these people carried across the land bridge from Asia more than ten thousand years ago, like some genetic imprint, patterns and colors no conquest can expunge. A man in tribal dress detaches himself from the crowd and asks the visitor, in passable English, if he realizes his Mayan ancestors invented the telephone, television and space travel, too? If that is so, he is asked, why did the Spanish conquer them so easily, why is Guatemala in its present state now?

"Temporary difficulties, temporary difficulties." He laughs, revealing a mouth full of rotted teeth. "All this is only an interruption."

Besides Guatemala City, Antigua, Lake Atitlan and Chichicastenango, visitors to Guatemala usually take an excursion to the temple-pyramids of Tikal, thus completing the cycle they began when they checked into their hotels. These giant monuments soar above the jungle. But the jungle is indifferent. It long ago consumed the unknown dreams, the inexplicable ambitions of those who caused these grandiose monuments to be created. Back in Guatemala City, one returns to a hotel shaped like a pyramid and, in an elevator, ascends to its summit. From the window at night, Guatemala City is as dark and silent as the Peten jungle. In this land of stunning ruins, one falls asleep in a room cool as an air-conditioned crypt. What Charles Gallenkamp wrote a few years ago could be written today, or could have been written in Monroe's time, or in Alvarado's time, or even before writing began:

> [T]hroughout the Maya realm . . . ageless prayers are recited, copal incense is burned on crude altars, farmers seek the favor of earth gods before planting their milpas, and rituals are enacted in sacred shrines.

Occasionally this world suffers its intrusions. Soldiers arrive, on horseback or in helicopters, to rape and pillage. Spanish troops burn crops, or American counterinsurgency officials direct search-and-destroy operations. But, to most of Guatemala's population, the rotating flags, the changing ideologies of the capital, mean nothing. Nothing history records has ever snapped the "threads linking them to remote depths of antiquity, to those unfathomed mysteries buried in the shattered, jungle-shrouded cities of their ancestors."

In 1954 in Guatemala, as in El Salvador later, the United States acted as though the Soviet Union were the new Holy Alliance, and communism on the way to achieving a conquest of the Americas that had eluded the divine right of kings. But these notions were no more relevant to what really was happening in Central America than *The Federalist Papers* were back in 1823. The truth was that in Guatemala the twentieth century was only a veneer on the sixteenth century, which overhung a prehistoric void. Even the prayers of the Mayans only propitiated an indifferent universe, where jungles consumed pyramids no less than earthquakes laid low the churches of Rome.

How—all in the name of freedom—had a U.S. ambassador come to call down air strikes on this land which lived a little in the twentieth century, partly in the middle ages, but mostly in that realm where time does not exist at all?

Until 1944, Guatemala posed no threat to the American illusion that Central America, like the rest of the hemisphere, was only some corollary to our doctrines about ourselves. In Guatemala the periodic matanzas were more like seasonal storms, not the hurricanes of blood that, at much longer intervals, swept across El Salvador. Otherwise the situation there was little different from what it was across the border. Like General Martinez, in El Salvador, Guatemala's perennial dictator, General Jorge Ubico, managed to dominate his unruly country for as long as he did for three basic reasons.

First, Ubico was utterly ruthless in suppressing both political opposition and popular discontent. Second, he placed the apparatus of the Guatemalan state at the service of the local elite and foreign investors. Equally important, Ubico understood the Americans and was adept at catering to their fantasies. So in the 1930s he was as vigilant against the Mexican-Bolshevik menace as Somoza. Then, in the early 1940s, Ubico sensed the change of winds in Washington and became a dedicated anti-Nazi, as Gunther discovered.

Relations between the United States and Guatemala are in every way excellent, [he reported]. General Ubico has promised us any kind of facility in case of need, and his associates say frankly that they will be delighted to toss every German into a concentration camp if the United States declares war. . . .

Such policies served the interests of Guatemala's tiny elite, of the firmly entrenched American business, and of General Ubico himself, who throughout the Depression drew an annual salary of $150,000—twice that of the President of the United States.

But what was the effect on Guatemala? By World War II, another divergence of history was manifest. The United States, in the generations since independence, had grown into the most self-sufficient nation on earth. But in Guatemala, things had moved in the opposite direction. By then, Guatemala, economically speaking, was less a nation than a collection of plantations operated to enrich absentee landlords. More than 90 percent of Guatemala's exports were agricultural products, but the United States had long since replaced Britain as the chief exploiter of Guatemala's resources. More than nine tenths of all exports went to the United States; the United States supplied three quarters of Guatemala's imports. And nothing so completely dramatized Guatemala's lack of economic sovereignty as the power and wealth of the United Fruit Company.

In a country where 90 percent of the population owned less than 15 percent of the arable land, the giant company's holdings exceeded half a million acres. The company paid no Guatemalan taxes. Laborers on its banana plantations were paid a maximum of 50 cents a day, but United Fruit's stranglehold on the Guatemalan economy neither began nor ended with bananas. In a land where highways were little more than mule tracks, it owned almost all of

Guatemala's railroads—and charged the world's highest freight rates to use them. The company also owned Puerto Barrios, Guatemala's sole outlet to the Caribbean, through which almost all its foreign trade was conducted. By any objective standard, the American corporation possessed attributes of sovereignty—economic, military and political—that the republic of Guatemala almost entirely lacked.

Like Martinez in El Salvador and the Somozas in Nicaragua, Ubico generally won praise from foreign observers while he was in office. For on the surface, as Gunther noted, Guatemala was "orderly as an empty billiard table." But, underneath, revolutionary forces were building. As in Nicaragua and El Salvador, it was only a matter of time before the earth would quake. In 1944, time ran out for both Ubico in Guatemala and Martinez in El Salvador. In El Salvador the resulting "revolution" was chiefly cosmetic. Its new generation of military rulers did nothing to resolve the basic national conflicts that had produced the 1932 matanza and which would plunge that country into the matanza of the 1980s.

In Guatemala the results were different. By the end of World War II, a visitor to that country might have reported that there had been a signal triumph of American values. Within a year of Ubico's downfall, Guatemala had adopted a new, liberal constitution. The first completely free election in Guatemala's history had been held, and a schoolteacher and intellectual, Juan Jose Arevalo, had been inaugurated President. Guatemala now had a free press and a freely elected national assembly—which promptly enacted a flurry of social legislation reminiscent of Franklin Roosevelt's first hundred days.

These exercises in American-style democracy did little to change the two dominant facts of Guatemalan national life: most of Guatemala's people remained desperately poor; most of Guatemala's wealth remained in foreign hands or under the control of a small elite. Yet, seemingly out of nowhere, it was demonstrating that the freedoms the United States had proclaimed to the world during World War II could instill even a nation like Guatemala with hope. Officials of the Roosevelt administration expressed their delight when Arevalo took office, in March 1945. Everywhere that year, the dictators seemed on the road to unconditional surrender. If democracy could triumph over the Japanese and Hitler, perhaps it could conquer Central America, too.

It was a hope that events beyond the control of any Guatemalan government soon conspired to crush. Within a month of Arevalo's inauguration, Roosevelt was dead. And by the time Arevalo completed his six-year term, and Arbenz succeeded him, in 1951, the world was as deeply divided as Europe had become following the great victory over Napoleon at Waterloo. U.S. troops were dying in Korea. The Russians had blockaded Berlin and extinguished democracy in Czechoslovakia—and these events had produced the same effect in the United States that the Holy Alliance's invasion of Spain had in Great Britain a century and a quarter earlier. At the moment of

America's greatest power, the euphoria of total victory had been superseded by the phobias and psychoses of the Cold War. Enemies lurked not just in Moscow, but everywhere—even, the government in Washington ultimately would decide, in Central America.

*   *   *

How would America combat the conspiracy arrayed against it?

In March 1947, President Truman, on one level, responded to the crisis on the southeastern periphery of Europe created by Britain's decision to end its intervention in Greece in support of the right-wing, royalist faction. But, on another, he did what Wilson had done before him, and Nixon would do later: he mistook American myth for historical precedent, and responded to the difficult realities of the foreign world by trying to replicate the illusory triumphs of Monroe.

"One of the principal objectives of the foreign policy of the United States," the President declared in a dramatic message to Congress, "is the creation of conditions in which we and other nations will be able to work out a way of life free from coercion." Truman then proclaimed the doctrine that, for the next thirty years and more, would be used to justify U.S. military intervention in the internal affairs not just of Greece, but of nations all over the globe:

> [I]t must be the policy of the United States to support free people who are resisting attempted subjugation by armed minorities or by outside pressures.

Subsequent U.S. interventions in the internal affairs of Iran, Guatemala, Cuba, the Dominican Republic, Vietnam, Laos, Cambodia, El Salvador, Nicaragua and many other countries all would be justified in terms of creating "a way of life free from coercion." But what would really link them would be the essential axiom of the Truman Doctrine: that the United States did not have the right merely to defend nations of its choosing against "outside pressures," but to crush "armed minorities" of which the United States disapproved. After 1947, the real doctrine governing U.S. foreign policy was that the national sovereignty of others could be violated with impunity. It was not necessary for a foreign nation to actually attack the United States, or to oppose its interests in any way; the mere attempt to establish an internal government defying the American conception of what it should be was now sufficient to justify American intervention.

Monroe's cautious, ingratiating and equivocal statement of abstention had been metamorphosed into the Truman Doctrine of direct U.S. intervention in domestic conflicts everywhere in the world.

It was President Truman's contention, when he proclaimed his doctrine, that the civil war in Greece was part of the "Kremlin's conspiracy to take over the entire world." In fact, by Truman's time the Greek war of independence, of which President Monroe had been such a concerned spectator, had produced results not dissimilar from those of the Latin American struggles for emancipation. In the end, the Turks, like the Spaniards, had been driven out. But as is often the case with wars of national liberation, liberty was not triumphant even when the foreign oppressors were defeated. Instead, Greece, like Guatemala, quickly slipped into the orbit of British military and commercial power; thereafter great-power politics, not the wishes of the Greeks themselves, determined what form the country's modern destiny would take.

Great Britain's rationale for its intervention in Greece's internal affairs had been the same rationale that, simultaneously, the United States had developed for Central America and the Caribbean. The approaches to the Suez Canal, like the approaches to the Panama Canal, had to be protected from foreign rivals. And the way to keep the Germans or the Russians out of the Mediterranean was to stop them at the Aegean, even if this strategy involved treating countries like Greece as though they were no more than banana republics. In terms of internal politics, the result in Greece was the same as in Central America: a political elite grew up whose first loyalty was not to its own country, but to whatever foreign patron could assure that their privileges were not threatened by the wrath of their countrymen. During World War II, many Greek conservatives—hoping the Nazis would be patrons as useful as the British had been—collaborated with the Axis forces. The king and court, for their part, fled, as was the custom, to exile in London. Internal resistance to the Axis forces therefore fell to nationalist partisans whom the old regime had repressed, and many of whom were—like Tito in Yugoslavia and Ho Chi Minh in Vietnam—not only dedicated revolutionaries, but committed Marxists. And so, as later in Vietnam, the Allied decision to restore the old regime, in spite of the wartime promises of self-determination, produced a bitter civil war.

One finds additional similarities between Truman's military intervention in Greece and our military intervention in Indochina. Behind both these local melodramas a larger strategic drama was unfolding. Both the British and the French empires were in decline. The British were increasingly unwilling and the French unable to play policeman in the spheres of influence they previously had guarded jealously as their own. Would the Russia of the commissars, like the Russia of the czars earlier, be tempted to fill the resulting vacuum of power in the eastern Mediterranean?

Once again, as in 1823, a message from London—the announcement by Atlee's Labour government that it would no longer support the royalists against their guerrilla adversaries—drove the White House and the State Department to act.

The New World, on a scale unimaginable in the early-nineteenth century, was redressing the balance of the Old—and not just in Europe. Soon, under Truman's direction, U.S. weapons and money were pouring into Indochina to support France's vain ambition of restoring its lost empire there, and it was not just the French that we Americans had begun to supplant. In a vast Far Eastern triangle stretching from Thailand in the southwest to Korea in the north to Micronesia in the southeast, a new American sphere of influence was quickly replacing Japan's Greater East Asia Co-Prosperity Sphere. Before long, the United States would also supplant Britain in the Middle East as the arbiter of the internal politics of Iran, where the British-created dynasty of the Pahlevi shahs faced many of the same problems, for many of the same reasons, that Greece's British-supported monarchists did.

The British in general and Canning in particular, however, cared little about the internal nature of foreign regimes. Under the Pax Britannica, the Brazilians were free to have their Braganza emperor, the Argentines and Mexicans their military caudillos. Even we Americans were more than welcome to our republican Constitution—so long as France was not aggrandized. Even Metternich recognized that trying to impose particular forms of government on particular countries was a thankless business.

As for the United States, after World War II it fell prey to the fantasy that its powers—not just militarily, but ideologically—were without limits.

Later, many Americans would wonder why their attempts to "defend freedom" found them fighting so many freedom fighters. They little suspected the fundamental reason why our foreign entanglements were so complex and far-flung and so often had so little to do with the defense of liberty: In a matter of a few years following World War II, and with virtually no sense of either the strategic or the moral implications of what it was doing, the United States had rushed in to fill the power vacuums created by the collapse of the old colonial empires. On occasion our attempts to "resist Communist aggression" would lead to our fighting real Communists, though never the Russians we imagined directed and controlled them. But most of the "aggressors" turned out to be independent nationalists. Why should we Americans be killing such people, even when their philosophies were not the same as our own?

Without ever fully grasping the significance of the fact, the United States had decided to extend its own power over vast tracts of the imperial "balance of power" that had prevailed before World War II. For the next thirty years and more, under the guise of "counterinsurgency," the United States would go on fighting the colonial wars of the British, the French, the Japanese—even the Portuguese, the Belgians and the Dutch. From the 1950s through the 1980s, an unnoticed pattern linked most of our military interventions in the former colonial regions—that is to say, all over the Third World. The "aggressors," whatever their political stripe, would be the same partisans who had rescued our pilots, fought the Axis behind the front lines—in short stood by us during World War II. And the "friends of freedom"? Almost everywhere, they were the ones who had either collaborated with the Axis or had been the servants of the colonial regime—and who were now collaborating with us.

There was one more very important similarity to 1823: In 1947, Soviet military intervention in Greece was no more likely than an invasion of South America by the Holy Alliance had been 124 years earlier. Like Monroe's recognition of Russia's claims to Alaska, Roosevelt's negotiations at Yalta not merely had sanctioned Russian control over a vast region where Americans had dreamed that their own principles might prevail, but had also delimited the farthest extent of Russian power. Over the next thirty years, the Soviets would ruthlessly crush resistance to their control in the lands that fell under Russian military occupation during and immediately after World War II. But not once—in spite of all our alarums about the Soviet "onslaught"—would they overstep the great partition line that had emerged in Europe. An important reason, indeed, that the royalists prevailed in Greece and the Truman Doctrine came to seem, to so many U.S. officials, such an important model for "stopping Communist aggression" in other countries was that the Greek guerrillas received no significant help from the Soviet Union at all. What was true of much of the world over the next thirty-five years was equally true of Greece in 1947: had the Russians been half so bent on "enslaving" small countries around the world as we Americans were eager to "save" them, events there no doubt would have unfolded very differently.

As in most times when the center manages to hold, there prevailed, beneath all the doctrines proclaimed on both sides, the cold calculations of balance-of-power politics. Geopolitical reality, however, would have been little evident to anyone listening to President Truman in 1947. Like President Reagan's speeches on Central America, Truman's pronouncements read like theological invocations of the American destiny: "Communism" was stopped in Greece. U.S. money and weapons also helped transform the Turkish military into the largest standing army in NATO except for our own. But as subsequent events revealed, all that was quite different from conferring liberty on the Turks and the Greeks. Over the next thirty years, democracy in both nations would face a grave threat—from the military establishments the United States itself had helped to raise to dominance. The Greek colonels were the real offspring of the Truman Doctrine, which also helped assure the political preeminence of the armed forces in Turkey.

A year after Truman proclaimed his doctrine, the Soviet Union crushed democracy in Czechoslovakia. This time, the President let the Czech domino fall. If, as the Cold War orators already were claiming, the Soviets were the new Nazis, then this was the new Munich, and Truman was the new Chamberlain.

In fact it was all a replay of what had happened in Spain in the 1820s. In spite of his doctrine, Truman was as unwilling to counter Soviet actions in Czechoslovakia as Canning had been unwilling to counter the Holy Alliance's invasion of Spain. Though he never dignified it with that label, Truman had initiated still another "doctrine"—one all his successors would obey, no matter how stridently anti-Communist their speeches to Congress became. This was the doctrine of the double standard. Quite simply, the United States would resist "Soviet aggression" everywhere except where the Soviets really committed aggression; we would defend all countries except those countries that really did experience foreign Communist attack.

Since 1947, it is no exaggeration to state, U.S. foreign policy repeatedly has been based on the assumption that unleashing wars on foreign peoples not only could make them "free," but as Secretary of State Haig put it in 1981 in an attempt to justify our intervention in El Salvador, "moderate Soviet behavior around the world."

The main effect of the Truman Doctrine, therefore, was one that was little noticed amid the hysteria of the Cold War. It was that the model for U.S. foreign military intervention it provided was at best of hallucinatory relationship either to the real world or to the objectives the United States ostensibly had set for itself. Thus Eisenhower, enforcing his own doctrine, would land the Marines in Lebanon in 1956—and almost simultaneously the Russians would invade Hungary. In 1968, Soviet tanks moved into Prague precisely at the moment Lyndon Johnson's crusade to "defeat Communist aggression" was at its peak in Vietnam. In the 1980s, whatever President Reagan's own crusade in Central America achieved, it certainly did the Poles and the Afghans no good.

Wilson's Fourteen Points had exported the Monroe illusion to Europe; now, as Henry Steele Commager put it, "The idea that the United States was to underwrite the defense of free states against 'totalitarian regimes' was widely hailed as . . . a world-wide equivalent of the Monroe Doctrine." This fusion of American military might and American national fervor, in the coming decades, would profoundly affect dozens of foreign countries— though never so strongly as many Americans imagined. Truman's intervention in Greece, for instance, was hailed as an American triumph over communism. But most students of the Greek civil war agree that the guerrillas would have failed even had President Truman never proclaimed his doctrine.

Even when the United States was defeated, the result was not necessarily catastrophe. Although Laos and Cambodia did fall under Vietnamese control following our loss of Saigon, as they had fallen under French control when the French had been the masters of Vietnam, outside Indochina not a single domino toppled.

But what have been the consequences for the United States of fighting so many foreign "wars for freedom"?

Following proclamation of the Truman Doctrine, as Americans roamed the world "seeking," in Adams's words, "monsters to slay," virtually all our foreign policy and national-security institutions, whatever their ostensible purpose, succumbed to the military influence and power that Clay had singled out as "the greatest danger."

The Central Intelligence Agency is the most obvious example. Whatever the achievements of that secrecy- and ideology-obsessed bureaucracy over the past four decades, the dispassionate accumulation and objective analysis of intelligence is certainly not principal among them. To the contrary, the CIA has performed two completely opposite functions in dozens of foreign countries: the manipulation and misrepresentation of information, so as to justify the intrusion of U.S. military influence and power; and the actual violation of other nations' sovereignty by clandestine military means.

From the late 1940s, the rhetoric of liberty could not control, let alone reverse, a growing American obsession with power, even when that power was abused to crush the freedoms of others and, increasingly, to violate our own liberties here at home. In 1948, for example, the name of the Department of War—a title that had served presidents like Washington, Lincoln and Roosevelt well enough—was changed, at President Truman's behest, to the Department of Defense. Yet this change in title in no way impeded the real transformation that occurred at the Pentagon following World War II, which was the creation of an aggressively militarized U.S. foreign policy. Even now the actual defense of the United States is, at best, one of the more peripheral activities of the Department of Defense. Whether it is saturating Honduras with marines or trying to saturate the American Southwest with MX missiles, the activities of our military establishment persistently lack any real congruence with performing the traditional and legitimate function of the military, which is defending the lives and liberties of U.S. citizens. Instead, the ceaseless generation of new weapons systems and of new foreign interventions— that is, the survival and expansion of "military power and influence"—has become an end in itself.

The National Security Council, established the same year the Truman Doctrine was proclaimed, is another of those government institutions whose chief historical effect has not been to protect our national security, but only to foster an insensible change in the fundamental maxims of our policy from liberty to force. Established outside the framework of the Constitution, and coming to exert a more powerful influence over the conduct of U.S. foreign policy than such constitutionally mandated institutions as the Senate, it has played a key role not just in subverting foreign governments, but in destabilizing the foreign-policy processes the Founding Fathers established.

Even when another of our foreign adventures comes to an end, we are left to live with a government system in which the J. Edgar Hoovers and Henry Kissingers are far more powerful than the senators and congressmen we elect. As in Latin America and the other parts of the Third World, power has increasingly flowed outside the ostensible channels of power. At crucial moments in our history after World War II, the Congress, in Washington, has had no more real authority than some banana-republic national assembly; the White House, the CIA and our national-security advisers have been as omnipotent and disdainful of the law as any Central American junta or head of the secret police.

The militarization of U.S. Government institutions, and hence of U.S. policy-making, following World War II was not limited to organizations dealing with military affairs. Under the Truman Doctrine, the American ambassador in Athens ceased being merely the diplomatic representative of the United States. He, like scores of American envoys elsewhere, became at times the most powerful participant in the internal affairs of the country to which he was accredited, and inside the embassy all distinction between diplomatic persuasion and military coercion broke down. The function of U.S. military attachés was no longer merely to observe the military situation in the country where they served. Their task was to directly influence—indeed often assume de facto command of—the local military, and the same was true even of U.S. Government agencies with no foreign mandate at all.

During the 1960s, the diplomatic roster of many an American embassy in the Third World was not complete without an envoy from the Federal Bureau of Investigation. These emissaries of J. Edgar Hoover, it turned out, had been dispatched to teach the local police forces the techniques of "interrogation." It seemed an anomaly at the time, but it was not: Just as the CIA had little time—any more—for gathering intelligence, and U.S. ambassadors were too busy calling down air strikes to engage in peaceful diplomacy, so the Federal Bureau of Investigation had more important tasks now than investigating violations of federal law. It had to teach the "friends of freedom" how to crush dissent—and, increasingly, the black arts the FBI taught the secret police of foreign countries were those the FBI also practiced at home, inside the United States.

Over the years, the capacity of the United States to conduct peaceful diplomacy became grossly compromised. CIA station chiefs were unlikely to provide objective reporting on struggles in which they themselves were direct participants. The political sections of American embassies were equally indisposed to provide dispassionate analyses of opposition groups the U.S. embassy itself was committed to eradicate. As the American effort to "defend freedom" assumed truly global proportions, U.S. officials more and more came to inhabit an increasingly closed system, in which even internal dissent was equated with external subversion. The U.S. commitment in and of itself "settled the issue of the importance of Vietnam," Henry Kissinger wrote more than twenty years after the Truman Doctrine had decided the importance of Greece. Once the doctrines are proclaimed, "commitments" made, what is reality except one more threat to U.S. policy?

Of all the consequences of the United States' "seeking dragons to slay," the most important was not that the United States would support so many foreign dictators; it was that the American presidency itself would acquire so many of the characteristics of the foreign leaders it befriended.

Although words like "colonialist" and "imperialist" still stick in the American throat, "imperial presidency" has become a staple of the American political vocabulary—and with far better reason than many people who use the term suspect.

In the beginning, the bargain the Senate and people of Rome made with their *imperatores* seemed like an astute one. While the Senate and the other republican institutions were left supreme in Roman Italy, the emperor and his legions were given full power to impose Rome's power on the rest of the world. The Romans imagined what we Americans, much later, supposed: that they could preserve republican liberty at home while enjoying imperial power abroad. But, in both cases, freedom turned out to be surprisingly indivisible. The Romans had empowered their emperors to subdue the Lusitanians, the British, the Jews and other unruly, untutored and "underdeveloped" peoples. In the end, they found themselves treated like some conquered race. The Roman Republic, having conquered the world, became no more than an imperial province. In the end, even the emperors themselves were no more than pawns of "a military power and influence," as a palace guard of mercenaries and courtesans turned what was left of the old, self-reliant republic into an effeminate and vicious despotism in the oriental style.

A couple of millennia later, the defenders of the imperial presidency on occasion would summon up the terrible specter of the Roman Empire's decline and fall. We must support our President—lest the barbarians overrun Saigon, Singapore, New York. Even during Watergate, they seemed unmindful of the real precedent. If the United States, in due course, does not wind up like Rome, it will be because we Americans have managed to maintain, even during the worst moments in our history, a strong sense that liberty is more valuable than power, and that military influence cannot be allowed to overwhelm the rule of law.

Both the Truman Doctrine and our subsequent "victory over Communist aggression" in Greece would have enormous influence on two generations of U.S. officials. By proclaiming his doctrine, President Truman had meant to foster liberty overseas. But his main accomplishment, by no means unintended, was to initiate a profound reorientation of our own foreign-policy institutions—away from the noninterventionist principles of Roosevelt's Good Neighbor Policy in Latin America, and away from the democratic principles that had prevailed globally during World War II. It was easy enough for a country rich and powerful as the United States to destroy foreign political movements, even to overthrow foreign governments which incurred its disapproval. But as the next thirty-five years would show, it was far more difficult to control an American diplomatic-military establishment whose habitual response was to blame the "Communists" for every foreign-policy problem the United States faced, and to propose U.S. subversion of foreign governments as the solution to every ill.

During the next several decades, the scene would change frequently: from Greece to Iran to Guatemala, to the Congo and Indochina, and then back to Latin America again. But the American actors would remain the same. CIA agents and military attachés who had "stopped communism" in Greece or Iran would find new, even more fertile fields of mayhem to till in Latin

America, in the Middle East, above all in Indochina. And because bureaucracies tend not merely to organize themselves around static, simplistic notions, but also to reproduce themselves without limit so long as their resources and powers are not limited, each new U.S. "defense of freedom" would incubate new generations of U.S. officials eager to repeat the mistakes they and their predecessors had made in Iran and Guatemala, in Laos and Vietnam.

By the beginning of the 1980s, Central America was certainly "the next Vietnam" in that it had become a kind of new frontier for scores of officials who had been at loose ends ever since the termination of the Indochina War. John Negroponte, a veteran of the disastrous "pacification" campaign in Vietnam, was U.S. proconsul in Honduras, charged with using that country to fight "the Communists" in neighboring Nicaragua and El Salvador, much as Vietnam itself had been used to expand the fighting into neighboring Cambodia and Laos. And if the supposed beneficiaries in El Salvador of the State Department's land-reform program increasingly resembled the terrified peasants of Vietnam a decade or two earlier, there was good reason for it. The Salvadoran program had been devised by Roy Prosterman, an American "counterinsurgency expert" who had developed an equally disastrous attempt to "take the revolution away from the Communists" in Indochina, and whose published credentials for conferring freedom on Central America included a tract entitled "Turning the Tables on the Vietcong."

So far as the catastrophe which befell democracy in Guatemala in 1954 is concerned, only one of these intercontinental careers in "stopping communism" need be mentioned. In 1953, the official most eager to be President Eisenhower's ambassador to Guatemala was also the official who, until recently, had been President Truman's proconsul in Greece. As a result, Guatemala and Greece soon would have something more in common than the fact that independence, back in the early-nineteenth century, had led to generations of internal repression and foreign abuse.

What was the result when an American ambassador like John E. Peurifoy, who, as Schlesinger and Kinzer point out, "spoke no Spanish and knew nothing about Guatemala," but as President Eisenhower later put it, was "familiar with the tactics of the Communists in Greece," injected himself into the complexities of a volatile, divided and troubled Central American nation?

"Peurifoy soon reached definite conclusions on the nature of the Arbenz government," Eisenhower later wrote in a passage Reagan also could have written about the proconsuls he would send to Central America. Peurifoy's conclusion was "that unless the Communist influences in Guatemala were counteracted, Guatemala would within six months fall completely under Communist control." "Something had to be done quickly," the President decided.

The Truman Doctrine could "save" countries like Greece from Communists, but not from those—many of them tainted with Nazi collaboration and profoundly antagonistic to democratic values—whom we chose to support.

Nor, even more important, could it save our own officials from acquiring their values. For Americans like Ambassador Peurifoy, the "lessons" of Greece to be applied in Guatemala would be the same "lessons" of Indochina our officials are still trying to apply in Central America today: if only we Americans give the right weapons to the right people, then both American security and American liberty would prevail.

Greece itself, after 1944, suggested some very different conclusions. Nearly 160,000 people had been murdered there; the country was devastated. But the Truman Doctrine had failed to reverse the flow of Greek political history. In 1974, twenty-seven years after the United States had thrown its support to the royalists, nearly 70 percent of the Greek electorate voted in a free referendum to abolish the monarchy. More than a century and a half after the outbreak of the Greek war of independence, republican institutions were at last reestablished on a permanent basis in the birthplace of democracy.

How would American security actually be affected if the Greeks were free to choose leaders who did not consider our Truman Doctrine interventions defenses of liberty—who in fact strongly denounced "the tactics used by the ruthless imperialist power of the West, the United States of America, to infiltrate, corrupt, subvert, colonize and subjugate" countries around the world? By the early 1980s the author of those harsh words, Andreas Papandreou, had been elected Prime Minister of Greece—in spite of decades of U.S. attempts to keep him and like-minded Greeks from power. Greece now had a government that was far less to Washington's taste than the previous, conservative governments—including the right-wing dictatorship of Colonel George Papadopoulos, which both the Johnson and the Nixon administrations had supported. But the strategic consequences of these long-delayed internal changes in Greece were nil.

In the end, 1948 did turn out to be a strategically decisive year in Eastern Europe. But this was not a result of either what we did in Greece or what the Soviet Union did in Czechoslovakia. Instead, the really decisive events of 1948 occurred in Yugoslavia, a country where neither the United States nor the Soviet Union has ever intervened.

During and immediately after World War II, the situation there had been similar to that in Greece. Yugoslavia's King Peter, like Greece's King George, had fled the country, and among Yugoslavia's right-wing extremists the Axis found, especially in Croatia, many willing collaborators. Internal resistance had fallen to Marxists like Tito and his partisans, who, like the Greek partisans, by the end of the war controlled most of the country.

There were important differences, however. Tito and his Communists, unlike the Communists of Eastern Europe, had not been installed in power by the Red Army; they had won, with crucial Allied support, their own battles. Of equal consequence was the fact that in Yugoslavia, unlike in Greece, neither the British nor the Americans made any attempt to restore the monarchy. In those years, Americans increasingly believed the world to be divided into two antithetical camps: the "Free World" and the Communists. Yet, from the beginning, there was an enormous difference between the Communist regimes in such countries as Poland, Hungary and Czechoslovakia and those in such countries as Yugoslavia, China and Vietnam.

This difference was not ideological; it was historical. In countries like Czechoslovakia, Marxist rule was imposed by Soviet force of arms; in countries like Yugoslavia, local Communists had won power through authentic wars of national liberation—independence struggles which, while fought for different philosophical reasons, were similar to our own. Did all this make any difference?

Even today, official U.S. doctrine asserts that it makes no difference at all. The Reagan doctrine for Central America is that the establishment of any Marxist regime anywhere is ipso facto an extension of Soviet power, and hence a threat to the United States, even when the Soviet Union is not involved in its establishment.

One of the greatest ironies of modern American history is that this thesis was being definitively rebutted by events even as our Truman Doctrine intervention in Greece was setting the stage for more than three decades of U.S. attempts to quell internal revolution in foreign countries. In fact, by 1948 it was clear the Yugoslavs were determined to demonstrate, like the Chinese later, that internal communism was not incompatible with external independence, and the strategic consequence was nothing less than decisive: the first great Communist schism of the postwar era had established a check on Soviet Communist expansion, in the form of an independent Communist Yugoslavia, that endures to this day. And as Tito's quarrel with the Russians expanded and he sought American friendship to counter Soviet hostility, other advantages flowed to the United States. All along, Stalin had been wary of the Greek guerrillas; already confronted with one Tito, Stalin had no desire to see yet another insubordinate revolutionary regime gain power in southeastern Europe. Instead, the Greek partisans' external support had chiefly come from Yugoslavia itself.

Such comradely solidarity among the guerrilla veterans of the anti-Nazi struggle did not long survive among the new realities of the postwar world. Instead, under Tito, Yugoslav national expediency soon prevailed. In July 1949, Tito closed his borders to the Greek guerrillas. Deprived of sanctuaries and foreign supply routes, they forfeited whatever chance of victory, even of survival, they had once had. The Greek revolution had indeed been "taken away from the Communists"—by a fellow Communist.

Though even now the late 1940s are remembered as the years when Stalin went on the offensive, it was a period—like most periods since World War II —when U.S. interests, if not American values, were enjoying a notable success. At the very moment that Cold War hysteria was approaching its peak in the United States, the external world was witnessing a triumph of nationalism, *Realpolitik* and expediency over the forces of ideology, conspiracy and doctrine. What was the real significance of the diverse events that overtook Czechoslovakia, Yugoslavia and Greece during those years?

It was a significance that Richard Rush, from his diplomatic vantage point back in 1823, would have had no trouble grasping, however elusive it was to envoys like Ambassador Peurifoy. The Czechs and the Yugoslavs had not been "made free," at least by our standards. Nor, for that matter, had the Greeks. But those events were secondary to the most important consequence. The Soviet Union was not aggrandized.

Soviet-style communism, as Tito's declaration of independence from the Kremlin had made manifest, was inevitable nowhere—not even in countries where Communists happened to gain power—except where the Red Army imposed it. After 1948, communism in the Russian manner ceased being a doctrine of any philosophical vitality, in spite of repeated American attempts to view global events as some Armageddon-like confrontation between the dark legions of communism and the forces of American light. In fact, 1948 is as good a year as any from which to date one of the major historical developments of our time—an ongoing process that the CIA is as loath to recognize as is the KGB. This is the steady repudiation by world history of orthodox Marxism-Leninism. One reason future historians no doubt will find the American obsession with the "Communist threat" so mysterious is that the last half of the twentieth century almost certainly will be remembered as the epoch when Stalin-style communism joined Hitler-style fascism, to say nothing of Metternich's divine right of kings, in that vast historical graveyard of failed ideological doctrines.

Hardly for the first or last time, therefore, the United States in the late 1940s set out to defend the world against a "threat" that, in the terms in which Americans defined it, simply did not exist. The real ideological question by then was not whether communism would sweep the world; the real question, still unanswered, was whether the Russians and their subject peoples would ever find a way to liberate themselves from their own ideological shackles. In Western Europe, after 1948, communism was in irrevocable decline, while in Eastern Europe, "defending socialism," like "defending freedom" in Latin America, became only a code term for foreign domination, imposed by foreign force of arms. Even today, however, many U.S. officials—notably U.N. Ambassador Jeane Kirkpatrick—continue to argue for our support of even the most vicious anti-Communist dictatorships. Any anti-Communist government, this argument runs, is preferable to any Communist (or merely Marxist or revolutionary) government, because while evolutionary improvements are possible under right-wing "authoritarian" regimes, "totalitarian" Communist regimes doom their peoples to permanent, unchanging bondage. In fact, contemporary history totally rebuts any such supposition. In Somoza's Nicaragua, the Shah's Iran and Diem's Vietnam, to cite only three of the most obvious examples, dictatorship certainly showed no tendency to wither away and be peacefully replaced by American-style freedom. Those dictatorships disappeared only in the face of violent revolution. As for communism, it has revealed, over the past thirty-five years, evolutionary tendencies as heterodox as Tito's communism, Dubcek's communism, and Deng Xiaoping's communism—to say nothing of Pol Pot's communism and Eurocommunism. Quite contrary to official American doctrine, communism has ceaselessly defied the efforts of both the United States and the Soviet Union to treat it as a unitary phenomenon whose form was irrevocably predetermined by Stalin, Lenin, Marx or anyone else.

That is not to say that the reverse of the Kirkpatrick thesis holds. A few U.S.-backed "authoritarian" dictatorships, notably Spain and Greece itself, have evolved, though seldom without upheaval, into democracies, just as many U.S.-backed democracies—such as the Philippines, Turkey and various Latin American countries—have become dictatorships. Nor have the internal evolutions of communism all been toward greater liberty.

Beneath this history of diversity, in fact, lies a very clear pattern that both the United States and the Soviet Union constantly go to enormous lengths to deny: Attempts to liberalize countries like Hungary, Czechoslovakia and Poland have not failed because of any inherent properties of communism, any more than efforts to liberalize countries like Nicaragua, Guatemala and El Salvador have failed because of any inherent properties of democracy. Instead, efforts to achieve greater human freedom in both parts of the world have failed for a reason that has nothing to do with ideology and everything to do with military influence and power: just as we have imposed our own Ulbrichts, Kadars and Jaruzelskis on Latin America, so the history of Eastern Europe since 1945 is the history of the Russians inflicting their own Trujillos, Somozas and Pinochets on that unfortunate part of the world. Today, the Kremlin denounces Walesa and Solidarity as the agents of capitalist subversion. Reagan and his men denounce the murdered clergy and tortured peasant leaders of El Salvador. But, beneath all the talk about "defending freedom" in El Salvador and "defending socialism" in Poland, both U.S. and Soviet officials make their denunciations into a mirror.

"[G]overnments which we recognize and support stay in power, while those which we do not recognize and support fall." Once again, Secretary Olds's maxim sums up the Brezhnev Doctrine as well as it defines the "Monroe Doctrine." In the end, the only real crime of the Sandinistas in Nicaragua is that we do not support them. And certainly the only real virtue of the regime in El Salvador is that we do—and the same is equally true of the Soviets' opposition to the Solidarity movement in Poland and its support for the corrupt, repressive and inefficient dictatorships it keeps in power in its part of the world. Future historians no doubt will be as impressed by the symmetry of the two superpowers' actions as they are bemused by the attempts, in both Washington and Moscow, to pretend that unprovoked aggression has an entirely different moral and political significance depending on whether it is we Americans who violate another people's sovereignty or the Soviets who do.

In each case, it is important to point out, the result is defeat—even when repression succeeds—for in both cases, the Russians and the Americans are only ensnaring themselves more deeply in the trap in which they, not just the Poles and the Salvadorans, are caught. Whether they admit it or not, the Russians desperately need the Dubceks and Walesas they periodically repress, if new experimentation is ever to permit the escape from failed ideological orthodoxy that Khrushchev and his successors have all sought with no particular success. The same is equally true of us Americans. For more than thirty years our leaders have also been seeking, without success, some—any— solution to the crisis of Third World poverty and instability that has so much of Latin America, and the rest of the world, in its grip.

Why do our leaders never seem to come up with any effective answers? One reason is that we—like the Russians—waste so much of our time, so many of our resources, trying to crush political and economic experimentation before it has a chance either to fail or to succeed. One of the most depressing characteristics of both leaderships is that even when they know their own doctrines are bankrupt, they still refuse to consider the possibility that Solidarity or the Sandinistas, far from being a problem, might become part of a solution that clearly neither Moscow nor Washington can devise on its own.

Another pattern in the recent history of communism and its interconnections with both Soviet and American power is also worth mentioning: for nearly forty years now, indiscriminate U.S. anticommunism has been the greatest ally of hard-line, orthodox Marxism outside areas of Russian military control. Our hostility to such Cambodian nationalists as Prince Norodom Sihanouk, more than any other external factor, helped deliver the destiny of that tragic land into the clutches of the Khmer Rouge. More than twenty years of both strategically and ideologically irrational American hostility toward China greatly strengthened the radicals there—and, not insignificantly, deprived us of the strategic advantages flowing from the Sino-Soviet schism for years after it occurred.

The great lesson of Deng Xiaoping's China, indeed, is the same as the lesson of many of our other strategic allies both formal and de facto. "National security," that is to say strategic advantage, has no necessary connection with "defending freedom," that is to say trying to make the internal politics of foreign countries correspond to our notions.

Friendship with the United States, however much we suppose the contrary, does not necessarily transform foreign governments into "friends of freedom," whether their authoritarianism is of the left- or the right-wing variety. On the other hand, decades of American hostility failed to transform the Chinese into pawns of the Russians. We Americans nonetheless possess two stupendous advantages, in our dealings with such countries, that the Russians lack. The first advantage is that our system, for all its faults, basically works.

The second advantage is that the Soviet system, for all its accomplishments, basically does not. It was nationalism and pragmatism—not the Truman Doctrine and the Nixon Doctrine—that led both Yugoslavia and China to reject the militarist, closed Soviet system of political repression and economic irrationality. We no doubt will find the Cubans and the Vietnamese equally revisionist if we can ever bring ourselves to make strategic pragmatism, not ideological partisanship, the basis of our relations with them.

Even today, the independence, stability and prosperity of Western Europe is the single most important geopolitical fact in the world. And although Americans may have believed that the Truman Doctrine had saved all of Europe from Soviet enslavement, Stalin and his successors certainly deserve an important part of the credit. Like the Holy Alliance earlier, the Soviets after World War II were simply much more cautious than the alarmists in Washington supposed. Marshall Plan dollars also made a vital contribution to the reconstruction of the economic foundations of European stability. But the greatest American contribution was that after World War II, we joined the United Nations and stayed in Europe—rather than precipitately withdrawing and creating the kind of power vacuum the Soviets might have been tempted to fill. As in the future, America's greatest successes came when it acquitted itself as a mature world power. And as in the past, its greatest failures would come when it imagined its first duty was not to protect its own national interests, but to give civics lessons to the world.

Later, in many countries, U.S. officials would argue there was no alternative to Greece-style U.S. interventions in foreign civil wars. Yet, as early as the 1940s, events revealed that there were many alternatives, if only the United States had been willing to consider them.

Cooperation with the independent-minded democracies of Western Europe proved highly effective in maintaining the postwar balance. Yet after 1948 the United States viewed the efforts of Third World nations to maximize their own independence with a hostility that was often thinly disguised at best. For long periods of time, we viewed democratic India and the nonaligned movement as nearly as great a "threat" as the Soviet Union and the Warsaw Pact. The United States not only had forgotten the real meaning of Washington's Farewell Address; it was incapable of perceiving in the newly independent nations of Asia and Africa the opportunity that Canning had recognized, more than a century earlier, in the independence of Latin America: even when their policies and systems of government differed from ours, even when they spurned formal alliance with us, the newly independent nations automatically contributed to maintaining the postwar balance of power by not contributing to the Soviet side of the balance. Far from being "surrender on the installment plan," nonalignment in fact served U.S. interests doubly: Nations that had just won their independence had no interest in becoming new colonies. In addition, their quite understandable desire to stand on their own two feet freed the United States itself from acquiring new political and military responsibilities in a world in which our "commitments" were already immense. Yet, for a quarter of a century, U.S. policymakers would regard the nonaligned movement as a nagging problem—not the strategic solution it really was.

Although cooperation with an independent Communist Yugoslavia had proved effective, the real lesson of Tito, like the real lesson of Greece, was not applied again for nearly twenty years. Instead of treating Mao's China as a potential ally, we treated it, even more than the Soviet Union, as a pariah— with tragic consequences for all concerned.

Finally there was the old Monroe option of abstention. Though such a policy was ideologically inadmissible in the United States after World War II, abstention in many cases was unavoidable in practice: even at the height of its power, the United States could not be involved in every struggle everywhere. What were the consequences when we Americans were not there to save foreign peoples from the Russians?

After World War II, more than one hundred new nations, by one means or another, managed to gain, and sustain, their independence—in most cases without the United States assuming command of the "forces of freedom," and sometimes over our opposition. Leaving the consequences of the Korean and Indochina wars aside, it is one of the dominant facts of contemporary history that not a single one of those newly independent nations has fallen permanently under Russian military or even under Russian-style local Communist control. To the contrary, many nations our leaders once said were "lost" or about to be lost to the Communists—Indonesia, Egypt, Somalia and Ghana are only a few examples—turned out not to be new provinces of the Soviet Empire after all. Indeed, in several very important cases they wound up closely associated with the United States. Yet our leaders still persist in assuming that the world is full of toppling dominoes, the scene of a constant, irreversible Soviet advance.

One of the most important reasons the international system, in spite of nearly forty years of endless crisis, has worked so well is that neither we nor the Soviets have been able to determine events to the extent officials in both Washington and Moscow imagined possible. In fact, the biggest strategic reverses both super powers have suffered have occurred when they believed their own rhetoric—and acted as though they could decide the destiny of China or Vietnam, Egypt or Cuba.

* * *

In 1949, Americans received an enormous shock. That year, Mao Zedong's peasant army gained full control of mainland China; Chiang Kai-shek, having squandered billions of dollars in U.S. aid, fled to Taiwan. Like Tito and his partisans and Ho Chi Minh and his guerrillas, Mao and his followers were Communists. But, like the Yugoslav and Vietnamese Communists, the Chinese Communists were in no sense anti-American. Like Tito and Ho, Mao and Chou En-lai had close and cordial relations with U.S. officials, notably members of the OSS, during World War II. And like the Yugoslavs, the Chinese were wary of the Soviet Union, for both historical and practical reasons. Stalin had scoffed at Mao's chances of winning a war of national liberation in a feudal nation that had not, in keeping with Marxist doctrine, achieved capitalism before attempting socialism. Accordingly the Comintern had maintained close links with Chiang's Kuomintang—links so close that Chiang's son and eventual heir as ruler of Taiwan, Chiang Ching-kuo, had married a Russian during his training in Stalin's Moscow, and spoke better Russian than he did English. Mao, for his part, visited the Soviet Union only once—long after he had gained power—and throughout his life was deeply suspicious of the great northern power which, over the centuries, had stolen so much Chinese land and inflicted on China so many humiliations. For Mao, the United States was no inevitable adversary; it was a potential counterfoil to Russia.

A quarter century later, when the Americans decided to reestablish contacts with him, Mao invited Richard Nixon to China. One of the most poignant scenes of Mao's senescence occurred following Nixon's disgrace, when the former President revisited Peking. By then the old revolutionary clearly did not have all his wits about him. But as he was presented to Nixon, Mao suddenly became animated and began to pump Nixon's hand, beaming, as he once had from countless revolutionary posters, on Mrs. Nixon and her daughter Patricia.

A few years afterward, I visited Mao's mausoleum, in Peking. The waxen effigy in the glass case in front of me was scarcely five feet long. It was astonishing to see this tiny figure that had remade China, and then, with his encounter with Nixon, remade the strategic reality of the world. By then, the Chinese Communist leader had become a figure far more admired in the United States than he was in his own country. So one watched American tour buses pull up in front of Mao's tomb, and package tours from middle America file respectfully past the body of the man who, well within the memory of these affluent businessmen and tourists, had been denounced in Washington as evil incarnate.

Had Mao Zedong, in the course of his long life, found any explanation for the absolute vilification, the unquestioning admiration, these powerful foreigners, all in the space of a quarter century, had directed toward him? The figure in the glass case had no answer. But as one strolled through Deng Xiaoping's Peking, with its youth obsessed with American fashion, with its bureaucracy obsessed with American technology, one discovered that the Chinese were not very different from us Americans: Here the disgraced Nixon was as admired by the Chinese as the disgraced Mao was admired back in the United States. The Chinese no more cared about the excesses of Watergate than the American tourists cared about the excesses of the cultural revolution: all that mattered to them was that Nixon had been a friend of China.

Why, in 1949, had the "loss" of China provoked such hysteria in the United States? The historian Walter Karp suggests that the Truman Doctrine was to blame for the highly emotional U.S. reaction to Chiang's defeat and for the even more emotional American reaction to the outbreak of the Korean War, the following year: by grounding his Aegean policy in a transcendant, universal doctrine of American good and Communist evil, the President had convinced the American people all too well that revolution everywhere, not just in Greece, was the manifestation of a conspiracy to destroy the United States.

Karp's perception is a shrewd one, because at bottom the Truman Doctrine was much more than a doctrine about the Aegean. Above all else, it was a doctrine about the United States. For generations prior to the proclamation of the Truman Doctrine, Americans had believed the "Monroe Doctrine" conferred on them both the right and the duty to order the affairs of the western hemisphere. In 1947, Truman had transformed manifest destiny into a doctrine that was no longer hemispheric, but global: every revolution everywhere was now like those insurrections in Latin America it had been our national custom, for so many generations, to crush. How to deal with these new Zeledons, these new Sandinos? Over the next thirty-five years, we would train Nicaraguan national guards on a global scale. The entire Vietnam War would be a gargantuan attempt to make of Southeast Asia what we earlier had made of Central America and the Caribbean.

The fundamental flaw in the Truman Doctrine was that conflicts in the world very seldom come down to clear-cut struggles between good and evil. But there was another, equally invalid premise: even at the height of American power, the world was no Latin America; Mao was no Sandino; and certainly China was no Nicaragua, to be "saved" by landing a few thousand marines.

So, for the same reason that he had done nothing as Stalin took Prague, President Truman did nothing as Mao took Peking. America lacked the capacity to control events there. Not even a million U.S. ground troops could have kept Chiang Kai-shek in power, and Truman knew it.

But what did the American people know? One thing they knew was that, less than three years following the proclamation of the Truman Doctrine, America's most cherished beliefs about itself seemed to be under assault everywhere. Whatever else, Mao's assault on Chiang's crumbling bastion was an assault on those fantasies about America's place in the world that, for a short time following the unconditional surrender of the Axis, had seemed nothing less than a universal reality. Mao's victory in China meant that American-style freedom was not destined to prevail in the world's most populous nation. Not only was Communist evil triumphant in China, American goodness had been shown to be powerless there as well. Could it be that we Americans were not destined to be to the world what we were to the western hemisphere?

A conspiracy of evil, as the President himself had revealed to the nation, explained why Stalin and Mao acted as they did. But what could explain the inaction in Washington—as, one by one, the dominoes fell? Could it be that Stalin's agents had taken over the State Department?

Mao Zedong not only had ushered in a new era in Chinese history; he had also inaugurated the McCarthy Era in the United States. In his attempt to win support for his Aegean policy, Truman had opened a Pandora's box of American nationalism. Now the Truman Doctrine for the world generated a domestic corollary: when communism was not stopped, when freedom was not defended, the man in the White House would be to blame.

All through 1949 and into 1950, members of the Truman administration labored to put the genie back in the bottle. The "loss" of China, they correctly argued, did not threaten the security of the United States. The President, the Secretary of State, even the joint chiefs of staff all had the same thing to say: America's natural "defense perimeter" did not lie on the mainland of Asia. It lay in the Pacific, and included the Asian offshore archipelagos such as Japan and the Philippines. Suddenly the author of the Truman Doctrine himself was proclaiming a new, and most equivocal, doctrine: "Freedom," at least in Asia, was not indivisible. All across the country, there was the pervasive sense that somewhere, somehow, America and its principles were being betrayed.

In January 1950, less than four months following Mao's victory in China, Secretary of State Acheson gave an address before the National Press Club, in Washington, that was shortly to become notorious. In fact, Acheson delivered the same "defense perimeter" speech many other officials had given many times before. His basic point was an entirely valid one: that U.S. national security did not require American land wars on the continent of Asia. Our naval supremacy in the Pacific and our land bases in Japan, he said, were sufficient to ensure that Pearl Harbor never happened again. Acheson's corollary was equally obvious: the United States would not embroil itself in Asian civil wars just because it found one side more ideologically congenial than another. This was a point on which all high-ranking officials agreed. More than ten months earlier, for example, in March 1949, General Douglas MacArthur, the U.S. commander in the Far East, also had excluded South Korea from the U.S. defense perimeter. The place to draw the line against aggression, if a line ever needed to be drawn, MacArthur told the press, would be in the great offshore Pacific arc stretching from the Philippines through Japan to the Aleutians.

In his speech, Acheson, like MacArthur before him, specifically excluded South Korea from his list of nations in the Far East the United States would defend in case of attack. He also excluded Taiwan and Vietnam from the American "defense perimeter." Three years after the proclamation of the Truman Doctrine, the real Monroe doctrine suddenly was alive in Washington again. At least in Asia, the United States would pursue a policy of abstention: the Koreans, the Chinese, the Vietnamese and the other Asians would be left to work out their own destinies in their own ways.

Acheson's speech nonetheless raised an important question: what would happen if Mao's forces tried to dislodge Chiang from Taiwan, if the Korean or Vietnamese Communists did seek the same kind of military victory Mao had achieved in China? Astonishingly enough, considering the expectations Mao's triumph had excited among revolutionaries all over Asia, no one in the Truman administration took such a possibility very seriously. In fact at the press club the Secretary of State treated the whole question as though it were entirely theoretical. Having vowed to defend Japan and the Philippines, Acheson turned to the question of South Korea and Taiwan:

> So far as the military security of other areas in the Pacific is concerned, it must be clear that no person can guarantee these areas against military attack. But it must also be clear that such a guarantee is hardly sensible or necessary within the realm of practical relationship. Should an attack occur —one hesitates to say where such an armed attack could come from—the initial reliance must be on the people attacked to resist it and then upon the commitments of the entire civilized world under the Charter of the United Nations which so far has not proved a weak reed to lean on by any people who are determined to protect their independence against outside aggression.

It was a fateful pronouncement—not because of what Acheson said, but because what he said so faithfully mirrored all the illusions and contradictions of U.S. policy.

In 1949, the United States had withdrawn its forces from Korea—creating the kind of power vacuum we had not allowed to develop in Europe. And to an extent rare in Europe, the opposing factions in Korea clearly needed only the slightest pretext to fly at each other's throats. All the American talk about "defending freedom" in fact raised a question about Korea that would recur in many other countries, including Vietnam and El Salvador.

What should the United States do in countries where there was nothing resembling freedom to defend? South Korea was ruled by the tyrannical Syngman Rhee. North Korea was under the control of the megalomaniacal Kim Il Sung. Both leaders not only were autocrats; their fanatical determination to reunite Korea by force totally outweighed any concern for the lives of the Koreans, let alone for world peace. So unsavory was the Rhee dictatorship, and so concerned were the Americans that Rhee might march north and ignite a major war, that the United States had steadily distanced itself from the South Korean Government.

Acheson's speech had been one more attempt to rid the Truman administration of another Chiang Kai-shek and so avoid "losing" another Chinese civil war. Nonetheless the question remained: what would happen—both in Korea and the United States—if some spark ignited full-scale war in one of the most volatile nations on earth? Uncontrollable forces were loose in Korea. And as the Truman administration would soon discover, they were also loose in the United States.

Over the next three years, 54,246 Americans would be killed and 103,284 Americans maimed in Korea, but these casualties were only flesh wounds in comparison to the other injuries the Korean War would inflict upon us. More even than Vietnam, Korea was the determinant tragedy of American history following World War II. No other event did more to coarsen the quality of our domestic liberties. No other event did more to militarize the conduct of U.S. foreign policy.

Up until June 25, 1950, the date when North Korean troops invaded South Korea, the Truman policy on Korea had been clear-cut and unequivocal: the national security of the United States was not at stake there, whatever happened. But as Kim Il Sung's troops swept southward, the Truman Doctrine overwhelmed the Truman policy.

So far as the Truman administration was now concerned, Kim Il Sung hardly figured at all; it was Stalin who had attacked, and his objective was no mere conquest of some distant Asian peninsula. If the Soviets "were to succeed," President Truman was convinced, "the United States would be numbered among their principal victims."

How could the President be sure this was an act of Soviet, not merely North Korean, aggression? A "secret intelligence report," Truman later told the nation, proved "the scheming rulers of the Soviet Union" had ordered the attack. "The Communists in the Kremlin," he asserted, "are engaged in a monstrous conspiracy to stamp out freedom all over the world."

Later, a revisionist theory of history arose to challenge the official U.S. doctrine that Stalin was the aggressor in Korea: the United States itself, it was suggested, had started the war as part of some inscrutable conspiracy of its own. A generation later, both these simplistic explanations of why the Korean catastrophe occurred remain unproved—no doubt because both are wrong. Truman clearly perceived no interest, either national or political, in the outbreak of a major war in Asia. In fact both the Truman policy and the Acheson address, disastrously counterproductive though they were, had been intended to minimize any possibility of U.S. military involvement on the mainland of Asia. The Truman administration must stand acquitted of any charge it deliberately started the Korean War.

What about Stalin? Unlike the impulsive Khrushchev, whom Americans always liked, Stalin—for all our hatred of him—was no military adventurer. After World War II, Stalin had failed to "save" the Greek Communists; he had turned on Tito; in Iran he had abandoned the Marxists of Azerbaijan. Though it was a truth both left-wing admirers and right-wing detractors of the Soviet Union refused to admit, cautious expediency, not revolutionary fervor, was the foundation stone of Soviet policy before, during and after

World War II. Did Stalin, in complete defiance of his habitual behavior, nonetheless "order" Kim Il Sung to attack?

We shall never know for sure, unless somehow, someday, the archives of the Kremlin are available for impartial examination. But no "secret intelligence report" produced by the U.S. Government has ever proved that Stalin gave the order. Any supposition that Stalin "ordered" the attack also goes against all we know of Kim Il Sung. Neither before nor after the Korean War was Kim anyone's puppet. Instead, his autocracy in North Korea, for more than thirty years, has maintained a prickly independence from both the Russians and the Chinese.

Soviet responsibility for the Korean War nonetheless remains onerous, for the partition of Korea was as much a part of the post-World War II arrangements as the European zones of occupation were. The Soviets, like us, had withdrawn their ground troops from Korea before the war started. They had established Kim's Communists in power north of the thirty-eighth parallel, and armed them, just as we had established and armed the Rhee administration to the south. Pending the peaceful reunification of Korea under Allied auspices, maintaining peace in a divided Korea was one of those responsibilities victory had imposed on both America and Russia, and which neither side could shirk.

Not even during the most hysterical phases of the Cold War would the United States "unleash" Chiang Kai-shek the way Kim had been unleashed, or tolerate the slightest suggestion that the West Germans be permitted to "liberate" the eastern part of their country. Had the United States allowed, or even failed to stop, a South Korean attack on North Korea, the whole world, quite rightly, would have held Truman responsible for a major threat to peace, and Stalin cannot escape a similar verdict.

But was the United States, as we Americans usually suppose our country is, totally blameless? The truth is that Kim's attack had directly flowed from one of the greatest foreign-policy blunders in American history. By failing either specifically to include or irrevocably exclude Korea from its Pacific "defense perimeter," the Truman administration had helped to assure that the United States would have to fight the very kind of long, bitter ground war in Asia that Acheson and Truman in their ambiguous rhetoric about "the entire civilized world" had hoped to avert. Thanks at least as much to diplomatic fumbling in Washington as to military aggression in Korea, American troops once again were dying on foreign battlefields, less than six years following the end of World War II. And as with Greece earlier, the official line from the White House was that Korea was a test of U.S. will and character, on which the survival of liberty everywhere depended.

Once again, President Truman's portrayal of a complex foreign crisis in one nation as "a clear and present danger to the security and independence of every free nation" was momentarily successful—but only at the cost of ensuring future disasters.

Appalling as the onset of the Korean War had been, one of its most important initial revelations was that the "monstrous conspiracy" was not nearly so formidable as it first had seemed. The North Koreans had attacked on June 25, 1950. Within six weeks, their offensive had stalled. By mid-September the North Koreans were in full retreat, and by early October U.S. forces had plunged deep into North Korea. Once again, Marxist inevitability had been stood on its head. The military question now was not whether the Communists would overrun Korea, let alone the world. The question was whether the Korean Communists would be totally routed.

Less than three and a half months after the war had begun, victorious U.S. troops were everywhere on the advance—and in some sectors the anti-Communist forces were less than two hundred miles from Vladivostok. Yet no Russian troops came to the aid of the retreating North Korean troops. Kim's forces had no Soviet air cover, no Soviet artillery support—even though Rhee's forces were getting all that, and much more, from the United States. Stalin clearly was no more willing to risk a military confrontation with the United States in the Far East than he was in Europe.

By November, Kim's forces had been driven from all but a thin band of Korean territory lying along the Chinese and Soviet frontiers. For some Americans, Kim's defeat opened up vaster horizons for defending freedom. With almost all of Korea freed of Communist control, why stop at the Yalu? Suddenly quite another kind of Armageddon seemed at hand—one in which we Americans could win a short, quick, decisive and total victory over evil.

Why not "liberate" China from Mao Zedong? Beyond Korea and China lay the soft underbelly of Russia—with its subject peoples eager to join the great crusade against Stalinist evil. For a brief moment around Thanksgiving 1950, it seemed anything was possible.

While nothing could have been so dramatic as the U.S. military victory in Korea, the months following the outbreak of the war had witnessed, back in the United States, a victory for U.S. principles that was also impressive. At the United Nations, in New York, "the entire civilized world" had not rallied to the cause of resisting aggression in Korea. But the Soviets seemed as paralyzed diplomatically, following Kim's attack, at the Security Council as they were militarily in the Far East. The outbreak of the war in fact found the Soviet Union boycotting the UN Security Council, and even as the United States marshaled its forces, both in the Far East and at the United Nations, the Soviets continued to avoid all involvement in the UN debate.

Though the evidence is circumstantial, Soviet inaction implied that Kim's offensive may have surprised Stalin as much as it had Truman. Though we tend even now to assume Moscow totally controls events everywhere within its sphere of power, the truth is that the Soviet Union later would lose complete control of events for considerable amounts of time in Hungary, Czechoslovakia and Poland—and it would permanently forfeit its ability to influence developments in China. It is at least possible that the United States was not the only superpower suddenly to find, in June 1950, that events in Korea had gotten out of hand.

Whatever its causes, the Soviet Union's inaction at the UN allowed Secretary Acheson to achieve an important symbolic success. Among the foreign anti-Communist forces in Korea, Americans would do almost all the fighting, and the United States would pay an ever larger proportion of the bills. But the military fiction that Korea was a United Nations "police action"—not an American war—nonetheless bespoke an important world reality.

As the North Koreans were driven back across the thirty-eighth parallel, not a single nation—Communist or non-Communist—either defended North Korean aggression diplomatically at the Security Council or joined Kim Il Sung militarily in his crusade to impose communism on Korea by force.

By the autumn of 1950, the drama that had begun in Korea at the end of June was over. Both the United States and the "civilized world" had proved themselves more than equal to the task of turning back military aggression. The postwar international system had survived; indeed it had prevailed over the most serious attempt yet made to overturn it.

But as one drama was ending, a far vaster one was beginning, almost unnoticed—and this was one melodrama to which no one would find a happy ending. American "military influence and power" could save Korea from Kim Il Sung. But what could save the United States from the consequences— foreign, but above all domestic—of unleashing General Douglas MacArthur?

Other military men in our history have achieved, even surpassed, the stature in American national affairs that MacArthur commanded by 1950. But no other general—not even Andrew Jackson—ever embodied, in so unalloyed a manner, the military impulses of American millennial nationalism. As U.S. troops advanced toward the Chinese border in 1950, General MacArthur's very person seemed to constitute genetic, not just military, political and philosophical proof that we Americans were destined to be the historical masters not just of our own country or even of the western hemisphere, but of all Asia and the rest of the world.

MacArthur's own father had been the U.S. military commander in the Philippines; now the son was ruler of a much vaster empire in the Far East. From the western front during World War I to his triumphal return to the Philippines at the climax of World War II, MacArthur's whole career seemed living proof of one of the most cherished doctrines of American nationalism: that American conquest is only a synonym for the liberation of others.

For five years following the end of World War II, MacArthur had been military ruler of Japan, and even the Japanese agreed he was one of the most enlightened despots in Japan's history. Now the Land of the Morning Calm, not just the Empire of the Rising Sun, had been added to MacArthur's dominions. Did not destiny decree that such a brilliant sunrise, such a glorious morning, must lead inevitably to a triumphant sunset of total victory?

In the Empire of the Setting Sun, Mao Zedong less than a year earlier had installed himself, after decades of struggle, as master of the Forbidden City. Now in Peking, as MacArthur's troops swept northward, an alarming question posed itself: was MacArthur's army, with its United Nations flags, only the latest incarnation of the international forces of "civilization" that, just fifty years earlier, had advanced on Peking and crushed the Boxer Rebellion? In 1900, General Arthur MacArthur had sent the following petition to his civilian superiors in Washington: "As paramount situation has for time being developed in China, request permission to proceed thereto in person to command field operations. . . ."

Unlike his father, Douglas MacArthur was not in the habit of asking the civilians in Washington for permission to do anything.

By the autumn of 1950, an imponderable question hung like a storm cloud over the government of China. What were the real intentions of General Douglas MacArthur? Revealingly enough, the identical question by then cast an equally dark shadow over the government of the United States: having nearly lost Korea to Kim Il Sung, had the Truman administration now lost control of U.S. policy in the Far East, and perhaps much else as well, to its Asian *imperator?*

From the beginning, Truman's war in the Far East had raised the gravest questions about the constitutional balance of power inside the United States. Korea was the first major foreign war in American history that Congress did not declare. Did Truman's undeclared war in Asia, wondered Senator James Kem, a fellow Missourian, mean that the President "arrogates to himself the power to declare war"? Such questions, initially at least, were drowned out by the outpouring of congressional and public support the President's decision to send troops to Korea elicited. But, in less than six months, that question had been superseded by an even more serious question.

Could civilian supremacy over the U.S. military be maintained during an undeclared war?

In October 1950, the constitutional Commander in Chief of the United States invited the commander of U.S. forces in Korea to confer with him, and suggested Hawaii as the most convenient site for the meeting. But Hawaii was too long a journey from his Tokyo headquarters for MacArthur's convenience. The general, the White House was informed, "would be delighted to meet the President on the morning of the fifteenth at Wake Island." This message was not the only sign that the American constitutional system of checks and balances was becoming one of the casualties of Korea. On October 4, MacArthur had demanded that Kim Il Sung surrender unconditionally or face "such military action as may be necessary" to destroy his forces entirely. On October 9, aircraft under MacArthur's command had attacked a Soviet air base more than sixty miles inside Soviet territory. But the most alarming messages of all, by then, were coming from China. The same day that MacArthur had demanded Kim Il Sung's capitulation, Chou En-lai had sent a message to Truman: if U.S. troops menaced China's security, Mao's Foreign Minister announced, China would not "stand idly by." China had done nothing to prevent U.S. forces from driving the North Koreans out of South Korea. But if MacArthur's forces attempted to conquer all of North Korea, too, China would enter the war.

Less than ten months earlier, Acheson's rhetorical imprecision had made it seem, at least to Kim Il Sung, that he could reunify Korea by force without any American consequences. Now Chou En-lai was making sure he did not repeat the Acheson mistake.

On October 15, 1950, a groaning propeller plane, after some twenty-four hours in the air, landed on Wake Island; Truman alighted, and a quonset hut on that distant tropical atoll, more than nine thousand miles from the White House, witnessed the spectacle of the American President paying court to the American generalissimo.

We seem no more likely to ever know with certainty exactly what transpired between Truman and MacArthur during that two-hour meeting in October 1950 than we are likely to know what transpired between Stalin and Kim Il Sung earlier that year. Later, amid the bitterest recrimination, Truman's partisans and MacArthur's partisans would provide completely contradictory accounts of what happened. Both symbolically and substantively, however, the significance of the Wake Island encounter was beyond dispute: civilian, constitutional control over the conduct of the Korean War was severely eroded, if not entirely forfeited. The American constitutional mechanisms of war, for the moment, had been stood on their head.

MacArthur returned to Japan. Truman flew back to Washington. In New York, the Soviet Union finally had returned to the Security Council. A Soviet veto now blocked further U.S. efforts to rally the support of "the entire civilized world." But the United States still commanded a large majority in the General Assembly. In early October the United States, buoyed by MacArthur's victories, successfully urged the General Assembly to pass another Korea resolution. Composed by the State Department, it called for the establishment of "a unified, independent and democratic" Korea under UN—that is to say, U.S. military—supervision.

A war to prevent the reunification of Korea by force had become a war to reunify Korea by force. The resolution not only marked a radical escalation of U.S. war aims in Korea, it contained the seeds of a constitutional nightmare.

Was General MacArthur, who bore the title of UN commander, under the command of the President? Or did he owe a higher allegiance, to the United Nations? Or was MacArthur a sovereignty unto himself?

On November 24, 1950, the general launched what he called his "final" offensive, designed to completely destroy all remaining North Korean forces. "The war," MacArthur announced, "very definitely is coming to an end shortly."

Forty-eight hours later, thirty-three Chinese divisions smashed through MacArthur's lines. A victorious Thanksgiving gave way to one of the bitterest Christmases in American history. By New Year's Eve, another Chinese offensive was underway, and soon Seoul, for the second time in seven months, fell to a Communist army. A quick victory in Korea had turned into one of the longest and most inconclusive wars in American history. What both sides had imagined would be a short war to reunify Korea would last three years, one month and two days and leave Korea as divided—and far from freedom —as ever. Yet, by the end, it was, as with many melodramas of American foreign policy, as though nothing had happened. Syngman Rhee still ruled in the South, though he eventually was replaced by a series of military rulers. Kim Il Sung still ruled in the North—where in due course there would occur another permutation of communism unforeseen by U.S. doctrine.

By the beginning of the 1980s, the North Korean autocrat's son, Kim Jong Il, had been installed, with regal pomp, as his father's officially designated successor. Marxism, planted in the strange soil of Korea and fertilized with decades of blood and repression, had produced its strangest hybrid yet: the world's first Communist hereditary monarchy.

When it happened in North Korea, Moscow pretended it was "socialism." When the Somoza family ruled in Nicaragua, we Americans called it "freedom."

What were the lessons of Korea? So far as many Americans, including their presidents, have been concerned, only a "monstrous conspiracy" could explain such monstrous events. Even more than the events in Europe, the Korean War convinced more than a generation of Americans, on a thoroughly bipartisan basis, that the world, and everything in it, did come down to a confrontation between Soviet conspiratorial evil and American democratic good.

What was the objective of "Soviet policy"? President Eisenhower later asked. Over the years, the men in the White House would change, but not the words from the White House. "Their basic aim is to conquer the world," Eisenhower said. "The Communist goal of conquering the world has never changed." The object of "the Communist conspiracy," President Kennedy added, was "a final enslavement." "The Russians and Chinese [were] totally mobilized for the advance of the Communist system." Their aim: to have the United States, and all else who opposed them, "swept away with the debris of history." The Communist "aim in Vietnam," President Johnson added in 1965, "is not simply the conquest of the south, tragic as that would be. It is . . . endless conquest."

One of the most fateful strategic consequences of the Korean War was that the valid concept of a Pacific "defense perimeter" in the Far East was totally abandoned. From that time on, it became U.S. doctrine to "stop communism" everywhere on the mainland of Asia that either revolution or war broke out. Vietnam? Laos? Cambodia? All were now as vital to U.S. national security as South Korea. If South Vietnam were lost, Lyndon Johnson wrote to John F. Kennedy in 1961, "the island outposts—Philippines, Japan, Taiwan—have no security and the vast Pacific becomes a Red Sea." The United States, he added, would have to "pull our defenses back to San Francisco."

Too much American blood had been shed in Korea for U.S. policymakers to confront the real question. Did the Korean War really have any relationship to our national security? Or had it been fought for reasons that really had little or nothing to do with our national interests at all?

Though Americans scarcely noticed it, the United States actually fought two quite distinct wars in Korea: a short, victorious war against North Korean aggression, and a long, unsuccessful war in which China successfully checked MacArthur's attempt to reunite the peninsula by force. The first war was one of the most dramatic victories in U.S. military history; the second war, in spite of the eventual cease-fire, was essentially an American defeat.

Why had the President, with all the resources of the United States at his disposal, been unable either to speak clearly to Kim Il Sung, or listen intelligently to Chou En-lai? Just as the United States, after World War II, had doctrinized the conduct of its foreign policy, so it also had ideologized the conduct of diplomacy itself. After World War I, opponents of U.S. membership in the League of Nations had tapped a wellspring of American nationalism that went all the way back to the "Monroe Doctrine" and Washington's Farewell Address. Was not the great danger of associating ourselves with the corrupt diplomatists of the Old World that we would be corrupted too? Far better, this argument ran, for the United States to remain in virtuous isolation than to risk the contagion of diplomatic cooperation.

After World War II, the United States did join the United Nations, but the belief that to treat diplomatically with an adversary is to be suborned by evil dies hard. Indeed, for many Americans, the idea of diplomacy in general, and the United Nations in particular, providing mechanisms by which nations with fundamentally antagonistic views must actually compromise with each other remains subversive and illicit. The purpose of the UN, like the purpose of American foreign policy, has to be to "defend freedom" and "stop communism" if it is to have any legitimate purpose at all. Thus the United States, following the outbreak of the Korean conflict, moved—without even grasping what it implied for possibilities of a diplomatic settlement—to transform the United Nations from a forum for settling international disputes into a mechanism for the United States' prevailing in such disputes.

But what if those who disagreed with us wished to make their voices heard at the UN, or even to communicate with us directly, by opening an embassy in Washington?

Nearly two weeks before the Wake Island rendezvous, the Indian ambassador to Peking, K. M. Panikkar, transmitted through his government, in New

Delhi, a message to the Truman administration that was of crucial importance.

Chou En-lai, in a meeting with the Indian diplomat, had explicitly and unequivocally set out the Chinese position on Korea. If MacArthur's "forces crossed the thirty-eighth parallel China would send in troops to help the North Koreans. However, this action would not be taken if only South Korea crossed the thirty-eighth parallel." China was clearly attempting to prevent a wider war that would bring it into conflict with the United States. China, Chou's message left no doubt, would not impede restoration of U.S. control in South Korea. It would not even intervene in North Korea, so long as the fighting there was limited to fighting among the Koreans themselves.

China's Korea policy in fact was the same as America's had been before the Administration's decision to drive northward: it would fight no war in Korea to reunify that country for ideological reasons, but it would fight to preserve its strategic interests there if they were threatened.

Why did Washington disregard the Indian message? As Truman and his advisers saw it, the Indians were really no different from the Chinese or the North Koreans. All were pawns of the Soviet conspiracy. "Mr. Panikkar had in the past played the game of the Chinese communists," Truman later wrote in his memoirs. The message from New Delhi was "no more than a relay of communist propaganda," or as Truman later explained, "a bald attempt to blackmail the United Nations. . . ." Once again, the Truman administration had totally, fatally misread the situation.

What might have been the consequences if the United States had taken a more conventional and conservative approach to the conduct of diplomacy? What if it had recognized the fact that the Communists now were the government of China—if it had opened a U.S. embassy in Peking and not clung, at the United Nations, to the diplomatic illusion that Chiang Kai-shek, not Mao Zedong, spoke for China?

Certainly one of the great unnoticed threats to peace all through 1950 was that the United Nations, from the U.S. perspective, was working all too well. At the very moment the Security Council should have been the place where the contending sides in Korea conducted a war of words, Stalin's emissaries were sulking in silence. The United States, however, bore an even greater responsibility for the fact that, in 1950, no diplomatic solution for Korea was found. At U.S. insistence, Mao's government was excluded from even speaking at the United Nations. The North Koreans were excluded too.

With one side of the Korean conflict effectively barred from the diplomatic debate, it is not surprising that diplomacy, in 1950, failed to avert war. In fact, the war was wider, longer, and far more destructive than either side had initially wanted. The most important diplomatic lesson of Korea was that when we Americans refuse to meet with our adversaries at the negotiating table we only increase the danger that we shall meet them on the battlefield.

Nevertheless, after 1950 the United States continued to exclude China and other nations with governments we opposed from the United Nations, and also to reject normal diplomatic relations with them. Nonaligned nations, such as India, fared little better. For the Eisenhower administration, even more than for the Truman administration, nonalignment was only "surrender on the installment plan." Those who were not for us were against us—as much a part, wittingly or unwittingly, of the Kremlin conspiracy as Russia itself.

In the postwar world, however, as much as Americans refused to accept it, national interest and balance-of-power politics—not ideology—continued to be the mainspring of international relations, both in the "free world" and behind the "iron curtain."

Korea, China, Japan and the Soviet Union all would be deeply affected by the Korean War. But the conflict produced the biggest changes in the country that considered itself, at the height of the Cold War, the one unchanging, fixed point of decency, rationality, consistency and resolve in an otherwise anarchic world. Domestically, in fact, the Korean war was the dominant event in the postwar history of the United States.

As the war dragged on through 1951 and 1952, the popularity the President had enjoyed in the first months of the conflict turned into mounting public scorn, which totally precluded any chance of Truman's seeking reelection, and which increasingly eroded his ability first to lead and ultimately to govern. Truman hardly was the worst President in our history (as many Americans believed then), but neither was he the great President apologists for the imperial presidency later pretended. Truman's greatest historical achievement in foreign affairs was that, even as he demonized the Soviet Union in order to win support at home for UN membership, the formation of NATO and the Marshall Plan, he avoided war with the Soviet Union.

Why did Truman allow Korea to consume his presidency? The sad truth was that Truman at no point had any more real understanding of Korea, and what consequences his actions there might entail, than Lyndon Johnson later had of Vietnam. Events in Korea simply could not be made to fit into the grand, easy American patterns he had used so effectively to win support for his actions in places like Berlin and Greece. Like his successors in Indochina, Truman found himself pushing buttons and pulling levers that connected only with a deepening void.

Korea also proved the nemesis of General Douglas MacArthur. On Thanksgiving Day 1950, MacArthur was the most powerful man in Asia outside China; he was one of the commanding figures of the world. Six months later, he was a dismissed ex-general who commanded nothing—except the adulation of a hysterical claque that imagined its hero not only would have conquered Korea, but "liberated" the whole of Asia, were it not for the perfidy of Truman and Stalin.

Hailing MacArthur as a conquering hero, however, could not change reality: MacArthur's military career had ended with a major, humiliating, avoidable, self-inflicted defeat. How had thirty-three Chinese divisions managed to enter Korea and poise themselves for assault without the UN commander's even noticing it? What sort of military "genius" squandered real victory, as MacArthur had, in pursuit of an illusory victory far beyond his military capacities?

These questions, for a time, were drowned out by the thunderous applause that greeted the homecoming general President Truman had fired. But, in the long run, MacArthur's sonorous simplifications ("There is no substitute for victory") served him no better than blaming everything on the Kremlin's "monstrous conspiracy" served Truman. MacArthur did not escape accountability for the fact that he militarily—like Truman diplomatically—had been hearing only what he wanted to hear and seeing only what he wanted to see. Once the ticker tape stopped flying, no great American crusade propelled him into the White House. As the years passed, the old soldier faded away.

What accounted for MacArthur's decision to snatch defeat from the jaws of victory? Some suggest that behind the shining American millennialism MacArthur so strikingly personified there lies a darker American impulse that explains our Koreas, Vietnams and El Salvadors—an American impulse not toward universal triumph, but toward our own dishonor and defeat.

Whatever the case, MacArthur's behavior following his dismissal demonstrated what his retreat from the Philippines a decade earlier also had shown. This was one American who reveled at least as sensuously in the embrace of disaster as he responded to the caresses of good fortune. Like Richard Nixon, MacArthur was in the most fundamental sense "a man of destiny"—a figure who seemed, at the most crucial moments, not to be in control of his actions and what they produced.

It reveals something about the quality of American nationalism that the most ardent admirers of both Truman and MacArthur revered these two antithetical figures for the same reason. Both men were supposed to be great Americans because they were "decisive"—as though any decision can be judged independent of its consequences, and the mere capacity to decide is an attribute of greatness.

In fact, both the Wake Island meeting and the whole Korean War were catastrophes of indecision. Truman did not know when to say no, and MacArthur did not know when to stop. William Manchester's epitaph for the Wake Island meeting sums up the consequences of the entire disruption of the constitutional chain of command the Korean War had produced: "Many men would pay for it with their lives." And even after they were dead, the living would go on paying for it too.

Of all the American casualties of the Korean War, one of the most important was the foreign policy of the United States. China had been "lost," Truman had ordered the development of the hydrogen bomb, the first U.S. advisers had landed in Vietnam, and many another die had been cast, before

North Korea invaded South Korea. But the Korean War determined that specific instances of friction between the Soviet Union and the United States, which were inevitable immediately after the end of World War II, would become institutionalized into a system of permanent hostility that would dominate both the international relations and the domestic affairs of the United States for more than thirty years.

Was there any alternative to an endless Cold War? Back in 1947, when George Frost Kennan wrote his famous "X article," so called because it was published anonymously, most of the great initial melodramas of the U.S.-Soviet confrontation had not yet occurred. In the article, which was entitled "The Sources of Soviet Conduct" and appeared in *Foreign Affairs,* Kennan proposed that the United States adopt a policy involving "the adroit and vigilant application of counterforce at a series of constantly shifting geographical and political points, corresponding to the shifts and maneuvers of Soviet policy."

Translated from Washington bureaucratic into standard English, this meant that if Stalin attempted to upset the postwar balance of power in Europe, the United States should try to stop him. Kennan had an even pithier description for what he was proposing: "containment."

At that time, Kennan's approach to deterring possible efforts by Stalin to expand Soviet military influence certainly was worthy of serious consideration, but even then it was of only limited applicability. What could the United States do when Stalin, for example, crushed democracy in Czechoslovakia—which, lamentable as the action was, did not upset the strategic balance? In one sense, the United States doing to Greece, Iran or Guatemala what Stalin was doing to Eastern Europe was an "application of counterforce." But it was an exercise in U.S. power that did nothing for the Czechs, did nothing to Stalin, and achieved nothing for us. From the beginning, "containment" posed a serious threat to the general conduct of our foreign policy. To transform our foreign policy into a series of reactions to Soviet policy was in essence to let Moscow, not Washington, determine what U.S. policy was, to forfeit both tactical and moral initiative to the Soviet Union. And even if our "adroit and vigilant application of counterforce" succeeded, the danger was that we would stop the Russians only by becoming more and more like them.

Both at that time and later, Kennan discounted these drawbacks in his proposal for a valid reason: he no more intended that the "X article" govern U.S. policy universally and in perpetuity than President Monroe had intended, back in 1823, that his message to Congress dictate U.S. policy on a permanent basis.

Nonetheless, the "X article" became to the Cold War what the "Monroe Doctrine" was to our hegemony in Latin America and what the State Department's White Paper later became to the Reagan intervention in El Salvador:

suddenly an American pronouncement made history simple, comprehensible —above all, controllable.

Twenty years after he wrote the "X article," Kennan was still stunned and appalled by the results his modest proposal had helped to produce. In a lament Adams might have written more than a century earlier, Kennan wrote in 1967 that his article

> soon became the center of a veritable whirlpool of publicity. . . . The term "containment" was picked up and elevated, by common agreement of the press, to the status of a "doctrine," which was then identified with the foreign policy of the administration. In this way there was established— before our eyes, so to speak—one of those indestructible myths that are the bane of the historian.

As Kennan watched "containment" become nothing less than the doctrine justifying the permanent militarization of U.S. foreign policy on a worldwide basis, he felt "like one who has inadvertently loosened a large boulder from the top of a cliff and now helplessly witnesses its path of destruction in the valley below, shuddering and wincing at each successive glimpse of disaster."

After 1947, the American "boulder"—which is only another word for the American domino—would fall on, and crush nations, from Laos to Guatemala, that could not have been more remote from the Soviet Union.

"There is today no such thing as 'communism' in the sense that there was in 1947; there are only a number of national regimes which cloak themselves in the verbal trappings of radical Marxism and follow domestic policies influenced to one degree or another by Marxist concepts," Kennan pointed out in 1967. A year before the Tet offensive, no one in Washington listened. Kennan's successors at the State Department were too busy containing the Soviet Union by fighting the Vietnam War to pay much attention to what he said. Here was one prophet with entirely too much honor in his own country: even when the prophet disclaimed his prophecy, his followers continued their ritual dance of death. "In the years that have passed since that time," Kennan ruefully conceded, "the myth of the 'doctrine of containment' has never fully lost its spell."

Whatever Kennan's article revealed about "The Sources of Soviet Conduct," the reaction to it revealed much about the sources of American conduct. Though the ostensible subject was Stalinist Russia, the "X article" was most important for the vision it propounded of the United States. For "The Sources of Soviet Conduct," while providing virtually no factual information about the Soviet Union, propounded as strategic principles for the nuclear age two of the oldest and deepest tenets of American nationalism.

Kennan's first thesis had been that Stalin's Russia was no normal nation. Instead, like all America's adversaries—Nazi Germany, Tojo's Japan, Mao's China, Kim Il Sung's Korea, the guerrillas in El Salvador today—the Soviet Union was profoundly aberrant. From this perspective, the Soviet Union did not pose a "threat" because it happened to be a great power or even because it was a great power whose interests and ambitions sometimes conflicted with those of the United States; the Soviet Union was a threat precisely because it was not a normal great power, but one bent on conquest for Communist ideological, not Soviet national, reasons.

Even in 1947 this was a view of the Soviet Union that was disputed. "I cannot agree in drawing the conclusion," wrote Philip Mosley, of Columbia University, that year, "that the Soviet government operates blindly on the basis of philosophical assumptions." Kennan, however, took the other side of this debate among the Sovietologists. As Daniel Yergin observes in *Shattered Peace,* his study of the outbreak of the Cold War, Kennan's article "made the case that the United States was dealing not with a Great Power pursuing imperial goals, but principally with a messianic religion, an ideological force, for which co-existence was always a threat." In Kennan's own words, Stalin's Russia was out to fill "every nook and cranny available to it in the basin of world power."

Though Kennan later emphasized he was offering a judgment only on Stalinist Russia as it existed in 1947, not passing some permanent judgment on the Soviet Union whoever led it and whatever it did, his article could not have appealed more successfully to the American belief that evil, far from having been defeated in 1945, had only changed residence—from Hitler's bunker in Berlin to Stalin's apartments in the Kremlin.

What could stop the Soviet Union from taking over "every nook and cranny"? Behind "the Kremlin's challenge to American society," Kennan discerned nothing less than the immutable unfolding of a divine plan. Americans should "find no cause for complaint" in Stalin's actions, he informed his readers. For even Stalin and the Soviet Union were fated to be only stepping-stones on the way to a universal triumph of American good. Kennan concluded his article by urging his countrymen to welcome this "test of national quality" and

> experience a certain gratitude to a Providence which, by providing the American people with this implacable challenge, has made their entire security as a nation dependent on their pulling themselves together and accepting the responsibilities of moral and political leadership that history plainly intended them to bear.

The "X article" is one of the most important documents in the history of American foreign policy—not because of what it revealed about Soviet communism, but because of what it made so clear about America and America's continuing vision of itself and of the world. Having set out to analyze what he called the "mystical, Messianic movement" behind Soviet actions, Kennan, like so many other Americans throughout our history, had wound up reasserting America's own deep faith that the United States was itself a "mystical, Messianic" force. He may have intended no doctrine for the Soviets, but he proclaimed a doctrine for the United States. Americans everywhere embraced the Kennan doctrine not merely with "a certain gratitude to . . . Providence," but with a sense of rediscovering something about their country and themselves they had always known. Thanks to the Soviet Union's "implacable challenge," the whole world now would be the stage where Americans assumed the "moral and political leadership that history plainly intended them to bear."

The effects of the "X article" and many other events in the United States during the late 1940s, including the Truman Doctrine itself, revealed a strong American predisposition, even before the outbreak of the Korean War, to see the world as a place in which only American military power and influence could assure the survival of good. Americans as diverse as Harry Truman and Douglas MacArthur, George Frost Kennan and Joseph McCarthy had one characteristic of American nationalism in common: Like President Reagan later as he surveyed Central America, they needed the Soviet Union, in order to make the postwar world intelligible in American terms. For if the Soviet Union were not evil, and if Soviet evil did not explain every untoward event, then the world would no longer be a testing ground "of the over-all worth of the United States," and Americans would be cheated of the destiny "history plainly intended them to bear."

It is possible, as a number of critics of our Cold War foreign policy have argued, that the deep American need to fight a global struggle against a global enemy would have produced endless confrontation with "Soviet aggression" even if there had been no Korean War. But, for most Americans, the Korean War turned what the "X article" had argued was diplomatically desirable into an undebatable military necessity.

Soviet force must be met by American counterforce everywhere—even in places where, to an even greater extent than in Korea, "Soviet aggression" was a wildly simplistic, often totally erroneous label for what actually was happening. Just as Mao's victory in China had "proved" that Stalin aimed to conquer Asia, so the fact that American boys were being killed in Korea showed that the Soviet Union would, and therefore the United States should, stop at nothing.

Of all the defeats the United States inflicted on itself in Korea, perhaps the greatest defeat was cognitive: in fact, the Korean War did in a general way to America's capacity to understand the world what the earlier "loss" of China had done to our capacity to objectively analyze events in that country. Because Mao had driven Chiang from the mainland, America's most perceptive China watchers were driven from the State Department. Now, because Kim Il Sung had attacked South Korea, the ideologues took the offensive in the CIA, the Pentagon, the State Department, the universities, the think tanks— wherever Americans were charged with the difficult, crucial task of trying to understand foreign events. This was the period when the study of "totalitarianism" began to acquire the same vogue in our universities that the doctrine of "containment" did in the practice of our foreign policy. As a result, not just the mechanisms, but the mind of U.S. relations with the Soviet Union was militarized, ideologized. Nazi Germany and Soviet Russia, Mussolini's black shirts and Ho Chi Minh's guerrillas in black pajamas—since all were totalitarians, the U.S. response to them all must be the same.

Later, on television, "M*A*S*H" would reflect the great truth of Korea much more accurately than the official scholarship ever did. That long-running war, like the long-running TV series, had no villains and no heroes—only various human personalities fated to play roles in the same macabre joke. Yet even when we elected a Hollywood actor President, the script would not change in Washington.

"President Truman's words are as apt today as they were in 1947, when he, too, spoke before a joint session of Congress," President Reagan said in April 1983. "The countries of Central America are smaller than the nations that prompted President Truman's message," he added. "But the political and strategic stakes are the same. Will our response—economic, social, military—be as appropriate as Mr. Truman's bold solutions to the problems of postwar Europe?"

The Korean War had a kind of Doppler effect on public discourse in the United States: the whole pitch of debate was permanently shifted. The notion that the Soviet Union was a conventional great power, not a "mystical, Messianic movement," now became inadmissible in respectable American foreign-policy debate. Indeed, to press such a view vigorously tainted those Americans who held it with the suspicion that they were a "security risk." The notion that a great evil conspiracy threatened the world no longer needed to be argued. Even in the Congress of the United States it was now acceptable simply to proclaim the existence of such a conspiracy—even to allege that its agents were manipulating events not merely in Moscow, but in Washington itself. One of the many things the United States lost in Korea, and even today has not entirely regained, is the capacity for dispassionate and objective discussion of foreign-policy issues.

If, after 1950, the basic question in the United States was no longer whether Moscow's "monstrous conspiracy" existed, the question nonetheless remained of how to combat it.

Even at the time, Kennan, in his own words, had gone "to great lengths to disclaim the view . . . that containment was a matter of stationing military forces around the Soviet borders and preventing any outbreak of Soviet military aggressiveness. I protested, as I was to do on so many other occasions over the course of the ensuing eighteen years, against the implication that the Russians were aspiring to invade other areas and that the task of American policy was to prevent them from doing so."

Yet the United States would premise its applications of the "doctrine of containment" on another American doctrine: that only American military might, both conventional and nuclear, could "deter Soviet aggression."

The consequence was that the United States, at enormous expense, would do exactly what Kennan had said it should not do. We would ring the Soviet Union with military bases and target nuclear warheads on every Soviet city. There would be permanent U.S. garrisons not just in Europe, but all over Asia, from Turkey to Japan. Nor was NATO enough. We needed CENTO (and hence the Shah) in the Middle East; we needed SEATO (and hence Diem and Thieu) in Southeast Asia to stop the Russians from starting another Korean War. We also needed hydrogen bombs, not just atomic bombs, and intercontinental ballistic missiles, not just B-52s, if our "deterrence" was to remain "credible." Just as terror begat terror when the death squads struck in Guatemala, so nuclear terror begat nuclear terror, after 1950, all across the world.

"The Russians don't want to invade anyone," Kennan protested. "It is not their tradition." And with one single exception outside Eastern Europe—Afghanistan—the next twenty years proved Kennan right. Even under Stalin's successors, the great Soviet onslaught never came; Soviet foreign policy remained focused on the Soviet Union, not "endless conquest." Like those vigilant civil-defense volunteers who, during the most hysterical phases of the Cold War, stood on the rooftops of American skyscrapers scanning the skies through binoculars for Soviet bombers, all our missiles and nuclear submarines and bombers and battleships would spend year after year waiting for Soviet invasions that never came. Yet Kennan might have been Monroe trying to speak from the grave as the United States embarked on the biggest, longest, most self-perpetuating military buildup in human history.

One result was that the immense "military power and influence" the United States amassed was, in most cases, entirely irrelevant to its ostensible purpose of containing the Soviet Union. Another result, when the weapons could not be used against Russia, was that they generated other demands for their use. B-52s designed to drop bombs on Moscow would drop bombs on Laotian villages. Tanks designed to parry Soviet thrusts against NATO would roll across the countryside of Cambodia. "Counterterror" units trained to operate behind the advancing Soviet front lines would busy themselves mailing e..ploding cigars to Castro, assassinating political dissidents in South America, and unleashing reigns of terror in Indochina.

"We are at last beginning to understand the significance of the stockpiles," Senator J. William Fulbright observed during his Vietnam War hearings. It was one of the most perceptive statements of the entire war. By then, half the great arsenal of "containment"—both material and ideological—we had amassed to stop Stalin was being jettisoned, almost as an afterthought, on Laos, Cambodia and Vietnam.

Building up "military power and influence" proved irrelevant to containing Soviet evil, but what was the significance of the stockpiles for us?

Even now they oppress our nation like some occupying army which, however much it loots the national treasury, provides us no security. By 1984 the

United States and the Soviet Union had more than fifty thousand nuclear weapons aimed at each other, capable of destroying every city and town with more than five thousand people in both countries. Just one U.S. nuclear submarine carried sufficient missiles to destroy all two hundred forty cities in the Soviet Union with populations of more than one hundred thousand people. Yet, as even our leaders conceded, amassing these doomsday arsenals had not made us safe. President Reagan proposed a new, five-year military buildup, to "restore" America's military strength, that would cost no less than $2.7 trillion—or more than eleven thousand dollars, in a hungry and indebted world, for every man, woman and child in the United States.

It was the official contention, of course, that these weapons must be built precisely so they never would have to be used. But what if, in a world where catastrophe much more often flowed from miscalculation and malfunction than from conspiracy and evil, these weapons were unleashed?

In September 1983, thirty years after the killing in Korea finally stopped, that war of diplomatic miscalculation led to one of those small dramas that can bring on much vaster catastrophes. A Korean Air Lines passenger jet manufactured in the United States strayed over Soviet territory as it flew from the United States to Seoul. A Soviet interceptor shot it down.

President Reagan and most Americans drew the same conclusions from the attack on the Korean jetliner in 1983 that President Truman and most Americans had drawn from the attack on South Korea in 1950: the Soviets were aggressive, ruthless, disdainful of human life and human freedom—evil. The attack on the airliner, President Reagan told the nation, proved he had been right all along about the need for the MX, about the Communist threat in El Salvador and everywhere else. "Is it not time," he asked in one of his weekend radio addresses, "that we stop seeing the Soviets as we wish they were, and start seeing them as they really are?"

Behind these perceptions of the Soviet Union, however, lay facts President Reagan seemed determined to avoid. The American-made navigation system on the American-made Korean airliner unaccountably had misfunctioned. For hours, the civilian aircraft had flown, hundreds of miles off course, over a closed Soviet military zone. And in spite of Moscow's brazen attempts to justify its unjustifiable action, something else was clear: there had been a gruesome malfunction, technological or human, on the Soviet side as well.

What if the errant Korean airliner had been an errant U.S. bomber or missile? And what if, as it penetrated deeper and deeper into the Soviet air defenses, the "fail-safes" on the Soviet side had failed too?

In *The Fate of the Earth,* Jonathan Schell summed up one entirely possible end result of so many years of applying the "doctrine of containment":

A darkness in which no nation, no society, no civilization will remain; in which never again will a child be born; in which never again will humans appear on Earth—and there will be no one to remember that they ever did.

The effort to "stop Communist aggression" had created a new, infinitely more serious dilemma of containment. Could the missiles be "contained" in their silos? Having amassed sufficient weapons to destroy civilization, was there any way to be sure those weapons would not destroy civilization—that, unlike the B-52s in Indochina, they would not find some use, some day?

"To my mind, the nuclear bomb is the most useless weapon ever invented," Kennan declared in 1981. "It can be employed to no rational purpose. It is not even an effective defense against itself. It is only something with which, in a moment of petulance or panic, you commit such fearful acts of destruction as no sane person would ever wish to have upon his conscience."

Thirty-five years after writing the "X article," Kennan was still trying to stuff the genie of "containment" back into the bottle. His effort led him to ask a question of great relevance not merely to the Korean War or the Cold War but to the future of the human race:

How have we got ourselves into this dangerous mess?

Let us not confuse the question by blaming it all on our Soviet adversaries. They have, of course, their share of the blame [but] we must remember that it has been we Americans who, at almost every step of the road, have taken the lead in the development of this sort of weaponry. It was we who first produced and tested such a device; we who were the first to raise its destructiveness to a new level with the hydrogen bomb; we who introduced the multiple warhead; we who have declined every proposal for the renunciation of the principle of "first use"; and we alone, so help us God, who have used the weapon in anger against others, and against tens of thousands of helpless noncombatants at that.

It was time, the day the Korean airliner was shot down, as it had been time every day for more than thirty-five years, not just to see the Soviets as they really were, but to see us Americans as we really are, not as we imagine ourselves to be. Yet President Reagan, when he looked at the Soviet attack on the airliner, saw only what he saw when he looked at the El Salvador insurgency: he looked into a mirror of American good and saw a reflection of Soviet evil, which must be countered by the production of more and more weapons in the United States.

There were some American winners of the Korean War, and the most important of them was the Constitution. In the end, Truman did fire MacArthur—and MacArthur, like Andrew Jackson back in 1824, obeyed the Constitution even when it was used by civilians he despised to deprive him of what he believed was rightly his. One of the true glories of American nationalism is that not once in our history have any of our military heroes used their power and popularity to make war on the system of civilian supremacy. MacArthur, in Manchester's memorable phrase, was an American, not a

Roman Caesar. Whatever his other mistakes, he never made the one mistake that, in a democracy, is absolutely unforgivable in a military man. He never attempted to use the arms he commanded against the republic that had entrusted them to him.

In a less obvious way, the Constitution also triumphed over Harry Truman. Though it was a lesson Johnson and Nixon would not learn, Truman's undeclared war in Korea proved what the undeclared war in Vietnam would also demonstrate. When a President bypasses the constitutional procedures for making war, he may gain a momentary advantage over both his domestic adversaries and his adversaries on the battlefield, but he does so only by increasing the risks of long-term, strategic defeat. Even the most popular wars in time usually become unpopular wars; and when an unpopular war is also an undeclared presidential war, it is usually the President, and the President alone, who pays the price. The great disadvantage of undeclared wars is that they are both too easy to start and too difficult to sustain.

Since World War II, our presidents have tended to regard the Constitution as a great nuisance when it comes to their efforts to exercise American military power and influence around the world. Yet, like Watergate, later, the constitutional ramifications of the Korean War provide a source of legitimate, if inadvertent, American pride. Even when our leaders inflicted gratuitous disaster on both foreign peoples and themselves, the constitutional center held. MacArthur could conquer most of Korea, but this did not change the fact that when the President withdrew his approval, the general had no authority at all. Nixon, for his part, could ravage Cambodia, but he, too, learned what MacArthur had: the United States has a government not of men, but of laws.

The other American winners of the Korean War were less estimable. In the short run, the great winner was Senator Joseph McCarthy. The "loss" of China in 1949 had made this fire-breathing personification of the conspiracy theory a figure to be feared. But, as Eric Goldman points out in *The Crucial Decade—and After,* it was the Korean War that made McCarthy as commanding a figure in the United States as MacArthur had been in the Far East:

> The shocks of 1949 had given Senator Joseph McCarthy his start. The frustrations of 1950 and 1951 blasted wide his road to power. With America tangled in deadlocks at home and abroad, the man with the simple answer, the furious flailing answer, had his day.

And what was McCarthy's answer? His answer for America really was no different from the answer President Truman had been giving—to questions about Greece, Czechoslovakia, Berlin, China, Korea itself—for years. It was the same answer President Reagan later had for El Salvador. A "conspiracy so immense, an infamy so black, as to dwarf any in the history of man," as McCarthy told the Senate nearly a year after the Korean War began, explained everything. The conspiracy's object: to make the United States "fall victim to Soviet intrigue from within and Russian military might from without."

McCarthy might as well have found British rifles at Tippecanoe. His speech resonated with America past, and America future—with the Holy Alliance and the Bolshevik-Mexican and Cuban-Soviet conspiracies, John F. Kennedy's "Sino-Soviet bloc" and Ronald Reagan's "Moscow-Havana-Managua Axis." The same thing that explained Tecumseh and Sandino, the fact that so many Greeks disliked their king, so many Iranians disliked the Shah, so many Vietnamese disliked Thieu and so many Nicaraguans were willing to die to overthrow Somoza also explained why, over seven thousand miles from Washington, Americans were being killed in Korea.

"Responsible" Americans were of course disgusted—and frightened—by the demagogue from Wisconsin, though they would have been hard-pressed to give any convincing reason why. Certainly McCarthy was only doing what the most "responsible" American officials already had done many times before. McCarthy gave his "conspiracy so immense" speech on June 14, 1951—more than two months, to cite only one example, after President Truman, on April 11, had given his own "monstrous conspiracy" speech, complete with its own "secret intelligence report" that the real objective of the Communists in Korea was to "unify the people of Asia and crush the United States."

Why did McCarthy thrill so many Americans, and frighten so many others? Like Huey Long, Joseph McCarthy was not merely a demagogue. He was—at least when it came to foreign policy—a great democrat. Previously the imputation of evil, the discernment of the conspiracy, the proclamation of the doctrines, had been the preserve, in Washington, of a small elite. Only men of the caliber of George Kennan, Dean Acheson and Harry Truman had played the great game of dominoes. It was Joseph McCarthy's distinction to demonstrate that this was a game anyone could play. If Stalin was guilty of starting the war, was not Truman guilty of not winning it? If Kim Il Sung was part of the great conspiracy, was not Dean Acheson a part of it too?

In his totally irresponsible way, McCarthy had pointed his finger at the great truth "responsible" Americans could never admit, not even to themselves. Truman and Acheson indeed were, in their way, as responsible for the Korean War as Stalin and Kim Il Sung were. A great conspiracy—in Moscow and Washington, Pyongyang and Seoul—did explain the gruesome reality of the Korean War. Of course it was not McCarthy's conspiracy of "Soviet intrigue from within and Russian military might from without." It was only a conspiracy of ineptness, miscalculation and self-illusion that had led to so many people being killed and maimed for no reason, and to no result.

Senator Joseph McCarthy shouted in the Senate what no one dared whisper at the State Department and in the White House: there were people right here in America who were as responsible for the Korean War as Stalin and Kim Il Sung. For all the wrong reasons, McCarthy was right. For all the wrong reasons, tens of millions of Americans knew he was right. And for wrong reasons and right reasons, "responsible" Americans both hated him and feared him and, most important, dared not stand up to him, even when they lived in the White House.

Over the next decades, Harry Truman, Dwight Eisenhower and John F. Kennedy all would denounce foreign evil fearlessly. They would not hesitate to send Americans to foreign lands to die fighting "evil." Yet these presidents would go to their graves with one thing more in common: they never dared denounce, let alone fight, Senator McCarthy. Instead, Truman would let McCarthy defame his own subordinates, and not protect them. Eisenhower would spurn every appeal that he speak out against McCarthy and his witch-hunt. And Kennedy, then in the Senate, would evade taking a stand one way or another when the crucial vote on McCarthy's censure came.

Later, as President, Kennedy was fond of quoting Dante to the effect that the deepest pits in hell were reserved for those who maintained their neutrality at times of moral crisis. Yet long before foreign neutralists refused to support our war against evil in Indochina, a kind of nonalignment movement had swept Washington, D.C. Such Americans as Truman, Eisenhower and Kennedy would combat evil everywhere except in the nation's capital. Even as America roamed the world "seeking monsters to slay," the fundamental maxims were changing in America; as McCarthy's rise to power demonstrated, America was less and less "the ruler of her own spirit." So while MacArthur marched across Asia like an American Caesar, McCarthy turned the Senate into a Roman circus.

If asked to explain why they found McCarthy so irresponsible and so dangerous, informed Americans would have cited one example more than any other: McCarthy, to quote Goldman, had accused "General of the Army George Marshall, the over-all architect of victory in World War Two [and] one of the most generally esteemed figures in the United States," of being part of the "conspiracy so immense."

This indeed was a truly outrageous, irresponsible and dangerous allegation. But was it any more outrageous, irresponsible and dangerous than alleging that every Greek guerrilla was Stalin's handpicked agent, than purporting that every Korean, Vietnamese, Guatemalan or Salvadoran we killed was part of a conspiracy so immense its object was nothing less than the destruction of the United States? McCarthy ruined the lives of thousands of Americans. But millions would die because our presidents, when it came to the complex workings of the foreign world, had the same explanation that McCarthy had for the complex workings of the government of the United States.

Of all his many crimes, McCarthy's greatest, in official Washington, was that he violated the doctrine of the double standard. "Responsible" Americans did not accuse their domestic adversaries of being evil conspirators; they reserved such allegations for their foreign rivals. Men like Kennan, Acheson and Truman did not find Reds under beds inside the United States; it was only in foreign countries that they let their ambassadors and CIA station chiefs conduct the kind of witch-hunts McCarthy let Roy Cohn and David Schine conduct inside the United States. The Korean War proved what the Vietnam War also would prove—and what, back in 1823, both Adams and Clay already had known: "domestic" affairs and "foreign" affairs cannot be separated; what we Americans do in foreign countries, what we do to others, are part and parcel of who we are and what we do to each other.

Back in 1947, Kennan had explained why the "Russians don't want to invade anyone." "They far prefer to do the job politically with stooge forces," he said. Now McCarthy was finding Communist stooges not just in Greece and Korea, but in the State Department and the U.S. Army. The Truman Doctrine had come home to haunt President Truman in the form of the McCarthy hearings, just as the Nixon Doctrine would come home to haunt President Nixon in the form of Watergate.

No one in Washington would ever really stop Senator McCarthy, any more than anyone in Washington would ever really stop the Vietnam War. Instead, both would simply escalate and escalate—and finally self-destruct. It is revealing that, far more often than we refer to the Truman or the Eisenhower, or the Johnson or the Nixon Era, we Americans refer to the McCarthy Era and the Vietnam War Era. Both labels are appropriate, for in both periods the dominant fact in the United States was not the identity of the President; it was that a destructive flood tide of American nationalism had been unleashed, which no one in the White House could really control.

As the 1952 elections approached, the chance to change presidents nonetheless seemed—as it did again in 1968—also to offer the chance of ridding the nation of the frustrations produced by a presidential war in Asia. Truman had led the nation into Korea. Whom would Americans choose to lead them out?

If Truman and MacArthur were the thesis and antithesis in national affairs, Dwight David Eisenhower—with his politician's smile and soldier's bearing —was the synthesis.

"I Like Ike" in 1952—like "Nixon's the One" in 1968—was an astonishingly substanceless presidential slogan in a nation traumatized by internal dissension and foreign war. If Eisenhower did have a plan to rid America of its albatross in Asia, it was a plan that he, like Nixon sixteen years later, did not choose to confide to the voters of the United States. Yet Eisenhower's vast popularity was another indication that the center was holding. Americans were sick of Truman, but that did not mean they wanted a caudillo like MacArthur. It had been a long time in the United States since anybody had really liked anyone. Whatever else he represented, Eisenhower stood for amiability, and that was a quality Americans badly wanted restored to their national life.

The Eisenhower candidacy nonetheless had one drawback: at the height of the McCarthy era, not even Eisenhower was anti-Communist enough for some Americans, notably those in the right wing of the Republican party. What better way to "balance" the GOP ticket headed by the fatherly, middle-of-the-road soldier-diplomat than by nominating some young, fire-eating, card-carrying anti-Communist for Vice President?

Countless miscalculations on all sides had inflicted the Korea crisis on America. Now a casual decision at the Republican convention in Chicago determined that Richard M. Nixon would be a one-man American national crisis for the next twenty-two years.

While McCarthy was the great short-term winner, Richard Nixon turned out to be the great long-term winner of the Korean War. Nixon's Red-baiting in the House of Representatives had made him, like McCarthy, a national figure before the fighting started. But were it not for the trauma of Korea, Nixon might not have been elected to the Senate in 1950, and he almost certainly would not have been nominated for national office in 1952.

In those poisonous times, Joseph McCarthy was a boil festering on the face of America. But Richard Nixon proved to be the more serious affliction; for decades he would circulate through the political bloodstream of America like some undiagnosed toxin. Here was one infection that could not be removed by lancing; in the end it would take a general crisis of the system to purge it.

Both careers described the same orbit: conspiracy, demagoguery, power, intrigue, corruption, disgrace, defeat. This was because neither McCarthy nor Nixon could escape the gravitational pull of power for its own sake. To a greater extreme than any other American leaders of their time, they personified the American impulse to power, and hence also the American repudiation of liberty.

The fact that power meant so much and liberty so little to both these Americans no doubt helps explain why the careers of these two famous "anti-Communists" were so intimately intertwined with communism: However inadequate his "conspiracy so vast," his "infamy so black" was to the events of Korea, it perfectly described the black, conspiratorial events that unfolded inside Joseph McCarthy. The temperament of Richard Nixon, too, was oddly in consonance with the evasions, the half-truths, the intellectual dishonesty, that some victims of the House Un-American Activities Committee brought with them to the witness chair. The great, sad truth about American communism by 1950 is that it long since had turned a certain number of former idealists into left-wing Richard Nixons. For years the party had demanded that its members hail Stalin's pact with Hitler one day, accuse the bourgeoisie of not being sufficiently antifascist the next. To call the Moscow purge trials "justice" and Soviet military oppression in Czechoslovakia "people's democracy," you had to work—like Richard Nixon—on the assumption that the means mean nothing; the end is all.

At the great inquisition in Washington, many poor heretics therefore found in Richard Nixon a most intuitive grand inquisitor. He thought as they thought, and this was a symmetry that would provide one of the great dominant themes of Richard Nixon's entire career. He began by denouncing the intrigues of Stalin; by the end, Nixon's own regime in Washington was embroiled in conspiracy to an extent that was truly Stalinesque, and it was only in Moscow and Peking that Nixon felt at home—only with autocrats like Brezhnev and Mao that he could communicate.

Maneuver was all. Brezhnev understood Nixon because Nixon had invaded Cambodia for the same reason Brezhnev had invaded Czechoslovakia. Mao understood Nixon because Nixon had unleashed the B-52s on Hanoi for the same reason Mao had unleashed the Cultural Revolution on the Chinese countryside. Even the destruction of whole nations was only an incident in the pursuit of power and the maintenance of power for its own sake. It is no accident that in Moscow and Peking, more than in any other foreign capitals, Watergate provoked alarm, consternation and dismay.

Brezhnev suspected it was all a conspiracy hatched by the enemies of détente. Mao was absolutely convinced, he told Imelda Marcos and other visitors, that Watergate was an anti-Chinese conspiracy designed to benefit Taiwan and the Soviet Union. In the final days of his presidency, Nixon flew off to Moscow as if in search of refuge, and following his disgrace he journeyed to Peking, where he was welcomed, like some latter-day MacArthur, as a conquering hero. Along the well-policed boulevards of those capitals, no passing cars honked at him, as cars passing the White House did. No one shouted, "Resign!" or refused to shake his hand when he offered it. Instead, at the official banquets the well-rehearsed speeches lauded the repudiated American President, and when Nixon spoke, the assembled minions applauded on cue.

The Russians and the Chinese were right to be alarmed by Watergate. It was one more defeat for their notion, not just Nixon's notion, that doctrines can explain, and power control, events everywhere. Marxism purported to define the laws of history, and hence to provide control over its forces. Yet just as the Truman Doctrine and the Nixon Doctrine had only alienated their authors from the realities of Korea and Vietnam, so the rulers of the Soviet Union and China now found themselves face to face, in the United States, with an upheaval to which all their theorems were simply irrelevant. Something profoundly "subversive" was unfolding in Washington: Americans, like Vietnamese and Salvadorans, were demonstrating that human beings possess a disconcerting capacity, when they choose, to topple even the grandest doctrines, the mightiest potentates, as though they were no more than dominoes.

The rise and fall of Richard Nixon; the rise and fall of Lyndon Johnson, of Joseph McCarthy, of Douglas MacArthur—after World War II, these individual Americans only personified a much larger American national pattern. Truman's grand doctrine for the Aegean led as surely to the frozen mass graves of Korea as Kennedy's thrilling invocation of American destiny led to My Lai and the Tet Offensive.

In this epic, the illusion of light tended toward a reality of darkness: the great revelation of the McCarthy Era in particular and the Cold War in general was that even when events in places like Greece and Korea did not come down to contests between good and evil, a Manichean struggle between liberty and power nonetheless dominated the mind of America. Nixon was no "aberration" in American domestic politics, just as the Vietnam War was no "mistake" in terms of America's dealings with the world. Instead, both were only the most extreme examples of an American national tendency that is all the more remarkable because Americans so consistently and successfully avoid confronting it. Whatever the conspiracy theory explained about Moscow or Peking, it clearly had the capacity—in the Senate, in the House Un-American Activities Committee, in the State Department and in the White House—to determine events in Washington.

Many Americans welcomed the McCarthy Era, and many more welcomed the Cold War Era, for the same reason that Kennan had welcomed Stalin's "implacable challenge" and President Reagan later welcomed the "Communist threat" in El Salvador. In a time of total change, these events seemed to prove that America's destiny was changeless. It was still his destiny, Richard Nixon proclaimed in his Checkers speech, to fight "the crooks and Communists in Washington," just as it was America's destiny, as President Truman had proclaimed in his doctrine, to fight them everywhere.

At the very moment that Americans willingly, eagerly took up the burden of global power, they willingly, eagerly put down the burden of self-knowledge. There was no further need for questions, for explanations. Korea and the other postwar crises had explained it all. All across the nation, Americans, already weary of so many complexities, were rediscovering that things were really very simple after all.

We need mention here only one such American, and his rediscovery. Earlier, he had supported Franklin Roosevelt; after World War II, he had opposed Richard Nixon and others who shared Nixon's beliefs. But about the time the Chinese were invading Korea, Truman was dismissing MacArthur, and McCarthy was unearthing his Communist conspiracy in Washington, this paradigmatical American underwent a paradigmatical transformation. Ronald Reagan, at that time president of the Screen Actors Guild, discovered what he considered "a Communist plot to subvert the film industry."

The great defect of the "X article" was not what it proposed for the Soviet Union; it was that neither Kennan nor anyone else, during those fateful years, devised a policy to check the "mystical, Messianic" impulses of the United States.

* * *

By the beginning of the 1950s, the McCarthy Era had become institutionalized in the Cold War bureaucracy of the United States Government.

As President Eisenhower assumed office, in 1953, nothing more epitomized this fact than the elevation of John Foster Dulles and Allen Dulles to supreme command of the State Department and the Central Intelligence Agency. Not since the days of Coolidge had the conduct of our foreign policy been entrusted to men so prone to detect a single, sinister conspiracy lurking behind the most far-flung and unrelated events. Not since Woodrow Wilson had America's relations with the world been seen so starkly in terms of a confrontation between good and evil. And not since the days of Theodore Roosevelt had an administration in Washington been more implicitly committed to a policy of violation of the sovereignty of foreign nations.

In 1954 in Guatemala, as in El Salvador nearly thirty years later, the basic thesis of U.S. intervention was that the United States was only responding to events, that we acted as we did because events there had the capacity to "menace" the rest of the hemisphere, and us. To use Kennan's idiom of "containment," the United States was only engaging in an "adroit and vigilant applications of counterforce . . . corresponding to the shifts and maneuvers of Soviet policy."

In fact, Latin America's role in our foreign policy during Eisenhower's administration was the same as it had been in Monroe's time. Latin America, as always, had been completely peripheral to the central drama of our foreign relations, unfolding in Europe and the Atlantic, and in Asia and the Pacific. It had been even more remote from that great drama of American nationalism that perpetually unfolds inside our own minds. Yet by the early 1950s, it was a most unwise Latin American leader who did not take note of the sea change that had occurred in Washington and trim his sails to the gale-force winds of anticommunism. As the Cold War hurricane bore southward, it was as though the Nazis never existed. All the political prisoners, all the campesinos who were machine-gunned, the U.S. Government was assured, were "Communists" now.

But what of a country where there were no political prisoners—where national policy was something more than a communiqué ghostwritten by the American ambassador and broadcast from the presidential palace?

What if a nation as small, as weak, above all as close to the United States and dependent on it as Guatemala, took a position at variance, at times even at odds, with that of the United States? In Washington at that time there could be only one explanation.

"Communism," as President Eisenhower put it, "was striving to establish its first beachhead in the Americas by gaining control of Guatemala." A word to the CIA, to the State Department, to the Department of Defense, was sufficient. It was in such a manner, and for such reasons, that the death warrant of Guatemalan democracy was signed.

Arevalo, Arbenz, Diaz and their Guatemala, like Archbishop Romero and his El Salvador, and Augusto Sandino and his Nicaragua, today belong only to the potential Latin America—to that hemisphere of the imagination that might have existed had we Americans not helped to turn so many patriots into cadavers, so many hopes into bitter despair. One might as well ask what would have become of Antigua Guatemala had there been no earthquake, as ask what Guatemala would be today were it not for the CIA.

Historically, however, two things are indisputable: Those who ruled Guatemala from 1945 until 1954 were not Communists and were in no way the agents of the Soviet Union. And their policies, however much they offended Guatemalan conservatives, did not threaten the security of the United States, or even its economic interests.

Under Arevalo and Arbenz, indeed, Guatemala had the kind of government that, a few years later, the Kennedy Alliance for Progress would have supported, and which the Reagan administration says it is trying to achieve for El Salvador today.

But 1954 was not 1963 or 1984. The United States was combatting a hallucinatory conspiracy. And in such a struggle, were not illusory acts of aggression in Central America as insidious as massed infantry assault in Korea?

When Stalin died, in January 1953, and the Guatemalan national assembly held a memorial service for the Soviet dictator, the State Department reacted as though Guatemala had joined the Warsaw Pact. Yet when Ambassador Peurifoy demanded an explanation, President Arbenz had a ready answer. Only recently even the Americans had lauded Stalin, along with Roosevelt and Churchill, as saviors of the world from fascism, the Guatemalan leader pointed out. Guatemala had honored Roosevelt when he died, Arbenz added, and no doubt would honor Churchill when his time came. It was this conversation that convinced Ambassador Peurifoy that President Arbenz of Guatemala "thought like a Communist and talked like a Communist, and if not actually one, would do until one came along."

"[I]t is only a matter of time," the ambassador also concluded, "before the large American interests will be forced out completely." But Guatemala's economic aggression, like its political aggression, was only illusory.

The truth is that under Arevalo and Arbenz, United Fruit continued to enjoy privileges no corporation had in the United States. True, this was the first Guatemalan Government ever to impose taxes upon it—though the taxes in 1953 amounted to no more than $150,000. But the government made no move to confiscate the company's railroads, or to nationalize Puerto Barrios or even to take over its banana fields, even though such Latin American countries as Mexico and Venezuela had nationalized similar foreign holdings long before.

Instead, the reforms of the Guatemalan Government were much more modest: United Fruit had immense landholdings that were not even cultivated. What better way to provide productive land for Guatemala's landless peasants than to purchase and redistribute this unused acreage?

Such was the nature of the political and economic "menace" the United States confronted. Eight years of democracy had not emancipated Guatemala's poor; least of all had it emancipated Guatemala itself from the form of international peonage that went back to the beginning of its history. But, for the first time in Guatemalan history, a freely elected President had served out his full term and then peacefully transferred power to another freely elected president. This experiment in democracy in Central America had one major achievement to its credit: it had survived.

Now democracy was under assault. And as so often in Latin American history, the conspiracy against freedom had been hatched by the United States itself. The State Department, the Pentagon, the CIA, the U.S. Information Service—there was hardly an American agency that did not have some role to play under the Eisenhower-Dulles destabilization program. By the time Truman left office, plans to overthrow Arbenz were already in the works in Washington.

After proclaiming the Truman Doctrine, in 1947, the United States had gone on, in keeping with the doctrine of "containment," to organize the whole of Latin America into a unified military alliance against the Communist "threat." As a result of the 1947 Rio Treaty, the Organization of American States became the equivalent, in the western hemisphere, of NATO in Europe and CENTO and SEATO in Asia. Stringing the dominoes together with acronyms fulfilled a deep need, among officials in Washington in those days, to perceive American order imposing itself on a disorderly, threatening world. Senator Vandenberg called the formation of the OAS "the greatest advance ever made in the business of collective peace."

But the production of these alliances—like the production of B-52s and H-bombs—raised an important question: what could they be used for in a world where, as Kennan pointed out, the reality was that the Russians were not coming? The maintenance of NATO no doubt was, and still is, a prudent measure, but the situation in the western hemisphere was entirely different. The Soviets were no more able to threaten the military security of the western hemisphere in 1947 than the Holy Alliance had been back in 1823.

Almost all the independent nations of the western hemisphere joined the American alliance for two very good reasons. First, it was always prudent to do whatever the United States wanted. The second reason was that, whatever its relevance to Europe, the Truman Doctrine's pledge to help allied governments resist "attempted subjugation by armed minorities or outside pressures" offered the Latin American dictators what they had always wanted from the United States, within the framework of a formal, binding, military alliance. This was a standing U.S. commitment to help them put down whatever rebellions their repression provoked, whenever they arose. At a stroke, the "doctrine of containment" provided Latin American autocracy both internal and external safeguards. By signing the Rio Treaty, Somoza's Nicaragua, Papa Doc's Haiti, Trujillo's Dominican Republic and all the others took out a double-indemnity insurance policy on which premiums were never collected but claims were always paid. The external threat of U.S. intervention was averted; more than that, every uprising against every caudillo was now a

Soviet threat to "hemisphere security," which the United States would help repulse.

Of all the independent nations of the western hemisphere, only two declined to sign the Rio pact and subsume themselves within the great acronym the United States had erected to parry the anticipated Soviet thrust. And in both cases, interestingly enough, this decision made in 1947 derived directly from the historical fact that, back in 1823, the United States had never taken the stand against Old World colonialism on behalf of New World liberty later generations of Americans imagined it had.

The first and by far the most important nation to refuse to join the western hemisphere alliance was Canada. Ever since the War of 1812, Canada's independent survival had rested on the twin principles of maintaining close ties with Britain and as much distance as possible from the United States. Membership in NATO reaffirmed the first principle; it was as much a reassertion of Canada's transatlantic ties with its two parent nations, Britain and France, as it was an alliance with the United States. Rejecting membership in the OAS reaffirmed the second principle of Canadian independence: that it steer clear of all U.S. schemes smacking of manifest destiny. Even today, the neighbor most vital to our national security is not a member of the U.S. system of "hemispheric security."

Guatemala, unlike Canada, did join the OAS. But there was a sticking point for Guatemala: it could not ratify the entire treaty for the same historical reason Canada would not ratify it—which was, quite simply, that after 1823, Canning's and Britain's grand design for the Americas, not the American principles of Monroe and Adams, had prevailed. By signing the Rio Treaty, in 1947, Guatemala would have had to renounce the use of force in the settlement of territorial disputes with its neighbors—and thus also have renounced, in the name of the U.S. crusade against "Soviet aggression," its right to undo the "aggression" Great Britain had committed back in 1836. Guatemala would have had to solemnly foreswear any attempt to retake British Belize.

This was a renunciation of Guatemalan pride that no government there—either before or after 1954—has ever been willing to make. Even today the stoutly "anti-Communist" military rulers of Guatemala refuse to recognize either Britain's previous rights to Belize or the independence Britain ultimately granted that territory. Why did the "pro-Communist" Arbenz have the same policy? Arbenz could not have recognized the British claims even if that had been his wish, because, unlike most of the Latin American leaders lining up to sign the treaty, Arbenz was no dictator. In a democracy, such as Guatemala, national decisions are taken nationally, not just by the man in the presidential palace. Guatemalan public opinion was strongly against any capitulation on Belize, and so was the Guatemalan congress. Quite simply, Arbenz did not have the votes.

In Washington such factors meant nothing. Guatemala's quibblings about

Belize, its quibblings over the Rio Treaty, were just additional signs that the agents of the worldwide Communist conspiracy were well on the way to fulfilling their subversive schemes. The U.S. response was straightforward: if the Guatemalans would not sign the U.S. treaty, then the United States would not sell Guatemala arms.

Therefore a fantasy of American nationalism joined with a fantasy of Guatemalan nationalism to doom the Arbenz government. No one in Washington doubted that the "Monroe Doctrine" gave the United States the right to "defend the hemisphere" by attacking any Latin American country it chose. Yet precisely because the Monroe Doctrine was only a myth—because Monroe and Adams never had defended, and never had intended to defend, countries like Guatemala—the Arbenz government, 131 years after the fact, lacked the arms to defend itself, let alone to undertake some fantasy reconquest of Belize.

Theoretically speaking, Arbenz was as free to purchase arms from powers other than the United States as Zelaya had been to invite some other nation to build a Nicaraguan canal half a century earlier. But what happened when a small Central American nation actually attempted to put the theory of sovereignty into practice?

In early 1954, President Arbenz committed the kind of aggression against American doctrine that not even the most supple Central American dictator might have been able to survive. Following fruitless efforts to purchase arms in Western Europe, he authorized the purchase of more than $1 million in arms from Communist Czechoslovakia.

By then, Arbenz needed arms wherever he could find them. Both the State Department and the CIA were deeply enmeshed in a campaign of violent subversion against Guatemala. The United States already had forced through the Organization of American States the resolution President Eisenhower later called the "charter for the anti-Communist counterattack that followed." Even before the Czech arms arrived, the United States already had organized and emplaced just over the Honduran border the U.S.-paid and -directed mercenary force that would invade the country the following month, and chosen Carlos Castillo Armas, a protégé of the United Fruit Company, to lead it.

The arms themselves, which had been transported in a Swedish vessel under charter to a British firm, consisted mostly of obsolete British, German and Czech army-surplus weapons dating from World War II. The Guatemalans had no foreign military advisers; there was not even a Soviet embassy in Guatemala City.

But, by purchasing the weapons, Arbenz might as well have delivered his country into the hands of the Inquisition. The shipment allowed U.S. officials to convince the press, our allies and public opinion—above all to convince themselves—that "proof" at last had been discovered that all their darkest suspicions were true.

The Czech arms had reached Guatemala on May 15, 1954. By June 27, Arbenz had been forced from office. And by the third of July, Castillo Armas —the head of the CIA force and a traitor to his country by any juridical standard—had been flown to Guatemala City in the American ambassador's private airplane and installed as leader of the republic which, just twenty-six days earlier, on U.S. orders, he had attacked.

By any objective standard, the government of Guatemala had fallen prey to precisely the kind of aggression the Truman Doctrine had been intended to deter. The government of a "free people" had suffered "subjugation by armed minorities" as the result of "outside pressures." More than that, the entire American-devised system of "hemispheric security" had been violated, grossly and with impunity.

Twenty-seven years later, in its White Paper, the State Department would accuse "Cuba, the Soviet Union and other Communist states" of carrying out a similar "well-coordinated, covert effort to bring about the overthrow of El Salvador's established government and to impose in its place a Communist regime with no popular support."

Whatever its lack of relevance to what was happening in El Salvador in the 1980s, the State Department formulation described perfectly what had happened in Guatemala in the 1950s.

The Czech arms shipment, the United States purported, "far exceeded any legitimate, normal requirements for the Guatemalan armed forces." But subsequent events made clear that that assertion, like so many of the assertions from Washington, was only a fantasy. In his own resignation speech, Arbenz made a point that has been valid since the time of President Monroe.

"The truth," he told a national radio audience, "is that the sovereignty of a people cannot be maintained without the material elements to defend it."

By 1954, Americans like Eisenhower, Dulles and Peurifoy were not the only ones acting out a fantasy. Guatemalan democrats like Arevalo, Arbenz and Diaz were also in the grip of an illusion: that American-style democracy not only could survive in the face of American hostility but prevail in a nation so alienated from the sources of democracy. By 1954, Guatemala's subjugation to foreign economic interests was no mere matter of the banana plantations United Fruit owned, or even of its control of Guatemala's national infrastructure. The centuries had created a system of foreign vassalage that had stripped Guatemala of everything except the symbols of independence.

Like the Somozas and Martinez, General Ubico had maintained the façade of sovereignty so successfully, because he had never been foolhardy enough to attempt to exercise it. But after 1944 all that had changed. Arevalo and Arbenz acted as though the votes of their countrymen actually conferred on them a sovereignty those far more powerful than they, including the United States, would be obliged to respect.

Like the skyscrapers of the capital, like the baroque ruins of Antigua and like the pyramids of Tikal, Guatemalan democracy was a most attractive edifice. But who was there in Guatemala to defend this fragile monument against the earthquakes, the volcanic lava, the rushing walls of water that periodically assault everything there?

In attempting to reform Guatemalan society by peaceful, democratic and gradual means, Arevalo and Arbenz made powerful and implacable enemies. Even more important, they failed to win the committed support of the many. Their very commitment to constitutional processes in fact gave them the worst of both worlds. Their democratic principles did not prevent their adversaries from denouncing them as "Communists," and treating them accordingly. But the fact that they were not Communists assured that the armed forces and other centers of power in Guatemala were not ruthlessly subordinated to their will. Most important, it meant that—in contrast to truly revolutionary states—the unlettered masses of Guatemala's urban slums and rural barrios were never turned into an implement of political power. Under Arbenz and democracy, as under Ubico and dictatorship, most Guatemalans, especially the country's Indian majority, remained as isolated from the politics of the capital as they had been in the time of Alvarado.

As a result, the crisis of 1954 was notable not merely for the speed with which some things happened, but for the things that never happened at all.

The Guatemalan armed forces may have been ill equipped. But their lack of supplies was never tested, because the Guatemalan Army made no attempt to defend the nation the CIA army had invaded. Nor did the people of the capital take to the streets in support of the government they themselves had elected. And in the countryside, the vast majority of Guatemala's peasantry was as indifferent to the catastrophe that had overtaken democracy as the jungle was indifferent to the ruins of Tikal.

Assaulted from without, democracy in Guatemala had collapsed from within—demonstrating another truth we Americans sometimes like to proclaim. Democracy is indeed a most fragile institution, one that requires the most careful nurturing if it is to survive in a violent and selfish world. Several generations of assiduous U.S. support there might have allowed such a vulnerable transplant to take root in Guatemalan soil. Instead, that country's sole experiment in constitutional rule and peaceful reform had been gratuitously crushed, and for no real reason at all.

It was, by all accounts, one of the most exuberant Fourth of July parties ever held in Guatemala City. With Arbenz and Diaz gone, and Castillo Armas in the saddle, hundreds of Americans and their Guatemalan friends converged on Ambassador Peurifoy's residence. On the surface it was the kind of revel that must have preceded John Quincy Adams's address, exactly 133 years earlier. Who could not be proud to be an American on such a day? There were tears in the eyes of more than one U.S. official when hundreds of Guatemalans sang "The Star-Spangled Banner." These Guatemalan military men and landowners, these businessmen and executives of U.S.-owned companies, had good reason to sing our national anthem: outside the American ambassador's residence, all across that other Guatemala, their estates and bank accounts and villas once again were "safe"—not merely from "communism," but from social accountability of any kind.

As in El Salvador later, the lyrics were all of freedom, but what of the substance underneath? A little more than a week earlier—a few hours before Ambassador Peurifoy had ordered the bombing of Guatemala City—a different kind of American-Guatemalan gathering had occurred. In the national palace, President Diaz had received a visit from the CIA station chief, John Doherty, and one of his assistants, Enno Hobbing.

Even at that late moment, Diaz had imagined it was possible to reason with the Americans. The Guatemalan President was speaking of the need for social reform when the following exchange occurred. It is taken from Schlesinger and Kinzer's account, though Doherty might have been the Grand Inquisitor, Hobbing some factotum of the Inquisition, and Dostoevsky the author of what follows:

"Wait a minute, Colonel," Hobbing suddenly interjected. "Let me explain something to you," he said sternly, pointing a finger at Colonel Diaz. "You made a big mistake when you took over the government."

Hobbing paused to let his words sink in. Then he continued: "Colonel, you're just not convenient for the requirements of American foreign policy."

Diaz was taken aback. "But," he stammered, "I talked to your ambassador. He gave me his approval."

"Well, Colonel," Hobbing said, "there is diplomacy and then there is reality. Our ambassador represents diplomacy. I represent reality. And the reality is that we don't want you."

"You mean I can't stay in office?" Diaz meekly asked.

Hobbing shook his head.

So President Arbenz had been punished for his crime, which was the heresy of believing a government of Guatemala could act in the interests of Guatemala without incurring the wrath of the United States. And now President Diaz, like some character in *Nineteen Eighty-four,* was being secretly accused and tried, convicted and punished by omnipotent, faceless men.

Among the "Communist propaganda" that Castillo Armas, a few days after the Fourth of July party, ordered confiscated and burned were the works of Dostoevsky. But outlawing *Crime and Punishment* could neither change the nature of nor save the United States from the kind of victory it had inflicted on itself.

With U.S. support, Castillo Armas outlawed labor unions, political parties and peasant cooperatives. Three quarters of Guatemala's voters were disenfranchised, and freedom of the press was ruthlessly expunged.

The American-chosen leader also inaugurated one of modern history's most sweeping land-reform programs, though it ran in reverse. Peasants were driven from their subsistence plots; immense estates were given to wealthy Guatemalans, influential foreigners and American corporations, and what the CIA coup began, Castillo's successors continued. By 1982, only 1 percent of Guatemala's population controlled 60 percent of Guatemala's arable land. Rural standards of living were lower than they had been thirty years earlier, under Arbenz, and as in El Salvador, the institutionalization of such repression produced the usual results. By then, the Guatemalan Army was killing some 450 peasants a month, the better to defend the country from the latest "Communist" threat. After nearly 160 years, Guatemala's grim tapestry of feudal exploitation and medieval violence was unchanged.

If anything, thanks to U.S. intervention, history had marched backward. "[N]ever in our history," Guatemala's conference of Catholic bishops noted in 1982, "have such extremes been reached, with the assassinations now falling into the category of genocide."

During the Arevalo and Arbenz years, many idealistic Latin Americans were drawn to Guatemala. Among them was a young Argentine doctor named Ernesto Guevara. His eyewitness view of the destruction of Guatemalan democracy, he later stated, was a main factor in convincing him that the system of dictatorship and exploitation the United States supported in Latin America could be defeated only through armed struggle. Guevara also derived another lesson from Guatemala: that even after the struggle was won, democracy was a luxury no revolution could afford: complete control of the economy and the apparatus of the state, a veritable dictatorship, would be necessary if the Americans were not to use the armed forces and local elites to subvert other nations the way they had Guatemala.

Some bitter contagion seemed to have been unleashed, by the destruction of democracy in Guatemala, from which neither we nor the Latin Americans were immune. "The rest of Latin America was not in the least displeased," President Eisenhower later purported. Displeasure, however, was a mild epithet for the reception Richard Nixon received in Latin America less than three years later. What could account for the howling, taunting mobs that besieged the Vice President of the United States practically everywhere? "Communist agitation" was Nixon's explanation, and though this generalization was unwarranted it nonetheless contained a kernel of truth. After 1954, "Che" Guevara's dark vision was of incalculable influence not just in Cuba, but throughout Latin America. Over the next twenty years, violent revolutionary movements would spring up throughout South and Central America. Wherever they arose, the United States would oppose them. And as in Guatemala the results were the same: all over Latin America, with U.S. support, "decent democratic regimes" were subverted and destroyed.

Within twenty years of Arbenz's overthrow, indeed, the domino theory had worked in reverse in Latin America. A tidal wave of U.S.-supported right-wing dictatorship had swept the region. By September 1973, when Allende was overthrown in Chile, there were only three multiparty democracies left in the whole of Latin America: oil-rich Venezuela, Colombia, and tiny Costa Rica. Nixon and Kissinger, like Eisenhower and Dulles nineteen years earlier, proclaimed a triumph of American principles. But just as Castillo Armas had been only another Somoza, so Pinochet was just another Castillo Armas. Following the U.S.-supported coup, thousands of Chileans were murdered and all left-of-center political parties were outlawed. Even moderate and conservative groups were banned. Chilean democracy was destroyed, root and branch, as Pinochet pursued his campaign to "exterminate Marxism." Lest Allende, like Arbenz, destroy freedom, the United States had destroyed freedom itself.

So far as the politics of Latin America was concerned, the chief effect of the Guatemala coup was not merely to radicalize some advocates of reform, but to deeply divide all those who sought change. On one side were Guevara and many others like him, who argued that only armed struggle could bring liberation. Others, such as Allende, retained their faith in the possibility of peaceful, constitutional, democratic change.

In October 1967, six years before Allende's murder, Guevara was captured and murdered, in Bolivia, as part of a U.S.-planned counterinsurgency campaign. It said much about the Latin American condition, but it said much more about the national condition of the United States, that the fate of Guevara and Allende should be identical. Whether it was violent revolution or democratic change such Latin Americans sought, it made no difference in Washington. Both efforts were destined to incur our implacable opposition. The foreign policy of the United States had been radicalized. After 1954, it was not merely in Guatemala that those like Castillo Armas reigned supreme; in the CIA, the State Department and the Pentagon, the extremists were in control too.

John F. Kennedy summed up the closed circle in which the United States had trapped itself, in a discussion of the crisis in the Dominican Republic that was to fester throughout the first half of the 1960s. "There are three possibilities in descending order of preference," he told Arthur M. Schlesinger, Jr. The three possibilities, as Kennedy perceived them, were "a decent democratic regime, a . . . Trujillo regime or a Castro regime. We ought to aim at the first, but we really can't renounce the second until we are sure that we can avoid the third." There is no need to recapitulate the long and shameful history of U.S. support for the Trujillo dictatorship, because it is a history identical to that of our support for the Somozas in Nicaragua. There, too, the

United States sent in the Marines. There, too, an early rehearsal for the Vietnamization program placed control of the local armed forces in the hands of an unscrupulous flatterer of the Americans who seized power as soon as the Marines pulled out. One of Gunther's observations is illuminating on a number of levels:

> The United States Marines liked Trujillo . . . and he built his career largely on their favor. They said, "He thinks just like a marine!" One American officer, a Major Watson . . . "created" Trujillo much as—in a faraway part of the world—the British General Ironside "created" the present Shah of Persia.

Gunther added: "Trujillo, it seems, is content to let Americans control 60 percent of the country's business, provided he is free to do what he likes with the remainder."

After World War II, what really linked Diem and Trujillo, the Shah and Somoza, and so many other of the "dominoes" the United States attempted to shore up, was not a crisis of external subversion, but a crisis of internal legitimacy.

What no American President, with the possible exception of Jimmy Carter, understood after 1954 was that Kennedy's three options had been only a fantasy. For by refusing to "renounce" support for dictatorship, as Kennedy had put it, the United States was implicitly allying itself with dictatorship— and thus strongly reinforcing the vicious circle of repression followed by revolution, followed in turn by new cycles of dictatorship and upheaval that still grip much of Latin America and the rest of the Third World today. The lesson of Castillo Armas and Guatemala was also the lesson of Pinochet and Chile, of both Nicaragua in 1927 and El Salvador today: alliances with repression, even in "the defense of freedom," are inseparable from alliances against freedom.

Like the earlier U.S. attempt to "save" Nicaragua and the later attempt to "save" El Salvador, the Guatemala intervention had resulted only in the perpetuation of a nightmare that in the end consumed not just our adversaries, but those in whose "defense" we acted as well. Within a few years, indeed, it would have been difficult to decide who were the greater victims of U.S. fantasy: those we had deposed or those we had placed in power.

After 1954, President Arbenz faced a life of exile. But his fate seemed benign in comparison to the fate that lay in store for Carlos Castillo Armas, the joint candidate of the CIA and United Fruit for "liberator" of Guatemala.

For nearly three years, Castillo Armas lorded it over Guatemala as though General Ubico had never left office. But he proved far less adept at the techniques of dictatorship than his predecessor. With his administration mired in corruption, and his repression of "Communist agitators" steadily alienating even those who had opposed Arbenz, Castillo Armas was gunned down inside the presidential palace on his way to dinner one evening in July 1957.

Official American grief was as unstinting for the fallen Guatemalan dictator as it had been for the elder Somoza, who had been assassinated under similar circumstances the previous year. President Eisenhower lauded Castillo Armas as "a farseeing and able statesman" who "enjoyed the devotion of his people." The official explanation was that Castillo had been a martyr of freedom—gunned down by a Communist fanatic. But this was an interpretation of Castillo's life and death that eventually even the Pentagon discarded. An official U.S. summary of the Castillo Armas presidency, prepared in 1968, not only explains why this particular Guatemalan dictator, like so many others, died as he had lived; it also provides an epitaph for all the American illusions that had raised him to power:

> Castillo Armas headed a junta until he was confirmed in the presidency by plebiscite. He ruled until July 1957, when he was assassinated by one of his palace guards. During his term illiterates were disenfranchised, thus canceling the voting rights of the Indians, who made up more than half the population. Expropriated lands were returned to former owners. The Constitution of 1945 was abolished and . . . [a]ll political parties left of center were disbanded, and only those approved by the Government could function.

The most appropriate American epitaph for Castillo Armas and dozens of figures like him, however, had to wait for John F. Kennedy's inaugural address. Speaking to the leaders of "those new states whom we welcome to the ranks of the free," the American President who soon would launch the Bay of Pigs invasion and involve the Green Berets in foreign civil wars from Laos to Bolivia asked them "to remember that, in the past, those who foolishly sought power by riding the back of the tiger ended up inside."

Kennedy's words were meant to alert the world to the dangers of communism. But like so many of our doctrines about others, these words from Washington unintentionally revealed a great truth about the United States. Like the Somozas, Diem, the Shah and so many others, Castillo Armas had ridden to power on the back of the American tiger. Like them, it was his fate, sooner or later, to be devoured.

After 1954, in Guatemala it became more and more difficult to distinguish predator from prey. Guatemala's next "strong man," General Miguel Ydigoras Fuentes, certainly came in like a tiger: he gained power by hijacking an airplane and threatening armed revolt when he lost a presidential election. But, in the end, the fate of Ydigoras was only the fate of Diem. An Alliance for Progress counterinsurgency program designed to shore up the Guatemalan leader had the opposite effect. The Americans grew tired of "saving" Ydigoras from "communism," so they overthrew him themselves. According to some accounts, President Kennedy personally approved the ouster of the

Guatemalan President; whatever the exact circumstances, there is no doubt that the 1963 coup in Guatemala City, like the one in Saigon, had the support of the United States.

Thereafter it was politics as usual in Guatemala. The leading presidential candidate was gunned down in 1966. The real winner of the 1974 elections was prevented from taking office. By 1980 not even the highest officials of the republic were immune from terror: That year the Vice President of Guatemala himself fled the country lest he, too, fall victim to his own government's "counterterror" campaign. Finally General Fernando Lucas Garcia, the President responsible for the terror campaign, was ousted in another coup, only to be replaced by still another general, who, the New York *Times* reported in June 1982, "believes that his authority to rule comes from God."

General Rios Montt [the *Times* elaborated] is a born-again Christian who belongs to the Christian Church of the Word, a fundamentalist group based in California. "I have confidence in my God, my master and my king, that he will guide me," the 59-year-old general shouted. "Only he can grant and take away power."

In August 1983, as a series of U.S. naval flotillas patrolled both the Caribbean and the Pacific coasts of Central America, power was taken away from General Rios Montt—though what role, if any, God played in the latest Guatemalan coup d'état was not immediately ascertainable.

These U.S. naval task forces were led by such gargantuan vessels as the aircraft carrier *Coral Sea* and the battleship *New Jersey*—leviathans, like the B-52s, that had been constructed to fight other wars, other enemies. The day before Rios Montt was overthrown, the Guatemalan Minister of Defense, General Oscar Umberto Mejia Victores, along with other Central American ministers of defense, had been summoned to the aircraft carrier *Ranger*. The *Ranger* costs $15 million a month to operate, and General Mejia and the others had been invited there to see for themselves the kind of military power and influence the United States was bringing to bear in their part of the world.

The objective, as one U.S. spokesman put it, was to show "the bad guys in Nicaragua and Cuba that we are positioned to blockade, invade or interdict" if they tried to overthrow "free" governments like the one in Guatemala. But this display of American military resolve seemed to have another effect: after being flown back to Guatemala City in a U.S. aircraft, like Castillo Armas twenty-nine years earlier, General Mejia overthrew the Guatemalan Government himself.

After General Mejia's coup, President Reagan's Assistant Secretary of State for Inter-American Affairs called for renewed U.S. military aid to Guatemala, just as U.S. officials had, following the overthrow of Lucas Garcia.

"The implications of a Marxist takeover in Guatemala are a lot more serious than in El Salvador," Lieutenant General Wallace H. Nutting, the commander of U.S. forces in Latin America, had explained earlier. Accordingly it was "imperative" that the United States play "essentially the same role" that it already was in El Salvador. "[U]ntil understanding and will increase," the American general explained, "the guerrilla will persist."

Americans paid little attention to Guatemala after 1954. With communism "stopped" in Central America, Kennedy and Johnson, like Wilson before them, sought a more grandiose and far-flung stage on which to act out their illusion that agencies like the CIA, in collaboration with figures like Castillo Armas, could make the world safe for democracy. Yet Guatemala's full catastrophe, and our own participation in it, had scarcely begun.

Operation Success, as Nixon's 1958 visit to Latin America demonstrated, had only deeply embittered those we imagined we were defending. The following year, when Castro entered Havana, something else became evident: Destroying democracy in Guatemala had not stopped communism in Cuba.

The Guatemalan military had stood by while the CIA invaded their country in 1954. But by 1960 the use of Guatemalan bases for operations against Castro, including training for the upcoming Bay of Pigs invasion, outraged many Guatemalan military officers. In spite of so many national humiliations, a tradition of national pride persisted. In late 1960, in response to our manifold violations of Guatemala's sovereignty over the previous six years, there was a military uprising.

The U.S. response was straightforward. Any event that might impede the approaching invasion of Cuba must be crushed. CIA bombers, this time piloted by Cuban exiles, soon were bombing Guatemala again.

With the military uprising crushed in Guatemala, the United States was free to proceed with the Bay of Pigs adventure—and so soon would face all the consequences that act would entail. In Guatemala the long-term results were equally disastrous. A number of officers involved in the failed revolt fled to the countryside and raised the banner of insurrection. The country now had a real guerrilla war on its hands—headed by men trained not in Moscow or Havana, but in American bases in the United States and the Panama Canal Zone. Their objectives, as these Guatemalan officers explained them, were straightforward: The U.S. use of Guatemala for its Cuban adventure, they pointed out, was only the latest demonstration that the government of their country was only "a puppet" of the United States. "Democracy vanished for our country long ago," one of their manifestoes added.

Thanks to the U.S. intervention of 1954, peaceful, democratic change in the manner of Arbenz had been destroyed as an option in Guatemala. As a result of the U.S. intervention of 1960, the more traditional Guatemalan means of overthrowing dictatorship—military revolt—had been eliminated too. With all other alternatives closed to them, these American-trained military men turned to armed insurrection in an effort to restore their country's sovereignty.

Even more than Castro's initial success, the failure of the Bay of Pigs profoundly shocked the United States: it was to the Vietnam Era of U.S. counterinsurgency wars what Kim Il Sung's attack had been to the Korean War Era of "containment." The Bay of Pigs "proved" to many Americans what they already had wanted to believe: not just Southeast Asia and the Middle East, but our own hemisphere was under Communist assault. With Cuba "lost," dared the Kennedy administration let the Communists take over Guatemala, too? By 1961 our quest to "save" Guatemala had created, in the jungles and mountains of Central America, a mirror image of that fantasy world our policymakers inhabited. But by then Guatemala was not alone. So far as the foreign policy of the United States was concerned, much of the world was a hall of mirrors.

In Asia, one of the many mirrors was called Laos. That medieval kingdom made no pretense to the political sophistication of a Guatemala. But in 1955 a prince of Luang Prabang named Souvanna Phouma became Prime Minister —and this descendant of twenty generations of Lao kings had some important things to say about the strategic realities of the nuclear age. Trying to enlist nations as poor, small and weak as Laos in the great crusade against communism, he argued, did nothing to "defend freedom" or to enhance the security of the United States; it only threatened to destroy such countries and embroil America itself in futile conflicts. It would be far better, the prince suggested, for the United States to agree to the neutralization of Laos. Only by detaching Laos's internal conflicts from the larger Cold War conflict, in the manner of Finland or Austria, was there any hope of solving those conflicts and sparing Laos involvement in a wider war.

No one in Washington listened; the U.S. ambassador to Laos, J. Graham Parsons, explained why: "We don't talk to neutralists," he told an American anthropologist, Joel Halpern; Souvanna Phouma, and Norodom Sihanouk in neighboring Cambodia, so far as the United States was concerned, were just Communist agents, like Mossadegh in Iran and Arbenz in Guatemala.

The Castillo Armas of Laos was a general named Phoumi Nosavan. In 1959 the CIA, using Phoumi, overthrew Souvanna Phouma in the same way that, five years earlier, they had overthrown Arbenz. In Washington once again there was talk of communism being stopped cold in its tracks. But in Laos, as in Guatemala, the consequence was completely different. In 1960, a young, nonideological but patriotic military man named Kong Le, shamed and appalled by what the Americans had made of his nation, revolted against the CIA-installed government, just as Guatemalan military men later would.

Kong Le and his troops had been armed and trained by U.S. advisers as part of the American embassy's Greece-style operation in Laos. For years, Kong Le said, the Americans had informed us that there were enemies ready to enter and cause agitation within our country. But I and my friends . . . have never seen such enemies coming to make trouble. We have only seen Lao killing Lao without cause.

He had acted, he explained, with the objective of "saving the nation and ending a war in which I never saw a foreigner die." As even a strongly anti-Communist observer of the crisis in Laos, Arthur Dommen, later recounted, Kong Le's objective was not to bring his country under Communist domination; it was to rid Laos of "a new form of colonization, this time under the United States."

"[N]o other assumption possible but that he outright Commie," Truman's Secretary of State, Dean Acheson, earlier had cabled the U.S. mission in Saigon about Ho Chi Minh. Now the outgoing Eisenhower administration made the same decision about Kong Le in Laos that it earlier had made about Arbenz in Guatemala. Even if he were "not actually" a Communist, Kong Le "would do until one came along." Later, when an interdepartmental task force of the Kennedy administration was asked to prepare an analysis of the "Communist 'master plan' to take over all of Southeast Asia," among the many manifestations of the conspiracy it enumerated was "Kong Le's coup in Laos."

Kong Le "was a lost soul and wholly irretrievable," President Eisenhower told President-elect Kennedy when they conferred following the 1960 elections. One President was replacing another President; responsibility for the safety of the United States in a dangerous world was being transferred from one administration to another. And at that crucial moment, two presidents of the United States considered the state of Kong Le's soul a matter of "national security" worth discussing in the Oval Office at the White House. The Soviet Union, Laos, the mighty armies of the Warsaw Pact, a ragtag band of military mutineers on the upper Mekong—all were integral "threats" to the United States of America and its survival.

CIA agents and Green Berets already were embroiled in a full-scale guerrilla war in the foothills of the Annamite cordillera—a kind of long-distance, slow-motion Bay of Pigs eleven thousand miles from Washington. As Charles Stevenson later wrote in *The End of Nowhere,* "the highest echelons of State Department . . . feared Kong Le might be another Castro."

In the early 1960s, Laos made the same kind of headlines El Salvador had twenty years later, though beneath the headlines nothing very important, and certainly nothing new, was happening: we Americans once again were ravaging a hapless, defenseless nation for no reason. Meanwhile, the Guatemala insurrection, as Washington saw it, was only another manifestation of the same conspiracy we were battling in Laos. "The message of Cuba, of Laos . . . in Asia and Latin America," as President Kennedy himself emphasized, "these messages are all the same." He added:

The communists move among them, disciplined, organized, subject to an international discipline, [seeking to impose] the iron grip of the totalitarian state . . . upon the population. . . .

Soon the tribesmen of Guatemala and the tribesmen of Laos had something more in common than the colorful patterns of their traditional dress. Earnest Americans, "all trained in Laos," as Schlesinger and Kinzer point out, moved among the Central American peasants, dispensing machine guns and antibiotics, teaching "interrogation techniques" and giving slide shows on the menace to freedom the Kremlin conspiracy posed.

The American techniques of subversion used to overthrow Arbenz in Guatemala had exported themselves to Indochina. Now the "counterinsurgency" tactics of Indochina were being recycled to Latin America. Thereafter the poison ceaselessly flowed in both directions, as the United States tried to turn Southeast Asia into an oriental vindication of the "Monroe Doctrine"—and treated every Latin American revolutionary movement as though it were some New World version of the Vietcong.

Though victory was claimed more than once, the insurrection in Guatemala was never really crushed. Instead, for more than twenty years now, it has simmered on in various forms, giving each successive U.S. administration the chance to "stop communism" in its own way. In the face of Stalin and the new menace of nuclear weapons, Truman had reverted to a fantasy of Monroe. In response to the Cold War, and the Third World's hunger for emancipation, Eisenhower had updated the gunboat diplomacy of Wilson and Coolidge. In his inaugural address, Kennedy had escalated the Eisenhower response into a global doctrine of American machismo: we (or at least the Special Forces) would fight "the long twilight struggle, year in and year out," even when it was not "the survival and success of liberty" that was at stake, only a few hilltops in the Laotian or Guatemalan back of the beyond.

What happened in Laos or Guatemala "directly affects the security of the people who live in this city," Kennedy told an audience gathered in a high school stadium in September 1963.

"This city" was Great Falls, Montana. Any suspicion that the complexities of the world were in any way distinguishable from the convolutions of the American mind had disappeared from the conduct of our foreign policy. So far as Kennedy's rhetoric went, most of the world was nothing more than a long row of Guatemalas.

What was the substance beneath the rhetoric? Kennedy's predecessors Truman and Eisenhower had not been quite so doctrinaire as most of their speeches and many of their actions made it seem. Truman had cultivated Tito, in spite of the Truman Doctrine, and had carefully "contained" the Korean War following the Chinese intervention there. Eisenhower had kept the lines of communication open to the Kremlin even at the height of the Cold War; the same year he had overthrown Arbenz in Guatemala he had refused to commit U.S. bombers and troops to the doomed French defense of Dienbienphu. Aside from the fact that the Soviets are not nearly so aggressive as Americans like to believe, the other, equally important reason there has been no World War III is that we Americans are not so reckless as either our own pronouncements, or those of our critics, often suggest.

By mid-1963 the Kennedy administration also showed some positive signs, among all the negative ones, of learning one or two lessons of history. The nuclear confrontation over Cuba, like the war in Korea, changed nothing locally: Castro remained in power, but Cuba did not become a forward position for Soviet offensive military operations. In an odd way, Cuba had become to the United States what Finland was to the Soviet Union. The internal nature of the regime, as a result of the U.S.-Soviet agreements that ended the Cuban missile crisis, was divorced from questions of the international balance of power. So a Communist government would rule in Havana, two hundred miles from Miami, just as a democratic government ruled in Helsinki, two hundred miles from Leningrad. The chief difference was temperamental and psychological, not political and military. The Russians maintained correct, even cordial relations with democratic Finland; we Americans would opt for a chronic policy of institutionalized spite toward Communist Cuba. Substantively, however, the result was the same: Finland, in spite of its contrary ideology, posed no threat to the Soviet Union. And Cuba, over the next twenty years, and for all our refusal to recognize the fact, would pose no threat to us. Just as one would never suspect, in somber, socialist Leningrad, that the consumer society lurked just beyond the Finnish border, a hundred miles away, so sybaritic Key West might be a million, not ninety, miles from Havana, so little has the "loss" of Cuba really affected our security.

The most important result of the Cuban missile crisis, in fact, was not in Cuba. It was in Washington, where the confrontation with the Soviet Union had starkly revealed the dangers of playing nuclear dominoes in the Third World. In July 1963, President Kennedy approved the limited nuclear test-ban treaty; in August, the Washington–Moscow "hot line," designed to reduce the risks of accidental war, was opened. A great threat seemed to have become apparent to the Kennedy administration: miscalculation and impulsiveness threatened the security, indeed the survival, of the United States at least as much as the shadowy guerrillas of Latin America and Southeast Asia did.

At the opposite end of the world, the Laos imbroglio had produced similar results: a war against "Communist aggression" there, it quickly became evident, was not just unwinnable; it was not worth fighting.

A Geneva conference was convoked, and Kennedy sent the unflappable, pragmatic Averell Harriman, who had been Roosevelt's wartime ambassador to Moscow, to negotiate a Laos settlement with representatives of the Soviet Union and eleven other nations, including Mao's China and Ho Chi Minh's Vietnam.

As the naysayers in Washington predicted, the Geneva talks were long and complicated; soon even the Soviets were publicly venting their frustration. "One cannot sit indefinitely on the shore of Lake Geneva counting swans," the Soviet Foreign Minister, Andrei Gromyko, complained. Yet beneath the delicate, interminable negotiations among the "rightist" prince, the "neutralist" prince and the "Communist" prince of Laos, something of potentially great significance was happening.

For the first time, the United States had committed itself to the neutralization of a divided Third World nation—rather than regarding that as "surrender on the installment plan." The United States was even talking to the Communists now. In July 1962, the willingness to talk paid off, when the three Lao factions and the twelve other nations represented at Geneva jointly pledged "to build a peaceful, neutral, independent, democratic, unified and prosperous Laos."

Declarations in Switzerland did not create Switzerlands in Southeast Asia. Laos's ultimate fate still depended on whether the much larger, much more intractable conflict in neighboring Vietnam would be resolved peacefully, or through war. But another American land war in Asia had been averted. The possibility that Laos might become a model of international cooperation, rather than a victim of ideological confrontation, now existed. Even more important, a precedent had been set, if the United States chose to apply it, for ensuring that other Laoses did not lead to other Cuban missile crises, to other U.S. military interventions even more destructive than in Guatemala and more frustrating than in Korea.

Like October 1950 at Wake Island, November 1963 in Washington might have been one of those turning points in history when many future catastrophes were averted. From Vietnam had come word that the U.S.-supported dictator in Saigon, Ngo Dinh Diem, was contemplating peaceful negotiations with Ho Chi Minh in Hanoi.

President Eisenhower had chosen Diem to be another Syngman Rhee, but by Kennedy's time it was clear Vietnam was not another Korea. Ho was no megalomaniac, like Kim; Diem, arrogant, aloof and unpopular as he was, lacked the cold rigidity of his South Korean counterpart. Vietnam was a land of languorous heat and pelting rain, not ice and snow; it offered the United States possibilities for diplomatic maneuver it never would provide militarily.

Another thing was clear by then: Ngo Dinh Diem had ample reason to seek peaceful accommodation, rather than fighting an endless war with Ho Chi Minh. Hundreds of millions of dollars in U.S. military aid and thousands of U.S. military advisers had failed to defeat the guerrillas, but they had produced a new, much more serious threat to Diem's position. The creation of an immense "military power and influence" in Saigon had turned the U.S.-trained, -armed and -paid South Vietnamese armed forces into a gargantuan version of the Nicaraguan National Guard.

What position should the United States take in regard to Diem's rumored contacts with Hanoi? Above all, how should the United States react if some Saigon general decided to make himself the South Vietnamese Somoza?

By 1963 the presence in Saigon of U.S. Ambassador Henry Cabot Lodge demonstrated an important truth about the foreign policy of the United States: there seems no discernible relationship between whom we elect and whom we do not elect, and whether we drop bombs and overthrow governments in foreign nations or not. Beneath the clash of domestic party politics in the United States, a truly "bipartisan" consensus did exist, which made it impossible even to question the U.S. commitment to conspiracy and subversion in foreign affairs.

Kennedy had defeated Lodge in his race for the Senate in 1952; he had bested Lodge again in 1960, when the Massachusetts Republican had been Nixon's vice-presidential running mate. Now Lodge held what was, for the moment, the single most crucial American diplomatic appointment anywhere in the world: the ambassadorship that could well decide not only the fate of South Vietnam, but whether the United States would become mired in another major Asian war.

From Saigon, Lodge's advice was unequivocal. Diem had become as much a "threat" to U.S. policy as Ho Chi Minh himself. Diem must go—and therefore a military coup must be supported. Only two years earlier, Lyndon Johnson had compared Diem to Winston Churchill. But now, so far as the United States was concerned, Diem was only another Arbenz.

"I want to know what is the attitude of the U.S.?" President Diem asked Ambassador Lodge, over the telephone, as the U.S. tanks surrounded his palace and the U.S.-supported overthrow of the South Vietnamese Government began. "After all, I am a Chief of State. I have tried to do my duty."

There were no official U.S. eulogies for Diem the next day, as there had been for Somoza and Castillo Armas. Several years would pass before a high-ranking U.S. official provided a definitive epitaph.

"In other words," he told a congressional questioner who had asked about Diem's overthrow, "he was at one time Prime Minister, and I would say fell from favor with the United States." Diem had ridden the American tiger and, as Kennedy had warned in his inaugural address, those who ride the tiger usually wind up inside.

When the possibility of an accommodation between Diem's South Vietnam and Ho Chi Minh's North Vietnam had arisen, U.S. officials had declared that the following scenario would be inevitable: Whatever the technicalities, such an accommodation would lead, sooner or later, to the reunification of Vietnam under Ho's control. And a unified, Communist Vietnam would exercise strong control, direct or indirect, over both Cambodia and Laos. In short, all of Indochina would be "lost"—which, of course, is exactly what, in due course, did happen.

As in Korea in 1950 and in Central America today, the United States lacked the capacity in Indochina in 1963 to change a number of unpalatable realities. But it did retain the option of confronting those realities realistically —and attempting to adjust peacefully to a situation it could not change even at the cost of a major war. If, in October 1963, President Kennedy had withheld U.S. support for a coup and had encouraged the Vietnamese to work out among themselves the same kind of settlement that had been negotiated among the Lao, the ultimate fate of Indochina might not have been any different. But what might the United States be like today without the legacy of the Vietnam War?

By the end of November 1963, President Diem's bullet-riddled, blood-spattered corpse haunted all our illusions about being able to "save" South Vietnam, just as the bullet-riddled, blood-spattered corpse of President Kennedy haunted all our illusions that America was a land of providential grace. For neither the first nor the last time, there had emerged a ghastly symmetry between what we did to others in the name of freedom, and what happened to us.

Was disaster avertable in Indochina following the killing of Diem? In retrospect, one thing is clear: Lyndon Johnson from the beginning rejected the peaceful alternatives to military disaster.

[Y]our mission is precisely for the purpose of knocking down the idea of neutralization wherever it rears its ugly head and on this point I think that nothing is more important than to stop neutralist talk wherever we can by whatever means we can,

President Johnson instructed his ambassador to Saigon in early 1964.

In pursuit of a military victory in Vietnam, the neutralization of Laos was also knocked on its head. With the outbreak of undeclared war between North Vietnam and the United States, Laos ceased being an irrelevant backwater and became an important theater of a full-scale Indochina War. Laotian mountaintops less than one hundred miles from Hanoi harbored U.S. clandestine military outposts; their electronic equipment was used to direct bombing of North Vietnam. The CIA also hired mountain tribesmen in Laos to run "intelligence probes" and "counterterror" operations in North Vietnam. Hanoi's approach was identical. As thousands of U.S. bombers flew over Laos to bomb North Vietnam, tens of thousands of North Vietnamese troops moved down the Ho Chi Minh Trail into South Vietnam. So soon after Laos had been neutralized at Geneva, it was transformed into a military crossroads where American high-technology warfare met Vietnamese guerrilla warfare.

Long before President Nixon's secret bombing of Cambodia, President Johnson was secretly bombing Laos. The bombing could not stop the North Vietnamese, and the Americans could not stop the bombing. The result was an aerial matanza that, for nearly nine years, turned that country into a high-technology El Salvador. In 1972, Fred Branfman published some oral accounts of life under the bombing, by Laotian peasants, that read like the later accounts, by Salvadoran campesinos, of the terror there:

> In the region of the Plain of Jars [one Lao villager recounted], there came to be a lake of blood and destruction, most pitiful for children, friends and old people. For there were airplanes and the sound of bombs throughout the sky and hills. . . . Every day and every night the planes came to drop bombs on us. We lived in holes to protect our lives. There were bombs of many kinds [and] shooting and death from the planes. . . . I saw my cousin die in the field of death. My heart was most disturbed and my voice called out loudly as I ran to the houses. Thusly I saw the life and death for the people on account of the war of so many airplanes . . . until there were no houses at all. And the cows and buffalo were dead. Until everything was leveled and you could see only the red, red ground.

"We give the impression not only to foreign people, but to many of our own people, that we are mad," Senator Fulbright observed some time after the Laos bombing had begun. "[W]hy don't we leave them alone?"

"[T]he problem of maintaining both the independence and the neutrality of Laos has faced us with very complex issues," the longtime U.S. ambassador to Laos, William H. Sullivan, explained to Fulbright in congressional hearings. "Independent of whom?" Fulbright wondered. Had the Soviets violated the 1962 Geneva accords, as we had? "The Soviets have not violated it," Sullivan conceded. Fulbright reiterated his question; Sullivan reiterated his answer. The United States must bomb Laos to defend the neutrality of Laos.

It was a dialogue of the deaf. Earlier, President Kennedy had said the United States had to be militarily strong enough not just to defend its allies, but to defend "the uncommitted nations" as well. Neutral nations like Laos, from this perspective, maintained their neutrality precisely by letting us unleash the same kind of devastation within their borders that we were unleashing in South Vietnam. Ambassador Peurifoy had begun by calling down a few air strikes on Guatemala in 1954; by the time the Laos bombing ended, in 1973, Ambassador Sullivan and his successors had called down more than two million tons of bombs on Laos. The United States had dropped nearly as many tons of bombs on Laos, which is smaller than Colorado, as it had dropped on Germany, Japan and all the other nations of the world during the whole of World War II.

It was the destiny of Lyndon Johnson in Latin America, as well as in Southeast Asia, to escalate the particular mistakes of his predecessors into a general catastrophe. In 1965, Johnson ordered the Marines to invade the Dominican Republic. Why had twenty-two thousand U.S. troops killed four thousand Dominicans? "Fifty-three known Communists," the Johnson administration revealed, had been plotting to take over the country. McCarthy's

Communist numbers game had become one of the fundamental maxims of the conduct of the foreign policy of the United States.

Johnson invaded the Dominican Republic in April 1965. By the end of June, he had authorized the 173rd Airborne Brigade to launch the first major U.S. combat offensive of the Vietnam War, and by the end of the year nearly half a million U.S. troops were in Southeast Asia.

This was indeed "escalation," though not in the measured, "counterforce" sense administration officials meant it. The unlimited Kennedy rhetoric was becoming the unlimited Johnson reality, just as the Truman Doctrine for Greece had become the Eisenhower policy in Iran, Guatemala and practically everywhere else. The American interventions in the Dominican Republic and Vietnam were not Lyndon Johnson's only wars. In 1966, Guatemala itself became the scene of a U.S. counterinsurgency war at least as intensive as the one fought in El Salvador later. Like Vietnam, Guatemala had a U.S. Military Assistance Program. U.S. troops directed search-and-destroy operations. And the U.S. Office of Public Safety gave more than thirty thousand Guatemalans training in "counterterror" techniques.

The insurrection in the countryside was not crushed. But urban terrorism and political assassination on a scale astonishing even for Guatemala now became the norm. Independent political parties, freedom of the press and the other mechanisms of peaceful politics had been destroyed long since in Guatemala. All through the 1960s and 1970s, the human substance of moderation was murdered as well. By the beginning of the 1980s there was no need in Guatemala for the kind of matanza unfolding in El Salvador: In uncounted thousands of shallow graves, the mutilated corpse of Guatemalan democracy already had been laid to rest.

About the time many Americans were wondering if El Salvador would be the "next Vietnam," I visited Guatemala, because others were predicting that it soon would become the "next El Salvador." By then the catastrophe that had overtaken the country in the years since the CIA invasion was evident even to U.S. officials. They conceded that the United States faced an unenviable choice.

"The government is antidemocratic and terrorist," one high-ranking U.S. diplomat explained when he gave me the usual off-the-record briefing. "The opposition is antidemocratic and terrorist. We would like to see democracy here," he added, unconscious that, twenty years after the fact, he was only reiterating Kennedy's fantasy options. "But we have no choice but to support the military. Otherwise the Communists will win. The problem with this country," he concluded, "is that Guatemala lacks a center."

To this official, the absence of a political center loomed as something more than an anthropological curiosity, or even a product of history. He took the extremism of the Guatemalans as a deliberate affront to the United States, and to himself: These Guatemalans were impeding the orderly exercise of U.S. foreign policy, with their penchant for the politics of murder. How could a Guatemala military aid appropriation ever get through Congress without some semblance of American-style democracy?

I mentioned Alvarado and Ubico, Peurifoy and Lyndon Johnson to this representative of the United States. "You journalists can deal with ancient history," he replied. "This embassy has to deal with the fact that the Communists are trying to take over Guatemala now."

* * *

To visit Central America in the 1980s was like visiting Southeast Asia in the 1970s. One couldn't help wondering how whole American presidencies might have turned out if only their foes had actually been the "Communists" —if they had not found themselves ensnared in the traps their predecessors had laid for them. What might have been the fate of the Kennedy presidency without the plans for the Bay of Pigs invasion that Eisenhower bequeathed him? Would Johnson and Nixon both have left office in disgrace were it not for the Tet Offensive and the Cambodia invasion, for the Vietnam "commitment" each inherited and then passed on in turn?

The presidency, like so much in America, seemed to contain not just an impulse to power, but an impulse to self-destruct. Would the dominoes ever stop falling?

Certainly Jimmy Carter had no success in shoring them up. Nixon dominoes, Eisenhower dominoes, even Coolidge, Wilson and Teddy Roosevelt dominoes kept falling on that unfortunate President, until he was entirely crushed. By the time Carter was repudiated, in the 1980 elections, he had a number of foreign-policy successes to his credit: He had normalized relations with China; he had negotiated the Camp David Accords. He was the first President in generations under whom not a single American soldier died in foreign combat.

Yet by then Carter had the reputation for being a pitiably inept statesman who had deprived America and the world of "strong leadership." He was the one who had "lost" Nicaragua and let the Iranians take our citizens hostage. By the end of his term, Carter had become a figure of such general derision that it was often forgotten just where and how the unraveling of his presidency, specifically, had begun.

The truth was that Carter's defeat, like so many American defeats, flowed from the great wellspring of American manifest destiny. In 1903, Theodore Roosevelt had set up one of the dominoes that would fall on Carter three quarters of a century later, when he wrested Panama away from Colombia, and then wrested the Canal Zone away from Panama. The fears of imperial aggression that had led Simon Bolivar, in 1826, to propose a Concert of the Americas had been fulfilled. "The inevitable effect of our building the Canal must be to require us to police the surrounding premises," wrote Roosevelt's Secretary of State, Elihu Root, in 1905.

"It became an early version of the domino theory," observes Walter

LaFeber in his study of the Panama Canal crisis Jimmy Carter would later face. "[I]f unfriendly, powerful Europeans settled in one part of the Caribbean, their influence could spread until the Canal would be endangered." No "powerful Europeans" ever did endanger the canal, but soon after construction of the canal began, President Roosevelt, in two messages to Congress, ostensibly addressed the strategic questions raised by construction of the canal.

But just as the Truman Doctrine had not really been a doctrine for the Aegean, and Kennan's "X article" not really about the sources of Soviet conduct, Roosevelt's messages were not really about the Caribbean.

They were a reaffirmation of the American doctrine of manifest destiny. The United States, Roosevelt proclaimed, not only had the right and duty to defend the western hemisphere against outside aggression, should it ever occur; the United States had the right and duty to intervene in the internal affairs of its Latin American neighbors in order to punish "chronic wrongdoing" and establish "the ties of civilized society."

America, Roosevelt concluded, using a phrase that later American presidents would use to justify their wars in Korea and Indochina, was entitled "to the exercise of an international police power."

In the United States, in 1904, this was a revolutionary statement—nearly as revolutionary, in terms of the long-standing principles of American foreign policy, as Wilson's proclamation of the Fourteen Points for Europe would be, fifteen years later. All through the nineteenth century, and well into the twentieth, the real Monroe doctrine—the doctrine of abstention—died hard. However flagrantly Americans, before 1904, had intervened in the internal affairs of their neighbors, no American President had presumed to declare as a matter of principle that we Americans had the same right in the western hemisphere that the European imperialists proclaimed for themselves in Africa and Asia. Our military interventions in Latin America had been justified, however groundlessly, on the need either to liberate our neighbors from foreign rule or to defend the hemisphere or ourselves against military aggression.

But now the President declared that the backwardness of the Latin Americans would "ultimately require intervention by some civilized nation," and that that nation must be the United States.

Roosevelt had the military power to "take" Panama and any other prize he wanted in Latin America. But his radical new policy nonetheless confronted him with a classic dilemma of American leadership: How was he to reconcile the reality of American conquest with the illusion of American liberty? How could he square his new imperial policy with the cherished American faith that the United States was destined forever to remain a nation apart, a nation above the corruptions and avarice of other great powers? How, above all, was Roosevelt to reconcile this clear repudiation of the "Monroe Doctrine" with the American necessity to believe that all America's doctrines are inviolate, immutable?

Roosevelt did what Truman did forty-three years later. He presented his new policy as the fulfillment of a heritage nearly as old as America itself.

The "adherence of the United States to the Monroe Doctrine," the President informed Congress, not only justified his actions; it made them necessary.

At the heart of the "Roosevelt Corollary to the Monroe Doctrine," as it was called, there lay, however, an entirely different doctrine of American nationalism: that no possible contradiction can exist between American force and the liberty of others. "Our interests and those of our southern neighbors are in reality identical," Roosevelt emphasized. "In asserting the Monroe Doctrine," the President added, ". . . we have acted in our own interest as well as in the interest of humanity at large."

But what if "our southern neighbors" disagreed? Roosevelt proclaimed the same doctrine Ronald Reagan, eighty years later, would use to justify his own war of subversion against Nicaragua, his own invasion of Grenada.

"Any country whose people conduct themselves well can count upon our hearty friendship," Roosevelt announced. But "in flagrant cases of such wrongdoing" as the United States opposed, such peoples, Roosevelt made clear, could count equally on a U.S. overthrow of their government, and a Marine Corps occupation of their country.

"[E]very nation, whether in America or anywhere else, which desires to maintain its freedom, its independence," the President added, "must ultimately realize that the right of such independence can not be separated from the responsibility of making good use of it."

Once again, in the American mind, the independence of others had become only a synonym for American sovereignty—the sovereign right of the United States to define "decency in social and political matters" not merely for itself, but for the world.

The Roosevelt Corollary had nothing to do with the "Monroe Doctrine." But it was an epochal event in a parallel and no less illuminating history. This is the expansion, over the past two hundred years, of the American illusion that the growth of U.S. power is necessarily an extension of liberty—across North America, Latin America and the world.

Like Adams's Fourth of July address and Reagan's television speeches on El Salvador, the Roosevelt Corollary was also a classic proclamation of the doctrine of the double standard. The Roosevelt Corollary, Americans believed, both authorized U.S. military intervention everywhere and prohibited "outside" intervention anywhere. When we Americans invaded a country, it was "of benefit to the people of the country concerned." But when others acted as we Americans did, such actions constituted "flagrant cases of wrongdoing."

The Roosevelt Corollary centered on the western hemisphere. Later presidents would assure us that Soviet support for North Korea or North Vietnam violated the Truman Doctrine, the Nixon Doctrine. But what of our own, much more flagrant interventions in South Korea and South Vietnam? They, as President Nixon later explained it, were justified, because they fulfilled the American commitment to "peace, a better life for all Americans, a better life for all people on this earth."

Just as Theodore Roosevelt had transformed the Monroe doctrine of abstention into a doctrine of U.S. intervention, so modern presidents would transform the Roosevelt Corollary into a doctrine entitling the United States to combat what might be called "internal interference" in the western hemisphere and in the rest of the world as well.

President Reagan summed up this doctrine well in October 1983. Cuban involvement in Grenada was intolerable, the President asserted, because "a Cuban occupation of the island had been planned." This allegation was never proved. But to assume it is true raises an important question.

If it is invalid for one western hemisphere nation, Cuba, to plan to occupy Grenada, how can it be valid for another hemisphere nation, the United States, actually to occupy it? Few Americans would dispute that the military authorities of Grenada did wrong when they killed some Grenadians and imprisoned many more for political reasons. But, following the Reagan invasion, American television viewers could see U.S. troops rounding up political prisoners in Grenada.

Why was it not also wrong for us Americans to kill Grenadians, to imprison others without trial?

Ronald Reagan's explanation was Theodore Roosevelt's explanation: the United States not only had the right to invade a foreign country in order to defend "our own national security," it had the right to remove some Grenadians from power and to place other Grenadians in control so that the Grenadians "might have a chance at peace and freedom in their own lives and in the life of their country."

Theodore Roosevelt could no more change the text of Monroe's 1823 statement than Ronald Reagan could rewrite international law. But, like President Reagan later, he could exercise his power as commander in chief of the American imagination; he could use a presidential doctrine to close the circle of American fantasy. By presidential decree, U.S. conquest in Latin America had become "really of benefit to the people of the country concerned," just as, later, the Reagan invasion of Grenada would not be an invasion at all, but a "rescue mission."

Latin America did not have long to wait for the benefits of the Roosevelt Corollary. In 1904 the United States invaded the Dominican Republic, overthrew its government and imposed an administration of its own choosing. Later the Marines would return and occupy that country from 1916 to 1934 —setting the stage not merely for Trujillo but for the 1965 Johnson invasion. And that was only the beginning. As LaFeber puts it, the Roosevelt pronouncement triggered the most ignoble chapter in United States–Latin American relations. Believing, as TR said, that "a civilized nation" such as the United States possessed the right to stop "chronic wrongdoing," North Americans sent troops into a half-dozen Caribbean nations during the next twelve years, and within two decades dominated at least fourteen of the twenty Latin American countries through either financial controls or military power—and, in some instances, through both.

Eighty years after Secretary of War Calhoun had urged President Monroe to sound the alarm, the independence of Latin America was under general assault, and it was this general American assault on the independence of Latin America that, far more than the "Monroe Doctrine," provided the real historical precedent for our interventions in Greece, Iran, Guatemala, Vietnam, Laos and so many other countries after World War II. "We talk of civilizing the lower races," William Graham Sumner noted at the time, "but we have never done it yet. We have exterminated them." The turn-of-the-century American sociologist had some other comments that would remain relevant long after the Roosevelt Corollary had been superseded by the Truman, Eisenhower and Nixon doctrines:

If you want war, nourish a doctrine [Sumner wrote in 1903]. Doctrines are the most frightful tyrants to which men ever are subject, because doctrines get inside of a man's reason and betray him against himself.

Somebody asks you with astonishment and horror whether you do not believe in the Monroe Doctrine. . . . You do not know what it is; but you do not dare to say that you do not, because you understand that it is one of the things which every good American is bound to believe in. Now when any doctrine arrives at that degree of authority, the name of it is a club which any demagogue may swing over you at any time and apropos of anything.

Naysayers like Sumner were as outnumbered in the nation in 1904 as opponents of the Gulf of Tonkin resolution were in the Senate in 1964. Like the Truman Doctrine, the Roosevelt Corollary in fact was a brilliantly successful domestic American political maneuver. At a stroke, in the eyes of Congress and public opinion, a radical new policy of U.S. military intervention was alchemized into a reverent fulfillment of American traditions almost as old as the republic. After 1904, all the contradictions in what Roosevelt had done, and what his successors were doing, vanished from the American mind.

A real threat to the Panama Canal did exist—and it was a threat no American "exercise of an international police power" could avert. By creating a U.S. Canal Zone bisecting the Republic of Panama, Theodore Roosevelt had created a standing affront to Panamanian nationalism. Inside the Canal Zone, generation after generation of "Zonians"—American colonialists who, even when they were born there and died there, spoke no Spanish and were above the laws of Panama—lived in imperial splendor in comparison to how the Panamanians lived. Any Panamanian in the western half of the country who wished to visit the eastern half had to traverse U.S.-administered territory, and the same was true in reverse. Panama's sole significant national asset was a negative one: Here the vastness of the Americas diminished to a narrow isthmus less than fifty miles wide. Yet even that slender advantage the United States had arrogated to itself. The great waterway, the ships flying all the maritime flags of the world, did not traverse Panama; they traversed the U.S. Canal Zone. More than anything else, a single symbol was a permanent act of aggression against Panama's every pretense to national dignity: Atop a hill dominating the capital, Panama City, but just within the Canal Zone, stood a flagpole. And twenty-four hours a day—in the tropical sun and at night, illuminated by klieg lights—on that flagpole flew an immense flag of the United States. There scarcely was a place in the capital of Panama where the Stars and Stripes could not be seen.

Less than two months following the Diem and Kennedy assassinations, there arose, in Panama, a threat to the vital interests of the United States of the kind Mossadegh and Arbenz, Kong Le and Castro had never posed. In January 1964 four days of warfare broke out between U.S. troops and Panamanians armed mostly with rocks and knives. By the time the fighting ebbed, four U.S. soldiers were dead and eighty-five wounded. And in keeping with the body count that usually prevails in such Third World confrontations, the Americans had killed twenty-four Panamanians and wounded nearly two hundred others.

This was one "act of aggression" not even the CIA and the White House could interpret as part of some Moscow master plan. Our weapons systems could only destroy the Panama Canal; they could not keep it open if Panamanian demonstrators chose to disrupt its operation. Like most real threats to our security, this was a situation in which the great arsenals of our military power and influence were useless.

The lesson of Dienbienphu had not been learned in Washington, but the lesson of Suez had not gone unheeded. The ensuing negotiations between the United States and Panama, which continued intermittently for thirteen years under four American presidents, were far more frustrating and difficult than the negotiations over Laos had ever been—though the source of the frustrations was not in Panama, but in the United States.

The general outlines of a settlement with Panama became clear very early in the negotiations: The immense American flag on the hill would be pulled down, and the flag of Panama raised in its place. But while the symbols changed, the substance would change hardly at all. Panamanians would gradually be trained to operate the canal; the Canal Zone itself would be reintegrated into Panama. But U.S. rights to use of the waterway as well as America's military interests would be completely safeguarded. Panama would remain, in fact, America's major foreign base in the Caribbean at least until the end of the twentieth century. In Washington there was completely bipartisan agreement that such a settlement was not only acceptable, but desirable.

Presidents Johnson, Nixon and Ford all supported such a solution. But they were as loath to pull down the flag in Panama as Truman, Eisenhower and Kennedy had been to stand up to Senator McCarthy—and for the identical reason: Everywhere else in the world by then the Europeans were pulling down their colonial flags. But talk in the White House and in the State Department of the United States doing the same thing aroused the same dark suspicions in many quarters that the "loss" of China had. Once again the boys in pinstripes were opting for surrender on the installment plan. Would Johnson forsake the Roosevelt Corollary, would Nixon betray the "Monroe Doctrine"? Presidents who did not hesitate to bomb Laos, to invade Cambodia, to land whole U.S. armies in Vietnam, recoiled from the domestic political consequence of "giving away our canal."

In 1977, Jimmy Carter bit the bullet. And unlike President Wilson, President Carter did get his treaty through the Senate—though only through a gargantuan expenditure of political capital, so reluctant were even normally "responsible" senators to risk the wrath of the voters by supporting the canal treaties.

In late 1980, after Ronald Reagan had defeated Jimmy Carter by a bigger margin, in the electoral college, than Franklin Roosevelt had defeated Herbert Hoover, I went down to Panama to take a look at the canal. Just as they should see a space shot, all Americans should see the Panama Canal at least once, because the Panama Canal is one of the great technological triumphs of our civilization. As American presidents have proved over and over again, it is all too easy in Latin America to foment a coup, or send in the Marines. But it took a cooperative endeavor of real genius to build those locks, which lift, every day, dozens of oceangoing ships over the mountainous spine of Panama, and carry them from ocean to ocean. It took genius, too, to grasp, seventy years ago, that eradicating malaria and yellow fever were as much a part of the work of building the canal as leveling mountains. Where the Spanish had never tried, and the French had failed, the United States had triumphed. Both Americans and Panamanians agreed the canal was working as smoothly as ever. The canal had been "neutralized"—that is, successfully removed from the battlefields of international confrontation. It was now free to go on being, as it had been for so many generations, a great constructive American contribution to the peaceful development of the world.

The chief change the treaties had brought to Panama was visible from my hotel-room window in downtown Panama City. An immense Panamanian flag now flew on the hill where the U.S. flag once had flown, but Panama was still a place where American influence was far more pervasive than it ever was in Korea, Vietnam or El Salvador.

American dollars, not Panamanian currency, were the medium of exchange. The long American occupation also had tainted Panamanian society with an overt racism rare in Latin America. Just as the Zonians had looked down on the brown-skinned Panamanians, the Panamanians looked down on the black-skinned West Indians whose great-grandfathers had been imported to work on the canal. If Panama City had its Park Avenue sections, the town of Colon, at the Caribbean terminus of the canal, resembled a Central American Harlem. Unemployed black youths lounged on street corners; muggings were as common there as political murders in El Salvador.

As in Nicaragua, Guatemala and the Dominican Republic, the chief political consequence of so many decades of U.S. military power and influence was that there, too, military power and influence was dominant. In a little-noticed provision, the treaties had provided $50 million in "military assistance" for Panama's National Guard, as well as $295 million in other aid the military would control. This was indeed a "giveaway," but its main effect, as LaFeber noted, was not to diminish U.S. influence in Panama, but to "tighten relations between the two countries, especially between the Pentagon and the National Guard." As a result of "giving away our canal," Panama would continue to be one more "free world" nation where military power and influence, not democratic liberty, was dominant.

Even after the Panama Canal treaties were passed, Panama seemed most notable not for what had happened to the canal, but for what Panama showed about the United States. There, perhaps more than anywhere else in the world, the American capacity for enormous accomplishment and the American capacity for astonishing failure were juxtaposed. We Americans had built a canal, but not built democracy, in Panama. We had eradicated yellow fever in Panama, but not the militarization of its national life.

The Panama Canal treaties changed nothing in Panama, but in the United States the dominoes fell. Suddenly the right wing had a foreign-policy issue as visceral as the "right to life" was in social affairs. Who was to blame for the "loss" of our canal?

One problem for the "responsible" leaders in both parties was that Nixon, Ford and Carter were all as deeply implicated in the "loss" of the canal as Truman, Marshall and Acheson had been in the "loss" of China. As opponents of the Panama Canal "giveaway" saw it, this was no matter of an individual President betraying our nation. The entire power elite in Washington was responsible—and therefore a general purge was necessary. This was the time when the Political Action Committees, years in advance of the 1980 elections, began targeting members of the Senate for attack. And a key qualification for inclusion on the "enemies lists" of the PACs was a vote in favor of the Panama Canal treaties.

The Panama Canal settlement aroused strident opposition to President Carter, but even before the treaties were passed, the issue also had overshadowed the contest for the 1976 Republican presidential nomination. With "moderate" Republicans like Ford and Bush as committed to giving away "our canal" as liberal Democrats, where were truly patriotic Americans to turn for strong leadership? Would no one stand up for our "rights" in Panama?

Ronald Reagan would. More than four years before he finally became President, Reagan had discovered that the Panama Canal issue possessed a tremendous capacity to mobilize public support and presidential votes. "People sense in this issue some way, after Vietnam, and Watergate, and Angola, of reasserting the glory of the country," one Reagan campaign adviser observed. "People once more see a chance for Americans to stand up as Americans." Reagan himself saw the Panama Canal as the issue that made "all the other issues possible" on his conservative agenda.

How far would President Reagan go to retain the canal? "How far would we go to stop someone from taking the state of Alaska?" Reagan replied. The Canal Zone, he elaborated, "is sovereign United States territory just the same as Alaska is and as the part of Texas that came out of the Gadsden Purchase and the states that were carved out of the Louisiana Purchase."

The Canal Zone, Reagan emphasized, "is ours and we intend to keep it." It was a classic Reagan pronouncement for many reasons, not the least of which was the ignorance of both U.S. and Panamanian history it revealed. The Canal Zone had not been ceded to the United States the way Louisiana, Texas and Alaska had. Equally significant, in terms of the grasp of America's own historical realities that Reagan would bring to the White House, no part of Texas had come out of the Gadsden Purchase, though parts of New Mexico and Arizona had.

Reagan's comments excited a national response nearly as strong as Nixon's Checkers speech had earlier. Here was one presidential candidate who would chase the crooks and Communists out of Washington. As LaFeber notes, Reagan used the Panama Canal issue "to catapult himself into contention for the Republican presidential nomination" in 1976. President Ford was given a bad scare that year at the Republican convention. But Ronald Reagan's curious relationship with Central America—as odd in its way as Nixon's long relationship with Asia—was only beginning.

After passage of the treaties, in 1977, Reagan ran as hard and far with the Panama Canal "giveaway" as Nixon had ever run with Whittaker Chambers's pumpkin. Later, after Reagan was elected President, in 1980, his Central America policy was mysterious to many who were familiar with the realities of Central America. The President clearly knew very little about Central America; but how could even he believe, and act on the assumption, that American security was threatened there by a great Communist conspiracy? Why was the President so insistent on involving himself in a deepening crisis that, but for his desire to turn Central America into a "test case," might easily have been forgotten?

President Reagan may have known very little about El Salvador, but he knew a great deal about the United States. More than any other single issue, the Panama Canal "giveaway" had propelled him toward the presidency. And more than any other factor, it was his unswerving "anticommunism" that provided the bedrock of his continuing political support.

In and of themselves the Panama Canal treaties did not destroy the Carter presidency. But in the struggle to make the Senate agree to let the Panamanians fly their flag over the canal, Carter had expended political resources he would never again be able to muster for much more consequential struggles: The SALT treaty would never be ratified. By then too many senators had too many PACs after them for the Senate to repeat the Panama Canal mistake. Carter's real problem, however, was that all dominoes, sooner or later, must fall. After the Teddy Roosevelt domino had fallen on Carter, in Panama in 1977, the Sandinistas took over Nicaragua and the Coolidge domino fell. But heaviest of all was the Eisenhower domino that fell in Iran. Back in 1953, Ike had overthrown Mossadegh the way he later overthrew Arbenz, and installed the Shah as the Castillo Armas of Iran. Now, as the ayatollah toppled the Shah, the final catastrophe of the Carter presidency began. How could it be, Americans asked themselves, that those Islamic hordes could overrun our embassy, take our diplomats hostage—and still our President did nothing? The hostage crisis was like the Panama Canal crisis; the problem was that all our weapons were irrelevant. Carter could have bombed Tehran (and been cheered for his "strong leadership" if he had). But that would not have freed the hostages; it would only have killed them.

As Carter conducted those excruciating negotiations with the Iranians that ultimately brought every one of the hostages back home alive, the conviction spread throughout the nation: here was a truly contemptible President. Teddy Roosevelt had taken Panama; Carter gave it away. Even Eisenhower and Coolidge had stood up for our rights in Iran and Nicaragua; now Jimmy Carter was letting America be kicked around from Tehran to Managua. And so Ronald Reagan charged toward the presidency the way Teddy Roosevelt once had charged up San Juan Hill. Who cared, in America, that on the other side of the hill lay the corpses of El Salvador?

By 1984, there was scarcely a place in Central America where our interests were not being threatened as a result of President Reagan's determination not to repeat Jimmy Carter's mistakes. There was one place, however, where the United States faced no "threat"—where our military bases were safe, where our investments were unmolested, where the government neither opposed us nor asked our help to oppose its own people.

That place was Panama.

Over the past thirty years, the list of foreign leaders the United States has destabilized, overthrown or helped to overthrow has never ceased to lengthen. But what figures ranging from Jagan in Guyana to Lumumba in the Congo and from Sihanouk in Cambodia to Bosch in the Dominican Republic all had in common was that their fragile regimes, which proved so vulnerable to American subversion, could not have corresponded less to the "totalitarian" dictatorships we imagined we were combatting.

After 1954, therefore, the Bay of Pigs approach to the conduct of U.S. foreign policy was informed by an immense contradiction, and an even more stupendous irony. The contradiction was that the "anti-Communist" tactics developed in Greece, Iran and Guatemala were really only effective against "enemies" who were not really Communists at all.

The resulting irony, of even greater dimensions, was that such tactics were, for the most part, utterly useless against those who really did happen to be Communists. Over the next twenty-five years, the failure of the United States to stop figures like Castro and Ho Chi Minh, and the inability of the United States to prevail in countries like Cuba and Vietnam, where, for better or worse, the contest really was one between Communists and their adversaries, demonstrated the real fantasy behind the American assumption that the United States could "stop communism" by unleashing the Castillo Armases of the world.

Over the years, a kind of network came to link all the places around the globe where our ambassadors made and unmade governments, our CIA station chiefs plotted coups and countercoups, and our military attachés paid mercenary armies to fight endless wars against faceless foes. Whether they were the tribesmen of the Mekong uplands, the Congo basin or the Andean altiplano, these people were all, the embassy briefing officers always emphasized to the visiting journalist, committing aggression against us. In Laos and Cambodia, in the late 1960s and early 1970s, one would encounter AID directors and CIA functionaries who spoke fondly of the days, back in countries like Guatemala, when we had not had to fight with one hand tied behind the back. A few years later, one would arrive in Iran, and discover that Ambassador Sullivan, who once had been charged with saving Laos, now was expected to "save" the Shah. Then, one day at the end of 1980, I entered the U.S. embassy in San Salvador and found I was not in Central America at all.

I had only reentered some endless, self-repeating cyclorama of falling bombs and fleeing peasants which, no less than the Guatemalan soldiers and peasants on the road to Chichicastenango, it was also the destiny of us Americans ceaselessly to act out, again and again.

In the darkened room, with the maps and pins, the American colonel was saying the same things about "defeating Communist insurgency" I had heard in half a dozen countries. I scarcely needed a notebook—I had been given the same briefing over the past twelve years in Asia, in the Middle East, Africa and elsewhere in Latin America.

What made the scene surreal was that it was the same American officer, a man named Eldon Cummings, who had given me the same briefing twelve years earlier in Vientiane, the capital of Laos. In the intervening years, in countries like Laos and El Salvador, several million people had died because of the United States. The life of this American journalist and the life of this American soldier, like the power and destiny of the United States itself, had spanned the globe. Yet the journey, which had begun in violence and chaos, seemed to know only one itinerary: the road to more violence, more chaos. Colonel Cummings and I, no less than some Salvadoran peasant, seemed cast in some malign pageant whose plot we were powerless to change, perhaps even incapable of understanding.

Even the dialogue was changeless: "These Salvadoran guerrillas are real Pol Pot types," Colonel Cummings told me. "This is a limited commitment. We are only doing what we did for the Lao: helping the Salvadorans do the things they cannot do for themselves." Even the map of El Salvador, in the embassy briefing room, might have been the map of Laos, except that where Laos runs north to south, El Salvador runs west to east. The red blobs imperiling Chalatenango and Morazan might have been those oozing out of Samneua and Phongsaly, toward the Mekong, a dozen years earlier. The American helicopter gunships, the M-16 rifles, the "struggle to contain Communist aggression," as Cummings called it, were all the same.

Outside the American embassy in San Salvador, it had started to rain—though I didn't realize it until, following the interview, I renegotiated the embassy security checks and went outside. It must have been the combination of Colonel Cummings and not knowing it was raining that made me recall a similar incident in Laos in 1969. The monsoon had just broken when I arrived at the U.S. compound in Vientiane for a briefing in a room with no windows. I was dripping wet, and the secretary eyed me with suspicion. Then she dialed a complicated code on her telephone. After a few seconds, a voice answered.

"Is it raining?" she asked. Only after the discrepancy between my rain-soaked clothes and the interior of this American world, where no natural light penetrated and the temperature never varied, had been subjected to official verification was I allowed to proceed—into the closed world of utter certainty that lay beyond the door with the combination lock.

Over the years, I occasionally had pondered the parable of the windowless command center and the rain. Now the question of Laos came back to me, in the form of El Salvador.

The Americans always said there were no windows in order to keep our secrets. But at times I wondered if the world outside did not contain some larger secret—which we had determined to keep from ourselves.

"El Salvador isn't another Vietnam," the colonel assured me as we parted. "We've learned the lesson of Vietnam." Cummings' most important contribution to our intervention in El Salvador, however, turned out to be in Washington. Even before Defense Minister Garcia passed his documents about Communist interference in El Salvador to Jon Glassman and the State

Department, he had given them to the U.S. embassy's chief military attaché. And this first batch of documents, the New York *Times* later reported, "was sent to the Defense Intelligence Agency by Col. Eldon Cummings, then head of the United States military mission in El Salvador." The DIA had circulated the Garcia documents to other agencies in Washington. And it had been the resulting supposition in the Department of State that Garcia had proof that the guerrilla insurgency in El Salvador was really the work of Moscow, that had led to the Glassman mission, to the white paper—to the Reagan administration's decision to publicize U.S. intervention there as a clear-cut "test case" of American resolve in the face of Communist aggression.

On the way back to the hotel, it occurred to me I would never see Colonel Cummings again. The passage of the years had transformed me from a youth into someone who, before too long, would be forty, and it had transformed Cummings from one of those bright young American officers who knew, if only the right counterinsurgency techniques were used, that the Indochina War could be won into a man who is about to receive a pension. He had enlisted in the great American war to defend freedom back when Arbenz and Mossadegh and all the others were threatening us: soon his thirty years would be up.

As it happened, I did see Colonel Cummings once again, on film. He was retiring, and it seemed every Salvadoran colonel and major who had ever burnt a crop or machine-gunned a crowd of fleeing campesinos or bombed a village had driven down to the international airport from San Salvador to give him a warm good-bye *abrazo*. Defense Minister Garcia headed the reception line as, one by one, dozens of Salvadoran military men embraced this American military man, and he embraced them in return. The Pathet Lao, the Islamic Guards, the Khmer Rouge, the Catholic peasants of El Salvador— they were all the same to this diligent American officer, who never doubted the justice of what America did, just as Thieu and the Shah and Lon Nol and the Salvadoran colonels and everyone else we befriended were, by definition, the friends of freedom.

The film in which Colonel Cummings appeared was called *Roses in December*. It was about the life and death of Jean Donovan and the three other American churchwomen Garcia's forces had murdered. By then it was clear that justice would never be done, because it might impede the war to stop communism in El Salvador. Ambassador White and most other U.S. officials who shared his views on the case had been purged from the State Department and replaced by other officials, who were more reliably "anti-Communist." The echoes of China and Korea still resonated in the corridors of power in President Reagan's Washington. El Salvador, by then, also had become a replication of the American past.

It was at this same airport that Jean, Dorothy, Ita and Maura had arrived;

V
Unmanifest Destiny

Like all American wars, it was not a war of aggression. It was a struggle to
defend and expand "the area of freedom." All along, freedom had been menaced by a far-reaching conspiracy—a conspiracy which, as one of the President's supporters in the Senate put it, had "well-nigh enslaved the world."

Then the President himself had come to Congress with even more shocking
news. Conspiracy had been followed by brazen, unprovoked aggression
against the United States. Self-defense and our commitment to liberty dictated that the United States stand up to the aggressors; but there was another
reason why there could be no question.

"[T]he principle avowed by Mr. Monroe," the President reminded Congress, gave the United States no alternative but to fight.

Events in Washington, once the fighting began, followed the familiar, the
forgotten pattern. Initially the President rode high on a wave of militant
nationalism. But "[o]nce the hysteria began to abate" and the war grew more
and more unpopular, the President was "castigated . . . for exceeding his
authority" and "opponents who feared being dubbed 'treasonous' [when the
war began] were less than a year later charging their president with war
crimes."

"The President's war was a violation of "every just consideration of national dignity, duty and policy," one senator wrote. In the House of Representatives, the President was accused of murdering "unarmed peasants." Another congressman called the war "unholy, unrighteous and damnable."

The President's attempt to defend freedom abroad had spawned a new
conspiracy theory at home: The war was part of a plot in the White House to
subvert the Constitution, to destroy America's liberties. "We charge the president with usurping the war-making power," a Georgia congressman announced. What was the "value of this constitutional provision," a New
Hampshire colleague asked, "if the president of his own authority may make
such military movements as must bring on war?" A young congressman from

Illinois called the war unnecessary and pronounced the President guilty of "the sheerest deception."

Steadily opposition assumed the dimension of a nationwide protest, challenging not just the worth of the war, but the validity of America's own institutions.

The war, a young Harvard graduate wrote in a manifesto that gained wide attention, proved that the "government itself" was "abused and perverted."

"How does it become a man to behave toward this American government today?" he asked:

[W]hen . . . a whole country is unjustly overrun and conquered by a foreign army, I think that it is not too soon for honest men to rebel and revolutionize. What makes this duty the more urgent is the fact that the country so overrun is not our own, but ours is the invading army.

A war to extend liberty abroad had provoked a crisis of liberty at home. The nagging general question behind the increasingly bitter debate was a question of morality: Did the United States have the right to extend "the area of freedom" through force? The specific questions about the President's conduct, however, were identical to the later questions of Watergate. Had the President deliberately deceived Congress and the public? In his pursuit of military victory abroad had he violated the Constitution at home? Or did "the principle avowed by Mr. Monroe" entitle the President to act as he had?

There was another similarity to the Vietnam War Era: Much as the war divided the nation, it also produced unexpected alliances of principle. On the surface, the dissident congressman from Massachusetts and the conservative senator from South Carolina had nothing in common. Yet their common opposition to the war insensibly transformed them into allies in one of the great, continuing controversies of American history.

Can the President's authority in foreign affairs be effectively limited? And if it is not, is there any way to prevent the President from arrogating to himself unlimited domestic powers, too?

"Allow the president to invade a neighboring nation whenever *he* deems it necessary," the Illinois congressman told his colleagues, "and you allow him to make war at pleasure. Study to see if you can fix *any limit* to his power in this respect after you give him so much as you propose."

It was the South Carolina conservative in the Senate, however, who most strongly rebutted the President's claims that the "principle avowed by Mr. Monroe" gave him the right to intervene in other nations.

There was "not one word" about U.S. military intervention in Monroe's message, he pointed out. "There is nothing said of it; and with great propriety it was omitted." What Monroe had said or not said, however, was beside the point, he emphasized, because no presidential doctrine could lay down "our established policy." Under the Constitution, the southern senator reminded the President, everything must be decided according to the circumstances. . . . Declare war when necessary. Negotiate when this may fulfill your aims; make modifications; act, in brief, as your conception of the political interests of the country may advise you to do it. . . .

Above all, he urged, the United States must avoid "getting entangled in formulas."

Why had the President tried to get debate over his policy entangled in the Monroe formula? The President was pursuing a radically new and controversial policy, and by cloaking it in the Monroe mantle, had hoped to bypass the Constitution and turn presidential declarations, as the South Carolina senator put it, into "the settled policy of this country": "What, the declarations? 'Presidential declarations' are not policy," he exclaimed, "and cannot become settled policy." Such decisions of war and peace "belong to us—to Congress."

The Illinois congressman had summed up the threat to domestic liberty such foreign wars for freedom presented. Now the South Carolina senator defined the threat in foreign affairs, both to the United States and others, contained in the President's invocation of Monroe: to accept the President's argument that the White House was entitled to intervene unilaterally in foreign countries was not merely to misrepresent history and to disregard the Constitution, it was to empower our presidents to make war at pleasure, and thus

make us a party to all their wars; and hence I say if this broad interpretation be given to these declarations, we shall forever be involved in wars.

History lessons could not stop the President's war. But votes in Congress could make his position untenable at home. The same young Illinois congressman who accused the President of making "war at pleasure," demanded the full details of the supposed attack that had provoked U.S. retaliation. Where, when and in response to what U.S. military provocations had the alleged act of aggression occurred? Would the President hand over his papers?

By an overwhelming majority, the House also demanded that the President provide its investigators with the classified documents relating to the President's diplomatic efforts.

The President invoked executive privilege. "National security," he contended, prevented him from heeding the congressional resolution. Only after long delays would the White House finally relent. But the President's very refusal to share U.S. official documents with Congress corroborated what Americans already knew by then. The President and his advisers had conspired to involve the United States in war long before the supposed "aggression" occurred; the White House had seized upon an isolated military incident to stampede Congress into a declaration of war.

By a narrow majority, the House of Representatives declared that the war had been "unnecessarily and unconstitutionally commenced by the president." There was talk of impeachment. But national elections were less than ten months away and it was already clear that the war had assured that the man in the White House would be a one-term President.

Three years earlier, he had entered office with commanding majorities in both houses of Congress. Now Americans were denouncing him as a tyrant and a liar. Ill and exhausted, the President chose not to attempt reelection, but not even his own abdication could save his party. It already had lost control of Congress. In the next elections it would lose the White House as well. Within four months of leaving office, the President himself would be dead. Much of the nation would react to the news with indifference, nor would posterity vindicate his war to extend "the area of freedom." His contemporaries had reviled him; posterity would forget him. So far as future generations were concerned, it was as though he scarcely had occupied the White House at all.

The consequences of the war, however, were not limited to politics. Increasingly the trench warfare in Washington was replicated across the nation. As dreams of a quick, decisive victory gave way to the reality of protracted fighting, neighbor turned against neighbor, American against American. Never before had the nation been so bitterly divided.

It was a classic American war in the sense that an American military effort to extend "the area of freedom" abroad was generating a growing crisis for democracy at home. Even the reports of victory in foreign battles could not dispel the pervasive sense that America, in its eagerness to combat foreign "aggression," had wound up declaring war on itself.

When military honors were proposed for the commanding generals it was just another routine vote on the war for many members of Congress. But the proposal raised one more issue of principle that could not be shirked by the old dissenter from Massachusetts. He opposed the measure, one bystander noted, "with an uncommonly emphatic tone of voice."

Then, a little later, the old man rose, once again, from his desk in the House chamber, and prepared to speak. His colleagues had heard the same arguments many times: This war was an offense against American principle, not a defense of liberty. The war was no fulfillment of traditional American policy; it was a repudiation of all the fundamental maxims President Monroe had really espoused. Honors for a dishonorable war? It was as though even he, after so many years, finally was face to face with an absurdity that was unspeakable. His lips moved, but no words could be heard. A fit of apoplexy convulsed his body, and he collapsed.

It was one of the great revealing moments of American history—one of those instants when the reality of American history rises up in an attempt to rebut America's illusions about itself.

John Quincy Adams, principal author of President Monroe's message to

Congress twenty-five years earlier, had collapsed protesting the war the President claimed was legitimized by "the principle avowed by Mr. Monroe."

The year was 1848. The war that had turned America against itself, destroying the President's position this time, was President James Knox Polk's American war of conquest against Mexico.

More than a century later, in keeping with "the doctrine of containment" of the Soviet Union, Americans would kill more than one million people in Asia—no matter how often George Kennan pointed out that such wars totally violated the actual policy he had proposed. Yet there was nothing new in that. A century before the Truman Doctrine was proclaimed, the fate of Adams and his "moderate and conciliatory" foreign-policy statement of 1823 was the fate of George Frost Kennan and his "X article" of 1947. Americans were slaughtering Mexican civilians, bombarding Mexican cities, and simultaneously creating a great crisis of liberty in their own country—all because, no matter how much Adams protested, they believed their President when he told them that "the principle avowed by Mr. Monroe" ordained such "an extension of the area of freedom."

John Quincy Adams was not the only one to protest. The young Harvard graduate who urged his fellow citizens to "rebel and revolutionize" was Henry David Thoreau. He wrote his "Essay on Civil Disobedience" 120 years before the first draft card was burned. The New Hampshire congressman who questioned the value of the Constitution if it allowed the President, "of his authority," to "bring on war" was Daniel Webster.

The South Carolina senator who accused the President of going "infinitely and dangerously beyond Mr. Monroe's declaration" spoke, like Adams, with especial authority. For it was John C. Calhoun, Monroe's Secretary of War in 1823, who denounced President Polk for imputing to President Monroe's statement "an entirely different meaning and tendency" from what President Monroe had intended.

Later it would be considered somehow un-American to criticize the President during time of war. Yet the young Illinois congressman who accused the President of "sheerest deception," who called the war unconstitutional and who demanded that the President prove his allegations of foreign aggression was Abraham Lincoln.

Now, as Adams lay dying, it was as though two Americas stood by, mourning. Adams's old rival Henry Clay grasped his hand. Abraham Lincoln would help make the funeral arrangements for the man who once had been the confidant of George Washington. Two days later, as that new invention the telegraph carried the news of John Quincy Adams's death across the nation, church bells began to ring solemnly.

Although in 1848 Adams was the most prominent opponent of slavery in Washington, and Calhoun slavery's staunchest defender, it was Calhoun who summed up best the dramatic changes the Mexican War had produced in America.

The war had led to a great military victory for the United States, Calhoun conceded. But it also had led to a great defeat for the principles of "justice, moderation and wisdom" at home. "In the early stages of our government the great anxiety," he said, "was how to preserve liberty." Now, Calhoun lamented, "the great anxiety is the attainment of mere military glory."

It was as though not just John Quincy Adams, but something else, had died in the nation: the last human link connecting the Founding Fathers and their principles of liberty with a new age of American power, with a new America founded on conquest, had been snapped. It was as though the nation were mourning some general loss, within America itself.

With the conquest of Mexico in the name of "the principle avowed by Mr. Monroe," the New World had become, like the Old World, a continent where might made right, where aggression was its own reward. Perhaps that was why, even as they delighted in his conquests, Americans hated President Polk so much.

They called it "Mr. Polk's war," as though he alone were culpable for the crime the United States had committed. They called the President himself "Polk the Mendacious"—as though he were the only one to tell the great lie of American nationalism, that so long as we Americans did the conquering, even conquest itself was only "an extension of the area of freedom." Even in victory the nation faced a dilemma, the dilemma of how to reconcile the reality of what we had done with our imagination of who we were. What better way, in America, to transform a war of aggression into a triumph of American virtue, than by myth?

The year had begun in mourning, in division, but by the end of 1848, America was united in celebration: by then, Americans told themselves, the conquest of another nation and the annexation of half its territory, as ordained by President Monroe, was manifest proof of America's goodness.

In March 1848, the month after Adams died, the Senate had ratified the treaty that completed the U.S. seizure of 905,994 square miles of Mexican land. By November there was more cause for rejoicing. General Zachary Taylor, the conqueror of Mexico, had conquered the White House as well. Soon "Polk the Mendacious" would be gone.

With liberty everywhere triumphant, only one question remained to be answered: how could a destiny so beneficent to us be so unkind to others, if Americans did inhabit a world where rightness and virtue were destined to prevail? A New York newspaper resolved this contradiction for its readers in a commentary that might have been lifted from the "X article" a hundred years later. Like all else in American history, the war with Mexico had been ordained by Providence, so that America might prevail in a test of its national quality:

The aborigines of this country have not attempted and cannot attempt, to exist independently alongside us [the editorial explained]. The Mexicans are aboriginal Indians and they must share the destiny of their race.

So the church bells rang; the American armies kept advancing. In the churches there were, in Adams's honor, eulogies on liberty; in Mexico there was scarcely a province that had not been "unjustly overrun and conquered."

Soon the protests of Adams and Calhoun, the misrepresentations of Polk, would be forgotten. Soon the war itself would be only another forgotten link in an unnoticed chain—connecting the "Monroe Doctrine" to the "doctrine of containment," binding the America of the B-52 to the America of the Trail of Tears.

Like the fate of Nicaragua in 1927, of Guatemala in 1954 and of El Salvador later, the fate of Mexico in 1848 illustrates what is, by far, the most consequential of the divergences separating the history of Latin America from our own.

After the early-nineteenth century, no foreign power ever again threatened either the form or the substance of our independence. The United States enjoyed the vital luxury every developing nation needs if it is, in Washington's words, "to settle and mature its yet recent institutions": it escaped involvement in other people's wars.

One of the many myths of the "Monroe Doctrine" had been that it somehow ordained an inviolable separation of the New World from the Old when it came to the strategic balance of power. The truth was the opposite: our security remained completely integrated with the balance of power in Europe. The most important reason the United States was not involved in a general European conflict for so long was that, between the end of the Napoleonic Wars and the outbreak of World War I, there was no general European conflict. Canning's grand design not only prevailed in the Americas; it gave Europe nearly a century of peace as well. What, nonetheless, would happen if a major threat to the balance of power did arise in Europe?

Between 1812 and 1914, battleships replaced men-of-war, and cavalry charges gave way to trench warfare. Yet the industrialization of warfare had not changed geopolitical reality: in Woodrow Wilson's time, as in the time of the Founding Fathers, a general war in Europe inevitably became a general war in the Atlantic.

Neither Washington's Farewell Address nor the "Monroe Doctrine" could repeal one of the governing laws of American history: From the beginning, our security—our very survival as a nation—has been connected intimately with the great questions of war and peace in Europe. Once such a war began, President Wilson was no more able to keep the United States out of it than President Madison had been.

During the nineteenth century, the abstentionist principles of Washington and Monroe nonetheless served the cause of American nationalism well for internal reasons. For even without foreign intervention in our internal affairs, and American enmeshment in the perennial rivalries of Europe, what Washington called America's endeavor to gain "command of its own fortunes" proved far heavier in "cares, labors and dangers" than perhaps even he could have imagined.

After 1823, fate had many unpleasant surprises in store for Americans, the most important of which was that Monroe's Era of Good Feeling was not the natural American condition, only a temporary aberration. Many members of Monroe's own Cabinet lived to experience firsthand a bitter truth. This was that our internal divisions posed a far greater threat to the security and survival of the United States than the Holy Alliance ever had. In the years after Monroe left office, the United States was on the march—not toward some New World utopia of liberty, but toward the first mass slaughter of modern history. Only after America had traversed an abyss of gore and human suffering would Americans, once again, be able to imagine it was our destiny to incarnate the inevitable triumph of liberty.

Even today the Civil War makes all our other wars seem like only minor national disturbances. Yet the killing was less appalling than what caused it. This single greatest of our national catastrophes was not the work of any foreign aggressor, or external conspiracy. The blood flowed from our own rivalries, suspicions and hatreds.

Civil war was no stranger to Latin America, either, in the years following the end of European rule. But there, to the traumas of internal conflict, another catastrophe of history was added. In Latin America, the age of foreign domination never ended.

Even today in much of Latin America, sovereignty is only an illusion— whether it is the sovereignty of the state, or of its leaders, or that sovereignty of the individual over his own life which we call human rights. It is that condition which, more than anything else, establishes the abyss separating a country like Nicaragua from a country like the United States, a President like Arbenz from a President like Eisenhower—which distinguishes the fate of the Salvadoran campesino today from the fate of Americans like you and me. For all of them, independence in the national, political or human sense, 160 years after Spanish colonialism ended, is still only an unrealized dream.

In Guatemala the orchids always bloom; the soldiers permanently interrogate the peasants at gunpoint. And so also, unchangingly, do our presidents hand down doctrines, our colonels give briefings—while still others of us inform presidents, sometimes whole nations, whether their independence, even their survival, is "convenient for the requirements of American foreign policy."

Why should the fate of liberty in Latin America have been so entirely different? So far as the external causality is concerned, the answer is that after 1823, Americans replaced Europeans as the autocrats of the New World.

What we are doing now in Central America is only a cameo of what we have done to Latin America generation after generation, because what President Polk began in 1846, in the name of Monroe, has never ended. Contrary to all our illusions, it has been the historical destiny of the United States to conjure up an American system of Dostoevskian darkness in the western hemisphere, in the name of freedom.

This continuing saga of oppression, in which we replace the Spanish and the helicopter gunship replaces the sword, poses one of the most important questions not just about Latin American history, but about the unfolding of our own national destiny.

How was it that the United States, which so identified its history, its cause, its fate, with the fate of liberty, had become by 1846 the single most important enemy of liberty in Latin America?

How, in only one generation, had the "fundamental maxims" of American policy undergone such an astonishing change?

Thomas Jefferson had believed that even when Americans became masters of a nation the size of Europe, they would remain sylvan, pure, uncomplicated, unindustrial—unlike Europeans. When Jefferson looked West, he saw an endless frontier which would provide a limitless refuge from the complexities and corruptions of the Old World he knew so well. New Connecticuts, new Marylands, new South Carolinas would spread westward, but America's principles would remain changeless, because America itself would not change.

Anti-Jeffersonians such as Alexander Hamilton knew better. They looked West and saw factories, mills, canals, mines, fortunes—wealth and power to stagger the imagination of Europe, the biggest real estate bonanza in human history.

It was in the quest to build an America "separated by nature and a wide ocean" from the exterminating havoc of Europe, to fulfill the dream of "possessing a chosen country, with room enough for our descendants to the hundredth and thousandth generation," that Jefferson had purchased Louisiana and sent Lewis and Clark to explore the empty vastness of North America all the way to the Oregon coast. But the fur trader, John Jacob Astor had staked his own claim to the wealth of the West. In 1811, only six years after Lewis and Clark had reached the mouth of the Columbia, Astor founded Astoria there. By the time he died, in March 1848, the same month the Senate approved the annexation of California, Astor had amassed a personal fortune of no less than $30 million.

Jefferson had died in debt, but not before his dream of egalitarian liberty in the West had produced an entirely new kind of American: the New York plutocrat whose western holdings generated the kind of wealth old New England and Virginia aristocrats like the Adamses and the Jeffersons had never dreamed of possessing. Soon the silver of Nevada, the gold of California, would produce American riches that might have made even John Jacob Astor gasp. But long before then it had become clear that the human and moral substance, not just the geographical form, of the United States was changing.

In 1824, less than a year after President Monroe had enunciated his for-eign-policy principles, Adams and Clay had vied for the presidency. Who would inherit the Era of Good Feeling—the abstentionist aristocrat or the interventionist frontiersman? The answer is that both these orators of liberty lost the election. For while Adams and Clay had been debating the liberty of Latin America, new forces—forces of power—had remade the political land-scape of the United States. Andrew Jackson—slave owner and scourge of the Indians, the marauder of Spanish Florida, the "victor" of New Orleans, a hero of force if America ever produced one—finished first, both in the popu-lar vote and in the electoral college.

Following Jackson's victory at the polls, Adams and Clay—adversaries for so long—united to deny him the White House. With no one candidate having received a majority in the electoral college, the House of Representatives named Adams President. The Constitution was followed to the letter, but the aggressive new spirit of the American people was clearly transgressed.

These maneuverings only deferred the Jacksonian revolution. The debates on liberty would never stop in America, but already the future belonged to the prophets of force. Today Adams and Clay are dimly remembered, almost antique figures, while Jackson remains as quintessentially American as the face on the twenty-dollar bill. Modern developments as diverse as Sunbelt shift and counterinsurgency warfare are only elaborations of what Andrew Jackson began.

Years before Jackson entered the White House, one American nationalist wrote: "Spain has possessions upon our southern and Great Britain upon our northern border. It is impossible that centuries shall elapse without finding them annexed to the United States."

"It is a physical, moral and political absurdity," the writer concluded, "that such fragments of territory . . . should exist permanently contiguous to a great, powerful and rapidly-growing nation."

It reveals much about the unquenchable impulse to power that always has defined American nationalism that the author of those lines was John Quincy Adams himself. Decades before the phrase "manifest destiny" came into use, Adams had proclaimed "our proper dominion to be the continent of North America."

Adams managed to resolve the contradiction between his nationalist ambi-tions and his abstentionist principles through a kind of socioeconomic deter-minism. As our population multiplied and our wealth and power grew greater and greater, the United States would absorb its neighbors through a process of organic coalescence. It was "unavoidable that the remainder of the conti-nent should ultimately be ours," Adams believed—"not that any spirit of encroachment or ambition on our part renders it necessary. . . ." Others, notably Jackson, were more inclined to trust to the sword, but however they differed on means, Americans agreed on ends: In the fullness of time, the United States would outgrow its borders—with Canada and Mexico, and at the Rockies—the way a strapping frontier youth outgrows his breeches. Inevitably the country would don the apparel of greatness. The Atlantic and the Pacific, the Arctic and the tropics, all would be ours—no matter what, or who, stood in the way.

Our acquisition of Florida, under President Monroe back in 1819, in fact had provided an instructive demonstration of just how united Americans were in pursuit of their ambitions even when they disagreed on tactics. Jackson had marauded across Spanish Florida the same way he had pillaged and sacked the Indian lands of the Mississippi Valley. Adams had preferred the more genteel coercions of diplomacy. But neither Boston Brahmin nor son of the Tennessee frontier had sensed any contradiction between the seizure of foreign lands and the territorial expansion of American liberty. Even under Monroe, America's commitment to the liberty of others had tended to end where our own ambitions began.

With the United States preordained to mastery of a continent, what were Canada and Mexico, the Caribbean and Central America, except nations that were, like the Indians, as doomed to extinction as we Americans were fated for greatness?

From the beginning, this belief that a destiny not just of liberty but of dominion awaited the United States, raised the most important questions about the American view of the external world. In any age, how we perceive ourselves is inseparable from how we perceive—and treat—others. Even during the Era of Good Feeling, as Samuel Flagg Bemis notes, others "seemed profoundly impressed with the idea that Americans were an ambitious and encroaching people."

The decades following Jackson's election did nothing to change that impression. Earlier, the French, the British and the Spanish had been the objects of our encroachments. The Age of Jackson would see quite a different branch of humanity fall victim to our ambitions.

The superficial similarities and the enormous differences between the Indian wars in Latin America and the Indian wars in the United States were noted earlier. Yet here two additional observations seem necessary.

The first is that, like the War of Independence, the Mexican War and the Civil War, the Indian wars were a test, and ultimately a triumph, of American force. To the extent that this single most shameful of all episodes in our history made any principle manifest, it was only a principle as old, in human affairs, as the Roman sack of Carthage.

The second observation concerns that perpetual antithesis in American history: our tendency to transform our crimes into mythical triumphs of virtue. But some crimes are so immense that not even time and the human imagination can work such a metamorphosis upon them, and such certainly is the case with the historical fact of our pursuit of the Indians to the brink of extinction.

The dispossession of the Indian, like the enslavement of the African, is one of the most important determinants in our national identity. More than any other single factor, it explains why, racially and socially, we in the United States are so very different from most of the other peoples of the western hemisphere. In a crucial sense, we are what we are today because of what was done to the Indians.

In Latin America the Indian provides a central theme, indeed constitutes almost a thematic obsession in philosophy, literature, art, war and politics. But what of the role of the Indian in our own intellectual, cultural and moral life—in the way we Americans understand our past and interpret ourselves? We all know the Indian of James Fenimore Cooper, of Remington's paintings and the Hollywood Western. But in any deeper sense the Indian—above all the American national experience of genocidal slaughter of the Indian—is nearly nonexistent.

It is easiest to illustrate this point and its significance simply by contrasting the role of the Indian and the role of the African in the evolution of our national consciousness—and conscience. For 350 years we Americans have pondered, debated and fought over the role of race relations in our national life. Even today, attitudes on race provide one of the principal standards by which Americans define themselves and judge each other. Ask an American today about busing or affirmative action. And—like Tocqueville a century and a half ago when he asked Americans about slavery—you will receive an answer that interconnects with every other fissure and cleavage in our national life.

In the history of the United States, however, no Henry Ward Beecher denounces our crimes against the Indian from the pulpit. No John Brown takes up arms in the Indians' defense. For that matter, no John C. Calhoun bothers to build a philosophical system around the dispossession of the Indian. Instead, in the moral sensibility of America there is only a void, and one can sense the dimensions of that void by trying to imagine a Civil War fought over the Indian question—or Lincoln proclaiming an Emancipation Proclamation on their behalf. For Americans of all moral and political tendencies, the Algonquin and the Sioux were to the advance of American liberty only what Canada and Mexico were in the grand scheme of manifest destiny—and what, much later, Sandino was to Secretary Olds and the Vietcong were to Lyndon Johnson. They were not human beings; they were only obstacles to the inexorable triumph of American virtue, who must be swept away to make room for a new reality of American freedom.

There was from the beginning an American consensus on the Indian that was so implicit in every aspect of our nation's foundation and growth that it rarely aroused discussion, let alone provoked the national divisions and controversies slavery did. This consensus, quite simply, was that our own solemnly proclaimed rights to life, liberty and the pursuit of happiness totally superseded the rights of the peoples whose lives, liberties and happiness we were expunging from the face of the earth. From the beginning, therefore, the morality of America was as selective as its ambitions were boundless.

Even now the prevailing image of the Indian, in our popular culture, is the same as it was in the nineteenth century. The Indian is the aggressor who surrounds the wagon train, who scalps innocent women and children, who attacks the frontier outpost of civilization. Will the aggressors triumph? Or will the Americans successfully defend themselves? In a thousand Hollywood Westerns, as in countless children's games, the aggressor is also, always, the loser: the attack on the wagon train is turned back; the cavalry rides to the rescue, because it is preordained that we Americans will reach Oregon or California—whatever destination we set for ourselves—whatever stands in our way.

"Most of the literature on the Indians is highly romantic and historically worthless," Morison and Commager note. Besides their factual worthlessness, these mythic tales of American virtue triumphant over a recalcitrant but inevitably yielding "frontier" have much in common with both the parallel iconography of the "Monroe Doctrine" and with the official versions, handed down by President Eisenhower and President Reagan, of our "defense of freedom" in places like Guatemala and El Salvador.

Is the murder of an Indian in 1814, or the murder of a Salvadoran in 1984, really an act of virtue simply because we Americans commit or condone it?

What links the "red peril" of the nineteenth century with the red peril our officials later conjured up in Central America is more than a coincidence of language. In both cases, the definition of the aggressors is that we have attacked them. Our triumphs are liberty's triumphs, our enemies the enemies of freedom, because liberty and freedom are only subsidiary terms, synonyms for America itself.

Our attempt to resolve the unresolvable contradiction between the ideology of liberty and the reality of force is one of the great themes linking the crises of our distant past with the crises of today, and tomorrow. One result is that in the Mississippi Valley or El Salvador, in the nineteenth century or today, we Americans often find ourselves simultaneously fighting two separate wars.

The first war is the one that makes the headlines and produces the body counts. It unfolds in the jungles of Indochina, or in the mountains of Central America, or at Tippecanoe or along the Little Big Horn. The second war unfolds at closer quarters. But it, too, is a war for "freedom," in this case the struggle to free the American mind from any sense of its own contradictions.

El Salvador, as much as any incident in our history, provides a paradigm of these twin struggles. On the ground there, one war unfolds in a straightforward manner; it is a campaign to kill all those we oppose, conducted with unspeakable barbarism. The second war is more complicated. It consists of the perpetual American struggle to convince ourselves that even when we support terror and pursue a policy of mass slaughter, "[i]t is not our power but our will and character that is being tested," as President Nixon put it when he invaded Cambodia in 1970. Our attempts to transmute our crimes against others into triumphs of American virtue in large part explain why the reports from places like San Salvador or Saigon and the reports from Washington so often seem as though they are describing completely different conflicts, as though they flow from completely different, and fundamentally antagonistic, realities.

The news from Central America or Southeast Asia is always the news of death; yet the headlines from Washington are always the headlines of liberty. Our intelligence agencies manufacture "proofs" of subversion and aggression and, following each new massacre, the State Department detects another advance for democracy. Our presidents continue to conjure up shared destinies of freedom. In this sense, Reagan's war in El Salvador is Johnson's war in Indochina, just as Eisenhower's war in Guatemala was Coolidge's war in Nicaragua—and all of these are only continuations of the oldest war in American history—the war of extermination we have successfully pursued to eliminate what we have done first to the Indian and then to many other peoples from all our systems of politics, thought and morality.

By the time Andrew Jackson and his followers overran Washington as though it were only one more Cherokee encampment, a whole new America really had been wrung into existence—an America with a capacity, and with an appetite, for conquest that would have astonished the Founding Fathers. As William Graham Sumner later put it, Jackson was the "typical man of his generation." He not only had "the frontiersman's contempt for the Indian," he had a rough-and-ready contempt for the niceties of law. At New Orleans, Jackson's abuses of civil liberties were so conspicuous he was fined for contempt of court. While President, he defied the Supreme Court when it ruled that encroachments on Indian lands violated their treaties with the federal government. To the new, conquering America, Jackson was a hero, because he turned what already had been the governing national fact into explicit presidential policy: even the Constitution of the United States meant nothing when the liberties of others impeded the advance of American liberty.

One reason John Quincy Adams was so unpopular in the Age of Jackson was not only that he respected the Indian treaties, but that he had what now seemed an effete and contemptible devotion to the letter of the law. But was there any fundamental difference between Americans like Adams and Americans like Jackson?

It was Adams's great contention, made in the same Fourth of July speech in which he pointed out the danger force posed to liberty, that we Americans inhabited a New World that was morally superior to the Old World not because of America's geographical distance from Europe or even because of its recent settlement; the United States, he believed, was superior to all other nations because it possessed "the only *legitimate* foundation of civil government."

Where other systems of government were based on "the oppressions of power," Adams argued, in the United States "all was voluntary." Because the establishment of the United States flowed from "a social compact . . . in which conquest and servitude had no part," our American form of government was morally superior to "all governments founded upon conquest."

Yet even as he lauded America as the incarnation of liberty, Adams did so in a nation that condoned human slavery. He stood, as he made his Fourth of July speech about the dangers of power corrupting liberty, on land stolen from its original inhabitants. In his Fourth of July oration Adams did with these twin original sins of American nationalism what the State Department white paper would do with the Salvadoran matanza 160 years later. The Secretary of State totally subordinated reality to the task of defending the American illusion that even when Americans conquered, their conquests were necessarily a triumph of liberty. Addressing the subject of the American settlers' "relations with the aboriginal inhabitants of the country," Adams offered his audience the following astonishing version of events:

> The first settlers . . . immediately after landing, purchased from the Indian natives the right of settlement upon the soil.

> Thus was a social compact formed upon the elementary principles of civil society, in which conquest and servitude had no part. The slough of brutal force was entirely cast off: all was voluntary: all was unbiased consent: all was the agreement of soul with soul.

Here was an interpretation of American history so hallucinatory as to make all our later hallucinations about the "Monroe Doctrine" seem mere misprints of fact. But even more revealing was the fact that no American, in 1821, saw any reason to disagree.

Americans, however, were not the only ones who gathered in Washington to hear Adams speak that day. The diplomatic corps had also been invited to the House of Representatives to hear the Secretary of State's oration on liberty. What did the Europeans make of this American pretension that the United States, "because of its principles," was "the genuine Holy Alliance?"

One hundred twenty years later, modern scholarship provided an answer that was as pertinent to the Cold War Era as it was to the Age of Jackson. Adams's speech had been printed and copies distributed to the assembled dignitaries. In the course of preparing his study of *John Quincy Adams and the Foundations of American Foreign Policy,* Samuel Flagg Bemis asked the State Department to ascertain from the Soviet Government if a copy of the oration happened to be in the official archives of the czars. Presently there arrived from Stalin's Moscow a photocopy of the text of Adams's speech that had been given to Pierre de Poletica, the Russian minister to Washington back in 1821. Bemis was surprised to discover that the printed text of Adams's discourse on liberty, after more than a century of war and revolution in Russia, "remained buried to this day in the archival tombs of St. Petersburg and Moscow." The text itself provided even more cause for surprise. For, as Bemis notes, the Russian minister not only had listened carefully to Adams's version of the establishment of the United States; he had penciled his own comments in the margin:

> "How about your two million black slaves," the Russian marked against Adams' boast that American independence had presented . . . the only lawful foundation of government. "How about your two million black slaves who cultivate a great expanse of your territory for your particular and exclusive advantage? You forget the poor Indians whom you have not ceased to spoil. You forget your conduct toward Spain."

How about our black ghettos? How about Hiroshima? How about the Un-American Activities Committee of the same House of Representatives where Adams had given his address?

Bemis's study was published in 1949. By then, all sorts of Americans—our MacArthurs and our Trumans, our McCarthys and our Kennans—had the same answer to such questions that our Adamses and our Jacksons had back in 1821. Since ours was the "only *legitimate*" form of government, all that our government did must be uniquely legitimate too.

Perhaps no other President personifies so well the moral streak in American nationalism as John Quincy Adams. Yet the "corrupt bargain" that won him the White House in 1824 was a fitting metaphor for the larger bargain with history that assured the foundation of our country, and its expansion across a continent to world power. From the beginning, we Americans have been not only a moralistic but a legalistic people—taking as great pains with our colonial charters and our proprietary leases as Adams and Clay took with the letter of the Constitution to deny Andrew Jackson the White House. Even today we remember that we "purchased . . . the right of settlement" of most of a continent—as though Peter Minuit's trinkets could both compensate the original inhabitants and free us from any responsibility for the general extermination that was soon to follow. Yet the paperwork of our history can no more change its substance than some presidential doctrine can turn the incineration of some Asian or Latin American village into an act of liberation.

The original colonies had been established by force, and expanded beyond the Appalachians by force. Our national union had been born of war; by the same means it would be extended to the Pacific. And only through the most terrible war in all American history would that union be preserved. The contradiction between the illusion of virtue and the reality of conquest had pursued the earliest settlers across the Atlantic. In the nineteenth century it pursued Americans across a continent.

In the twentieth century it would pursue us Americans, quite literally, to the ends of the earth.

Although most nineteenth-century Americans might have agreed with Adams that it was "unavoidable that the remainder of the continent should ultimately be ours," our national territory had not increased by so much as a single square inch a quarter century after Monroe's annexation of Florida. To the contrary, the most important practical result of Monroe's policy was the legitimization of European colonialism in the New World. In 1824 the Russians were confirmed in their possession of Alaska. After 1823, Spain, for all its feebleness, held on to Cuba and Puerto Rico, as the other continental powers did to their Caribbean colonies. Elsewhere in Latin America, from the Falklands through the Guianas to Belize, it was Britain, not the United States, whose territories were expanding.

As noted earlier, Russia, Spain, the Holy Alliance, all had been the beneficiaries, to a greater or lesser extent, of the mildness of President Monroe's measures. But no nation had gained more than Great Britain. And it was from the British, more than any others, that Monroe and Adams had hoped for a quid pro quo. The Oregon country, and much else besides, might inevitably attach itself to the United States through what Adams called "the law of political gravitation"—if Britain, as Monroe's message had requested, refrained from "future colonization" in areas where "the rights and interests of the United States are involved."

But what if the British did not? It is one thing to avow principles to the universe, quite another to assure they are respected in one's own backyard.

By 1843, the British were more powerful than ever in Oregon; the chances of its peaceful annexation to the United States seemingly never more remote. By then, indeed, the United States was even more encircled, geopolitically, than it had been during the War of 1812. The age of colonialism was supposedly long gone, the fulfillment of America's destiny supposedly at hand. But the Russian, British and Mexican flags flew the length of the Pacific from the Bering Straits to Central America.

The Latin Americans had experienced no difficulty blocking European reconquest even before President Monroe had composed his message. By the 1840s, however, the "Monroe Doctrine" did pose a major question—about the United States. Was the erstwhile protector of the hemisphere capable of halting European colonization on lands it claimed were its own?

How should Americans react to this glaring discrepancy between their principles and their ambitions—between their illusions about themselves and the reality of the world? Abstentionists like Adams might be content to let "centuries" elapse before North America finally coalesced into a single nation. But most Americans were not so patient. Would our Pacific destiny be deferred forever? Virtue, Americans began to realize with exasperation, was not merely its own, but in this case its only, reward.

Still, neither faith in American liberty nor national frustration was sufficient to rouse American nationalism to its full fury. Some other development
was necessary. This "development," as Albert K. Weinberg points out in his
classic study of *Manifest Destiny,* was the emergence of that "danger from
abroad" that Americans also had seen lurking in Europe back in the 1820s,
and which they would discover again at the end of World War II.

Suddenly, in the early 1840s, both the conspiracy theory and the domino
theory were rediscovered to possess transcendant validity. Soon the principle
of abstention "avowed by Mr. Monroe" would be plucked from oblivion and
transformed into an American doctrine of conquest. Fittingly enough, the
progenitor of this "Monroe Doctrine" of conquest was Andrew Jackson. In
1837, as he left the White House after two terms, Old Hickory had looked
back on the tumultuous epoch that had seen both him and the nation achieve
unprecedented power. From the battle of New Orleans, from his Florida
invasion, from all his conquests, Jackson drew a conclusion few Americans,
either then or later, ever doubted. Providence, Jackson told the nation in his
Farewell Address, had singled out us Americans to be "the guardians of
freedom to preserve it for the benefit of the human race."

Less than a decade later, when freedom seemed, to many Americans, to be
everywhere under attack, Jackson had as ready an explanation for America's
frustrations as he had for America's triumphs. In a letter written in 1843, the
retired President blamed it all on British intrigue. It was a conspiracy by
Great Britain, not the Holy Alliance, this time, that stood in the way of the
United States' "extending the area of freedom." And so far as many Americans were concerned, the object of the British conspiracy was not merely to
deny us new lands that were rightfully ours; its goal was nothing less than the
destruction of the United States.

Jackson had made his comments in a private letter to a man named Aaron
V. Brown. Yet his call for an "extension of the area of freedom" to counter
British "intrigue" soon became as nationally famous as Kennan's call for
"containment" in *Foreign Affairs* would be later. Suddenly the cause of all
America's problems was clear—and so was the American response those
problems demanded.

The question was no longer whether American ambition could be recon-
ciled with American principle, or whether we would follow a policy of power
or a policy of liberty. It was our will and character that were being tested.

In 1846, for no morally or strategically justifiable reason, the United States
attacked a foreign nation, overthrew its government, devastated its lands,
terrorized its people and, in this case, stole nearly a million square miles of its
national territory.

Yet, as Weinberg demonstrates, this was not how many Americans saw
things. In fact, President Jackson's view of the British and Mexican "threat"
was identical to President Reagan's view of the Soviet and Central American

"threat." So far as Jackson was concerned, events "in adjacent countries appeared to threaten not merely economic and strategic interests but also the security of democracy."

Our attempt to defend ourselves against the British conspiracy by attacking Mexico also had strong resonances with our later attempts to "contain the Soviet Union" by overthrowing the governments of countries like Iran, Guatemala and Chile. As Weinberg explains, Jackson's

> conception of an "extension of the area of freedom" became general as an ideal of preventing absolutistic Europe from lessening the area open to American democracy; extension of the area of "freedom" was the defiant answer to extension of the area of "absolutism."

Or as one prowar senator put it seventy-two years before the establishment of the Soviet Union, it all came down to "a question between two great systems."

Later, when the Anglo-American "special relationship" transformed Britain into America's closest ally, Americans would do what they often do when the facts contradict their beliefs about themselves. They would forget entirely that Britain, for much of the first half of our history, occupied the same place in the official American demonology that the Soviet Union has for most of the past forty years.

Another parallel with the future existed. "There was never definitive proof of Britain's 'plot' to disrupt the United States," as Sidney Lens rather mildly puts it. The truth, however much Americans refused to accept it, was that from Canning's time onward it was much more British policy to appease than to contain the territorial ambitions of the United States—as the events of the 1840s would reveal most dramatically.

Not that these mild truths would have been acknowledged by Americans at the time. By the election year of 1844 the United States was in the grip of a war fever not witnessed since 1812—and seized of a virulent Anglophobia such as this nation would never experience again.

The Era of Good Feeling was gone; force and dissension were superseding liberty and consensus everywhere in the United States. An age of American violence was at hand, which would find its culmination in the Civil War. Yet history had so accelerated that, even as the United States entered a new era of conquest, most of the great protagonists of the Era of Good Feeling, excepting Monroe himself, were, as we have seen, still alive, indeed active as ever in national affairs.

John C. Calhoun, who, as Monroe's Secretary of War, had feared a European invasion of Latin America, had gone on to serve as Vice President under both John Quincy Adams and Andrew Jackson. Then he had represented South Carolina in the Senate and briefly been President Tyler's Secretary of State; by 1844 he was back in the Senate again. As for Adams, the former Secretary of State had been unhappy in the White House. But that had not prevented him, following his defeat in the 1828 presidential elections, from beginning a new, far more successful phase of his public life. As Bemis later put it, both elegantly and aptly:

In one lifetime John Quincy Adams had two notable careers, separated by an interlude as president of the United States. The first career was that of diplomatist and continentalist, the second a crusader in the House of Representatives against the expansion of slavery.

For decades, Adams, the quintessential New Englander, and Calhoun, the paradigmatical Southerner, had been cabinet colleagues, shared the two highest offices in the land, and now the two were congressional colleagues. Yet the passage of the years had done to the two of them what it had done to the nation as a whole. Time had widened immeasurably the political distance between North and South, between the son of Massachusetts and the son of South Carolina—and diminished both men from national figures into spokesmen for sectional interests and sectional ideological agendas.

Calhoun and Adams were not alone. By 1844, events also had diminished Andrew Jackson into a sectional figure. "After he left Washington," Sumner records, "Jackson fell into discord with his most intimate old friends, and turned his interest to the cause of slavery, which he thought to be attacked and in danger."

Least of all was Henry Clay gone from the scene, though 1844 proved to be his last hurrah. For the last time that year Clay would be nominated for the presidency, and for the last time the office would elude him in a national election. Clay had first come to Congress as a "War Hawk," determined to have his War of 1812. Later, a war for the freedom of all Latin America had been his objective. As men grow older, however, they grow cautious. They dream, in their final years, of at last reconciling their principles and their ambitions. Above all, they lose touch with the passions of youth. In the presidential campaign of 1844 Clay found himself playing the role Adams had twenty years earlier. The old hawk was now the candidate of the doves, counseling against rashness, arrogance and war.

Clay, like Adams, was no enemy of manifest destiny. He was not opposed to our annexation of either Oregon or Texas, where American settlers also wanted admission to the union. But he favored territorial expansion in the manner of Jefferson and Monroe—through diplomacy and compromise. The boundaries of both Texas and Oregon were ill defined. The British already had indicated their willingness to partition Oregon; it was Britain's refusal to capitulate to all our demands, not any unwillingness to negotiate, that so outraged many Americans. As for Mexico, it long since had lost control of Texas to its American residents, and might be persuaded, in due course, to recognize formal annexation of the Republic of Texas to the United States, if only because by then, like so many underdeveloped countries today, Mexico was strapped for cash.

"Annexation and war with Mexico are identical," Clay forthrightly declared in April 1844. "I certainly am not willing to involve this country in a foreign war for the object of acquiring Texas."

Nor was high-minded statesmanship, in 1844, limited to Henry Clay. President Van Buren had been defeated for reelection, in 1840, by William Henry Harrison. But the "hero of Tippecanoe" had died a month after taking office, and his widely detested successor, John Tyler, was a President without a party. Now, in 1844, Van Buren confidently expected both to win the Democratic nomination and to return to the White House. The same month Clay said Texas was not worth a war, Van Buren announced that he, too, opposed the immediate annexation of Texas. Annexation threatened to lead to war, the former President pointed out, and even if it did not, it would saddle the federal government with Texas's debts.

More than six months before the presidential election, the two front-runners for the two major parties' presidential nominations had taken the two most responsible positions on the two most important national issues: the territorial expansion of the United States, and the territorial expansion of slavery within the United States.

But, like "responsible" American statesmen during the McCarthy Era, Clay and Van Buren had failed to reckon with two other factors: the national passions of the American people, and the capacity of other politicians less "responsible" than they to cater to those passions.

For established national leaders like Clay and Van Buren, Oregon and Texas were what the Canal Zone was to Ford and Carter a century and a quarter later. They were only complex foreign-policy imbroglios that were best left to professionals like them to solve.

But that was not how millions of American voters saw it. For more than a quarter of a century, Americans had been told it was their manifest destiny to possess the North American continent. For just as long, their leaders had been explaining the failure to fulfill America's ambitions in terms of a conspiratorial "danger from abroad." Now the two men most likely to become the next President of the United States were telling the nation that America's manifest destiny must be deferred for yet another presidential election.

Suddenly, bipartisan consensus at the top was overturned by upheaval at the bottom. Would no candidate stand up for our "rights" in Texas and Oregon? Would no leader defend us against the British peril?

James Knox Polk would. If he was elected President, Polk proclaimed, he would never "permit Great Britain or any other foreign power to plant a colony or hold dominion over any portion of the people or territory of either" Texas or Oregon. Years earlier, Clay had declared he "would rather be right than President." As for Van Buren, he might have said he would rather be right than the Democratic nominee. Polk, previously an obscure figure, suddenly became the embodiment of unashamed American nationalism, the man destined to fulfill America's destiny. In rapid succession, Polk defeated Van

Buren for the Democratic nomination and Clay for the presidency. With Van Buren cast aside, the Democrats had declared U.S. sovereignty over "the whole territory of Oregon" to be "clear and unquestionable"; they called also for the immediate annexation of Texas—and reaped a harvest of American chauvinism at the polls.

The nomination and election of the first "dark horse" presidential candidate in American history constituted one of the greatest triumphs of popular democracy in the history of the United States. Like Jackson earlier and Reagan later, Polk at first was not even taken seriously as a presidential candidate by "responsible" political leaders. But James Knox Polk had plucked a chord in the heart of American nationalism. As much as any presidential election in our history, the election of 1844 was a clear-cut referendum on principles, not a contest of personalities. Would America pursue a policy of liberty, abstention and peace? Or would America pursue a policy of power, intervention—and war?

As Polk's victory demonstrated, Adams's "law of political gravitation" was working in quite a different way from what he had intended. Before Jackson's election, Virginia and Massachusetts had monopolized the White House. Now, in just fifteen years, Tennessee had produced three presidents: Jackson, Polk, and President Sam Houston of Texas. The political balance of power within the United States had shifted fundamentally, and the new America the Indian wars had helped create was hungry for further conquest.

Months before the November election, the outgoing President Tyler announced his decision to annex Texas. The mere knowledge of his intention opened up the national fissure that, three years later, would grow into an unbridgeable chasm during the Mexican War. Many Americans, like Clay and Van Buren, opposed Tyler's plan of annexation because they believed it would mean war with Mexico. Many other Americans, like Polk, demanded annexation even if it did mean war.

Yet the main effect of Tyler's plan, like so many unilateral presidential initiatives on behalf of "liberty," was to raise an internal question about American principle that overshadowed even foreign-policy questions of war and peace: by what right did the President of the United States annex a foreign territory without the consent of that territory's rightful owners?

President Tyler soon received a straightforward answer: He had no such right. The Senate overwhelmingly rejected the president's plan of annexation. The President had proposed, but the Constitution had prevailed. "Mr. Tyler's infamous treaty, by which he hoped to rob Mexico of her province of Texas, against the consent of the people of the United States, to promote his political ends with the southern states, at the risk of plunging the country into an unjust and discreditable war," one opponent rejoiced, "has received its quietus. . . ."

"Quietus," however, was a most inapt term for the national uproar that ensued. Northerners were outraged—because they saw in Tyler's attempt to annex Texas a southern plot to extend slavery. Southerners were outraged—because they saw in the Senate's attempt to stop annexation a northern plot to deprive the South of its fair share of "the area of freedom." With the Civil War still seventeen years away, the cry "Texas or disunion" quickly replaced the cry for "Texas and liberty" throughout the South. Texas, as Calhoun himself observed, had become

> the all-absorbing question, stronger even than the presidential . . . the most important question, for both the south and the Union, ever agitated since the adoption of the Constitution.

Tyler's attempt to "extend the area of freedom," like Polk's later war against Mexico, had created a great crisis of liberty within "the area of freedom."

Presidents as eminent as Jefferson, Monroe and Jackson all had held back from attempting the kind of vast, additional territorial acquisitions in the Southwest that Tyler and Polk did not hesitate to grasp. In 1819, for example, Adams had been inclined to press the Spanish for Texas, in addition to Florida, but the President had restrained his Secretary of State. In a letter to Thomas Jefferson the following year, James Monroe had explained why: The growing national dispute over the extent of slavery within the Louisiana purchase had alerted him to the grave sectional dangers U.S. territorial expansion might produce. Annexing Texas, he feared, would create a national crisis to which no Missouri Compromise might be found. As Bemis puts it,

> Texas, in Monroe's view, would have fatally upset the historical sectional balance upon which the Union had rested ever since independence.

Similar considerations had also restrained Jackson during his presidency. By 1844, Jackson's call for extending freedom reverberated through the nation like a war cry. But while he was in the White House, his policy had been guided by his most famous maxim of all: "Our Federal Union, it must be preserved." So Jackson too had spurned the Texans.

Now, in the uproar over Tyler's attempted annexation of Texas, Monroe was proved right. "Manifest destiny" posed a far greater threat to the unity, security and survival of the United States than either British "intrigue" or Mexican "aggression." The Senate's rejection of the Texas treaty nonetheless seemed to defer another attempt to annex Texas—and further threats to "the historical sectional balance"—at least until a new President took office. But that was not the way things worked out.

In early 1845, following Polk's victory but before he took office, President Tyler tried a new tactic to secure Texas for the United States, and this one worked. The lack of a two-thirds majority in the Senate still blocked annexation by treaty. But, after much searching, Tyler had come upon another constitutional provision that seemed to suit his needs. The Constitution held that "new States may be admitted by the Congress into this Union." So, in clear violation of the intent of the Constitution and all previous practice, the

Tyler administration decided not to annex Texas as a foreign territory, but to admit it directly as a state by seeking a simple majority in both houses of Congress, rather than a two-thirds majority in the Senate.

The vote was close in the House, and the bill approving Texas statehood passed the Senate by only two votes. The entire operation was of the most dubious constitutionality, but this, too, was no innovation: the fundamental law of the nation also had been bent to the expediencies of American ambition back in 1803, when, in the interest of gaining a veritable empire, the United States had acquired Louisiana.

Once again, in 1845, the internal implications for the United States were as important as the external consequences: For just as the United States expanded at the territorial expense of its neighbors, so would the prerogatives of the presidency expand at the expense of the original intent of the framers of the Constitution.

Soon U.S. troops were pouring into Texas to "defend" it against possible Mexican "aggression." Yet Tyler's hasty annexation of Texas had proved both Van Buren and Clay wrong on one important count. Annexation of Texas and war with Mexico had proved not to be identical. So reluctant were the Mexicans to risk full-scale war that their forces retired deep into undisputed Mexican territory. A vast no-man's-land separated U.S. forces north and east of the Nueces from Mexican forces south and west of the Rio Grande.

As James Knox Polk took the presidential oath to "preserve, protect and defend the Constitution of the United States," he seemed an American leader doubly blessed by destiny. His willingness to fight for Texas had made him President. But now that he was President, Texas was already his—without recourse to war.

But what of the northwest? The new President solemnly and frequently reiterated his pledge that all of Oregon, from the forty-second parallel, which was the northern boundary of Mexican California, to the latitude of fifty-four degrees, forty minutes, which marked the southern boundary of Russian Alaska, must be annexed to the United States. The nation rang with the cry "Fifty-four forty or fight!" Yet London was completely unwilling to accept "Fifty-four forty."

It was amid a national sense of deep and irreconcilable crisis that President Polk, thirteen months after taking office, strode into the Capitol to address a joint session of Congress. His words epitomized the deep frustration many Americans felt over the British refusal to recognize the American claim to all of Oregon. Rousing Congress to a fever pitch of indignation, President Polk portrayed the United States as the innocent victim of willful aggression, a peace-loving nation that, over and over again, had turned the other cheek, only to have it slapped by a sinister foreign power:

We have tried every effort at reconciliation [Polk announced]. The cup of forbearance had been exhausted even before the recent information from the frontier. . . . But now, after reiterated menaces, [the aggressor] has passed the boundary of the United States, has invaded our territory, and shed American blood on American soil. She has proclaimed that hostilities exist, and that the two nations are now at war.

It was as though Lyndon Johnson was President and our ships in the Gulf of Tonkin had been attacked. A declaration of war was stampeded through Congress—not against the British "aggressors," but against our sister republic Mexico.

Soon half of Mexico was in flame as the United States engaged in what one American officer conceded was the "most unjust war ever waged by a stronger against a weaker nation." The words were important; even more so was the identity of the speaker, Ulysses S. Grant. Just as Central America, much later, would be the rehearsal hall for Woodrow Wilson's "crusade for freedom" in Europe, so Mexico was the training camp for the great generals, both Union and Confederate, of the Civil War.

Not even the American national mythology has been able to alchemize the attack on Mexico into a war of American self-defense, but most Americans do suppose that American conduct of the war was militarily gallant, if not legally justified. For that reason, two of the most decisive engagements of that long-forgotten conflict deserve mention. The following description of General Winfield Scott's attack on the Mexican port of Veracruz, taken from Meyer and Sherman's history of Mexico, requires no amplification:

Militarily sound, but morally questionable, the plan of attack called for a heavy bombardment of the city; coincidentally it meant that hundreds of innocent civilians with no possibility of escape would be sacrificed to the apparent exigencies of war.

For the next forty-eight hours Scott devastated the city and refused all implorations of foreign consuls to allow women, children, and other non-combatants to evacuate. He would countenance no manner of truce not accompanied by unconditional surrender. Another day of intense fighting with heavy bombardment ensued.

With military and medical supplies diminished, hundreds of civilian corpses building up in the streets, fires gutting buildings, hospitals destroyed, and the frightening specter of a yellow-fever epidemic mounting, Veracruz surrendered. . . . Sixty-seven Americans had been killed or wounded, while the toll of Mexican dead within the city was between one thousand and fifteen hundred. Civilian casualties outnumbered military casualties almost two to one.

A new chapter in American history was opening. But Mexican history was only repeating itself. "Veracruz surrendered on 27 March 1847," Morison and Commager note, "and the American army started for Mexico City along

the road Cortes had followed three centuries before." Having once been conquered by Spain in the name of God, Mexico was now being conquered a
second time, in the name of liberty.

Mexican resistance was finally broken—militarily and psychologically—
when the Americans overran Chapultepec Castle, in Mexico City, headquarters of the Mexican military academy, in hand-to-hand fighting. Its last defenders were teen-aged cadets who had just begun their military training.
They are remembered today in Mexico as the Niños Héroes—the Little Heroes. Today the battle of Chapultepec is nothing more than a name and date
in our history books. But in Mexico, September 13—the day the fortress fell
—remains an anniversary of deep and poignant significance. Many Mexicans
go there every year, even now, to lay wreaths at the monument to the Niños
Héroes. Especially revered is the memory of a youth named Juan Escutia:
Rather than surrender to the Americans, the young cadet wrapped himself in
the Mexican flag and threw himself off the fortress's two-hundred-foot-high
battlement.

The young Mexican's gesture established a permanent leitmotiv in U.S.-
Latin American relations. This is the pattern of U.S. actions driving Latin
Americans into situations in which even suicidal gestures become preferable
to utter capitulation to our arrogance. As for the U.S. artillery attacks on the
civilian population of Veracruz, they also established a constant theme in our
relations with the weak that continues even today. I am referring not just to
our tendency to attack those least capable of defending themselves, but also
the double standard we apply when it comes to "defending freedom."

More than thirty years after the "rockets' red glare" created by the British
naval bombardment of Baltimore had inspired "The Star-Spangled Banner,"
the United States was still loath, for all its belligerent rhetoric, to risk an
armed clash over Oregon, which might expose our cities, once again, to British attack. Less than two months after Congress legitimated President Polk's
attack on Mexico, it approved with equal docility the U.S. surrender of all
claims on half of the Oregon Country. A short time later, the President who
had defeated Henry Clay by vowing to get "Fifty-four forty or fight" signed
the treaty recognizing full British sovereignty over all of Oregon north of the
forty-ninth parallel, and over all of Vancouver Island, which dips beneath the
forty-ninth parallel, as well. Under this partition, approximately 260,000
square miles of land—today comprising the states of Oregon, Washington and
Idaho as well as parts of Montana and Wyoming—went to the United States.
In return, the United States solemnly recognized British sovereignty over
British Columbia, a territory 360,000 square miles in extent.

The synchronization of the U.S. attack on Mexico with the U.S. retreat
over Oregon in the dispute with Britain thus established certain themes in the
conduct of U.S. foreign policy that remain prominent even today. The conquest of half of Mexico was a small price to pay for "an extension of the area

of freedom"—so long as the Mexicans were too weak to threaten the United States itself. But with Britain, the United States was far more cautious, even though the U.S. claim to all of Oregon was far stronger than the totally fraudulent claims it had manufactured to justify the war against Mexico.

Polk's joint policy of aggression against Mexico and compromise with Britain violated American principle, violated American rights—and, no less consequentially, violated the campaign promises that had won him the White House. Yet it possessed an internal, not just an external, logic.

To understand why, it is necessary to return to the dominant fact of the first half of our national history, which is that by the 1840s the poison of sectionalism called into question the very survival of the United States. Everything in the United States, including foreign policy, revolved around the dominant national problem, which was the deepening hostility between North and South.

As a slave-owning Tennessean, Polk's personal sympathies were with the South in its long, losing struggle to maintain parity with the more populous, rapidly industrializing North. In fact, the chief reason war with Mexico was so popular with many Southerners was not that it seemed to offer quick, easy fulfillment of the national destiny; it was that the war seemed to offer sectional salvation. Texas had been admitted to the union not merely as a slave state, but with the option of subdividing itself into a total of four states, with eight members of the U.S. Senate. As many Southerners saw it, Texas was only the beginning. With the acquisition of New Mexico and California, slavery would surely continue to expand westward, as it had expanded west from Virginia and the Carolinas across the Appalachians and beyond the Mississippi. With the extension of the nation's territory to the Pacific, many Southerners believed, the division of the United States into slave states and free states would also extend itself from ocean to ocean. And so long as the admission of new slave states allowed the South to maintain parity with the North in the U.S. Senate, that region would retain an effective veto on national legislation. In a real sense, the Mexican War was not merely an unprovoked act of aggression against a foreign country; it was an attempt to vastly enlarge the scope of human slavery and thus preserve what the Southerners called their "freedom" within the constitutional framework.

In the South, war with Mexico aroused great expectations. But it aroused great apprehensions in the North. Polk, like Jackson, was not just a southern slaveholder; he was a fervent unionist; and back then the fundamental task of unionist policy was somehow to maintain balance between the sections even in time of war.

A war against Mexico was winnable, but only at the risk of losing the support of the North if territorial gains in the southwest were not counterbalanced by territorial gains in the northwest. Yet a war against Britain, however much it might serve northern ambitions, was by no means surely winnable.

And a two-front war against both Britain and Mexico could prove disastrous. What was President Polk to do?

As so often during the first half of our history, a combination of adroit diplomacy in London and expediency in Washington assured that British interests prevailed—while also fostering the illusion on this side of the Atlantic that America's national destiny was being fulfilled. Britain all along had been amenable to a partition of Oregon. The only question was where the line of partition would be drawn, and the two nations had been wrangling over various proposals for years. There is no doubt that if Clay had won the presidential election of 1844, Britain and the United States could have settled the dispute through quiet diplomacy.

Quiet diplomacy, of course, was not what the United States wanted then. It wanted a President who would fight for America's rights. Rejecting all possibility of partition, Polk audaciously confronted the British with a clear-cut choice: surrender of all of Oregon, or war with the United States. "The British proposition of compromise . . . can never for a moment be entertained by the United States," Polk declared, "without an abandonment of their just and clear territorial rights, their own self-respect, and the national honor."

The British responded to Polk's blustering with that classic tool of nineteenth-century imperial statecraft—a judicious bit of gunboat diplomacy. Soon a conspicuous British military buildup was underway. When the American minister in London inquired as to the purpose of these military preparations, he received a straightforward answer from Lord Aberdeen, the British Foreign Minister. If President Polk continued to oppose "any new proposition on the basis of compromise, and to concede nothing of the extreme demand" on Oregon, it would become necessary for Britain not only to defend its rights in that territory but to undertake "offensive operations." Accordingly Her Majesty's Government was ordering "the immediate equipment of thirty sail of the line, besides steamers and other vessels of war."

A word to the wise was sufficient. The President who would authorize the naval bombardment of Veracruz had no intention of risking the fate of James Madison during the War of 1812. Even as he prepared to attack Mexico, President Polk privately made an extraordinary demarche to the British. He not only invited the British to name their terms for an Oregon compromise, he pledged "to receive and to treat with the utmost respect" whatever terms the British might suggest. Clay had lost the election by seeming to be soft on the British. Now the man who had defeated him by pledging he would not let Great Britain kick the United States around was crawling, diplomatically speaking, to London on his hands and knees.

American domestic politics had not offered the British such brilliant opportunities since 1823—and Aberdeen proved no less adept at exploiting them than George Canning had been in the time of James Monroe. In fact Polk's determination to attack Mexico, even at the cost of forsaking our claims on Oregon, offered Whitehall an extraordinary range of possibilities. With U.S. troops tied down in Mexico, what was to stop Britain itself from launching a war of its own to resolve the Oregon dispute, on its own terms, once and for all?

The U.S. seizure of Texas, combined with the outbreak of full-scale war, also offered Britain brilliant opportunities in Latin America. Canning had called the New World into existence to balance the Old. Yet, twenty-five years later, the growing power of the United States was threatening to unbalance the entire western hemisphere. In France the Bourbons had been overthrown for the second and last time, in 1830. The Orleanist Louis-Philippe—the "Citizen King"—was now a constitutional monarch on the British model, and Britain and France were in the midst of one of their periodic ententes cordiales. Louis-Philippe's Foreign Minister, François Guizot, feared accurately enough that U.S. expansionism was upsetting the "balance of power" in the Americas. What better way to restore that balance than to reverse Canning this time, and have the Old World redress the balance of the New?

It bespeaks both the adroitness and the vision of nineteenth-century British diplomacy that Aberdeen rejected all suggestions that the Europeans side with Mexico in the face of this latest American act of encroachment. In truth, Aberdeen, like Canning, was playing a much bigger game, in which the object was not so much the curtailment of U.S. power, as it was the channeling of growing U.S. power to British purposes. Where the British might have been hostile, they therefore were friendly. Where they might have presented Polk with an ultimatum, they offered the President a deal—and he grabbed it. What better way to resolve the Oregon dispute once and for all, the British responded, than simply to extend to the Pacific the arbitrary line, along the forty-ninth parallel, that already divided U.S. and British possessions east of the Rockies?

This British offer not only was statesmanlike in its generosity, it cleverly exploited a well-known fact of U.S. diplomacy. Nearly twenty years earlier, President Adams and Secretary of State Clay had to partition the disputed territory along the identical line. Would President Polk risk war with a great power over all of Oregon? Or would he accept the kind of deal his opponent for the presidency had favored?

The outcome is well known, though at least in the United States its significance has seldom been fully appreciated. In London, the British Foreign Minister had taken a pencil and ruler and drawn an arbitrary line across the Oregon wilderness to an arbitrary point on the Pacific. In Washington the American President not only accepted this classic exercise in colonial cartography "with the utmost respect"; he altered not a jot or a tittle of this British line drawn across an American map. So, just as we have one British Foreign Minister to thank for many of the most important provisions of the "Monroe Doctrine," we have another to thank for Seattle, Boise, Yellowstone Park— for the fact that, seventy years after the Declaration of Independence, our "manifest destiny" was at last fulfilled, the "area of freedom" at last extended from sea to shining sea.

Not since 1823 had the British played an American card with greater finesse. After nearly three quarters of a century, the last major territorial dispute between the British and the Americans was now resolved, and the old American dream of annexing Canada was interred forever. Polk had gained the White House by threatening war with Britain over "the whole Territory of Oregon." But in the end his accomplishment was quite different: he wound up committing the United States to acceptance of the peaceful emergence of Canada as an independent nation, for the partition of Oregon completed the partition of the North American continent.

The Oregon settlement thus constituted formal U.S. acknowledgment that the contours of North America were not congruent with the territorial destiny of the United States after all. It was a major victory for the British. Strategically speaking, Canning had won back in 1823 what Britain had lost in 1783. In 1846 Aberdeen had expanded Canning's strategic breakthrough to the Pacific Ocean.

If one asks any American today what Polk's presidency achieved for us one receives a straightforward answer. Just as we suppose that President Monroe said "Hands off the New World" to the scheming Europeans, so in countless grade school history books "President Polk" and "Manifest Destiny" are interchangeable terms.

But all that is only another American illusion. In Polk's haste to trade away lands upon which we had legitimate claims, lest they complicate his plans for seizing lands to which we had no legitimate claim at all, Polk utterly forsook our "manifest destiny." And he did this not merely in the sense in which abstentionists like Adams had understood our national destiny, but in complete violation of the concept of manifest destiny as it was defined by Polk's own supporters, during Polk's own presidency.

The year before Polk attacked Mexico while letting Great Britain define our boundaries in the northwest, a New York journalist named John L. O'Sullivan both coined the phrase "Manifest Destiny" and prophesied what it would get us, in an editorial that became nationally famous.

Having annexed Texas, O'Sullivan predicted, the United States in time would also annex Oregon. California, in the fulfillment "of the manifest design of Providence," was bound to be ours as well. Territorially, O'Sullivan's prophecy was correct. But when it came to the means by which his prophecy was fulfilled, he could not have been more wrong. No corrupting attacks on the weak, no demeaning compromises with the mighty, he assured his readers, would be necessary to gain for the United States nearly a million square miles of another nation's land. Instead, he exulted:

All this [would be accomplished] without agency of our government, without responsibility of our people—in the natural flow of events, the spontaneous working of principles, and the adaptation of the tendencies and wants of the human race to the elemental circumstances in the midst of which they find themselves placed.

Never did the New World doctrine of American national and moral particularity receive a more precise definition. The essence of "Manifest Destiny" was that we Americans were not merely destined for redemption, but were to be spared original sin. It was this, above all, that made the New World a Garden of Eden, and Americans history's chosen people. We—unlike the corrupt, Old World empires—would never have to eat the fruit of the tree of knowledge of good and evil.

Our enemies would fall as President Eisenhower assured us Arbenz and Mossadegh fell—"without agency of our government." Whole peoples and nations would disappear to make room for our greatness, the same way we are told the matanza unfolds in El Salvador today—"without responsibility of our people." The "spontaneous working of principles" would get us what we wanted.

Most Americans, including President Polk, were of the opinion that by annexing the lands of others we not only fulfilled our own destiny, we did those whose lands we seized a great service. Were not the Canadians in almost all ways identical to us? Would not U.S. rule be welcomed by "the better sort" of Mexicans, by which Polk meant fair-skinned Mexicans, of European descent? From this perspective, by conquering Mexico we were "regenerating her decadent race."

Yet by 1846, as events clearly demonstrated, not even the English-speaking settlers of Canada—let alone the French of Quebec—had any desire to be incorporated into the aggressive and arrogant republic to the south. To the contrary, they regarded the British crown as their only sure guarantee against Yankee encroachment.

The same proved to be true even of the blondest, bluest-eyed Mexicans. For more than a year before attacking Mexico, President Polk, working through his agents in California, schemed to create a fifth column of local, Spanish-speaking merchants and landowners who, under the guidance of the U.S. consul at Monterrey, Thomas O. Larkin, would obligingly petition Washington for the privilege of U.S. rule, just as the Texans had, and thus relieve the United States of the onus of "aggression" when it annexed the territory.

But the Californians were no more interested in acquiring the privilege of U.S. rule than the Canadians. Americans were mystified, and asked the question we so often would ask ourselves in the future. How could a people be so ungrateful as not to welcome the progress and stability conferred by the U.S. Flag and Constitution? No American could imagine then, just as no one remembers now, that many more would die in our own Civil War than would perish in all of Mexico's internal upheavals combined.

The discrepancy between reality and what one might wish it to be is an affliction that falls on the powerful in ways quite different from the ways it falls on the weak. The weak usually have no choice but to accept the dictates of reality. The strong, however, have the option of attempting to coerce reality into conforming to their imaginations. What is so interesting about what happened in 1846 is that the United States, under President Polk, found itself simultaneously in a position of strength and a position of weakness. Thus the British soon received one kind of answer to the question the Oregon dispute posed about the nature of American nationalism, and the Mexicans quite another kind of answer when it came to Texas and California. Though President Polk himself would have denied it, and subsequent generations of Americans have entirely forgotten it, it was Polk's own personal destiny, therefore, to demonstrate conclusively that the theory of "Manifest Destiny"—no less than the conspiracy theory of history and the domino theory—was only a figment of the American imagination. The United States indeed was on the road to greatness—but it was the same road all the empires of history had pursued: a road of force paved with expediency. Conquest of the weak, combined with compromise with the mighty, had made our national dream come true.

The conquest of Mexico, militarily speaking, was a straightforward task. But what of that second war almost all American presidents have to fight when they involve us in foreign conflicts—the war, here at home, to convince Americans that even their most aggressive wars of conquest are really defenses of liberty?

Like a number of our later presidents, James Knox Polk must stand acquitted of any charge he committed naked aggression. By the time he finally attacked Mexico, his aggression was fully cloaked in a whole wardrobe of lies, half-truths, misrepresentations and outright fabrications—all designed to convince Congress and American public opinion that the United States was only defending itself against the Mexican peril.

Yet, after more than a year of such efforts, President Polk faced a dilemma certain of his successors would also confront. What does one do with an aggressor who refuses to attack? When President Polk's own conspiracy of aggression failed to elicit the Mexican response he wanted, he did what Lyndon Johnson later did with the Vietnamese, and the Reagan administration did in El Salvador. He invented an act of aggression.

The southern boundary of Texas had been the Nueces River under both Spanish and Mexican rule. Following U.S. annexation of Texas, Mexican troops had withdrawn deep into Mexican territory and taken up positions south and west of the Rio Grande. Nothing in Spanish, Mexican, U.S. or international law suggested that the territory between the Nueces and the Rio Grande was a part of Texas, let alone a part of the United States. In his efforts to provoke the Mexicans, Polk had ordered U.S. troops to penetrate far beyond the Nueces, to the banks of the Rio Grande. He also had ordered U.S.

naval forces to blockade the mouth of the river—as indisputable an act of war, in terms of international law, as President Reagan's later minings of Nicaraguan ports.

Finally these U.S. provocations did goad the Mexicans into a response. It was a minor skirmish inside Mexico between Mexican and U.S. troops that permitted the President to rush to Congress with his allegation that "after reiterated menaces, Mexico has passed the boundary of the United States, has invaded our territory and shed American blood on American soil."

Julius Pratt's comment on the effect on Congress of Polk's war conspiracy might well be a comment on some much more recent presidential attempts to stampede both Congress and public opinion into supporting unprovoked military operations in foreign countries:

> The bulk of the message [demanding a declaration of war] was as Polk had planned it prior to the coming of the news from the Rio Grande—a summary of Mexican offenses against the United States, with emphasis upon her "breach of faith. . . ."

> [But h]ad Polk sent his contemplated message to Congress before the clash of arms on the Rio Grande was known, or had there been no such clash, there would almost certainly have been a long and bitter fight over the proposed declaration of war . . . [T]he shedding of American blood on "American soil". . . supplied the necessary emotional element to give Polk the war he desired. Within two days Congress, by a vote of 173 to 14 in the House and 42 to 2 in the Senate, had declared that a state of war existed "by the act of the Republic of Mexico," had authorized the President to call out fifty thousand volunteers, and had appropriated ten million dollars for military and naval expenditures.

> Thus to the American public, unacquainted with the deliberations in Polk's cabinet, the ostensible cause of the war with Mexico was the Mexican attack. . . .

A war to defend Texas could be justified by an attack on Texas, however spurious. But what could be used to justify the general assault on Mexico that followed, let alone the theft of half that country's territory?

Some deeper menace, above all some higher authority, would be necessary to transmute Polk's war of aggression into a crusade to extend liberty. The President provided an answer familiar enough in our own time: All this was necessary, Polk explained in a message sent to Congress less than six months before the attack, not merely because our national security required it; the hallowed principles of our forebears demanded it.

"Near a quarter of a century ago," Polk reminded Congress,

> the principle was distinctly announced to the world, in the annual message of one of my predecessors, that—"The American continents, by the free

and independent condition which they have assumed and maintain, are henceforth not to be considered as subjects for future colonization by any European powers."

Polk continued:

This principle will apply with greatly increased force should any European power attempt to establish any new colony in North America. In the existing circumstances of the world the present is deemed a proper occasion to reiterate and reaffirm the principle avowed by Mr. Monroe and to state my cordial concurrence in its wisdom and sound policy.

Polk's invocation of Monroe was portentous, but even at the time its meaning was mysterious. By the end of 1845, where, indeed how, could "any European power attempt to establish any new colony in North America"? The Russians already had Alaska; the Spanish retained Cuba. Britain's presence in Oregon, much as it vexed the Polk administration, was by no means new. Outside Central America and the Caribbean, all that remained of North America was the republic of Mexico. And as the Mexicans, along with everyone else, fully realized, by then the great threat there did not come from Europe. It came from the United States itself.

The fact of the matter is that President Polk had convinced himself that the British conspiracy threatened not just U.S. rights in Oregon, but Mexico's rights in California, too. Perkins explains:

Polk looked with dark suspicion upon the machinations of Great Britain in the Far West. Sinister rumors came from the American Consul at Monterey of British agents whose presence boded no good. . . . Polk definitely told Senator Benton of Missouri that he meant to reassert "Mr. Monroe's doctrine against permitting foreign colonization, and that in doing this he had California and the very fine bay of San Francisco as much in view as Oregon."

What better way to save California from the British than to conquer it ourselves?

Initially at least, even Polk's own administration was manipulated to imagine the United States was fighting a strictly limited and defensive war. Hardly was war declared, for example, than Polk's Secretary of State (and future President), James Buchanan, publicly proposed that Mexico and the United States speedily negotiate "a peace just and honorable for both parties." "In going to war," Buchanan informed U.S. diplomats in a confidential memorandum, "we did not do so with a view to acquire California or New Mexico or any other portion of the Mexican territory." But hardly for the last time did the Department of State find itself unaware of the real foreign policy of the United States. Polk not only had managed to deceive public opinion and Congress. Like Lyndon Johnson with the Gulf of Tonkin incident and Richard Nixon with his secret bombing of Cambodia, he had managed to dupe his own administration as well: with the declaration of war safely in his pocket, Polk curtly ordered his Secretary of State to delete all talk of "peace just and honorable" from his messages. Soon Buchanan, no less than some latter-day Washington survivors, was "on team," informing the Mexicans that their obduracy gave the United States no choice but "to prosecute the war with vigor." The United States pushed onward—toward a victory that would be both unjust and dishonorable.

When all the underlying historical causes of the Mexican War are given their full due, one is left with a very simple reason why the Mexican War occurred when it did, unfolded as it did and produced the results it did. President James Knox Polk, as his own diaries reveal, all along had intended it that way—and in a rehearsal for the problems created by the "imperial presidency" of much later times, he had used every tool of the presidency, both legitimate and illegitimate, to get the war he wanted.

Constitutionally, therefore, the Mexican War—as Americans as antithetical as Lincoln and Calhoun were quick to realize—was as much a war of presidential aggrandizement as it was a war of territorial aggression. Long after President Polk was forgotten, Polk's war, and all the other presidential wars that followed, continued to pose the question Lincoln had raised in the House of Representatives.

If the executive branch of the federal government can make war single-handedly, what can it not do? What effective check on its power can the other branches of government, let alone individual citizens, really have? "We have already given . . . one effectual check to the dog of war," Thomas Jefferson had written of the war-making provision of the Constitution, "by transferring the power of letting him loose from the executive to the legislative body, from those who are to spend to those who are to pay."

What was the result of Polk's upsetting not merely the strategic balance of power in North America, but the constitutional balance of power in Washington as well?

"[W]e shall forever be involved in wars." Even today Calhoun's prophecy never ceases to come true.

* * *

What is the meaning of freedom in a country like the United States, when being an American is no longer a matter of free choice, only the result of conquest? The existence of slavery and the dispossession of the Indians had always mocked this particular American "principle." And well before Polk conquered New Mexico and California, Jefferson, Monroe and Tyler, with their acquisitions of Louisiana, Florida and Texas, had certainly disregarded the fundamental law of American nationalism: that to be an American was to be a person (or a descendant of a person) who had chosen to be an American. The American illusion that the expansion of the United States is synonomous with the expansion of liberty all along has been rebutted by a largely forgotten fact. Not once in our history has the territorial expansion of this nation occurred with the consent of the people we Americans have chosen to govern. Like the inhabitants of Florida and Louisiana, the peoples of New Mexico, California, Oregon, Alaska, Hawaii, Puerto Rico and the Philippines would never be given the option of deciding to be Americans, or to live under American rule. Instead, the growth of the United States, like that of all other great powers, was "founded in conquest."

Yet for all its misrepresentations, Adams's Fourth of July epiphany to freedom had defined what was, and still is, the great glory of American nationalism, no matter how much events periodically tarnish that glory. Even when the territory of the United States was expanded by conquest, the government of the United States did not rest on a foundation of oppression, but on "the unalienable sovereignty of the people." The liberties of Americans, even when not all Americans shared those liberties, did not come "as a donation from their sovereigns." They flowed from a "single, plain and almost self-evident principle—that man has a right to the exercise of his own reason."

"Her glory is not *dominion,*" Adams had declared of the United States, "but *liberty.*" Of all the proud boasts Adams hurled at the Old World in 1821, the proudest was that the United States, unlike Great Britain and the Europeans, "without a single exception, respected the independence of other nations. . . ."

"GO THOU, AND DO LIKEWISE." With that injunction had the New World orator concluded his sermon on liberty to the monarchies of Europe.

Yet now, only twenty-six years later, it was the United States that had gone and done likewise. The war between the republics of Mexico and the United States completely rebutted the fantasy that revolution could overthrow the international system of perpetual rivalry that dominates world events in every age, whatever the ideology. The end of colonial rule in the New World had only unleashed the same nationalist conflicts that for so long had pitted the independent nations of Europe against each other. In the New World, too, the great tribalism that had governed events in Europe for so many centuries was destined to be the sovereign of events.

In California and New Mexico, the Americans, as in so many other places later, expected to be welcomed as liberators. Instead they soon found themselves embroiled in a war against the very people they imagined they were "saving." Within three months of the arrival of the Yankee conquistadors, all of southern California had risen against the Americans. A few months later, even stiffer resistance to the Americans arose in New Mexico. The American governor and other U.S. officials were killed in a popular uprising. There, as in California, "the area of freedom" was secured only by an American counterinsurgency campaign that terrorized the local population into submission.

As the Declaration of Independence itself proclaimed, free choice was the essence of Americanism. With his armed assault on the principle of self-determination, Polk not only had violated the principles of Monroe in the name of the "Monroe Doctrine"; in the name of expanding "freedom," he had trampled on the principles of the Declaration of Independence, thus raising a question that would be even more fateful for the United States than it was for Mexico.

If the President had the right to extend the Union by conquest, did he not also have the right to preserve the Union through war? Less than fifteen years later, the same Southerners who had so strongly supported "extending the area of freedom" by force would learn the answer to that question.

The precedents Polk's actions established for future U.S. actions clearly emerge from a consideration of the events of the 1840s. But it is useful to specify them here because, even though we seldom realize it, they play such a determining role in our current foreign military adventures.

Polk's foreign policy—a combination of arrogance toward the weak and accommodation with the mighty—in fact was an outgrowth of the divisions, tensions and debates inside the United States, rather than the product of any external "crisis" or "threat." Some Americans (mostly in the South) had the vision of the United States as a confederation of regions largely autonomous one from the other and capable of tolerating the greatest diversity of customs, including slavery. Other Americans (mostly in the North) believed in a much more integral form of union; they even believed that, at least at home, liberty really was indivisible and that a nation could not exist "half slave, half free."

As events ultimately would demonstrate, there was no philosophical or political answer to the question that sectionalism posed. There was only a military answer. But an entire generation of American nationalists tried to find an answer, and Polk was the quintessential American nationalist in that his foreign policy derived entirely from the exigencies of the overriding domestic political need in the United States in that period: somehow to satisfy and thus balance the ambitions of both the South and the North.

Similar internal disputes over the nature of our national identity underlay the foreign-policy debates of 1812 and 1823, and the same, if anything is even more true of the debates that periodically erupt between the "hawks" and the "doves" in our own time. Almost all our great national divisions over foreign military intervention are hardly limited to divisions over the nature of events in Vietnam or Nicaragua, Cambodia or El Salvador; they are debates over the nature of American nationalism.

Shall we be the policeman of Southeast Asia or Central America (that is, have "law and order" at home)? Shall we unleash the CIA on the "Communists" overseas (that is, shall we unleash the FBI on "subversives" at home)? Will we have "a strong defense" (that is, domestic economic policies that distribute wealth upward and into the hands of the "military-industrial complex")? Or will we pursue a policy of "human rights" (if not necessarily for foreigners, then at least for ourselves)? U.S. presidential politics provided the personification of one side of this permanent American debate in the 1972 candidacy of George McGovern—an antiwar candidate whose philosophical agenda was hardly limited to ending the war in Indochina. Presidential politics provided an equally striking personification of the opposite pole in American nationalism in the 1980 candidacy of Ronald Reagan—a President whose commitment to defending the privileges of economic and military elites against "communism" has hardly been limited to El Salvador.

The most interesting figures in our history, however, are not those who represent the ideological extremes of American nationalism. The most interesting ones are those who try to reconcile our contradictions.

Lyndon Johnson was to our time what James Knox Polk was to the period before the Civil War, with one enormous difference: Johnson failed in the short run, while Polk's failure became evident only with the passage of time. Johnson tried to satisfy the "hawks" with a war in Vietnam and the "doves" with a war on poverty at home. His reward was not merely the Tet Offensive, but the riots that scorched nearly every inner city in America. As for Polk, he proved that even when we conquer others we cannot conquer the divisions within ourselves. Militarily, Polk was one of the most successful presidents in U.S. history. But he was a failure where it really mattered: he failed to halt the tragic evolution of this country toward the Civil War.

In 1846, as in 1823 and 1965, 1812 and 1983, the domination of the conspiracy theory of history over the mind of official America was truly striking to behold. Why should Tecumseh oppose us in 1811, Sandino oppose us in 1927; why should so many others oppose what we Americans do in El Salvador and Grenada?

Changing the names of invasion, plunder and conquest does not change the nature of those actions—or disguise that nature to the victims. But, throughout American history, American doctrine has ceaselessly been challenged by a heretical, truly subversive fact: If we are good, and if it is the destiny of good to triumph, how is it that (even when we win) we Americans still find ourselves inhabiting a world of war, torture, terror, exploitation, cruelty? Like the Jehovah of Genesis, we Americans are both inherently omnipotent and oddly impotent. Since we are definitionally free of responsibility for the existence of evil, some other—some sinister, powerful and "foreign"—force must be to blame.

Such was the American explanation for the fact that the Indians and the Mexicans resisted us in the nineteenth century. And it is still the explanation our leaders give us today for the fact that others see only carnage, not redemption, in what we do.

The projection of conspiratorial evil on our adversaries has been one of the essential themes of American nationalism. But the domino theory has been no less indispensable in justifying our actions to ourselves. For even if those we oppose in places like El Salvador do happen to be evil, why should that concern us if their machinations pose no threat to the United States?

"Linkage," the phrase that enjoyed such vogue in the Nixon-Kissinger years, is what repeatedly has allowed our leaders, at so many points in our history, not only to violate our principles in the guise of defending them, but to violate them in areas where our national interests and security have not been engaged at all. Just as the supposed "machination of Great Britain" filled President Polk with "dark suspicion," so in 1983 President Reagan decided it was "no coincidence" that U.S. marines should simultaneously be in combat in Grenada and Lebanon. "The events in Lebanon and Grenada," the President told the nation, "though oceans apart, are closely related. Not only has Moscow assisted and encouraged the violence in both countries, but it provides direct support through a network of surrogates and terrorists."

"Whatever happens anywhere in the Americas affects us in this country," President Reagan declared.

If we do not act promptly and decisively in the defense of freedom, new Cubas will arise from the ruins of today's conflicts. We will face more totalitarian regimes, tied militarily to the Soviet Union; more regimes exporting subversion. . . .

But why should that be the case? What frailty lurks in other countries that dooms them to become "new Cubas" if we Americans do not act "promptly and decisively"?

Back in President Polk's time, America's right "to extend the area of freedom," as many Americans saw it, was more than a national right. Our "manifest destiny," it was widely believed, flowed from our racial superiority over those we conquered. "Liberty" was only another word for the triumph of the fair-skinned over the dark, for as one member of the House of Representatives proclaimed, "[T]he principles of civil liberty . . . march *pari passu* with the migrations of the Anglo-Saxon race." In our own time, overt racism is inadmissible. But assertions of inherent American national superiority are a different matter. As President Nixon put it in 1970, the United States,

because of its strength, its history and its concern for human dignity . . . occupies a special place in the world. Peace and progress are impossible without a major American role.

Yet not even the combination of belief that our adversaries are evil and that the United States "occupies a special place in the world" really suffices to explain why the "loss" of Vietnam or El Salvador should imperil the whole world, including us. Some other factor is necessary to sustain the inner logic of such actions.

"We did not choose to be the guardians at the gate," Johnson said in 1965 after he had escalated Kennedy's Vietnam intervention into a full-scale war, "but there is no one else."

It is this deep American conviction that "there is no one else"—the incapacity to perceive others as human beings at all except to the extent they are extensions of us—that, more than any other factor in our national consciousness, links our earliest nationhood with our conduct today as a superpower. What connects the "reds" of the American frontier with the "reds" of El Salvador is that so far as the United States is concerned, killing them is not really a crime at all, because, at bottom, our victims, by opposing us, have forfeited any possibility of acquiring human rights, which can flow only from us.

"There is no alternative to United States leadership," Johnson advised Kennedy, and this was a deep conviction Johnson brought to the conduct of his own presidency—and his own war. But if there really is "no alternative" to us Americans, a very important question arises: what if we Americans are not there "to control, plan, direct and exact results"? In 1965, Johnson conjured up the same dark catastrophe that later haunted Nixon, which Reagan later invoked. "The battle would be renewed in one country and then another country," Johnson predicted.

> If we are driven from the field in Vietnam, then no nation can ever again have the same confidence in American promise or in American protection . . . and an Asia so threatened by Communist domination would certainly imperil the security of the United States itself.

The conspiracy theory and the domino theory are so completely intertwined in the American view of the world that it is impossible to separate them in practice. Yet, in order to understand why the United States acts as it does, it is necessary to understand that they are two quite different things.

The conspiracy theory flows from the doctrine of American virtue: since we Americans define goodness, those who oppose us are definitionally evil.

The domino theory flows from the doctrine of American superiority: since there "is no alternative to United States leadership," even those who do accept our leadership are inherently inferior.

The conspiracy theory explains why we project such hostility on our adversaries; the domino theory explains the contempt that so consistently colors our relationships with our friends. The Salvadorans and the Vietnamese, the Organization of Eastern Caribbean States and NATO—all are really the same, since none of them means anything unless we Americans are there "to control, plan, direct and exact results."

In Asia, after World War II, why did the United States not only imagine that the Soviet Union was capable of communizing the immensity of Asia, but that U.S. troops and firepower could "save" it? The whole objective of the Asian liberation movements—whether they were led by Marxists, as in China and Vietnam, or by non-Communists, as in India and Indonesia—was to terminate, not cast into new forms, centuries of overlordship by outside powers. But, once again, we were unable to grasp that leaders like Mao, Ho Chi Minh, Sukarno and Nehru were not "against" us, only that they had fought, and were continuing to fight, for causes of their own.

As we have seen, the "loss" of China, more than any other single event, convinced Americans not only that the Soviets were conspiring to impose on all Asia the "intolerable . . . new imperialist colonialism of communism," as John Foster Dulles called it, but that the Asians were incompetent to stop them. Yet, in 1960, even before we began our war in Indochina, China expelled its Soviet advisers, and within four years China exploded its first atomic bomb—a weapon clearly aimed at the Soviet Union, not the United States. Far from being the first "domino" to fall into Moscow's hands, China had become a continental counterweight to Soviet influence in Asia, and a gargantuan shield separating the Soviet Union from the rest of Asia. The Soviet expulsion from China was possibly the single most important geopolitical event since the end of World War II—and it cost the Soviet Union immeasurably more than our own "loss" of Indochina ever could cost us. After World War II, Asia was highly resistant to control by either superpower, and as events also demonstrated, the domino theory did not work even among the Asians themselves.

Instead, China and India, Indonesia and Vietnam all became, in spite of their differing ideologies, regional powers with regional concerns and influence. Less than a decade after the Vietnam War, an impressively stable international system had taken hold in the Far East—even though U.S. troops and bombers were gone from the scene. The non-Communist nations of Southeast Asia were enjoying remarkable "peace and progress," although that was supposed to have been "impossible without a major American role." Meanwhile China iteslf had become, in strategic terms, a de facto ally of the United States. It was the U.S. defeat in Indochina that finally gave the natural balance of power in Asia the chance to reassert itself.

If Europe, with its nearly forty years of general peace, demonstrates the irrelevance of the conspiracy theory and Asia the irrelevance of the domino theory, the continuing travails of Latin America reveal something else: not only how impervious these two great doctrines of American nationalism are to correction by reality, but how thoroughly our actions are still infused with a deep American faith in our neighbors' inferiority.

Both in 1846 and later, America's "destiny" really did hinge on the outcome of the foreign-policy disputes in Washington—though not in the sense either Polk or Nixon intended. For both John C. Calhoun in 1823 and James Knox Polk in 1846—as for Lyndon Johnson and Ronald Reagan later—the Holy Alliance and the British, the "Sino-Soviet bloc" and the Vietcong, the Russians and the Cubans were more than adversaries. They were what made events intelligible. If only "they" could be stopped, then events in South

America and California, in South Vietnam and Central America, all would unfold exactly as America imagined they should.

Fortunately such an approach to the world, for all its appeal in the United States, seldom has gone uncontested in this country. Indeed, at times, proponents of an entirely different philosophy of world affairs have achieved notable success. In 1823, no "Monroe Doctrine" was proclaimed, precisely because Adams and Monroe refused to act on the assumption that the Holy Alliance was the kind of "mystical, Messianic movement" Kennan later claimed the Soviet Union to be. During the Mexican War, Abraham Lincoln's "spot resolutions"—so called because they demanded that Polk reveal the exact spot where the alleged aggression had occurred—epitomized the critical response the executive claims of foreign conspiracy have provoked in Congress during most of our presidential wars. Nixon's great success in China, where he was able to cast aside the conspiracy and domino theories, was the obverse of his great failure in Indochina, where he was never able to free himself from doctrine.

Whether it is the question of who "lost" China or who started the Korean War, whether the United States should "defend freedom" in Central America or Indochina, or whether the United States should pursue a policy of détente or "containment" toward the Soviet Union, most of the great debates in U.S. foreign policy in fact come down to a philosophical, indeed an epistemological question.

In order to act effectively in a place like El Salvador, do we Americans have to understand El Salvador? Or are the complexities of such places irrelevant to a single, immense and very simple factor: what President Reagan, for example, sees as the menace of "a larger imperialistic plan"?

Whatever the ostensible subject, it became clear as Reagan's presidency unfolded that almost all his foreign-policy statements really dealt with only one subject: the same Soviet "threat" that at one time or another he has seen lurking behind, and explaining, phenomena as diverse as the Panama Canal treaties and Islamic terrorism in the Middle East.

From such a viewpoint, all that matters is that "Soviet conspiracy" stands in the way of what the United States has the right to do in the world. All else is meaningless, and to suggest otherwise not only is to confuse the issue, but to aid and abet America's enemies as well.

President Reagan's ambassador to the United Nations, Jeane J. Kirkpatrick, summed up this view well in late 1983, when she addressed a meeting in New York held to honor Lech Walesa. Unsurprisingly, no one at the meeting praised what the Soviet Union had done in Poland. But, for Ambassador Kirkpatrick, as for President Reagan, Soviet actions in Poland really had very little specifically to do with that country. They were merely a particular manifestation of a universal—and unquestionable—axiom: that the Soviets were determined to destroy freedom everywhere. Nicaragua, Angola, Benin, Ghana, the Congo, Mozambique, Guinea-Bissau, Cuba, South Yemen, Syria and Ethiopia—events in all those countries, Kirkpatrick contended, demonstrated that the Soviet Union's commitment to terrorism, repression and conquest was limitless. As she saw it, the PLO and Libya, as much as East Germany and Bulgaria, were "parts of the Soviets' worldwide empire."

Ambassador Kirkpatrick's list of countries nonetheless raised an important question: if the Soviet threat really was as pervasive as she contended, how—and why—was it that so many of the countries she named had not wound up under Soviet domination at all? Of all the Third World nations she mentioned, only Cuba was tied militarily to the Soviet Union in the sense that the Warsaw Pact nations are.

Ambassador Kirkpatrick replied only indirectly: even to ask such questions, she suggested, was illegitimate. "The record is clear," she told her audience. "There is no reasonable room today for misunderstanding that record." She went further. The "greatest single obstacle" to an effective anti-Soviet policy in the United States was "an intellectual confusion that surrounds the moral worth of our own society and an intellectual confusion that surrounds the nature of our greatest adversary, the Soviet Union."

Why, throughout American history, does one so often encounter not merely an unwillingness to make distinctions, but the conviction that to make distinctions—between Ghana and Poland, between Bulgaria and the PLO—is in itself an "obstacle" to effective U.S. foreign policy?

One answer is that the doctrine of absolute American good and its necessary corollary, the doctrine of our opponents' absolute evil, really is a doctrine. And as is the case with all absolutist doctrines, to entertain the possibility that the doctrine does not apply universally is to accept the possibility that the doctrine may not apply at all. If Soviet evil does not explain the insurgency in El Salvador, is it possible that Soviet evil also does not explain events in Guinea-Bissau and Syria? And if, in fact, Soviet evil does not explain much of anything anywhere, why are we spending a quarter trillion dollars a year to "contain" the Soviet "threat"?

Questions about the "moral worth of our own society" are even more subversive. Could it be that our involvement in the matanza in El Salvador is morally indefensible, that our invasion of Grenada violates international law? Could it be that we Americans, no less than the Russians, are a worldwide menace to the independence of others? Could our own unremitting hostility help explain why Cuba and Vietnam, to a greater extent than any other Third World countries, have tied themselves to the Soviet Union?

Even to tolerate the admissibility of such questions starts the dominoes toppling, until one is forced to ask, Could it be that most of what we do to "defend freedom" around the world is usually irrelevant, and often detrimental both to the cause of freedom and to the national defense of the United States as well?

The fact that the conspiracy theory of history cannot explain history does not mean that real conspiracies never arise or that they never have an important influence on events. The limitations of the domino theory do not mean that small events do not sometimes cast very long shadows over much larger developments.

Back in the early 1940s, as we have seen, Americans were as vigilant against Nazi subversion in Latin America as they would be against "Communist subversion" there later. Yet at that time we were blind to a real anti-American conspiracy that was unfolding—not in Nicaragua or Mexico, but in Tokyo. This conspiracy would find its fulfillment in the attack on Pearl Harbor.

In 1981, as El Salvador and "Communist interference" there came to dominate foreign-policy discourse in Washington, a real Soviet conspiracy to destroy freedom was afoot. But it threatened Poland, not El Salvador.

Eastern Europe lies deep within the Soviet sphere of influence, just as Central America clearly falls within the sphere of influence of the United States. Nonetheless a coherent U.S. policy toward Poland might have had some marginal influence on the survival of the freedoms the Solidarity movement briefly established. Instead, the United States, while tilting at windmills in Central America, played into the hands of the Soviet Union in Eastern Europe. Poland's problems, officials of the Reagan administration said over and over again, should be solved "by the Poles themselves." Yet when the Soviets took this as a cue that the Soviet-controlled Polish Army and secret police were free to crush Solidarity, there was, as always, a sense of betrayal in Washington—followed by no substantive U.S. reprisals of any kind.

Killing Salvadorans had not liberated Poland. Nor had gunboat diplomacy done anything to advance the peace process in the Middle East—as the charred bodies of the U.S. marines killed in Beirut revealed with sickening clarity in 1983.

A less charitable interpretation, of course, holds that our leaders are better off obsessed with the Grenadas and El Salvadors of the world, because events there lack the capacity to threaten us in any really serious way, as our long Vietnam adventure wound up proving: had our national security, let alone our national survival, actually depended, to the extent our leaders pretended, on the outcome of what we did in Indochina, the United States would be in a most perilous situation now, if indeed we still existed as an independent nation at all.

Whether the year is 1984 or 1846, the President Reagan or Polk, history repeatedly demonstrates the costs to the United States of a foreign policy founded upon undiscriminating doctrine. No number of invocations of "Manifest Destiny" could defend the United States against the fundamental threat of President Polk's time, which was the deepening sectionalism that soon would cost hundreds of thousands of Americans their lives.

The same is true today: Will our time be remembered, for all its chaos and inequities, as an age of greater plenty and freedom than the world previously has known? Or will it be remembered, if there is anyone to remember it, as the moment when Icarus fell and Prometheus was consumed by his own fire? Whatever the fate of our struggle to "save" Central America, it will not save us from the real threats—notably the threat of nuclear catastrophe—that darken the horizon of our own era. That work of redemption will require quite a different kind of "commitment," should our leaders ever find time for it: a commitment to confronting the real threats to our security, to our very survival, even if the price is that our doctrines be shattered.

In that sense, we Americans really are a people of destiny.

Since the world, in fact, is full of complexities and ambiguities, the periodic attempts of our leaders to explain—and justify—everything in terms of sinister conspiracies and toppling dominoes establishes another theme linking Polk's war with so many other presidential wars. This is the question of our leaders' integrity.

Surely President Polk knew the British had no designs on California. Surely Lyndon Johnson knew he was lying when he purported that if Saigon fell the rest of Asia would fall too. Surely even Ronald Reagan knew the insurrection in El Salvador was not invented in Moscow, and shipped there, via Cuba—and that mass murder supported and condoned by the United States would not be justifiable even if it were.

Such statements are heard whenever our presidents set out to battle the conspirators and prop up the dominoes.

With the possible exception of Richard Nixon, Polk may have been the President with the least compunction about using the White House as a platform for the most outrageous deceptions. Yet we have no reason to suppose that Polk himself regarded his war of aggression, and all that flowed from it, as anything less than an unalloyed triumph of American liberty.

Like Polk in 1846, Nixon in 1970 made an irrevocable commitment to force in the attempt to fulfill his particular vision of the United States.

"I would rather be a one-term President and do what I believe is right than to be a two-term President at the cost of seeing America become a second-rate power," Nixon said in April 1970, when he announced the Cambodia invasion:

If, when the chips are down, the world's most powerful nation, the United States of America, acts like a pitiful, helpless giant, the forces of totalitarianism and anarchy will threaten free nations and free institutions throughout the world.

For Polk the fulfillment of our national destiny was a matter of territory: once Oregon and California were ours, America's moral and spiritual principles inevitably would prevail. By Nixon's time, the dominoes in Southeast Asia had merged with the dominoes of the American psyche. If the United States did not continue the Indochina War, Nixon declared in late 1969,

Southeast Asia would be lost. "Far more dangerous," he said, "we would lose confidence in ourselves."

As with Polk, we possess no evidence suggesting that Nixon ever deviated from the belief that we fought in Vietnam for a just and honorable cause—or that he ever doubted that the key to American success lay in how we dealt with the conspiracy he perceived behind the conflict. In the 1950s, as Vice President, he had favored direct U.S. military intervention in Indochina long before it occurred. In the 1960s, during his long march across the political wilderness, Nixon repeatedly made it clear that he believed the road to "peace with honor" ran through such neutral countries as Cambodia, just as Polk had believed the road to manifest destiny ran through Veracruz.

In April 1964, for example, at a time when Lyndon Johnson's "limited" war in Vietnam still barred U.S. military operations in neighboring countries, Nixon told a New York audience that "catering to neutrals" would never win the war. Only by attacking the "sanctuaries," he said, could the United States defeat the Vietcong and Hanoi. "Nixon Asks Raids on Reds in Asia," the New York *Times* dutifully reported on an inside page.

Yet six years later, when first the Cambodia invasion, then Nixon's Laos invasion, covered the front pages of every newspaper in this country, Americans felt deceived, betrayed. Nixon's secret "plan to end the war" was only a plan to win the war by prolonging it and expanding it.

Like Polk, Nixon was certainly guilty of concealing the contradictions of his policy: No less than the paeans to "Manifest Destiny," the talk in the Nixon White House about "peace with honor" really amounted to an effort to convince the American people that, even after My Lai, there was no contradiction between our principles and our ambitions—that we still somehow could achieve victory without dishonor. The Vietnamization program was a classic case of American fantasy in action: We could both "bring the boys home" and "save" South Vietnam—if only we let President Nixon do what he wanted.

By the time Nixon left office, the American tendency to explain all we dislike in terms of a sinister conspiracy no longer was directed outward: the White House had replaced the Kremlin as the font of all that was deceitful, unprincipled—evil—in the world.

Yet the character of Richard Nixon cannot explain the success with which he deceived the nation, however much it contributes to an understanding of how he deceived himself. Even as he was running for President in 1968, with his "plan to end the war" in Vietnam, the Nixon record made it manifest he had never confronted the fundamental contradiction in what we were attempting there.

The same was true of Ronald Reagan. Prior to his election there was nothing in his public record to suggest that he perceived the manifold complexities of El Salvador and the rest of the world as anything other than vindicating the simplistic, black-and-white, good-versus-evil universe he conjured up in his campaign speeches. Indeed, as had been the case with Polk, that was the principal reason Reagan had been elected President of the United States.

We really should not be surprised when our presidents actually behave, in such places as El Salvador, as though there were no contradiction between killing people and liberating them, because those of us who elect such leaders also demonstrate a deep aversion to confronting such contradictions—and an equally deep aversion to voting for politicians who remind us of them.

It may be no exaggeration to say that Reagan's essential function—certainly his most obvious skill—as President has been that of convincing millions of Americans that there was no antithesis between illusion and reality and, as the President's television performances have made clear, this was a task he performed with great success.

On President Reagan's orders, we aided and abetted terrorism in the name of "antiterrorism." We attacked sovereign nations in the name of defending national sovereignty. We spread chaos and suffering in the name of decency and progress.

Yet all these contradictions were wafted away whenever President Reagan spoke. On the television screen there flickered an illusion of rationality and principle in the conduct of our foreign affairs—and for millions of Americans, perhaps a majority of them, this fantasy has been far more real than the cadavers and vultures would ever be.

It no doubt is revealing that, in the age of television, we Americans should have chosen an actor for our President. Yet in his carefully scripted performances, Ronald Reagan did no more or less than what John Quincy Adams did in his performance in the House chamber back in 1821.

The truth—and it is a very important one about the United States—is that we Americans historically have shown a strong preference for leaders who are careful to nurture our illusion of virtue, even as they fulfill our ambitions by violating the principles we suppose they are defending.

The really great revelation of the Pentagon Papers, the Watergate tapes and the Freedom of Information Act is not how often our leaders have deceived us, but how often they have deceived themselves.

* * *

Another continuity linking the Age of Manifest Destiny with our own is that on both occasions it has been the fate of Latin America to be a kind of kaleidoscope which our leaders twist and turn, and hold up to various lights, until they find the pattern they want.

"Manifest Destiny" was what Americans wanted to perceive in 1846. Even as Polk invoked the principles of Monroe, he had only a policy of American conquest in Latin America, combined with a complementary policy of accommodation with the British. In fact, even as Polk feigned reassertion of Monroe's principles, he withdrew from Latin America even Monroe's rhetorical endorsement of hemispheric independence. As Polk himself explicitly put it, it was his "policy that no future European colony or dominion shall with our consent be planted or established on any part of the *North* American continent [emphasis supplied]." He thus made explicit the self-centeredness that had lain at the heart of the Monroe policy. Should the nations of South America find themselves the victims of European aggression, they could count on no help from the United States.

Central America, of course, is "part of the North American continent." And in 1846, as Perkins relates, the Nicaraguans, following Polk's lead, invoked "the spirit of the Monroe Doctrine" and asked for U.S. support against British encroachment along the Miskito Coast. The same year, the Colombians, fearful of British encroachment in Panama,

> called attention to the repeated declarations of American statesmen with regard to European intervention and colonization in the New World, and urged the United States to assume the leadership of an American confederation, opposing to the avaricious proposals of Europe the human and disinterested principles of the young democracies of the New World.

It bespoke the essence of the "Monroe Doctrine," as applied not only by Polk but by most of his successors, that the United States did not bother to respond to the Nicaraguan appeal at all.

The Colombians fared little better. In 1846, President Polk did take a few moments off from his war intrigue against Mexico and his secret diplomacy with Britain to sign, following considerable hesitation, a treaty with Bogota. But if Colombia (then still called New Granada) had hoped the treaty would commit the United States to the defense of Panama against outside aggression, President Polk proved it wrong. The President had been rattling sabers over Texas and Oregon for months. But when it came to Panama, Polk proved more abstentionist than Monroe himself.

The treaty contained no U.S. commitment to help defend the isthmus; nor did it contain even the general statement against European "interposition" that the 1823 statement had. But in return for a U.S. pledge to respect both the territorial integrity of New Granada and the neutrality of any canal built there, President Polk did gain for American citizens the same rights of transit across Panama that the Colombians themselves enjoyed. Even here, U.S. self-interest was not merely the dominant theme in all Polk did; it was the only theme, so far as Latin America was concerned.

What role did Latin America itself play in Polk's grand design? It played the same role that Latin America does today in the Reagan administration's foreign policy—that is to say, no substantive role at all.

In 1846 President Polk, as his private conversations and own diaries make clear, wanted not just Texas, but California and everything between the two territories. Mexico's sole function, then, was to provide the excuse, any excuse, for the course of action Polk already had determined to undertake.

When the Reagan administration took office in 1981, its policymakers knew little of events in Latin America, and they cared about them even less. Yet just as Polk was determined to fulfill our "Manifest Destiny" during his four years in the White House, so the Reagan administration took office with a deep commitment to achieving a quick, dramatic "victory over communism" that would dramatize the new ideological agenda it intended to bring to both U.S. foreign and domestic affairs.

The same has been true throughout most of our history. Corpses can litter the streets of Veracruz, corpses can litter the garbage heaps of San Salvador; the White House and the State Department remain unconcerned. On the contrary, in almost every time, the two main sources of our "Latin America" policy have not been in Latin America at all.

The first source of U.S. policy has always been situated thousands of miles away from Latin America—in our preoccupation with our main transatlantic rival of the moment, whether Great Britain in 1823 and 1846 or the Soviet Union in 1954 and 1983.

As for the second source, it is even more remote—being inside the mind of America, in that swirling compound of American illusions and American ambitions that so often blind us to the rights, even the existence, of others.

The myth of the New World always has been a myth; the reality of great-power balance-of-power politics always has been a reality. British rockets could incinerate American cities in the early-nineteenth century just as Soviet missiles can vaporize them today. In both cases the fundamental task of American statesmanship is clear: to manage our disputes, however grave and intractable, with the power in question in such a way as to avoid military consequences that would utterly outstrip any possible political gain.

What is utterly misplaced is to purport that Latin America does have some transcendental significance for us—while simultaneously treating it as a mere extension of our relations with our principal European rival. El Salvador is a classic case of letting our myths rob our actions of relevance—of the United States pursuing a policy that is not merely entirely destructive but which at bottom really has nothing to do with our own national interest, with the Soviets, and least of all with the realities of El Salvador itself.

That is the main reason for our past and present failures there. And that is the main reason our future relations with that part of the world no doubt will be characterized by continuing failure, no matter how much money and ammunition we expend.

Excluding the War of Independence and the Civil War, the United States has fought eight major wars over the past two hundred years. And with the exception of the War of 1812, not one of those wars has been fought against an enemy that was stronger than the United States. What the Indian nations, the Mexicans, the Spanish, the North Koreans and the Vietnamese all had in common was that they all were, or at least at first seemed to be, pitiably impotent in comparison to us. Only after the Chinese intervened in Korea, and the Tet Offensive demonstrated that Hanoi was a far more formidable adversary than the government in Washington had imagined, did it become clear that the United States had blundered into Asian land wars that were not easily winnable—indeed not winnable at all.

Even in those instances, the United States remained immensely more powerful than its opponents, which makes the American response to the failure to win quick, easy victories in Korea and Vietnam especially illuminating. As during the War of 1812, the prospect of the kind of "long twilight struggle" Kennedy evoked in his inaugural address did not evoke, in the American nation, a determination, as Lyndon Johnson urged, to "stay the course" until victory was won; the fruits of military stalemate were dissension and recrimination.

The two world wars, by different means, also rebuke the notion that we Americans are always the first to leap to the defense of liberty. During World War I, Germany, mighty as it was, by no objective standard was more powerful than the United States. Even during World War II the combined might of the Axis did not exceed our own. And of course there never was any question of the United States fighting those powers single-handedly.

Yet those wars, most especially World War II, raised real questions about the American commitment to defending freedom. Would the United States stand aside while the Nazis raped Austria and Czechoslovakia and then overran Poland, Denmark, Norway, the Low Countries, France, the Balkans and Greece? Would it rise to the "test case" presented by Japan's assault on China?

We all know the answers to those questions. The United States only entered World War I years after the German advance on the western front had been halted and a clear-cut German victory was beyond the realm of military possibility. Even today, no revision of history has yet moderated the judgment that Hitler came as close as any leader to incarnating absolute evil in the world. Yet only the Japanese attack on Pearl Harbor was sufficient to involve the United States in one of the few wars in history where the fate of freedom may actually have hung in the balance.

This reluctance to fight wars in defense of freedom is matched, in American history, by a quite unrealistic expectation of the kinds of freedoms that can flow from war, when we Americans finally do fight them and win them. The illusion that war can lead not just to victory, but to an "extension of the area of freedom," was not just the great American illusion of the Mexican War; it is one of the permanent illusions of American foreign policy.

Of all the major powers involved in World War I, the United States fought the least, suffered the least, and paid the least, in proportion to its population and wealth, in lives and money. Again, during World War II, our sacrifices, while much greater, were minor in comparison to those endured by our allies.

Yet on both occasions Americans acted as though the outcome of war was

—or at least should be—not merely the defeat of the common enemy, but the creation of an American-style global utopia. Linking the negative American reaction to victory in both world wars—a reaction of hysteria, feelings of betrayal and irrational isolationism following World War I; a reaction of hysteria, feelings of betrayal and irrational interventionism following World War II—is an inability to understand that victory, like freedom, legitimately can mean something else to others than it means to us. The Fourteen Points, no matter how earnestly Wilson proclaimed them, could not change the fact that the Allies had not fought a long and arduous war to make Europe "safe for democracy." They had fought longer, harder and suffered much more than we had for reasons and objectives of their own. The same was true following the Second World War. All the Truman, Eisenhower and Nixon doctrines could not change the fact that such leaders as Stalin, Mao Zedong and Ho Chi Minh had fought the Axis to defend their own, quite different principles.

Most Americans, of course, did not see things that way. In fact by the 1940s the American view of the world was not very different from the American view of the western hemisphere in the 1840s. Following World War II, at the very moment when American principles were supposed to be universally triumphant, Americans found themselves confronting a quite different reality, and so also found themselves seized, to the point of national hysteria, by the same subversive doubt that had gripped the nation in 1844: perhaps our manifest destiny was not so manifest after all.

Considering the totality of the evil which the United States imputed to the Soviet Union following World War II, one is tempted to say about Russia what President Polk said about Great Britain: Compromise with such an aggressor could "never for a moment be entertained by the United States without an abandonment" of America's "own self-respect, and the national honor."

Yet the parallel with the past was not limited to the imputation of conspiratorial evil to our main transatlantic rival. Just as no conflict with Great Britain followed Polk's loud denunciations of that country, so in our time, beneath decades of rhetorical denunciation of the Soviet Union, lies a parallel military fact: as we have seen, not once have Americans, in the nearly forty years since the end of World War II, engaged in combat with the armed forces of the Soviet Union.

All power—American and Russian, "free world" and Communist, in 1846 and today—tends to expand, at the expense of the liberty of others, unless it is "contained." But there is another, equally valid truth about power. When "it finds unassailable barriers in its path," American power, not just Russian power, tends to accept "these philosophically and accommodates itself to them," as our own history repeatedly shows.

Beneath all the rhetoric of "Manifest Destiny," there is a very simple reason why President Polk conquered California but would not go to war for "the whole territory of Oregon." It is that in 1846 Mexico was very weak and Great Britain was very strong.

The same is no less true today. In 1983, Grenada, with less than one eighth the territory and less than one seventh the population of Rhode Island, presented the kind of "test case" the United States, with its more than three and a half million square miles of territory and its population of nearly 240 million, has historically found irresistible. Grenada was not invaded because it was a "threat": it was invaded because it was so manifestly incapable even of defending itself.

In comparison to Grenada, Nicaragua was a nation-state of substance—and so the Sandinistas did not have to face an American invasion, only U.S. military, political and economic harassment. And in comparison to Nicaragua, Cuba was a superpower—so Cuba faced no U.S. military harassment at all—only a continuation of the diplomatic and economic boycott begun under President Kennedy. And the Soviet Union? Not even economic sanctions, in the Reagan White House, were considered an appropriate response to Soviet "aggression." Rhetorical denunciation was the great weapon the President of the United States unleashed on Moscow.

The realities of power explain much, and ideology explains very little, of what has happened in Europe and Asia since the end of World War II. The same has been even more true of the western hemisphere for nearly 140 years.

The great importance of Polk's conquest of Mexico, so far as our relations with Latin America are concerned, is that, with the American victory, any possibility of a functioning balance of power among the nations of the New World was forfeited. After 1846, the growing power of the United States created a permanent imbalance of power in the New World that endures even now.

Few Americans—whether they support or oppose our actions in places like El Salvador or Grenada—doubt that, for better or worse, an irrepressible American impulse to "pay any price, bear any burden, meet any hardship, support any friend, oppose any foe" lies at the heart of the foreign conflicts in which we so often find ourselves embroiled. The facts of our history suggest a contrary conclusion: There may be many more "Vietnams," or at least El Salvadors, or at least Grenadas. But we Americans are most unlikely to start World War III, or any other war that involves fighting any enemy capable of posing a real threat to ourselves. Instead the missiles will soar skyward, holocaust will befall the world only because of some fateful forgetfulness.

* * *

Why has James Knox Polk been so forgotten? We Americans have always expected our presidents not just to fulfill our ambitions for us, but to vindicate our faith in our own virtue. A "Monroe Doctrine" served this double purpose well, because it allowed Americans to imagine they were really exporting the Era of Good Feeling even when they inflicted great pain on others. But a "Polk Doctrine"? Like Joseph McCarthy, later, Polk embodied the darker impulses of American nationalism all too well. And so for future Americans it was as though James Knox Polk, like the Indians, had scarcely existed.

Forgetting Polk could not change the massiveness of what he had wrought, for both good and ill, and for both the United States and the rest of the world. From the twin events of 1846—attack on Mexico, settlement with Britain—in fact flow most of the great themes that still dominate America's interaction with the world today.

By gaining for America not just the rather isolated northern window on the Pacific the United States had claimed in Oregon, but an immense Pacific coast nearly as long as its frontage on the Atlantic, Polk's conquest of California revolutionized America's strategic relationship with the world. From a second- or third-rung Atlantic power, really no more consequential than Brazil or the Netherlands, the United States was transformed into a Pacific power second only to Britain itself.

In 1853, only seven years after Polk's attack on Mexico, an even more consequential nation found itself fundamentally transformed as the result of the intrusion of American power. Commodore Perry, at the head of a U.S. fleet, sailed into Yokohama Harbor, ending centuries of Japanese hermitage, commencing Japan's own astonishing ascent—and intertwining the destinies of the two greatest Pacific powers as irrevocably as the Mexican War had merged our destiny with that of Latin America.

Polk was the real author of America's Pacific—and Asian—destiny, and that destiny manifested itself with astonishing speed.

The settlement over Oregon was equally important, because it was another milestone in the emergence of the Anglo-American "special relationship." That the two great English-speaking nations did not go to war in 1846 even today can be described as one of the determining events of modern world history. There is hardly a single major event of the past century—including the outcome of World War II and the development of nuclear weapons—that has not been shaped by the fact that, after Polk's time, an American war with Britain was no longer a real possibility, and that the two countries, once enemies, more and more were willing collaborators.

But of even more pervasive importance than any specific event was the fact that as British power steadily ebbed over the next century, and U.S. power steadily increased, an astonishingly smooth transfer of power occurred from Britain to the United States.

This was not the transfer of power over a specific territory, region or sphere of influence. It was the transfer of power over an entire world system from Britain to the United States. Across the century bracketed by the two dates 1846 and 1946, which on the surface appear to have nothing in common, this transfer of power was the single most important event in the history of the world. Beginning with the Oregon settlement in 1846, U.S. power first supple-mented and then gradually replaced British power almost everywhere, until, exactly a century later, the process—as was manifest in 1946—was complete. From the Middle East and Western Europe to the Far East and the South Pacific, an entire world that once had been patrolled by the Royal Navy, conducted its business in the King's English, and settled its accounts in pounds sterling, was now a world of American GIs, American slang, U.S. dollars—and American nuclear weapons.

All that, however, even now remains secondary to the most important consequence of Polk's presidency: he unleashed changes inside the United States even more dramatic, more fateful and more enduring than the changes America itself, over the next century, would unleash on the world.

The nature of this internal American metamorphosis became ominously clear almost as soon as the war with Mexico started. Polk, like Clay before him, had imagined that "a successful war" would unite the nation, even at the cost of creating "a military power and influence." Polk's grand design had possessed, if nothing else, the gargantuan logic of simplicity applied on a continental scale. The acquisition of Oregon, he calculated, would satisfy the North, while the annexation of California would fulfill the ambitions of the South. And with both sections satisfied, the United States would fulfill its continental destiny. Thanks to the Mexican War, the American nation would extend from ocean to ocean—united, yet divided, from the Atlantic to the Pacific, between slave states and free.

Polk had calculated well in his dealings with Mexico and Britain. But like some other wartime presidents, he had left a most volatile factor out of his equation: the passionate divisions within the United States his war was sure to arouse. Barely had the war to "extend the area of freedom" begun when the United States was divided by the oldest, deepest, darkest division in American life, the division over slavery.

Even after the Mexican War, "respectable" politicians—including John Quincy Adams and Abraham Lincoln—still considered slavery, as Lincoln himself would put it in his 1861 inaugural address, an institution that the federal government had "no lawful right" to circumscribe "in the states where it exists."

But what of the new states to be formed out of the territories seized from Mexico? Lincoln summed up the crisis of American nationalism that Polk's war against Mexico had provoked:

> *May* Congress prohibit slavery in the Territories? The Constitution does not expressly say. *Must* Congress protect slavery in the Territories? The Constitution does not expressly say.

Even as U.S. forces seized New Mexico and California, many Northerners saw no triumph for liberty, no fulfillment of our "Manifest Destiny"—only a betrayal of American principles and the triumph of a southern plot to expand the moral abomination of slavery to the Pacific coast.

"They just want this Californy/So's to lug new slave-states in," ran James Russell Lowell's bitter verse. And, it must be added, most Southerners saw things exactly the same way. No one, North or South, denied that the object of conquest was "bigger pens to cram with slaves." It was only the significance of this objective that tore America asunder. The South saw salvation shimmering in southern California. But in those vast new conquests, Northerners like Lowell perceived only "a grand gret cemetary/Fer the barthrights of our race."

Who was right? In his eagerness to fulfill America's "Manifest Destiny," Polk had touched off one of the most fateful disputes in American history—a dispute all the more illuminating because, from beginning to end, it was grounded on utter fantasy on both sides.

Fourteen years before the electoral votes of California would help elect Lincoln President, Northerners like Lincoln opposed Polk's war because they believed annexation of California would intolerably strengthen the South's power in national politics. Sixteen years before the gold of California would help finance the North's war against the South, Southerners like Polk wanted California because they believed its resources would help redress the North's power in national affairs.

Had human beings, in 1846, possessed some insight into the future, some rational capacity to act in their own interest, the North would have supported Polk's war for the same reason the South would have opposed it: no previous event in American history did more to assure the national dominance of the North; none did more to doom the cause of the South, and of slavery. But, hardly for the last time, reality was cast aside in the United States; self-illusion became the dictator of events.

As a result, the government of the United States was first divided, then paralyzed, and finally shattered by a controversy that seems as fantastic today as all our disputes about whether communism can be stopped in Central America no doubt will seem to future generations.

Would slavery be permitted to prevail in Hollywood, in Las Vegas, the Grand Canyon—in all those other lands so recently stolen from Mexico, yet destined, in little more than a century, to attain the purest fulfillment in thousands of split-level suburbs, freeway interchanges and franchise shopping malls of the American Dream?

Or would slavery be contained in the South?

No less than during the Cold War, Americans had been conquered by the domino theory. If slavery were not stopped at Texas, they believed, it would overwhelm New Mexico, Colorado, Arizona, Nevada, California. Was there no one who could see things straight?

John C. Calhoun, like John Quincy Adams, today is considered an antique and irrelevant figure. For a related reason, they remain two of the most crucially relevant figures of American nationalism. Both could see realities invisible to other Americans.

As early as 1821, as late as 1848, Adams recognized the contradiction built into America's growing power in the world: American liberty and American force were antithetical. Adams could offer no resolution to this antithesis except to call for abstention, which was, at bottom, only to express the faith that American virtue somehow could manage to control American power. It is a hope that America's actions in the world, even now, ceaselessly excite and ceaselessly disappoint.

Calhoun was doomed—there is no other word for it—to an even more fateful insight: to conquer Mexico was not to fulfill America's "Manifest Destiny"; it was to destroy the United States of the Founding Fathers and conjure into existence an entirely new kind of America, an America "founded in conquest," completely different from the nation Calhoun and Adams, Polk and Lincoln all knew.

Like many people capable of startlingly original perception, Calhoun could see so much because he had a blind spot. More than any other major public figure of his time, he grasped the enormous national and global transformations the Mexican War was unleashing, precisely because he was incapable of imagining the South as anything but the semitropical, semifeudal, overwhelmingly agricultural, slaveholding oligarchy it was in 1846.

In a nation, in a world, destined for stupendous change, Calhoun believed the South must be preserved exactly as it was, forever. It was Calhoun's inability to imagine a South without slavery, and a United States without a southern veto in the Senate, that allowed him to perceive with such utter clarity the real consequences of Polk's war. This was that a Union expanded by force—by presidential war and by national armies—would inevitably become a Union within which force—presidential war, national armies—would reign supreme.

Not merely would the United States be aggrandized territorially beyond recognition; the very substance of American nationalism, Calhoun foresaw, would be transmuted. The system of federal liberty devised by the Founding Fathers would inevitably give way to a system of federal supremacy, in which the states, no longer sovereign, would be little more than provinces, and the power of the central government, especially the power of the presidency, would dominate all. The carefully crafted republic of the Founding Fathers would become a mere democracy. Presidents would become demagogues. Congress, no longer an institution of deliberation and sectional consensus, would become the mere mouthpiece of the majority.

And in such a nation, Calhoun saw, the rights of the South—doomed to a permanent minority—would be as defenseless against the onslaught of big government and the recurring fanaticisms of the majority as Mexico itself had been against the onslaught of the U.S. Army and the American battle cry of "Manifest Destiny."

It was thus Calhoun's fate to see in 1846 what would become apparent to most other Southerners only in 1861. If the President could make war "at pleasure" on Mexico, the President could make war on the South. If U.S. troops could conquer California, they could conquer South Carolina. Calhoun could see that the bombardment of Veracruz was a rehearsal for the burning of Atlanta.

Calhoun grasped all this because he could see something else about the interrelationship of war and politics that few other Americans did either then or later. This was that while armies can win wars, wars cannot determine the form peace takes, no matter how mighty the conqueror is.

Instead, for most Americans in 1846 the question of slavery in New Mexico and California was like the question of "freedom" in Vietnam and El Salvador later. Few Americans, North or South, doubted that the United States could impose slavery on the Southwest if it wished, just as few doubted that the United States could impose democracy on Indochina later.

And so the dispute, they believed, came down to a test of America's will and character, not reality. Would the United States ban or guarantee slavery in the new lands?

Calhoun would be one of the most illuminating figures in American history even had he never held high office, because he saw the stark reality behind this hallucinatory debate in Washington. He understood that slavery, like "freedom," was not some abstract concept. Like democracy, slavery was not merely a peculiar, but a practical, institution, which thrived in some social, historical, political and geographic settings—but which could not be established in other environments, no matter how strong was America's military might.

Calhoun also recognized something about the newly conquered lands that few of his contemporaries perceived. These territories were not the blank spots Americans saw on their maps in 1846. As much as the North and the South, the West had its own peculiarities, within which its own peculiar institutions would take root, whatever was ordained in Washington.

Thus where his fellow Southerners looked West and saw new Virginias, new Mississippis, Calhoun pored over the official maps of those lands, still only partially surveyed, and saw what a trip across Texas still reveals today.

Once crosses the Sabine River from Louisiana into East Texas, and finds one is still in the South. But with the passage of each successive river—the Trinity, the Brazos, the Colorado, the San Antonio—the sense of the South diminishes; the presence of the West grows more powerful. There is no sharp dividing line, but even before one reaches the Nueces, the South has been left behind forever. Austin, on the Colorado, and San Antonio, a little to the southwest, are not much more than an hour apart on the interstate freeway. Yet even today they still belong to different worlds, just as they did back when the Nueces divided Texas from Mexico.

Austin—named for the first U.S. settler of Texas—faces east. Its domed state capitol is a monument to one of the great trains of human migration that has made Texas the meeting ground of differing cultures it is today. This is the train of migration from the United States that has so speedily transformed eastern Texas from a Mexican province into an American state in the past century.

In San Antonio one is in a different world. There the most famous landmark is the Alamo—a Mexican monument to a Mexican victory. San Antonio belongs to the Hispanic West as totally as Austin belongs to the English-speaking South, and that is just as true today as it was in 1846.

Polk's armies could redraw the political maps, but they could not change the human contours of North America. Nearly a century and a half later, it is still at the Nueces—not at the Rio Grande—where one world ends and another begins. It seems no accident that, within sixty years of Polk's conquest of Mexico, this sectional no-man's-land should produce a figure so transitional, so divided, so obsessed with America's, and his own, identity and lack of it in the world, as Lyndon Johnson.

In the midst of a bitter national dispute in which "slavery" and "California," like "freedom" and "Vietnam," were only code words for America's internal divisions, Calhoun looked at that reality without flinching. And so he came to a judgment all the more illuminating because, to most of his countrymen, it illuminated nothing at all.

Slaves were no more likely to pick cotton in the Mojave Desert than the Bill of Rights is ever likely to prevail in El Salvador. The South ends in Texas, Calhoun understood, and no number of conquests in California and laws in Washington could change that reality. Far from becoming an extension of the South, the West—like the North and the new plains states—was destined to become a powerful region of its own, a region which, on the question of slavery, was bound to side with the North, against the South. Far from restoring the old sectional balance, Calhoun recognized, Polk's conquests would destroy it totally. As a result, he also foresaw, the South would be doomed, and probably the Union, too.

The President's entire grand design, Calhoun warned Polk in December 1846, was based on a fantasy, because slavery would "probably never exist" in California and New Mexico. "Calhoun's clear vision," note Morison and Commager, "foresaw that the conquest of more territory would upset the sectional balance and revive the dangerous question of slavery in the Territories."

He might as well have been trying to tell Lyndon Johnson that B-52s could not implant freedom along the Mekong, or warning Richard Nixon that invading Cambodia would lead to Watergate. Americans, North and South, were caught up in one of the great fantasy melodramas of American nationalism.

Would the South's "right" to extend slavery into the new territories prevail? Or would the North counter Polk's conspiracy, as one Massachusetts congressman put it, to "give the South a perpetual preponderance in the councils of the nation"?

In August 1846, Polk asked Congress to appropriate $2 million to purchase lands from Mexico, on the erroneous assumption that America's initial battlefield victories would lead to a quick, easy triumph. Instead the Mexicans would resist for another two years. Polk's request, however, turned out to be a turning point in American history far more important than our eventual defeat of Mexico.

Congress gave the President his $2 million—but only after a Pennsylvania congressman, one of the President's own Democrats, had attached an amendment to the appropriation that even today most Americans vaguely remember from their high school history books. The amendment provided, "as an express and fundamental condition to the acquisition of any territory from the Republic of Mexico by the United States," that neither "slavery nor involuntary servitude shall ever exist in any part of said territory."

The Wilmot Proviso passed the House of Representatives, but not the Senate, and President Polk would have vetoed it even if it had. The fact that the measure never became law, however, is beside the point.

For, with the Wilmot Proviso, an entire era in American history ended, and a fateful new epoch—the epoch of the Civil War—began. For decades, sectionalism had been eating away at America's national unity like some slow-growing cancer. Now, because of the Mexican War, the cancer metastasized.

Samuel Eliot Morison describes the terrible defeat the United States had inflicted on itself, even as it utterly vanquished a neighbor:

> The state of the American Union in 1848 may be compared with that of Europe in 1913 and 1938. Political and diplomatic moves become frequent and startling. Integrating forces win apparent victories, but in reality grow feebler. The tension increases until some event that, in ordinary times, would have little consequence, precipitates a bloody conflict.

There had been only 1,733 American battle deaths in the entire Mexican War—but the real American body count had not yet begun. At Bull Run, Antietam, Gettysburg and the other Civil War battlefields, some three hundred thousand Americans would be killed—nearly as many as in the two world wars combined.

One thing united all Americans, even during the Civil War: they all believed they were fighting for freedom, as all Americans always have.

But what was freedom? For the South, freedom was slavery, just as conquest had been freedom for President Polk. For the North, freedom was preservation of the Union, even if it meant that the Southerners—like the Indians, blacks and Mexicans before them—were to remain Americans whether that was what they wanted or not.

In April 1864, President Lincoln made an observation that might have been made during the Mexican War, the Vietnam War—or today. "The world has never had a good definition of the word liberty," he told an audience in Baltimore, "and the American people, just now, are much in want of one."

The Civil War, like all such events in American history, in due course would be transformed into a triumph of liberty, but for the moment the only reality was the reality of death, the reality of disunion, the reality of devastation—and it all had come from attempting to "extend the area of freedom" by force.

"Mexico is for us the forbidden fruit," Calhoun had warned fifteen years earlier; "the penalty of eating it would be to subject our institutions to political death."

Now the America Calhoun and Adams had known was dead, though death, as always in American history, would be followed by transfiguration.

Calhoun had handed down the prophecy. It was Morison's fate to write the epitaph for the Polk doctrine, and the American catastrophe it had made inevitable.

Had there been no "Mexican war," he pointed out a century later, "there would have been no Civil War, at least not in 1861."

Polk's war to unite America had fatally divided it. His war to fulfill our "Manifest Destiny" had raised the most fateful question in the whole of our history. Did the United States have a destiny at all?

It was the single most instructive metamorphosis in the whole of American history.

In 1864, two weeks before he made his comment on the need for a definition of liberty, Lincoln proclaimed a truth Lyndon Johnson and Richard Nixon would never have the courage to face.

"I claim not to have controlled events," Lincoln wrote, "but confess plainly that events have controlled me."

Lincoln was only stating what by that time was the obvious. Once again, war and fate were working their transformations—creating changes in America neither victor nor vanquished could avert or control.

Insensibly the war to preserve the Union had become—against Lincoln's own intentions—a war to free the slaves. The war to preserve the Constitution had become a war in which the powers of the President exceeded the power of the Constitution itself. Lincoln, who had once condemned Polk for making "war at pleasure," now found himself wielding war powers on which no one, not even he, could "fix any limit." Yet even here fate held in store the ultimate rebuke: even the most total presidential powers could not stop an assassin's bullet.

"*Sic semper tyrannis!*" Like Jackson and Harrison, Polk and Lincoln, McKinley and Wilson, Lyndon Johnson and Ronald Reagan, John Wilkes Booth was a paradigmatical American.

He, too, killed in the name of liberty.

*   *   *

As always, it was the destiny of Latin America to be the historical victim of the extraordinary changes overtaking the United States, and the nature of its relations with the rest of the world.

Gold was discovered in California even before the war with Mexico formally ended. The immense wealth of the West would flow into U.S., not Mexican, coffers, and help finance our industrial development, not the development of our neighbors. Because the transcontinental railroads would not be completed until after the Civil War, the need to maintain communication with California by sea suddenly gave U.S. relations with the Caribbean and Central America an importance unimaginable in the past. It was thus also Polk—not Theodore Roosevelt—who made the Panama Canal, and all the U.S. entanglements building and defending the canal would entail, a historical inevitability, rather than the utopian scheme it had been until then.

One notable result of the new importance to the United States of the transit routes across Central America was that, thirty years after Monroe had sent his abstentionist message to Congress, the "Monroe Doctrine" finally, actually became a historical reality.

Not even Polk had presumed to use the word "doctrine" to describe the policy he falsely had attributed to President Monroe. But now a figure of American nationalism no less commanding than Millard Fillmore was in the White House and, so far as more and more Americans were concerned, it was now their nation's manifest destiny not just to conquer, but to proclaim doctrines to the world.

As Thomas A. Bailey explains:

Texas, Oregon and the Mexican cession territory—an imperial domain—had fallen into the outstretched hands of the United States within the short space of three years. One would think that the American people . . . would be content. But this was far from being the case.

The swift and relatively easy victories of the Mexican War, operating as a heady intoxicant, caused the United States to rise to the full height of its "exulting manhood."

The adolescence of America was over. But where would America spend its "exulting manhood"? By the 1850s, Americans had found a suitable object for their ardor:

Let no technical impediment be thrown in the way of our Americanizing Central America [declared Representative Anderson of Missouri at the end of the decade]. Humanity, philanthropy and Christianity demand that it shall be done at no distant day. Such is our manifest destiny; and why should we be afraid to proclaim it to the world?

The "fall" of Mexico had unleashed a domino effect. All through the 1850s, Americans—ranging from magnates like Cornelius Vanderbilt to adventurers like William Walker—turned Central America into a new frontier.

For those who dreamed of "Americanizing Central America," these usurpations of Central America's sovereignty and wealth were no acts of aggression. Instead, Vanderbilt was the new John Jacob Astor, just as Walker was the new Sam Houston. As Congressman Anderson saw it, it was not just we Americans who would replicate our destiny in Central America; as part of the divine plan of Providence, the Central Americans would share the fate of the North American Indians:

> Wave upon wave of immigration will roll in upon that country, until, ere long, its internal wars, ignorance, superstition, and anarchy will be supplanted by peace, knowledge, Christianity and our own Heaven-born institutions.

Impediments, and not just technical ones, nonetheless stood in the way of "Americanizing Central America," the chief one being the impediment Walker himself encountered in the form of Costa Rican armies and a Honduran firing squad—the same impediment Ronald Reagan would encounter, 130 years later, in the Salvadoran guerrillas and the Sandinistas in Nicaragua.

The Central Americans themselves had no desire to be "Americanized" the way the Indians had been in Louisiana and Florida, and the Mexicans had been in Texas and California. But not only local subversives stood in the way of fulfilling our manifest destiny; hardly had the Mexican War ended, when a foreign conspiracy in Central America was discovered—the same conspiracy of British intrigue that earlier had presumed to oppose us in Canada and Cuba, Oregon and California.

One reason the British were so strong in Central America by the 1850s was that no "Monroe Doctrine" had been applied anywhere in Latin America after 1823. Monroe and Adams had done nothing to prevent British "interposition" in Belize. Jackson and Polk had done nothing to prevent the British from expanding their control to the Bay Islands, off Honduras, and to the Miskito Coast of Nicaragua, and since President Fillmore had no more intention than his predecessors of risking war with the dominant power of the nineteenth century, he, too, tried to strike a deal—and, like his predecessors, found London more than willing to accommodate the United States.

Under the Clayton-Bulwer treaty, the two English-speaking powers—without so much as consulting the Central Americans—agreed to share control over any canal built across the isthmus.

For the British, the Clayton-Bulwer Treaty was only another manifestation of the policy, going back through Aberdeen to Canning, of appeasing American ambitions while containing U.S. threats to Britain's vital interests.

But, in the United States, the treaty aroused the same kind of outrage the Panama Canal treaties later would. Did not President Fillmore realize he had betrayed the legacy of President Monroe? Suddenly Fillmore's treaty, even though it had been overwhelmingly approved by the Senate, was discovered to violate a higher law. It was in the uproar following the Anglo-American compromise over Central America, as one diplomatic historian notes, that "Monroe's pronouncement was for the first time consistently referred to in Congress and in the press as a 'doctrine.' "

As with future American doctrines, the sudden discovery not only that a "Monroe Doctrine" existed but that it barred the British from Central America, had almost nothing to do with foreign affairs—and everything to do with the internal politics of the United States.

After four years in the political wilderness following Polk's retirement and their defeat in the 1848 elections, the Democrats were eager to regain control of the White House. For them, the "Monroe Doctrine" was to the 1852 election what "Manifest Destiny" had been to the election of 1844, the issue that made all other issues possible. Riding high on charges that Fillmore had violated the "Monroe Doctrine," the Democrats recaptured the White House in the 1852 elections; they would keep it until the outbreak of the Civil War.

The Clayton-Bulwer treaty in fact marked a significant advance for the principles of President Monroe. Under the treaty both the British and the Americans jointly pledged that "neither will ever . . . occupy, or fortify, or colonize or assume, or exercise any dominion over . . . any part of Central America." Twenty-seven years after Monroe had announced U.S. opposition to future colonization "as a principle," his abstentionist approach was finally embodied in a treaty obliging both nations to abstain from "future colonization" in Central America. Had the Clayton-Bulwer Treaty actually been respected, the future of Central America no doubt would have been much different—and much happier.

The Democrats, however, denounced the treaty as invalid for two reasons: It implicitly accepted the colonial establishments Britain already had in Central America. Even more important, it pledged the United States itself to respect the sovereignty of the nations of Central America—a pledge which, so far as many Americans were now concerned, violated both the "Monroe Doctrine" and the doctrine of "Manifest Destiny."

In consequence, President Pierce not only recognized Walker's usurpation of Nicaragua; he purported that both the "Monroe Doctrine" and the Clayton-Bulwer Treaty obliged Britain to abandon the territories it already controlled in Central America.

Legally speaking, the U.S. position was as untenable as the earlier claim that the Louisiana Purchase entitled us to Texas. The pledge not to "colonize . . . any part of Central America" had been stated in the future tense. Neither the 1850 treaty nor any known principle of international law suggested that Britain, by pledging to abstain from future colonization in Central America, had somehow also pledged to abandon its existing colonies there.

Not that the letter or the spirit of the law stood in the way of either Pierce or President James Buchanan after Polk's former Secretary of State succeeded Pierce in the White House.

"These Yankees are most disagreeable fellows to have to do with about any

American question," Lord Palmerston complained, in 1857, in a comment many a Latin American leader might have made. "They are . . . totally unscrupulous and dishonest, and determined somehow or other to carry their point."

Just how disagreeable the United States could be had been demonstrated three years earlier. Americans might consider Britain's protectorate on the Caribbean coast of Nicaragua an intolerable violation of the "Monroe Doctrine," but it was quite popular with the local inhabitants—English-speaking blacks and Miskito Indians—because they, like the Canadians, considered the British crown their best protection against encroachment by their neighbors, in this case the Spanish-speaking majority in western Nicaragua.

How unpopular the "Monroe Doctrine" really was there, the American consul discovered in July 1854, when, in the course of a melee involving the local inhabitants, his face was cut by a broken bottle. Bailey's description of what followed might be the description of many a future U.S. "defense of freedom," and not just in Latin America:

> An American naval officer demanded reparations, and when it was not forthcoming bombarded and destroyed the town.

Greytown, Nicaragua, seems to have been the first foreign city in history the United States found it necessary to destroy in order to save. More than thirty years after the fact, George Canning's effort to entice President Monroe into issuing a statement opposing military intervention in Latin America had borne ironic fruit: the "Monroe Doctrine," as Americans now understood it, entitled them to wage undeclared war not just against the Latin Americans, but against the British themselves.

The British, not without moments of vexation, held to their traditional policy: U.S. ambitions were to be accommodated, not crushed, because American interests—however bumptious—served British interests.

Britain, *The Times* of London declared in 1856, should "look with great resignation and even pleasure" on U.S. expansion in Central America. The *Economist* explained why: Central America *"exploité* by Anglo-Saxons will be worth to us tenfold its present value."

"[W]e possess no interest in Central America," Lord Clarendon candidly informed President Buchanan. And "so far from wishing to create one," he added, "we would not accept . . . Central America if it could be offered to England as a gift."

The British for years had been willing to abandon the Bay Islands of Honduras and to withdraw from the eastern coast of Nicaragua. But they intended to keep Belize, which Guatemala claimed. In an 1859 treaty—with Honduras, not the United States—Britain accordingly relinquished its claims to the Bay Islands. In 1860, a similar treaty with Nicaragua ended the British presence there. But the British held on to Belize. In fact British troops, in utter defiance of the "Monroe Doctrine," are still there today.

In the United States these events were heralded as a great triumph for the "Monroe Doctrine," which hereafter I shall no longer render in quotation marks, because it was under Pierce and Buchanan that the "Monroe Doctrine" at last became, in both substance and name, the Monroe Doctrine we know today.

Presidents Pierce and Buchanan, the real authors of the Monroe Doctrine, had made themselves the grand arbiters of the Miskito Coast. But even now their names are synonymous with presidential impotence. They had "saved" Central America from the British, but they were powerless to save America from itself. At the very moment when Americans first explicitly handed down doctrines to others, America's command over its own destiny was forfeited. Less than two years after the halls of Congress rang with the rhetoric about the United States conferring "peace . . . and our own Heaven-born institutions" on Central America, the United States itself was mired in internal war and anarchy.

It was an American illusion that the Monroe Doctrine had been vindicated in Central America. We only replaced the British as the dominating foreign power there and throughout the rest of Latin America. "Outside domination" did, indeed, largely end—but only as a by-product of the establishment of a new system of internal domination of the western hemisphere, by the United States.

Just how jealous the United States was of its growing hemispheric dominion the British themselves would discover by the end of the nineteenth century. Neither Britain's withdrawal from the Miskito Coast nor its continuing role in Belize had altered the essential provisions of the Clayton-Bulwer Treaty regarding control of the Central American canal. But as construction of the canal more and more became a technological possibility, Americans discovered they faced yet another "threat." The United States not only wanted a canal; it wanted exclusive dominion over it. And it wanted the canal itself to be a bastion of American military power. But the Clayton-Bulwer Treaty stood in America's way.

By the turn of the century, "Dishonor be damned" had replaced "Manifest Destiny" as the war cry in the United States. But, in 1901, as in 1846 and 1850, neither war nor dishonor proved necessary—thanks to supple diplomacy in London. In the Hay-Pauncefote Treaty, negotiated at the end of that year, the British agreed "that the canal may be constructed under the auspices of the government of the United States." They also ceded to the United States "the exclusive right of providing for the regulation and management of the canal."

Once again, in the United States, a great victory for the Monroe Doctrine was proclaimed, but—as in 1823, 1846 and 1850—the British saw things differently. Bailey sums up the logic behind the British action:

Why not, concluded Downing Street, permit the United States to build the canal—a canal that would double the power of its navy and enable it to guarantee the status quo in America against Britain's rivals, notably Germany?

Nearly seventy years after Canning had sought to redress the balance of power in the Old World by calling a New World into existence, Germany had replaced the Holy Alliance as Britain's main rival in world affairs. But the British calculus had not changed. What did it matter if the Americans were allowed to build, even to regulate and manage, the canal?

Germany was not aggrandized.

Britain thus gained all the strategic benefits of a canal, just as, earlier, it had gained all the strategic benefits of Latin American independence, without having to commit itself to any new expenditures, or saddling itself with any new military or colonial obligations.

Nearly a century earlier, every British soldier tied down fighting Andrew Jackson at New Orleans had been a soldier who might have fought Napoleon at Waterloo. Now British ships that otherwise would have had to patrol the Caribbean would be free, during World War I, to fight the Germans in the Battle of Jutland.

A new chapter in the "special relationship" had opened, which, forty years later, under Franklin Roosevelt's Lend-Lease program, would see the United States assume Britain's remaining imperial commitments in the Caribbean even before the United States entered World War II.

So far as Latin America and the Caribbean are concerned, this is a chapter in Anglo-American relations that still has not entirely ended, though surely President Reagan wrote one of its final paragraphs when he invaded Grenada. By the beginning of the 1980s, the United States had long since supplanted the British even in such former British possessions as Jamaica and the Bahamas. But along with Belize and the Falkland Islands, the island states of the eastern Caribbean were one area where British influence still predominated. As late as 1969, Britain had intervened on the tiny island of Anguilla when Grenada-style turmoil had broken out.

Like the U.S. bombardment of Greytown 129 years earlier, President Reagan's assault on Point Salines marked yet another brash American assault on yet another remnant of the former British empire—which was the principal reason Prime Minister Thatcher reacted with nearly as much initial vexation, and ultimate resignation, as Lord Palmerston earlier had.

Our continuing failure to enforce the Monroe Doctrine except when it suits U.S. expediency nonetheless still contains the potential for at least one more international crisis. What will happen when Britain ultimately withdraws its troops from Belize, leaving that corner of Central America undefended against a century and a half of pent-up Guatemalan nationalism? Thirty years after the CIA overthrow of democracy there, Guatemala remains one of the most volatile nations in the western hemisphere. We should not be too surprised if, one of these days, Americans wind up dying to "defend freedom" in Belize—this time against Guatemalan "aggression."

Certainly this would be a fittingly ironic outcome of Monroe's injunction against "future colonization," for the history of the Monroe Doctrine is in fact the history of the United States's violating all Monroe's principles, all in Monroe's name.

Monroe's principle of abstention in Latin America, of course, had been turned into a dead letter by Polk's attack on Mexico. With the Spanish-American War, the U.S. pledge that it would not interfere with "the existing colonies or dependencies of any European power" was totally violated too. And with U.S. entry into World War I, Monroe's most important principle was also cast aside. Thereafter the United States would be deeply involved in "the wars of the European powers."

But what of that provision of the Monroe message that, even now, Americans consider the cornerstone of our hemispheric policy? I am referring to his statement that the United States would not view "with indifference" the attempts of outsiders to "extend their political system to any portion of either continent."

Less than twenty years after U.S. forces bombarded Veracruz, that gulf port became the beachhead for the third great foreign invasion of Mexico in recorded history. Along the same route from Veracruz to Mexico City that Hernan Cortes and Winfield Scott had traversed, Emperor Maximilian now advanced toward his own New World destiny.

Unlike his Spanish and American predecessors, however, the Austrian was no conquistador on horseback. French troops already had occupied Mexico City. Maximilian and his Belgian consort, Charlotte, made their way toward Chapultepec Castle in a caravan drawn by eight mules. At Veracruz, *zopilotes,* great black birds of carrion, had greeted the self-proclaimed sovereigns of Mexico; these scavengers were the harbingers of all that was to come.

Maximilian's rococo adventure need not detain us. But the reaction in Washington to this flagrant act of European "interposition" in the Americas is important, because it set the stage for one of the most illuminating episodes in the whole of U.S. foreign policy.

Less than twenty years earlier, the internal divisions within the United States had made a U.S. attack on Mexico seem expedient in the White House. Now the greatest internal division in American history—the Civil War— dictated that the United States do nothing at all to help defend its neighbor's independence. Mexico's nationalist forces, under Juarez, were left to fight Maximilian and the French alone.

U.S. abstention from involvement in the Mexican struggle no doubt was unavoidable until the Civil War ended, in 1865. But expediency cannot explain U.S. actions following the end of the Civil War, for even then U.S. forces never came to Mexico's defense. Instead, in this—the only significant instance, after 1823, of European military intervention in the Americas—the United States adopted a policy of official neutrality.

More than that, neither President Lincoln nor his Secretary of State, William H. Seward, who continued to guide U.S. foreign policy following Lincoln's assassination, ever invoked the Monroe Doctrine in connection with Mexico. French forces stayed in Mexico, and Maximilian remained on Mexico's throne until 1867, when Juarez's forces finally captured and executed him.

Maximilian's fate had become the fate of William Walker—not because the Monroe Doctrine had preserved the liberty of the western hemisphere, but because the Mexicans, like the Central Americans before them, had successfully defended their own independence.

Why had the United States not invoked the Monroe Doctrine?

As usual, the internal politics of the United States, not the realities of Latin America, provide the answer. Just as "extending the area of freedom" actually had been a program for extending slavery, so in the 1850s the Monroe Doctrine was principally a southern and Democratic tenet, aimed at counterbalancing the power of the North by the expansion of southern interests in the tropics. Lincoln was the heir of Adams, not of Polk, when it came to foreign policy, and so was as opposed to a Monroe Doctrine approach as Monroe himself would have been.

Like Franklin Roosevelt's Good Neighbor policy, seventy years later, the Lincoln policy in some ways amounted to a return to the Monroe-Adams policy of abstention, which the United States had followed during the Latin American wars of independence.

As in 1823, there was no doubt where America's sympathies lay. Lincoln and Seward repeatedly made it clear to Maximilian and the French that they opposed the cause of European intervention and monarchism. They made it equally clear they considered Juarez and his forces to be fighting for America's own principles of national independence and republican liberty. But, as in Monroe's time, these expressions of American principle were not matched by any American military commitment. Instead, as Monroe had put it, the United States remained the "anxious and interested spectator" of Mexico's struggle to free itself from foreign military intervention.

The consequences, for all concerned, in the end were very positive. Direct U.S. military intervention would have hastened the withdrawal of the French and the downfall of Maximilian—but only at the cost of poisoning U.S. relations with France and, even more important, depriving the Mexicans of one of the great, decisive triumphs of their nationalism.

In many ways, Maximilian's intervention defined a new kind of imperialism: the "neocolonialism" many nations, including the United States, would practice in later times. In contrast with earlier European interventions in the New World, France aimed at no formal annexation of Mexico. Instead, beneath the rhetoric about France uplifting and civilizing Mexico, the objective in supporting Maximilian was similar to the later U.S. objective in supporting such figures as the Shah, Somoza and Diem. The French hoped to create a client regime, under Maximilian, that would "stabilize" the country, allow their interests to prevail there, and eventually become strong enough for their own forces to be withdrawn.

Juarez thus led one of the first modern wars of national liberation. And in 1867, this struggle produced a result of great significance for Mexico, Latin America and the rest of the Third World. The largely Indian forces of Juarez, himself a full-blooded Indian, defeated the forces of Maximilian, the very personification of the divine right of kings. Not only a Hapsburg archduke was cut down by Juarez's firing squad; the notion that the "aboriginal" races were inevitably fated to fall under the rule of the white race died then too. The outcome of the Mexican uprising thus provided a striking vindication of the principles Monroe and Adams had affirmed forty-four years earlier: the Mexicans had proved that liberty was a principle strong enough to prevail even when we Americans did not "go abroad seeking monsters to slay." It was one of the great formative events of modern Latin American history.

The same year Juarez defeated Maximilian, abstentionism prevailed again when Secretary of State Seward negotiated the purchase of Alaska from Russia. Less than fifty years after the supposed conspiracy of the Holy Alliance had so agitated some Americans, "future colonization" by the czars in the New World not only had been checked; it had been reversed.

Patience and diplomacy had led to a notable triumph for U.S. principles in Mexico—and to an equally notable territorial aggrandizement for the United States in Alaska. More than that, Juarez's victory taught an important lesson: foreign armies cannot create internal legitimacy; and even the most "underdeveloped" peoples can achieve notable victories if they believe their cause is just.

It was a lesson that the United States was destined not to learn. Like the Monroe Doctrine and Kennan's "X article," Juarez's victory was quickly transformed into only one more vindication of the essential doctrine of American nationalism. "Mexico owes her liberty to America more than to anyone else," proclaimed the New York *Tribune.* "Juarez would never have been victorious without the help of the United States," General Philip Sheridan wrote later. One Mexican official, summed up the situation more accurately:

We have obtained our victory by our own efforts without the aid of any foreign nation—in spite of the moral influence of Europe and the material force of France and the continental powers. We have opposed this gigantic combination with nothing more than the suffering and patriotism of our people and the firm sympathy of the United States.

The United States had no reason to be ashamed of its actions during Mexico's second war of independence. Our "firm sympathy" had played a contributing role in the Mexican victory—though it was not remotely comparable to the contribution France itself had made, ninety years earlier, to the achievement of our own independence.

The Mexicans were not the only ones to discover the limitations of the American commitment to liberty. While Juarez was fighting Maximilian and the French, an even more blatant violation of the Monroe Doctrine occurred. In 1861, the Spanish restored colonial rule in the Dominican Republic—the only instance, in the entire history of the western hemisphere, of an "outside" power actually terminating the independence of an American nation. The United States did nothing. Instead, the Dominicans—like the Mexicans— were left to fight for, and restore, their own sovereignty, which they did in 1865.

Then, in 1868, an even more important "test case" of the United States commitment to hemispheric liberty arose. The year after Juarez defeated Maximilian, a war of independence broke out in Cuba. For forty-five years, Spain's continuing control of that nearby island had been a standing rebuke to the notion that, back in 1823, President Monroe had terminated the era of European dominion in the New World.

Now the Cubans had taken matters into their own hands, and Spain moved ruthlessly to crush the insurrection. Though Spain's counterinsurgency war off the coast of Florida certainly did not violate Monroe's original policy, it was, like the French intervention in Mexico, an assault on the Monroe Doctrine as most Americans understood it by then. U. S. Grant was now President; the Civil War had turned the United States into a formidable military power. If U.S. forces had come to the aid of the Cubans the way the French had come to our aid during our own War of Independence, liberation would have been assured.

Once again, the United States remained "the well-wisher to the freedom and independence" of its neighbors, but "the champion and vindicator only of her own." War with Spain was as carefully avoided as it had been during the earlier Latin American wars of independence. The Cubans fought on alone for ten years—until 1878, when Spain finally crushed the revolt. Fifty-five years after the supposed proclamation of the Monroe Doctrine, a European power had fought and won a full-scale war against the cause of American liberty.

Was the Monroe Doctrine dead? The truth was that the spirit of President Polk was only dormant. The cries for war, the cries for liberty, in due course would shake America, the hemisphere and the world once again.

*　*　*

"Action, Action, Action! Jackson, Jackson, Jackson!" clamored the New York *World.* The year was 1898, not 1844, but it was an appropriate tocsin. Once again an illusory past was being invoked to justify future dishonors, and a passion for war was loose in the land. Next only to the Mexican War, the war with Spain would be the greatest war of unprovoked aggression in American history. The New York *Sun* defined the choice starkly: would America fight for "human lives and the liberty of human beings, for *Cuba Libre*"? Or would it let oppression prevail ninety miles off our shores?

The war fever of 1898 caught President McKinley nearly as unawares as the war fever of 1844 had caught Van Buren and Clay. No such clamor for war had followed the first Cuban insurrection. Why now had Cuba become the new Oregon?

"[T]he currents of destiny flow through the hearts of the people," President McKinley observed. "Who will check them? Who will divert them? Who will stop them?"

Certainly not President McKinley. A political cartoon of the era shows the hapless President, like some latter-day Canute, trying to turn back the war tide surging in his direction from Congress and from the American people.

"The march of events rules and overrules human action," the President conceded as U.S. forces seized Cuba, Puerto Rico, Guam and the Philippines from Spain.

As it had been with the Mexican War, so it was with the war against Spain: the territorial changes the war produced were far less important than the internal consequences for the United States and the external changes in America's relations with the rest of the world. Like the War of 1812 and the Cold War, the Spanish-American War produced a kind of political revolution inside the United States. Cautious, old-style politicians like McKinley lost control of events. Even after the war was won, McKinley struck many Americans as far too stodgy and passive to lead the United States in this new, exuberant era of its national expansion. What could McKinley do to assure reelection in 1900?

Like Eisenhower's choice of Nixon fifty-two years later, McKinley's choice of Theodore Roosevelt for Vice President was an agile exercise in "balancing" the Republican ticket. It also proved to be a fateful choice for American history, as destiny soon would demonstrate in a characteristically American way. In September 1901 an assassin's bullet killed McKinley—and made Teddy Roosevelt President of the United States. Not since Andrew Jackson, had the contradictory American impulses toward force and liberty found a more perfect presidential incarnation.

Of no less consequence was the entirely new U.S. relationship with the cause of independence, not just in Latin America, but around the world, which the Spanish-American War established. Prior to the Spanish-American War, the United States had been the well-wisher, if not the champion, of the cause of independence everywhere. But the war for *"Cuba Libre"* quickly worked a characteristic American metamorphosis.

As a result of the war to free Cuba, the United States itself became a colonial power. Like Spain, the United States soon would find itself the enemy of independence, not just in the Caribbean, but in faraway Asia as well.

Ostensibly the Spanish-American War had been a crusade against imperialism, for liberty and independence. But not even in Cuba was that the result. Following its defeat, Spain did not grant independence to Cuba. It only renounced its own sovereignty there, and handed Cuba over to occupation by the United States. Nowhere in the peace treaty was the principle of independence mentioned at all. U.S. forces would occupy Cuba from 1898 to 1901, and again from 1906 until 1909. In fact, U.S. forces never left the island. Following the war, the Cubans were obliged to hand over Guantanamo Bay to the United States. It remains under American military control even now—a quarter century after Castro took power.

Guantanamo was not all *"Cuba Libre"* was required to render unto its American liberators. In 1901, as the price for the end of the U.S. military occupation of their country, the Cubans were obliged to acknowledge in their own national constitution that U.S. "liberty" superseded Cuba's own sovereignty. Under the Platt Amendment, written by U.S. officials, the Republic of Cuba ceded to the United States implicit control over its economic, military and foreign affairs. The Cubans were even obliged to renounce the most fundamental of all national rights: the right of self-defense.

The United States, the Platt Amendment provided, was "at liberty to intervene for the purpose of preserving order and maintaining Cuban independence."

It was a classic American attempt to equate force with liberty. Cuba would not become fully independent, technically speaking, until 1936, when Franklin Roosevelt, as part of the Good Neighbor Policy, abrogated the Platt Amendment, but changing the law would not change the substance.

The war to free Cuba had led to the most complete U.S. domination of a supposedly independent foreign country in our entire history. By the beginning of World War II, Americans owned 85 percent of Cuba's sugar mills and dominated the rest of the economy. American holdings in Cuba were four times as great as those in the entire Far East, including the American-owned Philippines, greater than in any other Latin American nation. To economic bondage was added the burden of political oppression. With U.S. support, Cuba was abused by a series of unsavory, at times sadistic, dictators. For the Cubans, the dream of *"Cuba Libre"* had turned into a historical nightmare.

The long history of our abuse of Cuba's sovereignty did not end with Castro's revolution; it only entered a new phase, in which the Cubans found themselves obliged to accept dependency on the Soviet Union as the price for independence from the United States, just as earlier they had been obliged to accept dependency on the United States as the price for independence from Spain. Real independence for Cuba will become possible only when we Americans finally are able to face up to the fact that independence in such countries means independence not only from others, but from us.

The long, unhappy history of U.S.-Cuban relations nonetheless has one utility. It calls attention once again to an extraordinary historical fact.

Not once in our history, in spite of the Monroe Doctrine mythology, have we Americans directly intervened either to save or to definitively establish the independence of a nation in the western hemisphere. In that sense at least, the policy of abstention was never abandoned. The illusion that we freed Cuba is, like all our other "defenses of freedom," part of a truly hemispheric fantasy.

Our continuing hostility toward the Cuban Revolution, like our continuing hostility toward revolution everywhere in Latin America, calls attention to another equally extraordinary fact: although it has been seldom noticed in the United States, the only three successful revolutions in modern Latin American history—in Mexico, Cuba and Nicaragua—have occurred in the three countries where U.S. violation of independence was not merely a major, but the dominant, historical theme.

Our conquest of Cuba in 1898, like the conquest of Mexico, made inevitable a new Latin American quest for independence—from us.

President McKinley's famous explanation for his decision to turn the Philippines into an American colony is to be found in every American history book. But it is worth quoting again here, because of its striking similarity to the same explanations most later presidents, including President Reagan, would give for their violations of the sovereignty of other foreign peoples.

McKinley, it is hardly necessary to be reminded, was on his knees in the White House, praying for divine guidance on what to do with the Philippines when, suddenly, his prayers were answered:

> [O]ne night late [McKinley later explained] it came to me this way—I don't know how it was, but it came: (1) that we could not give them back to Spain—that would be cowardly and dishonorable; (2) that we could not turn them over to France or Germany—our commercial rivals in the Orient—that would be bad business and discreditable; (3) that we could not leave them to themselves—they were unfit for self-government—and they would soon have anarchy and misrule over there worse than Spain's was. . . .

Would the United States choose cowardice and dishonor? Would it let the Philippines fall to our rivals? Providence, in its beneficence, had revealed to McKinley the same solution other presidents would discern from Nicaragua to Cambodia:

> [T]here was nothing left for us to do but to take them all, and to educate the Filipinos, and uplift and civilize and Christianize them, and by God's grace do the very best we could by them, as our fellow-men for whom Christ also died.

God had neglected to tell William McKinley that the Filipinos were already Christians. Even more important, He had not informed the President that the Filipinos, far from being "unfit for self-government," already had proclaimed their independence and, like the Cubans, had been fighting the Spanish for years. The Filipino independence forces, under Emilio Aguinaldo, like the Vietnamese independence forces, under Ho Chi Minh forty-seven years later, had welcomed the Americans as liberators.

But what would happen if the Americans turned out not to be liberators at all?

The United States had suffered only 385 battle deaths in the entire war with Spain; more than 4,000 Americans would die fighting, and crushing, the cause of Filipino independence. Thousands more would die of tropical disease. The United States, following the end of the war, paid Spain $20 million for the Philippines. The United States would spend more than $600 million, an immense sum in those days, on the war to impose U.S. rule there.

McKinley's decision to "uplift and civilize and Christianize" the Filipinos, however, would produce an even more illuminating statistic. Between 1899 and 1903, Americans would kill at the minimum 220,000 Filipinos—nine tenths of them unarmed civilians.

"It has been a splendid little war," John Hay wrote Theodore Roosevelt, following Spain's defeat. But what price would we Americans pay, and make others pay, for such a victory? "Our soldiers took no prisoners, they kept no records," a congressional inquiry later established; "they simply swept the country, and wherever they could get hold of a Filipino they killed him." As in Vietnam later, the American troops were only following orders.

"I wish you to kill and burn," General Jake Smith told his men; "the more you burn and kill the better it will please me."

"This is not a jungle war, but a struggle for freedom on every front of human activity," Lyndon Johnson would proclaim about the Vietnam War sixty years later. He was only paraphrasing McKinley. The war in the Philippines, that President told his critics, was a war "for the happiness, peace and prosperity of the Philippine Islands."

McKinley, in his turn, paraphrased Polk. The United States, he argued, was not committing aggression in the Philippines; it was only defending itself against Filipino aggression. The islanders had "assailed our sovereignty"; therefore the United States had no choice but to fight.

In his own country McKinley was accused of being an "insatiable murderer." Mark Twain, taking up the cudgels of Henry David Thoreau, proposed that, in keeping with America's new role in the world, the skull and crossbones replace the stars on Old Glory.

There was equal outrage expressed over our occupation of the Philippines after the war. U.S. troops had taken Manila only after the cease-fire with Spain had come into force. By what right did the United States annex an Asian nation, seized from its rightful owners, against the will of its people, after the fighting had stopped? Strong opposition to annexing the islands arose both in Congress and among the public. In the end, the peace treaty ceding the Philippines, Guam and Puerto Rico to the United States passed the Senate by only two votes—the same margin by which, fifty-four years earlier, the Senate had approved the annexation of Texas.

If anything, the ultimate consequences of this new annexation were even greater. Even Theodore Roosevelt recognized that the distant Asian archipelago, far from being vital to U.S. security, was a "heel of Achilles," strategically speaking. It was a perception that would become reality forty-one years later, when the Japanese would repeat Dewey's naval assault on the Philippines, and the U.S. forces, under General Douglas MacArthur, would be routed the same way the Spanish had been. As would become manifest later in Korea and Vietnam, overextending U.S. power in Asia did not extend the area of freedom; it only risked involving the United States in unnecessary wars.

Long before that, however, our "splendid little war" would start reshaping the fabric of American life. It had been easy enough to invade and colonize Puerto Rico and the Philippines. But how was the United States to cope with the counterinvasion—as millions of Puerto Ricans and hundreds of thousands of Filipinos established their own colonies inside the United States?

Back when the United States had conquered Mexico and "taken" Panama, Puerto Rico and so much else in Latin America, people had spoken of our expansion as a "demographic conquest," because we Americans so greatly outnumbered our neighbors. But by 1984 the demographic tables had been turned. Latin America's population of 390 million exceeded that of the United States by two thirds and was expected to be double that of the United States by the beginning of the twenty-first century. As the growing Latin Americanization of the United States demonstrated, the forces of "demographic conquest" were now advancing in the opposite direction.

Just as the Indian wars had been the training ground for the Mexican War, so the Americans engaged in the "pacification" program in the Philippines were, quite literally, the fathers and grandfathers of the Americans who would fight in Korea and Indochina. In the Philippines, free-fire zones were first established and the Filipino population was herded into "reconcentration camps"—successors of the Indian reservations, forerunners of the strategic hamlets. Torture, like murder of unarmed civilians, became U.S. standard procedure.

The U.S. Commander, General Arthur MacArthur, explained the war in the Philippines in terms his son might have used to explain the Korean War half a century later. Americans were killing Asians, he said, "to plant in the Orient . . . the idea of personal liberty." But, as in the future, one notable consequence was a rising American "military power and influence" that threatened the American constitutional chain of command. In rehearsal for the Truman-MacArthur controversy, fifty years later, General Arthur MacArthur vied with the American civilian governor for control of the islands.

As in the future, the Constitution held. Civilian supremacy over the military was asserted—in this case by William Howard Taft, the future President and father of Senator Robert Taft. The consequence—more than twenty years before our war against Sandino—nearly seventy years before Richard Nixon announced his own plan for peace with honor in Vietnam—was a familiar one.

"In this country," Taft had decided, "it is politically most important that Filipinos should suppress Filipino disturbances." Taft, rather than Henry Stimson, seems to have been the original author of the Vietnamization program. Soon Filipinos were being trained to kill Filipinos, and, in Taft's ample shadow, what he called his "little brown brothers" were being taught American-style democracy. It was only the beginning. For more than forty years, the United States would Americanize the Philippines.

In the Philippines, to a greater extent than anywhere else, the United States acted out the El Salvador fantasy: that oppression can create freedom, and that by imposing a regime of our own choosing on a foreign nation, we Americans can confer democracy on a conquered people. The history of that country, as a result, remains of enormous importance to U.S. foreign policy even today.

The consequence was that the Philippines became an Asian Nicaragua, but on a much larger scale. The forms of democracy prevailed while the United States was in charge; indeed they survived for some time following Philippine independence, in 1946. But in the end the creation of a political-military elite founded on collaboration with the Americans only produced a new Somoza for the Filipinos—and a new domino for the United States—in the form of the Marcos dictatorship.

By 1984, Marcos—like Somoza and the Shah before him—was teetering. The question was not whether, only when, this latest domino would topple, and whether the United States would repeat the Nicaraguan mistake once more.

The Spanish had killed at most 100,000 in their war to crush the independence movement in Cuba; we Americans killed more than twice that many human beings to crush the independence movement in the Philippines. Earlier, Americans had denounced Spain as "the brute, the devastator, the outrager of women, the exterminator of men . . . running riot with tortures and infamies of bloody debauchery." "And now we have come to it," exclaimed the Baltimore *News*, two generations in advance of the My Lai massacres.

We Americans had wound up murdering the very people we had set out to save. Yet as in the future this unsettling discovery produced no fundamental reappraisals, only the discovery in Washington that America dared not dishonor its commitment.

There was no alternative to fulfilling America's "obligations . . . to remain in the Philippines," declared one of the war's supporters. "[W]e will not come away, because we cannot come away . . . unless we write dishonor across the forehead of the American people."

It would take four years, and more than 120,000 U.S. ground troops to "pacify" the Philippines in the name of liberty. Armed resistance would continue into the 1920s.

In the end, Senator George Hoar's epitaph for the war for the Philippines might have been delivered by John Quincy Adams—had he lived long enough to see the end of the Vietnam War:

> You have wasted six hundred millions of treasure. You have sacrificed nearly 10,000 American lives, the flower of our youth. You have devastated provinces. You have slain uncounted thousands of the people you desire to benefit. Your generals are coming home from their harvest, bringing their sheaves with them, in the shape of other thousands of sick and wounded and insane. . . .

The United States, he concluded, had turned a friendly foreign people "into sullen and irreconcilable enemies, possessed of a hatred which centuries cannot eradicate."

Like most historical realities that contradict our national illusion of ourselves, it was the destiny of this first full-scale American war in Asia to be expunged entirely from the national consciousness and memory.

Generations of Americans would remember Commodore Dewey's gallant victory over the Spanish at Manila Bay. Generations of Americans would forget the burnt crops, the burnt villages, the charred cadavers of the Filipinos. Just as the Mexicans owed their liberty to us, even when we failed to defend them, so our attack on the Philippines, Americans would not doubt, also was a gallant gift of American liberty.

This national forgetfulness of our first full-scale war in Asia would prevail in the White House as well as the schoolroom. More than sixty years later, Presidents Johnson and Nixon would cite many precedents for their Indochina "commitment" in the attempt to explain why they, like Presidents McKinley and Roosevelt, had no choice but to fight their own ground war in Southeast Asia.

But just as no President would ever invoke the "Polk Doctrine" to explain our invasions of Latin America, so no President would invoke the "McKinley Corollary" to explain why he, too, was unleashing a maelstrom of American firepower on a terrorized Asian people who had done us no harm.

Between 1898, when the United States declared war on Spain, and 1903, when the Philippine insurrection was crushed, the United States traversed a watershed no less important than the one it had traversed, with the acquisition of Texas, Oregon and California, between 1845 and 1848.

Once again the foreign policy of the United States had been revolutionized. And as always with presidential warfare, the strategic balance abroad was inseparable from the constitutional balance at home.

"[If] this precedent be not reversed," Calhoun had warned, "nothing can prevent the executive power from overshadowing the constitution and liberties of the country." What was true of the Mexican War was no less true of the war in the Philippines. Roosevelt was not only the first occupant of the "imperial presidency" when it came to fighting undeclared land wars in Asia; his "trust busting" and federal regulation of the economy inaugurated, for both good and ill, the current era of presidential domination in our domestic affairs.

Within fifteen years, the reconcentration camps of the Philippines, like the Mexican War crisis, had been entirely forgotten. America's past, America's present—America's future—once again was a seamless web of fantasy in which the Founding Fathers proclaimed our independence and James Monroe proclaimed his doctrine.

Lincoln was the Great Emancipator, and Teddy Roosevelt handed down his Corollary to a grateful hemisphere. Now Woodrow Wilson was off to Europe to make the whole world safe for democracy.

It was the beginning of a crusade that has not ended yet. Neither at Versailles nor anywhere else would Americans ever find "a good definition of the word liberty." But that would not stop them from fighting for freedom on the Marne and on the Mekong, from killing Nicaraguans and Cambodians for the same reason they had killed Mexicans and Filipinos—and each other.

Our wars in places like Korea and El Salvador nonetheless raised the same question our wars in places like Mexico and the Philippines had. If it really is the destiny of us Americans to win wars for freedom, how is it that, over and over again, we keep finding ourselves ruled and overruled by events?

The answer, in at least one respect, was a rather simple one. How could a nation that had forgotten the paradox of Veracruz and the reconcentration camps of the Philippines be expected to remember the paradox of the strategic hamlets and the bombing of Hanoi? Why should an America oblivious to the realities that produced its own War of Independence, its own Civil War, not also be oblivious to the struggles of other peoples, both against others and against themselves?

All through the twentieth century, our presidents would act out the myths of Monroe, of Lincoln, of Theodore Roosevelt—and so they would find themselves becoming the new Polks, the new Buchanans, the new McKinleys. They would bombard new Greytowns; they would become the masters of countless Miskito Coasts.

But they would no more be able to resolve America's own inner contradictions than their predecessors had been able to contain the American impulse toward the Civil War.

The events of 1846 had revolutionized America's relationship with the Pacific basin, and hence with Asia. They had revolutionized America's relationship with Britain and hence with Europe. And Polk's war produced yet another revolution—in America's relations with what we call the Third World today.

The Mexican War had forged the doctrine of U.S. abuse of the weak, which, by the 1850s, had begun to expand itself to the rest of Latin America. Now, as a result of the war with Spain, the Monroe Doctrine—like the United States itself—had outgrown even the western hemisphere. Just as the destiny of Mexico had become the destiny of the Philippines, so in the new century—the American Century—the fate of the Philippines would become the fate of nations all over Asia, and the rest of the colonial world.

From these events in turn derived a development of even greater importance. This was the realization of an American destiny even more grandiose than that proclaimed by the cult of "Manifest Destiny." The United States would become arbiter not just of the New World, but of the whole world, as a result of what Polk had begun.

If not the father, that forgotten President is certainly the godfather, of the American Century.

* * *

As the great American flotilla sailed west across the Pacific, toward Asia, "Freedom" might have been emblazoned on every prow.

Battleships had replaced sailing ships. But these U.S. Navy vessels might have been named the *Santa Maria* and the *Mayflower,* for they were acting out the very illusion that had wrung America itself into existence: If you sailed west far enough, you not only could reach the East; you could discover "a special place with a special destiny."

An editorial in the Washington *Post* took note of this seeming paradox, sending battleships and destroyers to implant freedom in Asia. "A new consciousness seems to have come upon us," the newspaper observed, "a consciousness of strength—and with it a new appetite. . . ."

Actually there was nothing new in either the consciousness or in the appetite. Only the locale was new for this latest reenactment of an old American story.

Though it was 1898, it could have been 1945, 1950 or 1965—the U.S. troops bound for Hiroshima, the Yalu River or My Lai—because the truth, in any time on this earth, is that if you keep pushing in one direction far enough, hard enough, you wind up where you started.

Not for the last time, Providence had chosen the Washington *Post* to reveal something important about America.

"The taste of empire is in the mouth of the people even as the taste of blood is in the jungle," the editorial noted.

Then it summed up what our first century of conquest had produced for America, what in the course of our second century—the twentieth century, the American Century—Americans would discover all around the world.

"We are face to face," the editorial concluded, "with a strange destiny. . . ."

VI
An Empire of Evil

As the "frontier" retreated, the fleeing Indian nations of the Southwest gave way to the nations of Latin America; beyond the wide horizon of the prairies lay the limitless horizon of the Pacific Ocean, and all the lands beyond it. The Appalachian wilderness, the immensity of the Great Plains, the western deserts and the stupendous physical barrier of the Rocky Mountains did not halt—they scarcely slowed—the onward march of American destiny. Why should that destiny stop at the Pacific, be limited to only one hemisphere?

"We take up the task eternal," exulted Walt Whitman about the time U.S. firepower leveled Greytown. "We will not grow tired," Lyndon Johnson vowed 110 years later.

The Vietnam War lasted a very long time—so long that, by stages, Americans forgot why it was being fought. But there were recurring moments, at least in the White House, when both the war and America seemed to have some definable purpose.

One such moment came at the end of April 1970, when President Richard Nixon announced the invasion of Cambodia. He had ordered the attack, the President explained, to ensure "the survival of peace and freedom." The forces of "totalitarianism and anarchy" were threatening "free nations and free institutions throughout the world," he said, and only "the American people" could stop them.

"I know it may not be fashionable to speak of patriotism or national destiny these days," Nixon had conceded a little earlier. "But I feel it is appropriate to do so on this occasion." Justifying his escalation of the Indochina War, he went on:

> Two hundred years ago this Nation was weak and poor. But even then, America was the hope of millions in the world. Today we have become the strongest and richest Nation in the world. The wheel of destiny has turned so that any hope the world has for the survival of peace and freedom will

be determined by whether the American people have the moral stamina and the courage to meet the challenge of free world leadership.

"Cambodia," the President later emphasized, "is the Nixon Doctrine in its purest form."

Between Cambodia and earlier American attempts to "extend the area of freedom," there was an unnoticed continuity.

In June 1898, when the U.S. cruiser *Charleston* had trained its guns on Guam, the Spanish had quickly surrendered the little island colony. Like so much else, Guam had fallen to America as though it were a gift of Providence. Over the decades, the little American bastion in the far Pacific—nearly five thousand miles southwest of California and more than fifteen hundred miles from the mainland of Asia—had been transformed, along with Okinawa, to the north, into a main anchor in what Acheson had called America's "defense perimeter." By 1969, however, the "defense perimeter" had undergone a metamorphosis of its own. It had been turned into an American offensive perimeter for U.S. attacks on the mainland of Asia.

In July 1969, Air Force One, bearing President Richard M. Nixon, landed on Guam. In most places, the presidential jet was an impressive aircraft, but there Air Force One was overshadowed by the long lines of B-52s. A military honor guard saluted the Commander in Chief. Everywhere he went on that tropical island, the President was flanked by high-ranking officers in crisp uniforms. In the most important event of the presidential visit, the press was summoned to a military briefing room.

President Nixon began by speaking of what he called his "very consuming interest in Asia." Then he came to his main point.

"[W]hether we like it or not, geography makes us a Pacific power," the President began, "and when we consider that Guam . . . is in the heart of Asia . . . we can all realize this."

Eight months earlier, he had been elected President promising to end the Vietnam War. But now Nixon propounded a different doctrine: of permanent U.S. involvement in the conflicts of Asia.

"Look at Asia," the President emphasized. "It poses . . . the greatest threat to the peace of the world, and for that reason," he stated, "the United States is going to continue to play a major role in Asia."

At first it was called the Guam Doctrine, but seven months later, in a February 1970 message to Congress, the President himself gave it a new name. *"Peace Through Partnership—the Nixon Doctrine."* Nixon made it explicit that he was acting with a strong sense of historical precedent.

"The postwar era of American foreign policy," the message said, "began . . . with the proclamation of the Truman Doctrine." Now, because "the world has dramatically changed," a new presidential doctrine was needed for a new era in world affairs.

"[T]here would be no more Vietnams," the President had pledged at Guam. Yet the United States nonetheless would go on "meeting our responsibilities, protecting our interests. . . ."

In truth Guam, when Nixon visited there, might have been some prism of America, separating the illusion of light from the reality of darkness, and recapitulating a contradiction old as America itself.

For while the President had been publicly proclaiming his doctrine of "peace and freedom and justice," a parallel American drama—of destruction, self-delusion and corruption—was unfolding on Guam, concealed even from those who acted it out on that little island. It was from the same runways where Nixon's plane had landed that, for more than thirteen months before the U.S. invasion of Cambodia, the B-52s had been taking off to bomb Cambodia secretly. One of the Cambodian bombing campaigns was called "Freedom Deal": It was as though Americans had but to call death liberty for conquest to become a triumph of American principles.

The paradox of Guam—publicly proclaiming peace while secretly making war—was thus also the paradox of the entire Vietnam policy, which would give both America and Indochina nearly six more years of desolation and bitterness. How was it possible "to end the war and win the peace," as the President promised, by expanding the devastation of Vietnam into other countries?

The final answer to that question would come only in 1975 as the Khmer Rouge overran Phnom Penh and Saigon fell to the North Vietnamese Army. It had not been possible to "win the peace" by widening the war. The Nixon Doctrine had been only another American fantasy.

Long before those much vaster catastrophes were played out, however, the secret bombing of Cambodia contained a mystery of its own. What were the B-52 strikes expected to achieve?

The heaviest bombing campaign in the history of warfare had not prevented the Tet Offensive, a year earlier, or saved Lyndon Johnson from its consequences. The U.S. military, even before the Cambodia bombing had begun, had concluded, as the Pentagon Papers later revealed, that even more intensive bombing could neither deter nor prevent Hanoi from continuing the war.

While bombing Cambodia offered no shortcut to victory in South Vietnam, it did contain a serious danger for the United States. This was that the bombing would drive the Vietnamese deeper into, not out of, Cambodia, the last country of Indochina to escape involvement in the war, and so thrust one more "domino" into North Vietnam's hands. If "peace with honor" ever was going to be achieved in Southeast Asia, it could come only by turning Laos and South Vietnam into new Cambodias—not by transforming Cambodia into another American free-fire zone.

What could justify the risk that bombing Cambodia would embroil the

United States in still another full-scale war, in still another Southeast Asian nation?

It was a question not even the crews of the B-52s, on their long flights from Guam to Cambodia, asked themselves—because it had been decided that not even those who dropped the bombs should know where they fell. On presidential orders, the crews were given false bombing coordinates and told they were bombing South Vietnam.

Others from whom it was kept secret that the U.S. Air Force was bombing Cambodia included the Secretary of the Air Force and the U.S. embassy in Cambodia. But that was only the beginning. Even top-secret military documents were falsified. Almost no one in the Pentagon and the CIA was told what was happening, and the entire State Department was deceived as well. Not only was the United States not bombing Cambodia, U.S. officials were assured, it was U.S. policy not to violate Cambodia's neutrality in any way.

In secret testimony, Congress was told the same lie—though for the most part the high officials did not know they were lying to Congress, because the White House had lied to them, too. Three years later, the Senate Armed Services Committee would discover that, even as Richard Nixon had taken office, an entire conspiracy had begun to unfold—a conspiracy designed to make it possible for the President of the United States to make war in a foreign country without the government of the United States knowing it.

On one level, the conspiracy was a success. Between March 1969 and May 1970, the B-52s flew a total of 3,875 secret bombing missions over Cambodia; they dropped 108,823 tons of bombs there.

"We could hear the explosions in Phnom Penh," Lloyd M. Rives, the American chargé d'affaires in Cambodia, later remarked. "But we believed the bombs were falling on Vietnam."

The secret bombing was no secret in Hanoi, and even in Washington it quickly became clear that the most elaborate deception in the history of presidential warfare was not working. The bombing had begun on March 18, 1969. On March 26, the New York *Times,* in a story by its Pentagon correspondent, William Beecher, reported that the U.S. command in Saigon had requested the White House to approve air strikes against Cambodia. In early May, in another *Times* article, Beecher confirmed that "American B-52 bombers have raided several Viet Cong and North Vietnamese supply dumps and base camps in Cambodia. . . ."

These reports attracted almost no attention in Congress. They had no effect on events in Indochina. But they turned out to be milestones in the modern constitutional history of the United States.

How had the most closely kept secret of the Indochina War wound up being published in the New York *Times?* In the White House, the President came to the same conclusion about the American press he already had reached about Vietnam: only a counterconspiracy could explain events that displeased the Administration.

Following publication of the Beecher reports, Nixon and Kissinger ordered wiretaps and other acts of espionage against members of the press; they ordered wiretaps and spying on their own staff members as well. Nearly a year before the Cambodia invasion, the secret war there had insensibly transposed itself into a secret presidential war against the First Amendment and the war-making provisions of the United States Constitution. Richard Nixon had taken the first steps down the road to Watergate, and for him, there would be no turning back.

While the bombs were falling secretly, a secret American ground war also was being fought. During 1969 and 1970, on presidential orders, U.S. troops launched no less than 1,031 secret ground operations in Cambodia. Simultaneously there were nearly 2,000 secret helicopter gunship attacks and 1,239 secret U.S. tactical air strikes.

Thousands of U.S. troops participated in these operations. The soldiers were threatened with imprisonment and heavy fines if they revealed where they had fought, and even when twenty-seven Americans were killed, the deception continued. On government orders, the families were told that their sons and husbands had been killed in "Southeast Asia" or "along the border." Only in 1973, as the Watergate investigations gathered momentum, would their families learn where and how these Americans had died; even then they would not be told why.

Cambodia had become a place where Americans now disappeared, just as the bombs fell, into a nameless void. Yet the secret ground war, like the secret air war, contained a mystery that went beyond the secrecy. What were these attacks intended to achieve?

In terms of intelligence, they only confirmed what one could read in the Washington *Post* or hear in the cafes of Phnom Penh. As virtually the whole South Vietnamese border had become an American free-fire zone, the North Vietnamese and the Vietcong had dug in along a narrow strip of territory on the Cambodian side. Later, congressional investigations showed these forays had provided no information that could not have been obtained by other means. Much of the "intelligence" these military probes gathered turned out to be spectacularly false.

Nor did the operations have any military utility. Half a million U.S. ground troops had failed to win the war in South Vietnam; not even a thousand raids into Cambodia—not even a full-scale U.S. invasion, as events ultimately would show—could destroy the sanctuaries there.

The question of Guam and the White House was thus also the question of the Cambodian jungle. What secret was the secrecy designed to conceal? What was it, just across the border, that President Nixon was so determined to find and destroy?

A year after the Tet Offensive in South Vietnam, the fascination with Cambodia was not confined to the White House. Within the U.S. headquarters in Saigon, known universally by the acronym MACV, Cambodia was the object of a secret operation as well. MACV—a series of sealed, air-conditioned, underground bunkers near Saigon airport—was the closed mind of the American war in Vietnam. And all through 1969, and into 1970, in those underground chambers where the temperature never varied and no natural light ever penetrated, analysts worked around the clock, piecing together what was called an intelligence "mosaic" of Cambodia.

What riveted the attention of MACV and the White House, and beckoned toward it the B-52s and the Special Forces could not fail also to excite the attention of the CIA and its kindred institutions.

About a month after President Nixon took office, according to a former member of Naval Intelligence named Samuel R. Thornton, "the highest level of government" in Washington gave "blanket approval to take any and all measures" to overthrow Prince Norodom Sihanouk, the neutralist ruler of Cambodia.

One of the plans developed in Saigon and approved in Washington, according to Thornton, was "to insert a U.S.-trained assassination team disguised as Viet Cong insurgents into Phnom Penh to kill Prince Sihanouk." The objective, he added, was to bring into power a new Cambodian Government, which would "issue a public request for U.S. military intervention. . . ."

Both Sihanouk's position and Cambodia's neutrality already were most precarious. Every day, the Vietnam War, like some rising sea of devastation, lapped a little farther into Cambodia. Sihanouk's—and Cambodia's own— worst enemies, however, were not foreigners. As future events would reveal with sickening clarity, they were Cambodians. By the beginning of 1969, Sihanouk's own Minister of Defense, General Lon Nol, was plotting to overthrow him. What made the plotting all the more dangerous was that Lon Nol and his associates fully appreciated that they could achieve power only at the risk of plunging their country into full-scale war.

Since Lon Nol, not Sihanouk, controlled the Cambodian military, mounting a coup would not be difficult. But what would happen if the Cambodian peasantry rose up on Sihanouk's behalf—and the North Vietnamese supported the effort to restore him to power? Could Lon Nol count on President Nixon's support if his coup ignited a Cambodian civil war? Or had the United States finally learned the real lesson of Vietnam, and so many of our other foreign interventions: that U.S. embroilment in such conflicts helped neither us nor others?

In secret communications with the Americans in early 1969, Lon Nol asked for U.S. weapons, ammunition and money. The Americans also had something else Lon Nol needed. For twenty years, the CIA had maintained close links with Son Ngoc Thanh, an exiled Cambodian leader who had attempted many times, with U.S. support, to overthrow Norodom Sihanouk and replace his government with one that would support the U.S. war effort in Indochina.

These attempts all had failed. But Son Ngoc Thanh nonetheless had wound up playing an important role in the American war in Vietnam. With his help, the United States had recruited its own Cambodian force, known as the Khmer Krom, from ethnic Cambodians living in South Vietnam.

These forces had fought well in South Vietnam, and the fact had not gone unnoticed in Phnom Penh. If Lon Nol did overthrow Norodom Sihanouk, would the United States send the Khmer Krom troops to Phnom Penh to protect him from the consequences? According to Thornton, the "highest levels of government" also approved "a request for use of Khmer Krom mercenaries . . . to infiltrate key Cambodian Army units stationed in Phnom Penh in order to support the first stages of the coup."

The scheme to kill Norodom Sihanouk never unfolded, because General Lon Nol, quite correctly, rejected it as "silly," and made a counterproposal. Thornton's version of it is worth quoting in its entirety, because it outlines the actions Lon Nol took exactly a year later, in March 1970. Lon Nol proposed

> to lead a coup when Prince Sihanouk left the country on one of his periodic rest cures . . . in the south of France. [It] was felt by the general and his advisers that by confronting the Prince with a fait accompli when he was cut off from direct access to his resources they could discourage him from attempting to mount a countercoup, to them a very real and frightening possibility based on their assessment of the profound support he enjoyed among most Cambodians, excepting themselves.

By April 1969, Henry Kissinger had drastically reorganized the National Security Council, and it appears that the White House, too, by then had concluded that the plans in Saigon to kill Sihanouk were "silly." When Lon Nol's counterproposal was relayed to the National Security Council, the "response," according to Thornton, "was surprisingly cool considering the original carte blanche authorization."

Officially, Lon Nol was "told that while the U.S. would support in principle the accession to power of a Phnom Penh regime more sympathetic to U.S. interests in the region," the Nixon administration could make no advance promise of support. Instead, "the U.S. would have to base a decision for the commitment of U.S. forces in support of such a regime on the circumstances which obtained at the time the new regime came to power."

By back channels, however, Lon Nol was sent quite a different message:

> Unofficially, he was . . . told that, although he could in fact expect the requested support, he must understand that the U.S. was sensitive to international criticism on this point, so that he must be prepared for a show of vacillation and great reluctance on our part to his initial, public requests for military assistance.

Lon Nol, Thornton adds, "indicated an understanding of this problem and an eagerness to go forward on these terms. He also expressed great interest in the possibility of using Khmer Krom [troops], but insisted that he must first have discussions with the Khmer Krom commander, an exiled veteran of Cambodian politics."

Though Thornton was cited "for outstanding performance of duty," and his account was corroborated by events in Phnom Penh and Washington, it is based solely on his personal experiences in Saigon between May 1968 and May 1969. What happened next, however, is more amply documented. In Phnom Penh in 1971, Son Ngoc Thanh, the "exiled veteran of Cambodian politics," himself confirmed that, through him, Lon Nol had requested, and the CIA had approved, a U.S. pledge to send the Khmer Krom troops to support Lon Nol in the event he overthrew Norodom Sihanouk.

Lon Nol was not the only Cambodian receiving assurances of support from Washington. Less than a month after the secret bombing of Cambodia began, Sihanouk himself received a letter from President Nixon pledging that his administration "recognizes and respects the sovereignty, independence, neutrality, and territorial integrity of the kingdom of Cambodia within its present frontiers."

Simultaneously U.S. officials were violating Cambodia's neutrality and pledging respect for it—both cultivating Norodom Sihanouk and encouraging Lon Nol to overthrow him. Well before the phrase came into use at the Paris peace talks, the Nixon administration was following a "two-track" policy in Cambodia. In Washington, Lon Nol was considered "pro-American," just as, later, the Khmer Rouge would be imagined to be "pro-North Vietnamese." But, for Sihanouk, Lon Nol and Pol Pot alike, the American war in Indochina was only one chapter in a millennium-old history of Cambodian enmity with Vietnam to which ideology was totally irrelevant, in which passionate nationalism was all.

Lon Nol dreamed U.S. troops and bombs could rid Cambodia of the Vietnamese, just as Pol Pot imagined a radical revolution could. Norodom Sihanouk differed from them in only one respect. He saw with painful clarity what was invisible to Nixon: expanding the Vietnam War into Cambodia would not defeat North Vietnam; it would only destroy Cambodia and its independence. But Sihanouk was no more pro-Communist than Lon Nol, as President Nixon was certainly aware.

So by mid-1969 it seemed, to the President and the handful of his advisers who actually knew what U.S. policy was, that the United States could not lose in Cambodia. If one track led Sihanouk to acquiesce in the secret bombings, or at least not to officially protest them, that was good.

And if another track led to Lon Nol's overthrowing Sihanouk and establishing a "Phnom Penh regime more sympathetic to U.S. interests in the region," that was even better.

Only Sihanouk, as this double game of secrecy unfolded in Washington and Cambodia, seemed to have any sense that the result was not going to be "peace with honor" in Vietnam, only war in Cambodia and dishonor in the United States.

Ten days after the secret B-52 strikes started, as rumors circulated that Cambodia was turning toward the United States, Sihanouk addressed the fundamental question that the Nixon Doctrine of "peace and partnership" raised.

"What does 'turn to America' mean?" the prince asked in the course of a Phnom Penh press conference. "It means that Cambodia will become a second Vietnam, that there will be mourning . . . throughout Cambodia."

It was as though Sihanouk recognized that his country at last was face to face, in the form of President Nixon and his doctrine, with an American destiny not even his agility could avert. He might have been an astute Mexican, in 1846, explaining to his countrymen why the Americans not only destroyed, but destroyed without guilt.

"[T]he Americans will reason their intervention is legitimate," he said. How would Sihanouk react if the U.S. invaded? "I will become a turncoat if necessary," he announced, fourteen months before he allied himself with the North Vietnamese and the Khmer Rouge in order to resist the American invasion.

"[T]he Sihanouk era," he predicted, "is near an end." He also predicted the result of the Americans expanding the Vietnam War into Cambodia: only "Cambodians will . . . be killed, because the Vietnamese are skillfully camouflaged."

It would be better, the chief of state of Cambodia added, for the Americans to "kill me instead of my countrymen." And this, too, in the following years would be transformed by events from a personal assertion into nothing more controversial than a statement of fact.

Invading Cambodia would not defeat North Vietnam; it would only kill Cambodians, and drive first Sihanouk, then Cambodia itself, into the arms of the Communists. Such, a year before the Nixon invasion of Cambodia, were some of the truths an American President could learn by reading the public transcripts of Radio Phnom Penh. But what did the secret bombings, the secret ground missions, the growing "intelligence mosaic" of Cambodia at MACV reveal?

All through 1969 and into 1970, from their secret vantage points, Americans gazed into Cambodia, trying to find the answer to a question about themselves. What could explain the manifest failure of the United States, after so many years, to defeat the Communist conspiracy and instill freedom in South Vietnam?

Neither then nor later, within this closed world that kept so many small secrets from others and so many immense secrets from itself, would the fundamental paradox of the Nixon Doctrine, the fundamental paradox of America, ever be confronted: the faith that an American war of conquest could confer freedom on others. Some other, outside, un-American explanation must be found for all that had gone wrong.

As the intelligence mosaic at MACV pieced itself together, Cambodia ceased to be a country. It became, like so much of America's own past, only an invention. By then, even the names the Americans gave their secret reflected what had happened. The code name for the secret U.S. military ground operations was "Daniel Boone." Once again, Americans were preparing to lash outward, rather than confront America's own contradictions, and as the Nixon administration grappled with the "threat" it perceived there, Cambodia more and more resembled a new frontier.

As the American destiny assumed a Cambodian incarnation, a secret computer program seemed to be determining events.

The secret bombing had begun on March 18, 1969. A year to the day later, Sihanouk was overthrown. A script a year old was being acted out, exactly as it had been written in Phnom Penh, Saigon and Washington. Sihanouk had gone to France. Lon Nol had ousted him. And the Nixon administration—publicly making "a show of vacillation and great reluctance" following the coup—quickly dispatched both the Khmer Krom troops and the promised weapons and ammunition to Lon Nol.

Events followed the script in another way. In a rehearsal for the later, much vaster Cambodian catastrophe, the countryside rose up against the city. Peasants carrying Sihanouk's portrait marched on the capital. Lon Nol's troops gunned them down. Less than two hours' drive from Phnom Penh, the border between South Vietnam and Cambodia—between war and peace—was dissolving. U.S. bombs were falling deeper and deeper inside Cambodia. Hoping to restore Sihanouk, North Vietnamese troops seized a town only a few miles from Phnom Penh. But suddenly, in the midst of the fighting, the firing stopped.

Two Buddhist monks in saffron robes appeared, like a dream in the midst of a nightmare, and traversed the no-man's-land. Would the Lon Nol coup hold? Would Sihanouk return, like a vengeful god? Or could some mysterious, sudden apparition stop the killing and save Cambodia from full-scale war?

Cambodia's fate was decided in Washington, as Sihanouk had prophesied. Three years later, Senator Stuart Symington explained what happened next: "[W]e supported [Sihanouk's] overthrow when he was out of the country. When that overthrow appeared to be failing . . . we invaded his country on the ground as well as bombing it from the air."

"This is not an invasion of Cambodia," the President told the nation on the night of April 30, 1970, as tens of thousands of U.S. and South Vietnamese troops launched their offensive.

"American policy . . . has been to scrupulously respect the neutrality of the Cambodian people," Nixon added. "The United States had neither connection with, nor knowledge of," Sihanouk's overthrow, the President later asserted.

President Nixon's direct involvement in the secret air and ground operations in Cambodia later was fully documented by Congress. But just as no direct link ever would be established between the President and the actual Watergate break-in, no documentary evidence so far has been found to prove that Nixon personally authorized the pledges of U.S. support for the plot against Sihanouk.

There is no doubt those assurances were given, no doubt, either, that the President personally authorized them fulfilled once Sihanouk was overthrown. But a shadow of a doubt nonetheless remains. Had U.S. intelligence agents, like the Watergate "plumbers" later, interpreted general policy in the White House as authorization for actions of which the President was not personally informed? Or did Nixon succeed in covering up in Cambodia what he later failed to conceal during the Watergate crisis?

"The United States had absolutely nothing to do with the overthrow of Sihanouk in 1970," the administration claimed during later congressional investigations. Nixon's closest associates, however, were far less adamant in their denials. After he left office, Henry Kissinger declared that the United States had played no role in the Cambodia coup, "at least not at the top level." Melvin Laird, Nixon's Secretary of Defense, chose his words even more carefully: "I have no direct knowledge," he ultimately told William Shawcross, "that the approval of Sihanouk's overthrow was made."

William Colby, CIA director at the time, was even more equivocal: "Lon Nol may well have been encouraged by the fact that the U.S. was working with Son Ngoc Thanh," he told Shawcross. "I don't know of any specific assurances he was given, but the obvious conclusion for him, given the political situation in South Vietnam and Laos, was that he would be given United States support."

"[N]o direct knowledge," no "specific assurances," "at least not at the top level." By the time the United States invaded Cambodia, not only was secrecy power within the government of the United States; to know things only indirectly, to give only unspecific assurances, to avoid direct knowledge of what you have known all along—all these were essentials of the black art of wielding immense power while evading personal responsibility for the abuse of that power. Colby's account in fact corroborates Thornton's account of the instructions received from the White House. While Kissinger and the National Security Council avoided giving Lon Nol "any specific assurances," the unofficial assurances he received, quite possibly with President Nixon's personal authorization, led to "the obvious conclusion," as Colby later put it, "that he would be given United States support."

"Deniability" is always an essential in such clandestine exercises, but deniability in Washington could not absolve the United States from responsibility for the consequences in Cambodia. According to Son Ngoc Thanh, the pledge of U.S. support was the crucial factor in the decision to overthrow Norodom Sihanouk. "Only after I was able to provide assurances that the U.S. would send the Khmer Krom troops," he told me, "did Lon Nol act."

Lon Nol's brother Lon Non, who played a crucial role in the coup, said the same thing: "We would not have done what we did," he told me, "had we not been absolutely sure President Nixon would support us." Among Lon Non's actions, just before the coup and weeks before the North Vietnamese and the Vietcong took any hostile actions, was directing an unprovoked Cambodian attack on the North Vietnamese and Vietcong diplomatic missions in Phnom Penh. Lon Non's men had wrecked the two missions, stolen files and money, and desecrated the Vietnamese flags.

Just after the coup, Lon Nol took an even more fateful step. He served an ultimatum on the Vietnamese—ordering them to remove all their troops from the country within seventy-two hours. Simultaneously, Cambodian troops murdered hundreds of civilian Vietnamese residents of Cambodia.

The message to Hanoi was clear. This was no mere internal change of leadership in Cambodia. Lon Nol was determined to transform Cambodia into a military ally of the United States.

What accounted for this virtual declaration of war on a country immeasurably more powerful than Cambodia? By 1969, Sihanouk was unpopular with Cambodia's tiny urban elite. But only by transforming Sihanouk's ouster into a crusade against the Vietnamese—only by deliberately exciting Cambodia's ancient, smoldering nationalist passions—could Lon Nol hope to rally nationwide support for his coup.

"It would have been madness to antagonize the Vietnamese the way we did," Lon Non remarked more than a year after the coup, "unless we were sure of U.S. military support." Now the madness of Khmer nationalism had been unleashed. It would consume millions of Cambodians, including Lon Non himself, murdered by the Khmer Rouge in 1975.

At first, the President spoke of his Cambodia invasion as though it were the decisive battle of the Vietnam War. The invasion, Nixon asserted, would "guarantee the continued success" of U.S. operations in South Vietnam. More than that, it would make possible "a just peace in Vietnam and the Pacific. . . ."

But, almost immediately, U.S. officials began to drastically downgrade their military assessments. Soon it was clear that the will and capacity of North Vietnam to win the war had not been destroyed as a result of invading Cambodia. No capacity, in South Vietnam, to survive without permanent and unlimited U.S. military intervention had been created.

Instead, the invasion had produced only a tactically minor and strategically meaningless result, as Nixon himself made clear only eight days after the invasion began.

The invasion, the President said, had gained for the United States "at least six months and probably eight months of time" in a war the North Vietnamese had been winning, and their adversaries losing, for twenty-five years. In Saigon, President Thieu had an even more realistic assessment of what the invasion had achieved. The North Vietnamese and the Vietcong, he told the press, could be back in the sanctuaries in as little as two or three months.

One more monsoon and perhaps one more dry season had been purchased for the military mandarinate of Saigon and its American patrons. But at what price for the people of Cambodia? And at what price for the United States?

In truth, the military results of Nixon's invasion were trivial in comparison to its main result. Nixon's invasion had unleashed two dark dramas of nationalism, one in Cambodia, the other in the United States, and before these dramas were played out one nation would be rocked to its foundations—and another nation would have even its foundations destroyed.

The American drama erupted almost before President Nixon finished speaking. All along, the paradox of the Nixon Doctrine had posed a question not just about Vietnam, but about America.

How would the President act, how would the nation react, when events demonstrated that the Nixon Doctrine had no relation to reality? Less than ten weeks after his message to Congress about "peace and partnership," Nixon's announcement of the invasion answered one part of that question. The speech was long and emotional, but the President summed up his real policy in only five words.

"We will not be defeated," the President declared. Behind this latest doctrine, too, was a hidden presidential agenda, and now that secret objective—victory, not peace—was starkly revealed. He had no intention, the President declared, "to see this nation accept the first defeat in its proud, 190-year history."

Suddenly it was as though Polk were back in the White House, Calhoun and Adams still in Congress—and Henry David Thoreau reincarnated, a thousand times over, at Kent State.

He not only wanted to end the war, Nixon said later,

> but to end it in a way that will strengthen trust for America around the world, not undermine it; in a way that will redeem the sacrifices that have been made, not insult them; in a way that will heal this nation, not tear it apart.

It was an honorable aspiration, but the President's war intrigue in Cambodia already had destroyed any possibility of its ever being fulfilled.

At a stroke, the Cambodia invasion had divided America and assured that the bitterness that had destroyed the Johnson presidency would poison the Nixon presidency too. The obsession with Cambodia, the obsession with secrecy, the obsession with force, already had guaranteed that trust in America would be undermined around the world, that the sacrifices Americans had made would be insulted, that in the end the American nation would not be healed, but torn apart.

Meanwhile, beneath the passionate American divisions that the invasion had aroused, the President's secret bombing campaign, his willful deception of Congress, the tapped telephones, ticked away like time bombs under the White House.

What would be the result when it was discovered that the President not only had violated Cambodia's neutrality, but violated the Constitution? March 18, 1969—the day the secret Cambodian bombing began—was an important date in American history. Seldom so deliberately, and never so thoroughly, had an American President conspired to violate the war-making powers of the Constitution. August 15, 1973—the day the Cambodia bombing finally stopped—proved to be no less significant a date. For, following the revelation of the secret bombing, Congress moved forcefully to reassert its constitutional powers.

It ordered the bombing halted. For the first time in decades, Congress had specifically limited the President's ability to make war.

Cambodia had been ravaged, but once again the U.S. Constitution had prevailed. The bombing, which had begun with an unprecedented executive usurpation of the war-making power, would end with an unprecedented reassertion of congressional authority. Just as the Nixon Doctrine led to military defeat in Indochina, so also would it produce, in Washington, results the exact opposite of those the President had intended.

The congressional bombing halt was by no means the most dramatic consequence the secret bombing would produce. In 1973, after details of the secret bombing campaign and its attendant deceptions of Congress and violations of civil liberties were made public, a Massachusetts congressman named Robert Drinan rose in the House of Representatives and made a proposal that would earn him a footnote in history.

As much as the B-52s, Drinan himself, the only Catholic priest ever to serve in Congress, embodied the metamorphoses of America. His district abutted John Quincy Adams's old district, and as he denounced the President's war, Drinan spoke with the moral fervor of some Puritan divine. Over the generations, the human waves crossing the Atlantic had ceaselessly remade America, just as America, pushing westward, had wound up remaking the world. But some themes in America are changeless.

The President, Drinan charged, had

> authorized, ordered, and ratified the concealment from the Congress of the facts and the submission to the Congress of false and misleading statements concerning the existence, scope and nature of American bombing operations in Cambodia in derogation of the power of the Congress to declare war, to make appropriations, and to raise and support armies. . . .

For these presidential violations of the Constitution, Drinan proposed a constitutional remedy. "[S]uch conduct," he argued, "warrants impeachment and trial and removal from office."

Drinan's proposal would never win full congressional approval, but the presidential war in Cambodia now had its Wilmot Proviso; 128 years after Polk's war intrigue had made inevitable the greatest crisis of American nationalism of the nineteenth century, Nixon's war intrigue had produced the greatest constitutional crisis of the second century of our independence.

As always in America, the symmetry of past and present was entirely forgotten. As the Watergate crisis more and more obsessed America, another parallel was also ignored: it was seldom noticed that the questions raised by what Nixon called "a second-rate burglary" were the same questions posed by what had turned out to be a second-rate invasion.

What secret possibly could have lurked, inside Democratic headquarters, inside Cambodia, to justify the White House taking such a risk? And once the secret, illegal operation became public, what possibly could have led the President to imagine he could get away with a cover-up? What, above all, were the consequences, for the President and his own administration, when the President opted for a policy of deception not only without, but within?

Militarily, the Cambodia invasion had hurt the North Vietnamese no more than, politically, the Democrats would be hurt by the Watergate break-in. But in his determination to defeat his enemies, the President had made defeat inevitable for himself.

The most important single result of the invasion, in fact, had been to saddle the United States with a third strategic albatross in Indochina. Like Laos and Thieu's Saigon republic, Lon Nol's Khmer Republic was no asset. It was an irredeemable liability that no American commitment could "save," and the consequences would not be limited to Cambodia. At the very moment Nixon was pledging to end the U.S. combat role in Indochina, he had saddled the dwindling American forces there with a wider war. He also had ensured that, after the American soldiers went home, South Vietnam's U.S.-trained troops would be fatally overextended.

In early 1971 the Cambodia invasion was repeated in Laos; South Vietnamese and U.S. forces attempted—and failed—to cut the Ho Chi Minh Trail, just as they earlier had tried and failed to destroy the Cambodian sanctuaries.

Once again the rhetoric was of peace and partnership. This was no invasion, no escalation of the war, the President said. It was only part of his secret plan to end the war and bring the boys home. The South Vietnamese code word for the Laos invasion, however, summed up the real objective. It was *Lam Son*—Total Victory—that President Nixon had hoped to find in the jungles of Laos.

Like Cambodia, Laos was only another stepping-stone to total defeat. The South Vietnamese and their American advisers were routed. The stage was set for North Vietnam's 1972 spring offensive in South Vietnam—and for all the other Tets that, in the end, would see Thieu's immense, American-made military apparatus collapse from within.

Like Watergate, Cambodia had set the dominoes toppling, and they would not stop toppling until the result, in both Saigon and Washington, was total dishonor, total defeat.

What conclusion, so many years later, can one draw from these symmetrical catastrophes? Six months before he invaded Cambodia, Nixon himself wrote the epitaph for both the Nixon Doctrine and Watergate.

"North Vietnam cannot defeat or humiliate the United States," he told the nation. "Only Americans can do that." Over the next four and a half years it would be Richard Nixon's fate to vindicate that statement more totally than any other President in our history.

Cambodia resembled Watergate in another way: there, too, the totality of the catastrophe revealed itself only in stages. Yet the omens nonetheless were visible from the beginning, for those who could perceive them.

As the chaos of war spread across Cambodia, one saw things never seen, even after decades of conflict, in Laos and Vietnam: the tortured cadavers of women and children, their hands tied behind their backs, floating down the Mekong River; Vietnamese children, shot but not killed by Cambodian troops, and left to bleed to death.

Why had the body of a North Vietnamese soldier, his eyes gouged out, been hung from a tree? Cambodian villagers grinned proudly when asked, and said they had done it. As war became the general condition in Cambodia, the Khmer smile never disappeared, even when the atrocities became general. Smiling Khmer children in uniform returned from battle carrying severed heads; others smiled as, over an open fire, they grilled the livers of those they killed, and ate them.

From the other side of the lines came other stories, too often discounted, of a Catholic priest torn apart; of "pro-Lon Nol" members of the National Assembly locked inside a house that was then set ablaze; of villages the Khmer Rouge "liberated," then razed to the ground. In the first few months of the Cambodia War, more than twenty foreign journalists disappeared; only a handful were ever again seen alive. The pattern was there, even when the pattern was not perceived: all those apprehended by Cambodians had been murdered; only those fortunate enough to fall into the hands of the North Vietnamese survived.

As Watergate became a national obsession in the United States, Cambodia became the scene of a parallel revelation: There, too, the President's intrigue had unleashed a hitherto unsuspected national capacity for psychosis.

In December 1970, President Nixon described his support for Lon Nol as "in my opinion, probably the best investment in foreign assistance that the United States has made in my political lifetime." In February 1971, a year after he had announced his doctrine of "peace and progress," Nixon sent another message to Congress. "Cambodia is, in short, a concrete illustration of Nixon Doctrine principles," it announced. "I can report," the President told the nation two months later, "that Vietnamization has succeeded." The "success of the Cambodia operation," he added, proved it.

No other official in the world had access to so much information, had so many men and machines at his command. Yet, in both Indochina and Washington, the President seemed doomed to act out fantasies. One question not even the most sensational revelations answered later was how a President of the United States could have made such stupendous, self-destructive errors in judgment.

Two years before the Watergate burglary, four years before the House of Representatives voted to impeach the President, Cambodia provided one answer: By then all the fantasies of America had been institutionalized, not only in the immense power of the American Government, but in the minds of those who controlled it. Force and secrecy no longer were merely the fundamental maxims of America's policy; they had become ends in themselves, even when force led only to impotence, and secrecy to self-deception.

The secret plans to invade Cambodia, for example, had been no secret in Hanoi. The North Vietnamese Government had known about the invasion weeks in advance, and its commanders along the border had copies of MACV's assault plans days before the invasion began. It was only his own allies in Cambodia, his own embassy there, that the President had deceived. The American chargé, in consequence, learned of the invasion from a Voice of America news broadcast. He rushed to Lon Nol's residence to inform him, but Lon Nol, too, possessed a radio, and so already knew, from the same VOA newscast, that his country had been invaded without his consent.

What were the consequences of U.S. actions that perpetually deceived our own allies, our own government officials, but never America's adversaries? Of what value were all the "intelligence" assessments of Indochina if U.S. officials did not know what their own government was doing? Of what use, later, were even the most astute political assessments of the opposition at home, if the President's advisers did not know what the President was doing?

Over the next four years, the President's men in Indochina and the President's men in Washington came to have more and more in common. And what they had in common most of all was that they were always the last to know. The most important victims of the secrets, however, were those who kept the secrets, and of those, without doubt, the most important victim was the President of the United States.

How might the fate of the Nixon Doctrine, of Nixon himself, have differed, had the White House consulted the American embassy in Cambodia—had the United States asked the permission of the government of Cambodia to invade Cambodia?

Lon Nol had wanted a full-scale U.S. commitment to the defense of his country, not a hit-and-run invasion. By early 1970, U.S. diplomats in Phnom Penh knew what Lon Nol also knew: such an invasion would neither curtail North Vietnamese operations there, nor defeat the tiny and hitherto completely unsuccessful Khmer Rouge insurgency. It would only give Hanoi a free hand all over the country and give Cambodia's radical revolutionaries an historical chance they had never had before.

Had Richard Nixon respected American and international law, instead of violating it, there would have been no secret air war in Cambodia and hence no cover-up in Washington. Had the President kept his pledge to respect Cambodia's neutrality and sovereignty, Sihanouk quite possibly would never have been overthrown and Cambodia, almost certainly, never invaded. The outcome of the Vietnam War would not have been very different; but both the United States and Cambodia would have been spared national ordeals that, in the end, made the "loss" of South Vietnam seem minor in comparison. A couple of telephone calls to Phnom Penh, would have alerted the President and his national security adviser to the disaster they were unleashing.

Instead, within the closed world of official secrecy, knowledge itself had become an intolerable "security risk." As both Watergate and the Nixon Doctrine again and again would reveal, the right hand of government did not know what the left hand was doing; the eyes sought only to blind others, and so were blinded themselves.

And the mind? The President's "mind," one congressman observed, "taxed beyond its power, is running hither and thither, like some tortured creature on a burning surface. . . ."

As the Vietnam War Era insensibly transposed itself into the Watergate Era, Lincoln's description of Polk became a more and more apt description of Nixon.

Like America itself, the President had set out to master history with a doctrine. And so it was his fate to be a prisoner of fantasy, from which no amount of destruction—except self-destruction—could provide an escape. More than any other presidential war in American history, Nixon's war in Cambodia was destined to become a case study in the catastrophes the President inflicts not only on others, but on himself, when he disregards the Constitution.

The bombing of Cambodia went on, in total, for nearly four and a half years, before Congress stopped it. Every bomb created a crater, and soon Cambodia became a land of so many craters that no human mind, only the computers at MACV, could keep count. In early August 1971, people in Phnom Penh gathered on balconies and looked up into the sky. The monsoon night, unaccountably, was cloudless. The moon was full, and distance did to the moon what time does to war. It made the craters invisible. On one rooftop, a group of Cambodian refugees, their villages long since destroyed by the American bombing, stared in wonder at that distant, bright, smooth disk.

Americans had landed on the moon. More than half a century earlier, in Central America, Americans had divided the land and united the oceans. Now Americans were touching the stars. As for Cambodia, within that shrinking perimeter the Khmer Rouge did not control, it more and more resembled some banana republic; generals were growing rich collecting American paychecks for phantom soldiers, and cabinet ministers were growing rich selling President Nixon's aid shipments on the black market. The

American PXs of Saigon provided a limitless supply of contraband, just as the refugee camps provided a limitless supply of whores.

At MACV, the Cambodia "mosaic" showed the Communist supply lines running from Moscow and Peking to Hanoi, and then from Hanoi down the Ho Chi Minh Trail in Laos to the Khmer Rouge. But in Phnom Penh one could buy an American M-16 rifle for less than twenty dollars. The country was being saturated with American weapons, but not even the Khmer Rouge could eat bullets. Malnutrition was becoming common; night blindness and other vitamin-deficiency ailments were being reported for the first time in Cambodian medical history. Malaria returned to the lowlands as agriculture ceased and irrigation systems turned into fetid swamps.

Cambodia under President Nixon prefigured El Salvador under President Reagan in another way: Among the guerrillas, as much as among Lon Nol's general staff, among the street peddlers as much as the foreign correspondents, the U.S. embassy and the American officials within it had become the objects of fascinated speculation. Would the American ambassador approve the new Prime Minister? What would the military attachés do about the latest guerrilla offensive? What would the U.S. aid officials do about the rising price of rice?

In the shadow of Angkor Wat, the founding illusion of American nationalism now passed for self-evident truth among people who had never read the Declaration of Independence, or heard of James Monroe.

Destiny, few Cambodians doubted, had chosen these foreign-service officers and CIA agents, these colonels and aid officials with masters degrees in development economics—these Americans—to know things no Cambodian could know, to direct events that, for Cambodians, long since had ceased to have any understandable direction.

Why had their country been plunged into war? Would the war never end? As the Cambodian matanza came to be measured in years, not months, its victims to be counted by the thousands, and then by the hundreds of thousands, these were questions which, as one refugee put it in his grade-school French, "surpassed Cambodia." Yet even among the poorest and most illiterate of Cambodians, it was as though they had read the speeches of Jackson and John Quincy Adams. Surely this capacity for destruction had been entrusted to the Americans for some good purpose?

In fact the U.S. embassy already had become to Cambodia what the White House was becoming to America in those years. Behind the gates and the guards and the security checks, the secret documents contained countless secrets; those with access to them controlled wealth and weapons beyond the imagination of those outside.

Yet this inner American world connected with nothing. The money and weapons, like the bombs, disappeared into a void. Every month in Cambodia, America's friends grew weaker; those America had chosen for its enemies grew stronger. Except for the craters, except for the dead, it was as though all

America was doing there had no relation to reality at all. What could account for the continuing power of the North Vietnamese, the growing power of the Khmer Rouge in the world beyond the embassy walls?

Neither inside the embassy nor inside the White House were these questions ever seriously explored; instead, in both places America's immense power seemed only to create a greater and greater sense of threat, to conjure up new enemies even more threatening than the Communists.

How was the United States Government to defend itself against these new —these American—enemies?

In the White House the enemies list was drawn up, and the "plumbers," like the B-52s and the Special Forces before them, were dispatched on their secret missions: in due course, the Cambodia break-in would be followed by another break-in, of the office of a psychiatrist with a patient named Daniel Ellsberg.

Why was Ellsberg an "enemy"? As early as October 1969, the former Defense Department official had made public the secret which, more than any other, the Nixon Doctrine sought to conceal. "Short of destroying the entire country and its people," he wrote in a letter published in the Washington *Post,* "we cannot eliminate the enemy forces in Vietnam by military means. . . ."

For Ellsberg, as for many other Americans, the Cambodia invasion, six months later, became a turning point. In Senate hearings, he outlined the threat the President's invasion posed—not to Cambodia, but to the United States.

> I am afraid that we cannot go on like this [he told Senator Fulbright] and survive as Americans. There would still be a country here and it might have the same name, but it would not be the same country.

"[I]f this goes on," Ellsberg warned, there would be "a change in our society as radical and ominous as could be brought about by our occupation by a foreign power."

The presidential war in Indochina had produced another of its great, unnoticed metamorphoses in America; 124 years after Polk's intrigue against Mexico, the spirit of John C. Calhoun had been reincarnated on Capitol Hill.

Ellsberg was not the only one to recognize that Cambodia was the forbidden fruit, and now that the President had plucked it, our political institutions were menaced. In 1945, the Hiroshima year, Arthur M. Schlesinger, Jr., had published *The Age of Jackson*—a *roman à clef* in which the activist presidency of modern times was the real hero. But now it was 1970, year of the My Lai massacre revelations; soon Schlesinger might have been Sumner denouncing the Filipino reconcentration camps, as he thundered against *The Imperial Presidency.* Even New Deal Democrats now were saying what Calhoun had said all along. Unchecked presidential power was a threat to American liberty, no matter how you defined liberty.

In the spring of 1971, as the President lauded "the success of the Cambodian operation," Ellsberg took a leaf from Thoreau. He gave the Pentagon Papers to the New York *Times*. The administration would go to a remarkable extreme in its attempt to prevent publication of the Defense Department study. But neither then nor later was the most remarkable aspect of this drama really noticed: neither Nixon nor Kissinger seems ever to have bothered to read the Pentagon Papers, and so, in Washington as well as in Indochina, they remained untouched by the threat of reality. All over America the dominoes were toppling themselves, years before Phnom Penh and Saigon fell.

* * *

The U.S. embassy had one advantage the White House lacked: the U.S. Constitution did not apply in Phnom Penh. For more than three years, embassy officials systematically deceived the public, the press and Congress about the full extent of their involvement in the bombing of Cambodia, and when deception failed, the embassy—like the White House—resorted to other tactics.

In April 1973, when James G. Lowenstein and Richard M. Moose, two staff members of the Senate Foreign Relations Committee, visited Phnom Penh, they found themselves free to wander around the city. But, inside the U.S. embassy, they were treated like prisoners. U.S. marines were ordered to confine the two U.S. officials to the embassy lobby unless they were escorted by embassy personnel. All offices inside the embassy were locked, to prevent the two staff members, who had high-level security clearance, from entering them. It was also decided, Lowenstein and Moose reported to Congress, "that we should not be permitted to be in the embassy building corridors and stairways even though all the doors were locked."

It was as though the embassy of the United States of America had become one of Borges's labyrinths. Scheduled briefings on the bombing by U.S. military attachés were canceled. "Instead, embassy officials responded to our questions," they reported, ". . . in vague and general terms leaving the impression of a minimal embassy role in the air war. . . . We were told that the embassy possessed only limited information regarding tactical air operations and the locations of B-52 strikes."

Everywhere outside the embassy, the paradox of the bombing was evident: wherever the American bombs fell, the Khmer Rouge were winning. What secret could be so secret that access to the embassy of the United States by officials of the Congress of the United States constituted a "security risk"?

An American journalist named Sylvana Foa, working for UPI and *Newsweek*, proved able to provide Congress with more reliable information than the CIA, the Defense Department and the Department of State. Listening to her sixteen dollar transistor radio, the two congressional investigators could hear U.S. military transmissions, in plain English. And so they learned what the North Vietnamese and the Khmer Rouge no doubt had known for years: The U.S. embassy had ceased to be a diplomatic mission. Its principal function was that of an instrument of American military power and influence. Here, too, as in Washington, the constitutional separation of powers had broken down. What had begun with Ambassador Peurifoy in Guatemala in 1954 had, by 1973 in Cambodia, been escalated, quite literally, a millionfold. Hundreds of thousands of tons of bombs were being jettisoned on Cambodia, now that the stockpiles were no longer needed in Laos and Vietnam. And the chief function of U.S. diplomats was to find, in the country to which they were accredited, targets for the B-52s.

At the insistence of the U.S. embassy, Sylvana Foa was expelled from Cambodia—an action which, like all the others, did nothing either to stop the Khmer Rouge or to strengthen Lon Nol. If these representatives of the United States had ever understood their duty to be the representation of American principles in countries like Cambodia, that understanding had long since vanished. Instead, American journalists and American employees of Congress were—like the North Vietnamese and the Khmer Rouge—only more enemies to be put on a list, and dealt with accordingly. Just as U.S. officials now decided which Cambodian villages were to be incinerated, they now also decided which Americans were entitled to report the destruction of Cambodia, and which were not. Like Cambodia's sovereignty, the First Amendment had become another casualty of the question for "peace with honor."

Later one of the U.S. officials who had obstructed the activities of the two envoys from Congress and insisted on the American journalist's expulsion defended his actions strongly. Her reporting, he told a congressional committee, had been "tendentious."

The name of the official in question was Thomas Enders. He surfaced again in early 1981, when the Reagan administration decided the time was ripe for a strong stand against communism in Central America. Who would manage the flow of arms to El Salvador, the influx of U.S. troops into Honduras, the secret destabilization war against Nicaragua?

Like Peurifoy earlier, Enders had a reputation for standing up for America, so he was named Reagan's assistant secretary of state for the region. The Truman Doctrine had begot the Nixon Doctrine. Now the poison of Cambodia, the fantasy of Cambodia, would recirculate to the birthplace of our doctrines, and in due course Thomas Enders would undergo an American metamorphosis of his own.

Enders and other U.S. officials in Cambodia had violated the rights of U.S. citizens, but they could not be accused of singling them out for unequal treatment. For by then it was standard procedure to obstruct even members of the embassy who asked too many questions, and to expel even U.S. officials who told too many truths.

As early as 1970, some U.S. officials in Phnom Penh recognized what many members of Congress and the press also did: The Nixon invasion had "saved" neither South Vietnam nor Cambodia; it had only made U.S. defeat more inevitable. Just as quickly, another truth became manifest. American officials who tried to warn the White House of the impending disaster in Cambodia found themselves on the enemies list. As a result, there soon were echoes of the McCarthy Era and the "loss" of China, within the U.S. embassy. When U.S. officials too persistently suggested that Lon Nol was only another Chiang Kai-shek, that the Cambodian slaughter was achieving nothing, jobs were abolished from under them; they were shunted into dead-end positions, as critics of the Reagan involvement in the Salvadoran slaughter would later be.

The message from Washington was loud and clear: it was not the function of America's representatives in Cambodia to report reality to Washington, even through secret channels; the embassy's function was to act out the fantasies ordained in Washington. And so in Phnom Penh, as in the White House, Americans of honesty and integrity increasingly found themselves locked out of offices, banned even from the corridors of power, while the fate of Cambodia, like the fate of America itself, steadily was entrusted to those for whom truth and honor were, like so much else, only enemies.

There was another parallel with the future. In the face of growing public criticism of U.S. actions in Cambodia, Kissinger fostered the impression of seeking a peaceful, negotiated settlement for Cambodia, just as the Reagan administration later would apparently seek a settlement in Central America.

Those within, however, knew for a fact what those outside suspected: the talk of negotiations was only a maneuver to dampen public criticism of the real policy, which was to continue the war whatever the costs. Kissinger and Nixon rejected all attempts at serious negotiations with both Sihanouk's exiled nationalists and the Khmer Rouge, even when the U.S. ambassador to Cambodia, Emory Swank, urged them as the only possible alternative to total defeat.

Once again, the American commitment—not Lon Nol, not Sihanouk or the Khmer Rouge, not even the North Vietnamese—had decided the importance of a foreign country. And once the President had made a commitment, a mistake could not be admitted. Instead, the commitment must be honored, the mistake covered up, lest the President's enemies—America's enemies—triumph.

In September 1973, as Ambassador Swank prepared to leave Phnom Penh, it was as though even the United States ambassador, as he looked around him, was face to face with a disaster too manifest to be kept secret any longer. At a farewell press conference, Swank lamented the futility of the war. He also publicly rebutted Kissinger's pretense that the United States was seriously seeking peace.

In retaliation, Swank's career, like those of the China experts earlier, was ruined. Like the American ambassador to El Salvador later, the American ambassador to Cambodia was exiled to the State Department's own version of Siberia, in this case by being appointed, on Kissinger's orders, U.S. adviser to the NATO fleet in Norfolk, Virginia. No U.S. official ever again publicly criticized the Nixon-Kissinger policy in Cambodia even when, two years later, the Khmer Rouge overran Phnom Penh.

Of all the careers that the Indochina and Watergate disasters would bless, the most spectacular was that of General Alexander M. Haig, Jr. As Cambodia steadily disintegrated, Haig became almost as familiar a figure in Phnom Penh as he became in Washington during the disintegration of the Nixon presidency.

By August 1974, as the President found himself powerless and the U.S.-backed regimes in Indochina edged toward collapse, General Haig was one of the most powerful men in the world. What accounted for this stunning rise to eminence? More than any other figure of his time, Haig combined a capacity for unswerving loyalty to his superiors with an incapacity to perceive alternatives to the policies they pursued. None of Haig's missions to Indochina ever produced any questioning of the American disaster unfolding there, just as none of his actions in the White House ever questioned the disaster unfolding there. So Haig—like Lon Nol—was rewarded with the favor of the President of the United States and his closest advisers.

The Nixon Doctrine was working—though not in the manner its author had intended. Just as the White House more and more resembled, with its intrigues and corruptions, the presidential palace in Saigon, so, three years after Nixon's decision to defend "free nations and free institutions" by invading Cambodia, the conduct of U.S. foreign policy had been Cambodianized.

How thoroughly corrupted U.S. operations in Cambodia had become was revealed even before Swank left Phnom Penh. It turned out that the embassy harbored an even more illuminating secret than that U.S. diplomats were choosing targets for the B-52s: The targets they chose, like the policy itself, bore no relation to reality.

"[T]he embassy," a congressional report stated in April 1973, "did not have current photography on proposed target areas which would permit the identification of new or relocated villages." Over the previous three years, the Cambodia that had existed in 1970 had been scattered to the winds. Millions of villagers had been uprooted. Where once there had been towns, now there were only ruins; where once there had been empty fields and forests, there were, on both sides of the lines, masses of hungry, terrorized people.

Yet the "maps being used by the embassy" to select the targets "were several years old," that is to say completely inaccurate, completely useless for selecting targets.

It was one of the most important revelations of the Indochina War, and like so many similar revelations, its implication never really penetrated the American consciousness: in April 1973, the month this report was made public, U.S. planes dropped nearly three times the tonnage of one Hiroshima atomic bomb—50,000 tons of explosives—on Cambodia without American officials knowing, or evidently caring to know, where the bombs really fell.

Americans had learned to fly so high they could not see the people they killed, and so as the B-52s poured down bombs on their illusory coordinates, as embassy officials pored over their illusory maps, it was as though those the Americans killed had never lived, as though the charred cadavers did not exist at all.

Americans only knew that the killing, like America itself, must go on forever if the Nixon Doctrine, like all our doctrines about ourselves, was to prevail. He "did not want to speculate on North Vietnamese motives," Kissinger told the press in January 1973. "I have too much trouble analyzing our own."

America never would analyze its motives in Cambodia. And so the Cambodian people, like so many others, became another forgotten revelation in the history of the American people. It would be Cambodia's destiny to be transformed into the most unmitigated, irredeemable, unnecessary and complete human catastrophe an American doctrine has ever produced.

For the time being, however, the American "commitment" continued—unchanging, unquestionable, even as the Nixon presidency itself teetered before the blast of the Watergate revelations.

"Your job," Kissinger, now Secretary of State, instructed the U.S. ambassador to Cambodia, John Gunther Dean, in 1974, "is to improve the military situation. . . ." Once the Khmer Rouge had been stopped, Kissinger informed the embassy, he then would "negotiate from strength."

Like Swank, Dean knew this was a fantasy. But, like Enders, he knew how to defend his career. For another year the American ambassador would charge around Cambodia like some Marine Corps instructor exhorting his recruits to kill. In Washington, the Vietnamization of the White House was now total, as Richard Nixon fled, like some overthrown Saigon mandarin, to his sunny place of exile. The condition of the United States and the condition of Indochina had converged to the extent that even the names had become interchangeable. More and more, the latest, and last, U.S. ambassador to Lon Nol's Khmer Republic emphasized his middle name, to distinguish him from the other John Dean, the Watergate John Dean, on the other side of the world.

It made no difference. The John Dean in Phnom Penh and the John Dean in Washington—like Watergate and Cambodia—were only differing manifestations of the same, self-inflicted American catastrophe. There was another similarity: even in disgrace and defeat, both Deans would prosper, one as a Watergate celebrity, the other as a high-ranking State Department official whose career would flourish as a result of having defended the U.S. commitment to the bitter end. As Cambodia's torment deepened, there were no real American losers, except for those Americans who tried to avert it.

Phnom Penh would not fall to the Khmer Rouge until April 1975. But even by the time Kissinger had given Dean his instructions, Cambodia had ceased to be a nation; it was only a slaughterhouse specked with refugee camps, the largest of which was the city of Phnom Penh.

The refugees had fled the American bombing for years. But more and more, even after the bombing stopped, the eyes of these human beings reflected a terror even more terrible, impossible as that was to conceive, than the bombing.

What could explain that terror?

It was another of those questions that was never asked, let alone answered in the secret memoranda, because Cambodia, for the President and his closest advisers, still did not really exist, even after hundreds of thousands of people had been killed there.

Cambodia was still only an American code word, because, so far as these Americans were concerned, all that happened there, for both good and ill, derived from what America and America's enemies, not what Cambodians, did.

For the Cambodians, Cambodia had become, as Sihanouk had predicted, a second Vietnam. The same was true for Nixon and Kissinger. Even when Cambodians not only died, but killed each other by the millions, they were still only dominoes. And this was true not only of the Cambodians we supported, but of those we opposed. Like Lon Nol, it was believed, the Khmer Rouge were only inconsequential ciphers, with no real will or identity of their own. They were only the tools of North Vietnam, just as Lon Nol was the instrument of U.S. policy.

From this perspective, there was no Cambodian problem. There was only a North Vietnamese problem in Cambodia. "[T]his is no civil war, it has no aspect of a civil war," Nixon declared in 1970. It was the old fantasy of Greece, of Guatemala, of El Salvador later. The Cambodians were not really people, capable of as much rage, as much madness, as any American. Instead, "fatalism" was a national characteristic. Their fate would be determined either by North Vietnam or us—not by themselves.

"[P]eace is at hand," Henry Kissinger announced on October 26, 1972. Not since April 1971, when Nixon had reported that "Vietnamization has succeeded," had such a high-ranking official made such a hallucinatory statement about Indochina. Ahead lay Nixon's Christmas bombing of Hanoi, and when, the following January, the peace settlement was finally signed, it was only a paper peace.

Even then, however, the settlement involved a conspicuous anomaly. For Cambodia, there was not even a piece of paper.

Why had the North Vietnamese and American negotiators at Paris not been able to reach a settlement for Cambodia, even though they had worked out complex settlements for Laos and Vietnam?

The North Vietnamese secretly told Kissinger and his aides what the U.S.

embassy in Phnom Penh also had tried to tell him: they could not control the Khmer Rouge.

"We could not believe it when the North Vietnamese told us they could not deliver a Cambodia settlement," William Sullivan, who had assisted Kissinger at the talks, later told me. Sullivan had been ambassador to Laos, then to the Philippines. In his last ambassadorial post, in Iran, Sullivan himself would try to tell the Carter White House what Swank had tried to tell the Nixon White House: the ayatollah and his Islamic revolutionaries were as uncontrollable as the Khmer Rouge—the Shah as incompetent to stop them as Lon Nol had been to stop the Khmer Rouge. As a result, Sullivan's fate would become the fate of so many other U.S. officials who told the President and his national security adviser what they did not want to hear. The ambassador to Iran was purged from the State Department. The White House was free to plunge into another foreign-policy debacle, to set the dominoes toppling not only overseas, but in Washington, too.

All that, however, would come much later. At the Paris talks, Sullivan—like Nixon and Kissinger—believed the North Vietnamese were lying about Cambodia. "We had lined up Lon Nol," Sullivan recalled. "We could not understand why Hanoi would not line up the Khmer Rouge."

For generations, the conspiracy theory and the domino theory had shaped the official mind of America. And now the belief in the dominoes, the faith in the conspiracy, had produced its most illusory result of all.

At last the United States really was face to face with total evil, with a conspiracy whose objectives were truly unspeakable. But this horror—the horror of the Khmer Rouge—was invisible to these officials, because for them the Khmer Rouge, like all America's enemies in Indochina, were only the creations of what President Nixon called "the international outlaws of North Vietnam."

Even after the Khmer Rouge had rejected any settlement, even unconditional surrender, this illusion continued to determine U.S. policy. Since neither the United States nor North Vietnam had anything to gain, any more, from the killing in Cambodia, it was assumed the Cambodian killing would stop.

"[A] de facto cease-fire will come into being," Kissinger predicted after the Laos and Vietnam accords were signed, in January 1973. Two months later, Nixon repeated the same fantasy. Getting Hanoi's forces out of Cambodia, the President said, was the "key thing." Once that happened, "the chances for a viable cease-fire in Cambodia will be very substantial."

"I am convinced that under your vigorous leadership," Nixon wrote Lon Nol as late as February 1974, "and that of your government, the republic will succeed. . . ."

Such was the illusion; the reality was that, under the Nixon Doctrine no less than under the Monroe Doctrine, it remained America's destiny to be a sorcerer's apprentice. For years, as the bombs fell, it had been as though the sky had gone mad, and now it was as though each bomb had been some seed of evil, each crater a garden of madness. For every innocent Cambodian killed, a dozen Khmer Rouge fanatics had sprung up.

No American could be accused of having created this Khmer madness; it had some dark genesis all its own. Nixon and Kissinger were guilty only of nourishing it with their war, of assuring it grew until it consumed an entire nation.

No one fully appreciated it yet, but the American madness of the bombing had finally met its match.

"Destroy! Destroy!" Even after his overthrow, Sihanouk did not lose his gift for perceiving reality. In 1973, I had gone to Algiers to interview him, and in the course of our talk, he told the truth of Cambodia, the truth of America.

"The Americans and the Communists," he said, "they love to destroy." True Khmer that he was, Sihanouk smiled as he said that.

The place Cambodia came to occupy in the American imagination was best captured in the film *Apocalypse Now,* which was Francis Ford Coppola's Americanization of *The Heart of Darkness.*

In that film, Cambodia is a black, frightening place—a world completely alien to the bright, familiar American world of exploding napalm just across the border in South Vietnam. It is an area of darkness that Americans enter only at the price of being consumed by darkness themselves.

This sense of American metamorphosis, of creeping degradation, of deepening corruption, is expressed not only in the plot and locations, but in the film's casting. When Marlon Brando is discovered in his lair in the Cambodian forest, most American audiences are shocked. Across the years of war, Brando—like America—has been transformed. The handsome young ideal of American innocence who starred in *The Quiet American* has become a fleshy, grotesque personification of American evil.

Over the years, the nature of the American quest has been transformed too. The war that began so long ago, to confer liberty on Indochina, has become a quest to seek out and destroy another American. As both Brando and his pursuers move toward their preordained destiny of murder and death in the Cambodian jungle, these Americans also move toward the last of Indochina's dark revelations.

It is not the Communists we have been fighting there; the mind and soul of America have been at war with themselves.

To many film critics, *Apocalypse Now* proved that Coppola was an American out of control. The director seemed unable to direct his own film. The images he had created took on an uncontrollable, destructive will of their own.

Americans who had known Cambodia did not like Coppola's film either. It did not portray the realities of Cambodia, they complained.

It was only an American fantasy.

Apocalypse had long since engulfed Cambodia, but even then the great revelation both of the film and of the great American adventure it did not so much portray as reenact, was invisible to most Americans.

It all had been fantasy. America had never fought a real war; Americans had never killed or died for any real purpose. There had been no real crisis in Cambodia, only some crisis inside America, as President Nixon himself had made explicit the very night he announced his invasion.

"If we fail to meet this challenge," the President had said on April 30, 1970, ". . . the United States, when a real crisis comes, will be found wanting."

It was now February 24, 1975; there was a real crisis in Cambodia, and the question before the Foreign Assistance and Economic Policy Subcommittee of the Senate Foreign Relations Committee was whether the United States would be found wanting.

"[T]here is going to be the worst bloodbath we can imagine in Cambodia," Representative William Chappell of Florida told the senators. He and other members of the House of Representatives recently had visited Phnom Penh; they had been deeply shaken by what they had seen. It was not that Phnom Penh was about to fall, the way Saigon, too, was about to fall. Other dominoes had been "lost" before.

It was that something else, even more important, already had been forfeited there. Civilization itself had vanished.

Lon Nol's "Cambodian army is pursuing the practice of taking no prisoners," Representative Paul N. McCloskey of California reported. On the "Communist side," he added, all opponents "were shot or killed with hoe handles or ax handles or hammers."

"In my experience, which has not been inextensive," said Bella Abzug of New York, "I have rarely seen such terrible human suffering." She spoke of "the starvation and the destruction of souls."

What could explain this catastrophe? What could end it? Lon Nol by then had at least one cause for satisfaction. The "domino" in Phnom Penh had managed to hold out longer than the domino in the White House. But though Nixon was gone, Kissinger remained the master of U.S. policy.

It was the result of North Vietnam's decision "to organize, muster, arm, train and cadre what is now known as the Khmer Rouge," the State Department informed the members of Congress, that Cambodians were killing Cambodians with ax handles and hammers. The Khmer Rouge, it was added, were "completely dependent" on supplies coming "into Cambodia from Hanoi and Communist China."

The official U.S. remedy was also changeless. In fact, Kissinger already had presented his ultimatum, not to the Khmer Rouge, but to Congress: give Lon Nol $222 million in more weapons, or take responsibility for the "loss" of

Cambodia itself. Even now, for Kissinger, Cambodia remained an abstraction.

If Congress failed to meet his demand, he announced, he would not be held responsible for the ensuing "defeat for American foreign policy."

There would have been no way for more American guns, more American bullets, to reach Phnom Penh even if Congress had complied with his demand, and Kissinger knew it. The capital's overland connections to the sea had been cut; the Mekong River was under Khmer Rouge control. Soon the Khmer Rouge advance would close the airport.

It was only in Washington that the fighting now made any difference. Would the Secretary of State fall with Phnom Penh? Or could "deniability" be maintained? In America, at least, there was a happy ending. Kissinger had survived Watergate; Cambodia would not scathe him either. "Cambodia," Kissinger later emphasized in his memoirs, "was *not* a moral issue. . . ."

In Phnom Penh, the intrigues in Washington no longer mattered. Nothing mattered.

While the starving refugees stared with blank eyes at the advancing Khmer Rouge, Lon Nol and many of his courtiers were leaving for America and France, with suitcases stuffed with gold.

But avarice and corruption had never been the real story in Cambodia. The real story in this conflict that Americans saw as a clash of ideologies had been the continuing capacity of the tribalism of nationalism to destroy whole nations. Dozens of Lon Nol officials, even those with Swiss banks and French villas, elected to stay.

It was as though some primeval voice of Khmer nationalism, after all the betrayals of their nation, still called to them. So they, too, waited in their palaces, in their ministries, for the Khmer Rouge to come to kill them. Prince or Prime Minister, it no longer mattered. All Cambodians were refugees now, which perhaps explained the calmness in Phnom Penh those last days and hours. There was no place left to run.

In the Phnom Penh hospitals, where the wounded civilians lay in their own blood and ordure, however, the famous Khmer smile was still to be seen. The doctors smiled on their patients; not even the stench could stop those smiles.

They had broken out the morphine and, as if to kill all the pain around them forever, they had begun to inject themselves.

In the U.S. embassy, there was no need for morphine. The Americans, as always, had escapes of their own, though in Ambassador Dean's case the American role in Cambodia's catastrophe was not ending, only moving toward a new incarnation. In 1979, after four years of Khmer Rouge terror, the Vietnamese would invade Cambodia, and so the final revelation of what the Nixon Doctrine had produced there would be at hand.

The Cambodians would greet their old enemies as friends, as heroes, as saviors.

How should the United States react to this latest case of Communist aggression? By 1981, John Gunther Dean was American ambassador to Thailand, and in Washington, too, it was as though time was meaningless. Through Thailand, U.S. food and medicine were channeled to Pol Pot and his Khmer Rouge guerrillas. It was "humanitarian relief," the embassy explained. The CIA-supported arms shipments to the Khmer Rouge were not explained.

They were only denied, and as with our simultaneous support for the death squads of El Salvador, this was a bipartisan American policy. It began under Carter; it continued under Reagan. Were not the Vietnamese friends of the Soviet Union and therefore our enemies?

Were not the Khmer Rouge now enemies of the Vietnamese and therefore friends of freedom? "You must wonder when it is all going to end," John F. Kennedy had told an audience in Montana in 1963.

"Well, it isn't going to end. . . . If the United States were to falter, the whole world, in my opinion, would inevitably begin to move toward the Communist bloc."

On April 12, 1975, as the Americans boarded their helicopters in Phnom Penh, a crowd of Cambodians gathered to observe the spectacle. A few of them waved. Some of them called out the only words in English they knew.

"Bye-bye. Bye-bye." The noise of the rotors drowned out the voices of Cambodia; as the Americans soared higher and higher, the children, the city, a nation, disappeared beneath them.

"Our long Vietnam nightmare is over," President Ford announced a little later. But this, too, was only another false prophesy from the White House.

The nightmare was still with us; it always had been with us, in one form or another. It only awaited another incarnation.

* * *

It was Flag Day 1983 in Sarasota, Florida. In front of many of the houses surrounding the Meadows Country Club, American flags were flying over the neatly clipped lawns, as if standing guard over the shining Buicks and Lincolns and the glistening turquoise swimming pools.

Two years and seven months had passed since all those Americans had gathered, in the clearing in the Salvadoran forest, around the bodies of Jean Donovan, Dorothy Kazel, Ita Ford and Maura Clarke. Like some little nation, they now were scattered in countless places. Ambassador Bob White was living in Alexandria, Virginia, but about to move to Medford, Massachusetts. His consul Patricia Lasbury soon would be posted to Barcelona, after two years at the Department of State. Father Schindler was now a parish priest in Akron, Ohio, not far from Cleveland, where Dorothy Kazel had been buried. The journalists and photographers, except Ian Mates, mostly had gone on to other assignments, other wars.

Like Ita and Maura, Ian had been buried in El Salvador. Some others were still where they had been that day the bodies were recovered. Colindres Aleman and his fellow guardsmen were still living in El Salvador. General Garcia, who had denounced the missionaries at the presidential palace, had retired as Defense Minister. The U.S. embassy had found him lax in combatting communism; he had been succeeded by another general, named Carlos Eugenio Vides Casanova.

In Washington, too, there had been some changes in personnel, but the passage of time had not changed either the direction or the substance of events. "Nicaragua, Cuba, and, yes, the Soviet Union," President Reagan had told Congress a little earlier, were responsible for the continuing matanza in El Salvador, which by then had claimed some forty thousand lives. He later would suggest that many of the killings committed by right-wing death squads there actually were committed by Communists disguised as anti-Communists.

In Sarasota the shopping malls were crowded, and there, as in many other parts of the country, the President remained very popular. With the economy reviving, the President's chances for reelection seemed good. Those chances would be enhanced, a few months later, by the President's strong stand against communism in Grenada.

Officials who shared the President's view of the world were also prospering, notably Ambassador Jeane Kirkpatrick, who had called the slain women "agents of the Frente." She still represented the United States at the United Nations, though that was only the beginning of her importance. Since December 1980, she had become one of the most popular and effective spokespeople for the Administration's Latin America policy, and one of the most important shapers of what she described as the Administration's effort to "help peoples resisting incorporation in the Soviet bloc."

As for Jean Donovan, Father Schindler had taken her home to her parents, Patricia and Ray Donovan, and they had buried her not far from their house in Sarasota. Wearing a sports shirt, a pair of green golf slacks and a pair of white leather shoes, Ray Donovan drove me, in his air-conditioned Oldsmobile, to see Jean's grave. Not far from the former winter headquarters of the Ringling Brothers and Barnum & Bailey Circus, this grave was quite different from the one in Santiago Nonualco. Near an old shade tree, a simple headstone rose out of the green grass. It read:

A ROSE IN DECEMBER
Jean Marie Donovan
April 10, 1953–December 2, 1980

"Don't feel sorry for Jean," Ray Donovan said as we drove back to the house. "She's where we're all trying to get." By that, Mr. Donovan clearly did not mean a Florida cemetery. He meant Heaven. I asked him if his faith was as literal as that.

"Yes it is," he answered, "and I'm not ashamed of it."

The Donovans' living room, with its perfectly white wall-to-wall carpet, the expensive bric-a-brac and the off-white sofas, opened onto the golf course; the sliding glass doors, with the barbecue just outside, seemed to frame some fulfilled vision of America. At the Meadows Country Club, Patricia Donovan, aged fifty-nine, and Ray Donovan, sixty-five, are a popular couple. When Jean's body was brought home and scores of people from around the country attended the funeral, many of their neighbors, overwhelmingly Protestant and conservative, spontaneously offered to put the visitors up as house guests.

"One neighbor took his house guest out to play golf," Ray Donovan remembered. "Later he asked, 'Who was that woman? She was a natural pro.' When I told him she was a mother superior from Cleveland, he couldn't believe it."

One thousand miles to the north, in the inner suburb of Cleveland where Dorothy Kazel's parents live, the backyard view was different, but it, too, seemed to reflect the fulfillment of a kind of American dream. Plastic windmills turned in the hot, late-afternoon breeze, and a plaster leprechaun looked on as Dorothy's mother, seventy-two-year-old Malvina Kazel, poured pink lemonade for family members and friends.

Here neighbors talk over back fences, and every family knows every other family's children by name. The facts of Dorothy's death were known to the Kazels, but from the perspective of this American backyard, they still contained a great mystery. "She was our sunshine," Mrs. Kazel said of her murdered daughter. "If the Salvadoran Government didn't want those girls there, why didn't they just put them on an airplane and send them home?"

After so many years of speeches about the conspiracy, the threat, the whole of America still seemed like some tranquil, well-tended summer lawn in comparison to places like El Salvador. Not far from the White House, a group of Americans sat in an elegant garden—the women in flowery dresses, some of the men in seersucker suits—enjoying the summer dusk. In this case, the paradigm of America was the Washington elite taking its ease. A well-known author who was writing a political novel chatted with an Asian princess. The hostess helped direct a philanthropic foundation. A pretty young woman who was involved in urban policy arrived, beaming, with an old boyfriend, and introduced him to an intelligence analyst at the Department of State. In one corner of the garden, a lean, white-haired man was talking with a journalist.

It seemed such an anomaly that, here as well, a vision of horror should intrude. But, for Bob White, too, the clearing in the forest might have been here and now, not nearly three years and two thousand miles away. His memory was identical to what Father Schindler and the others who had been there remembered, except for one detail. White did not remember using the word "bastards."

"What I said at the grave site," White related, as canapés and gin tonics were passed, "was, 'This time they're not going to get away with it. This time they're not going to get away with it. . . .' "

As the U.S. "commitment" in Central America had deepened, those whose lives were touched by Jean and Dorothy and Ita and Maura had become a kind of extended family. And whether you talked with Bob White in Washington, or Father Schindler in Cleveland, or any of the scores of other people who knew the four women, they all agreed on one thing.

"They've gotten away with it," said Michael Donovan, Jean's brother, when I visited him that summer in Danbury, Connecticut. There was no anger in Michael's voice as he described what had happened since December 1980. "Rage is not a permanently sustainable emotion," he explained.

There was only a detached sense of incredulity. "It isn't the fact that the soldiers who murdered my sister and the others have not been punished, have not even been tried, and may never be," he said. "It's not even that the higher-ups—the colonels and generals who ordered the killings or have been involved in the cover-up—haven't been touched and never will be.

"The thing that's so hard to accept," Michael Donovan emphasized, "is that our own government should support these murderers and help them get away with it."

In Cleveland, James Kazel, forty-seven, spoke of his dead sister the same, quiet way Michael Donovan spoke of his. There was no rage, only sad wonder in his voice. "I guess our government thinks it's doing something constructive in El Salvador," he said. "But they're just letting those murderers make a fool out of our government and our country."

"I was raised as a middle-American. I was taught to love this country," added Martha Owen, the Ursuline nun who had climbed the Salvadoran mountain with Dorothy Kazel and helped her raise the flag of America there. "It's very disturbing to see us violating our principles in order to cover up a crime like this."

Down in Sarasota, I had asked Ray Donovan what, for his family and the families of the other slain women, would be a satisfactory outcome of the various "investigations" by the Salvadoran and U.S. governments, all of which, even after the passage of years, still had produced no trials, no convictions—no justice.

"Oh, hell," he replied, "it doesn't matter whether something happens or does not happen someday in some Salvador courtroom. What matters is that what was done to Jeanie and the others gave us a chance to really examine what we are doing in the world."

"We could have learned so much from this tragedy," Mrs. Donovan added. We had talked so long, gone over the facts so many times, that there seemed nothing to talk about any more. Yet, as he dropped me at the airport, Ray Donovan, too, still found himself confronting a mystery the facts could not explain.

"I voted for Reagan, my family voted for Reagan," he said, "and after three years I really have only one question: Why is President Reagan rewarding the murderers of our daughters?"

It all might have been some parable of America. Out of that hole in the ground, out of that void near Santiago Nonualco, two diametrical series of events had radiated, like expanding shock waves, creating two differing, opposite stories. One of those stories was a tale of the triumph of evil; the other, equally simply, was the story of the triumph of the American capacity for goodness. Each story was revealing, but it was the juxtaposition of the two that brought complete illumination, because the deaths of the four women, like their lives, had turned out to illustrate the great paradox of America—which is that we Americans have such an extraordinary capacity both to sow mayhem and to instill hope in the world.

Though the details were complex, the plot byzantine, the events at times grotesque, the first story was easily enough told. "We haven't had justice," said Michael H. Posner, a New York attorney who headed the legal committee that represented the families of the four women in the case. "We've had an obstruction of justice, a travesty of justice."

As Ray Donovan put it, the murderers had not been punished; they had been rewarded. The attempt to investigate the murders and bring those responsible to justice had degenerated, in Ambassador White's words, into "a joke." The triggermen had not been tried or punished. Far more important, those who ordered the triggers pulled had been assiduously protected, as the highest-ranking authorities in the U.S.-backed Salvadoran Government engaged in a massive campaign to obstruct the course of justice.

This cover-up involved the intimidation of witnesses and juridical authorities. It included, on the part of the Salvadoran authorities, a policy of adamantly blocking pursuit of the case. But that was not the whole truth or even the most important part of it. Key Salvadoran figures in the case had been provided sanctuary from justice inside the United States, and most astonishing of all, a fifth U.S. citizen had been murdered—after he appeared at the U.S. embassy in San Salvador offering to provide evidence identifying those responsible for the murders of the four women.

And while one cover-up had proceeded in El Salvador, a second cover-up also had unfolded. This second cover-up involved the concealment, either deliberate or through incompetence, of crucial evidence, including documents believed to bear the fingerprints of Salvadoran officials involved in the murders. It involved the censorship of official U.S. Government reports and the deliberate misrepresentation of the status of the investigation into the murders to Congress and to the American public.

It included defamation of the murdered women and attempts to extract more than thirty thousand dollars in payments from their families. And beyond all that, this second cover-up—relatives and friends were convinced—

involved violation of their constitutional rights, including wiretaps of their homes and spying on them. Simultaneously, U.S. officials opposing those actions and favoring a full, fair and impartial investigation into the murders had been fired, transferred or ordered to desist.

A familiar metamorphosis had occurred: originally the main source of pressure on the Salvadoran Government to investigate the murders and bring those responsible to justice, the U.S. Government steadily had become the chief accomplice in the Salvadoran effort to assure that justice never would be done.

The second cover-up had been mounted by the U.S. Government itself. "There are basic values in our country," said Posner. "One of those values is that people shouldn't be raped and shot with impunity. Over the past three years, that value has been traduced."

The second story was even easier to tell, yet at the same time deeply complex and luminously mysterious. It was a story of the human spirit triumphant—of the capacity of quite ordinary people like Jean Donovan, Dorothy Kazel, Maura Clarke and Ita Ford to bequeath hope and joy to the world even when they are deprived of everything, including the inviolability of their own bodies, and their lives.

"We never imagined it could happen," said Patricia Donovan. "But the death of Jean and the others has touched and reaffirmed the faith of millions, and helped to educate them about the reality of El Salvador."

Malvina Kazel, too, spoke with a kind of awe of the ongoing miracle that, three years after her daughter's death, still filled her family's life and the lives of those around them. "We have received over five thousand letters," she said, "full of consolation and support from people of all religions. Some Jewish people wrote and said they had planted a tree in Dorothy's honor in Jerusalem. Other people want to know how they can help continue their work, how they can help the poor people of El Salvador, how they can stop the killing. Their deaths touched the whole world."

It was at the funerals of the four women that their families first began to sense that their story was only beginning. "People were reaching out and touching us," remembered Marietta Kelly, whose husband, Don, is one of the Donovans' Cleveland cousins.

"I am a convert to Catholicism and until then I had never understood all the saint stuff. Then, when I saw the reaction of people, I understood. It wasn't about plaster statues and medieval martyrdom.

"Human beings have a strong need to know ordinary people are capable of heroic goodness in the face of extraordinary evil."

"Maybe it's because they were women, or nuns, or Americans," said James Kazel, "but there has turned out to be something in their story people can't ignore."

No doubt precisely because she was not a nun—because in her case any thought of vows of poverty, chastity and obedience would have been an absurdity—Jean Donovan in particular had become, in death, a living presence to millions of people.

"Saint Jean the Irrepressible" read the headline in one of the hundreds of magazine articles and newspaper stories on the life of Jean Donovan, who was twenty-seven when she died. In the living room of her parents' Sarasota home, there hung a colorful oil painting which also was part of the growing legend. It showed an idealized Jean Donovan playing the guitar in an attractive jungle setting to a group of appreciative campesinos. It was the illustration for her profile in *Reader's Digest,* which was read, in dozens of languages, by tens of millions of people. A widely acclaimed documentary on her life— *Roses in December,* by Ana Carrigan and Bernard Stone—was broadcast several times on public television, and in December 1983 a full-length television film on Jean's life was also shown. Like many such accounts, this fictionalized version of Jean Donovan's life told the dramatic story of a fun-loving young woman with a taste for fast motorbikes, hard liquor and handsome men—who finally found, in good works among the terrorized Salvadoran campesinos, a kind of inner fulfillment money and pleasure cannot provide.

The legacy of Jean Donovan, however, did not end with these video images. Following his own murder, Archbishop Oscar Romero's prophecy came true. He was reincarnated in his people. Everywhere in El Salvador, photographs of the slain primate were venerated like icons and, increasingly, this Latin American holy man was flanked, in this hagiography, by four fair-skinned, smiling North American angels. It was on a poster hanging in a Nicaraguan church that I saw the most striking rendering of the American face that also had smiled out from the pages of *Reader's Digest.* In this depiction, a serene and fulfilled Jean Donovan, along with Dorothy, Ita and Maura, was striding confidently toward paradise—as if to show the whole of Central America, and perhaps the United States, too, the way from terror and destruction to love and peace.

When Jean and the others are proposed for canonization, as no doubt will happen in due course, the careful investigators of the Vatican will point out that mere martyrdom is insufficient for sainthood. Miracles are required. Following the murders, it became clear that at least one miracle had occurred. The truth was that these were brave and good women who took great joy in helping some of the most wretched, abused human beings on earth. The miracle was that somehow this essential truth had survived violation and death, and prevailed over even the mutilations time, emotion, memory— above all video images and printed words—ceaselessly inflict on the truth of things.

People who knew the four women saw it; sometimes people who never had met them saw it even more clearly. "Every time we visit Dorothy's grave we find new flowers there," Mrs. Kazel said.

As time passed, the families and friends of the four women discovered that though their loved ones had been taken from them, much else was being given in return. Nothing can replace a vanished daughter—but that did not make the compassion of thousands of others any less moving. Friends of the families inevitably talk about how these women's parents, brothers, sisters, nieces and nephews have "grown" since their deaths.

"It has been an astonishing transformation," said a friend of the Ford family who had come to know the other families as well. "You sense they want to be equal to the legacy that has been left to them. They haven't buckled or broken or had time for self-pity. They recognize these terrible events presented them, too, with a big challenge."

The challenge was not limited to them. But, for the authorities in El Salvador, the nature of the challenge was different—somehow to sustain the illusion that the deaths of the four women, like their lives, meant nothing.

It had been easy enough to kill four unarmed women; it was not much more difficult to protect their killers. But how does one counter the "threat" to a whole policy of murder, to an entire system of injustice, posed by four martyrs—by four saints?

Following the discovery of the bodies at the Hacienda San Francisco, this was the threat Jean, Maura, Ita and Dorothy posed to El Salvador.

And as with all the other threats it perceived in El Salvador, it was a threat the Reagan administration quickly would transform into a threat to itself.

"A chief cannot be held responsible for the actions of a subordinate," President Jose Napoleon Duarte announced a few days after the women were murdered.

In Washington, Duarte was considered the Salvadoran embodiment of American principles; he impressed both the Carter and the Reagan administrations more than any other. But Duarte had defined the Salvadoran approach to the murders that would prevail in El Salvador no matter who held office in all the months and years to come.

The following "investigation" would establish only one fact beyond a reasonable doubt: none of the many leads that existed at the time of the murders was ever seriously investigated. After nearly four years, and the expenditure of some $750 million in the effort, as President Reagan put it, to create "an orderly and democratic society" in El Salvador, Ambassador White's initial assessment remained valid.

"What we had from the beginning," he later recalled, "was a cover-up, not an investigation." In investigating any conspiracy case, especially one involving murder, the crucial task is to prove linkage. What was true of the Watergate burglary was true of the murder of Jean, Dorothy, Ita and Maura. Even if the hit men were apprehended, the threat to the higher-ups could be "contained," so long as no link could be established connecting them to those who committed the crime. It was thus of potentially crucial importance from the beginning to ascertain the real chain of command in the murders. Only by doing that could the guilt—or innocence—of higher authorities, including the

Chalatenango and La Libertad commanders, and of the Defense Minister himself, be conclusively established.

Who, for example, was Colindres' immediate superior at the airport on December 2, 1980? Much later, after Colindres and the others finally had been arrested, an interesting discovery was made: The link in the chain of command directly above Colindres Aleman was missing. Colindres' immediate superior on the day of the murders had disappeared—though not in the way most Salvadoran *desaperecidos* do. Instead, the Lawyers Committee for International Human Rights reported in July 1982, Colindres' "commanding officer, a sergeant whose name is being withheld by the State Department, has subsequently retired and is living in the United States."

By early 1983, more details had become known. The officer in question was named Sergeant Dagoberto Martinez Martinez. Less than a month following the murders, he had resigned from the Salvadoran National Guard. He had been provided a U.S. entry visa and an air ticket and emigrated to Los Angeles—where he lived under an assumed identity and with no known means of support.

But that was only the beginning. Martinez was finally interviewed by the FBI in February 1982, more than a year following the murders. He had an extraordinary story to tell: He implicated Colindres Aleman in the murders. He claimed that at a special meeting of National Guard commanders held shortly after the women had been killed, Colindres had walked up to him and said, "Sergeant, the problem with the nuns is me." Martinez had advised Colindres to inform the director general of the National Guard of what he had done, but not to disclose the crime publicly and damage the reputation of the National Guard.

Did Colindres, who was not arrested until nearly five months later, follow Martinez's advice? Did the National Guard director then protect Colindres for more than four months—until intense political pressure in the United States and the threat of a possible cutoff of military aid in Congress forced the Salvadoran Government to announce at least some arrests? Above all, why did Martinez resign? Who paid his way to Los Angeles and paid his expenses there? Why was Martinez's crucial evidence never entered into the official record of the investigation? And why, when the Lawyers Committee presented the Martinez evidence to Salvadoran Government prosecutors, did they "profess ignorance of it, and . . . express no interest in examining Martinez or seeking his extradition to El Salvador"?

Martinez's statement, the Lawyers Committee concluded, strongly suggested that he, and possibly also the director general of the National Guard, were part of a cover-up.

In the spring of 1983—long after the U.S. Government was aware of the director general's alleged role in the Martinez affair—General Garcia resigned as Minister of Defense. With strong U.S. support, the National Guard director, General Eugenio Vides Casanova, was named to succeed him as the commander of the entire U.S.-supported military effort in El Salvador.

After repeated certifications to Congress that El Salvador was making steady and significant progress in human rights, President Reagan's effort to ensure that "the Salvadoran people's desire for democracy will not be defeated" had produced one small amelioration of conditions there. The forces the United States armed and paid were no longer under the command of a general suspected of ordering the murders of U.S. citizens. They were only under the command of a general suspected of protecting the murderers of those U.S. citizens.

Martinez's disappearance from El Salvador—and eventual reappearance in the United States—also brought into question the role of the U.S. embassy in El Salvador, and that of the State Department. Who issued Sergeant Martinez his U.S. visa? If it was a tourist visa and he overstayed it, why was Martinez not deported or detained—like thousands of other Salvadorans who have sought refuge in the United States? If Sergeant Martinez was issued a residence visa—which usually is granted only following a personal investigation—what U.S. official made the decision, and on what grounds?

To all these questions, and the many others the Martinez affair posed, the State Department had a ready answer.

"When we asked," Posner recounted, "we were told all consular files are routinely destroyed after eighteen months.

"We were told all the files on Martinez had been burned."

The questions raised by the Martinez incident, however, were trivial in comparison to those raised by the Thomas Bracken affair. Bracken, then forty-six, was a U.S. citizen—an ex-police officer and private detective from Nevada who, by December 1980, had been living off and on in El Salvador for more than three years. Ideologically a violent anti-Communist, Bracken had played a role in local politics back home, but it was in El Salvador that he seems to have found his niche. There he was a paid consultant to the Salvadoran National Police, the most indiscriminately "anti-Communist"—and murderous—of all that country's many armed forces. Bracken originally had come to El Salvador hoping to sell customized armored cars, but when his business venture failed, he found work with the National Police, whose chief, Colonel Lopez Nuila, had aroused Ambassador White's suspicions with his queries about what clothes the missing American women were wearing. Bracken's main job, before the U.S. military aid mission started shipping weapons to El Salvador, seems to have been to run guns from the United States to the National Police and instruct Nuila's men in how to use them.

Less than two weeks after Jean, Dorothy, Ita and Maura were murdered, Bracken walked into the U.S. embassy in San Salvador and "explained that he had important evidence relating to the death of the missionaries," Ambassador White later testified to Congress—evidence about the Salvadoran military's involvement in the killings.

Like many volunteer witnesses in such cases, Bracken wanted something in return for his evidence. In March 1980, a U.S. warrant had been issued against him for smuggling arms from the United States to Mexico. The charges had not prevented him from returning to the United States, but on one occasion, he had been arrested, in Brownsville, Texas.

Somehow, however, he had escaped. Commenting on Bracken's brief incarceration, North Las Vegas Assistant Police Chief Thomas Fay, who had worked with Bracken for thirteen years, later told Pat Williams, of the *National Catholic Reporter:* "They had him and he escaped. He was a good cop. He would have been a good CIA man or something like that." Whatever the exact circumstances of Bracken's brief detention in Texas and his subsequent reapparition in San Salvador, the gun-running charges interfered with his work for the Salvadoran National Police. Bracken accordingly offered the U.S. embassy a deal: if they would arrange for the gun-running charges to be dropped, he would provide "important evidence" on the murders of Jean Donovan and the nuns.

The fundamental rule of any successful murder investigation is that any lead, however self-serving the motive of the person who provides it, must be exhaustively pursued. Bracken visited the U.S. embassy twice. And things might have turned out differently had White, Lasbury or any of the other professional foreign-service officers in the embassy met with Bracken. Instead, the ex-cop from North Las Vegas was referred to U.S. military officers and FBI officials who had been sent to El Salvador to assist in investigating the murder of the four women.

They decided, following Bracken's second visit, on the sixteenth of December, that Bracken's evidence was "inconsequential," and rejected his offer.

It was a judgment no one might have questioned, except for one fact.

The next day, Bracken himself was murdered by Salvadoran troops.

Following Bracken's death, the Salvadorans offered two completely contradictory accounts of how he met his end. According to the first account, he died on the afternoon of December 17 while searching for a kidnapped Salvadoran businessman with a police patrol. The patrol entered a house, and Bracken was killed by a "wounded subversive." According to this version, no one was apprehended (not even the "wounded subversive"), and no one else was killed.

The second account was even less convincing. It purported that, the same afternoon, Bracken and some others were driving a jeep in one direction, while a jeep carrying Jose Morales Erlich, a civilian member of the ruling junta, approached from the opposite direction. A grenade went off and, according to this version, Morales' bodyguards opened fire—killing Bracken, and Bracken alone.

These cover stories convinced no one in San Salvador, but they seem to have satisfied the State Department. When, more than two years after Bracken's death, Williams pieced together the story and asked why the U.S. Government had sought no investigation, the official response was that there was nothing to investigate.

"In times of military conflict," State Department spokesman John Caulfield told Williams, "it is not unusual for someone to be caught in a crossfire." U.S. officials in El Salvador at the time had a quite different reaction. When they learned that no one else had been killed in the purported incident, they drew the obvious inference.

The Salvadoran authorities watch comings and goings from the U.S. embassy as thoroughly as they spy on suspected "subversives." When Bracken's visits to the embassy were noticed by his co-workers, they believed, he was "set up," apparently by Nuila's National Police, in order to silence him.

"Having killed four U.S. citizens," concluded White, "they killed a fifth U.S. citizen because he knew too much."

But what, exactly, had Bracken known? The families of the slain women requested that their attorneys be provided records on Bracken's two visits to the embassy. The Reagan administration refused, and at the beginning of 1984, the matter was still before the courts.

If Bracken's information was so "inconsequential," why was the U.S. Government fighting a legal battle to keep that information secret? For that matter, if Bracken knew so little, why was he killed? The mysteries surrounding Bracken's death did not stop there. Bracken's personal possessions (which possibly could have contained clues about what he knew) were never recovered, in spite of requests from his family in the United States that they be returned.

Bracken's body disappeared too. "I believe at that time he was an employee of the National Police, and he was buried by them," Patricia Lasbury later told Pat Williams. No friend or relation of Bracken ever identified the corpse the National Police said was his. In fact it was never ascertained where Bracken was buried, and the location of his body today is unknown, and perhaps unknowable.

Within a month of the murders, it was clear beyond doubt, as Ambassador White later told Congress, that "there was no serious investigation into the death of the nuns, and as far as I am concerned there never has been." And this was something both the State Department and the White House knew too. "During that time," White added, "our reporting from the embassy consistently showed that there was . . . no serious investigation under way."

It in fact had been illusory from the beginning to imagine there was any chance the Salvadorans themselves would seriously investigate the killings and then try to punish those responsible. No serious investigation, no trial and no punishment had occurred earlier, when Archbishop Romero had been gunned down while saying Mass. Indeed, years later, all the U.S. Government claims of progress in human rights in El Salvador were still rebutted by an extraordinary fact: although at least forty thousand people had been mur-

dered there, not one single government soldier had ever been tried and convicted of murdering Salvadoran civilians, even though literally thousands of
such murders had been amply documented.

The question never had been whether the government of El Salvador would
make sure "they're not going to get away with it." The question was whether
the government of the United States would face up to the fact that the very
forces it supported in El Salvador were murdering U.S. citizens, and act
accordingly.

Even before President Reagan took office, the State Department announced
a resumption of U.S. military aid to the Salvadoran armed forces, which had
been suspended following the murders. The Salvadoran authorities, the State
Department announced, had taken "positive steps" in the investigation of the
killings.

Many events would flow from the murders at Santiago Nonualco. Many
lives would be touched, and changed forever, as a result of what had happened to Jean, Dorothy, Ita and Maura. Now one of the most significant
personal transformations was beginning. For years, Ambassador White had
had the reputation of being an ace careerist—a foreign-service officer with a
knack for upward mobility. But, in a way, White had been changed forever as
he stood staring down into that pit at the Hacienda San Francisco.

White strongly protested the State Department action. There followed, by
long-distance telephone, a dialogue in its way as bizarre as the exchange
between General Garcia and the little boy.

"We believe there is a serious investigation," said White's boss in Washington, acting assistant secretary of state for inter-American affairs John Bush-
nell. White reiterated his own judgment: only a cover-up was occurring.

White might have been in Phnom Penh in 1973 or in Tehran in 1979, not
sitting in an office, with a big American flag beside his desk, in San Salvador
in 1981. Once again the government of the United States and the ambassador
of the United States—fantasy and reality—were on a collision course. The
Department wanted to "believe there is a serious investigation" and was
telling Congress and the public there was. Its own ambassador was saying
there was not and refusing to go along with the cover-up.

White put down the telephone. On what basis, he wondered, could the
Department believe a serious investigation was occurring? Was the U.S. Government so determined to pump weapons and ammunition to the Salvadoran
military that it was willing to implicate itself in the cover-up of the murders
of U.S. citizens?

On January 21, 1981, White went public with his opposition to the misrepresentation of the facts of the investigation, in an interview with Juan de Onis
of the New York *Times.* "As far as I am concerned, there is no reason to
believe that the government of El Salvador is conducting a serious investigation," Ambassador White declared.

"I am not going to be involved in a cover-up," he said.

In Washington, a new administration was taking power. But, in the Department of State, it was as though Phnom Penh had never fallen and the administrators of the Nixon Doctrine were being rewarded for defeating the Khmer Rouge. Alexander Haig was no longer Kissinger's emissary; he was now Secretary of State himself. The years of the Cambodian apocalypse also had been generous to Thomas Enders. In 1974, citing his "grossly misleading" statements, the Senate Foreign Relations Committee had censured Enders for his "conscious effort" to deceive Congress about the U.S. embassy's role in the Cambodian bombing campaign. But this rebuke seemed only to enhance Enders' reputation for loyalty to his superiors and to increase his value to them. Kissinger first promoted the former Phnom Penh chargé d'affaires to the post of assistant secretary of state for economic affairs. Then, in 1976, as he prepared to leave office, Kissinger had named Enders ambassador to Canada. So it was from the vantage point provided by our democratic northern neighbor that Enders had sat out the Carter presidency and its "human rights" approach to Latin America.

"International terrorism will take the place of human rights," Haig announced a few days after White had denounced the cover-up of the terrorist murders of U.S. citizens in El Salvador.

During his tenure as Secretary of State, Haig's tortured syntax often would provoke confusion. But for once he had defined U.S. policy with precision. In Central America at least, under the Reagan administration, support for terrorism would take the place of support for human rights. As Haig assembled his team, it was like a Watergate reunion on the top floor of the Department of State. President Reagan, one incoming official explained, had decided to "send a message to Moscow" via El Salvador. Enders, named assistant secretary of state for inter-American affairs, was chosen to send it.

These were the heady, early days when, so far as President Reagan and his administration were concerned, every dictatorship everywhere might have been a telegraph office. Assurances of support soon were flowing to the Argentine generals, who, a year later, would be emboldened to attack the Falkland Islands, and to General Zia of Pakistan, who had authorized the execution of his predecessor and replaced his country's Western-style penal code with Islamic justice, including beheadings for adultery and the severing of hands for theft. Following Enders' appointment, John Gunther Dean was named U.S. ambassador to Thailand. "U.S. Decides to Back Resistance Groups Active in Cambodia," the New York *Times* reported. The decision attracted little notice; instead, Americans were wondering if El Salvador would become a "second Vietnam."

The Russians were not the only ones on the Reagan administration's Central America enemies list. Four years later, the guerrillas in El Salvador would be stronger than when President Reagan took office; the Sandinistas would still rule in Nicaragua. But within two months of taking office, the

Reagan administration had one clear-cut victory to its credit: it had completely routed those in the State Department with any Central American expertise.

Many of these officials, who had been dealing with hemispheric affairs, under various administrations, for decades, were summarily but quietly dismissed. Others were simply transferred as far away from Central America as the State Department personnel office, and the circumference of the globe, would allow. The official who had been American chargé in San Salvador at the time of the October 1979 coup d'état, for example, was exiled first to Harvard, then to Kathmandu, Nepal. The American deputy chief of mission in El Salvador at the time the four women were killed was transferred to Rangoon, Burma.

If, later, U.S. actions seemed as unrelated to the reality of Central America as the State Department's white paper, there was a straightforward reason for it. By February 1981, when the white paper was published, U.S. policy was under the control of four officials—Reagan, Haig, Enders and Under Secretary of State William Clark—who had no previous experience of Central America and no personal or professional knowledge of conditions there. As a result there never would be an El Salvador policy or a Nicaragua policy; only, as Professor Enrique Baloyra put it, in his study of the Salvadoran catastrophe, a series of "American fantasies."

Of all its enemies in Central America one especially had attracted the new administration's ire. Even before the Carter administration left office, he in fact had committed the two most serious offenses the world of security clearances knows.

First he had refused to lie when the State Department had wanted him to join in the official effort to convince the press and Congress that there was "a serious investigation" into the El Salvador murders.

Then he had committed the only worse crime: he had told the truth, when he said there was "no reason to believe the government of El Salvador is conducting a serious investigation."

White's crimes were Swank's crimes; so White's punishment would be Swank's punishment too. In February 1981 he was summarily dismissed as ambassador to El Salvador and offered a post even more demeaning than Swank's position with the NATO fleet in Norfolk. White was told the only new job available to him was in the Foreign Service Inspection Corps, a traditional dumping ground for career officers singled out for retribution. When White declined this assignment, he was informed that he would be dismissed from the Foreign Service, in keeping with an obscure bureaucratic regulation.

The most intractable myth of American nationalism is that there are intrinsically good guys and bad guys. While he was actually ambassador to El

Salvador, many critics of U.S. policy had portrayed White as an ogre. Following his dismissal, he, no less than Jean Donovan, underwent a metamorphosis; White was venerated as some kind of foreign-policy saint.

In fact the story of the decision in Washington to ruin White's career was much more instructive of what the United States was doing, both to Central America and to itself, than that.

In reality, the ambassador of the United States was not very different from some Central American campesino. His main objective, in the beginning, was to avoid confrontation with the powerful men in Washington. But the attempt to humiliate him had pushed him too far.

"The Reagan people weren't smart," White said later. "They would have caused themselves far less trouble had they not been determined to provoke a confrontation," he added, not intending to sum up the entire Reagan policy in Central America. "They should have tried placation."

For a Salvadoran peasant, placation was as simple as the soldiers, the helicopter gunships, not burning his fields, not strafing his house, not constantly terrorizing him. For Bob White, with three college-age children, no personal income except his State Department salary, and no other professional experience except the foreign service, an ambassadorship to one of the smaller European countries would have sufficed.

Instead, confronted with the choice of humiliation or unemployment, White chose resistance. The new administration was barely a month in office, but already a striking symmetry between the intrigues of San Salvador and the intrigues of Washington was manifesting itself. By murdering the four churchwomen, the Salvadoran military had not defeated "communism." They had only transformed Jean Donovan and the others into far more powerful symbols of the moral bankruptcy of the Salvadoran Government than they ever could have been in life. The same was true of White. By treating him as an enemy, the Reagan administration had turned him into an enemy—just as, over the next four years, U.S. actions would turn hundreds of thousands of Salvadorans into enemies too.

With White and the others purged, the decks seemed cleared for the Administration to confront its other enemies. "The decisive battle for Central America is under way in El Salvador," Enders announced.

In fact quite another battle was soon under way—on Capitol Hill. In late February 1981, when Senator Carl Levin, a Michigan Democrat, asked the Reagan administration to outline its view of Central America, Ambassador Jeane Kirkpatrick, as she often would in the future, undertook the task.

She derided fears of U.S. escalation in Central America. "Nobody [in the administration] is worried that we are about to put our foot down on that slippery slope that led to Vietnam," she said. The United States, she added, was not interfering in El Salvador. The "outside intervenors in Central America," she emphasized, were "the Soviets by way of the Cubans." "We are confronted with two policy questions: whether we do anything at all, or whether we leave the government unsupplied while Cubans or the Soviet Union supply the guerrillas."

Kirkpatrick's view did not go uncontested. "To the extent that you emphasize a military solution in El Salvador," White told the same group, "you are going to be buttressing one of the most out-of-control, violent, bloodthirsty groups of men in the world." He strongly contested Kirkpatrick's assertion that the Salvadoran military must be supported because there was no alternative.

"The idea that Latin Americans are not capable of democracy," he added, "is just racist nonsense . . . but if we place ourselves . . . on the side of an oppressive military, then democracy is going to fade away."

Suddenly the distinguished, white-haired American with the ambassadorial manner seemed to be everywhere: at congressional committee meetings, on network newscasts, speaking before audiences all around the country. And everywhere Bob White spoke he had the same thing to say: The Reagan policy of supporting the military would not, as Kirkpatrick contended, produce a situation in which "the people of El Salvador can choose their own government." Instead, he argued, the Reagan emphasis on "the military component" would only strengthen the forces of repression and encourage a Salvadoran shift to the right.

"And that way," he warned, "lies disaster." White seemed to know El Salvador so well, to speak with such authority, and to have such a sensible approach to Central America that, at one congressional hearing, he was asked why he had been fired.

If you have . . . a ready-made doctrine which asserts that the solution . . . lies with the introduction of large quantities of armaments and military advisers, then your first priority becomes the removal of an ambassador who may complicate the application of your doctrine,

White explained. In its effort to crush dissent within the State Department, the Reagan administration had transformed White into the most effective and credible of the public critics of its El Salvador policy.

White's view of the murders and the investigation all along had been a minority view in the Department of State. For him the murders created a real test, not just for the Salvadorans, but for the United States.

If the Salvadoran military was determined not to investigate and punish the murderers, White believed, the United States, quite simply, should reassess its policy and not support the murderers of U.S. citizens. Not even White, at that time, thought the unthinkable: that the United States, faced with a government of massacre in that country, should withhold all support from the Salvadoran regime. But he considered the military component in El Salvador relatively minor, and in his debate with Kirkpatrick, he explained why.

"There's no way the leftist forces can take over El Salvador," White pointed out, and in early 1981 this judgment was entirely correct. At that time, almost all Salvadorans—except for the right-wing extremists and very much smaller numbers of left-wing revolutionaries—did not want to fight some war to the finish, either to "eradicate communism" or to achieve "national liberation." They wanted the slaughter, which already had produced such gruesome results, to stop before it consumed even more of El Salvador and its people.

"One of the real misanalyses—or lack of accurate, objective intelligence—has been this myth that El Salvador is ripe for falling to leftist extremists," White argued. And because he understood that fact, he understood an even more important truth about El Salvador: Emphasizing a military solution not only would have the principal result of strengthening the worst of the right-wing terrorists; as the matanza drove more and more Salvadorans into resistance, it was bound eventually to conjure up a real threat of El Salvador's "falling to leftist extremists" as well.

From this viewpoint, not only justice, but the national interest of the United States demanded a full and impartial investigation into the murders, because such an investigation would reveal, in the clearest possible way, whom the United States should support, and not support, in El Salvador.

The majority in the State Department, even while Carter was still President, but overwhelmingly so after Reagan assumed office, had an entirely different view.

To them, the murder of Jean, Dorothy, Ita, Maura and the other Americans was not a question of right and wrong, crime and punishment. The murders were only unfortunate complications that might impede funding in Congress for a successful counterinsurgency war against Communist aggression in Central America. From this perspective, it did not matter whether an investigation really occurred, or whether justice was ever done.

All that mattered was that the threat posed to U.S. policy by the murders be "contained"—that U.S.-supported officials like Garcia, Vides Casanova and Lopez Nuila stay in power, so as to be able to continue the war; and that Congress and public opinion be sufficiently satisfied that something was being done about the murders so that continued funding for the El Salvador military was not imperiled.

Within this majority view, in turn, were two separate tendencies. The first, epitomized by Thomas Enders, was that justice—for tactical, not legal or moral, reasons—must appear to be done. A semblance of an investigation should occur in order to satisfy Congress, the families and public opinion inside the United States, while care was taken to ensure that the boat was not rocked in El Salvador. From this perspective, the ideal "solution" was for a long, but carefully limited, investigation, ultimately to lead to the trial, and if possible the conviction, of the triggermen, while all others involved in the murders went untouched. In essence, this approach sought to allow the State

Department to have the forms of an exercise in "human rights" in El Salvador while retaining the substance of a military crusade to murder that nation into submission.

The second tendency, which ultimately prevailed, was personified by Ambassador Kirkpatrick, and it was a much harsher approach than the approach of "pragmatists" like Enders. From this viewpoint, Jean and the nuns got what they deserved. They had no business riling up the campesinos in El Salvador. Their actions, intentionally or not, had served the guerrillas—and hence Cuba and the Soviet Union. It was quite understandable, from this point of view, why they had been killed. Certainly the U.S. Government should not distract itself from its real task—crushing the Communist conspiracy in Central America—by doing anything on behalf of four dead subversive American women.

This was an approach, as we saw at the very beginning of this book, that Kirkpatrick made explicit even before she and the rest of the Reagan administration took office. Kirkpatrick's words, when published in the Tampa *Tribune* on Christmas Day 1980, conveyed the administration's approach to Central America more clearly than any subsequent statement. Everyone and everything that impeded the effort to turn Central America into a "test case," the Kirkpatrick interview made clear, were now to be considered enemies.

A tape recording of Ambassador Kirkpatrick's allegations—"The nuns were not just nuns. The nuns were also political activists. We ought to be a little more clear about this than we actually are"—also exists, and these spoken words are even more illuminating than the printed word, for two reasons.

First, of course, Kirkpatrick's comments were a classic example of a high official totally misrepresenting the facts when the facts happen to contradict policy.

But the Kirkpatrick tape is revealing for an even more important reason. On the tape, Kirkpatrick speaks with a kind of condescending, hard-edged arrogance that, for anyone familiar with the realities of El Salvador, is nothing less than terrifying. Simple-minded, gullible people, Kirkpatrick's tone of voice implies, may be duped into supposing that Salvadoran troops actually murder innocent Americans. They also may be foolish enough to believe that the four women were only nonpolitical missionaries.

But Americans like Jeane Kirkpatrick know better. The Salvadoran Government cannot be held responsible for the murders, justified as they might have been, and the "nuns were not just nuns," but "political activists on behalf of the Frente," for the same reason: it is Americans like Kirkpatrick herself, and no one else, who are entitled not merely to determine events, but to determine their meaning. Kirkpatrick's tone of voice communicates, more effectively than all the statistics and photographs of the matanza, the American wellspring of the catastrophe that would continue to consume El Salvador in the following years. Tens of thousands of human beings would die because, in Washington, it would never be doubted that events must necessarily vindicate a preconceived American notion of the world and the way the world works.

Hardly for the first time in this book, we are face to face with events that it is impossible to recount without asking the question: how is it that Americans like Kirkpatrick and Enders, all in the name of freedom and democracy, could so easily commit themselves to the support of oppression, of terror?

To ask that question, of course, is to confront not just an American contradiction, but one of the great and perhaps irresolvable paradoxes of human nature. Yet, in practical terms, the answers are dismayingly uncomplicated.

In the ideological, doctrinal American approach to foreign affairs that Kirkpatrick personifies, the only moral absolute is the absolute evil of the adversary, in this case the Soviet Union and its host of worldwide incarnations. Hence everything else—even the murder of unarmed American women —is the lesser of two evils, so long as it facilitates the continuation of the struggle against "communism." "The Reagan administration would like nothing better than to see a civilian democratic government in El Salvador," Kirkpatrick said in her debate with White, and there is no reason to doubt her sincerity.

But that was never the question in El Salvador. Instead, the question of El Salvador was the question of Korea, of Cambodia, of Iran—and dozens of nations: what should the United States do in situations in which the choice is not between "a civilian democratic government" and its opponents, in which the old American choice between freedom and slavery simply does not exist? As Kirkpatrick herself put it, it still came down to one of "two policy questions." The United States must either support "authoritarians" like the death squads, or permit "totalitarians," that is to say, Soviet evil, to prevail.

By those lights, supporting the murderers of U.S. citizens—even defaming the American victims of the matanza—was not merely an easy choice; it was the only choice.

In the "pragmatic" approach, epitomized by officials like Enders, such actions become not only possible, but necessary for a quite opposite reason: because no moral absolutes exist at all.

Even years after their deaths, the families of the slain women still seemed not so much angered, as completely mystified, by the treatment they received from the Reagan administration. "Can't they see the issue here?" Michael Donovan asked, at one point, in exasperation.

The answer, very simply, was no. Officials like Haig and Enders had perceived no moral issue in bombing Cambodia with inaccurate maps, in expelling journalists from Cambodia, in locking congressional officials out of embassy offices—in deceiving Congress itself. The U.S. Constitution had not applied in Phnom Penh; why should the rule of law impede U.S. policy in El Salvador? From this viewpoint, too, a cover-up was not only justifiable, but necessary. The destruction of the whole of Cambodia, from the point of view of "pragmatism," had been only an administrative detail. Why should the rape and murder of four American churchwomen provoke some reappraisal of America's actions, when the Cambodian apocalypse had not?

At first the families reacted mostly with puzzlement. Surely Ambassador Kirkpatrick had not meant what she said. Not the murders, not even the Kirkpatrick statement, changed the families' basic view, which was that the United States was the best nation on earth. It was a long time before the Donovans even began to regret they had voted for Reagan. Even today Michael Donovan says, "My faith in our government system is even greater than before. I may disapprove of certain people, but I still have faith in the system."

Yet the Kirkpatrick incident turned out not to be isolated. In the future, even higher-ranking officials would engage in even worse defamations of the dead women. And, in truth, Ambassador Kirkpatrick was not the first official who seemed to regard the women and their families not as victims, entitled to the aid and protection of the U.S. Government, but as "threats" to the conduct of the foreign policy of the United States.

Several weeks earlier, the telephone had rung at Michael Donovan's house in Connecticut. Michael had picked it up, and a voice, without identifying itself, had said, "Will you people please get the hell off our backs?" When he asked, the person on the other end of the line identified herself as Joyce Gunn, a State Department official who had been handling details concerning the transport of Jean's and Dorothy's bodies to the United States. After giving her name, the State Department official reiterated her demand: "I'd like you to get the hell off our backs."

In the aftermath of the murders, congressmen and members of the press were besieging the State Department—wanting to know when and how the murderers would be apprehended and tried. And the State Department, increasingly, was annoyed.

The State Department not only wanted the Donovans off its back. It wanted thirty-five hundred dollars from the family. Michael Donovan was mystified by this demand, since the Catholic Church was paying the expenses involved in transporting the bodies back to the United States.

"That's our charge for cutting the red tape in El Salvador," Gunn explained when Donovan asked.

Over the following months and years, these incidents coalesced into a pattern. Gradually a thought began to occur to the families far more appalling than the thought that government forces of El Salvador murdered people, even U.S. citizens, as a matter of course.

They began to realize that the U.S. Government itself was one of the principal obstacles to justice—that so far as most U.S. officials were concerned, the whole affair of the slain women was at best an irritating nuisance, and at worst a "threat" to the successful conduct of U.S. policy which must be eliminated, one way or another.

In the months ahead, State Department officials would lie to the families. Their letters to high officials, including Kirkpatrick, would go unanswered and, in the case of President Reagan, be intercepted. Their dead relatives would be slandered by the U.S. Government, which also would conceal crucial evidence in the case. Some family members would be followed by government agents. There would be demands from the State Department for even larger sums of money. And according to the Donovans, their telephones for a time would be tapped.

"All those things you see in the movies," recalled Michael Donovan, a calm and reasonable man who is a certified public accountant, "they started happening to us."

The State Department cover-up was best documented in its own official "Chronology of the Investigation into the Deaths of the American Churchwomen."

The chronology is a cheerful document, not unlike the prognoses of human-rights progress in El Salvador the Administration routinely passed on to Congress when it wanted more money for military purposes there.

The entry for December 3, 1980, for example, reads: "Salvadoran Government establishes a Special Commission to investigate the murders." No mention is made of Duarte's statement about military chiefs not being held accountable for the actions of their subordinates.

"Dec. 14–17 The Salvadoran Commission requests that autopsies be performed on the two bodies buried in the US." No mention is made of Bracken's visits to the embassy, or of his murder.

"Dec. 19 The Embassy's evaluation of investigation [is that] Commission's work to date . . . is progressing reasonably well." This entry, an outright fabrication, makes no note of the fact that White was reporting exactly the opposite to Washington at the time.

"Dec. 20–Jan. 5: Christmas vacation in El Salvador delays work of the Commission." No mention is made of Martinez's departure for the United States.

The State Department chronology rolls on, month after happy month. One would gain no suspicion, from reading it, that the United States Government itself was now actively attempting to suppress relevant information, and to deceive the families, Congress and public opinion.

The first documents the Reagan administration moved to suppress were Ambassador White's own reports from San Salvador. When White began testifying to Congress that the investigation was going nowhere, State Department officials professed mystification. White's testimony, a high-ranking administration official declared, "baffles the imagination." Lest any of the bafflement be resolved, the State Department quickly classified White's own cable traffic to the Department—even though what White happened to think about the investigation clearly in no way could compromise the national security of the United States.

More documents were soon consigned to secrecy. In the aftermath of the murders, FBI investigators had been sent to El Salvador. Although the FBI is not empowered to investigate crimes committed in foreign countries, the Bureau had gathered much evidence on the case—ostensibly in order to assist the Salvadoran prosecutors. As months passed and the Reagan administration clung to the position that the murders had been committed by low-level Salvadoran troops acting alone, the question of what the FBI had discovered assumed more and more importance. Did the FBI's findings concur with the administration's position that Colindres Aleman had acted alone? Or did the investigation indicate what every other independent enquiry into the murders did: that the murderers seemed to have been acting on the orders of higher officials?

As the months passed, the families made an important discovery—though it was not about the murders. It was that the Administration was doing everything it could to prevent them from obtaining access to information on the case. Early in 1983, the Lawyers Committee, in its third formal report on the case, summed up the situation that had prevailed since early 1981:

> Regrettably, the U.S. government has obstructed attempts by the churchwomen's families to monitor the case. Since December 1980, the U.S. Embassy in San Salvador has had access to a substantial amount of evidence pertaining to the investigation. Moreover, the FBI has, at a number of stages, provided technical and advisory services to the Salvadoran government. Yet repeated efforts by the families to obtain information in the possession of the U.S. government have been vigorously resisted.

Beginning in June 1981, the families commenced efforts to obtain, under the provisions of the Freedom of Information Act, access to the FBI's findings, and also access to State Department, CIA and Defense Intelligence Agency files on the murder case. The other three agencies adamantly refused even to reply, let alone provide any information. But at the end of June 1982, after ninety-one members of Congress joined in the families' appeal, FBI Director William H. Webster did personally respond to the request for information.

In a letter to a member of Congress, Webster refused to release any documents of any kind relating to the murders. In support of his refusal, Webster invoked two sets of reasons for keeping the FBI findings secret. First, he argued, its findings could be withheld because they were "classified in the interest of national defense or foreign policy." The second possible reason he cited for refusing to make public the documents was that "to release information would impede the ability of law enforcement personnel to conduct a thorough examination and effective prosecution, and might well preclude a fair and impartial trial."

In the Catch-22 world in which the families and their attorneys now found themselves operating, Webster did not indicate which reason justified his refusal to release the FBI's findings. But a process of elimination suggested a logical inference. "National defense" certainly could not be imperiled by revealing what the FBI had found. Nor was it very likely that releasing the "information would impede the ability of law enforcement personnel to conduct a thorough examination and effective prosecution," since the FBI personnel concerned were not empowered to enforce the law in El Salvador in the first place. "A fair and impartial trial" also had been unlikely in El Salvador from the beginning. Certainly, releasing information to the families in the United States was quite unlikely to influence what happened or did not happen in El Salvador after more than a year and a half of failures to have "a fair and impartial trial."

The only compelling reason to keep the information secret was that it had been "classified in the interests of . . . foreign policy."

In the years following the murders, in fact, "the interests of . . . foreign policy"—that is the policy of providing military support to the Salvadoran military, no matter whom it kills—would provide the only consistent thread in a tapestry of U.S. Government misrepresentations, evasion and outright lies.

"From the beginning," said James Kazel, "they tried to make us believe justice was proceeding, when nothing was being done." Added Michael Donovan: "They have lied to us again and again."

Early in the case, for example, State Department officials assured the families that autopsies had been performed in El Salvador—even though White himself had informed the State Department of the refusal, by Salvadoran forensic surgeons, to perform autopsies, and this had been recounted in the State Department report to the White House.

On another occasion, the families were assured that the white Toyota van that the four women were in when they were abducted "was in the custody of the FBI." But this, as Michael Posner discovered inadvertently more than two years later, was simply not true.

"I was in San Salvador," Posner recalled, "and I happened to mention the van, because it remains an important piece of evidence. I was informed it had been sitting in an open parking lot in El Salvador for more than two years."

The attempts to gain access to the FBI's investigation had not produced any new evidence on who ordered the killings of the four women. But they did reveal a pattern in the FBI investigation that, if one is to be charitable, must be described as incompetence, and which in fact seemed to amount to a deliberate refusal to pursue leads that might prove politically embarrassing in the case.

Among the Lawyers Committee findings: The FBI "neglected to analyze the fingerprints of area security forces, thereby leaving unidentified 12 of the 13 prints found on the churchwomen's Toyota van." In FBI-assisted polygraph examinations of the six arrested guardsmen, only one, Sergeant Colindres, was questioned regarding the involvement of higher officials. Neither U.S. nor Salvadoran investigators ever interrogated the commander of the airport military district. "The FBI failed to question rigorously the sergeant who was Colindres Aleman's commanding officer." There was never any investigation into how Colindres came into possession of his five thousand dollars.

While these were only a few examples of what the FBI had failed to investigate, in 1983 an even more extraordinary failure to pursue the investigation came to light. A death threat against Ita Clarke and Maura Ford, it was discovered, had been in the FBI's files for more than two years.

Yet this document never had been tested for fingerprints. The Salvadoran prosecutors had not even been informed of its existence.

To the families, the truth seemed clear: the U.S. Government was opposed to any investigation that might implicate any Salvadoran officials other than those who pulled the triggers in the murders.

In May 1981 the State Department—in pursuit of its own agenda—did achieve one thing: it got the Salvadorans to arrest the triggermen. But thereafter, in spite of all the headlines and maneuvers, nothing else happened. The Salvadorans continued to refuse to try the arrested men, let alone investigate who ordered them to murder the four women. The families were stonewalled in their efforts to obtain more information and to revive the investigation. The administration and the State Department, while steadily escalating U.S. intervention in Central America, continued to purport that the Salvadorans were making "steady progress" in human rights.

"For a long time," recalled Michael Donovan, "every six months, when the Administration once again had to certify to Congress that there was human rights progress in El Salvador, we'd act out a kind of minuet. Enders would invite us down to Washington, and we'd have a long discussion. Someone in San Salvador would say trials were just around the corner.

"Then they'd go to Congress and certify progress was being made."

In the spring of 1982, the minuet took a turn that was bizarre, even by State Department and El Salvador standards. Members of the families and their attorneys were ushered into an office in the State Department and introduced to an anonymous Salvadoran. Informing the family members that the Salvadoran's identity could not be revealed, State Department officials asked the families to pay him thirty thousand dollars. Although they refused to provide any detailed information, the State Department officials said the Salvadoran was a competent attorney who had consented—if he was paid that amount of money—to act as *acusador particular,* or private prosecutor, in the case.

As the State Department officials presented it, hiring the *acusador particu-*

lar was absolutely essential. According to them, the *acusador particular* could "present evidence, file appeals, and participate in the trial." (In fact, as the State Department later conceded, such a lawyer cannot present evidence, argue before the jury or cross-examine witnesses.) The State Department officials impressed on the families that hiring such an attorney could be "the deciding element in a successful prosecution." (In truth, under the Salvadoran legal system, the *acusador particular* plays no decisive role.)

Family members began to question the anonymous Salvadoran, who, to his credit, made no effort to deceive them. Could he guarantee that the trial would be held, in return for the thirty thousand dollars? Not at all, the Salvadoran replied. Least of all could he assure a conviction. If he was retained as *acusador particular,* would he pursue the investigation and find out who ordered the murders?

"I wouldn't investigate," the Salvadoran replied. "That would be too dangerous. The people who ordered them killed would have me killed too."

"Gradually it dawned on us," said Michael Donovan. "The only thing this guy could do was maybe, just maybe, get Colindres Aleman and the others put on trial. We were being asked to pay thirty thousand dollars up front to help the State Department sustain the illusion of 'progress.' Our money was to be used to help the cover-up."

Instead, as Donovan put it, "We decided not to give this anonymous Salvadoran thirty thousand dollars and made a counterproposal." The families requested the State Department to provide them with a list of Salvadoran attorneys willing to consider taking the case.

More than two years later, they were still waiting for a State Department response.

Beginning in late December 1980, friends and relatives of the slain women made repeated attempts to contact Ambassador Kirkpatrick and seek a clarification of her statements.

Sister Sheila Marie Tobbe, for example, in January 1981 wrote to Ambassador Kirkpatrick, Secretary of State Haig and President Reagan. A deeply pious woman who teaches at the Beaumont School for Girls, in Cleveland Heights, Ohio, Sister Sheila Marie much more corresponds to the old stereotype of a Catholic nun than to the more recent model of the socially committed Catholic churchwoman. Yet she had visited El Salvador, seen all four of the slain women at work and, following Kirkpatrick's statement, felt compelled to do something. "It was so wrong to say they were agents of the Frente," she later said. "You know, that just wasn't true."

In her letter to President Reagan, she wrote:

From first-hand information I know that all four of these women were performing works of mercy for poor refugees: feeding, clothing, finding shelters and medical supplies for them; in short, trying to provide some modicum of decency of life in a situation of turmoil, inhumanity and fear. Is this political activity? Is it political to take the Gospel seriously and live by its values?

She concluded her letter to the President, almost apologetically, with a series of requests: She asked President Reagan to "reconsider" Kirkpatrick's appointment to the UN. She asked the President to "give very careful consideration to our foreign policy in the entire Central American region. In accord with the requests of the various churches in Central America, I would beg for a discontinuance of all military aid."

Sister Sheila Marie is not the kind of woman to go behind someone's back with criticism. So, after writing to the President, she also wrote to Kirkpatrick, enclosing a copy of her letter to the White House. In her letter, the voice of a nun pointing out a mistake to an erring pupil mingled with the hope that even the errant could see the light.

"I hope in the future that you will exert more care in discerning the sources of your information before you make statements about others," she wrote. Sister Sheila Marie apologized for requesting that Kirkpatrick's appointment be reconsidered; "however, under the circumstances I would find it difficult to have confidence in your judgment of world affairs." Sister Sheila Marie closed with a blessing upon Ambassador Kirkpatrick: "May you experience Christ's blessing on the new year as we struggle to discern the truth of our world and its crisis."

President Reagan and Ambassador Kirkpatrick never replied personally to any of the scores of sincere—and at times naively charming—letters they received attempting to explain to them the real significance of the four women's deaths. Occasionally, though, some secretary would return a form letter. Sister Sheila Marie got one, indicating that no one had bothered to read what she had written. And when Michael Donovan and Ita Ford's brother William, a Wall Street lawyer, sent a detailed letter to Kirkpatrick, they, too, got back a form letter, which ended: "Again, thank you for sharing your thoughts with me on this vital issue."

By then Michael Donovan, like the State Department, was keeping a chronology. And in spite of his careful, CPA-type methods, it increasingly read like Kafka's *Castle:*

IV. CONTACTS WITH THE STATE DEPARTMENT BETWEEN DECEMBER 22, 1980, AND MARCH 19, 1981

A. I receive a copy of a news article.
1. Received from Tommey Sue Montgomery, together with her letter to Ambassador Jeane Kirkpatrick
2. Quote from Kirkpatrick claims that Jean and the others were political activists
3. See copy of article, enclosed

B. I attempt to contact Amb. Kirkpatrick
1. My letters are unanswered
2. I am unable to get an appointment
a. I went to the U.S. mission at the U.N. without an appointment
b. Unable to speak with the Ambassador
3. I accidentally find myself on an airplane with the Ambassador
a. I attempt to speak with her
b. She refused to speak with me.
C. My telephone calls to the State Department are unanswered, or I speak
to someone who knows nothing.

Later, sitting on the backyard deck in Connecticut, I asked Michael Donovan what it had been like to approach Ambassador Kirkpatrick on the airplane.

"I was flying back to New York from Washington when I noticed she was on board, so I went up, introduced myself and explained who I was.

"She didn't say anything," Michael Donovan remembered. "She looked right through me, as though I wasn't there."

A few months later, Ambassador Kirkpatrick did grant Michael Donovan an appointment. But when he arrived from Connecticut at the U.S. mission to the United Nations in New York, accompanied by two other persons, he was informed that Ambassador Kirkpatrick would not be seeing him after all. A receptionist led Donovan and his friends into a room on the first floor of the U.S. mission and told them to tell him what it was they wanted to say to Ambassador Kirkpatrick.

After some time, Michael Donovan noted the receptionist was not taking notes, and mentioned the fact. "There's no need," the low-level official replied. "We're being taped. Everything said in this room is recorded. Ambassador Kirkpatrick will hear everything exactly as you said it."

Down in Florida, Ray Donovan was beginning to wonder why no responses came from the White House, not even form letters. "Some kid wins a spelling bee," he later said, "and the White House sends a letter. We must be the only people in the United States to write to President Reagan and not get an answer."

This, too, in time was explained: "All your letters to the White House are intercepted," a State Department official sympathetic to the families told them. "The President never sees them."

Efforts to contact Ambassador Kirkpatrick never succeeded, but in the spring of 1981, in response to congressional inquiries, she did make a statement. In a letter to the two ranking members of the Senate Foreign Relations Committee, Charles Percy and Claiborne Pell, Ambassador Kirkpatrick claimed her statements had been taken out of context. She wrote:

My point was that order had broken down in El Salvador, that murders were being committed . . . and that more and more people were polarized and drawn into the civil war. Under these circumstances any kind of identification or perceived identification with one of the contending sides involves one in the conflict. . . . Thus the nuns, two of whom I said were reported to have just returned from Nicaragua and to have ties in the Santanista [sic] junta, were perceived not just as nuns teaching schoolchildren but as political activists on behalf of the Frente.

Ambassador Kirkpatrick's explanation was notable for several reasons, the most important of which was that what she now claimed she said was completely different from what she actually had said. She had not said, the previous December, that the nuns were "perceived . . . as political activists on behalf of the Frente." She had asserted as a fact that they were activists on behalf of the Frente. Yet now Ambassador Kirkpatrick added an entirely new allegation: that the nuns "were reported to have ties in the Santanista junta," by which she presumably meant the Sandinista junta ruling Nicaragua.

This was an allegation that never had been made, let alone "reported," before. Ambassador Kirkpatrick concluded:

I think I have some sense of Mr. Donovan's anguish at the death of his sister, and I am happy to take this opportunity to assure him and you that my words, spoken as a political analyst attempting to describe dispassionately a tragically violent scene, were in no sense intended as a smear.

To this conclusion, the UN ambassador appended a request: "Since I do not know Mr. Donovan's address, could you please ask someone in your office to forward the enclosed copy of this letter to him?"

It was a strange act of discourtesy, considering that the Donovan family had contacted Ambassador Kirkpatrick's office on numerous occasions and that Michael Donovan's address in any event easily could have been ascertained with a few telephone calls.

Yet Kirkpatrick's "clarification," like her original statement, nonetheless cast valuable illumination on the approach she and other high Reagan-administration officials continued to take toward the question of the murders, El Salvador and U.S. policy in Central America as a whole.

The ambassador did not know how to spell "Sandinista." But "as a political analyst," she continued to know best. "It is hardly surprising," she wrote of the four slain women, "that persons who perceive themselves as involved in the struggle for political and economic 'justice' should be so perceived by others."

By then, the quest of the Donovans and the other families for "justice" (to put it in quotation marks, as Ambassador Kirkpatrick did) had not produced any serious effort to obtain new information in El Salvador. But another kind of inquiry appeared to be under way.

In Connecticut, Michael Donovan noted squeaks and hisses on his telephone. Often the telephone would ring once, but when it was picked up, no one would be there. On one occasion, when Michael Donovan addressed a meeting at Fairfield University, he was followed on his way home. Sensing he was being tailed, he lured the pursuing car into a cul-de-sac, where it was obliged to turn around and follow him.

Similar things were happening down in Sarasota, so Ray Donovan contacted an old Connecticut friend who was a telephone executive. He put Donovan in touch with an executive at the telephone company in Florida, who in turn promised to take care of the matter. Telephone-company personnel arrived at the Donovans' house, tested their telephone equipment and promised to report back later.

Eventually Ray Donovan heard from the Florida executive.

"The only thing I can tell you," he said, "is that I can't tell you anything."

Curious, the Donovans contacted a lawyer familiar with wiretapping procedures, and he explained: Normally the telephone company would be obliged to confirm or deny whether the telephone was tapped and take legal action if it was. But in "national security" cases involving the federal government, it was forbidden even to tell those involved that their telephone calls were being monitored.

Later an even stranger incident occurred. William Ford, Michael Donovan and some others met at a Maryknoll house in New York City. It was hoped that this meeting would lead to a contact with a Salvadoran who had some important evidence in the case. But this was just another lead that never developed. Instead, both men would remember this meeting about their dead sisters for an entirely different reason.

A short time after they arrived at the Maryknoll house, it was noticed that a van with antennas on the roof had pulled up outside and parked directly in front of the door. The men went to the window and looked out, and then Ford—who also does criminal law—suggested they go outside to see exactly what was going on. With the others following, Ford walked up to the van and tapped on the closed window, wanting to talk to the driver.

"The driver looked straight ahead, pretending nothing was happening," remembered Donovan. "As soon as there was an opening in the traffic, he took off."

Ford, Donovan and the others returned inside. The room where they were meeting overlooked a back alley. Suddenly they noticed four or five men in the back alley. So they opened the window and asked what they were doing there.

"They said they were from the telephone company," Michael Donovan said. "But they didn't seem to be installing anything. They were just crawling around."

Why should the U.S. Government be spying on the families of four churchwomen killed in El Salvador? Even to the family members, the possibility seemed absurd at first.

Yet by the spring of 1981 the Donovan family, Bill Ford and his family, the

Kazels, and members of Maura Clarke's family had become—like Ambassador White—major embarrassments to the Reagan administration's El Salvador policy. The embarrassment did not lie so much in what the families said (many people were critical of U.S. actions in Central America by then). Instead, the "threat" was posed by who these Americans were.

For when they went on television or spoke to church groups or lobbied Congress, Ray and Pat Donovan had what Bob White also had when he testified before the Senate Foreign Relations Committee: absolute credibility.

The Donovans especially remembered a visit to Colorado Springs. After the usual radio, TV and church appearances, they had wound up answering questions at a coffee house near the U.S. Air Force Academy. A film crew had accompanied them, and when the television lights went on, the cadets all hid their faces.

"But they stayed," Pat Donovan recalled. "They sensed they weren't getting the truth from the government. They wanted to hear what we had to say."

These people were no long-haired leftists. In an utterly convincing way, the Donovans, the Fords, the Kazels and the others were mainstream America itself. And by then, the families were asking questions no one in the administration could answer—no matter how they spelled "Sandinista." Why was the United States making excuses for the murderers of American citizens? Why was it pretending there was progress in human rights when tens of thousands of people were being slaughtered? "I am only one person," Pat Donovan said on more than one occasion. "What about the ten thousand women in El Salvador who have had their sons and daughters killed?"

After Haig left the State Department, the telephone taps and surveillance seemed to stop. What, the families wondered, had been the purpose of these actions? Michael Donovan became convinced that, even more than the government wanted to discredit the families, "They wanted to get something on the women. They wanted to discredit them in some way."

It seemed an astonishing supposition. Yet Michael Donovan's judgment, which others involved in the case came to share, by then had a certain logic.

The Administration was caught in a dilemma. The Salvadorans, clearly, were not going to see that justice was done. Equally clearly, President Reagan was not about to forsake his confrontation with Communist aggression in Central America—even if it necessitated shipping weapons and hundreds of millions of dollars to the murderers of citizens of the United States. Yet Congress was increasingly wary of giving the White House a blank check. Indeed, every six months, when the question of certification on human rights came up, the same question still plagued the State Department: What about the four murdered women? When would there be indictments, trials, convictions—justice?

There was one conceivable way to get this problem "off our backs." If only there were some way to make Jean, Dorothy, Ita and Maura seem responsible for their own murders, then the entire problem would be resolved.

For Ray Donovan, especially, even to consider such possibilities was to subvert the commitments of a lifetime. For more than thirty-five years, he had been a card-carrying member of the military-industrial establishment. As chief design engineer for Sikorsky Aircraft, he had shepherded whole generations of helicopters from design, through Pentagon contract, to deployment. And with Reagan's victory, it seemed that Ray Donovan's kind of people were firmly in the saddle.

Alexander Haig, for example, had been President of Sikorsky's parent company, United Technologies, before Reagan tapped him to be Secretary of State. At Haig's going-away party, another executive had taken him aside and explained that one of the women killed in El Salvador was Ray Donovan's daughter. "You ought to contact Ray when you get to Washington," the executive suggested.

"I'll call Donovan," Haig promised, "first chance I get."

The chance, evidently, never arose. But, on March 18, 1981, Haig did have the chance to discuss the question of Ray Donovan's daughter's death with Dante Fascell, a Florida congressman. When Fascell asked Haig about progress in the murder investigation during hearings before the House Foreign Affairs Committee, Haig replied:

I would like to suggest to you that some of the investigations would lead one to believe that perhaps the vehicle the nuns were riding in may have tried to run a roadblock . . . and there may have been an exchange of gunfire. And perhaps those who inflicted the casualties sought to cover it up.

Haig's allegations created a sensation on Capitol Hill and in the press. From "political activists on behalf of the Frente," Jean, Dorothy, Ita and Maura had been escalated into pistol-packing nuns who "tried to run a roadblock," engaged in an "exchange of gunfire" and thus, Haig seemed to argue, had wound up as legitimate battlefield "casualties."

The consternation inside the State Department was, if anything, even greater. By chance, a meeting already had been scheduled with the families for the following morning, at which Michael Donovan took careful notes. After being challenged by family members either to substantiate its "slander [of] the memory of our sisters" or make a public apology, Assistant Secretary James Cheek conceded that "the State Department has no documents, either classified or unclassified, which state, or in any way suggest, that the four women ran a government roadblock, that the four women ever had weapons of any kind, or that the four women had ever engaged in any activity inconsistent with being peaceful religious missionaries."

Even the FBI official present at the meeting was so astonished by the allegations that he, too, began to point out the discrepancies in Haig's comments. According to Donovan's transcript of the meeting, this official

> stated that the FBI had no evidence to suggest that the women had run a roadblock, or that they had ever had weapons, and that they did have evidence to suggest that the women had not run a roadblock. "For instance," he said, "there was not even one bullet hole in the van." Furthermore, [he] pointed out, the roadblock theory does not explain the sexual attacks on the women.

The FBI official, however, seemed most concerned about where the Secretary of State might have gotten his information:

> [He] then stated that despite the Secretary's statement that this was the "most prominent theory," he, as the chief investigator from the FBI assigned to the case, had never before heard of this theory.

Though the FBI investigation later came in for heavy criticism, its decision to reject Thomas Bracken's offer of evidence being seen to have been especially ill-advised, the agency initially struck a number of observers—Ambassador White, the families, journalists—as sincerely trying to get to the bottom of the case.

But when initial inquiries clearly suggested a wide circle of official Salvadoran complicity in the murders, State Department officials, including Patricia Lasbury, were ordered to curtail their contacts with those interested in the case. The same thing apparently happened with the FBI. Initially forthcoming, FBI agents involved in the case eventually refused to comment at all, even in private, even to the families, though they, above all others, certainly had, to use the national-security idiom, a "need to know" what was happening. Once again, the families found themselves up against an appalling inference: the FBI had been ordered off the case. What else, they asked themselves, could explain crucial evidence like the death threat sitting, unexamined, in the FBI's files for two years—or the van being left to rust in a San Salvador parking lot?

Unlike Ambassador Kirkpatrick, Secretary Haig did retract his allegations. Indeed he treated it all as a joke. When asked, during Senate hearings, what evidence he had to prove that "the nuns were firing at the people," the Secretary of State replied, "I haven't met any pistol-packing nuns in my day, Senator. What I meant was that if one fellow starts shooting, the next thing you know they all panic."

This version of the murders also bore no relationship to any of the available evidence. But it did back up the official line, from which, in complete defiance of the known facts, the State Department never would budge: that the murders were an isolated, accidental incident in which no higher Salvadoran authorities were in any way involved.

Haig's retraction did not end allegations that the four women either had been Communist agents or had provoked their own deaths or both. In fact, since late 1980 a quite different interpretation of the murders from that suggested by the available evidence has circulated among right-wing groups strongly supporting the administration's policy in Central America.

> FOR IMMEDIATE RELEASE
> MURDERED NUNS IN EL SALVADOR SUSPECTED
> OF AIDING GUERRILLAS,

was the headline on one "news release" widely circulated by the Washington-based Council for Inter-American Security, known as the CIS. Mailed to thousands of people around the country in 1981, and since recirculated widely, the CIS statement contained numerous factual errors, and implied that the four women were part of a conspiracy, involving the smuggling of "vast quantities of arms," that was "working to overthrow the government in El Salvador." The press release accused the women's families, too, of being involved in supporting "a takeover by pro-Castro guerrillas." The statement added:

> United Nations Ambassador Jeane Kirkpatrick has said: "The nuns were not just nuns, they were political activists and we should be very clear about that."

> CIS is an independent foreign policy research and education organization in Washington, D.C.,

the "report" concluded.

In January 1982, President Reagan certified to Congress that the Salvadoran Government

> has made good faith efforts both to investigate the murders of the six United States citizens in El Salvador . . . and to bring to justice those responsible for those murders.

A year later, the State Department certified both that "there have been significant developments in the investigation and prosecution of the case" and that

> As of mid-January 1983, the overwhelming weight of the evidence demonstrates that the accused former guardsmen acted on their own and not pursuant to higher orders.

In late April, addressing a joint session of Congress, President Reagan justified his continuing military support for the Salvadoran Government on the grounds that

> the government of El Salvador, making every effort to guarantee democracy, free labor unions, freedom of religion, and a free press, is under attack

by guerrillas dedicated to the same philosophy that prevails in Nicaragua, Cuba, and, yes, the Soviet Union.

Then, at the end of 1983, there were two more important "developments" in the case. Congress passed legislation extending the requirement that U.S. military aid to El Salvador be conditioned on improvements in human rights there, including progress in the investigation of the murders of the four women. By then the legislation, which every six months required the administration to report on the human rights situation in El Salvador and to certify that improvements were being made, was about the only remaining incentive for either the Salvadoran or the U.S. Government to take any action on behalf of justice there. By extending the legislation, Congress was reaffirming the Reagan administration's own, frequently stated position that the U.S. objective was not merely to seek military victory, but to promote justice in Central America.

On December 3, 1983—the day after the third anniversary of the women's murders—Judge Harold Tyler presented the report of his own investigation into the murders to the Department of State. Tyler had been named by the White House to investigate the killings. Those who saw the Tyler report said it was notable for two reasons: It was an uncommonly thorough and dispassionate investigation into the facts, they said. And like all other independent inquiries, it led to the strong conclusion that justice was not being done, and was never likely to be done, in the case of the murdered Americans. There no longer could be any doubt in the Reagan administration. The investigator the Administration itself had chosen had reported what those whom the administration did not trust—including Ambassador White and the press—had made known years earlier: U.S. policy, as currently implemented, was not fostering justice in El Salvador at all.

In early 1984, the Lawyers Committee for International Human Rights, in an update of its own chronology of the "investigation," summarized the reaction of President Reagan and the State Department to these two developments:

On November 29, 1983, President Reagan vetoed legislation linking continued U.S. military aid with efforts to improve the human rights situation in El Salvador. One condition of the certification law was that there be "good faith efforts" to investigate the churchwomen's case and to prosecute those who are responsible.

On December 3, 1983, former federal judge Harold Tyler submitted his report on the case to the Department of State. The report was immediately classified by the State Department.

The message to the death squads was clear; and it was the same message President Reagan and his closest advisers had been sending since 1980. The authors of the matanza had committed government allies—not just in San Salvador, but in the White House, too.

In Central America, too, nothing really had changed since the Americans had gathered in that clearing in the forest—except that, thanks to U.S. actions, the State Department's dread scenario for Central America was in greater danger of coming true than seemed imaginable when President Reagan took office.

On the same trip that took me to Florida to see the Donovans, I also had returned to Central America for a visit. So many things had happened there since early 1981 that it was surprising, again and again, to find events recalling the official U.S. white paper on "Communist Interference in El Salvador."

One Central American republic, the white paper had alleged in February 1981, was the victim of "a well-coordinated, covert effort to bring about the overthrow of [its] established government and to impose in its place a . . . regime with no popular support." Still another Central American republic, it said, was being "progressively transformed" into a base for "indirect armed aggression" against its neighbors. In yet a third republic, the white paper had charged, armed terrorists were on the loose, killing thousands, violating every norm of civilized behavior. Their goal, the State Department had claimed, was nothing less than seizing complete control, "legitimizing their violence," and as the forces of decency were terrorized into submission, "to foster the impression of overwhelming popular support."

"In short," the white paper had concluded, Central America was "a textbook case of indirect armed aggression." None of these statements had been true in early 1981, but by early 1984 they had come to describe the situation in Central America quite well. It was also indisputable by then that a conspiratorial outside power was playing a "direct tutelary role" in the "political unification, military direction and arming" of the agents of subversion, chaos and terror. And it was equally true, as the white paper had argued, that these actions not only had "intensified and widened the conflict," but presented "a strikingly familiar case" of this outside power's "military involvement in a politically troubled Third World" region.

By then, indeed, it would have been worthwhile for the State Department, after correcting a few names, to reissue the white paper. For as a result of "United States Interference in El Salvador" many of the white paper's prophecies had come true.

In El Salvador the matanza not only had continued; thanks to U.S. support, the killers were as powerful as ever.

Under President Reagan, neighboring Honduras had been "progressively transformed" into a base for "indirect armed aggression." In this case the aggression was against Nicaragua. For more than two years, the CIA had been conducting "a well-coordinated, covert effort to bring about the overthrow of [its] established government and to impose in its place a . . . regime with no popular support."

Two or three years earlier, those involved in Central American affairs had tended to discuss the makeup of the Sandinista movement, the prospects for land reform in El Salvador, the economic crisis in Costa Rica, the Indian problem in Guatemala. But, over the years, the focus of their speculations had shifted northward. What new, unpredictable and destructive development, these diplomats, economists and politicians wondered, would sweep down on Central America from Washington next?

President Reagan himself inadvertently had summed up the questions that, as a result of his policy, now overshadowed Central America. Would U.S. actions destabilize the "entire region from the Panama Canal to Mexico, on our southern border"? Or would this effort "to destabilize our hemisphere" fail?

The answers Central America provided were oddly illuminating. Even there, the American capacity to determine events had proved to be as illusory as the American capacity to understand them. Indeed, considering the ordeal of intervention that Central America had experienced, the single most important fact was how impervious the dominoes remained to our nudges, even to our jolts.

Panama, Belize and Guatemala had been largely unaffected by the long U.S. effort to turn El Salvador into the "decisive battle for Central America." Even after Torrijos' death, in a 1981 airplane crash, the canal continued to operate without threat. The U.S.-funded National Guard had continued to dominate Panama—no matter which civilian was President, and how the Panamanians voted. After more than four years of Sandinista rule in neighboring Nicaragua, democracy showed no signs of toppling in Costa Rica. But Costa Rica was increasingly destabilized by CIA attempts to involve that country in the campaign against its neighbor. Democracy nonetheless seemed likely to survive in Costa Rica for a reason that had nothing to do with either U.S. intervention or "Communist subversion": the vast majority of all Costa Ricans, witnessing the military catastrophes of their neighbors, were determined not to repeat them in their own country.

Dictatorship and repression seemed sure to remain the norm in Guatemala, whether the regime there received direct U.S. military support or not, for a related reason. The bases of democracy long since had been destroyed in that country. If the possibilities for functioning democracy that had existed in 1954 ever were reestablished, it would be a most heartening, and most surprising, triumph for American principles. Following formal independence from Britain in 1981, Belize now had a national flag and a seat in the United Nations. But there, too, nothing fundamental had changed. It still was the British troops along the Guatemalan border, not the proclamations in Washington, that assured that Central America did not become the scene of a real international war of aggression.

"[D]emocracy is beginning to take root in El Salvador," President Reagan told Congress in April 1983; "the new government is now delivering on its promises of democracy, reforms and free elections." Reagan praised "the land reform program which is making thousands of farm tenants farm owners." The President also praised the work of the U.S. advisers in El Salvador: "The Salvadoran battalions that have received U.S. training," he said, "have been conducting themselves well on the battlefield and with the civilian population."

In fact El Salvador, even more than its neighbors, demonstrated the irrelevance of American doctrine to reality. After more than three years of deep, direct U.S. involvement in El Salvador's internal affairs, the elite, U.S.-trained units were committing atrocities that might have made General Martinez blanch. The constituent assembly, chosen in the U.S.-supported 1982 elections, had repealed land reform in all but name, an action a Reagan spokesman praised as "a positive step." In just three years, Ambassador White's 1981 prediction had come true. The decision "to emphasize the military component at the expense of the civilian component" had led to "disaster." By "buttressing one of the most out-of-control, violent, bloodthirsty groups of men in the world," the United States had helped to assure that whatever chances for peace and democracy El Salvador originally had possessed were "going to fade away."

In Washington, the El Salvador elections of 1982 had been heralded as a triumph for democracy. But elections had also been held fifty years earlier, to legitimize the 1932 matanza. After witnessing the elections, Enrique Baloyra, who is a professor of political science at the University of North Carolina, took them out of the context of American fantasy and placed them in the context of Salvadoran reality.

Far from strengthening the democratic forces in El Salvador, he pointed out, the American-sponsored election had grievously weakened them, while giving the terrorists—what he called the "disloyal Right"—new legitimacy.

The vote had expressed a deep "yearning for peace" and democracy in El Salvador. But El Salvador, he pointed out, had been yearning for peace and democracy "since 1932."

In fact, U.S. intervention had produced only two substantive changes: the Salvadoran military had been dramatically weakened, and the Salvadoran guerrillas had been notably strengthened. The paradox of Cambodia had become the paradox of El Salvador: the deeper America's commitment to its "friends" became, the stronger America's self-selected enemies grew.

As late as 1982, the war in El Salvador had remained a very one-sided affair. While government troops rampaged around the country killing tens of thousands, government casualties continued to be almost nonexistent. In spite of the U.S. advisers and the helicopters, this was war as it had been conducted in El Salvador for more than four hundred years—more a blood sport than a duel, in which the hunter runs no risks to himself even when he fails to kill his prey.

But what would happen when U.S. officials began insisting that a traditionalist Central American army subordinate its usual activities to the quite antithetical task of fighting and winning a counterinsurgency war?

By 1984, the United States had made no headway against the guerrillas. But it had done more to subvert the Salvadoran military—which, for all its defects, had been successfully quelling peasant uprisings for centuries—than the Nicaraguans, the Cubans and the Soviets had. First, with U.S. support, the Salvadoran officer corps had been purged of most of its truly reform-minded officers, because they were not considered sufficiently "anti-Communist." The most prominent victim was Colonel Adolfo Majano, one of the few Salvadoran officers who actually had tried to curb terrorism, most notably by attempting to arrest Roberto D'Aubuisson and other death-squad leaders. In a metamorphosis characteristic of the American intervention, Majano was exiled and D'Aubuisson became a principal player in the Reagan showcase of democracy.

With Majano gone, U.S. support for a time was concentrated on a quite different kind of Salvadoran military leader—the epitome of which was Defense Minister Garcia. General Garcia, of course, had been no champion of "peace, prosperity and freedom" even before the four American women were killed. But Garcia, by Salvadoran standards, did have the virtue of understanding the essentially feudal nature of the Salvadoran War. He also understood, and attempted to placate, the obsessions of the Americans.

So Garcia, unlike many rightists, not only talked about eradicating the Communist conspiracy, he gave speeches about land reform and human rights, if only because, as his U.S. mentors constantly reminded him, such pronouncements were the key to prizing more money and weapons out of Congress. Equally important, Garcia understood the danger of a real war against the guerrillas.

This was not merely that the guerrillas would not be defeated, but that the Salvadoran armed forces would disintegrate. Garcia's possible implication in the murders of U.S. citizens had never undermined his support among the Americans. But gradually a certain realization penetrated the U.S. embassy, the State Department, the White House: just as there was a charade of land reform, a charade of democracy, so, under Garcia, there was only a charade of a war. It was decided, as one U.S. official put it, that Garcia "had to go." The guerrillas had never managed to force Garcia from power, but now—in another familiar metamorphosis—the Americans had.

With Garcia gone, and Vides Casanova in command, there was much talk for a time in Washington about "shaking up the command structure" and "taking the war to the guerrillas." By mid-1983 the Americans were very optimistic about achieving a military "solution" in El Salvador, because Vides Casanova, unlike Garcia, seemed enthusiastic about implementing what the

U.S. embassy called the "national plan." Under the "national"—that is to say, American—plan, the Salvadorans no longer would fight a "nine-to-five" war. Just as we Americans had in Vietnam, the Salvadorans now would take the war to the people. In the summer of 1983, members of the White House staff began preparing a list of foreign-policy successes for President Reagan's 1984 reelection campaign. Prominent on the list was "stopping communism" in El Salvador.

"Salvador Rebels Make Gains and U.S. Advisers Are Glum," the New York *Times* was reporting by November. "The army," U.S. military sources complained, "seemed to be struggling with the same problems that have plagued it over the last four years: low morale, weak logistical support and divisions among its commanders. Some troops have fled their positions without putting up a fight." Following adoption of the "national plan," eight hundred Salvadoran officers and men had been killed, and four hundred prisoners, as well as immense quantities of American arms and ammunition, had been lost to the guerrillas. U.S.-trained Salvadoran troops were deserting, or refusing to reenlist; many of them were joining the massive flow of illegal aliens from El Salvador to the United States. Under the Reagan "commitment," more than a billion in flight capital had left the country; El Salvador's gross national product had declined by more than a quarter; per capita income had dropped by a third, to about $450 a year.

The result was that El Salvador, which lacked an economy and a political system, also increasingly lacked a military—and had to make do with an American imitation of one, conjured up in Washington, and exported, along with all bombs and bullets, via the U.S. training camps in Honduras. Increasingly, the Salvadoran armed forces became more and more of a mystery to their American mentors. Here were the guns. There were the guerrillas; why did the Salvadoran military not go off and kill them?

The more appropriate question was never asked: why should they? The U.S. insistence that the Salvadoran military subordinate its traditional pursuits of pillage, rape, massacre and self-enrichment to the conduct of war as Americans defined it had created a novel situation. For the first time in Salvadoran history, government troops were not just killing, they were getting killed. And they were not at all pleased with this new development. From the beginning, most Salvadoran military men either had actively opposed or been completely indifferent to the American agenda in El Salvador. They wanted villas and foreign bank accounts, not land-reform programs and counterinsurgency operations. And they wanted their careers to end in their Florida condominiums, not on some battlefield in the dirt-poor countryside, among the dirt-poor peasants they both feared and despised.

Instead, the military gradually had discovered, the U.S. embassy had come to pose at least as great a threat to their power and privileges—even to their lives—as the guerrillas did.

On the other side of the lines, the dominant fact was not that the guerrillas were winning. Barring some entirely possible collapse from within in San Salvador, they were not much more likely to overrun the capital than they had been in 1981. Instead, the great change the Reagan "commitment" had produced among the guerrillas was that they, unlike the original victims of the matanza, had learned how to survive. The guerrillas were increasingly battle-hardened and able to live off the land, as a result of their long ordeal. They clearly were ready and able to fight an open-ended war of attrition even if they received no outside help of any kind at all.

When President Reagan had taken office, the dominant military fact in El Salvador, as Ambassador White had put it, was that there was simply "no way that the leftist forces" could defeat the Salvadoran Army.

By the beginning of 1984, the dominant military fact in El Salvador had been reversed: now there was simply no way the Salvadoran Army could defeat the guerrillas—no matter how much U.S. money, weapons and advice they received.

Beneath the style of "strong leadership" in Washington, in fact, the substance of the U.S. intervention remained one of aimlessness and drift. In spite of the talk of building democracy and defeating communism, the Reagan administration never had possessed either coherent objectives or a coherent policy for achieving its objectives in El Salvador.

The guerrillas, at the absolute maximum, still numbered no more than eight thousand ill-equipped fighters. But with the Salvadoran armed forces increasingly apathetic about President Reagan's war, Vides Casanova showed more and more signs of playing Thieu to Garcia's Diem. Largely because of the attempt to force an American-style war on the Salvadoran military, President Reagan was closer than he seemed to imagine to the old Indochina choice: internal collapse or American escalation.

There was, however, one immense difference between Cambodia and El Salvador. From the beginning in Central America, we had supported the local equivalent of the Khmer Rouge. As a result of the ensuing avalanche of U.S. weapons into El Salvador, the original question posed by the matanza had become even more unanswerable.

How could the death squads be disarmed? How could the chronic militarization of Salvadoran politics be ended?

As the 1984 presidential elections approached, it seemed even the Reagan White House had rediscovered the political value of "human rights." More and more, from those surrounding President Reagan, one heard the same complaints heard from White House officials back in Jimmy Carter's reelection year. Didn't the Salvadorans understand that these killings were an embarrassment to the President?

By then, San Salvador resembled Phnom Penh in at least one significant way. Whatever Americans decided to do in Washington, it already was too late. Even a radical change in U.S. policy—away from killing and confrontation, toward placation and peace—could not stop the killers now. Indeed, some U.S. officials argued, to cease supporting the killers would run the risk of El Salvador's "anti-Communists" unleashing a matanza on the U.S. embassy itself.

Whatever happened in Washington, El Salvador had been "saved" for the politics of murder for many years to come; perhaps not even a guerrilla victory could end the bloodbath.

President Reagan, it was clear, had not repeated in Nicaragua his success in destabilizing El Salvador. As a result of the covert presidential war against the Sandinistas, perhaps a thousand Nicaraguans had died. These casualties attracted little attention in the United States. But in a nation of 2.7 million people, this was the equivalent of some eighty-five thousand Americans dying in the defense of their nation's borders. It might have been 1927 or 1912 or even 1855, as the Nicaraguan militiamen set out for the Honduran frontier to resist this latest American assault on their country's dignity and sovereignty. And in every village and barrio where, a few months later, the weeping women and silent men followed another coffin containing another young Nicaraguan killed by CIA-paid and -directed forces, Sandinista "propaganda" achieved another success. In early 1983, CIA sources were predicting that their forces, mostly recruited from former members of Somoza's National Guard, would drive the Sandinistas from Managua within a year. But, within six months, one heard the same complaints about these Nicaraguan "freedom fighters" one heard about the Salvadorans. They were undisciplined, the Americans complained. They were corrupt; they terrorized the very people they were supposed to liberate.

By early 1984, it was clear that President Reagan's undeclared war against Nicaragua was failing to overthrow the Sandinistas but by then the CIA destabilization campaign had produced one very important result: "The salient characteristic of the Sandinistas," a European diplomat in Managua observed, "is the stability of their joint leadership. Years of war and four years in power haven't divided them. And now President Reagan, by attacking them, is reinforcing their unity." It was a unity the Reagan invasion of Grenada had profoundly reinforced. The Administration had indeed taught the "Communists" an important lesson. It was that the kind of internal disputes and ideological inflexibility that had brought down Maurice Bishop and handed Grenada to the Reagan administration on a silver platter must be avoided at all costs.

My most illuminating interview in Nicaragua, however, unfolded inside the U.S. embassy. There, too, it was like going back to other times, other places, as the marine guards inspected my briefcase and I was ushered into the American ambassador's office. For there, too, was yet another American envoy whose essential problem was not "Communist aggression," but that no one in Washington wanted to listen.

The previous U.S. ambassador, Lawrence Pezzullo, had been most critical of the Sandinistas during my previous visit to the embassy. But he, too, had not been considered sufficiently "anti-Communist," and by now was long since gone from the State Department and working for Caritas, the Catholic refugee relief agency. I asked his successor, Anthony Quainton, what might be the consequences not only for Central America, but for the national security interests of the United States, if any of the scenarios in Washington for overthrowing the Sandinistas came true.

He conjured up a veritable catastrophe—not for the Sandinistas and the "Communists," but for the United States and its allies in Central America. A full-scale Honduran-Nicaragua war, he pointed out, probably would not destroy the Sandinistas. But it might well reduce Honduras to chaos, lead to direct Cuban military intervention in Central America and—if President Reagan attempted a Grenada-style U.S. "rescue mission"—create the biggest political crisis in Washington since Watergate.

It was the assessment of the U.S. embassy in Managua that the consequences of the CIA-directed forces advancing on the capital would be just as dire—as tens of thousands of well-armed Nicaraguans retreated into the hills to conduct protracted guerrilla warfare. "You really would have another Vietnam then," the ambassador noted. What about splitting the Sandinista leadership? "An excellent way to hand Nicaragua over to real Marxist-Leninists," the same official replied. "Fortunately it won't happen."

Ambassador Quainton was no Latin America "expert." But his previous posts in Asia and Africa seemed to have given him a sense of reality unusual in an American official of his rank.

"What we really need down here," he concluded, "is a decolonization policy."

I asked the ambassador why his views seemed to have so little relation to U.S. policy. "Oh, we're one source of input," he laughed. The telephone rang. It was Washington, and the call provided an example of the "input" the ambassador mentioned. A few days earlier the Nicaraguans had expelled three U.S. officials. They had charged that they were CIA agents who had plotted to assassinate the Nicaraguan foreign minister, a Jesuit priest named Miguel D'Escoto, by sending him a poisoned bottle of Benedictine. There was no way, of course, for State Department officials like Quainton to know what the CIA had or had not been doing, but now, in the White House, it had been decided to take "retaliatory" action.

"You might be interested to know," Quainton said as he put down the phone, "that someone in the White House has decided to close down three of the six Nicaraguan consulates in the United States." What had been Quainton's recommendation? The ambassador shrugged. "Oh," he replied, "we advised them to take 'firm and appropriate action.' "

Armed with my scoop, I dashed downtown to the Intercontinental Hotel, where low-level Nicaraguan officials and members of the local press corps told me what really had happened. The White House had closed down all six

Nicaraguan consulates and expelled their members from the United States. A few days later the consuls flew home—like the returning militiamen from the Honduran border—to a heroes' welcome. Once again, the U.S. embassy had been the last to know.

However trivial its accomplishments in Nicaragua, the CIA war did produce a characteristic metamorphosis—inside the United States. In April 1984, when Nicaragua announced its intention to bring action against the United States in the World Court because of the illegal mining of Nicaraguan harbors, the Reagan administration announced it would defy the court's jurisdiction. Once again an American crusade against "international outlaws" had transformed America itself into an outlaw. The fundamental maxims of American policy had insensibly changed from liberty to force.

A month later, in another address to Congress, President Reagan nonetheless announced another triumph for American principles. Jose Napoleon Duarte had won the presidential elections in El Salvador in a bitterly contested campaign against D'Aubuisson. Once again, following a masterful presidential performance, Congress narrowly approved increased U.S. aid for the ongoing matanza in El Salvador.

Yet it quickly became clear that the latest Salvadoran elections were chiefly another triumph for American power, not Central American liberty. The CIA had channeled more than $2 million to Duarte and other candidates it favored. The Left had been barred from the elections. D'Aubuisson and his supporters in the United States, notably North Carolina Senator Jesse Helms, accused the State Department and the Salvadoran military of rigging the elections, and there was little doubt that there was much truth in the denunciations made by both the Left and the Right. Once again the Salvadorans had voted for peace; once again the result was likely to be more war.

As the presidential campaign in the United States began in earnest, El Salvador was the scene of what President Reagan's supporters heralded as still another triumph of American principles. After more than three years of delay and obstruction, the five guardsmen accused of murdering the four American churchwomen were suddenly put on trial. The prosecutors were conducted to the courthouse in U.S. embassy vehicles. The windows of the courtroom were removed to allow unimpeded access by American television cameras. Guilty verdicts were quickly returned. As Julia Preston of National Public Radio reported, the judge "scrupulously excluded" all evidence suggesting that higher-ranking officers had been involved.

Once again the headlines in Washington were all of liberty; but in Central America the reality was of a continuing U.S. commitment to force as, almost simultaneously, a far less noticed item of news demonstrated: Quainton had been removed as ambassador to Nicaragua. What had the ambassador done to arouse the enmity of the White House?

"Quainton never had the right kind of answers," one U.S. official explained during a visit to Managua. So Quainton had gone the way of White and many others.

By simultaneously supporting Duarte and escalating the matanza, by convicting the triggermen while funnelling more weapons to their superiors, the Reagan Administration had engaged in a classic American attempt to reconcile the rhetoric of liberty with the reality of force. Election-year legerdemain, however, could not change the unenviable choice the Administration still faced in El Salvador: It ultimately could seek a negotiated settlement, and thus implicitly concede that all the slaughter had been for nothing. Or it could pursue the quest for a military "solution" indefinitely.

For El Salvador, the consequence was one that bore no particular relationship to ideology. "My country will be ravaged for no reason, to no particular result," a former Salvador cabinet minister, who had fled for his life, had predicted in Washington in 1981. By 1984, that prediction had come true, and in the United States, even older prophesies were being fulfilled.

In El Salvador, as Adams had foreseen, the United States had "involve(d) herself beyond the power of extrication, in all the wars of interest and intrigue, of individual avarice, envy and ambition, which assume the colors and usurp the standard of freedom."

By the end of 1983, U.S. prestige in Latin America was at one of its periodic lows. Margaret Thatcher's victory in the Falkland Islands—not either the Carter human-rights policy or the Reagan "antiterrorism" campaign —had finally restored democracy to Argentina. Pinochet, so many years after communism was "stopped cold" in Chile, was in deep trouble; he showed signs of becoming the Marcos of South America. The entire Organization of American States had been alienated by the unilateral U.S. invasion of Grenada, which, besides violating the OAS charter and the Rio Treaty, had revealed, like President Reagan's earlier support for Britain in the Falklands War, the reality of the American commitment to "hemispheric solidarity." Our most important allies in Latin America—the large, well-established democracies of Venezuela, Colombia and Mexico—also had been especially estranged by U.S. actions. For years, the Contadora Group, consisting of those three nations and Panama, had been trying to negotiate a peaceful settlement of the crisis in Central America. And, for all its expertise at seeming to favor a nonmilitary solution, the Reagan administration had blocked all their efforts—even when the Salvadoran guerrillas offered to negotiate with the United States, and the Nicaraguans had proposed a series of treaties by which the Sandinistas would formally pledge not to aid guerrilla groups in neighboring countries, in return for a pledge of U.S. respect for Nicaragua's sovereignty.

There was other news from Latin America as well, although it seemed to attract no attention in the White House. From Mexico to Argentina, Latin

America was reeling under an increasingly insupportable burden of debt, as prices for primary products failed to keep pace with the increases in prices for manufactured goods and oil. Some U.S. bankers feared that the shaky pillar of Third World indebtedness, if it ever toppled, could have a disastrous domino effect on the U.S. economy. One of the first actions of the new, democratic regime in Argentina, besides putting the heads of the death squads on trial, was to suspend repayment of Argentina's external debts. During the Reagan presidency, the Inter-American Development Bank reported in August 1983, Latin America's earlier economic gains had been reversed. During 1982, per capita incomes had declined in twenty-four of the twenty-five nations of Latin America and the Caribbean, including Jamaica, which the Administration had hoped to turn into a triumph of Reaganomics. About a third of Latin America's entire work force were unemployed or underemployed. Meanwhile, Latin America continued to have one of the largest population growth rates in the world. One result was that, every year, hundreds of thousands of impoverished Latin Americans continued to pour into the United States.

Nearly 140 years after Polk's conquest of Mexico, the demographic tables had been turned. The "biological conquest" of the United States by Latin migrants was more and more a reality. Three years after his speech to the Organization of American States, the "shared destiny" that President Reagan had proclaimed was being fulfilled, though it was not a shared destiny of American-style affluence and freedom. It was the destiny of poverty and violence that the barrios of East Los Angeles and San Salvador, the slums of Caracas and Spanish Harlem, all shared.

As always, the most telling metamorphoses were occurring in Washington. No constitutional crisis had grown out of the presidential war in Central America. But some Americans were disturbed by the attempts to control the U.S. press during the Grenada invasion; others noticed the Administration's unprecedented attempts to control press contacts with government officials and to make it impossible for U.S. officials to tell the truth about the inner workings of government even after they left office.

The CIA clandestine war in Central America had failed to topple the Sandinistas, yet it had raised, once again, the question of whether the CIA and its kindred agencies were subject to any constitutional check. But this was one threat, at least, that clearly evoked no alarm in the White House.

In late 1983, one small vignette seemed to sum up what the Administration's campaign to "defeat terrorism" and make America "more secure" had achieved, when surface-to-air guided missiles were installed at the White House. What previously had been unimaginable in America was now the reality: like the presidential palace in San Salvador, the White House now bristled with firepower. The stately old American mansion where President Monroe had once composed his message had been transformed, quite literally, into a bastion "of military power and influence."

It was in the Department of State, however, that the most revealing metamorphoses had occurred. In May 1983, Thomas Enders found himself undergoing the same transformation that earlier had overtaken Swank in Cambodia, Sullivan in Iran and White in El Salvador: White's successor as ambassador to El Salvador, Deane Hinton, was also fired.

Advisers close to President Reagan, led by Ambassador Jeane Kirkpatrick and National Security Adviser William Clark, it was reported, had considered Enders too soft on communism. He had appeared to seriously entertain the possibility of a negotiated settlement leading to "power sharing" with the Salvadoran opposition. Both Hinton and Enders had been ensnared by the same trap that had harmed the careers of many another U.S. foreign-policy official. In spite of all the security checks, they, too, had suffered the contamination of reality. "Enders was in a process of evolution," commented Senator Paul Tsongas of Massachusetts, following Enders' dismissal. "He was a real hard-liner two years ago. But now he's talking about a dual track of military and political solutions."

Hinton's offense turned out to be White's offense. He had lost the confidence of the White House by publicly stating in San Salvador that the right-wing death squads were at least as much a threat as the guerrillas. It was the circumstances of Enders' downfall, however, that were particularly illuminating. In 1983, the Administration had generated yet another white paper on Central America. And according to officials who saw the original draft, it was even more an exercise in fantasy than the first white paper had been.

Its allegations of a Soviet-Cuban terror conspiracy, State Department officials noted, were unfounded. If the paper was released, they realized, it would only provoke ridicule, not win any new adherents to the President's Central America policy. So Enders did what master bureaucrats often do in such situations: he pigeonholed the report, and when the CIA and the White House continued to insist it be published, he attempted to tone it down.

This action, military and intelligence sources later said, was the "last straw" so far as Kirkpatrick, Clark and Reagan were concerned. Several days later, he was fired: more than one Latin American specialist in Washington marveled that now even Enders had become a "good guy."

Another State Department official, however, pointed out the real significance of the Enders incident: "Enders kept responding to Clark and Kirkpatrick with pleas like 'It's not as simple as that.' " Whatever personal transformation had or had not overtaken the former Cambodia chargé d'affaires, Enders had made the mistake of informing the President and those around him of the real policy options they faced in Central America.

"One prerequisite for peace is that we be prepared to give military assistance in enough quantities, and long enough, to convince the insurgents they can't win," Enders later told the Council of the Americas. If the United States was not prepared to do that, he added, it should not rule out a negotiated settlement.

By then, not even hundreds of U.S. advisers in El Salvador—possibly not even a Cambodia-style American invasion—could have "convince[d] the insurgents they can't win." Enders's point was inescapable, though that would not stop the Administration from trying to escape it. El Salvador was simply not the quick, easy "test case" that Grenada had turned out to be. The United States faced only hard, dismal options there: another Vietnam War if it was seriously committed to military victory; or publicly admitting a mistake in an election year and accepting defeat, at least as the Administration itself had defined it, if it wanted peace.

Ambassador White had been the Majano of the State Department; Enders was its Garcia, and with Enders gone, the White House opted for the old Kissinger alternative: keeping the slaughter going as long as possible in hopes that if and when the "domino" finally fell, it would fall on someone else.

One result was that the State Department increasingly resembled the Salvadoran high command. Officials were divided, apathetic, demoralized. Former Senator Fulbright compared the damage to the harm earlier done by the State Department purges following the "loss" of China.

Yet I encountered at least one cheerful official in the Division of Inter-American Affairs. He had asked that we meet outside the Department, so he would not be seen talking to a journalist. He agreed with Fulbright's assessment. "Under Reagan," he said, "it's not just Central America that's been ravaged. The capacity of the United States to make intelligent Latin American policy has been greatly damaged."

I asked him why his morale was so high. He explained that, after more than three years, he was being transferred to a post "as far away from both Washington and Latin America as you can get.

"I survived," he said. It might have been the comment of a Salvadoran campesino.

As his first term in the White House drew toward an end, one of President Reagan's most notable skills remained not only the delegation of authority, but the delegation of responsibility. Even when public opinion strongly opposed specific Reagan policies, the voters seemed not to blame Reagan himself.

Yet, three years after Reagan had made his "commitment" to El Salvador, Haig was gone, Enders was gone, Hinton was gone. Even Clark had left—to become Secretary of the Interior—and Ambassador Kirkpatrick, it was reported at the time, was also planning to leave office.

One result was that President Reagan, and President Reagan alone, was really the only one who could take responsibility for what U.S. policy had produced in Central America. At every point when the advocates of compromise had faced the advocates of confrontation, the President had sided with the advocates of confrontation.

The "Reagan Corollary"—ceaseless turmoil and killing in Central America —was his, and his alone.

Another important result was that, by 1984, only the Central Americans themselves stood between disaster and even greater catastrophe for the United States in Central America. If there was no full-scale regional war, it would be because the Sandinistas avoided being goaded into one. If complete apocalypse did not engulf El Salvador, it would be because, in spite of everything the United States had done there, the matanza had yet to unleash among the Salvadorans the same suicidal bloodlust the matanza in Cambodia had among the Khmer.

If Honduras, too, did not become the scene of a self-fulfilling prophecy of chaos, it would be because the Hondurans, in spite of the growing U.S. military operations in their country, retained their old knack of somehow staying out of the quarrels of their neighbors.

As for chances of real peace, they depended on the slim chance that the Contadora nations or our European allies, all of which refused to support U.S. policy, might, somehow, come up with something. By choosing the death squads as its allies, the United States also had chosen, at least in Central America, to deny itself more principled allies. "Most U.S. presidents have asked allies to endorse their interventions . . . in the Third World," the respected French newspaper *Le Monde* noted. "This time—as in Vietnam— the U.S. is alone."

Following Enders' dismissal, the most stunning metamorphosis of all occurred: President Reagan exhumed Henry Kissinger—and charged him with finding a solution to the "threat" in Central America.

Once, Kissinger had spent four hours in Phnom Penh. Now, he spent a morning in San Jose, an afternoon in Tegucigalpa. Time seemed not to have changed Henry Kissinger; certainly it had not altered his star quality within the government, with the press and in Congress. Even journalists who had followed his progress across Indochina seemed dazzled by this new progress of the Kissinger career. His very apparition in El Salvador seemed to revive the belief that Americans, somehow, could square circles, work magic—that it was Kissinger's destiny, if not America's, to waft away reality and replace it with a triumph of America's illusions, through some feat of legerdemain.

Six weeks after the Reagan administration consigned Judge Tyler's report on the murdered American women to secrecy, it published, with great fanfare, the Kissinger report. Not since the release of the white paper nearly three years earlier had the White House and the State Department placed such emphasis on a Central America report.

Though it differed in some details from the general Reagan policy, the President had ample reason, as the New York *Times* noted, to welcome the Kissinger report, for "its basic contentions—that the United States indeed has a vital stake in Central America and that massive aid is needed to counter leftist revolutions encouraged by Moscow and Havana . . . are pure Reagan doctrine."

Some parts of the report emphasized the conspiratorial "threat." Others, without trying to reconcile the contradiction, emphasized the internal sources of Central America's ordeal. But what made the Kissinger report, for all its discrepancies, a seamless whole was that all its recommendations were founded on the same illusion: that revolution, poverty, dictatorship, everything that displeased Americans about the region, could all be wafted away if only the United States adopted the policy Henry Kissinger proposed. The report called for an $8-billion "Marshall Plan" for Central America. It also reiterated the Truman Doctrine emphasis on direct U.S. involvement in foreign civil wars.

No serious possibility of normalization of relations with Cuba was raised; nowhere was it suggested that, even if the United States did spend $8 billion there and greatly increase its military intervention, our actions might still remain simply irrelevant to what was happening in El Salvador and among its neighbors. In its quest to explain Central America, the Kissinger report had wound up replicating a fantasy of America. "Throughout history," it declared, "the U.S. policies toward the nations of the Americas that have succeeded [have linked] a variety of the different countries to a concept of the hemisphere as a whole."

It proposed that the United States, once again, make the same hemispheric commitment that had assured the success of the "Monroe Doctrine, the Good Neighbor Policy and the Alliance for Progress. . . ." Others, however, saw the report as the manifestation of a different kind of American historical continuity. By interpreting the Salvadoran conflict exclusively in terms of a conflict between American good and Communist evil, a spokesman for the Salvadoran primate, Archbishop Arturo Rivera y Damas, pointed out, "Mr. Kissinger has erred completely by ignoring the Christian forces, which are a vital force in the country." An archdiocesan spokesman said that Kissinger "has not listened to us" and reiterated their call for no more military aid, and for a dialogue with the guerrillas.

Kissinger also had failed to listen to Duarte and his Christian Democrats. "There can't be a simple military victory," a Duarte spokesman added. "We don't need a triumph which flattens the enemy but rather one that integrates him."

But Kissinger—like Glassman before him—evidently had listened carefully to the Salvadoran Minister of Defense, in this case Vides Casanova. The report accused the guerrillas of plotting to "create a totalitarian regime" and urged that the United States provide "much more in equipment and trained manpower" assistance to the Salvadoran military.

The Kissinger report did have one virtue: it stated explicitly what Enders, and White before him, also had said: Reagan's "limited" intervention was achieving nothing except the destruction of El Salvador.

"If present levels of expenditures, present efforts, are continued," Kissinger himself declared, "we will fail in both reform, both in economic and social progress, as we will fail in the security field. There will be a lingering disintegration with very grave consequences."

The difference was that Kissinger—faced with the choice between real policy change and military escalation—once again was opting for escalation. What if Congress refused to give the Administration its $8 billion for economic aid and a blank check for counterinsurgency war? Kissinger delivered the old Phnom Penh ultimatum: critics of the Reagan policy—not President Reagan and his supporters—would have to take responsibility for "paralysis in defending our national interests."

The lines seemed to have been drawn—in Washington, if not in Central America—for a long struggle between the proponents and the critics of America's latest presidential war. Yet even as the 1984 presidential campaign gathered momentum, it was clear that the greatest American fear about El Salvador all along had been groundless. El Salvador was no "second Vietnam."

It merely remained what it had been from the beginning: another Cambodia.

It was June 26, 1983, and it seemed as though some irreducible definition of what it means to be an American was to be found in the grand ballroom of the Bond Court Hotel, in Cleveland, Ohio. More than fifteen hundred persons had paid thirty dollars each to attend a luncheon meeting at which Jean Donovan, Dorothy Kazel, Maura Clarke and Ita Ford were posthumously given the first Robert F. Kennedy awards; according to the citations, "for their contribution to the struggle for human rights."

It might have been a political occasion, but neither President Reagan nor his opponents were mentioned; indeed, the crisis in Central America was not mentioned much, except as it related to the four women.

Instead, a kind of celebration unfolded—a celebration of the fact that, in a mysteriously savage and unjust world, these four vanished Americans should have been able to do something, as one speaker put it, on behalf of "justice, compassion, hope and love."

The mood in the big hall was not one of anger, or even sadness. Rather, a sense of joy and gratitude circulated—that so many people there actually had known Jean, Dorothy, Ita and Maura while they had the chance.

Joseph Kazel looked on with satisfaction as his son James accepted the award on his daughter Dorothy's behalf. "They're not going to forget those girls," he said. "They had such authenticity. No one believes it when the government says bad things about them. They'll go down in history."

Dorothy Kazel's nieces looked like homecoming queens. Ita Ford's niece Miriam was there, in pretty summer dress. Maura Clarke's twin nieces, Pamela and Patricia Keogh, accepted the award on her behalf, but as Pamela read the statement the two girls had prepared, she started to giggle involuntarily. It was her first public speech, she explained. Then she regained her composure and reached her conclusion.

"I think this is a very necessary thing," she said with a big smile. "The struggle for human rights gets right to the basics of life. The world is very much in need of freedom." The audience burst into applause, not so much because of what had been said, but because of the way the young woman had said it.

Why was all this so touching? It occurred to me that these affluent Americans had something some of the campesinos I had seen also had. They had a dignity—a faith in the rightness of what their relatives had done, in themselves and, evidently, a faith in God—that no amount of slander, or even violence, could take away.

Afterward, as waiters cleared away, Father Schindler talked about that terrible search of three years earlier. I asked him what he remembered most vividly, and like most people who knew the four women, he recalled the joy, not the pain.

"It was the day after we recovered the bodies," he said. "There was an all-night wake, and then, the next morning, it was time to move the bodies.

"When we took them outside, we found thousands of Salvadorans were waiting, lining the road. Then they all started applauding. Men were struggling among themselves for the privilege of carrying the coffins. The road was lined with applauding people."

The bodies started down the road, moving slowly past the applauding people. It was an old story being acted out once again there in El Salvador—older than the Americas, as old as the Bible.

Jean, Dorothy, Ita and Maura were passing through the valley of the shadow of death, bound—no matter how you define it—to a certain resurrection.

In March 1983, President Reagan urged his fellow Americans not "to ignore the facts of history and the aggressive impulses of an evil empire, to simply call the arms race a giant misunderstanding and thereby remove yourself from the struggle between right and wrong, good and evil." "Totalitarian darkness" threatened freedom everywhere, the President added; the Communists were "the focus of evil in the modern world. . . ."

"In summation," he told Congress a month later,

I say to you that tonight there can be no question: The national security of all the Americas is at stake in Central America. If we cannot defend ourselves there, we cannot expect to prevail elsewhere. Our credibility would collapse, our alliances would crumble, and the safety of our homeland would be put in jeopardy.

"Nicaragua, Cuba, and, yes, the Soviet Union," President Reagan said in the same speech, were responsible for the continuing *matanza* in El Salvador. "The guerrilla attacks," he explained, "are directed from a headquarters in Managua, the capital of Nicaragua."

Epilogue
The Search for COSVN

"I was born on the Fourth of July, 1776," the head of the U.S. military advisory team on the Cambodian border wrote on the twenty-fifth of December, 1970:

I am Washington, Jefferson . . . Abe Lincoln. I remember the Alamo, the Maine and Pearl Harbor. When freedom called I answered and stayed until it was over, over there.

Though his message took the form of Christmas greetings, the senior adviser of Chau Doc Province, in South Vietnam, was doing what Americans, from the very beginning, have always done in the most exotic settings.

He was proclaiming the syllogism of America. "God always has been on the side of those who are right," he wrote. "I am an American." Therefore, he concluded, "what we Americans are fighting for in Vietnam is right. . . . May I possess always—the integrity, the courage and the strength . . . to remain a citadel of freedom and a beacon of hope to the world."

"When men write the history of this nation, they will record that no people in the annals of time made greater sacrifices in a more selfless cause," President Nixon had said of the Indochina War nine months earlier, just before the Cambodia invasion.

Now that not just North America and the western hemisphere, but Asia and much of the rest of the world had become the stage where we Americans acted out our illusions, the persistence of our national rhetoric was striking. There was a new "red peril" now; there were new conspiracies, new "extensions of the area of freedom." Most of the globe had become a "new frontier." Our ancestors had conferred freedom on a continent; was it not our destiny to confer the great society on Indochina, too? Lyndon Johnson spoke of dams along the Mekong as though he were to Asia what both Andrew Jackson and Franklin Roosevelt had been to the Tennessee Valley. Once the killing was over—once the "red peril" was eradicated—America would illuminate the darkness with an Indochinese TVA.

And so, in the midst of the nuclear age, it was as though the adolescence of America was interminable. A single B-52 now carried more explosives than had been used to conquer the whole of the United States from Plymouth Rock to Los Angeles, but the American endeavor was changeless: America's relations with the weak were still characterized by the superimposition of an illusion atop a void.

The illusion was the illusion of Guatemala, of Vietnam, of El Salvador—of Monroe. The void was the emptiness of My Lai, the silence of the Salvadoran garbage dumps where the vultures scavenge. After World War II, it had become the American destiny to create voids in many places where our power took us. But these voids were nothing new. They were only re-creations of that first great void we Americans had created and then filled with our own boundless self-esteem.

Like all wars, the Indochina War had brought many changes. But, like all our wars, it left something unchanged, untouched, even among those Americans who could see the war with their own eyes.

"We of MACCORDS Advisory Team 64 . . . here on the Cambodian border are wholly dedicated," the Christmas message continued, ". . . to the effort that will bring the final victory."

For some Americans the perpetual quest for "the final victory" was a source of pride and inspiration. But, for others, it always had contained a darker mystery.

Back in Andrew Jackson's time, Alexis de Tocqueville had defined both the privilege and the great predicament of the American birthright: "The great advantage of the American," he wrote, "is that he has arrived at a state of democracy without having to endure a democratic revolution; and that he is born free without having to become so."

From the beginning, this privilege had made the American national experience essentially irrelevant to the experience of those who had to struggle to achieve their freedom. And, for that reason, our great national privilege also created a test of our national quality.

"Can a people 'born free' ever understand people elsewhere that have to become so?" the historian Louis Hartz asked in 1955, the year after Operation Success, in Guatemala.

"Can it ever understand itself?"

It was the question of the Mexican War, the Philippines, the question of El Salvador. In 1930, as the marines chased Sandino in Nicaragua, Reinhold Niebuhr had addressed it.

Americans tended to be "awkward imperialists," the theologian had decided, because their inability to understand themselves inflicted upon them such grave misapprehensions about others. The very privilege of having been born free, of enjoying by right what others often failed to achieve, even through struggle, led Americans to imagine "it is our virtue rather than our power which other nations envy." "From the earliest days of its history to the present moment," Niebuhr later wrote, during the Cold War, in a book called *The Irony of American History,* there had been a "deep layer of Messianic consciousness in the mind of America. . . ." But what lay beneath this layer?

Niebuhr found a "tremendous amount of illusion . . . in American culture," a "real schizophrenia afflicting American policy." Americans at once saw the world as both a vindication of themselves and as an intolerable threat. For Niebuhr, the result was an "ironic incongruity between our illusions and the reality which we experience."

America's immense power had led to the "discovery of the limits of power"; the fantasy that the whole world could be made to be like America had produced "an ironic refutation of some of the most cherished illusions" of American nationalism.

For Niebuhr, the greatest of the ironies was that, in its effort to combat a totalitarian conspiracy, American nationalism itself had become totalitarian, conspiratorial. Precisely because Americans were "incapable of recognizing [their own] corruptions of ambitions and power," because we Americans were so persuaded "that our society is so essentially virtuous that only malice could prompt criticism of any of our actions," Americans themselves had wound up generating the most "extravagant forms of political injustice and cruelty."

It was for these reasons, Niebuhr decided, that it was the destiny, over and over again, of "the most powerful nation on earth [to] suffer such an ironic refutation of its dreams of mastering history."

He called what Americans did to themselves and others an example of irony, rather than of tragedy or pathos, for a most revealing reason:

> Irony must be distinguished as sharply from pathos as from tragedy [he wrote]. . . . An ironic situation is distinguished from a pathetic one by the fact that a person involved in it bears some responsibility for it. It is distinguished from a tragic one by the fact that the responsibility is not due to conscious choice but to an unconscious weakness.

The result was that America's actions were not merely figuratively, but literally, quixotic. As they tilted at windmills in Central America or Southeast Asia, Americans were as "unconscious of the absurdity" of their actions as Don Quixote had been.

And so, at the moment of their greatest power, Americans were destined to deny themselves both pathos and tragedy, because they lacked both the innocence that defines pathos and the self-knowledge out of which true tragedy arises. Instead, they were fated to inhabit an intermediate world where Americans always bore "some responsibility" for what they did, yet where an "unconscious weakness" perpetually prevented them from coming to terms with the full significance of their actions.

Don Quixote had attempted to apply "the ideals of chivalry" in a world where feudalism already was dead; Americans were attempting to apply the ideals of the American mythology to a world which was not "born free," where the circumstances that made all the illusions of America seem real simply did not exist.

All along, America's peculiar worldview had been infused by "a contradictory combination of voluntarism and determinism." In consequence, the fate of Americanism had turned out to be not very different from the fate of communism, that is to say a destiny of both corruption and failure. "This American experience," Niebuhr wrote, "is a refutation in parable of the whole effort to bring the vast forces of history under the control of any particular will, informed by a particular ideal."

He thus defined the continuing irony of what America does in places like El Salvador, which is that the United States is simultaneously both much too powerful and all too impotent:

> The two aspects of our historic situation which tend particularly to aggravate the problems of American idealism are: (a) that American power in the present world situation is inordinately great; (b) that the contemporary international situation offers no clear road to the achievement of either peace or victory over tyranny.

Translated into the actualites of Cambodia or El Salvador, this meant simply that America had the power to destroy such countries, but no capacity to "save" them. It could kill millions—ravage whole nations—but the irony of ironies was that America, even then, was denied both the pathos of the Salvadoran campesino and the heroic stature of the truly tragic figure. To the contrary, the more Americans proclaimed, "I am Washington, Jefferson . . . Abe Lincoln," the more they became Polk, Buchanan—Richard Nixon.

By Christmas 1970, events had turned Niebuhr's intellectual construct into a historical reality. Never had the refutation of America's dream of mastering history taken more concrete form than the smoldering ruins of Cambodia. Yet even there, on the Cambodian border, Americans remained ironically "incapable of recognizing [their] corruptions of ambition and power."

* * *

"We can look back with pride [on] the long struggle," the Christmas message from the Cambodia border continued, "[and be] proud to say—I am an American." The officer who wrote the message was named John Virgil Swango, and before concluding, he posed a fundamental question.

"[W]hat is it," he asked, "about this great country of ours—these United States of America—that has inspired [it] to fight . . . for so many years?"

It was a question many Americans had asked, but few had answered, and for Senator Stuart Symington, at least, it was a conundrum that still troubled him three years after the Cambodia invasion.

"I have listened to many hours of testimony," Symington said in August 1973. "We discussed it with Dr. Kissinger, and I don't understand yet exactly what it is all about. . . . [W]hat I don't understand is why we supported [Sihanouk's] overthrow when he was out of the country. When that overthrow appeared to be failing, I don't understand why we invaded his country. . . ."

When the State Department replied, it provided no answer—only another demonstration of the continuing sovereignty, in America, of illusion over reality. By then, so far as the U.S. Government was concerned, Cambodia had never been invaded. There only had been "a brief incursion by United States ground forces in 1970 . . . directly connected with the withdrawal of U.S. forces from South Vietnam." The secret bombing, the invasion and America's subsequent acts of war in Cambodia, the State Department reply said, were not acts of aggression. They were authorized by the principle of "legitimate self-defense as permitted by the U.N. charter."

So Symington's question, like so many questions about America, went unanswered, but that did not mean there was no answer.

President Nixon himself had given it the night he had announced the Cambodia invasion. And in the course of the 1973 Senate hearings on Cambodia, several witnesses—usually without being asked—had volunteered the answer too. The reason it went unheard, unnoticed, was the same reason so many other answers about America went unheeded. It was lost in the immense stockpiles of words, reports, bombs, bullets, illusions, that had come to make up the war, and America itself.

"Incidentally, you might be interested in what the purpose of this whole thing was," General George J. Brown, chief of staff of the Air Force, had testified on July 13, 1973, "chasing what was known as COSVN headquarters, which was the communist headquarters in South Vietnam. They were functioning from just across the border. . . ."

This also had been the purpose of the invasion. "I think something sticks in my mind," Gerald J. Greven, a former Air Force captain, testified on August 8, 1973; "when we invaded Cambodia in 1970 [it was] the big headquarters we were looking for. . . ."

Though it was later largely forgotten, Nixon himself had said the same thing the night of the invasion: it had been his belief that by invading Cambodia he could destroy "this key control center" and so win the war.

* * *

What is dangerous to the world is not that nations should act . . . in accordance with their interest, but that they should act unreasonably, at the dictation of the reforming instinct, or of some megalomaniac dream,

an American author had written half a century before the first American killed the first Cambodian, about the American war in the Philippines.

But such warnings, in America, always had been forgotten, because, as

Ronald Steel later put it, during the Vietnam War, they betrayed a "deep-rooted instinct in our national character—an instinct to help those less fortunate . . . to emulate and perhaps one day achieve the virtues of our society."

"We are not a nation so much as a world," Herman Melville wrote more than half a century before the war in the Philippines. "We Americans are the peculiar, chosen people . . . we bear the ark of liberties of the world.

"While we are rapidly preparing for that political supremacy among the nations, which prophetically awaits us," Melville asserted two years after the conquest of Mexico, the time also had come "to carry republican progressiveness into Literature as well as Life. . . ." Calling on America's artists, no less than its generals and presidents, to take "a practical lead in this world," Melville exhorted the whole of American civilization to "breathe the unshackled, democratic spirit . . . in all things."

Yet Melville's "passionate defense of extreme American cultural nationalism" turned out to be as "haunted by the malevolence and horror of existence" as the Nixon Doctrine itself. The great American novel he wrote was a megalomaniac dream: the story of the projection of an American captain's hallucinations on the neutrality, the innocence, the pathos, of others. *Moby-Dick* had not "breathe[d] the unshackled, democratic spirit" its author had proclaimed. Instead, Melville's—America's—greatest work of literature had been insensibly transformed into the tale of a chained, autocratic psyche whose obsessive search for an external mirror of itself ensures self-destruction.

"Surely all this is not without meaning," Melville wrote—a century before the ceaseless flights, across all the oceans of the world, of Dulles, Johnson, Nixon:

And still deeper the meaning of the story of Narcissus. . . . Though I cannot tell why . . . the Fates put me down for this . . . voyage, cajoling me into the delusion that it . . . result[ed] from my own unbiased free will . . . chief among these motives was the overwhelming idea of the great whale himself. . . .

Such a portentous and mysterious monster roused all my curiosity [and so in pursuit of] undeliverable, nameless perils . . . I sail . . . forbidden coasts [and] am quick to perceive a horror. By reason of these things, then, the voyage was welcome . . . and in the wild conceits that swayed me to my purpose . . . there floated into my inmost soul . . . one grand hooded phantom. . . .

* * *

"During the invasion of Cambodia in 1970," as Frances FitzGerald later wrote, "American officials spoke of . . . the enemy's command headquarters for the south as if there existed a reverse Pentagon in the jungle complete with Marine guards, generals, and green baize tables. In fact . . . there was no such thing, but . . . the image kept returning."

Over the years, the center of the conspiracy increasingly had come to reflect the air-conditioned, windowless underground complex in Saigon where the Americans, using computers and earth satellites and electronic sensing devices "made mosaics of the general targeting system" and thus laboriously, secretly, constructed images of themselves.

The image that kept returning was an image of America. In its effort to define the enemy, MACV had reproduced itself in the form of COSVN. Like all the other search-and-destroy operations, the real objective of the Cambodia invasion was a mirror image of the America that launched it. The B-52s, the "Daniel Boone" operations, the invasion, on one level, were aimed at destroying COSVN. But the "still deeper" meaning was that America had set out to find, and destroy, some inadmissible truth about itself.

In late 1983, when Ambassador Kirkpatrick believed she perceived a pattern that was "by now discouragingly familiar: choose a weak government, organize a national liberation front, add a terrorist campaign to disrupt order and provoke repression to weaken an already weak economy, then intensify the violence," she imagined she was describing Communist tactics in El Salvador. She was, ironically, unconscious that she was really describing the Reagan policy toward Nicaragua. Nor had Polk understood, in 1846, when he told Congress about "the cup of forbearance" being exhausted, that he was only describing his own war intrigue.

The year before the Cambodia invasion, Senator Fulbright had held hearings in an attempt to gather some understanding of Vietnam. Instead, the Senate Foreign Relations Committee had wound up confronting "the meaning of the story of Narcissus."

The senator found himself intrigued, in a way astonished.

Is this really an extraordinary phenomenon or not? [Fulbright asked.] [I]ndividuals very often . . . accus[ing] someone with whom they are a rival of the very thing they have in mind themselves. . . .

I wonder if in these accusations made by Americans, especially the very prominent ones, who are in a position of power . . . if that isn't exactly what is happening.

"It is not our power but our will and character that is being tested tonight," Nixon said as he announced the invasion of Cambodia. "If, when the chips are down, the world's most powerful nation, the United States of America, acts like a pitiful, helpless giant, the forces of totalitarianism and anarchy will threaten free nations and free institutions throughout the world." "Have the elder races halted?" Whitman asked in 1854,

> Do they droop and end their lesson, wearied
> over there beyond the seas?

> We take up the task eternal. . . .

Whitman had begun with Melville's optimism, yet his voyage took him to the same destination. In 1873 he gazed out on the nation he once had celebrated as the incarnation of goodness—and found himself as appalled as John Quincy Adams earlier had been by the capacity of America's growing power to destroy America's principles of liberty:

> Shift and turn the combinations of the statement as we may, the problem of the future of America is in certain respects as dark as it is vast. Pride, competition, segregation, vicious wilfulness, and license beyond example brood already upon us. Unwieldy and immense, who shall hold in Behemoth? who bridle Leviathan?

Whitman asked.

Whitman, too, would become a myth—the poet laureate of the American destiny. "We take up the task eternal!" Even the end of that line would be forgotten, expunged from the mind of America.

"We take up the task eternal, and the burden and the lesson, Pioneers! O pioneers!" was what the poet really wrote.

As always the burden would be sloughed off, the lesson forgotten.

The national experience that began with the search for northwest passages in the arctic that did not exist, with the search for illusory cities of gold in the desert, with the universalist speculations of Thomas Jefferson subsidized by the slave-grown tobacco of Virginia, flowed on through time, unmindful of the realities it traversed, to the dream that America could avoid defeat and dishonor—if only it could find COSVN in the Cambodian jungle. The quest for the unattainable, for universal perfection, which because of its very nature must end in disillusionment and destruction, has been a permanent theme in the American experience. The refusal to confront America's own capacity for failure, for destruction—for evil—traditionally has been channeled into the search for an external causality to explain them, and so absolve America and its "special destiny" from responsibility.

"Tonight," Richard Nixon would announce, "American and South Vietnamese units will attack the headquarters for the entire Communist military operation in South Vietnam."

"[T]o my knowledge, we never got the headquarters," General Brown would testify.

"[T]he big headquarters we were looking for, to my knowledge it was never found," Captain Greven would testify. The "targets were not there, they could not be found, they were different from what people thought they were, they were a mile away, they didn't exist at all."

* * *

It was May 4, 1970, and where the MACV mosaics and the B-52 coordinates and the CIA intelligence analyses had said there would be COSVN, there was only a convergence of Americans.

There were dozens of them in that forest clearing—mostly soldiers and officers, but also journalists, photographers, TV crews. The soldiers lounged on their armored personnel carriers. Their officers spoke into the walkie-talkies, communicating with the planes overhead and with MACV. Some Cambodians had gathered to watch the spectacle of these Americans, who could go anywhere and do anything, and yet had chosen to come here.

There was a stench in the air. It was the smell of burning rubber. The Americans were defoliating the rubber plantation. Not far away, the Cambodian towns of Mimot and Snoul were burning. Few Americans, before now, had even known these places existed; now, as the American bombs fell, it was as though they never had existed.

The North Vietnamese were nowhere to be seen, but the Cambodians watching the Americans were like forest creatures; they had never seen Americans before, so they did not know to be afraid.

As quickly as the Americans had arrived there, they began to disperse. A lieutenant gave an order to his men. They turned their rifles on the Cambodians and shouted at them, in English, to raise their hands. Then they tied their hands behind their backs, tightly blindfolded them and roped them together. Their eyeless faces convulsed with indignation and terror, the Cambodians were led away. Millions of Americans would see those photos and read the wire-service caption that accompanied them. It said these Cambodians were "Vietcong prisoners."

It was as though America had converged in that forest clearing, looking for some explanation of itself.

Notes

Prologue   The Clearing in the Forest

pp. 1–18 Details of events and personal quotations in this section are based on interviews, in Central America and in the United States, between 1980 and 1984, with the following persons: Jean Donovan, Dorothy Kazel, Heather Foote, Peggy Healy, Mr. and Mrs. Robert E. White, Father Paul Schindler, Mr. and Mrs. Raymond Donovan, Mr. and Mrs. Michael Donovan, Mr. and Mrs. Joseph Kazel, Mr. and Mrs. James Kazel, Sister Martha

Owen, Michael H. Posner, Diane Orentlicher, James E. Zorn, Ana Carrigan, John Dinges, Jose Guillermo Garcia, Adolfo Majano, Ian Mates, Archbishop Arturo Rivera y Damas, Deborah Miller, Colleen Kelly and others who wished to remain anonymous.

pp. 1–3 Scene at grave site: "Special Report: Way of the Cross in Salvador," *Maryknoll* magazine, March 1981; *Time* magazine, December 15, 1980; *Miami Herald,* December 4–7, 1980.

pp. 2–3 "[T]his appalling crime": William D. Rogers, William G. Bowdler and Luigi R. Einaudi, *Report to the President of a Special Mission to El Salvador,* Washington, D.C., December 12, 1980.

pp. 3–5 Details of apparent plot: Lawyers Committee for International Human Rights, *A Report on the Investigation into the Killing of Four American Churchwomen in El Salvador* (September 1981); *Justice in El Salvador: A Case Study* (July 20, 1982); *Justice in El Salvador: A Case Study* (February 1, 1983); *Chronology of the Investigation and Prosecution of Those Responsible for Killing Four U.S. Churchwomen in El Salvador,* January 1984.

pp. 3–4 Rickelman interrogation: radio communication: John Dinges, "New Evidence on Missionaries' Deaths in Salvador Suggests Official Plot," Pacific News Service, July 11, 1981.

p. 5 "[D]river of a milk truck discovered the bodies" and other details at grave site: telegram from U.S. Embassy, San Salvador, to State Department, December 8, 1980.

p. 6 Mickey Mouse T-shirt: UPI photo, Washington *Post,* February 11, 1982.

pp. 7–9 Details in Lawyers Committee reports and Dinges reports for Pacific News Service.

p. 8 State Department allegations: Department of State, *Communist Interference in El Salvador,* Special Report No. 80 (February 23, 1981).

p. 10 "[N]o surgical masks were available": *Report to the President,* p. 6.

pp. 12–13 Alvarez Cordoba murder: Raymond Bonner, "In Salvador, the Unmaking of an Oligarch," NYT, December 14, 1980.

p. 13 Ita Ford quoting Romero: *From the Writings of Ita Ford, 1977–1980,* photocopy of excerpts from her letters to friends and family, p. 2.

p. 14 "Why does Jean's face remain so clear": T. D. Allman, "Rising to Rebellion: With the Guerrillas in El Salvador," *Harper's Magazine,* March 1981, p. 35.

p. 14 "Not mine dear friend": Jean Donovan letter quoted in Ana Carrigan and Bernard Stone, *Roses in December: The Story of Jean Donovan,* 2nd of December Films.

p. 14 "They too considered themselves idealists": Mike Sager, "Slain U.S. Adviser Had an 'Obsession' to Distribute Land," Washington *Post,* January 5, 1981.

pp. 15–16 Murdered women "agents of the Frente": John Hall, "Ambassador Kirkpatrick: Reagan-Appointed Democrat Speaks Her Mind on World,

Domestic Politics," Tampa *Tribune,* December 25, 1980; tape recording of Kirkpatrick's allegations, made by John Hall, and in sound track of *Roses in December.*

p. 17 Details on Hammer/Pearlman murder, Washington *Post,* January 5, 1981.

I The War Against the Children

p. 21 "[B]odies of 16 youths": UPI report, June 27, 1980, San Francisco *Chronicle,* June 28, 1980.

p. 21 "[M]ore than 13,000 people were killed": Raymond Bonner, "The Agony of El Salvador," NYT, February 22, 1981.

p. 21 "[L]ooking at the bodies": UPI photo, NYT, April 10, 1981.

pp. 21–30 Details of 1932 revolt in El Salvador: Thomas P. Anderson, *Matanza: El Salvador's Communist Revolt of 1932;* also Stephen Webre, *Jose Napoleon Duarte and the Christian Democratic Party in Salvadoran Politics 1960–1972,* pp. 7–10; Tommie Sue Montgomery, *Revolution in El Salvador: Origins and Evolution,* pp. 50–53.

pp. 22–23 *"[M]uy grande matanza":* Juan Vasquez, "For El Salvador, History Is a Nightmare of Guns and Gangsters," Washington *Post,* December 14, 1980.

p. 23 "[R]oadways littered with bodies": Anderson, pp. 131–34.

p. 24 Details of atrocities: NYT, February 19, 1981; February 7, 1982; February 1, 1982; September 21, 1982; October 3, 1982, among others. The reports of Raymond Bonner are particularly valuable; also American Civil Liberties Union/Americas Watch Committee, *Report on Human Rights in El Salvador,* January 26, 1982.

p. 24 "[C]ut off the palomita": Amnesty International, "Update on the 'Sumpul River Massacre,' " August 11, 1980, p. 3.

p. 25 Uprising a "godsend" for Martinez and other details: Anderson, pp. 145–46, 150.

pp. 25–26 Changes in the Church, popular organizations, coup: background described in Penny Lernoux, *Cry of the People;* Montgomery, pp. 97–116.

pp. 27–28 Gunther on El Salvador: John Gunther, *Inside Latin America,* pp. 126–30.

pp. 28–30 Details on Marti and Martinez: Anderson, pp. 64–82, 135–53.

p. 30 Criticism of Marti: Anderson, p. 146.

pp. 30–31 "[P]rospects for the Left are not very bright": Federico G. Gil, Enrique A. Baloyra and Lars Schoultz, *The Failure of Democratic Transition in Latin America: El Salvador* (December 1980 draft version of State Department report), pp. 103–6.

p. 32 "[M]ake Marti a legendary folk villain": Anderson, p. 138.

428

p. 32 "[S]cant evidence": U.S. Army, *Area Handbook for El Salvador* (1971 edition), pp. 14–17.

p. 33 "Soviet Union and other Communist states": State Department, *Communist Interference in El Salvador,* p. 1.

pp. 33–34 "[B]odies of 22 young people": "Salvadoran Troops Kill 22 Youths at House in Poor Area of Capital," NYT, January 11, 1981.

pp. 34–36 Details of matanza: Legal Assistance Department of the Archdiocese of San Salvador, *Repression Carried Out by the National Army of El Salvador; the Military Corps of National Security (National Guard, National Police, Rural Police) and Paramilitary Organizations (Death Squads, Secret Anti-Communist Army, ORDEN) Under the Protection of the Christian Democrat-Military Junta,* pp. 1–10; Amnesty International reports for El Salvador, August–December 1980; Legal Department of the Archdiocese of San Salvador, "Socorro Juridico Reports: Events from the 14th to the 19th of September," pp. 1–3.

pp. 37–38 Details on paramilitary organizations: Cynthia Arnson, "Background Information on the Security Forces in El Salvador and U.S. Military Assistance" (March 1980), Institute for Policy Studies, pp. 4–7.

pp. 39–41 Details of killings and disappearances: Amnesty International, El Salvador Packet (Amnesty International reports on El Salvador, March 1980–June 1981).

p. 42 Lempa River massacre: Warren Hoge, "Slaughter in Salvador: 200 Lost in Border Massacre," NYT, June 8, 1981; Amnesty International reports.

p. 43 Buckley estimate on government casualties: Tom Buckley, "Letter from El Salvador," *The New Yorker,* June 22, 1981.

pp. 44–45 Romero homily and letter to Carter: texts in Placido Erdozain, *Archbishop Romero: Martyr of Salvador,* pp. 77–80; Washington *Post,* February 19, 1980; Richard Millett, "Salvadoran Archbishop Romero: Martyr to Moderation," Washington *Post,* March 30, 1980.

p. 47 "I will rise again in the Salvadoran people": Erdozain, p. 75.

II The Last Domino

pp. 48–52 U.S. quotes on Central America, including Olds memorandum: Richard Millett, *Guardians of the Dynasty: A History of the U.S. Created Guardia Nacional de Nicaragua and the Somoza Family,* pp. 52–55.

p. 51 Coolidge on Nicaragua: Julius W. Pratt, *A History of United States Foreign Policy* (Second Edition), p. 368.

p. 51 Coolidge and Boston police strike: Samuel Eliot Morison, *The Oxford History of the American People,* p. 885.

pp. 51–52 "[D]anger of Bolshevism": Dexter Perkins, *A History of the Monroe Doctrine,* p. 337.

p. 54 "[S]hattered Nicaragua's hopes": John A. Booth, *The End and the Beginning: The Nicaraguan Revolution,* p. 30.

p. 55 Zeledon death: Millett, pp. 31–33.

p. 55 Sandino and Zeledon: Thomas W. Walker, *Nicaragua: The Land of Sandino,* pp. 19–20.

p. 56 "[D]ive-bombing attack": Bernard Diederich, *Somoza and the Legacy of U.S. Involvement in Central America,* p. 17.

p. 57 Borah on "Monroe Doctrine": Perkins, p. 338.

pp. 58–61 Stimson, Kellogg and other comments: Millett, pp. 113, 88, 55, 98, 148, 162.

pp. 61–62 FDR on Somoza; Somoza visit to United States: Diederich, pp. 21–22.

p. 62 Gunther on Somoza: *Inside Latin America,* p. 137

pp. 65–66 Description of Somoza: Diederich, p. 31.

p. 72 Somoza "worthy of support"; murderer "never convicted": Diederich, pp. 171–72, 296.

p. 72 "Somozism without Somoza": Walker, pp. 112–13.

pp. 75–77 Pierce and Walker: "Walker, William (1824–1860)," article in Encyclopaedia Britannica (Eleventh Edition), Vol. 28, p. 274.

p. 80 "[M]yth that revolution is inevitable": interview with Sister Peggy Healy, Managua, November 1980.

pp. 82–83 "[M]en with guns": interview with Ambassador Lawrence A. Pezzullo, Managua, November 1980.

p. 85 "[B]oring subject": interview with George Price in Belmopan, December 1980.

p. 85 "[B]etter life": interview with Jose Figueres, San Jose, November 1980.

pp. 88–89 White-paper assertions: Department of State, "Communist Interference in El Salvador" (Special Report No. 80), pp. 1–8.

p. 89 "[F]actual errors, misleading statements": Washington *Post,* June 9, 1981.

p. 89 "[G]uerrilla leaders . . . didn't write them": Jonathan Kwinty, "Tarnished Report? Apparent Errors Cloud U.S. 'White Paper' on Reds in El Salvador," *The Wall Street Journal,* June 8, 1981.

p. 89 "Rube Goldberg machine": John Dinges, "Did Haig Read His Own Intelligence Reports? Wide Disparity Between Salvador White Paper and Documents Behind It," Pacific News Service, March 14, 1981; "The Rube Goldberg Factor in the El Salvador Debate," Pacific News Service, August 26, 1981.

pp. 89–92 Glassman/Garcia encounter and development of white paper: ES-INFO El Salvador Information Office, "Unofficial Transcript of the Presentation Made by Mr. Jon. D. Glassman, Member of the Policy Planning Staff of the United States Department of State, at the 'New Administration

Series' Sponsored by the Center for InterAmerican Relations, New York, on May 20th, 1981," pp. 1–45.

p. 94 U.S. "plot": *Newsweek,* November 8, 1982, pp. 42–55.

p. 94 "Violence . . . Nicaragua's most important export": State Department, Current Policy No. 482, p. 3.

pp. 94–95 Nixon on Monroe Doctrine: Los Angeles *Times,* May 11, 1981.

p. 95 "It's Honduras": Bernard Weinraub, "Tied to Right for Reasons Gone Wrong," NYT, November 7, 1982.

p. 95 "[S]horter than their rifles": Alan Riding, "U.S. Is Looking to the Hondurans to Hold the Line," NYT, April 20, 1982.

pp. 96–97 Borges passages: Jorge Luis Borges, *A Personal Anthology,* pp. 15, 13–14.

III The Barren Gesture

pp. 98–99 Adams, Calhoun, Clay and Madison statements: cited in Samuel Flagg Bemis, *John Quincy Adams and the Foundations of American Foreign Policy,* pp. 373, 389, 384, 393–94.

p. 99 "[R]einstituting the 1823 Monroe Doctrine": Helms statement, Miami *Herald,* August 12, 1982.

p. 99 Phillips on "Monroe Doctrine": Miami *Herald,* July 24, 1983.

p. 99 Safire on "Reagan Corollary": NYT, April 22, 1983.

p. 101 Reagan comments: NYT, February 25, 1982.

pp. 103–4 Text of 1823 Monroe message: Henry Steele Commager, *Documents of American History* (Seventh Edition), Vol. 1, pp. 235–37.

pp. 104–5 "[L]egend and nothing more": Dexter Perkins, *A History of the Monroe Doctrine,* p. 54.

p. 106 "[C]ombined system of policy": Bemis, p. 382.

pp. 109–10 Calhoun and Clay statements: Bemis, pp. 389, 393–94.

p. 110 Text of Canning letter of August 20, 1823: Commager, pp. 234–35.

p. 110 Metternich and Chateaubriand statements: Perkins, pp. 51–55.

p. 110 Adams on Chimborazo: Bemis, p. 386.

pp. 110–15 For a useful overview of Latin America's problems, see Eric R. Wolf and Edward C. Hansen, *The Human Condition in Latin America.*

p. 116 Insurrection of 1832: Tommie Sue Montgomery, *Revolution in El Salvador: Origins and Evolution,* pp. 39–40.

p. 117 Britain "behind Tecumseh's confederacy": Samuel Eliot Morison, *The Oxford History of the American People,* p. 382.

pp. 117–19 Bailey and other quotes: Thomas A. Bailey, *A Diplomatic History of the American People,* pp. 130, 154.

p. 120 Reagan statement: NYT, February 25, 1982.

pp. 120–21 Adams statement: Bemis, p. 366.

pp. 125–26 Text of Washington's Farewell Address, of September 16, 1796, in Commager, pp. 169–75.

pp. 127–28 American fear of British: A. P. Whitaker, *The United States and the Independence of Latin America,* pp. 481–85.

pp. 128–30 Text of Canning letter of August 20, 1823: Commager, pp. 234–35.

p. 130 Jefferson statement: Perkins, p. 46.

pp. 130–31 U.S. reaction to Canning message: Bemis, pp. 385, 380.

p. 133 Text of Polignac memorandum of October 9, 1823; Monroe reaction; friendship of czar; Adams comments: Bemis, pp. 381, 386, 162, 387.

p. 142 "[N]o evidence": Perkins, p. 68.

pp. 145–45 Adams statement; Clay/Adams exchange: Bemis, pp. 387, 393–94.

p. 147 "[L]egend and nothing more": Perkins, pp. 54–55.

p. 147 "[H]earty agreement": Theodore Salisbury Woolsey, "Monroe Doctrine" article in Encyclopaedia Britannica (Eleventh Edition).

p. 149 "I called the New World into existence": "Canning, George (1770–1827)" article in Encyclopaedia Britannica (Eleventh Edition).

p. 151 "[B]arren gesture": Perkins, p. 32.

p. 153 Adams's reaction to South American revolution: Bemis, pp. 364–66.

p. 156 Wilson on "Monroe Doctrine": Woodrow Wilson, *A History of the American People,* Vol. 3, p. 265.

p. 157 Wilson on Monroe and World War I: Perkins, pp. 288–89.

p. 157 Nixon on Wilson: "Address by President Nixon on the War in Vietnam, November 3, 1969," WCPD, November 10, 1969, pp. 1546–55.

p. 157 "[F]orgot all about the American Constitution . . .": Harold Nicolson, *The Evolution of Diplomacy,* p. 114.

pp. 158–59 Adams/Clay conversation: Bemis, pp. 393–94.

p. 159 Reagan comment: NYT, February 25, 1982.

p. 160 "[F]unny feeling": Warren Hoge, "On the Scene—and Often on the Spot—in Salvador," NYT, February 28, 1982.

p. 160 "[N]o longer be the ruler of her own spirit": Address, p. 29.

IV From Liberty to Force

p. 161 John Foster Dulles, "The Threat of a Red Asia": DSB, April 12, 1954, p. 539.

Dwight D. Eisenhower, "Special Message to the Congress on the Mutual Security Program, March 13, 1959," PPP, 1959, p. 256.

pp. 161–62 Diaz and bombing message: Schlesinger and Kinzer, p. 209; David Wise and Thomas B. Ross, *The Invisible Government,* p. 193.

p. 162 "Monroe Doctrine": Schlesinger and Kinzer, pp. 142–43.

p. 163 "[T]ortures and murders": details in Amnesty International, *Gua-*

temala: A Government Program of Political Murder. 1981 Amnesty International Report.

pp. 164–65 "British domination": Ralph Lee Woodward, Jr., *Central America: A Nation Divided,* p. 129.

p. 166 "Indians . . . driven to join in the revolutions": "Guatemala" article in Encyclopaedia Britannica, Eleventh Edition (1910–11).

p. 167 "Maya realm": Charles Gallenkamp, *Maya: The Riddle and Rediscovery of a Lost Civilization,* p. 196.

p. 168 U.S.-Guatemalan relations: John Gunther, *Inside Latin America,* p. 126.

p. 169 "[O]rderly as a billiard table": Gunther, p. 118.

p. 170 Truman Doctrine: text in Henry Steele Commager, ed., *Documents of American History* (Seventh Edition), Vol. 2, pp. 524–26.

p. 174 Haig quote: Washington *Post,* March 9, 1981.

p. 174 "[W]orld-wide equivalent of Monroe Doctrine": Commager, p. 524.

p. 174 Guerrillas would have failed even without Truman Doctrine: Robert B. Asprey, *War in the Shadows: The Guerrilla in History,* Vol. 2, pp. 733–45.

p. 174 Adams-Clay comments: from Adams's *Memoirs,* cited in Samuel Flagg Bemis, *John Quincy Adams and the Foundations of American Foreign Policy,* pp. 393–94.

p. 176 "[I]mportance of Vietnam": Henry A. Kissinger, "The Vietnam Negotiations," *Foreign Affairs,* January 1969.

pp. 176–77 Roman *imperatores:* Edward Gibbon, *The Decline and Fall of the Roman Empire,* abridgement by D. M. Low, Vol. 1, pp. 42–52; Donald R. Dudley, *The Civilization of Rome,* pp. 124–42.

p. 178 Land reform: Roy Prosterman, "Turning the Tables on the Viet Cong," *Cornell Law Review* 53 (1967).

p. 178 "[S]poke no Spanish": Schlesinger and Kinzer, p. 133.

pp. 178–79 Peurifoy/Eisenhower conclusions: Dwight D. Eisenhower, *The White House Years: Mandate for Change,* pp. 505–6.

p. 179 "[R]uthless imperialist power": Andreas G. Papandreou, Introduction to Norodom Sihanouk and Wilfred Burchett, *My War with the C.I.A.,* p. 9.

p. 188 Acheson speech: quoted in Eric F. Goldman, *The Crucial Decade —and After,* pp. 153–54.

pp. 188–89 MacArthur on not defending South Korea: Manchester, p. 542.

p. 190 Truman speech: "President's Radio Report to the American People on Korea and on U.S. Policy in the Far East, April 11, 1951," PPP, 1951, p. 223.

p. 194 Arthur MacArthur request: quoted in William Manchester, *American Caesar: Douglas MacArthur, 1880–1964,* p. 35.

pp. 192–95 Wake Island meeting: Manchester, pp. 587–96.

p. 195 "[W]ar . . . coming to an end shortly": Goldman, pp. 177–78.

pp. 196–97 Dwight D. Eisenhower, "Address Before the American Society of Newspaper Editors, April 21, 1956," PPP, 1956, p. 423.

John F. Kennedy, "Address in Chicago to a Democratic Party Dinner, April 28, 1961," PPP, 1961, p. 340.

Lyndon B. Johnson, statement at the White House, May 4, 1965, DSB, May 24, 1965, p. 817.

p. 197 Lyndon B. Johnson, Memorandum to the President from the Vice President on "Mission to Southeast Asia, India and Pakistan," USVR, Vol. 11, pp. 159–66.

p. 198 Chou message and Truman reaction: Harry S. Truman, *Memoirs: Years of Trial and Hope*, pp. 360–65.

p. 200 "[W]ould pay for it with their lives": Manchester, p. 596.

pp. 201–4 Text of "X article": George Frost Kennan ("X"), "The Sources of Soviet Conduct," *Foreign Affairs*, July 1947.

pp. 202–6 Kennan complaints on misinterpretations of "X article": George Frost Kennan, *Memoirs 1925–1950*, pp. 354–67.

p. 203 Opposition to Kennan view of U.S.S.R.: Daniel Yergin, *Shattered Peace: The Origins of the Cold War and the National Security State*, pp. 321–24.

p. 205 Reagan on Truman Doctrine: Ronald Reagan, "Central America: Defending Our Vital Interests," Department of State, Bureau of Public Affairs, Current Policy No. 482, p. 3.

p. 207 Reagan on Soviets: Saturday radio address to the nation, September 3, 1983.

p. 207 "[D]arkness in which no . . . child will be born": Jonathan Schell, *The Fate of the Earth*, p. 178.

p. 208 Kennan on nuclear weapons: "A Proposal for International Disarmament," p. 2.

p. 208 Kennan on nuclear weapons: George F. Kennan, "A Proposal for International Disarmament," May 19, 1981.

pp. 209–12 McCarthy accusations and Goldman comments: Goldman, pp. 212–13.

p. 212 "[S]tooge forces": Kennan, *Memoirs*, p. 361.

p. 215 "Communist plot to subvert the film industry": Ronald Reagan campaign biography in Information Please Almanac 1981, p. 22.

p. 216 "[F]irst beachhead": Eisenhower, *Mandate for Change*, p. 27.

p. 217 Peurifoy/Arbenz meeting: Eisenhower, p. 506; Schlesinger and Kinzer, pp. 137–38.

p. 224 Guatemala bishops quote: "Message of the Bishops to the People of Guatemala," Guatemala Bishops' Conference, June 13, 1980.

p. 224 Latin America not "displeased": Eisenhower, p. 511.

p. 224 "Communist agitation": Julius W. Pratt, *A History of United States Foreign Policy* (Second Edition), p. 534.

pp. 225–26 Kennedy on Dominican Republic: quoted in Arthur M. Schlesinger, Jr., *A Thousand Days: John F. Kennedy in the White House,* p. 660.

p. 226 Trujillo and the Shah: Gunther, *Inside Latin America,* pp. 441–43.

p. 227 Eisenhower on Castillo Armas: *Mandate for Change,* p. 511.

p. 227 "Castillo Armas headed a junta . . .": U.S. Department of Defense, *Area Handbook for Guatemala,* p. 36.

pp. 227–28 Ydigoras ouster: Schlesinger and Kinzer, p. 242.

p. 228 Rios Montt interview: NYT, June, 1982.

p. 228 "Ranger" operating costs: *Central America Report,* August 5, 1983, p. 1.

pp. 228–29 U.S. quotes: *Time* magazine, August 8, 1983, p. 21.

p. 228 Rios Montt overthrow: "Exit Rios, enter Mejia," *Central America Report,* August 12, 1983, pp. 1–2.

p. 229 U.S. officials on Guatemala "threat": " 'It Is Not Too Late' for U.S. to Win in El Salvador," *U.S. News & World Report,* June 13, 1983; Alan Riding, "U.S. General Calls Guatemala Aid 'Imperative,' " NYT, August 22, 1982; NYT, May 10, 1981.

pp. 229–30 Guerrilla manifestos: Richard Gott, *Rural Guerrillas in Latin America,* pp. 75–77.

p. 230 Parsons quote: interview with Professor Joel Halpern, January 1984.

pp. 230–31 Kong Le/Dommen quotes: Arthur Dommen, *Conflict in Laos: The Politics of Neutralization* (Revised Edition), pp. 144–47.

p. 231 Acheson cable: USVR, Vol. 8, p. 196.

p. 231 Kong Le discussion: Clark Clifford, "Memorandum of Conference on January 19, 1961," in GRAVEL, Vol. 2, p. 637.

p. 231 Kong Le "another Castro": Charles Stevenson, *The End of Nowhere: American Policy Toward Laos Since 1954,* p. 93.

pp. 231–32 Kennedy quotes: PPP, 1961, pp. 306, 340.

p. 232 Americans "trained in Laos": Schlesinger and Kinzer, p. 242.

p. 232 Kennedy at Great Falls: PPP, 1963, p. 727.

p. 234 Gromyko "counting swans": Dommen, p. 210.

p. 235 Diem quote: GRAVEL, Vol. 2, p. 268.

p. 236 Johnson quote: Neil Sheehan and others, *The Pentagon Papers: The Secret History of the Vietnam War . . . as Published by the New York Times,* p. 285.

p. 237 "[L]ake of blood": Fred Branfman, editor, *Voices from the Plain of Jars: Life Under an Air War,* p. 127.

p. 237 Fulbright/Sullivan exchange: U.S. Senate, Committee on Foreign Relations, *United States Security Agreements and Commitments Abroad: Kingdom of Laos* (hearings), pp. 375–77.

p. 237 "Fifty-three known communists": Tad Szulc, *Dominican Diary*, p. 80.

pp. 239–40 Root/LaFeber quotes: Walter LaFeber, *The Panama Canal: The Crisis in Historical Perspective*, pp. 53–54.

pp. 240–42 Text of Roosevelt Corollary: Commager, *Documents of American History*, Vol. 2. pp. 33–34.

p. 242 Reagan comments: "Transcript of Address by President on Lebanon and Grenada," NYT, October 28, 1983.

p. 243 "[M]ost ignoble chapter": LaFeber, p. 53.

p. 243 "[T]he lower races": David Healy, *U.S. Expansionism; the Imperialist Urge in the 1890s*, pp. 151–53; cited in LaFeber, p. 56.

p. 243 "[N]ourish a doctrine": Sumner statement in "War" (1903), cited in "Forget the Maine," NYT editorial, July 24, 1983.

p. 246 Panama "giveaway": LaFeber, p. 206.

pp. 247–48 Reagan and aides' quotes: Washington *Post*, May 3 and May 9, 1976; cited in LaFeber, p. 190.

pp. 251–52 Cummings on film: Ana Carrigan and Bernard Stone, *Roses in December.*

V   Unmanifest Destiny

pp. 253–54 Congressional and other quotes: Sidney Lens, *The Forging of the American Empire*, pp. 124–34; Albert K. Weinberg, *Manifest Destiny: A Study of Nationalist Expansionism in American History*, pp. 100–29.

p. 254 "[W]hole country . . . unjustly overrun": Henry David Thoreau, "Civil Disobedience," Brooks Atkinson (editor), *Walden and Other Writings of Henry David Thoreau*, pp. 635–59.

p. 254 "Allow the president . . .": Lincoln quoted in NYT editorial, "Yankees, Bats and Nicaragua," July 26, 1983.

pp. 254–55 Calhoun comments: Dexter Perkins, *A History of the Monroe Doctrine*, pp. 90–92. Calhoun's comments were provoked by Polk's attempt, following the conquest of California and Texas, to send U.S. troops to the Yucatan on the grounds that Monroe's "principle" required him to resist supposed European encroachment there.

p. 256 "[U]ncommonly emphatic tone of voice": William H. Seward, *Life and Public Services of John Quincy Adams*, p. 333.

p. 259 "[A]borigines of this country": Pratt, *A History of United States Foreign Policy*, p. 138.

pp. 259–60 Text of Washington's Farewell Address: Henry Steele Commager, *Documents of American History* (Seventh Edition), Vol. 1, pp. 169–75.

p. 262 Adams comments: Samuel Flagg Bemis, *John Quincy Adams and the Foundations of American Foreign Policy*, p. 367n.

pp. 261–62 Jefferson comments: Samuel Eliot Morison and Henry Steele Commager, *The Growth of the American Republic*, p. 384.

p. 263 "[A]mbitious and encroaching people": Bemis, p. 366.

p. 265 "[L]iterature on the Indians": Morison and Commager, p. 837.

p. 266 Nixon comment: Background Information, p. 415.

pp. 266–68 Adams statements: Address, pp. 5–31.

p. 268 Bemis and Poletica comments: Bemis, p. 357.

pp. 270–71 "[D]anger from abroad" and Jackson letter: Weinberg, pp. 104–8.

p. 271 "[N]ever definitive proof": Lens, p. 114.

p. 272 Adams description: Bemis, p. ix.

p. 272 Sumner comments on Jackson: "Jackson, Andrew (1767–1845)," Encyclopaedia Britannica (Eleventh Edition: 1910–11).

pp. 272–73 Clay and Van Buren on Texas: Lens, p. 117; Thomas A. Bailey, *A Diplomatic History of the American People,* p. 253.

p. 274 Democratic platform: T. Harry Williams and others, *A History of the United States (to 1877)* (Second Edition, Revised), p. 517.

pp. 274–75 "Mr. Tyler's infamous treaty": Allan Nevins, editor, *The Diary of Philip Hone, 1828–1851,* p. 706, cited in Bailey, p. 256.

p. 275 Calhoun on Texas: Bailey, p. 257.

p. 275 Monroe on Texas: Bemis, pp. 351, 561.

pp. 276–77 "[C]up of forbearance had been exhausted"; Pratt comment: Pratt, p. 130.

p. 277 "[M]ost unjust war": U. S. Grant, quoted in H. L. Mencken, "The Anglo-Saxon," in Alistair Cooke (editor), *Mencken,* p. 129.

pp. 277–79 Battles of Veracruz and of Chapultepec: Michael C. Meyer and William L. Sherman, *The Course of Mexican History,* pp. 348–51.

pp. 277–78 "[T]he road Cortes had followed": Samuel Eliot Morison and Henry Steele Commager, *The Growth of the American Republic,* Vol. 1, pp. 595–96.

p. 280 Polk on Oregon: Pratt, pp. 109–10.

p. 282–83 O'Sullivan on manifest destiny: Williams and others, pp. 515–16.

pp. 283–87 Details of Polk's secret attempt to provoke war: R. R. Stenberg, "The Failure of Polk's War Intrigue of 1845," *Pacific Historical Review,* March 1935, pp. 39–69.

p. 285 Pratt on Polk message: Pratt, p. 130.

pp. 285–87 Polk "revival" of Monroe; Buchanan deception: Perkins, pp. 65, 77–81.

p. 288 Adams statement: Address, pp. 30–31.

pp. 288–89 California and New Mexico uprisings: Lens, pp. 127–28.

p. 291 Reagan on Lebanon and Grenada: NYT, October 28, 1983.

p. 291 Reagan quotes: text of February 24, 1982, OAS speech in NYT, February 25, 1982.

p. 291 "Anglo-Saxon race": Weinberg, pp. 125–26.

p. 291 "[S]pecial place": Richard Nixon, "United States Foreign Policy for the 1970s: A New Strategy for Peace. President Nixon's Report to the Congress, February 18, 1970," text in Background Information, pp. 381–400.

pp. 291–92 "[N]o one else": DSB, August 16, 1965, p. 262.

p. 292 "[N]o alternative": USVR, Vol. 11, p. 162.

p. 292 Johnson on domino theory: DSB, April 26, 1967, p. 607.

pp. 294–95 Kirkpatrick on Soviets: Richard Bernstein, "Mrs. Kirkpatrick Derides 'Confusion' Over Soviet," NYT, October 23, 1983.

p. 297 "[P]itiful, helpless giant": "Address by President Nixon on the Cambodian Strike, April 30, 1970," Background Information, pp. 415–16.

p. 306 Lincoln on extension of slavery: from Lincoln's First Inaugural Address (1861), text in *The Harvard Classics,* Vol. 43, *American Historical Documents,* pp. 334–43.

pp. 307–9 "Calhoun's clear vision": Morison and Commager, p. 592.

p. 311 Wilmot Proviso: Morison and Commager, Vol. 2, p. 589.

p. 311 "[S]tate of the American Union": Samuel Eliot Morison, *The Oxford History of the American People,* p. 568.

pp. 311–12 Lincoln on liberty: Address at Baltimore Sanitary Fair, April 18, 1864.

p. 312 "[F]orbidden fruit": Richard Hofstadter, *The American Political Tradition,* pp. 83–87.

p. 312 "[N]o Civil War" without Mexican War: Morison, p. 557.

p. 312 Lincoln controlled by events: Lincoln letter to A. G. Hodges, April 4, 1864.

p. 313 Quoted material: Bailey, pp. 281, 294–95n.

p. 315 Monroe pronouncement "doctrine" for first time: Richard W. Leopold, *The Growth of American Foreign Policy: A History,* p. 51.

p. 315 Text of Clayton-Bulwer treaty in Commager, *Documents of American History,* Vol. 2, pp. 326–27.

pp. 315–17 Palmerston statements and other quoted material: Bailey, pp. 281–302.

p. 321 New York *Tribune* and Sheridan quotes: Joan Haslip, *The Crown of Mexico: Maximilian and His Empress Carlota,* pp. 365, 504.

p. 321 Mexican victory "without the aid of any foreign nation": Alfred Jackson Hanna and Kathryn Abbey Hanna, *Napoleon III and Mexico: American Triumph over Monarchy,* p. 307.

p. 323 McKinley and other quotes: Bailey, pp. 511, 509, 516.

p. 324 Platt Amendment: Bailey, p. 549.

p. 325 McKinley on colonizing the Philippines: the original account of this famous statement was in the *Christian Advocate,* New York, January 22, 1903.

p. 326 "[N]o prisoners": *Congressional Record,* 58th Congress, Second Session, p. 4359.

p. 326 "[K]ill and burn": Philippine Information Society, *Facts about the Filipinos,* Vol. I, no. 10 (1901), pp. 41–50.

p. 326   "[N]ot a jungle war": DSB, August 24, 1964, p. 261.

p. 326   War for "happiness": Charles and Mary Beard, *A Basic History of the United States,* p. 674.

p. 328   Taft quote: Robert B. Asprey, *War in the Shadows,* Vol. 1, p. 196.

pp. 328–29   Taft quoted in U.S. Government, *Report of the Philippines Commission* (1900–3), cited in Robert B. Asprey, *War in the Shadows,* Vol. 1, 196–97.

pp. 329–30   Calhoun quoted in Perkins, p. 91.

p. 331   "[S]trange destiny": This famous editorial was first published in the Washington *Post,* June 6, 1898.

VI   An Empire of Evil

p. 332   Whitman poem "Pioneers! O Pioneers!": The Harvard Classics, Vol. 42, *English Poetry—Tennyson to Whitman,* p. 1486.

p. 332   Johnson quote: address at Johns Hopkins University, April 7, 1965, DSB, April 26, 1967, pp. 606–10.

pp. 332–33   Text of Nixon address announcing Cambodia invasion: Background Information, pp. 411–17.

p. 333   Cambodia "Nixon Doctrine in its purest form": Nixon press conference of November 12, 1971, WCPD, Vol. 7, no. 46, pp. 1511–15.

pp. 333–34   Text of Nixon remarks at Guam on July 25, 1969: *Congressional Record,* July 28, 1969, pp. S. 8637–40.

pp. 333–34   Text of Nixon's February 18, 1970, report to Congress: Background Information, pp. 381–400.

pp. 334–37   Details of secret bombing and ground operation in Cambodia: U.S. Senate, Committee on Armed Forces, *Bombing in Cambodia.*

p. 335   Rives quote: interview in "Vietnam: A Television History," P.B.S., December 1983.

p. 335   Beecher reports: NYT, March 26 and May 9, 1969.

pp. 337–39   Thornton statements: photocopies of Thornton letters describing his experiences, dated October 11, 15 and 27, and November 19 and 26, 1979.

p. 339   "[O]utstanding performance": photocopy of Department of Navy citation of May 26, 1969, signed by Vice Admiral E. R. Zumwalt, Jr.

p. 339   Son Ngoc Thanh confirmation: interview with Son Ngoc Thanh, Phnom Penh, August–September 1971.

p. 339   Nixon letter to Sihanouk: Background Information, p. 69.

pp. 339–40   Sihanouk statements at Phnom Penh press conference of March 28, 1969: text in *Bombing in Cambodia,* pp. 395–400.

p. 341   Symington statement: *Bombing in Cambodia,* p. 479.

p. 341   Nixon statements: Background Information, pp. 412, 432.

p. 342   "[N]othing to do with the overthrow of Sihanouk": *Bombing in Cambodia,* p. 480.

p. 342 Kissinger, Laird and Colby quotes: William Shawcross, *Sideshow: Kissinger, Nixon and the Destruction of Cambodia,* p. 122.

pp. 342–43 Lon Non statements: interview with Lon Non in Phnom Penh, June 1970 and September 1971.

p. 343 Nixon statements: Background Information, pp. 416, 420, 415.

p. 344 Nixon on ending war: April 7, 1971, address to the nation, quoted in DSB, March 31, 1972, pp. 367–69.

p. 345 Proposed article of impeachment because of Cambodia bombing: cited in Shawcross, p. 332.

p. 347 "Only Americans" can defeat the United States: WCPD, November 10, 1969, pp. 1553–54.

pp. 347–48 Nixon statements: WCPD, Vol. 6, no. 50, p. 1654; WCPD, Vol. 7, no. 9, p. 299; Background Information, p. 455.

p. 349 Lincoln on Polk: quoted in Sidney Lens, *The Forging of the American Empire,* p. 131.

p. 351 Ellsberg statements: Sanford J. Ungar, *The Papers & The Papers: An Account of the Legal and Political Battle over the Pentagon Papers,* pp. 59, 76.

p. 352 U.S. embassy obstruction of Congress and the press: details in U.S. Senate, Committee on Foreign Relations, Subcommittee on U.S. Security Agreements and Commitments Abroad, *U.S. Air Operations in Cambodia: April 1973.*

p. 354 Swank press conference: Shawcross, pp. 310–11.

pp. 355–56 Bombing without accurate maps: *U.S. Air Operations in Cambodia: April 1973,* p. 6.

p. 356 Kissinger on motives: Background Information, p. 513.

p. 356 Kissinger instructions to Dean: Shawcross, p. 323.

p. 357 "[N]o aspect of a civil war": WCPD, Vol. 6, no. 50, pp. 1654–55.

p. 357 "[P]eace is at hand": DSB, November 13, 1972, p. 549.

p. 358 Sullivan statement: interview with William H. Sullivan, New York, May 1981.

p. 358 "[D]e facto cease-fire": Background Information, p. 506.

pp. 358–59 Nixon statements: WCPD, Vol. 9, no. 9, p. 215; NYT, February 3, 1974.

p. 359 Sihanouk comments: interview with Norodom Sihanouk, Algiers, September 1973.

p. 360 Nixon on "real crisis": Background Information, p. 415.

pp. 360–61 Congressional and State Department comments on Cambodia: U.S. Senate, Committee on Foreign Relations, *Supplemental Assistance to Cambodia,* pp. 4–7, 47–52, 60.

pp. 361–62 U.S. support for Khmer Rouge: interviews with Thai and U.S. officials, Bangkok, December 1982.

pp. 362–414 Details of events and personal quotations in this section are based on interviews in Central America and the United States, between 1980 and 1984, with the following persons: Mr. and Mrs. Robert E. White, Mr. and Mrs. Raymond Donovan, Father Paul Schindler, Mr. and Mrs. Joseph Kazel, Mr. and Mrs. Michael Donovan, Mr. and Mrs. James Kazel, Sister Martha Owen, Michael H. Posner, Diane Orentlicher, James E. Zorn, Ana Carrigan, Colleen Kelly, Deborah Miller, Mr. and Mrs. Don Kelly, Heather Foote, Sister Sheila Marie Tobbe, Miriam Ford, Patricia and Pamela Keogh, and others who wished to remain anonymous.

p. 363 Reagan statement: "Central America: Defending Our Vital Interests," address to Joint Session of Congress on April 27, 1983, text in U.S. Department of State, Current Policy No. 482, p. 3, and in NYT, April 28, 1983.

p. 363 Kirkpatrick statement: NYT, October 23, 1983.

p. 369 Duarte comment: cited in Stewart Klepper, "The United States in El Salvador," *Covert Action,* no. 12 (April 1981), p. 5.

p. 370 Details on Martinez: Lawyers Committee for International Human Rights, *Justice in El Salvador: A Case Study* (July 20, 1982), pp. 27–28; February 1, 1983, update report, pp. 24–25.

pp. 371–73 Bracken murder: details in Pat Williams, "Did Salvador killing stifle evidence on slain women?" *National Catholic Reporter,* April 22, 1983.

p. 374 "[W]ent public": NYT, January 22, 1981.

p. 375 Haig comment; "send a message": Karen Young, "El Salvador: Where Reagan Draws the Line," Washington *Post,* March 9, 1981.

p. 375 U.S. support for Cambodian resistance groups: NYT, May 3, 1981.

p. 376 "American fantasies": Enrique Baloyra, *El Salvador in Transition,* p. 75.

p. 377 Enders statement: cited in *Time* magazine, June 6, 1983, p. 15.

pp. 377–78 Kirkpatrick/White debate: "Arms Aid and Advisers: Debating the New Policy on El Salvador," NYT, March 8, 1981.

p. 378 "[R]eady-made doctrine": "Ex-Envoy to El Salvador Says Views Caused Ouster," Washington *Post,* March 12, 1981.

p. 380 Kirkpatrick comments on nuns: Tampa *Tribune,* December 25, 1980.

p. 383 State Department Chronology: U.S. State Department, "Chronology of the Investigation into the Deaths of the American Churchwomen," submitted to Senate Foreign Relations Committee, April 9, 1981.

pp. 384–86 U.S. government obstruction; Webster letter; lack of full FBI investigation: details in Lawyers Committee for International Human Rights, *Justice in El Salvador: A Case Study,* July 20, 1982, report and February 1, 1983, update.

pp. 387–88 Letters to Reagan and Kirkpatrick: photocopies of letters written by Sister Sheila Marie Tobbe dated January 23, 1981.

p. 388 Kirkpatrick form letter: photocopy of April 2, 1981, Kirkpatrick letter to William P. Ford.

pp. 388–89 Attempts to contact Kirkpatrick: photocopy of Michael Donovan, "Chronology of Events Relating to the Death of Jean Donovan on December 2, 1980."

pp. 389–90 Kirkpatrick letter to Pell and Percy: photocopy provided by Senate Foreign Relations Committee.

pp. 393–94 Haig allegations: U.S. House of Representatives, Committee on International Relations, *Foreign Assistance Legislation for Fiscal Year 1982 (Part I),* p. 163.

pp. 393–94 FBI comments on Haig allegations: photocopy of Michael Donovan, "Notes on Meeting with Assistant Secretary of State James Cheek."

pp. 394–95 Haig retraction: Washington *Post,* March 20, 1981.

p. 395 "NUNS . . . SUSPECTED OF AIDING GUERRILLAS": Council for Inter-American Security, undated press release.

p. 395 "[G]ood faith efforts"; "guardsmen acted on their own": Lawyers Committee Report, p. 45; update report, p. 19.

pp. 395–99 Reagan comments: State Department, Current Policy No. 482, p. 3.

p. 396 Tyler report; Reagan veto: Lawyers Committee, January 1984 chronology of murder investigation.

p. 397 White-paper statements on Central America: Department of State, "Communist Interference in El Salvador (Special Report No. 80), pp. 2, 7–8.

p. 399 Baloyra, *El Salvador in Transition,* p. 184.

p. 401 "U.S. Advisers Are Glum": NYT, November 4, 1983.

pp. 403–6 Account based on interviews with U.S. officials in Nicaragua, June 1983.

p. 405 Details on CIA mining and Duarte election: NYT, April 15 and May 13, 1984.

pp. 406–7 Economic data: Lydia Chavez, "Rising Costs on Salvador's Second Front—the Economy," NYT, April 17, 1983; Bernard D. Nossiter, "What's the Bottom Line of Third World Debt?" NYT, May 25, 1983; Clyde H. Farnsworth, "Setback for Latin Economies," NYT, August 22, 1983.

p. 408 Enders "soft on communism": NYT, May 30, 1983.

p. 408 Tsongas on Enders; "not as simple as that": *Time* magazine, June 6, 1983, p. 15.

p. 409 Hinton on death squads: Washington *Post,* February 12, 1982; NYT, November 6, 1983.

p. 409 Enders on negotiations: Alfonso Chardy, "Enders' swan song: Don't count out talks with leftists," Miami *Herald,* June 3, 1983.

p. 409 "[L]ast straw," Miami *Herald,* June 1, 1983.

p. 410 *Le Monde* statement: cited in Washington *Post,* March 20, 1981.

pp. 411–12 Details on Kissinger Commission: NYT and Washington *Post,* January 8–15, 1983.

p. 413 "[F]ocus of evil": Reagan speech to evangelical conference, March 1983.

pp. 413–14 Reagan comments: State Department, Current Policy No. 482, pp. 3–5.

Epilogue The Search for COSVN

pp. 415–16, 417 "Christmas Greetings 1970–New Year's 1971 holiday greetings from Chau Doc Province Republic of Vietnam." Reproduced in Philip Jones Griffiths, *Vietnam Inc.,* p. 222.

p. 415 "[N]o people in the annals of time": "Statement by President Nixon of an Update Report on Vietnam, April 20, 1970," Background Information, pp. 410–11.

p. 416 Tocqueville and Hartz comments: Louis Hartz, *The Liberal Tradition in America,* p. 309.

pp. 418–19 Symington query and State Department response: *Bombing in Cambodia,* pp. 479–80.

p. 419, 422 Brown and Greven testimony: *Bombing in Cambodia,* pp. 502, 311.

p. 419 Nixon on "key control center": Background Information, p. 414.

p. 420 Melville statements: Jay Leyda (editor), *The Portable Melville,* pp. 409–11.

p. 420 "[H]aunted by the malevolence and horror of existence": Hans Kohn, *American Nationalism,* pp. 65, 152.

p. 420 "[T]he meaning of the story of Narcissus": excerpted from Chapter One of *Moby Dick.*

p. 420 "[N]o such thing": Frances FitzGerald, *Fire in the Lake: The Vietnamese and the Americans in Vietnam,* pp. 138–39.

p. 421 Pattern "discouragingly familiar": NYT, October 23, 1983.

p. 421 Fulbright comments: U.S. Senate, Committee on Foreign Relations, *Psychological Aspects of Foreign Policy,* p. 37.

p. 422 "[F]uture of America . . . as dark as it is vast": Whitman quoted in Samuel Eliot Morison and Henry Steele Commager, *The Growth of the American Republic,* Vol. 2, p. 9.

Bibliography

Adams, Charles Francis (editor). *Memoirs of John Quincy Adams, Comprising Portions of His Diary from 1795 to 1848* (12 vols., Philadelphia, 1874–77).

Adams, John Quincy. *An Address Delivered At the request of a Committee of the Citizens of Washington; on the occasion of reading The Declaration of Independence on the Fourth of July, 1821* (Washington: Davis and Force, 1821).

Alvarez, A. *The Monroe Doctrine: Its Importance in the International Life of the States of the New World* (New York: Oxford University Press, 1924).

Amnesty International. Reports on Central America, 1980–84.

Anderson, Thomas P. *Matanza: El Salvador's Communist Revolt of 1932* (Lincoln: University of Nebraska Press, 1971).

Asprey, Robert B. *War in the Shadows: The Guerrilla in History* (2 vols., Garden City, N.Y.: Doubleday, 1975).

Atkinson, Brooks (editor). *Walden and Other Writings of Henry David Thoreau* (New York: Modern Library, 1950).

Bailey, Thomas A. *A Diplomatic History of the American People* (New York: Appleton-Century-Crofts, 1946).

Baloyra, Enrique A. *El Salvador in Transition* (Chapel Hill and London: University of North Carolina Press, 1982).

Beard, Charles, and Mary Beard. *A Basic History of the United States* (New York: Macmillan, 1943).

————, and Mary Beard. *The Making of American Civilization* (New York: Macmillan, 1946).

Bemis, Samuel Flagg. *John Quincy Adams and the Foundations of American Foreign Policy* (New York: Knopf, 1949).

Bonner, Raymond. *Weakness and Deceit: U.S. Policy and El Salvador* (New York: Times Books, 1984).

Booth, John A. *The End and the Beginning: The Nicaraguan Revolution* (Boulder, Colo.: Westview Press, 1982).

Borges, Jorge Luis. *A Personal Anthology* (Secaucus, N.J.: Castle Books, 1967).

Branfman, Fred (editor). *Voices from the Plain of Jars: Life Under an Air War* (New York: Harper Colophon Books, 1972).

Carrigan, Ana, and Bernard Stone. *Roses in December: The Story of Jean Donovan* (New York: 2nd of December Films, 1982).

Commager, Henry Steele (editor). *Documents of American History* (2 vols., New York: Appleton-Century-Crofts, 1962).

Cooke, Alistair (editor). *The Vintage Mencken* (New York: Vintage, 1950).

Council for Inter-American Security. *Murdered Nuns in El Salvador Suspected of Aiding Guerrillas* (Washington, 1981).

Didion, Joan. *Salvador* (London: Chatto & Windus, 1983).

Diederich, Bernard. *Somoza and the Legacy of U.S. Involvement in Central America* (New York: Dutton, 1981).

Dinges, John. "New Evidence on Missionaries' Deaths in El Salvador Suggests Official Plot," Pacific News Service, July 11, 1982.

Dommen, Arthur J. *Conflict in Laos: The Politics of Neutralization* (New York: Praeger, 1965; revised edition, 1971).

Donovan, Michael. "Chronology of Events Relating to the Death of Jean Donovan on December 2, 1982"; "Notes on Meeting with Deputy Assistant Secretary of State James Cheek"; "Notes on Press Conference and Subsequent Telephone Calls from William Dyass, State Department Spokesman" (photocopies, 1981).

Dudley, Donald R. *The Civilization of Rome* (New York: Mentor Books, 1960).

Eisenhower, Dwight D. *The White House Years: Mandate for Change, 1953–56* (Garden City, N.Y.: Doubleday, 1963).

Encyclopaedia Britannica. Eleventh Edition (1910–11).

Erdozain, Placido. *Archbishop Romero: Martyr of Salvador* (Maryknoll, N.Y.: Orbis Books, 1980).

ES-INFO El Salvador Information Office. "Unofficial Transcript of the Presentation Made by Mr. Jon D. Glassman, Member of the Policy Planning Staff of the United States Department of State, at the 'New Administration Series' Sponsored by the Center for Inter-American Relations, New York, on May 20th, 1981" (photocopy, 1981).

FitzGerald, Frances. *Fire in the Lake: The Vietnamese and the Americans in Vietnam* (Boston: Little, Brown, 1972).

Ford, Ita. *From the Writings of Ita Ford, 1977–1980* (photocopy, 1980).

Gallenkamp, Charles. *Maya: The Riddle and Rediscovery of a Lost Civilization* (New York: David McKay, 1976).

Gibbon, Edward. *The Decline and Fall of the Roman Empire* (3 vols., abridgment by D. M. Low, New York: Washington Square Press, 1962).

Gil, Federico G., Enrique A. Baloyra, and Lars Schoultz. *The Failure of Democratic Transition in Latin America: El Salvador* (draft version of report to State Department, photocopy, December 1980).

Goldman, Eric F. *The Crucial Decade—and After: America, 1945–1960* (New York: Vintage Books, 1960).

Gott, Richard. *Rural Guerrillas in Latin America* (London: Pelican, 1973).

Griffiths, Philip Jones. *Vietnam, Inc.* (New York: Collier Books, 1971).

Gunther, John. *Inside Latin America* (New York: Harper, 1941).

Hall, John. "Ambassador Kirkpatrick: Reagan-Appointed Democrat Speaks Her Mind on World, Domestic Politics," Tampa *Tribune,* December 25, 1980.

Hanna, Alfred Jackson, and Kathryn Abbey Hanna. *Napoleon III and Mexico: American Triumph over Monarchy* (Chapel Hill: The University of North Carolina Press, 1971).

Hartz, Louis. *The Liberal Tradition in America* (New York: Harcourt, 1955).

Haslip, Joan. *The Crown of Mexico: Maximilian and His Empress Carlota* (New York: Holt, 1971).

Hofstadter, Richard. *The American Political Tradition* (New York: Knopf, 1948).

Kennan, George Frost. "The Sources of Soviet Conduct," *Foreign Affairs,* July 1947.

———. *Memoirs: 1925–1950* (Boston: Little, Brown, 1967).

———. "A Proposal for International Disarmament," New York: The Institute for World Order, 1981 (printed text of Kennan speech of May 19, 1981).

Kissinger, Henry A. "The Viet Nam Negotiations," *Foreign Affairs,* January 1969.

Kohn, Hans. *American Nationalism* (New York: Macmillan, 1957).

LaFeber, Walter. *The Panama Canal: The Crisis in Historical Perspective* (New York: Oxford University Press, 1978).

Lawyers Committee for International Human Rights. *A Report on the Investigation into the Killing of Four American Churchwomen in El Salvador* (September 1981); *Justice in El Salvador: A Case Study* (July 20, 1982); *Justice in El Salvador: A Case Study* (February 1, 1983); *Chronology of the Investigation and Prosecution of Those Responsible for Killing Four*

U.S. Church Women in El Salvador, (January 1984) (New York: photo-copies, 1981–84).

Legal Assistance Department of the Archdiocese of San Salvador. Reports on violations of human rights, 1979–84.

Lens, Sidney. *The Forging of the American Empire* (New York: Crowell, 1971).

LeoGrande, William M. "Drawing the Line in El Salvador," *International Security,* Vol. 6 (Summer 1981).

———, "Reply to the Kissinger Commission," *World Policy Journal* (Winter 1984).

Leopold, Richard W. *The Growth of American Foreign Policy* (New York: Knopf, 1962).

Lernoux, Penny. *Cry of the People* (New York: Doubleday, 1980).

Leyda, Jay (editor). *The Portable Melville* (New York: Viking, 1952).

Lippmann, Walter. *Early Writings* (New York: Liveright, 1970).

Manchester, William. *American Caesar: Douglas MacArthur 1880–1964* (Boston: Little, Brown, 1978).

Melville, Herman. *Moby-Dick* (New York: Signet, 1961).

Mencken, H. L. "The Anglo-Saxon." See Cooke, Alistair.

Meyer, Michael C., and William L. Sherman. *The Course of Mexican History* (New York: Oxford University Press, 1979).

Millett, Richard. *Guardians of the Dynasty: A History of the U.S. Created Guardia Nacional de Nicaragua and the Somoza Family* (Maryknoll, N.Y.: Orbis Books, 1977).

Mintie, Daniel. *Understanding Land Reform in El Salvador* (Seattle: Hunger Action Center, 1981).

Montgomery, Tommie Sue. *Revolution in El Salvador: Origins and Evolution* (Boulder, Colo.: Westview Press, 1982).

Morison, Samuel Eliot. *The Oxford History of the American People* (New York: Oxford University Press, 1965).

———, Henry Steele Commager. *The Growth of the American Republic* (2 vols., New York: Oxford University Press, 1954).

———, Frederick Merk, and Frank Freidel. *Dissent in Three American Wars* (Cambridge, Mass.: Harvard University Press, 1970).

Mowrer, Edgar Ansel. *The Nightmare of American Foreign Policy* (New York: Knopf, 1948).

Nicolson, Harold. *The Evolution of Diplomacy* (New York: Collier, 1954).

Niebuhr, Reinhold. *The Irony of American History* (New York: Scribner, 1952).

Nixon, Richard M. "Asia After Viet Nam," *Foreign Affairs,* October 1967.

Norodom Sihanouk and Wilfred Burchett. *My War with the CIA* (London: Penguin Press, 1973).

Perkins, Dexter. *A History of the Monroe Doctrine* (Boston: Little, Brown, 1955).

Pratt, Julius W. *Expansionists of 1812* (New York: Macmillan, 1925).

———. *Expansionists of 1898* (Chicago: Quadrangle Bks., 1964).

———. *A History of United States Foreign Policy* (Englewood Cliffs, N.J.: Prentice-Hall, 1965).

———. "John L. O'Sullivan and Manifest Destiny," *New York History,* July 1933.

Prosterman, Roy. "Turning the Tables on the Viet Cong," *Cornell Law Review* 53 (1967).

Schell, Jonathan. *The Fate of the Earth* (New York: Knopf, 1982).

———. *The Time of Illusion* (New York: Knopf, 1976).

Schlesinger, Arthur M., Jr. *The Age of Jackson* (New York: Mentor Books, 1963).

———. *The Bitter Heritage: Vietnam and American Democracy, 1941–1966* (Boston: Houghton, 1967).

———. *The Imperial Presidency* (Boston: Houghton, 1973).

———. *A Thousand Days: John F. Kennedy in the White House* (Boston: Houghton, 1965).

Schlesinger, Stephen, and Stephen Kinzer. *Bitter Fruit: The Untold Story of the American Coup in Guatemala* (Garden City, N.Y.: Doubleday, 1982).

Seward, William H. *Life and Public Services of John Quincy Adams, Sixth President of the United States, with the Eulogy Delivered Before the Legislature of New York* (Port Washington, N.Y.: Kennikat Press, undated).

Shawcross, William. *Sideshow: Kissinger, Nixon and the Destruction of Cambodia* (New York: Simon & Schuster, 1979).

The Senator Gravel Edition: The Pentagon Papers (5 vols., Boston: Beacon Press, 1971).

Sheehan, Neil, Hedrick Smith, E. W. Kenworthy, and Fox Butterfield. *The Pentagon Papers: The Secret History of the Vietnam War . . . as Published by The New York Times* (New York: Bantam Books, 1971).

Simon, Laurence R., and James C. Stephens, Jr. *El Salvador Land Reform.* (Boston: Oxfam America, 1981).

Steel, Ronald. *Pax Americana* (New York: Viking, 1967).

Sternberg, R. R. "The Failure of Polk's War Intrigue of 1845," *Pacific Historical Review,* March 1935.

Stevenson, Charles A. *The End of Nowhere: American Policy Toward Laos Since 1954* (Boston: Beacon Press, 1973).

Swango, John Virgil. "Christmas 1970–New Year's 1971 Holiday Greetings

from Chau Doc Province, Republic of Vietnam." See Griffiths, Philip
Jones.

Szulc, Tad. *Dominican Diary* (New York: Dell, 1965).

Thoreau, Henry David. "Civil Disobedience." See Atkinson, Brooks.

Thornton, Samuel. Letters and Personal Documents Relating to U.S. Clandestine Activities in Indochina, 1969–70 (photocopies provided by Laura
Summers).

Truman, Harry S. *Memoirs* (2 vols., Garden City, N.Y.: Doubleday, 1955–
56).

Ungar, Sanford J. *The Papers & The Papers: An Account of the Legal and
Political Battle over the Pentagon Papers* (New York: Dutton, 1972).

U.S. Government documents:
(All documents cited were published by the U.S. Government Printing
Office in the years indicated.)

U.S. Department of Defense:
(i) *Area Handbook* for El Salvador (1971), for Costa Rica (1970), for
Guatemala (1970), for Honduras (1971), for Nicaragua (1970), for Panama (1972).
(ii) *United States-Vietnam Relations 1945–1967* ("The Pentagon Papers," 12 vols., Washington, D.C.: U.S. Government Printing Office,
1971).

U.S. Department of State:
(i) "Communist Interference in El Salvador" ("white paper," Washington, D.C., February 23, 1981); *Communist Interference in El Salvador:
Documents Demonstrating Communist Support of the Salvadoran Insurgency* ("white paper supplement," Washington, D.C., February 23,
1981).
(ii) *Intervention of International Communism in Guatemala* (Washington, D.C., 1954).
(iii) *Department of State Bulletin,* 1950–84.
(iv) "Chronology of the Investigation into the Deaths of the American
Churchwomen," April 9, 1981.

U.S. House of Representatives:
Committee on International Relations, *Foreign Assistance Legislation for
Fiscal Year 1982* (Part I)

U.S. Senate:
(i) Committee on Foreign Relations Reports and Hearings:
  The Vietnam Hearings (1966).
  Kingdom of Laos (1969).
  Kingdom of Thailand (1969).
  Impact of the Vietnam War (1971).

Background Information Relating to Southeast Asia and Vietnam
7th Revised Edition (1974).
    U.S. Air Operations in Cambodia: April 1973 (1973).
    Psychological Aspects of Foreign Policy (1969).
    Thailand, Laos, Cambodia and Vietnam: April 1973 (1973).
    Causes, Origins and Lessons of the Vietnam War (1973).
    Supplemental Assistance to Cambodia (1975).
    (ii) Committee on Armed Services: *Bombing in Cambodia* (1973).
U.S. Government Periodicals:
Public Papers of the Presidents.
Weekly Compilation of Presidential Documents.
Congressional Record.

Van Alstyne, R. W. *The Rising American Empire* (New York: Oxford University Press, 1960).

Walker, Thomas W. *Nicaragua: The Land of Sandino* (Boulder, Colo.: Westview Press, 1981).

Webre, Stephen. *Jose Napoleon Duarte and the Christian Democratic Party in Salvadoran Politics* (Baton Rouge: Louisiana State University Press, 1979).

Weinberg, Albert K. *Manifest Destiny: A Study of Nationalist Expansionism in American History* (Baltimore: The Johns Hopkins Press, 1935).

Whitaker, A. P. *The United States and the Independence of Latin America* (Baltimore: The Johns Hopkins Press, 1941).

Williams, Pat. "Did Salvador killing stifle evidence on slain women?" *National Catholic Reporter,* April 22, 1983.

Williams, T. Harry, Richard N. Current, and Frank Freidel. *A History of the United States (to 1877)* (New York: Knopf, 1965).

Wilson, Woodrow. *A History of the American People* (5 vols., New York: Harper, 1908).

Wise, David, and Thomas B. Ross. *The Invisible Government* (New York: Random House, 1964).

Wolf, Eric R., and Edward C. Hansen. *The Human Condition in Latin America* (New York: Oxford University Press, 1972).

Woodward, Ralph Lee, Jr. *Central America: A Nation Divided* (New York: Oxford University Press, 1976).

Yergin, Daniel. *Shattered Peace: The Origins of the Cold War and the National Security State* (Boston: Houghton, 1977).

Index